HANDBOOK OF INDUSTRY STUDIES AND ECONOMIC GEOGRAPHY

Handbook of Industry Studies and Economic Geography

Edited by

Frank Giarratani
University of Pittsburgh, USA

Geoffrey J.D. Hewings
University of Illinois, Urbana-Champaign, USA

Philip McCann
University of Groningen, The Netherlands

Edward Elgar
Cheltenham, UK • Northampton, MA, USA

Published by
Edward Elgar Publishing Limited
The Lypiatts
15 Lansdown Road
Cheltenham
Glos GL50 2JA
UK

Edward Elgar Publishing, Inc.
William Pratt House
9 Dewey Court
Northampton
Massachusetts 01060
USA

A catalogue record for this book
is available from the British Library

Library of Congress Control Number: 2013938961

This book is available electronically in the ElgarOnline
Economics Subject Collection, E-ISBN 978 1 78254 900 0

ISBN 978 1 84376 961 3 (cased)

Typeset by Servis Filmsetting Ltd, Stockport, Cheshire
Printed and bound in Great Britain by T.J. International Ltd, Padstow

Contents

Contributors

Yuko Aoyama   Clark University, Worcester, MA, USA.

David Bailey   Aston University, Birmingham, UK.

Fiorenza Bellussi   University of Padova, Italy.

Gill Bentley   University of Birmingham, UK.

Mark Bokhorst   Vrije Universiteit Amsterdam, The Netherlands.

Frank Bruinsma   Vrije Universiteit Amsterdam, The Netherlands.

Kristy Buzard   University of California-San Diego, CA, USA.

Gerald Carlino   Federal Reserve Bank of Philadelphia, PA, USA.

Michael C. Carroll   Bowling Green State University, OH, USA.

Joyce Cooper   University of Washington, Seattle, WA, USA.

Lisa De Propris   University of Birmingham, UK.

Peter B. Doeringer   Boston University, MA, USA.

Elsie L. Echeverri-Carroll   University of Texas at Austin, TX, USA.

Chris Forman   Georgia Institute of Technology, Atlanta, GA, USA.

Pacey Foster   University of Massachusetts Boston, MA, USA.

Anne Gadwa Nicodemus   Metris Arts Consulting and University of Minnesota, Minneapolis, MN, USA.

Frank Giarratani   University of Pittsburgh, PA, USA.

Nancey Green Leigh   Georgia Institute of Technology, Atlanta, GA, USA.

Gene Gruver   University of Pittsburgh, PA, USA.

Geoffrey J.D. Hewings   University of Illinois, Urbana-Champaign, IL, USA.

Hiro Izushi   Aston University, Birmingham, UK.

Randall Jackson   West Virginia University, Morgantown, WV, USA.

Thomas Klier   Federal Reserve Bank of Chicago, IL, USA.

Stewart MacNeill   University of Birmingham, UK.

Ravi Madhavan   University of Pittsburgh, PA, USA.

Stephan Manning   University of Massachusetts Boston, MA, USA.

Ann Markusen   Markusen Economic Research Services and University of Minnesota, Minneapolis, MN, USA.

Catalina Martínez   Institute of Public Goods and Policies at the Spanish National Research Council (CSIC), Madrid, Spain.

Heike Mayer   University of Bern, Switzerland.

Philip McCann   University of Groningen, The Netherlands.

Ram Mudambi   Temple University, Philadelphia, PA, USA.

Raquel Ortega-Argilés   University of Groningen, The Netherlands.

Les Oxley   University of Waikato, Hamilton, New Zealand.

Ruth Rama   Institute of Economics, Geography and Demography at the Spanish National Research Council (CSIC), Madrid, Spain.

Neil Reid   University of Toledo, USA.

Aisling Reynolds-Feighan   University College Dublin, Ireland.

James M. Rubenstein   Miami University, Oxford, Ohio, USA.

Hong Shangqin   University of Canterbury, Christchurch, New Zealand.

Stephen Sheppard   Williams College, Williamstown, MA, USA.

David Terkla   University of Massachusetts Boston, MA, USA.

Introduction to the relationships between economic geography and industries: theory, empirics and modes of analysis

Frank Giarratani, Geoffrey J.G. Hewings and Philip McCann

The broad field of economic geography and spatial economics, comprising areas such as regional science, urban economics, new economic geography as well as traditional economic geography, is a research arena which has burgeoned since the early 1990s. Much of the current conceptual and methodological framework of the field has a long tradition dating back well into the mid-twentieth century. However, the renewed surge of interest in the field during the early 1990s was largely in response to the analytical work of various seminal authors including Allan Scott (1988), Michael Porter (1990), Paul Krugman (1991), and Edward Glaeser (Glaeser et al., 1992), as well as the empirical work of Luc Anselin (1988), whose ideas and arguments reignited investigations in all aspects of spatial-economic phenomena ranging from the role of cities and regions in economic growth, to factor mobility, knowledge spillovers and firm strategy.

As well as providing novel analytical arguments for numerous scholars to build on, the importance of the work of these commentators is twofold, namely awareness and timing. First, their arguments attracted the attention of a wide range of scholars from many different disciplines, and in particular: business and management studies; organizational studies; political science and sociology; as well as from the established audiences within economics and geography. As such, the potential interactions between geography and economics became topics for discussion and analysis from a greater variety of perspectives. A broader range of debates and an increased dissemination of ideas across broader constituencies all contributed to richer discussions, and also led to a greater awareness of these issues within both national and international policy-making circles.

Second, the timing of the work of these commentators was unexpectedly fortuitous. The onset of the modern era of globalization was driven by the enormous institutional and technological changes which took place between 1988 and 1994, including the creation of the EU Single Market, NAFTA, the fall of the Berlin Wall, the rapid institutional reform and opening up of China, India, South Africa, Indonesia and Brazil, and the invention of the World Wide Web (McCann, 2008). While the global transformations wrought collectively by these individual changes were obviously unforeseen by these various authors, the issues they raised and the questions they posed proved to be highly pertinent and timely with regard to the nature of many of the changes which were about to unfold. Many firms and industries in different parts of the world were catapulted into a fast-changing competitive environment for which many were prepared, but also for which many were not prepared.

As such, both awareness and timing played a key role in re-establishing spatial-economic phenomena as central to discussions of economic growth and development, as had been the case in the late 1950s and early 1960s. A greater awareness of the role played by geography in economic growth does not imply, however, that firms and industries are somehow less important in driving growth. On the contrary, the behaviour of firms is central to all of these discussions, but by the early 1990s the contextual and decision-making issues associated with geography were increasingly understood as being essential elements of any firm-level analysis. This line of thinking is consistent with the longstanding tradition within regional economics. Indeed, the growth role played by firms and industries and their interactions with geography has a long pedigree dating back many decades, based around the seminal insights of authors such as Ed Hoover (1948), Walter Isard and Bob Kuenne (1953), Robert Lichtenberg (1960), Raymond Vernon (1960) and Ben Chinitz (1961). In addition, outside of geography and also many areas of economics, the 1980s and early 1990s also saw important developments within international business and management studies which led to a renewed thinking of the nature of the growth role of firms and industries (Nelson and Winter, 1982; Piore and Sabel, 1984; Best, 1990; Williamson and Winter, 1991; Pitelis, 1993; Dunning, 2000). Moving away from idealized notions of a representative profit-maximizing agent, these lines of enquiry instead focused attention on the contemporary organizational and strategic challenges faced by different firms and industries in response to the new technologies on offer and the transaction costs and hierarchical systems within which firms operate. As such, these developments paved the way for much of the thinking of Scott (1988) and Porter (1990) in particular, and provided a complementary and alternative line of analysis to the more orthodox approaches of Krugman (1991) and Glaeser (Glaeser et al., 1992).

As noted above, the broad field of economic geography has burgeoned since the early 1990s, as evidenced by the enormous increase in the number of scholarly articles, journals and books published on these issues. New empirical approaches using micro-econometric techniques which aim to distinguish between firm- and geography-specific aspects have been developed. At the same time, it is possible to argue that the various lines of enquiry offered by Krugman, Porter, Glaeser and Scott have not converged, or at least not been integrated, quite to the extent that might have been expected at the time. The various lines of enquiry have tended to run alongside each other rather in parallel, at times complementing and at times somewhat conflicting with each other. Various possible reasons can be offered for this, including simply the internal sociology of the academic world. However, for our purposes, one such reason is that the fundamental organizational changes brought by the modern era of globalization – including outsourcing, offshoring and technological restructuring, all of which are central to discussions of geography – do not translate smoothly into the representative-firm construction characterized in formal economic models. Similarly, even where firm-specific heterogeneity is explicitly modelled (Melitz, 2003), fixed-effects-type regressions are unable to capture the reasons for the observed heterogeneity between industries and firms. The result is that in terms of the broad field of economic geography, the analysis of firm- and industry-specific issues tends to be something of a hybrid construction, drawing insights from various methodological approaches and traditions.

On the one hand, this multiplicity of approaches could be interpreted as a weakness of the field, undermining its ability to provide durable insights. On the other, however, this could also be interpreted as an opportunity to provide a deeper understanding of the issues at hand. Increasingly, in many fields of social science, 'big' issues such as the environment, well-being, governance, innovation and ageing, are increasingly understood as being inherently multidimensional in nature, and individual methodological frameworks are incapable of capturing all, or even a majority, of the features of the phenomena being investigated. As such, a multimethod approach offers insights which individual approaches may find difficult to realize, and this is also the case for the relationships among firms, industries and geography.

In terms of the variety of issues surrounding firm and industry behaviour and performance, the establishment of the Industry Studies Association[1] in 2008 was explicitly designed to spur more of a multi-thematic approach to firm and industry issues combining qualitative and in-depth case-study approaches to firm research with applied quantitative approaches, and to foster a greater awareness among scholars from many arenas as to the importance of industry- and firm-specific characteristics. The potential importance of this approach for economic geography research is obvious given the different lines of enquiry which are already evident in the field and indeed, this premise regarding the opportunities afforded by multidimensional research underscores the logic of this Handbook.

The individually commissioned chapters which comprise this volume are the product of a series of seminars and meetings which were co-convened between the Industry Studies Association and the North American Regional Science Association, and also between the British and Irish Sections of the Regional Science Association International and the Regional Studies Association. At these meetings the various authors discussed the issues facing the firms and industry they were examining, and also their ideas regarding how such issues can best be analysed. Importantly, all chapters are written by authors with a deep understanding of the specific mechanics and technological, organizational and strategic features of each industry, including the historical and technological evolution of the sectors. Many of the issues raised in this book will be entirely new to the majority of economic geographers, while at the same time many of the geographical issues uncovered here will be largely new to industry studies as well as to business and management scholars. Indeed, producing and editing this volume has been a deeply rewarding intellectual experience in its own right, demonstrating the importance of industry-specific knowledge in influencing spatial-economic behaviour, as well as the importance of geography in influencing firm- and industry-specific behaviour.

The Handbook comprises five parts made up of 20 chapters. The five parts reflect broadly different types of industries grouped around the themes of *Heavy Industries, Creative and Cultural Industries, High technology Sectors, Resource-based Sectors,* and *Knowledge- and Network-based Activities.* In terms of industrial classifications these groupings are neither exhaustive nor exclusive, but rather in thematic terms reflect the dominant types of characteristics, modes of operation, and key elements evident in groups of activities.

In Part I, which deals with what are traditionally often described as 'heavy industries', Frank Giarratani, Ravi Madhavan and Gene Gruver examine (Chapter 1) the economic and geographical evolution of the modern steel industry. Competition and niche opportunities offered by different types of technology, operations and infrastructure have transformed the modern steel industry, leading to fundamental processes of industry restructuring and locational adjustment. Similarly dramatic spatial recon-figurations are evident in the automobile industries of North America and Europe. The spatial-economic analysis of the US automobile industry by Thomas Klier and James Rubenstein (Chapter 2) and structural analysis of the European automobile industry by Gill Bentley, David Bailey and Stewart MacNeill (Chapter 3) demonstrate that a combination of the global changes in demand, emerging competition, excess capacity problems, and supply chain realignments both globally and locally, have driven enor-mous changes in the geographies of these sectors, changing the competitive advantage of different regions as potential production sites.

In Part II, a variety of sectors and activities which are nowadays often grouped under the common theme of 'creative and cultural industries' are examined. Peter Doeringer, Pacey Foster, Stephan Manning and David Terkla (Chapter 4) provide an in-depth examination of sectors which are characterized by project- and craft-based activities. Location is an essential element in these sectors, but the ways in which location matters differ according to exactly which operations and activities are being undertaken, and also result from the evolution of the industry itself. The importance of understanding an industry evolution is also discussed in detail by Yuko Aoyama and Hiro Izushi (Chapter 5), who show that within the video games sector, many of the current international differences in the sector result directly from the different domestic national conditions which fostered quite different historical evolutionary trajectories within broadly the same types of activities. However, as Ann Markusen and Anne Gadwa Nicodemus (Chapter 6) argue, many of these creative and cultural industries can be rather difficult to identify within standard industry classification schemes, so the empirical analysis of the scale and shifts in these sectors requires a careful decomposition and interpretation of the different activities, roles and services evident within these sectors. Similarly, in terms of the economic outcomes of these creative and cultural sectors, as Stephen Sheppard (Chapter 7) demonstrates, the impacts of cultural infrastructure investments may be multidimensional, impacting on both productivity and also amenity values.

Part III examines different types of high-technology sectors. High-technology sectors are extremely varied in their nature, activities, organization, behaviour and outcomes, but following on from some popular descriptions of Silicon Valley, much of the economic geography literature has tended to treat these sectors as being either largely a homogene-ous entity, or at least exhibiting an idealized typology towards which all high-technology subsectors should converge. This has been a rather unfortunate development in the lit-erature as it has tended to mask many of the interesting and important features of these sectors. Indeed, the mechanics of high-technology sectors differ markedly according to geography, nationality and history. Heike Mayer's analysis (Chapter 8) shows that the evolution of high-technology activities in so-called 'second-tier' regions develops along rather different lines from many of the popular descriptions evident in the literature. The interactions between history, geography and technology matter, and as both Ram Mudambi (Chapter 9) and Chris Forman (Chapter 10) demonstrate, this is also the case for the processes of international and national economic restructuring, as firms take advantage of the opportunities afforded by new technologies to reconfigure their activi-ties. Furthermore, the importance of high-technology sectors in the modern economy also means that historical and geographical differences in the evolutionary processes of these sectors have profound implications for aggregate economic performance. As Raquel Ortega-Argilés (Chapter 11) explains, many of the clues as to the productivity gap which emerged between the US and Europe are related both to the evolution of these sectors and also to their impacts on other non-high-technology sectors.

Part IV examines different aspects of resource-based sectors. In standard industrial classification terms these resource-based sectors represent a diverse group of activities and industries. However, they are sectors and activities which face common challenges in that environmental and natural resource management considerations dominate all aspects of their behaviour and underpin the logic of all of their actions. At the global scale, agribusiness is dominated by major international multinational companies linking suppliers to customers. As Ruth Rama and Catalina Martínez (Chapter 12) explain, the importance of global players in linking local and global suppliers and customers is particularly important in the food-related sectors, in which the development of systems of coordination are paramount. However, the research and policy intervention work of Michael Carroll and Neil Reid (Chapter 13) demonstrates that the development of such systems is also important at a local and regional scale, and the coordination challenges at this local scale for resource-based sectors are often at least as great as those at the international scale. At the same time, however, as environmental concerns are becoming important for many sectors, for resource-based sectors they also offer opportunities for the provision of new services with wider benefits across other sectors. This is clearly evident for the recycling and remanufacturing services examined by Joyce Cooper, Randall Jackson and Nancey Green Leigh (Chapter 14), and also for the case of the water management systems discussed by Frank Bruinsma and Mark Bokhorst (Chapter 15). Indeed, as environmental concerns move up the policy and competition agendas, the challenges and opportunities afforded by the emerging systems and services within resource-based sectors will become increasingly relevant for a wider range of sectors than the resource-based industries themselves.

Part V analyses different types of knowledge-related and network-based activities. It is now widely accepted that knowledge-related activities, sectors and modes of operation dominate the economies of developed economies, and increasingly so also in newly industrializing economies. Moreover, the geography of knowledge activities is complex, with many knowledge-related activities appearing on the one hand to be rather 'sticky' in certain places, exactly as Kristy Buzard and Gerald Carlino (Chapter 16) observe for US research and development activities, while also increasingly dispersed internationally via outsourcing and offshoring, exactly as described in the Latin American case by Elsie Echeverri-Carroll (Chapter 17). These spatial transitions reflect complex changes in the spatial patterns of communication possibilities and opportunities as mediated by key sectors such as the global airline industry. As Aisling Reynolds-Feighan (Chapter 18) demonstrates, the geography of these interaction and communication services exhibits clear hub-and-spoke-type features, leading to knowledge-related core and periphery structures which favour certain locations over others. As Hong Shangqin, Philip McCann and Les Oxley argue, (Chapter 19), this means that small and isolated regions face immense challenges in today's global economy, irrespective of the quality of the local and institutional environment and policy-setting arena. As national and international knowledge networks evolve, changing regional knowledge systems may also lead to newly emerging activities even within largely the same geographical and industrial structure, as is clearly documented for the case of Italy by Fiorenza Belussi and Lisa De Propris (Chapter 20).

Geography and industry are interrelated in many different ways, and the significant analytical and empirical developments over the last two decades have pushed our understanding forward markedly. However, as we move forward, more questions become uncovered, many of which are difficult to answer using orthodox models alone. In particular, different industries and firm types exhibit very different behaviour in terms of economic geography, and these are differences which are difficult to capture or categorize simply in terms of broad dichotomies such as the distinctions between urban and rural regions, or between diversified or specialized regions. Moreover, as globalization continues, the heterogeneity of places implies that many of these differences may well increase rather than decrease, and without a detailed understanding of the industries and firms we are dealing with, it is very difficult to generalize. Rather, a more varied and interdisciplinary approach is able to offer new insights and ways forward for understanding these relationships and as such, a more heterodox approach can complement more formal and orthodox approaches. This Handbook makes progress towards these goals by providing detailed industry-based analyses of the economic geography issues facing different sectors, and the impacts of different technologies, institutions and transaction cost challenges on the behaviour of the firms.

NOTE

1. For a history of the Industry Studies Association, see http://www.industrystudies.org.

REFERENCES

Anselin, L. (1988), *Spatial Econometrics: Methods and Models*, Dordrecht: Kluwer Academic.
Best, M.H. (1990), *The New Competition: Institutions of Restructuring*, Cambridge: Polity press.
Chinitz, B. (1961), 'Contrast in agglomeration: New York and Pittsburgh', *American Economic Review*, **51**, 279–89.
Dunning, J.H. (ed.) (2000), *Regions, Globalization, and the Knowledge-Based Economy*, Oxford: Oxford University Press.
Glaeser, E.L., Kallal, H.D., Scheinkman, J.A. and Shleifer, A. (1992), 'Growth in cities', *Journal of Political Economy*, **100**, 1126–52.
Hoover, E.M. (1948), *The Location of Economic Activity*, New York: McGraw-Hill.
Isard, W. and Kuenne, R.E. (1953), 'The impact of steel upon the Greater New York–Philadelphia industrial region', *Review of Economics and Statistics*, **35**, 289–301.
Krugman, P. (1991), *Geography and Trade*, MIT Press, Cambridge, MA: MIT Press.
Lichtenberg, R.M. (1960), *One-Tenth of a Nation*, Cambridge, MA: Harvard University Press.
McCann, P. (2008), 'Globalization and economic geography: the world is curved, not flat', *Cambridge Journal of Regions, Economy and Society*, **1** (3), 351–70.
Melitz, M.J. (2003), 'The impact of trade on intra-industry reallocations and aggregate industry productivity', *Econometrica*, **71** (6), 1695–725.
Nelson, R.R. and Winter, S.G. (1982), *An Evolutionary Theory of Economic Change*, Cambridge, MA: Belknap Press of Harvard University Press.
Piore, M.J. and Sabel, C.F. (1984), *The Second Industrial Divide: Possibilities for Prosperity*, New York: Basic Books.
Pitelis, C. (ed.) (1993), *Transactions Costs, Markets and Hierarchies*, Oxford: Blackwell.
Porter, M.E. (1990), *The Competitive Advantage of Nations*, New York: Free Press.

Scott, A.J. (1998), *New Industrial Spaces*, London: Pion.
Vernon, R. (1960), *Metropolis 1985*, Cambridge, MA: Harvard University Press.
Williamson, O.E. and Winter, S.G. (eds) (1991), *The Nature of the Firm: Origins, Evolution and Development*, Oxford: Oxford University Press.

PART I

HEAVY INDUSTRIES

1 Steel industry restructuring and location
Frank Giarratani, Ravi Madhavan and Gene Gruver

1.1 INTRODUCTION

Steel matters. As a material, it is critical to the infrastructure of economic development and the consumer durables and capital goods that fuel that development. As an industry, nations have used steel manufacturing as an instrument of economic, social, and regional policies. As an industrial base for regional economies, the steel industry has helped to define the character and identity of great cities. By examining critical periods of restructuring in this industry, the role of economic geography as a competitive factor is readily exposed. Moreover, the consequences of industry restructuring play out dramatically in terms of the well-being of regions. Whether examining the competitive factors linked to location or their consequences for regions, an important basis for explanation is to be found in steelmaking technology and related costs. The analysis offered in this chapter links technology-based competition, demand patterns, and managerial agency to describe and explain the process of restructuring in the American and global steel industries in terms of their economic geography.

Our analysis begins with a very brief explanation about how steel is made in order to help focus attention on some basic locational factors in the industry and provide a basis for explaining the relationship between alternative technologies and competition among steel firms. With this understanding, our analysis is framed by reference to long trends in industry restructuring as they play out for the geography of production in the United States. Subsequent sections of the chapter address the consequences of restructuring in terms of its spatial and regional dimensions. Our thesis is that technology-based competition, demand patterns, and managerial agency have been the primary drivers of the steel industry's fundamental restructuring. There are two related parts to our story: First, in Sections 1.2 to 1.6, we describe the transformation of the American steel industry in terms of the shift from the dominance of integrated steel to that of minimills. This shift in industry dominance was accompanied by a geographical shift away from the historical core of steel production in the Midwest to new locations closer to the growing markets of the South and Southeast. We argue that this dual shift was driven by an interlinked set of drivers, with technology-enabled changes in competition and the geographical displacement of demand being primary. The technology effects manifested themselves via two distinct pathways: changes in cost structures brought about by scrap-based steel production, and impacts on competition between minimills and integrated producers. However, the visible hand of managerial agency (Chandler, 1993) also played a role, in that decisions and investments by minimill managers – as well as by their counterparts in the integrated mills – served to hasten the shift.

Next, in Sections 1.7 to 1.9, we describe the transformation of the global steel industry which is still underway, in terms of the shift in production and demand from the Triad regions (North America, Europe, and Japan) to the rest of the world, and the rise of the steel multinational corporation (MNC) mainly through mergers and acquisitions (M&As). This shift, in turn, was driven by the same set of three factors, the most important of which were changes in demand patterns (manifested in the rise of China) and managerial innovation facilitated by new information technologies. The technology driver in this instance was not a production technology, but rather advanced information systems that greatly increased the geographical distance over which steel enterprises could be effectively managed. Managerial agency was manifested this time in aggressive growth seeking by steel firm managers, as they engaged in global M&A deals and other expansion efforts, in many cases newly energized by worldwide liberalization and privatization trends. Thus, the dramatic restructuring of the steel industry in the United States and also globally can be interpreted through the lens of technology-based competition, demand patterns, and managerial agency. Section 1.10 concludes.

1.2   MAKING STEEL

In many parts of the world, and certainly in popular images, steelmaking is defined by massive plant complexes that process material, beginning with iron ore, into semifinished steel products that are sold to other manufacturers or service centers for further processing. This image is true for part of the industry, but a competing recycling technology also helps to define the modern steel industry, especially in the United States, where more than one-half of all manufactured steel results from recycling ferrous scrap.

The concept of vertical integration in the steel industry was pioneered by Andrew Carnegie in the late nineteenth century. In 1890, the Carnegie Steel Company already included substantial holdings in coal, the primary energy source of steelmaking at that time, and Carnegie began to move, slowly at first, to acquire interests in the other key raw material, namely iron ore (Wall, 1989, p. 587). By the end of that century, Carnegie Steel also tied materials acquisition to manufacturing with its own extensive railway interests (ibid., p. 623).

Today, the concept of an 'integrated' steel company no longer relates to complete ownership in materials, transportation, and manufacturing, as it did for Carnegie. However, the fundamental process of integrated steelmaking remains largely unchanged in the sense that mill complexes include materials processing and iron- and steelmaking. Figure 1.1 shows a simple schematic of the integrated steelmaking process. The actual conversion of iron ore takes place in a blast furnace that uses coke as a reduction agent and a basic source of energy. The ore used in the blast furnace takes one of two forms: 'pellets' that are produced near the iron mine or 'sinter' produced at the steel mill by heating finely crushed iron ore along with coke powder and limestone (Hall, 1997, pp. 4–5). However, iron pellets are by far the largest form of iron used today in integrated mills (USGS, 1998). Blast furnaces are closed pressurized vessels that are designed to run continuously for years at a time. Depending on its design, the capacity of a blast furnace may be from 1.5 million to more than 3 million tons per year, and scale economies in such furnaces are critically important. The crude 'pig iron' produced in this process is transferred in molten form to the integrated mill's steelmaking operations, where carbon levels are reduced in a basic oxygen furnace or 'BOF'. In turn, while still in molten form, steel is moved in ladles from the BOF to secondary steelmaking facilities where steel

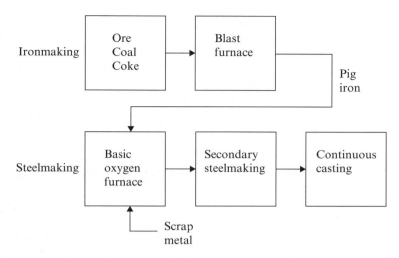

Figure 1.1   Integrated steelmaking schematic

chemistries and carbon content can be tightly controlled for specific end uses. Steel takes its first solid form in continuous casting operations, where the cast product is committed to flat shapes (slabs used to make steel sheet or plates) or long shapes (billets or blooms, which have cross-sections that are more nearly square or round).

The contrast between an integrated steel process and the alternative steel recycling process, which relies on the electric arc furnace (EAF), is dramatic, both in terms of complexity and, typically, the scale of operations. As shown in Figure 1.2, this alternative technology is much more direct. EAFs use post-consumer scrap metal such as old automobiles and appliances, and scrap metal which has been cast off in the manufacturing of steel products of many kinds. By melting the scrap metal from such sources, EAF producers recover steel that can be used to compete directly with ore-based mills.

The growth of electric furnace steelmaking in North America began to increase dramatically in the 1970s, and this was coincident with very important efficiency gains in this technology (Barnett and Crandall, 1986, pp. 56–7). The price of scrap metal was very low at that time, and it gave scrap-based producers a significant cost advantage in certain

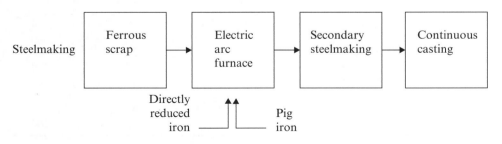

Figure 1.2   EAF steelmaking schematic

product lines. In the decades to follow, the scale of many electric furnaces in terms of annual capacities increased to over one million tons, which approaches the lower end of the capacity range of integrated steelmaking. Moreover, as experience has increased with electric furnaces and technologies have advanced, it has become common for the furnace 'charge' or input mix to include directly reduced iron (DRI) or pig iron. Input substitution between ferrous scrap and DRI or pig iron has greatly increased the product range of EAF producers by allowing them to more closely control the level of impurities in the scrap-based steels they produce.

1.3   LONG-TERM TRENDS IN INDUSTRY RESTRUCTURING

Perspectives on developments in steel technologies, such as the advancement of electric furnace steel production, and the competitive forces that they help to shape can be gained by reference to long-term trends in the economic geography of American steel production. The historical geographical core of steel production is defined by three state-based districts: Pennsylvania, including, of course, Pittsburgh, where integrated steelmaking began in the United States; Illinois–Indiana, where Chicago-Gary is by far the largest production center; and Ohio, especially the areas bordering the Great Lakes near Cleveland. The overriding core–periphery trend in American steel production is unambiguous. Table 1.1 shows that the historical core region's share of total steel production has declined monotonically for many decades, as the population and overall American manufacturing activity shifted southward and westward. However, while this trend in steel production is evident, the factors underlying it have evolved in terms of the technology and the nature of competition.

In the years immediately after the Second World War, the explanation for the historical core region's declining share meant, in practical terms, explaining why it was that Pennsylvania, and Pittsburgh in particular, was losing its share of national steel production. As indicated in Table 1.1, from 1940 to 1970 the historical core region's share of steel production declined from 72 to 62 percent, with Pennsylvania accounting for seven points of the 10-point decline over this 30-year period.

Table 1.1   Regional percentage shares of US steel production, 1940–2008

	OH	PA	IL–IN	Historical core region subtotal	All other states	Total (%)
1940	21	30	21	72	28	100
1950	19	28	20	68	32	100
1960	17	24	22	64	36	100
1970	16	23	23	62	38	100
1980	14	21	26	61	39	100
1990	17	12	29	58	42	100
2000	16	7	29	52	48	100
2008	15	6	29	50	50	100

Source: American Iron and Steel Institute (various years).

Pittsburgh's early advantage in American steelmaking in the mid- to late-nineteenth century was based on its proximity to Western Pennsylvania's coal resources as well as to the market position that Pittsburgh enjoyed when railroad systems began to move westward. Pittsburgh's distance from the source of the other great transferrable resource needed in steel production, namely iron ore, was of little disadvantage when integrated steelmaking began. North American iron ore travels primarily by boat or barge from mining areas in Michigan and Minnesota, and the transportation cost differentials related to iron ore simply did not offset the enormous advantage that Pittsburgh enjoyed by its proximity to metallurgical coking coal (Pittsburgh Regional Planning Association, 1963, p. 262). The other major steel-producing regions at the time in Ohio and Illinois–Indiana, all of which were located on the Great Lakes, had superior water access to iron ore, but suffered relative to Pittsburgh in their proximity to sources of coking coal.

Based on this historical advantage, explanations for Pennsylvania's relative decline focused on two sources: changes in technology that reduced the locational cost advantage in eastern production centers; and changes in the spatial distribution of the market. Isard and Capron (1949) explain the cost side by very substantial progress in fuel efficiencies that reduced the amount of coke required in blast furnaces to produce pig iron. This weakened the advantage of production centers, such as Pittsburgh, that are located close to the sources of coking coal (see also the Pittsburgh Regional Planning Association, 1963, p. 273). The market disadvantage of production centers in Pennsylvania and other eastern regions is also recognized as an important locational consideration by Isard and Capron (1949, p. 126) and by the Pittsburgh Regional Planning Association (1963, p. 278). Later, Hekman (1978) argues that changes in the geographical distribution of the market are the most important basis for explaining changes in the distribution of steel production among regions.

An argument can also be made that the effect of market growth on steel plant capacities in the Midwest was enhanced by the weakening and ultimate demise of basing-point pricing in the steel industry. Under basing-point pricing, steel customers pay the F.O.B ('free on board' or 'mill' price) price at a given steel plant plus transportation costs from a predetermined geographical basing point to the customer's plant location. Pittsburgh pricing, which prevailed until a Federal Trade Commission ruling in 1924, set the transport costs on the basis of the customer's distance from Pittsburgh – regardless of where the steel was actually produced. After that date the number of basing points used by the industry expanded to include Chicago and other cities (Rogers, 2009, p. 66), but the practice was not entirely eliminated until 1948 (Marengo, 1955, p. 509). The ability of Pittsburgh's mills to compete in markets located at the periphery of its market region was eroded when other cities were included in the multiple basing-point system. As the system was eliminated those other cities also lost the implicit market protection offered by this system. Consequently, the competitive position of steel plants located in distant regions was enhanced in geographical markets adjacent to their operations because of lower transportation costs, and the lower cost of delivered steel in these markets facilitated growth in steel-consuming operations.

While these geographical shifts were taking place after the Second World War, major investment decisions were undertaken by steelmakers in the United States and abroad that would profoundly affect the competitive balance among firms in years to come. The BOF, which is today a standard technology, emerged in the 1950s to compete with the dominant technology of that time, the open hearth (OH) furnace. Major expansions in steelmaking capacity were made in the United States, Europe, and Japan in the immediate post-war period. Throughout the 1950s, investments in new capacity in the United States were being made in OH furnaces; over 39 million net tons of OH capacity were added during that decade out of a total US capacity of 139 million tons (Hall, 1997, p. 40). In contrast, European and Japanese steelmakers invested in the emerging technology, BOF. A decade later, it was apparent that the BOF was superior, and OH furnaces began to be phased out of production worldwide.

Many factors, including investments in OH furnaces, combined during the 1950s and the 1960s to weaken the competitiveness of integrated steelmakers in the United States, and this long saga is well documented elsewhere (see, for example, Tiffany, 1988). Among these factors, labor issues were very important. In effect, the large integrated steel firms purchased labor peace at a very high price in the sense that negotiated labor settlements built in substantial cost disadvantages based on hourly rates, work rules, and retirement benefits (Hoerr, 1988, pp. 77–81; Hall, 1997, pp. 45–9). 'Big steel' emerged from all of this as being especially vulnerable to competition from foreign producers, and in 1960, the United States, which was still a major world producer, became a net importer of raw steel. In addition, anemic growth in steel demand after the Second World War along with the maturation of infrastructure investment in the United States (see Barnett and Crandall, 1986, p. 97) limited the opportunity to build new plants embodying new technology, without the closure of existing integrated mills.

Ironically, the replacement of OH furnaces with BOFs also helped to spur the growth of a new set of domestic competitors for US integrated steel producers. The OH technology, which accounted for the largest share of steel production in the United States through the 1960s, could accept up to 50 percent ferrous scrap in the furnace charge. While superior in other ways, BOFs by comparison could accept only much smaller amounts of scrap metal, and relied much more heavily on the pig iron generated by blast furnaces. Thus, the replacement of OH furnaces by BOFs in the 1960s drove down the market price of ferrous scrap. Small, independent steel producers emerged to take advantage of low scrap prices by using EAF technology, and these American 'minimills' would reshape the economic geography of steel production in North America.

Also in the 1950s, concern by integrated steel firms with the depletion of high-grade iron ore deposits stimulated major investments that further tied integrated firms to ore-based technologies. Costly investments were made in 'pelletizing' operations that could bring low-grade ores up to the high iron content levels necessary for steelmaking. In addition, integrated firms invested heavily to secure access to high-grade ores, especially in Canada and South America (Hall, 1997, p. 39). As a consequence of these locationally fixed investments, integrated firms were less able to respond to the opportunities presented by emerging scrap-based furnace production.

In addition to the technological and economic factors discussed so far, managerial factors also played a key role. Christensen (2000) has provided a rich analysis of the key managerial factors that may have differentiated between minimills and integrated producers in terms of their response to EAF technology. In Christensen's account, EAF technology was a 'disruptive' technology, one key characteristic of which is that, at its inception, it is markedly inferior to the prevailing technologies. In the case of EAF steelmaking, as indicated earlier, it was initially hard to control the chemical qualities of the steel produced, because the scrap that went into the furnace often varied in its metallurgical composition. Thus, the only markets open to EAF products were low-end applications, such as the production of construction industry rebars. In contrast, more demanding applications such as automotive steel required more precise control of chemical qualities. Focusing on their high value-added customers, integrated producers chose to cede the lower-end markets to minimills employing EAF technology. Given their lower cost structure, minimill companies were able to serve even the lower-end markets profitably.

However, a crucial characteristic of disruptive technology is that it gets better over time (ibid.). Bolstered by their profits, and incentivized by the prospect of moving upmarket, minimills such as Nucor and Chaparral worked hard to improve steel quality, as well as investing in the equipment to make larger shapes. By the mid-1980s, they had captured not only the entire rebar market, but also the lion's share of the market for bars, rods, and angles. Once again, constrained by their cost disadvantages and by the preferences of their existing customers, integrated producers retrenched from those markets, and now focused only on flat steel products that demanded the highest levels of purity. Christensen's analysis brings to light the process through which rational managerial decisions in response to real technological, economic, and customer pressures, led to the ascendancy of the minimill.

1.4 TECHNOLOGY-BASED COMPETITION AND INDUSTRY RESTRUCTURING

The profound effect of the minimill phenomenon on the economic geography of American steel manufacturing is revealed by reference to the long trends shown in Table 1.1. In the 30-year period from 1970 to 2000, the historical core region's share of national steel production declined by a further 10 percentage points, just as it had in the previous 30-year period. In the more recent period, however, integrated steelmakers were challenged by competitors on two fronts, both domestic and foreign, and Pennsylvania's declining share shows the consequences. By the end of the twentieth century, a steel era had ended, as Pennsylvania's share of national steel production declined from 23 to 7 percent, and at the same time, a rough parity in regional shares between the historical core and other regions ended the very concept of core–periphery distinctions.

The ascendance of EAF technology is evident in Table 1.2, which shows average annual steel production in the United States by furnace type for recent decades. EAF steel production doubled from the decade of the 1960s to the 1970s, and has continued a trajectory of steady growth to the present day – now accounting for well over 50 percent of raw steel production in the United States. OH technology, which was the focus of immediate post-war investments by US integrated steel producers, was phased out rapidly and replaced by BOF technology in the 1960s and 1970s. By the 1980s, OH furnaces were obsolete. Perhaps the most dramatic change revealed by Table 1.2 is the major decline observed in total steel production from the 1970s to the 1980s, all of which is accounted for by integrated steel firms.

The restructuring in the steel industry that is implied by these data – decline by ore-based integrated firms and growth by scrap-based EAF firms – has had a profound

*Table 1.2   Steel production by furnace type: average annual production for each decade,
1960s–2000s (millions of net tons)*

	Open hearth	Basic oxygen	Electric arc	Total (all furnaces)
1960–69	82.3*	24.4	13.0	119.7
1970–79	30.0	76.3	26.3	132.6
1980–89	6.9	56.0	31.3	94.2
1990–99	0.5	59.1	41.8	101.4
2000–08	0.0	49.7	55.7	105.4

Note: * Includes a small amount of production from Bessemer furnaces, which were completely
decommissioned in the United States by 1968.

Source: American Iron and Steel Institute (various years).

effect on the economic geography of US steel production. The 1981–82 economic recession experienced in the United States triggered a series of major plant closures and
capacity adjustments that reflected long-term strategic decisions taken by integrated
steelmakers. In 1974, 45 ore-based plants produced non-specialty steel, and by 1991,
ore-based capacity had been eliminated in 22 of these plants (Beeson and Giarratani,
1998, p. 425). Most of the plants involved were permanently closed; four remained open,
but only with EAF capacity. Mirroring the production data presented in Table 1.2, the
capacity of ore-based steel plants has also dropped very substantially in recent periods.
From 1974 to 1991, total ore-based furnace capacity decreased from 140.5 to 76 million
tons per year, a decline of 45.9 percent (ibid., p. 435).

Figure 1.3 shows the way that these reductions played out in terms of the spatial distribution of ore-based steelmaking capacity by focusing on total BOF capacity in state-
based regions during the 1970s, 1980s, and 1990s. Sharp declines in northeastern regions
(Regions 4 and 10) and in the West (Region 9) contrast vividly with relatively stable
capacity in other places, especially in the upper Midwest (Regions 1, 2, and 3).

The observed geographical patterns of ore-based capacity change are best understood
in terms of a partitioning of the product markets for steel. As explained by Ahlbrandt et
al. (1996), in the process of restructuring, ore-based integrated producers largely focused
the capacity of their plants toward flat products (steel slabs) and eliminated their capacities to produce long products (steel billets and blooms). At the time of this partitioning,
with a very small number of exceptions, the product range of EAF plants was limited to
the billets and blooms necessary to fashion products such as construction beams, steel
rods, and reinforcement bars. The cost advantage of EAF producers forced ore-based
integrated producers out of these markets, except in circumstances where the ore-based
firm produced bars or other long products with special characteristics in term of hard-
ness or other attributes that were beyond the metallurgical range of EAF mills (Barnett
and Crandall, 1986; Christensen, 2000). Inter-firm competition is not static, however,
and the relentless incursion of EAF producers into the markets served by integrated
firms continues to the present day.

The location of automobile plants and auto parts suppliers was an important consideration in restructuring by integrated steelmakers. In the 1980s, EAF producers had

Capacity (millions of tons)			
Region	1970s	1980s	1990s
1	22.1	22.6	23.6
2	11.4	9.9	7.7
3	15.3	14.5	15.8
4	15.1	11.7	4.0
5	0.0	0.0	0.0
6	9.7	4.8	3.5
7	6.5	6.5	6.0
8	4.0	3.7	3.2
9	5.1	1.0	2.5
10	8.9	4.8	3.9
11	0.0	0.0	0.0

No steel production

Source: Center for Industry Studies (2003).

Figure 1.3   *BOF capacity in state-based regions: annual average capacity in each decade, 1970s, 1980s and 1990s (millions of tons)*

limited or no access to the markets for automotive steel, and BOF producers made capacity decisions accordingly. Plant locations in Illinois–Indiana and Ohio served the strategic needs of integrated producers and the evidence for this is clear in Figure 1.3. The very dramatic declines in BOF capacities in Pennsylvania and other states are a consequence of the exit by integrated firms from the markets for long products, and the growth or stability in BOF capacities elsewhere. These are a consequence of the focus by integrated firms on the markets for flat products, and especially for steel sheet that is shipped in coils to manufacture automobiles and other goods (Beeson and Giarratani, 1998).

1.5   STEEL MINIMILLS AND INDUSTRY RESTRUCTURING

While the transport costs of materials and finished products are important in determining the profitability of steel minimills in the same way that these factors are important to integrated mills, the basic transferrable input used by minimills, which is ferrous scrap, is much more widely distributed than the iron ore and coking coal required by integrated mills. This suggests that regions where ferrous scrap is in surplus would be especially attractive for minimill locations, given the proximity of a plant location to product markets. It also suggests that transportation infrastructure, such as rail networks and barge access for scrap, and trucking for finished steel, will be important factors in plant

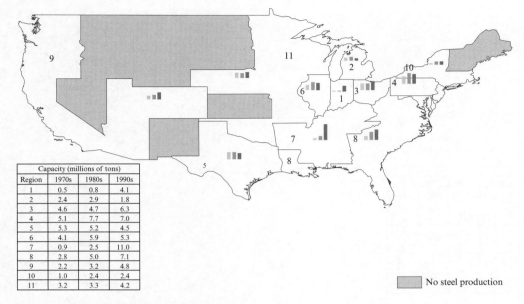

Capacity (millions of tons)			
Region	1970s	1980s	1990s
1	0.5	0.8	4.1
2	2.4	2.9	1.8
3	4.6	4.7	6.3
4	5.1	7.7	7.0
5	5.3	5.2	4.5
6	4.1	5.9	5.3
7	0.9	2.5	11.0
8	2.8	5.0	7.1
9	2.2	3.2	4.8
10	1.0	2.4	2.4
11	3.2	3.3	4.2

No steel production

Source: Center for Industry Studies (2003).

Figure 1.4   EAF capacity in state-based regions: annual average capacity in each decade, 1970s, 1980s and 1990s (millions of tons)

location. Furthermore, substantial electricity is required for scrap-based steel production, and the price of electricity is also a key locational factor.

Figure 1.4 shows the capacity of scrap-based steel production (EAF producers) in state-based regions during the 1970s, 1980s, and 1990s. In sharp contrast to the pattern observed for ore-based steel production (BOF producers), scrap-based plant capacity is widely dispersed and is steady or growing in most regions. Very substantial decade-to-decade growth is found in several regions, and especially in the southern and southeastern states – see Regions 7 and 8.

The contrast in locational patterns for ore- and scrap-based producers is displayed vividly in Figure 1.5, which maps specific plant locations for each technology in 2003.

One remarkable implication of EAF capacity growth is that it has changed the very concept of a 'steel region' in the United States. For most readers, the fact that the northeast corner of Arkansas, a very rural state, is home to one of the largest steel-producing counties would come as a great surprise. Yet, this location along the Mississippi River can claim two large scrap-based EAF steel mills and has a total steelmaking capacity that is greater than the current steelmaking capacity in all of Pennsylvania. Moreover, the plant capacity in Arkansas was built on two greenfield sites with one startup in 1987, Nucor-Yamato Steel Company in Blytheville, AR, and a second in 1992, Nucor Steel's facility in Hickman, AR. In order to understand this phenomenon fully, it is important to appreciate the process by which scrap-based EAF producers emerged as formidable competitors with ore-based integrated mills.

Although electric furnace steel production has a much longer history, the beginning

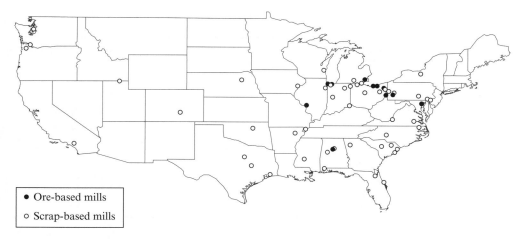

Source: Center for Industry Studies (2003).

Figure 1.5   Location of steel plants in the United States, 2003

of the market insurgence by steel minimills in the United States can be dated to the late 1950s and the early 1960s when a small number of firms used the cost advantages they enjoyed from scrap-based manufacturing to produce reinforcement bars for concrete used in the construction industry (Hall, 1997, pp. 154–7). The plants involved were often at the periphery of the market areas served by integrated steel producers and were buffered from competition by advantage in transportation costs (Barnett and Crandall, 1986, p. 19). In these locations, minimills enjoyed very significant advantages in production costs: ferrous scrap was abundant, easily accessible, and available at low prices; EAF mills had very low capital costs relative to integrated mills; and electricity costs were low (Ahlbrandt et al., 1996) in the peripheral locations. These advantages, and most particularly low capital costs, allowed minimills to exploit highly local markets for steel products in small-scale plants.

The most formidable challenges to ore-based producers began in the latter part of the 1960s and the 1970s, when minimill producers began building on their success and reinvesting profits to replicate successful mills within a multi-plant firm structure. Florida Steel Corporation began this pattern, while retaining its focus on producing steel products for the local construction markets (Hall, 1997, pp. 158–9). Nucor Steel was among the market entrants that followed the multi-plant pattern, but along with several other minimill producers, Nucor began to scale up plant capacities, to extend its product range beyond construction steels, and to serve much wider market areas (Barnett and Crandall, 1986, p. 19). Expansions in scale, product range, and geographical markets placed EAF producers such as Nucor in direct competition with integrated firms, and continuously improving EAF technologies added to the advantages of these insurgent firms over time. Beeson and Giarratani (1998) provide statistical evidence linking reductions in ore-based capacities across space and the closure of integrated plants directly to this minimill challenge.

The transformation of minimills from small-scale plants serving local markets to

Table 1.3   Size distribution of US steel minimills by plant capacity, 1978 and 2003

Plant capacity (thousands of tons)	1978 (no. of minimill plants)	2003 (no. of minimill plants)
1,000 or more	3	22
800–999	4	10
600–799	4	15
400–599	9	13
200–399	13	4
Less than 200	11	1
Total number of minimill plants	44	65
Total minimill plant capacity	20,293	61,089
Average minimill plant capacity	461	940
Median minimill plant capacity	350	750

Source: Center for Industry Studies (2003).

larger-scale plants serving broad markets explains the patterns observed in Figure 1.4, and this is plainly evident in Table 1.3, which documents the size distribution of minimills in 1978 and 2003. Over this period, the number of minimills increased by nearly 50 percent and total minimill capacity tripled. Median plant capacity increases from 350 thousand tons per year in 1978 to 750 thousand tons per year in 2003, and the average plant capacity begins to approach one million tons by the end of the period. Indeed, in 2003, nearly one-third of existing minimills have an annual capacity of one million or more tons.

1.6   MINIMILL COST ADVANTAGES

An important part of the cost advantage enjoyed by minimills was their early adoption of 'continuous casting' technology. In most modern mills, steel takes its first solid form only as it passes from the secondary steelmaking operations in a mill through to a continuous caster. The earlier technology required pouring molten steel into casts to create ingots that could be placed in an inventory for later use. Transforming ingots into billets, blooms, or slabs required re-melting before further processing in separate rolling mills. The costs of capital and energy required for ingot casting and re-melting are very substantial, whereas continuous casting is much more cost effective.

Scrap-based minimills began adopting continuous casting in the early 1960s, and the technology quickly became standard for minimills as EAF capacity expanded. By comparison, integrated mills adopted the technology only with a very substantial time lag, due in part to the challenges imposed by casting slabs at large volume (Warren, 2001, p. 256). Further, integrated producers may have experienced lock-in effects from the geography of their prior commitments: for example, at its Mon Valley plant, US Steel was constrained by the need to work with a furnace and a rolling mill which were situated 10 miles apart, a configuration which was consistent with existing casting technology (Ghemawat, 1997). The net result of this difference in adoption rates was a direct cost saving for minimills that may have approached \$40–\$50 per ton of steel (Rogers, 2009, p. 132).

Beyond these direct cost savings per ton, continuous casting technology was also a linchpin for the introduction of modern manufacturing techniques to the American steel industry. Ahlbrandt et al. (1996, pp. 89–90) explain that by investing simultaneously in continuous casting technology, human capital, and human resource practices that encourage the decentralization of decision making on the shop floor, steel manufacturers were taking advantage of important complementarities that had a tremendous impact on productivity. The basis for these gains was laid out clearly by Womack et al. (1990). In this widely read book on the automobile industry, the authors show how the elimination of inventories in production lines enables a process of lean manufacturing that provides a basis for substantial efficiency gains and quality improvements. The introduction of continuous casting in the steel industry had exactly these effects, and by doing so it enhanced the importance of human resource considerations in plant location decisions.

The importance of human resources in the link between technology and production efficiency is highlighted by the experience of Nucor Steel, which has served as a model for many other firms in the way that it ties together technology, human resources, and the process of production to enhance its competitiveness (Ghemawat, 1995, 1997). The heart of Nucor's labor model is a 'pay-for-performance' system keyed to quality-based production, but this is embedded in a much larger corporate culture that decentralizes decision making and encourages a 'get-it-done' approach to problem solving (Ahlbrandt et al., 1996, pp. 74–8). Nucor is not the only steelmaker with these characteristics, but its influence on the industry has been very important, and the kind of high-performance workplace that Nucor and other firms apply can result in substantial productivity gains (Ichniowski et al., 1997).

Minimill producers striving to implement Nucor-like work systems place a premium on labor flexibility in terms of cross-skilling. For example, most of these firms rely on a very limited number of job categories, so that workers in a given category have and use a number of different skills across a wide range of tasks. On a given day one worker might spend part of the day monitoring process controls and another part of the same day in maintenance activities. Because of the emphasis on decentralization in decision making, problem solving is valued and encouraged. This labor model encourages minimills to seek locations for new plants where workers could be trained in a flexible work environment. While many minimills are non-union and others are unionized, the spatial distribution of these producers strongly favors 'right-to-work' states.

The management of human resources was not the only area in which minimills followed sophisticated approaches that enhanced their competitive advantage. Staying with the example of Nucor, another key factor was the efficient management of capital, which was critical in the capital-intensive steel industry (Ghemawat, 1997). During its period of growth, Nucor demonstrated a cadence of building or rebuilding one plant a year, acting as its own general contractor in each instance. This approach provided not only significant knowledge spillovers in between plant construction and operations, but also superior capital efficiency, allowing Nucor to build its first thin-slab caster for an investment estimated to be 25 percent less than it would have cost its rivals, and to achieve an operating break-even point a year and a half sooner (ibid.).

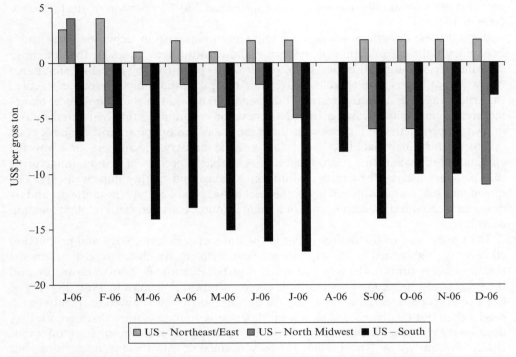

Source: Management Science Associates' (MSA) Raw Material Data Aggregation Service™ (RMDAS): http://rmdasindex.msa.com/.

Figure 1.6   Regional price differentials based on the RMDAS™ ferrous scrap price index: monthly price for prompt industrial composite, 2006 (delivered price – US weighted average)

In addition to labor factors, the locational cost advantage of EAF mills depends especially on the availability and price of ferrous scrap, which is the primary transferrable input for EAF steelmaking (Giarratani et al., 2006). Figure 1.6 shows clearly the cost advantage enjoyed by minimills away from the core Northeast and Midwest. Along with the lower electricity prices pointed out earlier, this factor further reinforced the attractiveness of production locations in what was previously the periphery. See Gruver and Giarratani (2005) for an analysis of the economic geography of ferrous scrap prices in the United States.

A summary of our key arguments is appropriate here as we conclude this Section. Over the decades, the regional structure of the American steel industry changed drastically as a result of three interacting drivers. The evolution of EAF technology changed the relative cost positions of industry players, propelling a significant growth in minimills. Economic growth in the South led to new markets for steel in areas which were away from the traditional industrial clusters of the Midwest, and minimills were able to situate themselves closer to those markets. Managerial agency intervened in the form of aggressive growth seeking by minimill firms such as Nucor, and a corresponding tendency on the part of integrated producers to retrench away from markets that were targeted by the minimills. Thus, technology-based competition, demand shifts, and managerial agency worked jointly to bring about the regional shifts we described in the American steel industry.

In order to provide the global context to our story, we now turn to the restructuring of the world steel industry. In addition to merely providing the context, however, we find that the same three drivers may explain the global restructuring that is currently underway. Demand shifts away from the Triad markets (US, Japan, and Europe), new information technologies that facilitate worldwide managerial coordination, and aggressive managers seeking to reconfigure the industry to their own advantage, were the three major drivers of the steel industry's globalization, much as they were in the case of the American steel industry.

1.7   THE GLOBAL DISPERSION OF DEMAND

Observers have noted that there have been three eras in the history of the global steel industry (for example, Laplace Conseil, 2003): the pre-war national era; the period from the Second World War to the 1970s' oil crisis; and the period since 1973, which is often viewed as culminating in the globalization of the steel industry. Two key developments underlying the globalization of the industry were liberalization (the freeing of political and strategic restrictions) and the attendant privatization of steel companies. Historically, governments around the world tended to heavily support their domestic steel producers, reflecting both concerns about preserving employment in a sector with powerful labor unions, and the entrenched view that the steel industry was 'strategic' for industrial and military reasons. In the 1980s, 60 percent of the world's steelmaking capacity was government owned (Wall Street Journal, 2005). Subsequently, however, reflecting the *zeitgeist* of liberalization as well as inability to continue to bear the economic costs of inefficient government-owned plants, much of this capacity was privatized, thereby bringing government ownership down to 40 percent of capacity by 2005 (ibid.). In the Triad nations, where government ownership was less of a factor, bankruptcy and restructuring facilitated the shedding of legacy costs such as pension obligations, leading quickly to the emergence of a robust global market for steel assets.

While the large-scale liberation of steel companies from government ownership and/ or the political strictures that kept them domestically oriented and owned was an important factor, the globalization of the industry is most apparent, however, if we examine the changes in the global demand patterns. In 1960, the United States accounted for 26 percent of world steel markets, and the Triad nations for 56 percent (Old, 1985). Parallel to the core-to-periphery shift noted earlier within the American steel industry, the world industry has also undergone a massive structural shift in terms of the geographical location of steel production, as we see in Figures 1.7 and 1.8.

Two observations are worth making here. Figure 1.7 demonstrates compellingly that Asia is now the center of gravity of steel production, accounting for over 60 percent of all steel produced. Figure 1.8 breaks down the Asian numbers even further, pinpointing simultaneously, the relatively stable role of Japan, the massive growth in China, and the significant room for growth in India. The well-known geo-economic shifts that comprise the slowing of growth in the Triad and the emergence of growth markets elsewhere (and

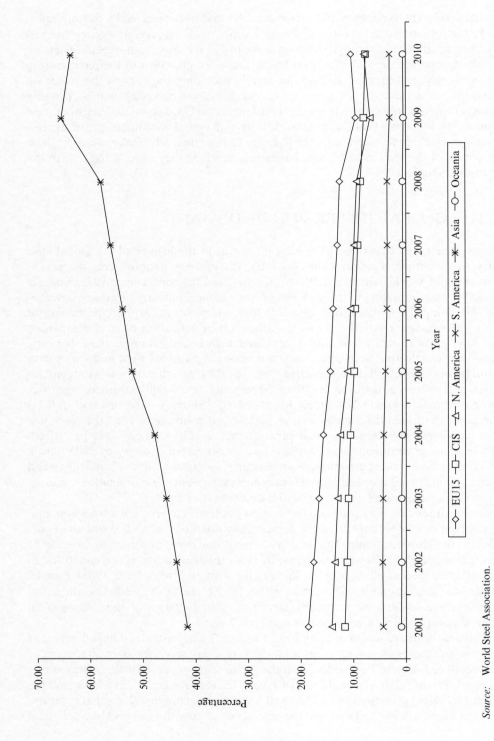

Source: World Steel Association.

Figure 1.7 The shift to Asia: crude steel production share across world regions

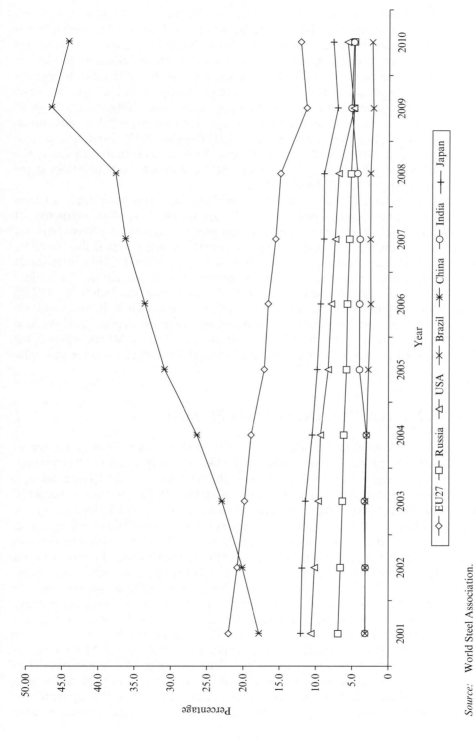

Source: World Steel Association.

Figure 1.8 The rise of China: crude steel production share in key markets

particularly the BRIICS nations of Brazil, Russia, India, Indonesia, China, and South Africa), are clearly the fundamental drivers of the shift toward regions that were hitherto peripheral. In particular, it is useful to note one factor that is here to stay: steel intensity declines in the developed world. Crude steel consumption has stabilized at 400 kg per capita in the developed world, and with low population growth and the shift to service-based economies, this steel intensity is not expected to increase. In contrast, however, China's steel consumption in 2010 was 450 kg per capita, and rising, driven by huge investments in infrastructure. Nor is China's hunger for steel expected to slow down any time soon, as suggested by two yardsticks (BHPBilliton, 2012). First, China's car penetration density in 2010 was 32 cars per thousand persons, compared to 423 in the United States. Second, China has only 32 square meters of urban residential floor space per capita, compared to 73 in the United States.

The second observation is that, as important as China is, this is not entirely a China story. The rest of the developing world (except China) consumed over 400 million tons of steel in 2010, and the 2000–10 average consumption growth rate was 5.6 percent (Arcelor Mittal, 2011). That there is even more room for growth outside China is illustrated by comparing steel intensity numbers. India, which is lagging behind China in terms of infrastructure investment and industrialization, consumed 60 kg per capita. The comparable number for other developing countries (apart from China and India) was 102 kg per capita. With a population base of nearly 5.5 billion, and driven by industrialization and urbanization, the emerging markets are therefore where the demand and demand growth are expected to be. For a firm-level illustration, at Arcelor Mittal, which is the world's largest steel producer, over one-third of current shipments go to the emerging markets (ibid.).

1.8 THE EMERGENCE OF THE STEEL MNC

Accompanying the demand and production shifts from the Triad nations to the emerging markets is the emergence of the steel MNC. Unlike similar or related industries such as aluminum or mining, both of which witnessed the emergence of MNCs decades ago, steel companies are latecomers to multinational operations. In fact, it was the merger of three European national steelmakers to create Arcelor in 2001 that heralded the rise of the large-scale MNC in the steel industry. The adoption of the MNC form can be seen as a natural response to the industry dynamics noted earlier. The large increased demand in China and more generally in Asia combined with the importance of operating on a global scale (global customers and global competition) led to the pressure for consolidation in a fragmented industry (IBM, 2007). Given the powerful economic rationale against creating new capacity in many regions of the world, M&As were the primary means of global expansion for the established steelmakers. Figure 1.9 and Table 1.4 lay out the extent and impact of M&A activity in the global steel industry.

At its peak in 2006–07, the steel industry witnessed a total of 323 M&A transactions over the two years, with a peak in dollar value of close to US$79 billion in 2006 (Figure 1.9). Although the number and size of deals has declined since then, the pace of consolidation continues. Table 1.4 demonstrates that the rankings of the top steel producers have been routinely upset by consolidation deals. For example, Arcelor became

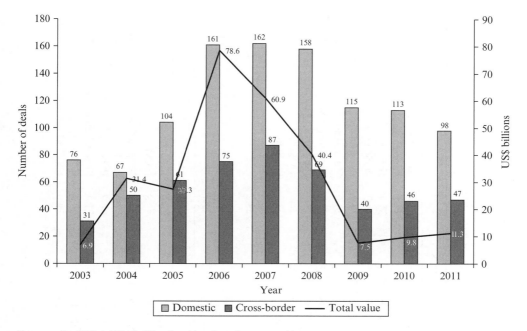

Source: PwC Metal Deals: Forging Ahead, various annual issues.

Figure 1.9   *M&A deal activity in the global steel industry*

the world's Number One steelmaker in 2001 as a direct result of the merger that created it. Similarly, NKK of Japan climbed from 8th position in 2002 to 4th (as JFE) following its merger with Kawasaki Steel. The appearance of new Chinese steelmakers on the top 10 list is also directly attributable to M&A transactions.

Table 1.4 also reminds us that, despite the considerable consolidation that has taken place, the steel industry remains highly fragmented. The total share of production accounted for by the top 10 (that is, C10) has barely changed during this period, in fact declining slightly from 0.25 in 2000 to 0.24 in 2010. By way of a rough comparison, the top five iron ore producers accounted for over 40 percent of the iron ore market (PwC, 2004).

One important implication of the cross-border M&A phenomenon was that the foreign ownership of steelmaking assets became, in reality, a far cry from the past preoccupation with domestic ownership of an industry that was widely held to be strategic in nature. At one point, it was estimated that foreign steelmakers owned 42 percent of steel capacity in the NAFTA region (Blume, 2008).

Thus, M&As played a critical role as an instrument of corporate restructuring that fundamentally reshaped the industry and impelled the emergence of the steel MNC. We view the prevalence of M&As in this context as an expression of managerial agency that took place in the context of demand shifts, but was distinct from it. A counterexample serves to make this point. Tiffany (1987) has noted that US Steel did not pursue the clear opportunity to expand in Europe when that continent's steel plants lay in shambles at

Table 1.4 How megadeals reshaped industry leadership: top 10 steel producers (million metric tonnes)

	2010		2009		2008		2007	
1	ArcelorMittal	98.2	ArcelorMittal	77.5	ArcelorMittal	103.3	ArcelorMittal	116.4
2	Baosteel	37.0	Baosteel	31.3	Nippon Steel	37.5	Nippon Steel	35.7
3	POSCO	35.4	POSCO	31.1	*Baosteel Gp.	35.4	JFE	34.0
4	Nippon Steel	35.0	Nippon Steel	26.5	POSCO	34.7	POSCO	31.1
5	JFE	31.1	JFE	25.8	Hebei Steel Gp.	33.3	Baosteel Gp.	28.6
6	Jiangsu Shagang	23.2	Jiangsu Shagang	20.5	JFE	33.0	*Tata Steel	26.5
7	Tata Steel	23.2	Tata Steel	20.5	Wuhan Steel Gp.	27.7	Anshan-Benxi	23.6
8	US Steel	22.3	Ansteel	20.1	Tata Steel	24.4	Jiangsu Shagang Gp.	22.9
9	Ansteel	22.1	Severstal	16.7	Jiangsu Shagang Gp.	23.3	Tangshan	22.8
10	Gerdau	18.7	Evraz	15.3	US Steel	23.2	US Steel	21.5
Total		346.2		285.3		357.8		363.1
World production		1,417.3		1,232.4		1,329.2		1,346.6
C10		0.24		0.23		0.28		0.27
C4		0.15		0.14		0.16		0.16

	2006		2005		2004		2003	
1	*ArcelorMittal	117.2	Mittal steel	63.0	Arcelor	46.9	Arcelor	42.8
2	Nippon steel	32.7	Arcelor	46.9	*Mittal Steel	42.8	LNM Gp.	35.3
3	JFE	32.0	Nippon Steel	32.0	Nippon Steel	32.4	Nippon Steel	31.3
4	POSCO	30.1	POSCO	30.5	JFE	31.6	*JFE	30.2
5	Baosteel Gp.	22.5	JFE	29.9	POSCO	30.2	POSCO	28.9
6	US Steel	21.2	Baosteel.	22.7	Shanghai Baosteel	21.4	Shangai Baosteel	19.9
7	Nucor	20.3	US Steel	19.3	US Steel	20.8	Corus Gp.	19.1
8	Tangshan	19.1	Nucor	18.4	Corus Gp.	19.0	US Steel	17.9

9	Corus Gp. 18.3	Corus Gp. 18.2	Nucor 17.9	ThyssenKrupp 16.1
10	Riva Gp. 18.2	Riva 17.5	ThyssenKrupp 17.6	Nucor 15.8
Total	331.6	298.4	280.6	257.3
World production	1,247.1	1,144.0	1,071.4	969.9
C10	0.27	0.26	0.26	0.27
C4	0.17	0.15	0.14	0.14

	2002	2001	2000
1	Arcelor 44.0	*Arcelor 43.1	Nippon Steel 28.4
2	*LNM Gp. 34.8	POSCO 27.8	POSCO 27.7
3	Nippon Steel 29.8	Nippon Steel 26.2	Arbed 24.1
4	POSCO 28.1	Ispat Int. 19.2	LNM 22.4
5	Shanghai Baosteel 19.5	Shanghai Baosteel 19.1	Usinor 21.0
6	Corus 16.8	Corus 18.1	Corus 20.0
7	ThyssenKrupp 16.4	Thyssen krupp 16.2	ThyssenKrupp 17.7
8	NKK 15.2	Riva 15.0	Shanghai Baosteel 17.7
9	Riva 15.0	NKK 14.8	NKK 16.0
10	US Steel 14.4	Kawasaki 13.3	Riva 12.8
Total	234.0	212.8	207.8
World production	904.0	851.1	848.0
C10	0.26	0.25	0.25
C4	0.15	0.14	0.12

Note: * Indicates a steelmaker that improved its top 10 standing by means of major acquisition(s) in that year.

Source: World Steel Association.

the end of the First World War. Tiffany attributes this to a judgment on the part of Wall Street financiers, the potential providers of expansion capital, that there were greater profits to be made by lending directly to Europeans to rebuild their own industry than by supporting US Steel's expansion. In such a view, managerial judgment may have led to the path (of internationalization) not being taken. However, in the late 1990s and then the 2000s, steel industry managers arrived at a different conclusion, and that has clearly led to a different set of outcomes.

It should also be noted that the M&A transactions did not emerge only from the established steel companies from the prior core, that is, developed world companies. Developed world steelmakers have indeed accounted for many large cross-border deals. However, steel producers from the emerging markets have also been active players, for example, Tata Steel's acquisition of Corus in 2007 and Gerdau's transactions in North America. In fact, arguably, one of the key instigators of the industry consolidation wave was a virtual outsider, Laxmi Nivas Mittal, who got his start running a small minimill in Indonesia (Ghemawat and Madhavan, 2011). Kumar and Chadha (2009) provide a useful comparative analysis of Indian and Chinese outward foreign direct investment in the steel industry.

The trend in domestic M&As is also similarly represented across the key nations. In China, for example, the fragmentation of the steel industry, with its implications for efficiency and competitiveness, is a matter of great concern to policy makers. In 2008, China's top 10 domestic steelmakers accounted for 42.5 percent of total output (that is, C10 = 42.5). According to the Chinese government's 2005 'Development Policies for the Iron and Steel Industry', the target C10 for 2020 is over 70 percent (KPMG, 2009).

One key aspect of the evolution of the steel industry relates to its interface with the mining industry. With the growth in demand for steel inputs such as iron ore and coal, as well as the increasing concentration in the mining sector, it is clear that ensuring access to raw materials is a key concern for steelmakers. One outcome has been vertical integration. Indeed, much of the value that Mittal saw in acquiring post-Soviet steel mills may have been in the captive mines that came with the factories rather than in their steel-making capacity (Ghemawat, 2007). This dialectical dynamic comprising concentrated market power on the part of the miners and the search for mineral self-sufficiency on the part of steelmakers, will have interesting results. For example, there may be more direct attempts to buy up mines, such as Arcelor Mittal's 2011 attempt to gain control of Macarthur Coal, and the emergence of 'haves' and 'have-nots' in the steel industry in terms of mineral self-sufficiency (Lichtenstein, 2011), with its attendant implications for valuation differentials that may in turn drive further merger activity.

In our description of structural changes in the US steel industry, technology played a key role, whereby minimills employed scrap-based production technology to direct great competitive pressure at integrated producers. Interestingly, technology also plays a parallel role in the ongoing restructuring of the global steel industry, although with an important difference. The US domestic story recounted earlier was driven by production technology, that is, the rise of EAF production. In the globalization case, we propose that it was not production technology, but rather the supporting organizational technologies that mattered; specifically, sophisticated information technology tools that triggered managerial innovations and which in turn facilitated the creation and ongoing management of the MNC form. Two examples serve to illustrate this: ThyssenKrupp's use of networked computer systems to bring about global integration, and Arcelor Mittal's coordination of interregional demand patterns through advanced information systems.

In ThyssenKrupp's case, we see how high-technology communication tools make possible a production chain that is dispersed over three continents (Wall Street Journal, 2010). ThyssenKrupp is a pioneer in stitching together a truly global steel supply chain, with a plant in Sepetiba, Brazil making steel slabs, which are then rolled and treated in Alabama for higher value-added applications. A small team based in Rotterdam uses networked computer systems to coordinate customer orders, slab production, and further processing efficiently. ThyssenKrupp sees itself as a 'virtual integrated steel mill' (ibid.). Industry accounts suggest that the company has been able to create significant efficiencies in production and logistics costs by virtue of this networking technology.

In Arcelor Mittal's case, the evidence suggests that significant managerial attention and the effective use of information systems (including knowledge transfer) has allowed it to leverage its resources globally as well as to respond in nuanced ways to regional differences in market needs. At the time of their merger in 2006, there was a significant difference in technological capability between Arcelor and Mittal Steel. While Arcelor and Mittal Steel were roughly the same size, Arcelor's annual R&D outlay was more than 10 times that of Mittal Steel, with the result that Mittal mills tended to lag their Arcelor counterparts in efficiency, reliability, and quality of steel (BusinessWeek, 2010). When you have a global company that demonstrates such stark differences in technology levels, leveraging advanced technology from the better units to the other units represents 'low hanging fruit', as compared to developing new technology. As evidence, consider how Arcelor Mittal's 2006 Activity Report (Arcelor Mittal, 2006, p. 61) opens its description of its R&D accomplishments: 'The merger has added a new dimension to the R&D effort by widening the range of potential applications for existing technical know-how and permitting the better use of this expanded R&D resource in order to accelerate project work'. A more graphic explanation of the technology transfer process is provided by Business Week (2010):

> To tap into that expertise, Burns Harbor recently dispatched a team of engineers to Sidmar, Arcelor's crown jewel, in Ghent, Belgium. The idea was to figure out why, with the exact same inputs, the Europeans were able to squeeze about 7% more steel out of their mills than the US plants could. The Americans relished the candlelight dinners in the old quarter of Ghent, but they were even more wowed by the advanced technology and shop-floor know-how they saw in Belgium. Now, they're gearing up to use a Sidmar device called a bomb that can be plunged into molten steel to sample its chemical properties and detect imperfections early on. The Mittals are pushing for just that sort of knowledge exchange across the company's global network, from Brazil to Kazakhstan. The many cultures now under the Arcelor Mittal flag provide 'an inexhaustible source of competitive advantage,' says Greg Ludkovsky, the company's chief technology officer for the Americas.

The main point here is that the Arcelor Mittal merger resulted in a much larger platform of application sites over which existing technologies could be leveraged. In other words, without the merger, each of these technologies would have suffered from a much smaller scope for application, thus reducing the return on investment for that particular technology.

A second aspect with regard to technology in the case of Arcelor Mittal, is represented by the company's approach to balancing global scale with responsiveness to local pressures. One specific aspect is that demand and product requirements for steel vary across markets, and Arcelor Mittal needed to view demand regionally in order to optimize production and customer service. However, internal data on approximately 200,000 customers were scattered across 30+ systems. With IBM's help, Arcelor Mittal developed an integrated system that provides managers with a unified view of regional patterns in demand (IBM, 2010).

To summarize the second part of our story, we propose that the geographical restructuring of the global steel industry should be understood in terms of the rise of steel production and consumption in the emerging markets as well as the rise of the steel MNC. The drivers of this fundamental shift, it turns out, are the same three drivers we noted earlier in the American industry's case; in other words, technology-based competition (although this time with a focus on information technology, not steel production techniques), demand shifts, and managerial agency.

1.9   PATTERNS IN THE RESTRUCTURING OF THE STEEL INDUSTRY

Before concluding the chapter, we would like to point out two features of the regional restructuring that we have described in the US steel industry and in the global industry. The first feature can be summarized as a shift from a core–periphery model to one of multipolarity; the second feature can be summarized as a regional model of globalization. Below, we briefly discuss each in turn.

In both the US domestic industry and at the global level, our analysis suggests the relative decline of the hitherto core and the ascendancy of the periphery. However, even more fundamentally, the data and trends perhaps suggest the irrelevance of the core–periphery model itself. Specifically, what we see is not merely a switch in the roles or the emergence of new cores and new peripheries, but rather a new structure in which different regions are much more equally balanced. Although it might appear that China is the new core and all other regions are peripheries, the steel intensity trends noted earlier suggest that this is not sustainable beyond the medium term. As emerging nations other than China gain speed on their own industrialization trajectories, we are likely to see a greater balance across the regions. More importantly, when assessed through the lens of global reach and the strategic capability of its steel companies, it is hard to describe China as the core. As a rough illustration, the companies in the list of top 10 steel producers in 2010 (see Table 1.4) represent China (three companies), Japan (two companies) and Europe, South Korea, India, United States, and Brazil (one company each). This raises the intriguing possibility that, rather than the core–periphery model, multipolarity may be more suitable as a description of the global steel industry of the future.

Experience also suggests that the globalization of the steel industry has not followed a 'flat earth' model, in which patterns of competition are uniform, but rather a semi-globalization model (Ghemawat, 2007) that is much more nuanced and complex. Despite the growth of China and the importance of steel MNCs, steel markets continue to be regional rather than frictionlessly global. A significant portion of steel exports consists of regional exports, and a steel producer in Germany is more likely to be in direct competition with a rival in Poland rather than one in Brazil. Ghemawat points out that regionally focused strategies are a discrete family of strategies that need to complement local and global initiatives. From the steel industry's standpoint, this exacerbates the organizational complexity associated with global footprints, in that strong regional hubs need to be created with the technological and managerial support for extensive knowledge-sharing both regionally and interregionally. Policy makers should take note as well; keeping up with the industry's restructuring implies developing new global approaches as well as closer regional coordination.

1.10   SUMMARY AND CONCLUSIONS

In this chapter, we proposed that technology-based competition, demand patterns, and managerial agency were the explanatory variables for the process of restructuring in the American steel industry in terms of its economic geography and in the context of sweeping changes in the industry's global structure. After the Second World War and leading through the 1960s, the industrial structure of the American steel industry was dominated by large integrated steel producers. During this period, competition was primarily among integrated firms and the location decisions taken during the period concerned individual production units within those firms. Subsequently, in the 1970s and on through the 1990s, steel minimills emerged in the United States to challenge the market share of integrated producers. Finally, with the turn of the century, world steel markets began to reshape, based on processes of globalization. Energized by industry liberalization and privatization in many parts of the world, and also supported by information technology and managerial innovations that increased spans of control, managerial agency manifested itself in the form of aggressive M&As to create the first large-scale steel MNCs. By examining these critical periods of restructuring in the American industry as well as in the industry globally, the role of economic geography as a competitive factor is exposed. In the process, we hope to have provided the context for understanding the regional and spatial implications of competitive adjustment.

REFERENCES

Ahlbrandt, Roger S., Richard Fruehan and Frank Giarratani (1996), *The Renaissance of American Steel: Lessons for Managers in Competitive Industries*, New York: Oxford University Press.
American Iron and Steel Institute (various years), *Annual Statistical Report*, Washington, DC: American Iron and Steel Institute.
Arcelor Mittal (2006), 'Activity Report 2006'.
Arcelor Mittal (2011), Untitled Presentation at the Citi Metals and Mining Nordic Symposium, December 6, 2011, available at: http://www.arcelormittal.com/corp/~/media/Files/A/ArcelorMittal/investors/presentations/investor-conference/2011/2011-12-Citi-Stockholm (accessed May 7, 2012).
Barnett, Donald F. and Robert W. Crandall (1986), *Up from the Ashes: The Rise of the Steel Minimill in the United States*, Washington, DC: Brookings Institution.
Beeson, Patricia and Frank Giarratani (1998), 'Spatial aspects of capacity change by U.S. integrated steel producers', *Journal of Regional Science*, **38**: 425–44.
BHPBilliton (2012), 'BHP Billiton Iron Ore – growth and outlook', Investor presentation, March 20, 2012, available at: http://www.bhpbilliton.com/home/investors/reports/Documents/2012/120320_AJMConference.pdf (accessed May 7, 2012).

Blume, Rick (2008), 'In the grip of globalization', BCMC 2008 Educational programs presentation, October 1, available at: http://2009.bcmcshow.com/images/2008/080910%20Blume%20presentation.pdf (accessed May 7, 2012).

BusinessWeek (2010), 'Mittal & Son: an inside look at the dynasty that dominates steel', *Business week*, available at: http://www.businessweek.com/magazine/content/07_16/b4030001.htm (accessed May 7, 2012).

Center for Industry Studies (2003), *US Steel Plant Database*, Pittsburgh, PA: University of Pittsburgh Press.

Chandler, Alfred D. (1993), *The Visible Hand: The Managerial Revolution in American Business*, Cambridge, MA: Belknap Press.

Christensen, Clayton M. (2000), *The Innovator's Dilemma*, New York: Harper.

Ghemawat, Pankaj (1995), 'Competitive advantage and internal organization: Nucor revisited', *Journal of Economics and Management Strategy*, **3** (4): 685–717.

Ghemawat, Pankaj (1997), *Games Businesses Play: Cases and Models*, Cambridge, MA: MIT Press.

Ghemawat, Pankaj (2007), *Redefining Global Strategy: Crossing Borders in a World Where Differences Still Matter*, Boston, MA: Harvard Business School Press.

Ghemawat, Pankaj and Ravi Madhavan (2011), 'Mittal Steel in 2006: changing the steel game', HBSP Case PG0002-PDF-ENG.

Giarratani, Frank, Gene Gruver and Randall Jackson (2006), 'Plant location and the advent of slab casting by U.S. steel minimills: an observation-based analysis', *Economic Geography*, **82** (4): 401–19.

Gruver, Gene and Frank Giarratani (2005), 'Modeling geographic ferrous scrap markets: regional prices and interregional transactions in the United States', *Journal of Regional Science*, **45** (2): 313–42.

Hall, Christopher G.L. (1997), *Steel Phoenix: The Fall and Rise of the U.S. Steel Industry*, New York: St. Martin's Press.

Hekman, John S. (1978), 'An analysis of the changing location of iron and steel production in the twentieth century', *American Economic Review*, **68**: 123–33.

Hoerr, John P. (1988), *And the Wolf Finally Came*, Pittsburgh, PA: University of Pittsburgh Press.

IBM (2007), 'Beyond the Familiar: Global Integration for Metals, Mining and Forest and Paper Companies', IBM Institute for Business Value report, available at: http://www-935.ibm.com/services/us/gbs/bus/pdf/g510-7885-00_beyondfamiliar.pdf (accessed May 7, 2012).

IBM (2010), 'Arcelor Mittal', IBM Software Information Management Case Study, available at: ftp://public.dhe.ibm.com/common/ssi/ecm/en/imc14604usen/IMC14604USEN.PDF (accessed May 7, 2012).

Ichniowski, Casey, Kathryn Shaw and Giovanna Prennushi (1997), 'The effects of human resource practices on productivity: a study of steel finishing lines', *American Economic Review*, **87** (3): 291–313.

Isard, Walter and William M. Capron (1949), 'The future locational pattern of iron and steel production in the United States', *Journal of Political Economy*, **57**: 119–33.

KPMG (2009), 'China's iron and steel industry amid the financial crisis', available at: http://www.kpmg.com/Global/en/IssuesAndInsights/ArticlesPublications/Documents/China-Iron-and-Steel-Industry.pdf (accessed May 7, 2012).

Kumar, Nagesh and Alka Chadha (2009), 'India's outward foreign direct investments in steel industry in a Chinese comparative perspective', *Industrial and Corporate Change*, **18** (2): 249–67.

Laplace Conseil (2003), 'The steel industry globalization trends: abstract of presentation to LME members', May 23, available at: http://www.laplaceconseil.com/LaplaceConseil/htdocs/admin/upload//File/LME%20Steel%20Globalization%20Trends.pdf (accessed April 28, 2012).

Lichtenstein, John (2011), 'Global steel's strategic imperatives', Remarks at Steel Success Strategies Conference XXVI, available at: http://www.accenture.com/SiteCollectionDocuments/PDF/Accenture-Global-Steels-Strategic-Imperatives.pdf (accessed May 7, 2012).

Marengo, Louis (1955), 'The basing point decisions and the steel industry', *American Economic Review*, **45** (2): 509–22.

Old, Bruce S. (1985), *The Competitive Status of the U.S. Steel Industry: A Study of the Influences of Technology in Determining International Industrial Competitive Advantage*, Washington, DC: National Academy Press.

Pittsburgh Regional Planning Association (1963), *Region in Transition: Report of the Economic Study of the Pittsburgh Region*, Volume 1, Pittsburgh, PA: University of Pittsburgh Press.

Pricewaterhouse Coopers (PwC) (2004), 'Forging Ahead: Mergers and Acquisitions Activity in the Global Metals Industry, 2004'.

Rogers, Robert P. (2009), *An Economic History of the American Steel Industry*, New York: Routledge.

Tiffany, Paul A. (1987), 'Opportunity denied: the abortive attempt to internationalize the American steel industry, 1903–1929', Working paper, The Wharton School, University of Pennsylvania.

Tiffany, Paul A. (1988), *The Decline of American Steel: How Management, Labor, and Government Went Wrong*, New York: Oxford University Press.

US Geological Survey (USGS) (1998), *Minerals Information: Iron Ore Statistical Compendium*, Washington, DC, US Geological Survey, available at: http://minerals.er.usgs.gov/minerals/pubs/commodity/iron_ore/stat/.

Wall, Joseph Frazier (1989), *Andrew Carnegie*, Pittsburgh, PA: University of Pittsburgh Press.

Wall Street Journal (2005), 'Mittal Steel plans plant in India after buying part of Chinese firm', *Wall Street Journal*, October 5, p. B3J.

Wall Street Journal (2010), 'Thyssen's high-tech relay; steelmaker uses computer networks to coordinate operations on three continents', *Wall Street Journal*, available at: http://professional.wsj.com/article/SB10001424 052748704681804576017692241019246.html?mod=googlenews_wsj&mg=reno-wsj (accessed May 7, 2012).

Warren, Kenneth (2001), *Big Steel: The First Century of the United States Steel Corporation, 1901–2001*, Pittsburgh, PA: University of Pittsburgh Press.

Womack, James P., Daniel T. Jones and Daniel Roos (1990), *The Machine that Changed the World*, New York: Rawson Associates.

2 The evolving geography of the US motor vehicle industry*

Thomas Klier and James M. Rubenstein

2.1 INTRODUCTION

Motor vehicle production involves two types of activity: the production of parts and the assembly of the finished vehicle. Several thousand parts makers supply the roughly 15,000 parts that go into a vehicle. The parts, some of which are already aggregated into modules or systems, are put together at the carmakers' assembly plants. The subsequent analysis of the industry's geography in turn considers assembly and parts plants, as well as how they relate to each other.

The motor vehicle industry in North America is highly clustered, as we see in Figure 2.1. In 2010 almost all assembly and most of the vehicle parts plants in the US and Canada were located in a region known as 'auto alley', as depicted in Figure 2.2. Auto alley is a narrow corridor, approximately 700 miles long and 100 miles wide, located in the interior of the United States between the Great Lakes and the Gulf of Mexico, extending northeast into Canada.[1] The spine of the corridor is formed by two north–south interstate highways, I-65 and I-75. East–west interstate highways, including I-40, I-64, and I-70, connect the two north–south routes like rungs on a ladder. Outside auto alley, the principal clustering of motor vehicle parts and assembly plants in North America is in Mexico. Some of these plants are in the interior of the country, centered on Mexico City, whereas others known as *maquiladoras* are strung out along the Mexico–US border.

This chapter describes the geography of US motor vehicle production for most of the twentieth century, explains reasons for the emergence of auto alley during the late twentieth century, and discusses key trends and internal patterns within auto alley in the early twenty-first century.

2.2 THE EARLY AUTO INDUSTRY GEOGRAPHY

For most of the twentieth century, the geography of North American motor vehicle production comprised two principal elements: (i) a central automotive district clustered around the southern Great Lakes where most parts were made, and (ii) several dozen branch plants dispersed across the United States where most vehicles were assembled.

This spatial pattern resulted from the concentration of production in the hands of the 'Big 3' carmakers, namely Ford Motor Company, General Motors Corporation, and Chrysler Corporation. Ford and GM, founded in 1903 and 1908, respectively, accounted for 75 percent of US sales in 1917. Chrysler, established in 1924, quickly joined Ford and

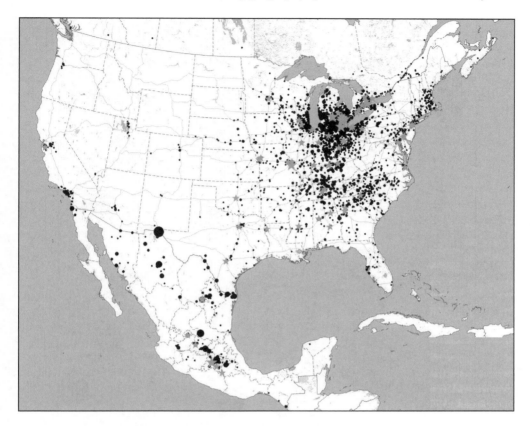

Note: Excludes assembly plants with capacity of fewer than 100,000 vehicles per year.

Source: Adapted by authors from ELM International and other sources.

Figure 2.1   Assembly plants and parts plants in North America, 2010

GM as one of the three sales leaders. At the peak of their dominance, during the mid-1950s, the Big 3 together accounted for 95 percent of US motor vehicle sales.

When commercial production began in the United States during the late 1890s, several hundred firms were building motor vehicles. More than half of these producers were located in the northeast, including New York City, Philadelphia, Springfield, Massachusetts, northern New Jersey, and several cities in Connecticut (Boas, 1961: 221–2). The first two vehicles to achieve annual sales of more than 1,000 were the Columbia in 1900 and the Locomobile in 1901, both of which were assembled in the northeast, in Hartford, Connecticut, and Tarrytown, New York, respectively (Bradley and Langworth, 1971: 138; Norbye, 1971: 112). Early producers of automobiles were also spread across the Midwest: Kenosha, Wisconsin; South Bend, Indiana; and Toledo, Ohio were among the major production centers in 1900 (Rubenstein, 1992: 27–8).

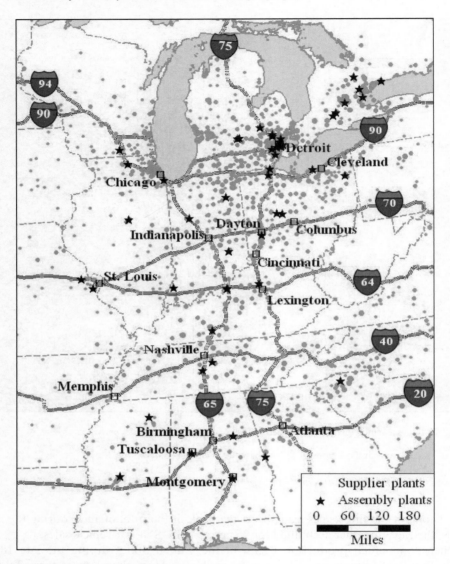

Source: Klier and Rubenstein (2008).

Figure 2.2   Auto alley

2.2.1   Production of Vehicles Clusters in Michigan

Southeast Michigan became the center of motor vehicle production in North America during the first decade of the twentieth century. Michigan accounted for 42 percent of US motor vehicle production in 1904, 51 percent in 1909, and a historic peak of 80 percent in 1913 (May, 1975: 333–4).[2] The Ford Motor Company was largely responsible for southeastern Michigan's dominance after 1900. In 1913, Ford alone accounted for more than one-half of Michigan's total.

Two economic geography factors help to explain Detroit's rapid dominance in the first decade of the twentieth century: (i) proximity to leading sources of inputs, and (ii) access to venture capital.[3]

Motor vehicle production clustered in Detroit in part because the leading suppliers of key inputs, such as engines and carriages, were already located there. At the top of the list of critical components for early carmakers was a reliable source of power for their products. In 1900, southeastern Michigan was the nation's center for production of gasoline engines. Once gasoline triumphed over steam and electricity as the preferred source of vehicle power for car engines during the first decade of the twentieth century, southeastern Michigan became the unrivaled leader in motor vehicle production (Klier and Rubenstein, 2008: 35).

- Leland & Faulconer Manufacturing Co., founded in Detroit in 1890, was the nation's largest producer of marine gasoline engines and became a leading supplier of precision-engineered motor vehicle parts into the twentieth century. Henry Leland became president of the Cadillac Automotive Co. in 1903, and Leland & Faulconer merged with Cadillac in 1905 (Hyde, 2005: 30; Klier and Rubenstein, 2008: 35).
- Dodge Brothers, founded in Detroit by brothers John and Horace Dodge in 1900, initially made marine engines and bicycle parts. When the Ford Motor Co. was established in 1903, it contracted with the Dodge Brothers for engines, gears, and other parts amounting to 62 percent of its cars' manufacturing costs. When Ford was unable to pay Dodge for the parts, John and Horace Dodge accepted shares of Ford Motor Co. (Hyde, 2005: 31).
- Olds Motor Works, based in Lansing, was the nation's leading producer of small stationary gasoline engines during the 1890s. Small stationary gasoline engines generated power on farms and in other rural settings that lacked access to electricity. Olds adapted his engine to motor vehicles in the late 1890s and produced the best-selling motor vehicles in the first three years of the twentieth century.

In addition, the availability of capital contributed to Michigan's emergence as the center of motor vehicle production in the early twentieth century (Flink, 1970). In 1900, the country's large banks, which were clustered in New York and other northeastern cities, were the main source of financing for industrial development. Given that the northeast was also the center of the market for motor vehicles, producers naturally looked to that part of the country for capital. However, eastern bankers were reluctant to invest in the motor vehicle industry.

In contrast, wealthy Michiganders, people who made their fortunes exploiting Michigan's resource-based industries, such as copper, iron, and lumber, were willing to gamble on the auto industry (Parlin and Youker, 1914). For example, Ransom Olds picked out a factory site in New Jersey to build cars, but when he failed to secure loans from New York banks he built a plant in Detroit, where he was able to get financing (Niemeyer, 1963: 27). James W. Packard started production in Cleveland but was unable to obtain sufficient financing in that city. Subsequently he received support from Detroit businessmen and moved production of his vehicles there (Smith, 1970: 31; May, 1975: 285–7; Wager, 1975: xiii; Rubenstein, 1992: 41).

2.2.2 Location of Parts Production

For most of the twentieth century, parts plants were arrayed in a 700-mile east–west region between upstate New York and southeastern Wisconsin along the southern rim of Lakes Ontario, Erie, and Michigan. A 1940 economic geography textbook called this area the 'central automotive district' (Colby and Foster, 1940, cited in Ballert, 1947). The central automotive district was home to nineteenth-century automotive parts pioneers, such as glassmakers in Toledo and tire makers in Akron. The Big 3 carmakers also built most of their parts plants in the central automotive district. In 1950 it contained 85 percent of the nation's parts plants (Hurley, 1959: 4).

A 1951 academic thesis documented the sources of parts at GM's Buick assembly plant in Flint, Michigan, at the time one of the world's largest assembly facilities, where 22,000 workers produced 2,000 cars a day (Henrickson, 1951). Henrickson found that 23 percent of Buick's suppliers in 1951 were located within 60 miles and 81 percent within 450 miles of Flint, arrayed in an east–west configuration along the southern Great Lakes (depicted in Figure 2.3).

2.2.3 Branch Assembly Plants

As demand for motor vehicles increased during the twentieth century, more assembly plants were constructed. Choosing their locations became an important business decision. A producer interested in serving the national market was faced with the task of finding the location for an assembly plant that minimized the cost of production. Production costs included the procurement of parts and materials, as well as the distribution of the finished vehicles to the dealers. In the case of a bulky consumer product, such as a motor vehicle, the cost of distribution is not trivial. While most parts continued to be produced in the central automotive district, new final assembly plants were beginning to locate elsewhere in the country as early as the second decade of the twentieth century.

Ford, the company most responsible for establishing southeastern Michigan's dominance in vehicle assembly, led the way in reducing it. Norval Hawkins, the company's first sales manager, came up with the idea of producing vehicle parts in Detroit and shipping them to so-called 'branch assembly plants' around the country (Rubenstein, 1992: 54). The concept of branch assembly accommodated a classic weight-gaining industry such as vehicle assembly, because it was cheaper to produce finished vehicles near the centers of population rather than to ship finished vehicles from a central location to many destinations across the country. Transportation cost economics provided the rationale: at the time the equivalent of 26 Ford cars could be shipped in knocked-down form in a railroad boxcar, compared to seven or eight fully assembled vehicles (*Dodge et al. v. Commissioner of Internal Revenue*, 1927: 62–3; Nevins, 1954: 500–501). The quickly growing motor vehicle industry was well-suited for a branch assembly plant system as production runs for the best-selling vehicles were large enough to support more than one assembly plant (Klier and McMillen, 2008: 247).

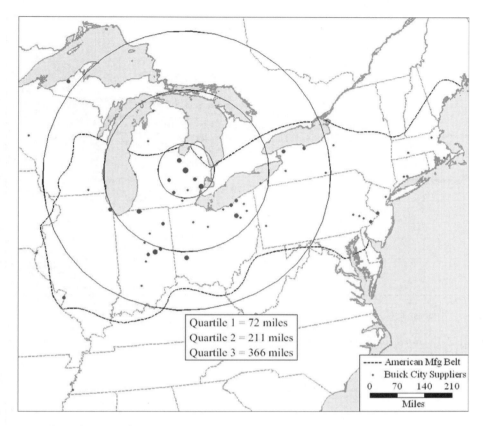

Quartile 1 = 72 miles
Quartile 2 = 211 miles
Quartile 3 = 366 miles

----- American Mfg Belt
· Buick City Suppliers

0   70   140   210
Miles

Source: Klier and Rubenstein (2008).

Figure 2.3   Suppliers to GM's Buick assembly plant in Flint, 1951

Ford opened its first branch assembly plant in 1912 in Kansas City. Within five years, the company operated 29 assembly plants outside of Michigan, and an all-time high of 31 in 1925, as we see in Figure 2.4. General Motors emulated Ford's assembly plant concept. As shown in Figure 2.5, by the 1950s, GM's Chevrolet and Buick–Oldsmobile–Pontiac divisions each had 10 assembly plants.

2.3   'AUTO ALLEY' EMERGES

The footprint of the US motor vehicle industry changed dramatically during the last two decades of the twentieth century. Two main influences drove this change. First, the system of branch assembly plants started to unravel once product variety was growing faster than the size of the overall vehicle market. As a result, individual assembly facilities needed to serve the national market as opposed to a regional market. Hence central locations became more attractive than coastal ones.

Source: Rubenstein (1992).

Figure 2.4   Ford final assembly plants, 1917

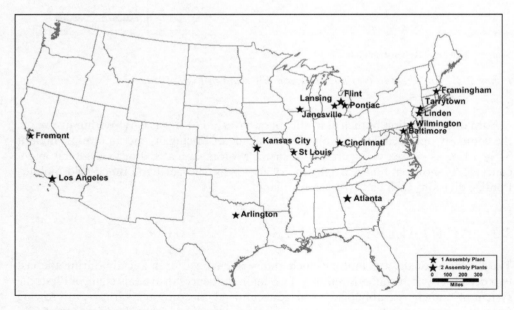

Source: Rubenstein (1992).

Figure 2.5   GM final assembly plants, 1955

In addition, foreign producers started setting up production facilities in North America. The foreign-owned assembly plants, which at the time were often referred to as 'transplants', located in the center of the country, away from traditional manufacturing locations and further south from where the Detroit carmakers had traditionally established their assembly plants. As the foreign producers increased their market share in North America they added production facilities, extending auto alley further south in the process.[4] Parts makers followed assemblers as they wanted to be within one day's drive of assembly plants. The logistics industry considers the maximum one-day shipping range to be 450 miles on Interstate Highways.

Meanwhile, the Detroit-based carmakers scaled back their footprint in response to their shrinking market share. By 2010, the Detroit 3, as they were now called, were more concentrated in the Midwest states of Michigan, Indiana, and Ohio than had been the case for most of the twentieth century.

As a result, auto alley[5] was firmly established as the location for nearly all US final assembly plants by the beginning of the twenty-first century. By 2010 all assembly plants in coastal locations were closed (of which there had been 12 in 1980). Parts suppliers and assembly plants were once again located within the same region.

2.3.1 Assembly Plants

In 1980, cars and light trucks were assembled at 57 assembly plants[6] in the United States. These assembly plants included 32 in what would become auto alley and 25 elsewhere in the United States. Of the 25 outside auto alley, eight were in the northeast, four in California, and 11 in the interior of the country, including four in the St. Louis area and three in the Kansas City area.

In 2010, 34 of 41 US assembly plants were in auto alley and only seven in other locations. In three decades, the number of assembly plants declined from 10 to zero in the northeast and from four to zero in California. Plants in interior locations other than auto alley declined to seven, including two each in the Kansas City and St. Louis areas and in Texas, all of which were relatively close to auto alley (see Table 2.1).

The southward movement of assembly plants occurred in two distinct waves. During the 1980s the industry started to reconfigure from a region with an east–west orientation to one with a north–south orientation. During the 1990s and early in the twenty-first

Table 2.1   Distribution of US assembly plants and assembly lines

	1980	1990	2000	2010
Total	57 (61)	57 (61)	54 (59)	41 (47)
Detroit 3	56 (60)	49 (51)	43 (43)	25 (25)
Other	1 (1)	8 (10)	11 (16)	16 (22)
In auto alley	32 (34)	38 (42)	36 (42)	34 (42)
Outside auto alley	25 (27)	19 (19)	18 (17)	7 (7)

Note: Assembly line count reported in parentheses.

Source: AutoInfobank, other sources.

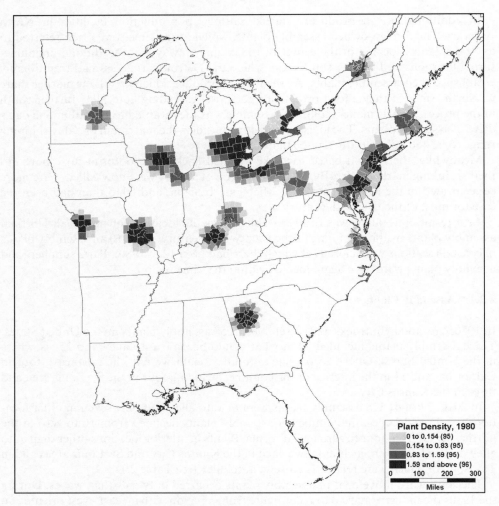

Plant Density, 1980
0 to 0.154 (95)
0.154 to 0.83 (95)
0.83 to 1.59 (95)
1.59 and above (96)
0   100   200   300
Miles

Source: Ward's AutoInfobank and other sources, authors' calculations.

Figure 2.6   Assembly plant density, 1980

century, the newly located assembly plants strongly pushed the edge of that auto region to the Deep South.

Figure 2.6 shows the density of light vehicle assembly plants in 1980.[7] For the eastern half of the United States it shows the geography of assembly plants operational that year. With the exception of a cluster in northern Georgia, which represents a Ford and two GM plants located in the Atlanta region, all assembly plants are located in a fairly compact region that extends south from the Twin Cities in Minnesota to Kansas City and from there all the way to the East Coast.

By far the highest density of assembly plants is found in southeastern Michigan: Wayne, Oakland, and Macomb counties are the only counties with a density value in

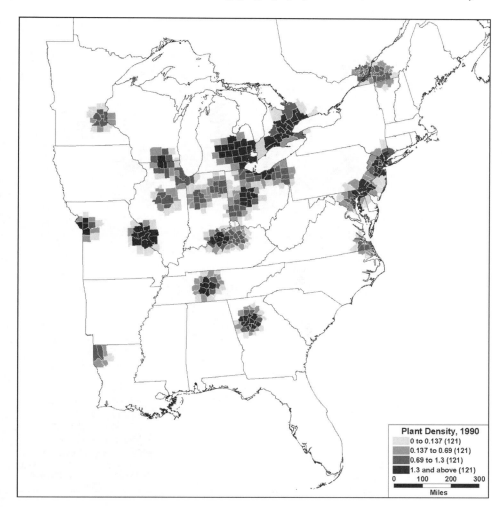

Source: Ward's AutoInfobank, authors' calculations.

Figure 2.7 Assembly plant density, 1990

double digits.[8] Secondary clusters, encompassing at least three assembly plants, are located near Chicago (including southeastern Wisconsin), St. Louis, Kansas City, northern Ohio, Delaware/Maryland, and New York.

During the 1980s, the number of assembly plants in the US remained unchanged. Underlying this summary statistic, however, is a substantial turnover: 12 assembly plants opened and 12 assembly plants closed during that decade. Figure 2.7 depicts the density of assembly plants in the year 1990. A comparison of Figures 2.6 and 2.7 shows two major changes in the east–west orientation of the auto region characteristic of 1980. The relative importance of the East Coast as an assembly location was being reduced by the closure of three assembly plants in Pennsylvania, New York, and Massachusetts.

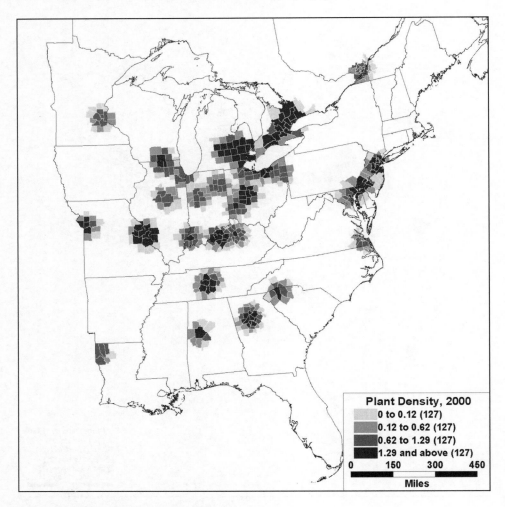

Plant Density, 2000
0 to 0.12 (127)
0.12 to 0.62 (127)
0.62 to 1.29 (127)
1.29 and above (127)
0   150   300   450
Miles

Source: Ward's AutoInfobank, authors' calculations.

Figure 2.8   Assembly plant density, 2000

At the same time, the newly opened assembly plants extend the area of auto assembly southward by GM and Nissan assembly operations in Tennessee and Louisiana. The majority of assembly plants opened during the decade, though, represented a filling-in of previously unoccupied areas in northern Illinois, Indiana, and Ohio.

The southerly extension of the vehicle-production region accelerated during the 1990s and the early twenty-first century (Figures 2.8 and 2.9). During the 1990s three assembly plants were opened and six existing ones closed. One new assembly plant opened in the heart of the industry, in Lansing, Michigan.[9] Other than this plant, the northernmost assembly plant was built in southern Indiana, a location which corresponds to the southern edge of the traditional east–west auto belt. By the same token, a second band

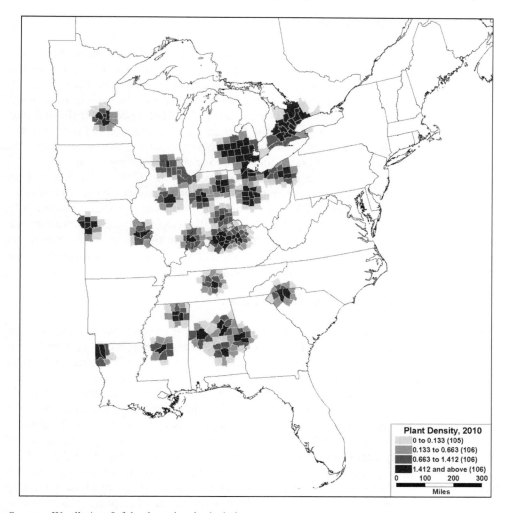

Source: Ward's AutoInfobank, authors' calculations.

Figure 2.9 Assembly plant density, 2010

of assembly lines was established at the far southern end of the auto corridor, reaching from central Mississippi to South Carolina. The assembly plants were built exclusively in 'greenfield' locations, that is in places where no major auto production or any other manufacturing facility had existed at the time.

During the first decade of the twenty-first century a substantial turnover and reduction of production capacity took place in the United States. Faced with rapidly declining market shares, the Detroit 3 closed several plants. Overall, 19 plants shut and six opened. By 2010, auto alley had substantially reinforced its dominance over the industry's geography. The region contained 83 percent of all assembly plants and 89 percent of all assembly lines.

2.3.2   The Detroit 3 Return to the Midwest

The forces leading to a restructuring of the auto industry geography began during the 1960s. In response to increased sales of smaller cars by foreign producers, such as the VW Beetle, US producers introduced a number of smaller platforms over the years, such as 'subcompact', 'compact', and 'intermediate' cars. As a result, the growth of product variety began to outpace the growth of overall demand. Rubenstein (1992) showed that the number of different models of cars and light trucks grew substantially faster than the overall market beginning in the mid-1970s. This development resulted in substantially smaller production runs of individual models, even for the best-selling models.[10]

In addition, in the wake of the recessions induced by the 1970s' oil crises and an increase in motor vehicle imports, domestic auto producers reduced capacity and shut down some of their production facilities. As the Detroit carmakers' share continued to fall, they further reduced their footprint (Klier, 2009). Assembly plants located on the coasts were increasingly abandoned in favor of locations in the center of the country as they could more effectively serve the national market. As a result, the location of assembly plants began to re-concentrate in the Midwest.[11]

2.3.3   International Carmakers Start Production

The share of US light vehicle sales held by foreign-owned companies has increased for several decades (ibid.). The market share loss of the Detroit carmakers declined especially rapidly during the early twenty-first century, falling from 67 percent in 2000 to 45 percent in 2009. Foreign carmakers began producing vehicles in the United States, starting with Volkswagen in 1979 (Table 2.2). Like the Detroit automakers they strongly preferred locations in the interior of the country. But the foreign producers extended the vehicle-production region to the south by opening plants in Kentucky and Tennessee, as well as even further south in Mississippi and Alabama. As a result, the footprint of the US auto industry changed noticeably (Mair et al., 1988; Klier and McMillen, 2006).

To avoid competing for labor with already existing assembly operations, foreign carmakers typically selected rural greenfield sites. In addition, foreign producers avoided locations with a strong union presence. As vehicle assembly plants represent large investments with a sizable employment, individual states offered substantial economic incentives trying to sway the location decision in their favor each time a new assembly plant was announced (see Molot, 2005).

Honda was the first Japanese carmaker to build an assembly plant in the United States, in Marysville, Ohio, where production began in 1982. Nissan followed with a plant in Smyrna, Tennessee, which opened in 1983. When in 1987 Toyota chose Georgetown, Kentucky, roughly midway between Marysville and Smyrna, for its first and largest US assembly complex, a north–south corridor of motor vehicle production began to take shape.

2.3.4   Site Location

Through the first two decades of investment in auto alley, the rule of thumb had been one international assembly plant per state (see Klier and Rubenstein, 2008). In order of

Table 2.2   *Arrival of foreign headquartered carmakers, by first year of production in the US*

Company	Year
VW[1]	1978
Honda	1982
Nissan	1983
Toyota[2]	1984
Mitsubishi, Mazda[3]	1987
Subaru	1989
BMW	1994
Mercedes	1997
Hyundai	2005
Kia	2009

Notes:
1. VW closed its Pennsylvania plant in 1989. It re-entered the US market with a plant in Chattanooga, TN, in 2011.
2. Toyota entered first via a joint venture with GM, called NUMMI.
3. Mazda entered via a joint venture with Ford, called AutoAlliance. Mazda pulled out of that plant during the fall of 2012.

Source: Ward's AutoInfobank, other sources.

opening, Honda picked Ohio, Nissan Tennessee, NUMMI California, Mazda Michigan, Mitsubishi Illinois, Toyota Kentucky, Subaru Indiana, BMW South Carolina, and Mercedes-Benz Alabama. The state 'captured' by a carmaker influenced the location of key suppliers, such as Honda's in Ohio, Toyota's in Kentucky, and Nissan's in Tennessee.

The one-international-assembly-plant-per-state pattern had a logical basis. International carmakers were reluctant to compete with one an other for qualified workers, subsidies, tax breaks, and training programs. It was also politically astute; each time international carmakers entered a new state, they expanded the number of public officials sympathetic to their distinctive needs and priorities.

Into the twenty-first century, with all states in auto alley occupied by an international carmaker, newcomers were forced to look for sites in already-occupied states. The principal objective when entering a previously selected state was to avoid competing for labor. The supply of qualified labor is relatively scarce in auto alley, especially in the southern end, because of below-average educational attainment. Furthermore, carmakers have discovered that their workers are willing to commute longer than the national average of 24 minutes to obtain good, high-paying jobs in the final assembly plants; one-hour commutes are common at plants in the rural portions of auto alley.[12]

To identify potential plant sites within auto alley, international carmakers first eliminated territory within two hours of existing assembly plants.[13] Carmakers then calculated whether the proposed site had a sufficiently large pool of labor surrounding it. A total population of 200,000 within the one-hour radius has been the minimum for carmakers to consider.

Toyota's consideration in 2007 of sites for an assembly plant illustrated the process of in-filling within auto alley. According to press reports, Toyota considered five sites:

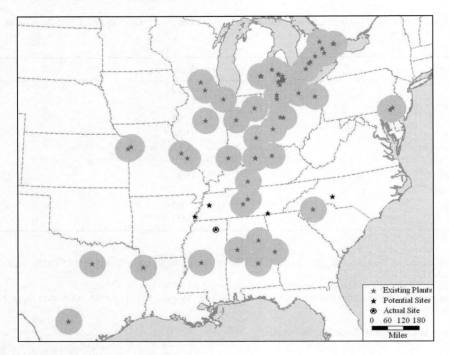

Source: Klier and Rubenstein (2008).

Figure 2.10   Laborsheds surrounding final assembly plants, 2009

Marion, Arkansas; somewhere in western North Carolina; Alamo and Chattanooga, Tennessee; and a fifth unnamed site (Shirouzo, 2007). A major overview of auto alley shows that all four named finalists were outside a 50-mile radius, corresponding to the one-hour commuting range surrounding all of the existing assembly plants (see Figure 2.10).

In the end, Toyota selected Tupelo, Mississippi, perhaps the fifth unnamed site. Tupelo was also beyond a 50-mile radius of existing assembly plants. A year later, Volkswagen selected the Chattanooga site that had been one of Toyota's finalists.

Similarly, Toyota and Honda located new assembly plants in portions of Indiana beyond the labor market area of the existing international plant operated by Subaru in Lafayette. Toyota went to the far southwestern corner of the state and Honda to the far southeastern corner. According to press reports, the runner-up for Honda's Greensburg, Indiana, plant was a site in eastern Illinois that was also beyond the 50-mile range of existing assembly plants. Honda and Hyundai also selected sites in Alabama, a state first staked out by Daimler-Benz, but beyond the 50-mile range of the Daimler-Benz plant.[14]

2.3.5   Parts Plants

Unlike motor vehicle assembly, the production of motor vehicle parts never left the Midwest.[15] The emergence of auto alley has pulled supplier plants southward (Glasmeier and McCluskey, 1987). Transportation infrastructure, especially highways, is a crucial factor for siting auto parts supplier operations (Woodward, 1992; Smith and Florida, 1994; Klier and McMillen, 2008). Klier and McMillen (2008) also demonstrate the importance of being near assembly plants.[16]

The geographical distribution of auto supplier plants displays a north–south orientation, with a concentration of plants along a corridor running from Detroit southward through Ohio, Kentucky, Tennessee, and into Alabama. The distribution of auto parts plants, which traditionally has been highly concentrated, remains so today. Yet the footprint of supplier plant locations changed noticeably during the last three decades. While plant openings have been concentrated in the area south of Detroit, the new location pattern mimics the distribution of existing plants in the area (Klier and McMillen, 2006, 2008).

2.4   CARMAKER–SUPPLIER NETWORKS IN AUTO ALLEY

Carmakers traditionally made most parts themselves and purchased the remainder through annual contracts with the lowest bidder. Now carmakers outsource entire integrated modules to suppliers on multi-year contracts.[17]

2.4.1   Production Linkages

Close linkages between an assembly plant and its network of suppliers is crucial for efficient operation in the contemporary environment of lean inventory with just-in-time delivery. Under mass production, parts were made in large quantities and stockpiled in final assembly plants. Under lean (or just-in-time) production, it is standard practice for most parts to arrive at the final assembly plant shortly before they are needed on the assembly line for installation in the vehicle.

Just-in-time starts with an order from a carmaker. Instead of producing according to a preset schedule, suppliers operate according to a so-called 'pull system', in which the flow of materials through the various stages of production is triggered by what is needed in the next production stage, and ultimately by the customer (Womack et al., 1990). For carmakers, maintaining a continuous and tightly controlled flow of parts allows for flexible modification of production changes in the demand for the product. Research has shown that the burden of accommodating just-in-time tends to fall to suppliers (Helper, 1991; Helper and Sako, 1995).

The introduction of lean manufacturing prompted some to wonder what it entails for the footprint of an assembly plant's supply chain (Estall, 1985; Mair, 1992). For a few suppliers, close linkage requires locating very close to an assembly plant. Seats are typically produced within a one-hour driving distance from the assembly plant. The seat plant receives an order from the carmaker for a truckload of specific styles of seats, which are subsequently assembled to order, loaded on trucks in the reverse sequence that they will be needed at the final assembly plant, and delivered within a few hours. The maximum distance between a seat plant and an assembly plant is constrained by the time needed to assemble the ordered seats, load them onto a truck, and drive them to the final assembly plant (Klier and Testa, 2002).

Few suppliers other than seat makers and some stamping and trim parts makers are within a one-hour drive of an assembly plant (Klier, 2000). The typical supplier only needs to be close enough to assure reliable delivery within one day. Approximately three-fourths of suppliers are situated within a one-day drive of their assembly plant customers. This pattern holds true regardless of where within auto alley the assembly plant is located (Klier and Rubenstein, 2008).

2.4.2   Network Analysis

Klier and Rubenstein (2008) have documented the footprint of supplier networks for individual carmakers. They have produced maps with concentric circles drawn around individual assembly plants. The concentric circles are chosen to represent quartiles of the distance from the suppliers to the assembly plant. The closest one-fourth of all suppliers to that carmaker were located within the inner circle, the next closest one-fourth were between the inner and middle circles, the third closest quartile were between the middle and outer circles, and the final quartile was beyond the outer circle. In other words, one-half of suppliers were within the middle circle and three-fourths within the outer circle. Thus, the radius of the middle circle represents the median distance for shipment of parts to the particular assembly plant.

Klier and Rubenstein have shown the footprint of the supplier networks of Chrysler, Ford, and GM to be nearly identical. One-fourth of the suppliers to each of the Detroit 3 were located within approximately 135 miles of Detroit, essentially southeastern Michigan plus small portions of western Ontario and northern Ohio. One-half of all suppliers were within 275 miles of Detroit, encompassing the Great Lakes region between Milwaukee and Buffalo plus southwestern Ontario. Another one-fourth of suppliers were located between 275 and 613 miles away, extending primarily into the southeastern United States. The most distant one-fourth of Detroit 3 suppliers were widely scattered, with the largest number in Mexico (Figure 2.11).

Honda, the first Japanese carmaker to assemble vehicles in the United States, put together a supplier base clustered tightly in western Ohio, near its Marysville and East Liberty assembly plants, which were constructed three miles apart from each other. One-fourth of Honda's North American suppliers were within 149 miles, one-half within 288 miles, and three-fourths within 449 miles of the west-central Ohio assembly plants (Figure 2.12). Most of the engines destined for Marysville and East Liberty were made in Anna, Ohio, 35 miles west. Transmissions came from a plant in Russells Point, Ohio, 25 miles west. For its Lincoln, Alabama, assembly plant, Honda built an engine plant right next door and a transmission plant in Talapoosa, Georgia, 60 miles east.

2.4.3   Logistics

The network of suppliers around an assembly plant can be rather loose because of efficient logistics. As a result, suppliers do not have to be bunched up in the immediate vicinity of an assembly plant, competing for the same labor supply and infrastructure investment. For a typical supplier, the most important unit of delivery time is one day, not one hour. A well-developed transportation infrastructure and modern logistics serv-

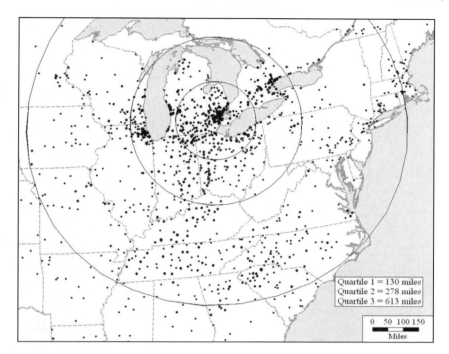

Quartile 1 = 130 miles
Quartile 2 = 278 miles
Quartile 3 = 613 miles

0   50 100 150
Miles

Source: Klier and Rubenstein (2008).

Figure 2.11   Ford parts suppliers

ices allow production facilities to be closely linked operationally without having to be physically close.

In addition, distribution centers have been built near assembly plants as staging areas to facilitate the timely arrival of parts at final assembly plants. Carmakers now require delivery of parts not merely on a just-in-time basis, but more importantly, in the correct sequence. This practice is referred to as 'just-in-sequence'. Klier and McMillen (2006) find evidence that suggests the possibility of stronger local effects of assembly plant openings on supplier plant location choices during the 1990s than during the previous decade. This tendency could be related to the increasing role of logistics and supplier functions having to be performed in proximity to the assembly location.

2.4.4   Linkages across Networks

Assemblers prefer to have multiple suppliers located nearby to ensure the reliable delivery of parts. Parts makers in turn prefer to be near several assembly plants to supply multiple customers. Only 10 percent of parts plants ship to a single carmaker.[18] The desire to have multiple sources and multiple customers has reinforced the spatial concentration of the US motor vehicle industry.

Linkages also exist across supply networks. For the 90 percent of parts plants with multiple customers, Rubenstein (2010) has identified the nationality of the assembly

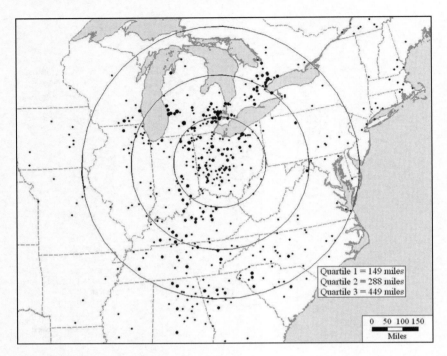

Source: Klier and Rubenstein (2008).

Figure 2.12   Honda parts plants

plant customers. Approximately 47 percent of parts plants supplied two or all three of the Detroit 3 carmakers and none of the foreign-owned carmakers, 41 percent supplied a mix of Detroit 3 and international carmakers, and 12 percent supplied at least two foreign-owned carmakers and none of the Detroit 3 (Table 2.3). In other words, 80 percent of the parts plants that supply an international carmaker also supply at least one Detroit 3 carmaker, and 88 percent of all parts plants ship to at least one of the Detroit 3. The dependency of the entire supplier industry on the Detroit 3 carmakers was a factor in the decision by the President's Task Force on the Auto Industry to rescue Chrysler and GM during the severe recession of 2008–09 (Congressional Oversight Panel, 2009).

2.5   NORTH–SOUTH DIFFERENCES WITHIN AUTO ALLEY

As the auto industry clustered in auto alley, important differences emerged between the northern (or Midwest) end and the southern end of the region. The tendency for new assembly plants, as well as new supplier plants, has been to locate farther south. In 1972 the seven southern states of Alabama, Georgia, Kentucky, Mississippi, North Carolina, South Carolina, and Tennessee together had 7 percent of all transportation sector employment. Thirty years later, the region's share had grown to 16 percent (Cooney,

Table 2.3   Extent of sharing of suppliers to Detroit 3 and international carmakers

Part system	Detroit 3	International	Both
Body	11%	21%	19%
Interior	14%	21%	15%
Chassis	15%	19%	17%
Engine	16%	15%	16%
Powertrain	22%	15%	18%
Generic	23%	9%	15%
N	1,793	446	1,589

Supplier to North American assembly plants owned by	Also supplier to N American assembly plants owned by		
	Detroit 3	Asia based	Europe based
Detroit 3 carmakers	100%	42%	15%
Asia-based carmakers	80%	100%	21%
Europe-based carmakers	81%	58%	100%

Source: Klier and Rubenstein (2008).

2007). On the other hand, the share of the nation's motor vehicle assembly and parts employment in Michigan had declined from 32 percent in 1990 and 29 percent in 2000 to 21 percent in 2008.

In 1980, only five of the 57 US assembly plants were in what would become the southern portion of auto alley. Two were in Louisville, only a few miles south of the Ohio River boundary between the 'Midwest' and 'South'.[19] The other three, in Atlanta, were relics of the Big 3's branch plants that once served customers in the southeast. The Midwest portion of auto alley had 27 assembly plants, including 20 in Michigan. Between 1980 and 2010, the number of assembly plants in the southern portion of auto alley increased from five to nine, and the number in the northern portion decreased by two to 25.

As discussed earlier in this chapter, the southward movement of assembly plants occurred in two distinct waves. During the 1980s, most of the new assembly plants were located in a relatively small area encompassing central Illinois, Indiana, and Ohio on the north and central Tennessee on the south. After 1990, the newly located assembly plants strongly pushed the edge of that auto region to the Deep South centered on Alabama and Mississippi. At the same time, new assembly plants were located in Indiana and Ontario, Canada.

The south's rise in importance can also be seen in the geography of parts plants, as shown in Figure 2.13. In the south, 67 percent of the parts plants were opened between 1980 and 2006, compared with only 40 percent in the Midwest and 39 percent in the rest of the United States. Conversely, only 19 percent of the parts plants in the south in operation in 2006 had opened before 1970, compared with 45 percent of those in the Midwest and elsewhere in the United States (Klier and Rubenstein, 2008: 223). The northern and southern portions of auto alley differ along these main factors: southern plants are more likely to produce different kind of parts from those in the north, and they are also more likely to be foreign owned and non-unionized.

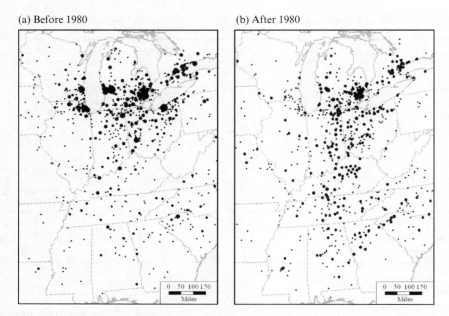

Source: Klier and Rubenstein (2008).

Figure 2.13   Parts plants opened before 1980 and after 1980

2.5.1   Nationality

Leading the move southward within auto alley have been foreign-owned carmakers and parts suppliers. A map of auto alley, Figure 2.14, shows the north–south split between US- and foreign-owned assembly plants opened in the United States between 1980 and 2010. US-owned plants cluster in the Midwest and foreign-owned ones in the south. The two groups overlap in southern Ohio and Indiana. The density of domestic assembly plants very closely assembles the traditional assembly region and its east–west orientation with Detroit at its center. In contrast, assembly plants operated by foreign-headquartered producers are neatly arrayed in a region that has a clear north–south extension to it, with Detroit being just one of many locations.

In 2010, the United States had 25 US-owned (Detroit 3) assembly plants and 16 foreign-owned ones. Seven of the foreign-owned assembly plants were in the southern portion of auto alley, seven in the northern portion, and two outside of auto alley. For the Detroit 3, the number in the northern portion was 18 compared to only two in the south and five elsewhere. The drift southward reflects the changing fortunes of various carmakers. Since 1980, the share of the US market held by the traditional Big 3 of Chrysler Group, Ford, and GM has declined from 80 to 45 percent. Most of the decline has occurred since 1995. Foreign carmakers have been responsible for opening 16 of 21 new assembly plants since 1980, excluding those designed to replace older ones in the same metropolitan area, and they have strongly favored southern locations.

(a) Detroit 3

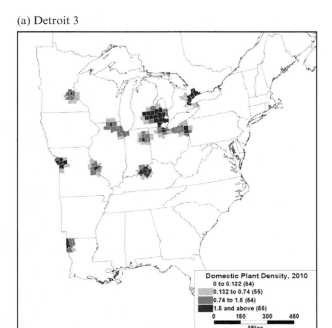

(b) Other carmakers

Source: Ward's AutoInfobank, authors' calculations.

Figure 2.14   *Assembly plant density for Detroit 3 and other carmakers, 2010*

To the contrary, as the Detroit 3 have closed most of their coastal and southern plants, they have pulled back to their traditional Midwest home. As a result, the corridor of motor vehicle production is increasingly divided into a northern portion dominated by domestic suppliers and Detroit 3 assembly plants and a southern portion dominated by foreign-owned suppliers and assembly plants. Should the market share of the Detroit 3 continue to erode, the Midwest will bear the brunt of plant closures and employment declines.

Exclusive Detroit 3 suppliers and exclusive suppliers to foreign carmakers locate in distinct patterns. Plants that ship only to the Detroit 3 have a much more northerly distribution than plants that ship only to the North American assembly plants of international carmakers, as is seen in Figure 2.15. In the Midwest, 76 percent of the parts plants were owned by US-based companies and 24 percent by foreign-based companies (Klier and Rubenstein, 2008: 224–6). In the south, only 57 percent of the parts plants were US owned and 44 percent were foreign owned. In other words, the Midwest had 58 percent of US-owned plants and only 44 percent of foreign-owned ones. The south had 36 percent of foreign-owned ones and only 20 percent of US-owned plants. Foreign ownership was especially high in South Carolina and Kentucky.

Parts makers based in Germany and Japan were responsible for most of the southern drift. Companies based in Germany and Japan each owned nearly one-fourth of all of the foreign-owned parts plants in the United States, but they each accounted for two-fifths of all parts plants in the south. Japanese- and German-owned parts makers both split about evenly between the Midwest and the South.

2.5.2   Distribution by Type of Part

Where a parts plant locates within auto alley depends to a great extent on the type of part being made (see Table 2.4).[20] Exterior suppliers have been heavily clustered in the Midwest because of a combination of proximity to inputs (especially integrated steel mills) and to customers (especially carmakers' stamping facilities and final assembly plants). Exterior parts are difficult to ship over long distances. Body panels and fascias are bulky and fragile and carmakers have retained much of the body stamping work as a core competency.

Powertrain production is also strongly embedded in the Midwest. As with the exterior, the powertrain depends primarily on proximity to iron and steel inputs, as well as carmakers' engine and transmission plants. Powertrain plants also depend more than other parts on skilled labor in the Midwest.[21] Interior suppliers invariably locate a seat plant within one hour of final assembly. However, the components that go into seat production, such as cloth, frames, foam, and electronics, may be produced further away. Chassis production has a mixed distribution. More than 60 percent of the plants making driveline and steering parts were still in the Midwest. Suppliers of wheel and fuel-handling parts were more likely to move southward in auto alley. Between these two were brake and suspension suppliers. Electronics plants were least likely to be in the Midwest. A large percentage of these suppliers have settled in Mexico.[22]

In summary, parts that are relatively expensive and fragile to ship are more likely

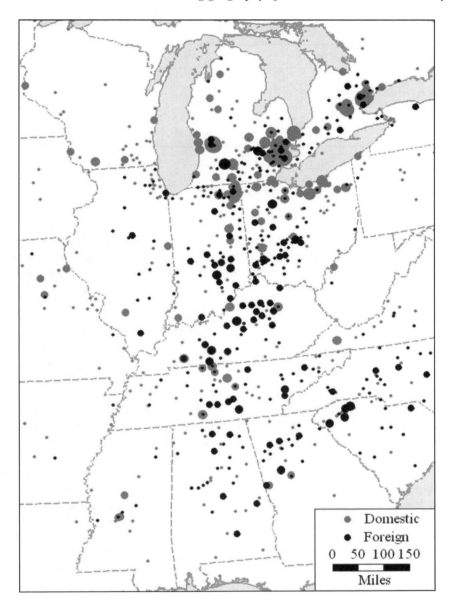

Source: Klier and Rubenstein (2008).

Figure 2.15 Distribution of US- and foreign-owned plants

to continue to be produced in the Midwest. In general, engines, transmissions, seats, and large body stampings tend to be produced relatively close to final assembly plants. Chassis and electrical components, as well as subassembly parts delivered to seat and powertrain plants, are more likely to be located further away.

Table 2.4   Location of parts production by type of part (median distance from Detroit)

System	Miles
Exterior	219
Powertrain	272
Interior	310
Chassis	366
Electronics	666

Source: Klier and Rubenstein (2008).

2.5.3   Labour

The auto industry has been moving south in auto alley in part because of labour considerations (See Klier and Rubenstein, 2008, ch. 21). Wage rates and union membership have been lower in the south than in the Midwest. As the auto industry has moved southward, it has been transformed within a generation from a high- to an average-wage industry. At the same time the level of unionization in the industry has declined.

Foreign-owned companies have been especially eager to avoid traditional concentrations of auto workers, especially unionized ones. The attitude of Japanese companies was captured in a letter from a Mitsubishi official to Representative Mary Rose Oaker (D-Oh): 'The rule of thumb we have been using in our site selection process is to avoid going right into the heart of any existing heavily automotive industrial region' (Jensen, 1985, quoted in Rubenstein, 1992: 232). Approximately 35 percent of all motor vehicle parts jobs were unionized in 2006, but at foreign-owned parts plants unionization was much lower, approximately 12 percent. The contrast is even more extreme at final assembly plants: all of the Detroit 3 plants were unionized, compared with only two of the 16 foreign-owned ones.

As recently as the 1980s, 90 percent of production workers in the US motor vehicle industry belonged to a union. Since then, the percentage of unionized motor vehicle workers has declined by 2 percent per year. The unionized workforce declined from about 1 million in 1980 to ¼ million in 2010. At the same time UAW[23] membership declined from a historic high of 1.5 million in 1979 to 431,000 in 2008 (Snavely, 2010).

Outsourcing by carmakers contributed to lower rates of pay and union membership. Two-thirds of the workers at carmakers were union members in 2007, compared to less than one-fifth at suppliers.

2.6   SUMMARY AND OUTLOOK

The geography of the US motor vehicle industry has experienced substantial change during the course of the last three decades. Assembly plants returned to the Midwest as the branch plant system of assembling motor vehicles outlived its rationale. Soon thereafter foreign-headquartered manufacturers started producing motor vehicles in North America. As they continued to gain market share there, they grew their production operations over the course of two and a half decades. In their wake a large number of foreign-headquartered parts producers entered North America. While the US auto industry as a whole prospered, a reallocation of economic activity took place southward from the traditional center of this industry in the states of Michigan, Indiana, and Ohio. By 2010 auto alley, a north–south-oriented industry cluster was firmly established.[24] In the course of about three decades the highly clustered auto industry had pivoted around Michigan, away from its traditional east–west orientation. Some suggested that this change illustrated the breaking up of the traditional Midwestern manufacturing belt (Krugman, 2008).

How will the next decade or two shape the auto industry footprint? Traditionally, most motor vehicles sold in the United States have been assembled in the United States from parts produced in the United States.[25] This is likely to continue in the future. Other manufacturing sectors, such as textiles and electronics, may have largely transferred production away from the US, but motor vehicle production is unlikely to do so. Motor vehicles have been and will continue to be bulky expensive goods to transport. Therefore the need to minimize the aggregate costs of transporting them to consumers throughout the US will continue to influence the locations of assembly plants.

Within the United States, auto alley will likely continue to strengthen as the hub of motor vehicle production because of transportation costs. 'Up for grabs' though are specific choices of locations as auto alley has fragmented into two subareas, a northern segment dominated by US-owned carmakers and parts makers, and a southern segment dominated by foreign-owned carmakers and parts makers.

The outlook for motor vehicle parts production is less clear. On balance smaller and more lightweight than finished vehicles, parts are less costly to ship over longer distances.[26] At the same time, just-in-time production constraints reinforce the regional agglomeration of production.

NOTES

*   The authors would like to thank Taft Foster and Vanessa Haleco for excellent research assistance.
1. The remainder of this chapter focuses on the US auto industry. For more detail on Canada see, for example, Sturgeon et al. (2007). See Weintraub and Sands (1998) and Carillo (2004) for a NAFTA perspective.
2. In comparison, in 2009 Michigan accounted for only 20 percent of US light vehicle production.
3. Economic geography factors were once viewed as insignificant in explaining the clustering of motor vehicle production in southeastern Michigan. 'At its formative stage, motor vehicle manufacturing was not tied to sources of materials or markets, transport costs were low and the industry was not yet capital intensive' (Bloomfield, 1978: 122–3). Automotive historians attributed the rise of Detroit to the accident of being the home of a remarkable collection of inventors. For example, 'With due allowance for the influence of economic and geographic factors, Detroit became the capital of the automotive kingdom because it happened to possess a unique group of individuals with both business and technical ability who became interested in the possibilities of the motor vehicle' (Rae, 1965: 59). Bicycle manufacturers contributed to the emergence of southeastern Michigan as the industry's hub by failing to recognize the automobile's potential (Rubenstein, 1992: 34). See also Klepper (2007) on the role of spinoffs within the auto industry in strengthening Detroit's role.
4. Foreign-owned carmakers represented 45 percent of US light vehicle production in 2009 (Ward's AutoInfobank).
5. 'Auto alley' is defined in this chapter as the states of Alabama, Georgia, Illinois, Indiana, Kentucky, Michigan, Mississippi, Ohio, and Tennessee.
6. A handful of assembly plants contain two separate assembly lines under the same roof. Figures 2.6

through to 2.9 utilize the number of assembly lines; data in the text and other figures refer to number of assembly plants rather than lines.

7. Klier and McMillen (2008) calculated the density of assembly plants using a tri-cube kernel density measure. The density of assembly plants near each county i is a function of the distance between each plant j and the county. The assembly plant location is measured by ZIP code, and the county location is measured as the county centroid. To compare identical geographical areas, a 50-mile radius was drawn around each county centroid. A cubic function gave more weight to plants near the center of a county. Plants located farther away than the radial distance do not affect the density measure. The density measure for each county is divided by all observations in the area of study. The share is then multiplied by 100. $j = 1, \ldots, J$ plants, D_i = density of plants around county I, d_{ij} = distance between county i and plant j, h = bandwidth:

$$D_i = 100\left\{\frac{1}{J}\sum_{j=1}^{J}\left[1 - \left(\frac{d_{ij}}{h}\right)^3\right]^3 I(d_{ij} < h)\right\}.$$

8. Essex County, Ontario, across the Detroit River from Detroit, represents the only other locale of equally high assembly density.
9. That plant replaced an existing facility very close by.
10. During the 1950s, at the height of the branch assembly plant system the best-selling vehicles had large production runs that utilized multiple assembly plants. Now, individual models rarely support more than one assembly plant (Rubenstein, 1992). The economic benefits of concentrated production in auto alley were reinforced by the introduction of new railroad equipment: Tri-level rack cars, introduced in 1960, permitted long-distance shipment of finished vehicles at a relatively low cost and eliminated most of the price advantage of shipping parts for assembly at branch plants. For example, the cost of shipping an assembled Chevrolet from Detroit in 1955 was $38 more than the outlay for transporting parts to the plants, but by 1966 the cost advantage was only $10 (White, 1971: 42).
11. The last assembly plant operating on the East Coast – GM's Wilmington, Delaware, facility – closed in 2009, and the last on the West Coast – NUMMI in Fremont, California – closed in 2010.
12. Information received by the authors from officials at several assembly plants.
13. Two hours represents the sum of the one-hour commuting range of the proposed plant plus one hour from the existing one.
14. The alternative location strategy – to look outside auto alley – was employed only once between 1980 and 2010, when Toyota built an assembly plant near San Antonio, Texas. Toyota justified the choice on the basis of Texas being the world's largest market for full-sized pickup trucks. During the 1980s, GM had considered sites in Texas for its Saturn plant but rejected them after calculating that freight charges would be $400–$500 higher, primarily because haul-away drivers would have to stop overnight more often (Rubenstein, 1992).
15. What goes into a vehicle can be sorted into a hierarchy: parts are typically small, individual pieces of metal, rubber, or plastic stamped, cut, or molded into distinctive shapes, such as knobs and levers. Components are several parts put together into recognizable features, such as radios and seat covers. Modules are several components combined to make functional portions of a motor vehicle, such as instrument panels and seats. Systems are groups of components that are linked by function into major units of motor vehicles, such as interiors and powertrain.
16. The variable used in their model accounted for the number of assembly plants within a 100-mile radius of each supplier plant.
17. The shift in responsibility from carmakers to suppliers is reflected in employment changes. In 1990, 239,000 assembly plant employees and 653,000 supplier employees produced 9.5 million light vehicles in the United States. In 2000, after a decade of record-high production, 237,000 assembly plant employees and 840,000 supplier employees produced 12.3 million vehicles.
18. According to Klier and Rubenstein (2008), the mean number of customers for a parts plant is four. They report 35 percent of supplier plants with two customers and 7 percent with more than six customers.
19. The northern half of auto alley consists of the states of Michigan, Indiana, Ohio, and Illinois. The southern part is made up of Mississippi, Alabama, Georgia, Kentucky, and Tennessee.
20. Klier and Rubenstein (2008) grouped parts into six systems: powertrain (including engine and transmission); chassis (including tires, wheels, brakes, steering, and suspension); exterior (including bodies, bumpers, glass, and paint); interior (including seats, instrument panels, doors, headliners, and carpeting); electronics (including engine management, passenger convenience, and safety); and generic parts (including bearings, brackets, and hinges). Twenty-two percent of plants make primarily parts for the powertrain, 19 percent for the chassis, 16 percent for generics, 15 percent each for electronics and the exterior, and 14 percent for the interior.
21. It is uncertain where alternative fuel powertrains will be produced and by whom.

22. Plants that supply only Detroit 3 carmakers tend to specialize in different types of parts than those that supply only international carmakers. The sharpest difference is the relatively high percentage of plants that supply the Detroit 3 with generic or bin parts, such as bearings, brackets, fasteners, gaskets, screws, seals, and springs (Table 2.4).

23. The UAW represents the United Automobile, Aerospace and Agricultural Implement Workers of America.

24. See Klier and Rubenstein (2012) on the impact of the bankruptcy-induced restructuring of GM and Chrysler.

25. Imported parts captured more than one-fourth of the US new vehicle market in the early twenty-first century, and foreign-owned factories in the United States more than one-fourth. That left US-owned factories in the United States with less than one-half. The 2002 US Census of Manufactures reported that 27 percent of the parts used at US assembly plants were imported (Klier and Rubenstein, 2006).

26. Parts production has become more dispersed than final assembly (Sturgeon et al., 2008). In 2002, 20 percent of vehicles sold in the United States were assembled overseas, whereas 44 percent of the parts were imported. However, data on the trade of motor vehicle parts do not distinguish between parts destined for assembly lines and parts for the so-called 'aftermarket'. That could explain the higher level of overseas imports for vehicle parts.

REFERENCES

Ballert, Albert George (1947), 'The primary functions of Toledo, Ohio', PhD dissertation, University of Chicago.

Bloomfield, G.T. (1978), *The World Automotive Industry*, Newton Abbot, UK and North Pomfret, VT: David & Charles.

Boas, C.W. (1961), 'Locational patterns of American automobile assembly plants', *Economic Geography*, 37: 218–30.

Bradley, J.J. and R.M. Langworth (1971), 'Calendar year production: 1896 to date', in Automobile Quarterly (eds), *The American Car since 1775*, New York: Dutton.

Carillo, Jorge (2004), 'NAFTA: the process of regional integration of motor vehicle production', in Jorge Carillo, Yannick Lung and Rob van Tulder (eds), Cars, Carriers of Regionalism?, Basingstoke: Palgrave Macmillan, pp. 104–17.

Colby, Charles C. and Alice Foster (1940), *Economic Geography*, Boston, MA: Ginn & Co.

Congressional Oversight Panel (2009), 'The Use of TARP Funds in the Support and Reorganization of the Domestic Automotive Industry', Oversight Report, Washington, DC, September.

Cooney, Stephen (2007), *Motor Vehicle Manufacturing Employment: National and State Trends and Issues*, Washington, DC: Congressional Research Service RL34297.

Dodge et al. v. Commissioner of Internal Revenue (1927), 'Petitioners Statement of Facts, April 18', Accession 96, Box 3, Archives and Library, Henry Ford Museum and Greenfield Village, Dearborn, MI.

Estall, R.C. (1985), 'Stock control in manufacturing: the just-in-time system and its locational implications', *Area*, 17 (2): 129–32.

Flink, J.J. (1970), *America Adopts the Automobile, 1985–1910*, Cambridge, MA and London: MIT Press.

Glassmeier, Amy and Richard McCluskey (1987), 'U.S. auto parts production: an analysis of the organization and location of a changing industry', *Economic Geography*, 63 (2): 142–59.

Helper, Susan (1991), 'How much has really changed between U.S. automakers and their suppliers?', *Sloan Management Review*, 15 (3): 15–28.

Helper, Susan and Mari Sako (1995), 'Supplier relations in Japan and the United States: are they converging?', *Sloan Management Review*, 36: 77–84.

Henrickson, G.R. (1951), *Trends in the Geographic Distribution of Suppliers of Some Basically Important Materials Used at the Buick Motor Division, Flint, Michigan*, Ann Arbor, MI: University of Michigan Institute for Human Adjustment.

Hurley, N.P. (1959), 'The automobile industry: a study in industrial location', *Land Economics*, 35: 1–14.

Hyde, Charles K. (2005), *The Dodge Brothers: The Men, the Motor Cars, and the Legacy*, Detroit, MI: Wayne State University Press.

Jensen, C. (1985), 'Mitsubishi–Chrysler ventures eye S. Ohio', *Cleveland Plain Dealer*, April 16: 1-E.

Klepper, Steven (2007), 'Disagreements, spinoffs, and the evolution of Detroit as the capital of the U.S. automobile industry', *Management Science*, 53 (4): 616–31.

Klier, Thomas (2000), 'Does "just-in-time" mean "Right-next-door"? Evidence from the auto industry on the spatial concentration of supplier networks', *Journal of Regional Analysis and Policy*, 30 (1): 43–60.

Klier, Thomas (2009), 'From tail fins to hybrids: how Detroit lost its dominance of the U.S. auto market', *Economic Perspectives*, **33** (2): 2–17.

Klier, Thomas and Dan McMillen (2006), 'The geographic evolution of the U.S. auto industry', *Economic Perspectives*, **30** (2): 2–13.

Klier, Thomas and Dan McMillen (2008), 'Evolving agglomeration of the U.S. auto supplier industry', *Journal of Regional Science*, **48** (1): 245–67.

Klier, Thomas and James M. Rubenstein (2006), 'Competition and trade in the U.S. auto parts sector', *Chicago Fed Letter*, 222.

Klier, Thomas and James M. Rubenstein (2008), *Who Really Made Your Car? Restructuring and Geographic Change in the Auto Industry*, Kalamazoo, MI: *The Upjohn Institute*.

Klier, Thomas and James M. Rubenstein (2012), 'Detroit back from the brink? Auto industry crisis and restructuring 2008–2011', *Economic Perspectives*, **36** (2): 35–54.

Klier, Thomas and William Testa (2002), 'Linkages across the border – the Great Lakes economy', *Chicago Fed Letter*, 179b.

Krugman, Paul (2008), 'The increasing returns revolution to trade and geography', The Sveriges Riksbank Prize in Economic Sciences in Memory of Alfred Nobel 2008 Lecture, available at: http://nobelprize.org/nobel_prizes/economics/laureates/2008/krugman-lecture.html (accessed June 5, 2011).

Mair, Andrew (1992), 'Just-in-time manufacturing and the spatial structure of the automobile industry: lessons from Japan', *Tijdschrift vor Economische en Sociaale Geografie*, **82** (2): 82–92.

Mair, Andrew, Richard Florida and Martin Kenney (1988), 'The new geography of automobile production: Japanese transplants in North America', *Economic Geography*, 20 (October): 352–73.

May, G.S. (1975), *A Most Unique Machine: The Michigan Origins of the American Automobile Industry*, Grand Rapids, MI: William B. Eerdmans.

Molot, Maureen (2005), 'Location incentives and inter-state competition for FDI: bidding wars in the automotive industry', In Loraine Eden and Wendy Dobson (eds), *Governance, Multinationals, and Growth*, Cheltenham, UK and Northampton, MA, USA: Edward Elgar, pp. 297–324.

Nevins. A. (1954), *Ford: The Times, the Man, the Company*, New York: Charles Scribner's Sons.

Niemeyer, G.A. (1963), *The Automotive Career of Ransom E. Olds*, East Lansing, MI: Michigan State University Business Studies.

Norbye. J.P. (1971), 'The race to produce: automobile manufacturing in the United States', in Automobile Quarterly (eds), *The American Car Since 1775*, New York: Dutton.

Parlin, C.C. and H.S. Youker (1914), 'Report of Investigation by Charles Coolidge Parlin, Manager, and Henry Sherwood Youker, Assistant Manager, Division of Commercial Research of Advertising Department, the Curtis Publishing Company', Accession 96, Box 3, Archives and Library, Henry Ford Museum and Greenfield Village, Dearborn, MI.

Rae, J.B. (1965), *The American Automobile: A Brief History*, Chicago, IL: University of Chicago Press.

Rubenstein, James M. (1992), *The Changing U.S. Auto Industry: A Geographical Analysis*, London and New York: Routledge.

Rubenstein, James M. (2010), 'Supply base interdependency', Presentation at Federal Reserve Bank of Chicago conference, Detroit, May 10, 2010.

Shirouzo, Norihiko (2007), 'Toyota revs up its push in U.S.', *The Wall Street Journal*, January 4: A:3.

Smith, Donald F. and Richard Florida (1994), 'Agglomeration and industrial location: an econometric analysis of Japanese-affiliated manufacturing establishments in automotive-related industries', *Journal of Urban Economics*, **36** (1): 23–41.

Smith, P.H. (1970), *Wheels Within Wheels: A Short History of American Motor Car Manufacturing*, 2nd edn, New York: Funk & Wagnalls.

Snavely, Brent (2010), 'New leadership tries to lead renaissance at UAW', *Chicago Tribune*, March 16.

Sturgeon, Timothy, Johannes van Biesebroek and Gary Gereffi (2007), 'Prospects for Canada in the NAFTA automotive industry: a global value chain analysis', Research Report, Industry Canada.

Sturgeon, Timothy, Johannes van Biesebroek and Gary Gereffi (2008), 'Value chains, networks and clusters: reframing the global automotive industry', *Journal of Economic Geography*, **8** (April): 297–321.

Wager, R. (1975), *Golden Wheels: The Story of the Automobiles Made in Cleveland and Northeastern Ohio, 1892–1932*, Cleveland, OH: Western Reserve Historical Society Publication 15.

Weintraub, Sidney and Christopher Sands (eds) (1998), *The North American Auto Industry under NAFTA*, Washington, DC: Center for Strategic and International Studies Press.

White, Lawrence (1971), *The Automobile Industry Since 1945*, Cambridge, MA: Harvard University Press.

Womack, James P., Daniel T. Jones and Damiel Roos (1990), *The Machine that Changed the World*, New York: Rawson Associates.

Woodward, Douglas P. (1992), 'Locational determinants of Japanese manufacturing start-ups in the United States', *Southern Economic Journal*, **58** (3): 690–708.

3 The changing geography of the European auto industry

Gill Bentley, David Bailey and Stewart MacNeill

3.1 INTRODUCTION

The geography of the auto industry in Europe is the outcome of a process of organizational change and changing production strategies. The chapter begins with an analysis of the process of restructuring and the theory of the spatial organization of the industry. In particular, we draw on Lagendijk (1997), who argues that there is a 'merging *filière*' in Europe, and Bordenave and Lung (1996) and Lung (2002) who suggest four models for the spatial organization of the industry, which take into account the relative location of original equipment manufacturers (OEMs) and supply chain firms. The extremes might be seen as a 'Swiss cheese' model and a 'Babybel'[1] model – in which the relative location of firms can be scattered or concentrated. The cluster model, however, has been increasingly referred to as describing the structure of the spatial organization of the industry (Porter, 1998; Blöcker et al., 2009). Therefore, the chapter first offers a general overview of the European[2] auto industry as a prelude to an examination of the geography of the industry as it is currently understood to be constituted. It then presents an analysis of the drivers to change in the industry and the challenges to the industry, in order to consider how far the geography of production in Europe will undergo further change.

It can be argued that in the pre-EU enlargement period in the early part of the twenty-first century, Western Europe was losing production capacity to new member states in Central and Eastern European countries (CEECs), and this was changing the geography of production in Europe. The CEECs are now integrated into the EU; the market has expanded and new production clusters have been created, with the auto producers and supply chain companies operating on a wider EU scale. As a result, considerable new production capacity has been set up in the CEECs (Stanford, 2010). The question is whether, in 2013, with new applicants (and/or associates) to the EU, including Turkey, the geography will undergo changes again, with a shift in production further east or to the southeast (such as Turkey), or North Africa, in search of lower labour costs. The challenge may also come from further afield, from China or even Russia. Europe may lose production capacity to producers in Russia or those in the Asian market, and in China in particular. Simultaneously, though, Russia and China are likely (and even need) to develop their domestic markets, in which case European-based producers may sell to these markets. However, it is likely that existing Chinese companies will nonetheless orientate towards developed markets such as those in Europe. It can be expected that they will make strategic alliances with existing European-based producers (as they are doing already), or may open production plants in the EU, just as the Japanese did in the early 1990s and South Korean OEMs more recently. However, it can also be argued that, as far as possible, European-based producers will adopt strategies to remain in business and will forge strategic alliances. This will sustain rather than threaten the auto industry in Europe. It will remain a distinctive world-region base for the organization of production, consumption and, since co-location is an advantage, with a geography of production characterized by clusters.

3.2   RESTRUCTURING THE ORGANIZATION OF PRODUCTION

Developments such as those taking place in the automotive industry can be characterized, according to regulation theory, as systems (or regimes) of accumulation. Regimes comprise the system of accumulation (or production) and the mode of regulation. The latter concerns the macro-level structure of consumption and encompasses general demand conditions for production, including government policy.

3.2.1   Changing Systems of Production

The system of accumulation refers to micro-level social relations of production, which have been changing (Wells and Rawlinson, 1994). Table 3.1 sets out the elements of different systems of production in the automotive industry. It is generally accepted that the industry has moved from the classic Fordist system of production to a post-Fordist system (Law, 1991; Wells and Rawlinson, 1994). The notion of lean production, or flexible specialization, characteristic of post-Fordism, and utilizing Japanese methods of production, is well documented in the literature (Womack et al., 1990; Wells and Rawlinson, 1994; Lagendijk, 1997). The industry has since been moving into what Lamming (1993) calls a 'post-Japanisation' phase. The characteristics of this phase are not entirely clear. Given recent and ongoing changes in the industry, it could be stylized as a 'Sinoism', so prominent are the Chinese as players in the global automotive market.

The restructuring process entails changes which are both internal and external to the firm. The changes within the firm encompass change in the organization of production (towards automation, teamworking, flexibility) and changes in its external linkages (strategic alliances and supply chain management linkages), as well as changes in products and markets.

3.2.2   The Spatial Organization of Production

Changes in the organization of production and in external linkages have an impact on the geography of production. The geography of Fordism is characterized as one of decentralization (Bloomfield, 1991). An internationalizing industry resulted in the major OEMs locating integrated production plants in different parts of the world, usually in low labour-cost countries but still near end markets, this dispersal aided by low transportation costs. The concentration of OEM production facilities in several locations resulted in a centralization of the firms lower down in the supply chain but, with time–cost distances not a threat to profitability, the location of supply chain firms and production plants was more dispersed on a global scale. Autos and parts were shipped around the world, with automotive production seen as a 'globalized' industry.

Table 3.1   Phases of production systems in the automotive industry

A CHANGING SYSTEM OF PRODUCTION

Fordism	Post-Fordism	Post-Japanization
Products and markets		
Mass	Small batch	Mass /batch
Standardized	Customized	Bounded choice
Quantity	Quality	Quality
Mass market	Niche market	Mass/niche
Parts	Components	Modules
Production technology		
Tools	CNC tools	CNC tools
Automation	Automation	Automation
Labour process		
Repetitive tasks	Multiple changing	Multiple changing tasks
Semi & unskilled	Skilled labour	Skilled & unskilled labour
Authoritarian	Teamworking	Contractual arrangements
Firm structure		
Multinationals	Transnationals	Hollow – marque holders?
Parts producers	Component producers	Module producers
National OEMs	Transnationals	Strategic Alliances
Operating principle		
Economies of scale	Economies of scope	Scale & scope
Supply chain management & supplier relationships		
Just in case	Just in time	JIT at supplier cost
Integrated plants	Disintegration	Devolution

AND A CHANGING GEOGRAPHY OF PRODUCTION

Decentralization	Centralization	Dispersal vs clusters?
Globalization	'Glocalization'	Regionalization?

Source: Adapted from Bentley (2000).

A key characteristic of the post-Fordist system, on the other hand, is the geography of proximity, this being fostered by the need for spatial proximity of OEMs and supplier firms (Lagendijk, 1997). This facilitates the development of production clusters, given rising transport costs (Storper, 1992). Local centres of production are in turn focused on 'national champions' (Lagendijk, 1997). Large firms benefit from the local sourcing of components, when just-in-time delivery, and shared problem solving, characteristic of Japanese systems for production, are necessary (Doel, 1997). The Japanese transplants in the UK – Nissan, Toyota and Honda – all sought over time to achieve higher local content, by adopting local sourcing strategies to secure local embeddedness, and by establishing a supply chain to achieve just-in-time delivery of components.[3] This represents a strategy of 'glocalization', or 'global localization', an internationalizing strategy where the inter-firm division of labour is set within the international division of labour (Solvell, 1988).

Bordenave and Lung (1996) concur with this argument. Looking at the impact of

Location tendency of component producers

Location tendency of auto assemblers	Polarization	Dispersal
Concentration	Unipolar agglomeration	Unipolar dispersed
Decentralized	Multipolar agglomeration	Continental integration

Source: Bordenave and Lung (1996).

Figure 3.1   Possible spatial configurations of the automotive industry

production reorganizations on the spatial configuration of activities in Europe, they considered that there are four possible forms of spatial organization that the industry could take (Figure 3.1). This classification is based on the activities of the automotive assemblers (whether they will decentralize to peripheral locations or concentrate in the European core), and the relative location of suppliers (whether they will polarize or disperse).

The spatial organization of what is thought to be the post-Japanization phase is one of decentralization and dispersal. Lagendijk (1997) describes this as a 'post-national' phase of development. In this phase, technological change is having an impact on the structure of the components industry and supply chain relationships. These production reorganizations are, in turn, changing the spatial organization of production. The changes threaten the development of local productive systems. Lagendijk considered that there is a 'merging *filière*' in Europe, brought about by the internationalization of component producers. Pointing to automotive component producers such as Bosch, Lagendijk found that these companies were dispersing production throughout Europe, to serve several national markets. Bordenave and Lung (1996) also considered that on the basis of trends observed in the mid-to late-1990s, the industry was moving away from this development path towards integration at the continental scale. Sadler (1999) in addition found that the auto assemblers and component producers were decentralizing production away from the European core area to what were then the new markets of Central and Eastern Europe (partly in search of low labour costs and partly to serve emerging new markets).

Sadler also considered whether the internationalization of automotive component production was leading to the hollowing-out of the automotive industry in Europe and whether Europe was simply becoming an auto assembly centre. There is some evidence of a shift in production and employment away from Europe to the rest of the world as the major OEMs continue to open production plants in other parts of the world.[4] A further development which raises the spectre of a 'hollowing-out' was that these developments involved outsourcing with the management of all stages of the production process being carried out by the brand/marque holder.

However, Sadler also argued that what is happening in Europe is rather a trend towards the regionalization or 'Europeanization' of the industry. Firms were orienting sourcing and sales on a European basis rather than on individual national markets. The idea of 'national champions' became much less significant since patterns of ownership were changing with mergers and acquisitions. For Van Tulder and Ruigrok (1993), this 'glocalization' represents a global strategy to produce vehicles for local markets, the 'local' market here being Europe. Production is thus dispersed internationally but concentrated within a world region and geared to production for those local (regional) markets and taste. As will be seen, the spatial organization of the European auto industry is based on a series of clusters: there is a pattern of multipolar agglomerations in the enlarged EU of 27 member states. The question is whether increasing global competition, overcapacity and the economic downturn of the late 2000s will in turn threaten this geography of production.

3.3 THE AUTO INDUSTRY IN EUROPE

Europe is the world's largest passenger auto producer, with an output of over 18 million units per year or 26 per cent of worldwide production (see Figure 3.2). The 'BRIC' grouping (Brazil, Russia, India and China) together account for 35 per cent of world

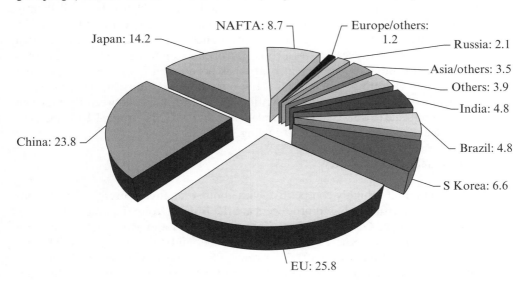

Source: ACEA (2011b).

Figure 3.2 Passenger auto production worldwide (% share), 2010

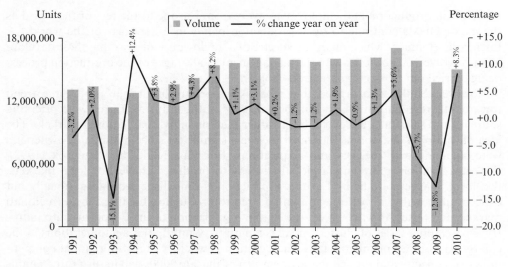

Units

Percentage

Source: ACEA (2011a).

Figure 3.3   Passenger auto production in the EU, 1991–2010

passenger auto production, more than Europe, but they actually represent distinct, different markets. China alone accounts for the lion's share of this figure (23.8 per cent) and clearly poses a competitive challenge to European producers and capacity.

Figure 3.3 shows trends in volume and year-on-year change in passenger auto production in the EU. As can be seen, production rose steadily from 1993 to 2000, fell slightly over the period to 2003 but rose again to reach a high in 2007. Thereafter it fell sharply, reflecting the onset in 2007 of the global financial and economic crisis which resulted in the worst recession for decades in Europe (European Commission, 2009a). There is some evidence of economic recovery in Europe as production levels rose 8.3 per cent between 2009 and 2010 to 15 million units, but ongoing uncertainty in the eurozone is leading to stagnating sales at the time of writing and a clear divide between the German OEMs which continue to do well and other players, notably GM Europe, FIAT, Peugeot Citroën and Renault, all of which are struggling.

3.3.1   Manufacturers by Country

The European market is highly competitive with about 40 manufacturers offering products. The 11 main European-based producers are the BMW Group, Daimler AG, FIAT SpA, Ford of Europe, General Motors Europe, Jaguar Land Rover, Porsche, PSA Peugeot Citroën, Renault SA, Toyota Motor Europe, and Volkswagen AG. The top three automakers are Volkswagen (21.3 per cent); PSA Peugeot Citroën (13.5 per cent) and Renault (10.4 per cent). There are a number of other smaller producers which are scattered around Europe. These and other major bus and truck manufacturers in Europe operate 169 vehicle assembly and engine production plants in 16 member states (ACEA, 2011b).

Table 3.2   Motor vehicle production by EU member state, 2010

	Cars	Vans	Trucks	Buses	Total
Austria	86,000		18,814		104,814
Belgium	313,520		24,340	430	338,290
Czech Republic	1,069,518	2,745	1,411	2,711	1,076,385
Finland	6,500				6,500
France	1,922,339	262,479	39,120	3,436	2,227,374
Germany	5,552,409	212,511	134,129	6,936	5,905,985
Hungary	165,000	2,760	130		167,890
Italy	573,169	254,290	28,770	1,130	857,359
Netherlands	48,025		44,764	1,317	115,487
Poland	785,000	73,953	2,015	4,487	869,376
Portugal	114,563	39,770	4,320	70	158,723
Romania	323,587	27,270		0	350,912
Slovakia	556,941				556,941
Slovenia	195,207	10,504			205,711
Spain	1,913,513	437,242	36,891	254	2,387,900
Sweden	177,084		30,000	10,000	217,084
United Kingdom	1,270,444	111,395	10,116	1,508	1,393,463
European Union*	15,068,473	1,426,518	377,106	32,339	16,904,436

Note: * Double countings are deducted from the totals.

Source: ACEA (2011a).

Germany, France, Spain, the Czech Republic and the UK produce the most autos in the EU. Germany is by far the largest auto producer, with 5.6 million units produced in 2010, 11.8 per cent more than in the previous year (see Table 3.2). France and Spain each manufactured 1.9 million units and performed similarly, as both countries increased their production by 5.7 and 5.6 per cent, respectively, compared to 2009. The UK expanded the most in 2010 (+27.1 per cent), with a total of 1.3 million units, up from 1 million in 2008/09, but still well down on a recent historical peak of just under 2 million units in 1998/99. For the first time, the Czech Republic produced over one million units, which was 9.5 per cent more than in 2009 (ACEA, 2012b).

3.3.2   Trade and Employment

The industry is a key part of the European economy with a positive contribution to the trade balance in 2010 of €54.4 billion, with exports of €76.5 billion and imports at €22.0 billion (ACEA, 2011a). These figures provide some evidence of recovery in the European economy since the trade surplus was €26.3 billion in 2009, exports having fallen considerably following the financial and economic crisis. The main trading partners which with the EU had a surplus in 2010 were the NAFTA countries where 29.3 per cent of EU autos were exported, the US importing 25.1 per cent of these, and China, which was the destination for 15.9 per cent of EU exports. The largest deficit

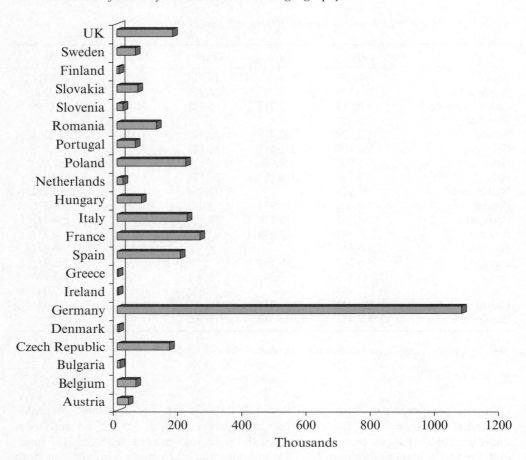

Source: Eurostat (online data code: ifsa_egan22d), European Commission (2012).

Figure 3.4   Employment in auto manufacturing by EU member state, 2010

was with Japan (€3.5 billion in 2010). The share of EU auto exports to Japan was 5.0 per cent, while a third of EU total imports came from Japan. The EU accounted for 12.4 per cent of the total auto exports of Japan in 2010. It is interesting to note that with the shift of assembly eastwards in search of lower labour costs, the 15 'old' EU member states now run a trade deficit in autos with the 'new' EU member CEECs (Stanford, 2010).

Employment in the industry is also significant. It is estimated that in 2010 about 2.84 million people were employed in the manufacture of motor vehicles and trailers, about 9 per cent of all manufacturing employment. The breakdown of this figure across the EU27 member states which have significant employment in the industry is shown in Figure 3.4.

Germany employs the largest number (1.1million or 38 per cent of the EU27 total). The next largest employer was France (258,200 or 9 per cent), with Italy having 218,700

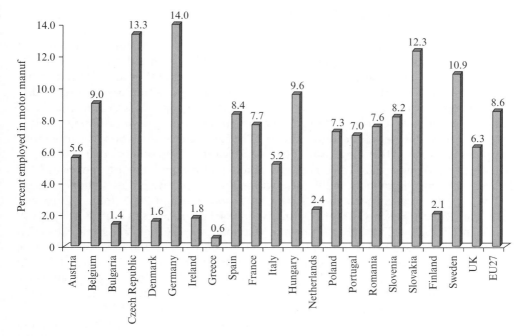

Source: Eurostat (online data code: ifsa_egan22.ifsa_egan2), European Commission (2012).

*Figure 3.5   Employment in vehicle manufacture as a percentage of manufacturing
employment in EU member states, 2010*

(7.7 per cent) working in the industry, Poland 214,200 (7.5 per cent), Spain 197,400
(7 per cent), the UK 174,500 (6 per cent) and the Czech Republic having 163,700 workers
in the manufacture of motor vehicles (6 per cent). Taken together, these seven member
states account for 81 per cent of employment. Adding in two of the candidate countries,
Croatia (with 5,200 employees) and Turkey (190,600), total employment in a wider
Europe in passenger auto production is 3.04 million. This does not include workers in
supply chain firms.

   That the industry is an important contributor to EU member state economies is demonstrated in Figure 3.5, which shows the number of people employed in motor vehicle
manufacture as a proportion of employment in manufacturing as a whole. In Germany
over 14 per cent are employed in the industry. The next largest proportions are in the
Czech Republic (13.3 per cent), Slovakia (12.3 per cent) and Hungary (9.6 per cent), all
Eastern European member states. In Western Europe, apart from Germany and Sweden,
the proportions are lower: Spain, France, Italy and the UK have less than the 8.6 per
cent average employed in the sector. This in part represents the shift and establishment of
automotive manufacturing plants in eastern EU member states, discussed further below,
but is also a reflection of the greater diversity in employment in other sectors found in
western EU member states.

3.3.3   The Auto Components Industry in Europe

Data on components industry firms which would give a fuller picture of automotive industry production and employment are less easy to obtain since the companies in the supply chain are in a variety of industries. The components industry includes companies whose business is metal or rubber processing or electrical and a number of other trades. Firms in these industries supply components or parts of components to industries other than the automotive industry, adding to the difficulties of properly attributing employment in these industries to the auto industry. The European Association of Automotive Suppliers (CLEPA, 2012) suggests that the industry is made up of more than 3,000 companies, employs more than three million workers and has an annual turnover of €300 billion, covering all products and services within the automotive industry supply chain.

The top 10 suppliers with their headquarters location and 2003 annual European sales are: Robert Bosch GBMH (Germany – €9.4 bn); Faurecia (France – €8.2 bn); Michelin (France – €7.6 bn); Continental (Germany – €7.6 bn); ZF Friedrichshafen AG (Germany – €6.1 bn); Johnson Controls (US – €6.1 bn); Valeo (France – €5.8 bn); Dupont Automotive (US – €5.6 bn); Siemens VDO (Germany – €5.5 bn); and Delphi Automotive Systems (US – €4.7 bn) (ILO, 2005). These data illustrate the dominance of European firms. These companies form part of the automotive industry clusters in Europe where supply chain firms operate in close proximity to the OEMs.

Within the EU, some 250 production lines are split between 16 member states, and every single member state is involved in the supply chain for manufacturing and the downstream chain for sales (European Commission, 2009b). The European Commission (ibid.) says that typically, there are around 50 upstream component suppliers for auto production spread all over Europe, and around 75 per cent of the value added of a new auto is generated by these suppliers. As a consequence, the value of intra-Community trade in automotive products is substantial, of the order of some €360 billion in 2007.

Taking into account employment in supply chain industries, it is estimated that total employment in passenger auto production is about 5 million across the EU (ACEA, 2012a). If all employment in downstream industries, including transport, is counted, it is estimated that about 10 million more jobs are accounted for by the industry and that over 12 million families depend on employment in the automotive industry in Europe; on this basis, each direct job creates at least another five related jobs (ibid.). Stanford (2010), citing extensive research, puts the general industry ratio higher, at 1:8. The overall trend, however, is thought to be a decrease in employment in the vehicle makers (OEMs) and an increase among the major suppliers, as a result of outsourcing and other changes in the production process which involve a greater role for first-tier or '0.5 tier' suppliers.

3.4   THE GEOGRAPHY OF PRODUCTION

The geography of production is shaped by the organization of production. It was observed that during the period of the Fordist system of production the pattern was one of decentralization. In the post-Fordist era and into a post-Japanization phase in recent times it has been argued that the pattern has been one of centralization both on a world-region scale and also at the subnational level. Instead of the idea of a global market, it has been argued that production and consumption is conducted on a world-region basis (see Bailey et al., 2010). Moreover, the geographical distribution of the main auto assembly firms in Europe had consolidated, with supply chain firms clustered around what could be seen as national champions. In the post Japanization era, however, changing patterns of ownership makes this term less meaningful. Moreover, cost and market pressures and the entry of the CEECs into the EU in 2004 have led to production plants being set up in these countries and a wider European geography of production, with a shift of production east in search of lower labour costs, to which we turn next.[5]

3.4.1 OEMs Shift East

Since the fall of communism, western auto manufacturers have invested €20 billion in the Czech Republic, Poland and Slovakia alone. Investment has also been made in Hungary, Slovenia and Romania. The new member states are attractive locations because of low labour costs, the availability of a skilled workforce, incentives and 'green-field' labour relations. The opening of new assembly plants has been followed by new supplier plants, often in close proximity on supplier parks. However, this is not the only reason why auto producers have moved to the CEECs; the CEECs offer access to new markets. Peugeot's move from Ryton in the West Midlands in the UK to Slovakia in 2003 was not only a cost-saving measure but also to be near to market; it had been importing kits from France, assembling the autos in the UK for trans-shipment to Eastern Europe (Bentley, 2007). Table 3.3 shows the increase in production in the new member states.

Initially, the plants primarily used parts assembled locally but manufactured in Western Europe. Finished autos were then imported back into Western Europe (with the latter now running a trade deficit on autos with Eastern Europe (Allen, 2001; Stanford, 2010). In the short term at least this implied a loss in employment and capacity to the traditional areas of production in Western European countries and a growing capacity in the new member states. However, these countries are now part of the EU and can be said to be integrated in a wider European production system and market and are part of the cluster map of auto production in Europe. Employment and production capability is distributed around the EU27.

Table 3.3   Central and Eastern European new member states: change in passenger vehicle production, 1990–2010

Production	Units 1990	Units 2002	Units 2010	% Change 1990–2010	% Change 2002–2010
Czech Republic	187,773	454,400	1,069,518	470	135
Hungary	na	134,600	165,000	na	23
Poland	283,890	309,900	785,000	177	153
Romania	90,000	70,300	323,587	260	360
Slovakia	na	235,700	556,941	na	136
Slovenia	na	106,000	195,207	na	84
Total	561,663	1,310,900	3,095,253	451	136

Source: ACEA (2011b).

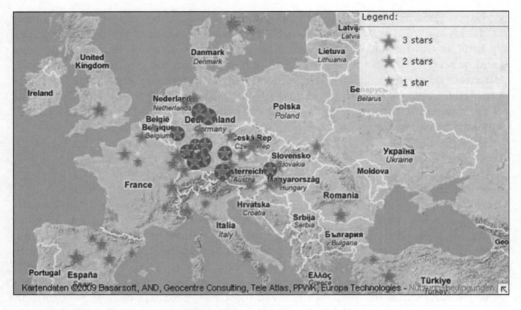

Note: The stars relate to scores in the categories of measures of employment in Table 3.4.

Sources: www.clusterobservatory.eu (accessed 13 August 2009); Blöcker et al. (2009).

Figure 3.6   Auto clusters in Europe, 2009

3.4.2   Automotive Industry Clusters

There are 48 automotive identifiable clusters in Europe (see Figure 3.6). Of these, 16 display the highest concentrations in employment, specialization and focus. Seven of the 16 clusters are in Germany, two in the Czech Republic and one each in France, Italy, Spain, Sweden, Romania, Turkey and the UK (see Table 3.4).

Each of these clusters is based around a major auto producer. This partial list also shows how ownership is intertwined:

- Stuttgart (in the state of Baden-Württemberg) is the location for Daimler (demerged from Chrysler) and Porsche (family owned; major shareholder in Volkswagen) and Bosch (component producer). Stuttgart is the area with the highest number of employees in the auto industry. Daimler is also based in Karlsruhe (in Baden-Württemberg).
- Braunschweig (Brunswick) is where Volkswagen (the number one auto producer in Europe, owning other brands including Audi, Skoda, Seat and Bentley, with integration with Porsche continuing) has three component plants, in Kassel, Salzgitter and Braunschweig. This locality displays the highest concentration of employment in the automotive industry within an area. VW-utility vehicles are produced in Hanover, Germany. (Volkswagen headquarters are in Wolfsburg in Lower Saxony.)

Table 3.4   Top specialized automotive clusters in Europe, 2006

Location of cluster	Employees	Size%[1]	Spec[2]	Focus%[3]
Germany				
Stuttgart	136,353	5.25	6.62	9.35
Oberbayern (Munich)	82,339	3.17	3.69	5.22
Braunschweig	79,997	3.08	10.7	15.16
Karlsruhe	40,694	1.57	3.03	4.28
Neiderbayern (Landshut)	37,960	1.46	7.44	10.51
Hannover	25,980	1.00	2.72	3.84
Saarland (Saarbrucken)	25,123	0.97	5.35	7.55
Czech Republic				
Severovychod (Hradec Kralove)	31,578	1.22	3.40	4.80
Stredni Cechy (Prague)	29,511	1.14	4.02	5.68
France				
Franche-Comte (Besancon)	24,767	0.95	5.38	7.60
Italy				
Piemonte (Turin)	85,915	3.31	3.49	4.92
Romania				
Sud-Muntenia (Ploiesti)	32,935	1.27	2.71	3.82
Spain				
Castilla y Leon (Valladolid)	27,136	1.04	2.07	2.93
Sweden				
Vastsverige (Gothenberg)	42,832	1.65	3.66	5.17
UK				
West Midlands (Birmingham)	37,913	1.46	2.26	3.20
Turkey				
Marmara (Bursa)	44,901	1.73	4.64	6.55

Notes:
1. Refers to share of total European employment.
2. This is a quotient. It compares the proportion of employment in a cluster category in a region over the total employment in the same region, to the proportion of total European employment in that cluster category over total European employment. It shows the degree of specialization.
3. This measure relates employment in the cluster to total employment in the region.

Source: Blöcker et al. (2009).

● Landshut (in Lower Bavaria) is where BMW (a private company which owns Rolls Royce and the MINI marque) is located, with Munich (Upper Bavaria) being the location for BMW headquarters.
● Saarland is the location for a Ford Europe plant; its European HQ is in Cologne.
● Sochaux in France in the region of Franche-Comté is where PSA Peugeot Citroën (largely family owned; majority shareholder in Faurecia component producer) has a production plant. Headquartered in Paris, it is the second-largest Europe-based automaker in Europe.
● The Czech regions of Stredni Cechy (near Prague) and Severovychod are locations for Skoda factories (owned by Volkswagen). These regions also have a high proportion of automotive employment.

- The Västsverige region in Sweden is where Volvo (now owned by the Zhejiang Geely Holding Group) is located, in the city of Göteborg (Gothenburg).
- The Piemonte region in Italy is the location for FIAT SpA (a joint stock company; owns Ferrari, Maserati; Chrysler and Magnetti Marelli, a component producer) and which is based in Turin.
- Sud-Muntenia (the city of Ploesti) in Romania is the location for a production plant for Renault (Corporation owns 44 per cent of Nissan and is in alliance with Daimler). It is headquartered in Paris, and owns the Romanian automaker Automobile Dacia and the Korean automaker Renault Samsung Motors, as well as Motrio (automotive parts).
- The West Midlands region in the UK is where Jaguar and Land Rover (the former Ford premium brands, now both owned by the Indian firm TATA) and a BMW engine plant are located.
- The Castilla y León a region of Spain is where Seat (a wholly owned subsidiary of the German Volkswagen Group) is based, at Valladolid.
- The Marmara Region in Turkey is the main location for the Turkish auto industry cluster and is home to Renault, PSA Peugeot Citroën, FIAT as well Turkish own-brand plants (Turkey produced 1,147,110 motor vehicles in 2008, ranking as the sixth-largest producer in Europe).

As Figure 3.6 indicates, there are other production clusters in Europe (Europe Innova, 2012). As Blöcker et al. (2009) point out, the regional concentration of employees in the industry mirrors the location of vehicle producers in Europe; there is no automotive region in Europe without an OEM. In other words, every region with a high proportion of employment in auto production[6] has an OEM located within it. This suggests that firms in the automotive supplier industries, unlike the OEMs, have not developed regional concentrations in the same way; none of the regions with a high concentration of employment in the industry is based round a supply chain firm. While data on employment in supply chains firms are not easy to find, it can be observed that broadly supply chain firms will locate in and around the regions in which OEMs are located. The locations are likely to be in auto supplier parks which have been developed in a number of locations in line with just-in-time delivery systems. These supplier firms will also supply businesses in industries other than the automotive industry.

3.4.3   A Sustainable Geography of Production?

It can be concluded that the geography of automotive industry production in Europe can be characterized as one of a series of production clusters. The co-location of OEM and first-tier supply chain companies is important since proximity minimizes transport costs (especially for bulky modules such as engines), a key consideration in the cost matrix of the production of autos. The core of the industry is in Germany (see Figure 3.6), which is home to several significant producers: BMW, Volkswagen, Porsche and Daimler AG. Nonetheless, PSA Peugeot Citroën in France and FIAT SpA of Italy are significant producers and are both loci and magnets for supply chain companies as well.

A critical question is whether this spatial organization of the auto industry will be sustained. It is clear that in the late twentieth and the early part of the twenty-fitst century,

OEMs have moved eastwards and OEMs have closed operations in Western Europe (notably in the UK), with an impact on the supply chain, to produce this geography of production (Bailey and Kobayashi, 2008). However, this spatial structure may change again. The candidate countries of the EU – Croatia, Montenegro, the Former Yugoslav Republic of Macedonia, Serbia and Turkey – may present new low-cost locations and market opportunities for OEMs; Turkey already has a developed cluster. But it is the BRICs that present a major challenge to the European auto industry. Of these, only Russia is physically within the European theatre and may offer a low enough cost location in turn to change the geography of production.

It is China and India, however, that may provide the major impetus to change the European geography of production. China has captured production capability from the UK, for example, in its takeover of the assets of MG Rover in the UK after the firm's closure, with the bulk of the plant and machinery being shipped to China in a 'lift and shift' operation (Bailey et al., 2008). China has been investing in an export-led strategy and is just starting to sell to Western markets, having concentrated so far on rapid growth in the domestic Chinese market (Donnelly et al., 2010). Nonetheless, China is still looking to export to the Europe market. Given the high transportation costs (linked to high fuel prices – which is likely to be a long-term phenomenon if the 'peak oil' hypothesis is correct), there is a question as to whether it will be economical to assemble autos in China for export to Europe, even with a large labour-cost advantage. Given this, over time it may well be the case that Chinese producers bring final assembly operations to Europe, as the Japanese and Korean producers have already done.

There are other possibilities for market entry available via takeovers. TATA's purchase of JLR has bought the Indian company prestigious brands and technology but has in turn also helped sustain the auto industry cluster in the West Midlands in the UK. Chinese companies might similarly buy up European companies to produce for the European (and in turn Chinese) market – such as in the case of Shanghai Auto/MG Cars, and Geely/Volvo.

The alternative for European OEMs, however, is through strategic alliances rather than direct takeovers.[7] There is evidence of increasing numbers of strategic alliances, both ways, with European companies entering into strategic alliances with Asian companies and vice versa. It may be that the existing spatial structure of the auto industry in Europe will be sustained in this way. Another dimension to consider is the EU setting challenging targets for environmental performance in the industry, which is both stimulating innovation and also effectively keeping out those foreign players unable to meet such standards (Wells, 2010). Indeed, such regulation is one feature of the industry being continually under pressure to change, and the next section discusses the drivers of change that shape the spatial organization of the industry.

3.5   DRIVERS OF CHANGE

Over the last decade in particular the automotive industry has experienced major organizational change. Also, there have been major changes in manufacturing and vehicle technology which, as noted earlier, can be characterized as leading to different

Table 3.5   Key drivers of change in the automotive industry

Key drivers		
Consumer demand	Oil polices/energy	Shifting lifestyles
Economy	R&D	Consumer Attitudes
Market segmentation	Manufacturing technologies	Personal identity
Legislation & regulation	Socio-demographics	Globalization
Environment	Urbanization	Emerging markets

Source: Paris et al (2009).

production systems (MacNeill et al., 2002). The overriding driver to change in the industry, however, is the need for firms to remain competitive and profitable in the global market in the context of excess global capacity and rising development costs; the reduction of costs is the key driver. The financial and economic crisis of 2008 and ensuing recession threatened the profitability (and even the survival) of many companies. This alone has forced firms to cut back production and take action to respond to a crisis situation. Looking beyond events and general trends, there are deeper underlying causal drivers to change to which companies respond in devising strategies for the management of change[8] (Paris et al., 2009). Table 3.5 lists what Paris et al. suggest are the key drivers of change.

Not all these are considered significant. It can be argued that the key drivers to change are: globalization; the economy and R&D, with these borne out in terms of competitive pressures; environmental issues and legislation; and personal mobility linked to shifting lifestyles, and consumer demand. The above issues very much represent the 'here and now' of the automotive industry (ibid.). The strategies adopted as a response can include internal restructuring, including consolidation; looking for new markets; designing new products; outsourcing, with its implications for the supply chain industries; the use of new production technologies including new patterns of work organization requiring a retraining of workers; job shedding and the closure of plant(s); or relocation. What can be said is that the automotive industry in Europe is constantly changing as a result of market trends, international competition, technological innovation and regulatory changes, but overriding this, costs. The key drivers we look at here are competitive pressures, environmental regulation and consumer demand.

3.5.1   Competitive Pressures and the 'Crisis of Cost Recovery'

Intense competition requires operations to be carried out with maximum efficiency if firms are to survive. In the mass market, the key is large-scale production to reduce the value of fixed costs per vehicle and, critically, to recover the costs of new model development, usually through platform-sharing approaches (Bailey and Kobayashi, 2008). The Premium segment is less cost sensitive, hence the success of companies such as Daimler, BMW, Audi (VW) and Jaguar and Land Rover. With increasingly sophisticated vehicles, and rising development costs, however, the optimum economic scale has increased

(Rees, 1999; Bailey et al., 2010). Companies have sought to achieve economies by maximizing volumes through platform sharing and standardizing parts across their model ranges. The outcomes are an investment in high capacity, the ongoing trend to consolidation through mergers and acquisitions, but also the increasing number of cooperative ventures to share, for example, R&D costs especially with regard to the environmental challenge (EUCAR, 2011).

One outcome of these drivers of change has been the increasing cost of genuinely new model development, in contrast with what was expected under the 'life-cycle' model of industry development. Rather, the 'crisis of cost recovery' facing automakers has intensified. In today's prices, the cost of bringing a genuinely new model can be of the order of $1 billion (Bailey et al., 2010). Consequently, large-scale production over different models and brands using a platform-sharing approach is seen as vital to generate the cash for future model development, and is set to be pushed even further by the large OEMs. The net effect has been a step-change in the underlying economics of the automotive industry; in earlier decades economies of scale were linked to individual models, and production of some 250,000 units per year could be enough for that model to break even for a producer. Today, however, economies of scale in the industry are rather linked to the underlying platforms and shared modules and components. This creates opportunities for firms to find ways to spread costs across models but also brings dangers in terms of undermining brands and risks to a whole range of models if a key component fails. This trend has also created a 'two-space' market, with one set of manufacturers 'leveraging' their brand portfolio and achieving economies of scale by platform-sharing platforms, and another set occupying the low-volume premium end of the market (Holweg et al., 2009). Firms which are 'stuck in the middle' (Saab and MG Rover being recent examples) find it increasingly difficult to generate the cash for new model development and hence to survive.[9] The trend has also driven consolidation and cooperation in the industry to offset rising development costs.

3.5.2 Consolidation and Cooperation

Throughout its history the industry has seen mergers and acquisitions (M&As). Notable M&As within the EU include the purchase of Seat (1986) and Skoda (1990) by Volkswagen plus the alliance between Renault and Nissan (1999) as well as the purchase of Rolls Royce by BMW (1998) and Bentley Motors by Volkswagen (1998). The Swedish marque Saab was owned by GM Europe until early 2010. Struggling to make Saab profitable, on the failure to secure a deal with a Chinese partner as it objected to the transfer of licences for patents and technology to a Chinese company, GM sold it to Dutch sports automaker Spyker GM. Renault bought 99 per cent of the Romanian company Dacia (1999).

The restructuring of ownership has included the acquisition of European auto producers by companies based in the developing economies, such as the takeover of Jaguar and Land Rover (2008) by the Indian company TATA motors and the acquisition of MG Rover by the Nanjing Automobile Group in 2005 (later taken over by Shanghai Automotive). Volvo passenger autos is now a subsidiary of the Zhejiang Geely Holding Group (2010). European manufacturers have also used M&As to enter existing and expanding markets, for example, such as the US, through Daimler-Benz taking control of Chrysler (1998) (and Mitsubishi in 2000) and by FIAT, through taking control of Chrysler in 2011 after Daimler AG divested itself of the company; second Korea, through Renault's purchase of Samsung (2000) and through GM's purchase of Daewoo (2003). Daewoo has since been rebranded as GM Korea (2011).

Not all consolidations have been successful. Well-known failures include the BMW purchase of Rover in 1994 that ended in 2000 with its sale to the Phoenix Consortium, and the Daimler acquisition of Chrysler in 1998 which ended in 2007. However, while the de-merged Daimler AG received US$1.35 billion from the buyers, Cerberus, it directly invested US$2 billion in Chrysler itself. Moreover, even after the split, the Chrysler Jeep in 2012 still shares a platform with Mercedes-Benz M class autos. As noted already, Chrysler has since been taken over by FIAT (2011). Some consolidations, however, have been successful such as the Seat (1990) and Skoda (2000) purchases by Volkswagen, where a platform-sharing strategy has worked well.

Alternative strategies, such as alliances on particular models or engines are commonplace. Examples include the 2002 agreement between Peugeot Citroën and Toyota to build a new small automobile in the Czech Republic, as well as the Renault–Nissan alliance (1999) and the subsequent alliance of this group with Mercedes-Benz parent company Daimler to swap engines (2010). Daimler AG joined this alliance for the increased sharing of technology and development costs on battery/electric technologies. PSA Peugeot Citroën and BMW also have a joint venture to develop and manufacture hybrid components including battery packs (2011). Another example was the planned FIAT investment in Poland for a FIAT–GM joint venture in powertrain production, producing multijet auto engines both for Fiat and GM models. In 2008 Bosch formed SB LiMotive, a 50:50 joint company with Samsung SDI to start production for hybrid vehicles in 2011 and for electric vehicles in 2012.

Some analysts have predicted that the number of independent vehicle manufacturers worldwide will fall from 13 in 2002 to 10 in 2015. One forecast is that only six global producers will survive – with two in Europe, two in Japan and two in the USA (ILO, 2005). This prediction might be coming true in Japan and the USA but, as observations of recent changes in ownership of OEMs in the European theatre has shown, there is not so much of a picture of consolidation in Europe but rather a pattern of merger and de-merger. The EU still retains six major European-owned auto producers: Volkswagen, PSA Peugeot Citroën, Renault, BMW, Daimler AG and FIAT.

It seems that a web of cooperative ventures has become a prevalent pattern for European auto assemblers, with alliances being made and unmade. However, as the ILO points out, this may mean that in fact the number of individual firms may fall, as alliances, similar to M&As, come to limit the effective independence of firms, regardless of majority ownership, in entailing cost-sharing commitments. Of course, the OEMs are also taking ownership of supply chain firms as a means of consolidation. For example, PSA Peugeot Citroën is the majority shareholder in Faurecia, which is one of the largest international automotive parts manufacturers, producing six types of auto modules: seats, cockpits, doors, acoustic packages, front ends and exhausts. Similarly, Magneti Marelli S.p.A, an Italian company, is a subsidiary of FIAT, and deals with development and manufacturing of systems, modules and high-technology components.

3.5.3   Supply Chain Trends

The above process, and the logic of scale, has also led to major consolidations in turn in the supply industry and the growth of major 'mega-suppliers'. Forecasts suggest the possibility of a 50 per cent reduction in the number of Tier-1 suppliers, from 5,600 in 2002, to 2,800 by 2015 (ibid.). A report by VDA (2011) found that 75 per cent of the supplier companies surveyed expected consolidation to increase, particularly among the small and medium-sized enterprises, so as to enable them to access knowledge and expertise and to create alliances to withstand price pressure from manufacturers. Consolidation has led to increasing specialization (Jürgens, 2003), with fewer global suppliers of certain modules such as safety systems, steering, lighting and seats. For example, TRW is dominant in supplying safety and steering systems; Bosch in engine control and injection systems, as well as brake technology; GKN in primarily front-wheel drives (where they are dominant); ZF in driveline, including gearboxes; while Faurecia specializes in seats and interiors.

Competitive pressures have led automakers to seek to cut costs by increasingly outsourcing to the supply industry but also by 'offloading' production and R&D costs onto supply chain companies. This is also a reflection of changing production technologies through the development of modules and systems rather than components.

3.5.4   Modularization and its Impact

Modules or systems are pre-assembled by the suppliers and delivered (just in time and just in sequence) to the auto factories (Chanaron, 2001). This makes assembly quicker and more convenient for the automakers and in addition transfers responsibility for quality and logistics to the suppliers. E-commerce is increasingly being used and has become an essential tool for purchasing transactions and for CAD (computer-aided design) communications to speed up transactions. European manufacturers have gone further in the move to modularization than their US or Japanese counterparts. In many cases module/systems suppliers have set up close to the assembly plants – for example, on supplier parks (Jürgens, 2003). The most advanced modular assembly developments include the Skoda Octavia plant in Bratislava (VW) and the Smart Auto plant at Hambach (Mercedes). Here the module suppliers have been integrated directly into the production process with organizational synergies and learning evident through such close proximity.

For the suppliers, module or system supply gives additional added value and a greater stake in innovation. The automakers benefit from cost savings but lose competence as jobs are lost through 'hollowing-out'. This is a potential threat and some companies resist too much outsourcing, in part for quality-control reasons. However, they gain from economies of specialization and scale. For maximum efficiency the whole supply system needs to be lean and each company in the value chain is required to organize logistics to buy, make and sell components 'just in time', and to minimize costs through flexible working and the elimination of waste.

This suggests that as modules become more complex, the local aspect of assembly of modules becomes essential (even if components making up such modules are sourced more internationally). It is unlikely, therefore, that there will ever be a wholesale transfer of assembly to low-cost locations and a scattering of production complexes. However, there is increasing pressure on the small lower-tier suppliers.

3.5.5   A Threat to Lower-tier Suppliers?

The biggest squeeze on suppliers has been in the lower size band among producers of single components. It has been difficult for these companies to find the resources to innovate as OEMs demand, and they lack the scale to address the high volume requirements of standardization. A continuation of the above trends could lead to large suppliers outsourcing more to subsuppliers. To some extent this has happened, but large suppliers have been reluctant to lose innovation and technological competences. They also tend to view the abilities of many of the lower-tier companies on quality, cost and delivery as inadequate. The use of e-commerce is also a challenge to lower-tier suppliers. Rapid responses are required as are high levels of expertise. Training, and finding the time and resources to train, is a significant obstacle that threatens many small companies.

3.5.6   Vehicle Technologies

On the vehicle itself one major change is a continued move to more electronics and telematics and a shifting value base from mechanical to electrical/electronic parts. There will be a revolution in vehicle telematics affecting both the 'in-vehicle' experience and mobility. The industry, along with planners and policy makers, are concerned about the waste of energy and additional costs to business, plus the inconvenience and irritation of congestion. Features likely to be introduced include more sophisticated route guidance, inter-model route planning, lane guidance and proximity radars for speed control and warning systems. Europe, with a lead in communications technology, is in a strong position. In-car entertainment systems may also become more common, although to date this market has been slow to take off (KPMG, 2012).

Second, work is well underway on the development of electric, hybrid and fuel cell drives, especially for city autos and fleet vehicles. However, the internal combustion engine (ICE) will continue to dominate in the foreseeable future as a reliable and well-proven technology with considerable lock-in effects. Further refinements will produce improvements to the efficiency of both diesel and petrol engines, for example through direct-injection petrol engines. A major interest is in alternative synthetic fuels that are made from biomass which would be (more or less) CO_2 neutral. They could also have wide-reaching consequences for the European agricultural environment.

The pressure to reduce emissions and fuel consumption is driving vehicle weight reductions through material changes such as the increased use of aluminium, magnesium plastics and composites. Materials changes will also facilitate cheaper modes of assembly, enhanced occupant and pedestrian safety and recycling, the latter the subject of environmental legislation.

3.5.7   Environmental Regulation

European regulation is a major driver of the industry. Emissions and recycling legislation have a strong impact on both vehicle technologies and construction.

EU emissions standards are compulsory in all member states. The European Commission proposed in January 2007 that the EU should pursue the objective of reducing emissions from automobiles with a view to reaching the Community target of 120 g CO_2/km by 2012 (European Parliament, 2009). The strategy was based on voluntary commitments from the industry, improvements in consumer information and the promotion of fuel-efficient lighter-weight cars. This, it was hoped, would create incentives for investment in new technologies to promote eco-innovation and the development of innovative propulsion technologies to secure the long-term competitiveness of the industry and more high-quality jobs.

The second main area is recycling and the End of Life Vehicle (ELV) Directive. This required member states to legislate to increase re-use, recycling and other forms of recovery of ELVs and components and phase out certain hazardous substances. About 25 per cent of each ELV goes into landfills and the target is to reduce this below 5 per cent by 2015. A further requirement is 'free take-back' of ELVs, which enables owners to take their vehicles to an authorized treatment facility at no cost to themselves. It is expected that the costs of compliance will be significant. Analysts estimate that the requirements of the ELV Directive results in an additional €20 to €150[10] per vehicle. A particular issue for manufacturers is the responsibility for achieving recycling and recovery targets. This will require partnering with downstream operators – and a number of consortia have been set up, for example by FIAT in the Turin area. A second line of approach is through the re-manufacturing of parts – probably more for the aftermarket than for new vehicles.

An additional effect of this attempt to 'green' the industry is that the pressures of cost recovery are intensifying as OEMs invest in new technologies. As noted, this has led to a wave of joint ventures and alliances (for example, Renault–Nissan–Daimler) as firms look to share costs and expertise. At the same time, existing firms may have to look to others; in what may be a shift to more 'open innovation' models in the industry (MacNeill and Bailey, 2010). Despite such possibilities, there are limits to 'openness'; conventional production modes will persist for some years to come because of scale, resources, and the fact that OEMs still control in a top-down manner global production networks and value chains.

3.5.8 Consumer Trends

Another key driver of change relates to changing consumer tastes. For example, there is a growing demand for more choice in respect of the options available on autos. As a result volume production has become more like that for premium autos, with more vehicles being 'made to order' with multi-option choice and with niche vehicles, although such a trend still has a long way to go. Another trend has been a move 'upmarket' in specifications and the inclusion of more on-board electronics and telecommunications systems. Through increased specifications, automakers have been able to extract higher margins. Premium producers, partly to meet fleet emission targets, have also been entering smaller vehicles segments – such as BMW with its MINI range and BMW 1 and 2 series, and Daimler via its Smart and A/B class Mercedes.

More generally, there is an increased eco-awareness of the carbon footprint of the manufacture and use of the auto. There is also a desire for greater fuel economy in Europe linked to high fuel prices. This is leading to increased demand for smaller, fuel-efficient autos, notwithstanding that the luxury auto market has been growing. Future thinking points to the provision of 'mobility services' by 2050; given that most people live in congested cities, a shift is envisaged towards auto *use* rather than auto *ownership per se*. A growing number of affluent young urban professionals already choose not to possess a vehicle and this could accelerate the development and use of alternative forms of traction, for example, shared, tracked electric vehicles (Deloitte, 2010; KPMG, 2012). Manufacturers are beginning to respond by selling 'mobility packages' rather than autos *per se*, giving the consumer the right to use a range of vehicles over a time period up to a certain limit.

In the short run, however, demographics and changing lifestyles continue to shape consumer demand. The increasing numbers both of women in the labour market and of older people in the population, is focusing attention on both occupant and pedestrian safety and ease of use, and these in turn are linked to safety and health. At the same time the need to express personality will ensure that manufacturers respond to the demand for increased customization in design (often via the internet) as well as the design and production of new models to satisfy consumer tastes.

3.6   CHALLENGES TO THE AUTO INDUSTRY

Responding to drivers to change should also lead to changes in the organization of production that ensure companies are competitive and actually stay in business. There is, however, a wider set of challenges to the industry: global competition, overcapacity and the global economic and financial crisis that has unfolded since 2007–08, and which has shown no sign of abating. By early 2012, the UK and other states on the EU periphery were back in varying degrees of 'double dip' recession, while France was stagnating and only Germany was growing strongly. The impact of austerity across Europe was a decline in the EU auto market, which was also affected by a 'pull forward' of sales under various auto scrappage schemes announced over 2008–10.

3.6.1   Global Competition

Intense global competition is one of the biggest challenges to the European automotive industry. The BRICs are already major centres of production, with capacity expected to increase in each of these theatres of production. BRICs will increase their global market share to 43 per cent in 2016; a rapid rise from 24 per cent in 2008 and the 2011 share of 36 per cent (KPMG, 2012). The expectation also is that they will export vehicles that will compete with established players in developed markets, with Geely and Shanghai Automotive the most advanced in beginning exports and assembling in Europe. China's newest automaker, Qoros Auto Co., is set to challenge established brands such as Volkswagen and Toyota when it starts sales in Europe (Grundhoff, 2012). Forecasts suggest that China will export a million or more autos by 2017 at the latest, with the Chinese government expecting one of its OEMs to be in the world's top 10 by 2016 (ibid.). India and Brazil are both expected to export one million or more vehicles between 2017 and 2022 (India is already the world's largest producer of 'A segment' superminis). Brazil is expected to export to North America. The ownership of UK-based Jaguar Land Rover by India's TATA, operating in the premium market, has given it direct access to markets in the EU and the US. Russia, on the other hand, has been concentrating on developing its domestic rather than export market.

But it is the competitive pressures that the industry in Europe is experiencing, from its lower factor cost rivals (most of which are also developing significant design, engineering and R&D capabilities, the last through strategic alliances) that is putting most pressure on the companies. Component producers in Europe are facing increased raw material costs as well as labour costs. Labour flexibility is also an issue as workers in the BRICs, unlike those in the EU, are not subject to social protection laws which govern conditions of work and which make labour costs higher and prevent labour flexibility in much of the EU. Turkey, which is outside the EU, is not yet subject to EU labour laws, and is an attractive location from this point of view. There is evidence that Chinese companies are building up production capacity in Turkey for sales in the European market (GlobalAutoIndustry.com, 2012; KPMG, 2012). Manufacturers plan capacity to achieve economies of scale but slowing demand, due to the recession in the second decade of the twenty-first century, and with the substantial investment in capacity in Central and Eastern Europe, has created sizeable overcapacity in the EU marketplace.

3.6.2 Overcapacity

The utilization of capacity in the short term is an issue for the European auto industry, and ultimately the result of cost pressures. Automakers need to run plants at about 80 per cent of capacity to break even and whereas capacity utilization has historically operated around this level, it dropped to 65 per cent at the beginning of 2009 (EC, 2009c). In part this may be because Europe saw far fewer plants closing during the downturn than in the US (three plants by 2011, as against 13 in the US with two more planned (Klier and Rubenstein, 2012). Not surprisingly, auto industry executives estimate that Europe has at least 20 per cent too much automaking capacity (Reuters, 2012). With production at 18.0 million and sales at 13.9 million (see Figure 3.7), it is estimated that there is an excess

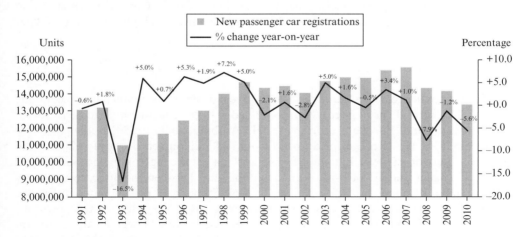

Source: ACEA (2011a).

Figure 3.7 New passenger auto registrations in the EU

of supply over demand in Europe of up to 4.4 million units (Reuters, 2012). Volume manufacturers predict a production (sales) volume needed to hit the market at a certain price but companies are often overconfident in sales predictions, an overconfidence that leaves them with unsold stock, while some underproduce and cannot meet demand (such as in the case of the MINI). Premium brands rarely have overcapacity issue. At the same time, however, demand is falling in general as a result of the recession in Europe. Almost all producers including Volkswagen, FIAT SpA and Renault-Nissan have seen sales fall over the 2011–12 period (ACEA, 2012b). Figure 3.7 shows the downward trend in new passenger auto registrations. A recent survey of automotive industry executives revealed that more companies expected overcapacity to emerge in key markets so that an export-led strategy will not reduce the excess of supply over demand in the European market (KPMG, 2012).

In the long term, however, the global market for motor vehicles is forecast to grow substantially, but given environmental and cost pressures this will be mainly in the market segment of smaller and low-budget autos (EC, 2009c). In principle, European manufacturers are well placed to take advantage of this market opportunity, with EU trade policy playing a supportive role in terms of enabling fair market access. Optimism about new markets has also led to investments in emerging markets, such as China and India. The continued investment in capacity by producers in China and India, however, makes it more difficult for Western Europe to export its production surplus, and in fact major OEMs such as GM Europe appear to be planning to shift production out of Europe to lower-cost locations such as Russia and then re-import significant volumes back into Europe. That in turn raises the spectre of further plant closures and restructuring.

The option that seems to be emerging is the intertwining of European and foreign firms in strategic alliances. While Chinese companies are looking for strategic alliances with companies in Europe to have a position from which to sell in Europe, European companies have a significant toehold in the Chinese market but need joint-venture partners under Chinese regulations in order to assemble in China. Consumer demand also needs to be preserved; GDP growth in China has fallen from its highs of 10.9, to 8.9 per cent in 2012.

3.6.3   Economic Downturn

The further challenge to the European automotive industry is the financial and economic crisis of 2007/08 and ensuing recession, combined with the enactment of austerity measures across much of Europe. According to IHS Automotive (Gott, 2010), the passenger auto market for Western Europe dropped from 14.8 million vehicles sold in 2007 to an expected figure of just over 12 million in 2012, which left the big-volume producers such as GM, Peugeot and FIAT with a serious imbalance between manufacturing supply and consumer demand. In addition, given that 60–80 per cent of new autos in Europe are purchased with the aid of credit, the financial crisis at the origin of the downturn hit the automotive industry particularly hard because credit has been harder to obtain (EC, 2009b). Moreover, the eurozone crisis in late 2011 added to the problem and with austerity budgets in operation in most EU member states, unemployment has risen and consumption fallen (as Figure 3.7 shows). While there were some signs of recovery in

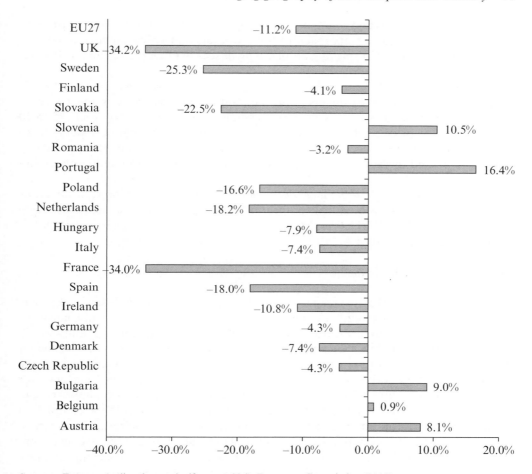

Source: Eurostat (online data code: ifsa_egan22d), European Commission (2012).

Figure 3.8 Percentage change in motor vehicle manufacturing employment, 2008–2010

2010/11, there were indications that the economic recovery was faltering in early 2012. The sales of autos in Europe were reported as having fallen 7.7 per cent in the first quarter of 2012 (ACEA, 2012b).

Employment in the auto industry has similarly fallen, by 317,000 (11.2 per cent), between 2008 and 2010 to 2.84 million (see Figure 3.8). Employment levels fell in almost all EU member states over the period. The largest decrease was in the UK where employment levels fell by 34.2 per cent (60,000 jobs) and in France where the fall was 34 per cent (89,000 jobs). Employment also fell in Sweden (25.3 per cent), Slovakia (22.5 per cent) and the Netherlands (18.2 per cent). Even Germany lost jobs (4.3 per cent). Employment levels rose only in Austria, Bulgaria, Portugal and Slovenia.

This overcapacity and the perceived need for restructuring has put the future of some plants in doubt, such as certain GM factories. GM Europe's core European brands are the UK-based Vauxhall and Germany-based Opel. GM Europe's strategy appears to have been a divide-and-rule approach to force workers and governments into concessions on costs and subsidies, playing off plants against each other (Bailey and de Ruyter, 2012).

To help the European auto industry, scrappage schemes were put in place by EU governments to persuade consumers to buy new autos and to put a floor under sales. It is estimated that the sales of passenger autos would have been lower by some 25 to 30 per cent, which is twice what they were had the scrappage schemes not been put in place (ILO, 2010).[11] Yet such schemes were likely to have had a knock-on effect by pulling forward sales, and thereby leading to a drop in sales once the scrappage incentives had finished.

More generally, though, there have been major differences in opinion regarding how to deal with the problems of global competition, overcapacity and the recession. Sergio Marchionne, the CEO of FIAT has been calling for a stronger EU level industrial policy to sustain the industry (ACEA, 2012a) and to assist with restructuring.

3.6.4   Industrial Policy in the EU

It is argued by many that overcapacity is the main issue for the industry in Europe. To address this will mean cutbacks and closures and job losses which will change the geography of production in Europe, if not globally, since production capability would further shift eastward (ibid.). China among the other BRICs is set to increase its market share. However, closures are costly, given EU labour laws on redundancy payments. Closing plants in general is expensive: to close PSA's Spanish factory at Villaverde, for example, would cost about €309 million (Reuters, 2012). The loss of jobs, however, can lead to a reduction in demand which further affects sales and results in the contraction of the economy. European producers looking instead to export their way out of crisis, will find this difficult, given that export strategies are being pursued by its global competitors aided by protectionist policies, which in turn reduces access to existing and new markets for European producers (EC, 2009b). As noted, however, other options are possible which could help in sustaining the industry in Europe, including government aid to support the development of the industry, such as measures to promote labour flexibility, and import restrictions in the form of 'planned free trade', to protect the industry.

However, it is ultimately the activities of the firms themselves that will have to sustain the industry in Europe. The growing number of joint ventures and strategic alliances is essential for ensuring that partners gain access to each other's markets and sustain businesses. Nonetheless, there is a need for state intervention to improve market access around the globe, and to ensure fair competition and reciprocity in trade relations (ACEA, 2012a). For example, ACEA suggests that the EU is too easily prepared to lower its barriers while allowing others to keep theirs in place. Measures also need to include policy for exchange rates since currency valuations affect trade. In particular it has been claimed that the Chinese RNMB is significantly undervalued, making China's exports cheaper and imports more expensive. China also restricts the foreign ownership of companies. There are also calls for a cluster-based industrial development policy that strengthens the industry and encourages innovation through R&D partnerships between governments, academia and corporations, and also for EU labour market policy to ensure flexibility in employment law which achieves a balance between the needs of workers and those of employers.

3.7   CONCLUSION

The geography of the auto industry in Europe is the outcome of a process of organizational change and the implementation of production strategies in the industry. It is clear that the current spatial organization is in the form of a large number of clusters around where the OEMs are located. The location pattern of supply chain firms is less easy to discern but it can be concluded that OEMs are surrounded by supply chain firms, with some located in supplier parks which have been built close to the OEMs, because proximity is important to reduce transport costs and satisfy the requirements of just-in-time production systems. It can be argued that in the pre-EU enlargement period in the early part of the twenty-first century, Western Europe has lost much production capacity to new entrants to the EU from the CEECs and this has changed the geography of production in Europe. However, the CEECs are now integrated into the EU; the market has expanded and new production clusters have been created, with the auto producers and supply chain companies operating on a wider EU scale.

The question is whether the geography of the auto industry will undergo significant change again, given the key challenges to the industry including: intensifying competition, overcapacity and recession/austerity in Europe; environmental pressures; the development of alternatively fuelled vehicles; and with new applicants to the EU. A competitive challenge may well come from further afield, from China or even Russia. Europe may lose production capacity to producers in Russia or those in the Asian market, and China in particular. At the same time, Russia and China may continue to develop their domestic markets, in which case European-based producers may sell to these markets (and locate production facilities there). However, it is also likely that Chinese companies will nonetheless want to continue to produce for the European market. It can be expected that they will make strategic alliances with existing European-based producers (as they are already), or may open production plants in the EU automotive cluster locations, just as the Japanese OEMs did in the early 1990s and the Korean OEMs more recently, in order to make sales in the EU market.

The *quid pro quo* will be that European companies will want to form strategic alliances with companies in China in order to sell autos in the Far Eastern market. As far as possible, European-based producers will also adopt strategies to remain in business and will forge strategic alliances among themselves, as GM and PSA plan to do (Reuters, 2012). This may be at the expense of ongoing job losses but if income levels are improved, this could serve to sustain rather than threaten the auto industry in Europe. As noted, there is a view in the auto industry that autos need to be made close to where they are sold (Bailey et al., 2010; Reuters, 2012). This suggests that Europe will remain a distinctive world-region base for both the production and the consumption of autos and, given that co-location is a major advantage, will continue to exhibit a geography of production characterized by clusters.

NOTES

1. A brand of cheese that is compact and ovaloid in shape.
2. The 27 EU countries as at 2012 are Austria, Belgium, Bulgaria, Cyprus, the Czech Republic, Denmark, Estonia, Finland, France, Germany, Hungary, Greece, Ireland, Italy, Latvia, Lithuania, Luxembourg, Malta, the Netherlands, Poland, Portugal, Romania, Slovakia, Slovenia, Spain, Sweden and the UK. Candidate countries include Croatia, Iceland, Montenegro, the Former Yugoslav Republic of Macedonia, Serbia and Turkey.
3. Although the effects of the Japanese earthquake and tsunami in 2010 indicated how such plants were still dependent on key components from Japan, especially in relation to electronics.
4. At the time of writing, GM Europe is thought to be considering shifting 300,000 units of production out of Europe to low-cost locations such as Russia for re-importing into Europe.
5. Klier and Rubenstein (2012) see a European 'auto region' as a compact rectangle extending southeast from the UK and comprising the UK, France, Belgium, Netherlands, Germany, Austria, Poland, Slovakia, Slovenia and Hungary. This 'core production region' continued to increase production share after 2007, but with west European states losing share (Germany being the exception).
6. Employment in NACE 34.
7. It is doubtful that German authorities would let their key automotive companies pass into foreign ownership.
8. Audi, Thyssenkrupp and Renault are identified as being good examples of undertaking a strategic management process.
9. Whether and how a possible shift to more specialized 'short-run' production will impact on development costs, economies of scale, and the nature of players involved in the industry, remains an open question.
10. End of Life Vehicle Directive, PwC, September 2002.
11. Such scrappage schemes led to the replacement of around 4 million vehicles, with the European Investment Bank providing some €3.8 billion in low-interest loans to member countries to fund the schemes (Klier and Rubenstein, 2012).

REFERENCES

ACEA (2011a), *The Automobile Industry: Pocket Guide 2011*, Brussels: ACEA Communications Department, available at: http://www.acea.be/images/uploads/files/20110921_Pocket_Guide_3rd_edition.pdf (accessed 10 April 2012).

ACEA (2011b), *European Union Economic Report*, Brussels: ACEA, available at: http://www.acea.be/images/uploads/files/20110927_ER_1105_2011_I_Q4.pdf (accessed 10 April 2012).

ACEA (2012a), 'Marchionne: "EU must counter economic headwind with a strong industrial policy"', *ACEA News*, 28 February, available at: http://www.acea.be/news/news_detail/marchionne_eu_must_counter_eco nomic_headwind_with_a_strong_industrial_polic/pr (accessed 10 April 2012).

ACEA (2012b), 'Passenger cars: registrations down 7.7% in first quarter 2012', available at: http://www.acea.be/news/news_detail/passenger_cars_registrations_down_7.7_in_first_quarter_2012/ (accessed 24 April 2012).

Allen, T. (2001), *The Automotive Industry and Candidate Countries, Statistics in Focus, Eurostat*, Luxembourg: Office for Official Publications of the European Communities.

Bailey, D. and A. de Ruyter (2012), 'Re-examining the BMW–Rover affair: a case study of corporate, strategic and government failure?', *International Journal of Automotive Technology and Management*, **12** (2), 117–36.

Bailey, D., A. de Ruyter, J. Michie and P. Tyler (2010), 'Globalization and the auto industry', *Cambridge Journal of Regions, Economy and Society*, **3** (3), 367–82.

Bailey, D. and S. Kobayashi (2008), 'Life after Longbridge? Crisis and restructuring in the West Midlands auto cluster', in M. Farschi, O. Janne and P. McCann (eds), *Industrial Regeneration and Regional Policy Options in a Global Economy*, Cheltenham, UK and Northampton, MA, USA: Edward Elgar, pp. 129–54.

Bailey, D., S. Kobayashi and S. MacNeill (2008), 'Rover and out? Globalization, the West Midlands auto cluster, and the end of MG Rover', *Policy Studies*, **29** (3), 267–279.

Bentley, G. (2000), 'The automotive industry: change and challenge for the RDAs', in G. Bentley and J. Gibney (eds), *Regional Development Agencies and Business Change*, Aldershot: Ashgate, pp. 125–50.

Bentley, G. (2007), 'Dealing with strategic change: A trio of automotive industry closures in the West Midlands', *Strategic Change*, **16** (8), 361–70.

Blöcker, A., U. Jürgens, H. Meissner and J. Paris (2009), 'Analysis of automotive regions, anticipation

of change in the automotive industry', Study 3, CLEPA Brussels, available at: http://www.anticipa
tionofchange.eu/fileadmin/anticipation/Studies/Study_3_Final.pdf (accessed 12 April 2012).

Bloomfield, G.T. (1991), 'The world automotive industry in transition', in Law (ed.), pp. 19–60.

Bordenave, G. and Y. Lung (1996), 'New spatial configurations in the European automotive industry',
European Urban and Regional Studies, **3** (4), 305–21.

Chanaron, J.-J. (2001), 'Implementing technological and organizational innovations and management of core
competencies: lessons from the automotive industry', *International Journal of Automobile Technology and
Management*, **1** (1), 128–44.

CLEPA (2012), 'European Association of Automotive Suppliers', available at: http://www.clepa.eu (accessed
11 April 2012).

Deloitte (2010), 'Auto Component Sector Report: Driving Out of Uncertain Times', Deloitte Touche
Tohmatsu, India, available at: http://www.deloitte.com/assets/Dcom-India/Local%20Assets/Documents/
Auto_Sector.pdf (accessed 22 May 2012).

Doel, C. (1997), '*The supply chain in regional development*', paper prepared for a Local Economic Policy Unit
(LEPU) seminar on improving competitiveness through supply chains and networks, Leeds, 21 October.

Donnelly, T., C. Collis and J. Begley (2010), 'Towards sustainable growth in the Chinese automotive industry:
internal and external obstacles and comparative lessons', *International Journal of Automotive Technology
and Management*, **10** (2/3), 289–304.

EUCAR (2011), 'Challenges and priorities for automotive R&D', EUCAR, Brussels, available at: http://www.
eucar.be/publications/Challenges_Priorities/view (accessed 13 April 2012).

Europe Innova (2012), 'Cluster Observatory', available at: http://www.clusterobservatory.eu/index.html#!vie
w=aboutobservatory;url=/about-observatory/about/ (accessed 13 April 2012).

European Commission (EC) (2009a), *Economic Crisis in Europe: Causes, Consequences and Responses*,
Luxembourg: Office for Official Publications of the European Communities.

European Commission (EC) (2009b), *Responding to the Crisis in the European Automotive Industry*, Brussels:
Commission for the European Communities.

European Commission (EC) (2009c), *European Industry in a Changing World Updated Sectoral Overview*,
Commission Staff Working Document. SEC(2009) 1111 final, Brussels: Commission for the European
Communities.

European Commission (EC) (2012), Eurostat, available at: http://epp.eurostat.ec.europa.eu/portal/page/
portal/eurostat/home (accessed 11 April 2012).

European Parliament (2009), *Regulation (EC) No 443/2009 of the European Parliament and of the Council of
23 April 2009 setting emission performance standards for new passenger cars as part of the Community's integrated approach to reduce CO² emissions from light-duty vehicles (Text with EEA relevance)*, Luxembourg:
Publications Office of the European Union

GlobalAutoIndustry.com (2012), 'Asian investments up, EU investments down in Turkey', available at
http://www.globalautoindustry.com/article.php?id=8130&jaar=2012&maand=4&target=Euro (accessed
22 May 2012).

Gott, P. (2010), 'New trends in the automotive industry: setting the scene', presentation at CLEPA Technology
Day, Brussels, 27 October.

Grundhoff, S. (2012), 'China's newest automaker takes aim at VW', *Automotive News Europe*, 19 March,
available at: http://europe.autonews.com/apps/pbcs.dll/article?AID=/20120319/ANE/303199861 (accessed
24 April 2012).

Holweg, M., P. Davies and D. Podpolny (2009), *The Competitive Status of the UK Automotive Industry*,
Buckingham: PICSIE Books.

ILO (2005), *Automotive Industry Trends Affecting Component Suppliers*, Geneva: International Labour Office.

ILO (2010), *The Global Economic Crisis Sectoral Coverage. Automotive Industry: Trends and Reflections*,
Geneva: International Labour Office.

Jürgens, Ulrich (2003), 'Characteristics of the European automotive system: is there a distinctive European
approach?', Research Paper, GERPISA, Paris.

Klier, T. and J. Rubenstein (2012), 'The economic downturn and the geography of vehicle production in
Europe and North America', paper presented at the 20th GERPISA colloquium, Krakow, Poland, May.

KPMG (2012), 'KPMG's Global Automotive Executive Survey 2012: Managing growth while navigating
uncharted routes', KPMG International Cooperative ('KPMG International'), Zurich.

Lagendijk, A. (1997), 'Towards an integrated automotive industry in Europe: "a merging filière" perspective',
European Urban and Regional Studies, **4** (1), 5–18.

Lamming, R. (1993), *Beyond Partnership: Strategies for Innovation and Lean Supply*, London: Prentice-Hall.

Law, C.M. (ed.) (1991), *Restructuring the Global Automobile Industry: National and Regional Impacts*, London
and New York: Routledge.

Lung, Y. (2002), 'The changing geography of the European automobile system', Research Paper, GERPISA,
Paris.

MacNeill, S. and D. Bailey (2010), 'Changing policies for the automotive industry in an "old" industrial region: an open innovation model', *International Journal of Automotive Technology and Management*, **10** (2/3), 128–44.

MacNeill, S., A. Srbljanin and G. Bentley (2002), *Developments in the Automotive Industry 2000–2015*, Birmingham: Centre for Urban and Regional Studies, University of Birmingham.

Paris, J.J., P. Loire, F. Piquard, N. Beech, G. Bowman, M. Dowling, S. Masrani, P. Mckiernan, H. Patrick, S. Singhal, U. Jürgens and H. Meissner (2009), 'Good practices of anticipation and management of change within companies and regions: anticipation of change in the automotive industry', Study 1, CLEPA, Brussels, available at: http://www.anticipationofchange.eu/archive/ (accessed 12 April 2012).

Porter, M. (1998), *The Competitive Advantage of Nations*, London: Palgrave Macmillan.

Rees, G. (1999), *Report on the Economic Prospects for the Automotive Industry in the UK and Europe and its impact on Ford of Dagenham*, Cardiff: Cardiff University Business School.

Reuters (2012), 'Europe closer to biting auto overcapacity bullet', available at: http://www.reuters.com/article/2012/03/02/europe-autos-idUSL5E8E22TV20120302 (accessed 23 April 2012).

Sadler, D. (1999), 'Internationalization and specialization in the European automotive components sector: implications for the hollowing out thesis', *Regional Studies*, **33** (2), 109–20.

Solvell, O. (1988), 'Is the global automobile industry really global?', in N. Hood and J.-E. Vahlne (eds), *Strategies in Global Competition*, London: Croom Helm, pp. 181–203.

Stanford, J. (2010), 'The geography of auto globalization and the politics of auto bailouts', *Cambridge Journal of Regions, Economy and Society*, **3** (3), 383–405.

Storper, M. (1992), 'The resurgence of regional economies: ten years later the region as a nexus of untraded interdependencies', *European Urban and Regional Studies*, **2** (3), 191–221.

Van Tulder, R. and W. Ruigrok (1993), 'Regionalisation, globalisation or glocalisation: the case of the world car industry', in M. Humbert (ed.), *The Impact of Globalization on Europe's Firms and Industries*, London: Pinter, pp. 22–33.

Verband der Automobilindustrie e. V (VDA) (German Association of the Automotive Industry) (2011), *Annual Report*, Berlin: Verband der Automobilindustrie e. V.

Wells, P. (2010), 'The Tato Nano, the global "value" segment and the implications for the traditional automotive industry regions', *Cambridge Journal of Regions, Economy and Society*, **3** (3), 443–57.

Wells, P. and M. Rawlinson (1994), *The New European Automobile Industry*, New York: St. Martin's Press.

Womack, J.P., D.T. Jones and D. Roos (1990), *The Machine that Changed the World*, New York: Rawson Associates.

PART II

CREATIVE AND CULTURAL INDUSTRIES

4 Project-based industries and craft-like production: structure, location and performance
Peter B. Doeringer, Pacey Foster, Stephan Manning and David Terkla

4.1 INTRODUCTION

Craft production, craft-based labor markets, and urban industrial districts were once central to the development of many US industries in the early nineteenth century (Jackson, 1984; Jacoby, 1991; Atack and Passell, 1994). In manufacturing these industries included meat cutting, brewing, clothing, printing, iron mills, and various kinds of non-electrical machinery. Outside of manufacturing, craft production was common in the maritime industry and the railroads as well as in construction. Craft-like production and craft skills, however, were subsequently replaced by large-scale firms using less-skilled labor, mass production technologies, and new forms of work organization that could more efficiently serve emerging mass markets (Stinchcombe, 1959; Chandler, 1962; Atack and Passell, 1994, chs 1, 17). As these industries matured, however, growth slowed in the latter decades of the twentieth century and often reversed as global competition and the international product cycle resulted in the transfer of much of US mass production offshore (Vernon, 1966; Dicken, 2011).

In an environment of debate about the future of industrial societies, Piore and Sabel (1984) advanced the provocative concept of 'flexible specialization' to describe a new manufacturing model for industrialized countries. The flexible specialization model was patterned after northern Italy's flourishing industrial districts, such as the manufacturing cluster of Emilia Romagna, where manufacturing is characterized by a high degree of product variety, small firms, highly skilled and flexible labor, and overlapping work and social communities that promote industrial performance through trust and cooperation. This form of 'craft-like' flexible specialization was seen as the modern counterpart of nineteenth-century craft production systems.

Flexible specialization presented a compelling logic for a new production model where small-scale firms could serve smaller, more volatile, and less-certain markets by exploiting the comparative advantages typically held by developed countries – advanced technologies, proximity to large industrial and consumer markets, educated and skilled labor, and the research and development capacity to produce innovative and high value-added products – and in some cases by drawing upon the externalities of local pools of labor and entrepreneurial talent. However, this model has not taken hold to any significant degree in the US manufacturing sector. Large firms have downsized, but they remain the dominant producers in most manufacturing industries; there is little evidence of a significant shift toward more fluid employment relationships (Copeland, 2010) despite major changes in the industrial and demographic composition of employment.

Craft-like production, however, occupies a dominant role in so-called 'project industries'. Project industries specialize in one-of-a-kind and customized products and in small batches of highly differentiated products. They often require a shifting mix of occupations and skills that must often be mobilized and coordinated on short notice by the firm that leads the project, and project industries often rely on complex networks of collaborating contractors. Employment relationships are often temporary, lasting for all or a part of each project, but the lead firms typically retain a core group of employees and contractors with greater continuity of employment and a greater knowledge of how to organize and conduct project-based production (for example, Lundin and Söderholm, 1995; Cicmil and Hodgson, 2006; Whitley, 2006; Manning, 2008).

Project-based production is common, for example, in construction, motion pictures and videos, software development, consulting, complex system development (see, for example, Eccles, 1981; DeFillippi and Arthur, 1998; Hobday, 2000; Grabher, 2004), as well as in manufacturing where examples range from prototype production for industrial and consumer products, to repeated cycles of small batches of innovation-based products (such as in fashion industries, advanced materials, biopharmaceuticals, and medical instruments), to one-of-a-kind samples and replacement parts supplied by small-scale machine shops (Hobday, 2000). Examples of project-based production can even be found in mass production industries such as autos, as illustrated by Midler's (1995) study of the tendency to 'projectification' at Renault.

We posit that project-based production, rather than flexible specialization *per se*, represents an important and enduring production paradigm for developed countries in the twenty-first century (Cicmil and Hodgson, 2006). Project-based firms in the United States have already established a track record for competing in global markets for products where scope economies, speed of production, and the ability to switch quickly from one project to another are more important than economies of scale, and they have also demonstrated a remarkable ability to adapt to changing market conditions and technologies.

Project industries often cluster in districts or regions because of the skills and knowledge required in design and production, the specialized materials and services provided by suppliers, and the imperatives of staffing project production and coordinating contracting networks when speed and flexibility are of paramount importance. Examples are high-tech firms based in Silicon Valley whose project-based production systems have co-evolved with strong regional externalities related to pools of skilled labor, career mobility, and knowledge spillovers among firms (see, for example, Saxenian, 1996).

This interaction between project industries and regional externalities has not been lost on local and regional economic development efforts. For example, several states have begun focusing on attracting creative industry clusters, and there has been increased focus on sectors of manufacturing, such as biopharmaceuticals and medical devices, which utilize project-based production practices. However, these state and local policies often treat these project-based industries in the same way as they would other types of industry clusters, while neglecting the distinctive micro-foundations of project-based clusters and the types of regional externalities that they require.

For example, education, training, and job-matching arrangements are often directed at larger employers that typically hire workers with relatively narrow skills and provide them with additional training as needed in skills that are relatively specific to the firm, rather than addressing the high-skill and mobility needs of more-fluid labor markets organized horizontally by occupations that typically characterize product-based production (Tolbert, 1996). Similarly, few regional development efforts recognize the fine-grained organizational relationships between the internal capacities of the firms that 'lead' project-based production and the myriad contractors that must be assembled and coordinated in order to meet the special production needs of one-of-a-kind and small-batch products.

This chapter reviews the relatively sparse literature on the structure, conduct, and regional clustering of project-based industries, followed by the more extensive micro-level literature on organizational and networking theories of project-based production. It then examines the organizational arrangements, internal employment systems, external labor market structures, labor-management practices, and regional externalities that define the project-based production paradigm. The chapter concludes with two case studies of project-based industries that provide concrete examples of the economic dynamics of such industries and their interaction with regional agglomeration advantages.

The first case examines the evolution of a traditional manufacturing industry with a relatively stable technology (women's wear) located in an industrial district (New York City) that has long provided substantial agglomeration externalities for women's wear manufacturing. Both the industry and the district have reached the mature stage of their life cycles and are hoping to survive the challenges of global competition by returning to an earlier form of small-scale, project-based production combined with new types of district externalities.

The second case looks at a project-based information industry (motion pictures, television, and videos) that has traditionally been concentrated in Los Angeles and New York City, both of which are 'creative' districts that have accumulated powerful externalities for serving the motion picture sector, television production, and related video industries (Christopherson and Storper, 1989; Christopherson et al., 2006). This industry has experienced significant changes in both its industrial structure and its technology that have lessened the importance of some of the agglomeration economies that kept production in Los Angeles and New York, and these districts are facing growing competition from other US regions and other countries that are offering production subsidies in hopes of establishing viable 'satellite' clusters of motion picture, television, and video production. The case study examines the initial experience in Massachusetts with creating an 'infant' production region that would have sufficient cost and agglomeration advantages to compete for an industry that is beginning to decentralize to new locations in the United States and abroad.

Each of these cases illustrates a distinctive set of organizational arrangements for project-based production and provides examples of how project-based industries improve their performance by creating and reinforcing regional production externalities. Collectively, the cases argue for the usefulness of studying economic development processes at the intersection of project-based industry and district externalities, and for taking a fresh look at federal and state policies for strengthening industrial performance in the context of local and regional economic development.

4.2   DISTRICTS, CLUSTERS AND PROJECT-BASED PRODUCTION: A REVIEW

Alfred Marshall is the most widely cited source for defining what makes an industrial district (Marshall, 1890). For Marshall, districts emerge when one or more key local externalities for firms are present: (i) human capital efficiencies from shared pools of labor with industrial skills and knowledge, (ii) transaction efficiencies of communication and transportation from proximity to specialized suppliers and buyers, and (iii) knowledge spillovers from production know-how, technological developments, and knowledge about customers and markets. These Marshallian externalities are freely available to firms that locate in the district, and are reinforced as firms locate and expand in response to the availability of regional market externalities. However, firms are seen as 'externality takers', rather than 'externality creators'.

Subsequent research has extended our understanding of what makes a district by introducing the concept of a network of interdependencies among industry sectors (Chinitz, 1961) and documenting the externalities of organizational relationships and district cultures as further sources of efficiency advantage. For example, Italian garment districts are well known for collaborative production relationships and the sharing of knowledge among local suppliers (Brusco, 1982; Bigarelli, 2000; Bigarelli and Crestanello, 2004); Saxenian's 'regional advantage' argument documented the role of regional business cultures in promoting knowledge spillovers (Saxenian, 1996); and Porter (1994) emphasized the importance of active competition among spatially concentrated clusters of firms. The mediating role of social relationships among workers and entrepreneurs in facilitating the blending of active cooperation with active competition has also been highlighted (Piore and Sabel, 1984; Couralt and Doeringer, 2008; Reid et al., 2008).

4.2.1   Gaps in the Theory and Literature

Major gaps remain in our understanding of industries that cluster, and of the districts that house such clusters. While we know that externalities and knowledge spillovers are critical elements of cluster performance, we do not know exactly how this happens and have little analysis of the internal organization of firms in relation to district development (Motoyama, 2008). Instead, there is a tendency to treat the clustering as a universal phenomenon, rather than recognizing the importance of industry- and region-specific conditions that are associated with particular aspects of cluster development (Doeringer and Terkla, 1995; Martin and Sunley, 2003; Motoyama, 2008).

The micro-foundations of Marshall's conception of externalities are rooted in the economics of atomistic markets in which individual firms have little independent influence on the formation of clusters and the development of the collective externalities of districts. Yet many modern districts are dominated by large firms, or by collective organizations (business associations of small firms, trade unions, and education and training institutions), that have considerable market power to shape local externalities (Doeringer et al., 2002; Lundequist and Power, 2002; Giarratani et al., 2007). Yet we know little about how strategic conduct and economic power affect clustering or the formation of district externalities.

Similarly, there has been insufficient exploration of the dynamic interactions between cluster development and district development – why and where clusters first develop, how they evolve, and why regions with similar clusters perform differently (Hill and Brennan, 2000; Newlands, 2003; Feser et al., 2008; Montana and Nenide, 2008). The few studies that exist are not enough to provide generalizations about the cluster development process (Lundequist and Power, 2002; Feldman and Francis, 2004; Motoyama, 2008). These gaps point to the need for longer-term studies of the origins and evolutionary paths of districts and their clusters of firms (Newlands, 2003).

4.2.2 Project-based Production

The literature that has come closest to addressing these gaps examines the organizational forms, organizational relationships, and production practices in the context of 'project-based production'. Projects are generally defined as a 'temporary endeavor undertaken to create a unique product or service' (PMI, 2000, p. 4) and project-based production is seen as an emerging paradigm that carries strong implications for US industrial performance and competitiveness.

The key elements of project-based production – time limitations, uniqueness and complexity, and the involvement of teams to accomplish project goals – require distinctive organizational forms, business practices, and organizational relationships (Lundin and Söderholm, 1995; Manning, 2008). These characteristics are also important for understanding the tendency of project firms to form clusters in regions that offer externalities that are tailored to project production, rather than to mass production.

The conventional economics literature has been largely silent about the role of project industries and project-based regional clusters in improving industrial performance and stimulating regional growth. However, there have been a handful of notable exceptions in regional economics and economic geography (see, for example, Grabher, 2002a, 2002b; Sydow and Staber, 2002) which have looked in particular at geographically concentrated 'project ecologies' around which creative industry clusters can form and be sustained. Project-based production has received considerable attention in a variety of other disciplines – systems engineering, innovation, and organizational behavior (see, for example, Hobday, 2000; Grabher, 2002a; Cicmil and Hodgson, 2006; Whitley, 2006).

One important aspect of this discussion is the relationship between flexible projects and the institutional context in which such production occurs. For example, using the case of cultural production, both Grabher (2002a) and Sydow and Staber (2002) make the point that in order for projects to be regularly initiated within a region there must be a certain amount of 'institutional thickness' embedded in interconnected local institutions, such as training and education organizations and funding institutions that can support project ideas, train professionals, and finance projects (Amin and Thrift, 1994). Regional economic and organizational studies have also pointed at the equally important role of flexible labor markets within regions as a source of innovation, knowledge spillovers, and the longer-term career opportunities of project professionals (see, for example, Saxenian, 1996; Grabher, 2004).

Project-based production has also been studied in a number of industries including: film and TV production (for example, 1989; Starkey et al., 2000; Windeler and Sydow, 2001; Manning and Sydow, 2011), advertising (Grabher, 2002b), theater and other cultural production (Haunschild, 2003; Uzzi, 2004); event management (Pitsis et al., 2003); construction (Stinchcombe, 1959; Newcombe, 1996; Berggren et al., 2001), complex product and systems development (Shenhar and Dvir, 1996; Gann and Salter, 2000; Hobday, 2000); and research and consulting (Hagedoorn et al., 2000; Lash and Wittel, 2002; Manning, 2010). Projects have also been recognized as the basis for important forms of production and business organization in various fields, including economic sociology and organization studies (for example, Lundin and Midler, 1998), innovation (for example, Cicmil and Hodgson, 2006), regional studies (for example, Grabher, 2002a, 2002b), and engineering (Shenhar, 2001). A number of scholars have also observed an increasing penetration of project-based organizational forms across industries (see, for example, Söderlund, 2000; Midler, 1995). The reasons include the relative flexibility and capacity of projects – compared to more continuous, routine-based forms of production – to mobilize resources within and across organizational boundaries in complex and novel ways (see, for example, Asheim and Mariussen, 2003).

In the organization and innovation literature, the focus of research has been largely on aspects of managing project-based production (for example, DeFillippi and Arthur, 1998; Hobday, 2000), the development of project-based relationships and networks (Starkey et al., 2000; Manning and Sydow, 2011), and the role of project-based learning and capability development (Davies and Brady, 2000). In sociology, important topics related to projects include the emergence of project-based careers (Jones, 1996), the functions of roles and status positions within and across projects (for example, Baker and Faulkner, 1991; Bechky, 2006), and the nurturing of creativity (for example, Burt, 2004).

One common theme that unites most studies, however, is the so-called 'temporary–permanent' dilemma of project organizing (Sahlin-Anderson and Söderholm, 2002). This refers to the challenge of maintaining practices, expertise, relationships, and employment beyond the end of any particular project. While the temporary and often unique nature of projects is seen as a major strength of this organizational form (for example, Lundin and Söderholm, 1995), it is also associated with several managerial, social, and economic challenges.

4.3   THE EMERGING INDUSTRIAL PARADIGM OF PROJECT-BASED PRODUCTION

The literature on project-based production provides a mosaic of findings about specific organizational structures and management practices that are found in project-based production, and a compendium of specific solutions that have been devised to address the challenges of such production. Nevertheless, this literature points to the outlines of a more general paradigm of project-based production as an industrial model for advanced economies. In this section, we show how the performance of project-based manufacturing firms depends on integrating three distinct sources of industrial efficiency: (i) the organization of production within and across firms, (ii) the relationship between craft-like occupational employment systems within firms and their counterpart external occupational labor markets, and (iii) the role of both traditional and 'created' regional agglomeration economies.

4.3.1   The Characteristics of Project-based Production

Project-based production involves products that are 'customized' in that they are pro-duced singly or in small batches and are typically part of a product portfolio that has enough variety to generate economies of scope in design, production, and distribution. Over time, project-based production depends heavily on economics of repetition (of certain project practices) and recombination (of resources) (Davies and Brady, 2000; Grabher, 2002b; Manning and Sydow, 2011). Project-based products occupy pivotal and often time-sensitive positions in various stages of the product life cycles of different industries. For example, project-based production is the starting point for prototypes of new products in a wide range of industries. It is the main mode of production in indus-tries with short product life cycles (as in 'quick fashion' apparel and motion pictures or various service industries, such as in the management information sector) and in indus-tries with seasonal production constraints (high-fashion apparel and construction), and it sustains a wide range of mature industries by providing customized equipment for mass production and by supplying replacement parts for older equipment.

A significant amount of project-based production is found, therefore, in sectors where there is considerable new product development that requires the manufacture of prototype products and small batches of samples (for example, Gann and Salter, 2000; Hobday, 2000). Examples include new materials and winterization techniques to extend working seasons in construction, greater use of information technologies and quick-response supply chain partnerships for production planning and logistics in the apparel industry (Abernathy et al., 1999), and electronic digitization in the motion picture industry.

The demand for project-based production is often intermittent and unpredictable and the mix of skills required may be hard to determine in advance of production, par-ticularly for prototype products using advanced materials and technologies. As a result, the skill composition and quantities of labor inputs needed may only be approximated during production planning and may need to be adjusted during the early phases of pro-duction as the specific needs of each project become apparent. This means that internal employment systems must be flexible enough to combine different skills in different ways and at different levels of scale, and that external labor market mechanisms must be designed to quickly respond to unpredictable demand for skilled and highly adaptable labor.

4.3.2   'Mingled' Occupational Systems

Urgent production, frequent product changes, use of new materials and technologies, and uncertain product demand require broad workforce skills and adaptable capital equipment in contrast to the dedicated equipment and narrowly specialized skills of mass production industries. In addition to broad vocational competencies and the know-how to quickly translate general knowledge into a wide variety of specific product applica-tions, workers must also have complex cognitive skills related to trust building, problem solving, and team working that allow them to exercise some discretion over how produc-tion assignments are completed (for example, Meyerson et al., 1996; Haunschild, 2003; Bechky, 2006).

Internal employment systems in project-based firms are typically stratified horizontally by occupation to accommodate these distinctive features of labor demand (Tolbert, 1996). However, occupational boundaries are often permeable or overlapping and groups of workers with different skills often interact with one another in different combinations depending on the needs of each project. This is true not only in project-based firms (Hobday, 2000) or 'adhocracies' (Mintzberg and McHugh, 1985), but also in matrix organizations where employees typically work on multiple projects under the direction of multiple bosses at the same time (Galbraith, 1971). Because of the fuzziness of occupational boundaries and the variety of ways in which occupations are combined within such internal employment systems, we call these 'mingled occupational systems' (MOSs).

By being employed on different projects and by multiple organizations, workers accumulate a wide repertoire of experience, skills, and problem-solving capacities. This enhances their productivity in an environment of rapid and frequent product change (Saxenian, 1996). Interactions among different occupational groups may be simultaneous (as in the filming stage of a movie) or sequential (as in the design, pre-production fabric layout and cutting, and assembly of apparel products), but either way they contribute to the broadening of occupational skills and the facilitation of team interactions. Project-based work also relies on and stimulates the accumulation of social capital (for example, Baker and Faulkner, 1991; Grabher, 2004).

In principle, MOSs are well-suited to accommodate adjustments in the occupational composition of project-based production resulting from changes in materials and technology. They can adapt flexibly to the introduction of new occupations and the shedding of obsolete occupations. When new technologies and new products require new or different skills, and especially when these changes cut across multiple occupations, it can be easier for firms to insert these new skills into a MOS-type occupational matrix without disrupting other occupation relationships than it is in vertical employment hierarchies, where skills are often developed sequentially.

Organizational forms of MOSs are varied. They can consist of independent occupations that are brought together to complete a single project as is common in residential and commercial construction and book publishing; of single firms that employ one or more occupations on a relatively permanent basis as is the case with small-scale 'artisanal' firms in *haute couture* apparel and some large-scale video game companies; or they may be multi-occupational teams that are brought together to complete a particular project and then shuffled again for the next project, either within a single firm or as a compilation of separate firms that collectively produce a project.

Although broad skills and complex cognitive competencies reduce the costs of direct supervision and monitoring under MOSs, special coordination problems arise in integrating production across different skills and organizational structures and ensuring efficient and timely production. Within firms, there can be coordination by management or self-coordination by teams. When production involves multiple firms, coordination arrangements are often managed by 'lead firms' and there are also examples of collective coordination within networks of firms linked by cooperative co-contracting arrangements (see, for example, Manning and Sydow, 2011).

However, the advantages of permeable occupational boundaries and flexible occupational composition can become liabilities if crafts and occupations seek to gain economic advantage by asserting jurisdictional control over particular tasks and technologies. For this reason, project-based production also requires organizational mechanisms for managing occupational conflict both within the MOSs of firms and across external production networks.

4.3.3 Occupational Labor Markets

MOSs draw their labor supplies from occupational labor markets (OLMs) that are similarly structured by craft and occupation. OLMs help project-based production to accommodate to time-sensitive production, new designs, materials, and technologies, and wide fluctuations in labor demand because there is neither the time nor the continuity needed for efficient employer-based training. Instead, firms engaged in project-based production rely on OLMs to ensure that occupational skills are up to date and that workers can reach full productivity quickly (Jones, 1996; Saxenian, 1996). OLMs must therefore establish close links with occupational education and training institutions and occupational certification procedures (Sydow and Staber, 2002).

When new technologies require new skills, established OLMs can incorporate new training links and new occupations. Common examples of such formal training institutions include apprenticeship programs for skilled crafts, technical schooling for science and engineering occupations, and arts and communications training for creative occupations. These types of formal occupational preparation are often combined with practical training in apprenticeship trades and through a variety of internship, cooperative education programs, and post-graduate training arrangements in other occupations.

OLMs also contribute to efficiencies in matching jobs and workers. Because much project-based production is for newly designed and highly differentiated 'one-off' products, labor demand by skill and occupation is inherently volatile and competitive bidding for project contracts can cause further shifting of demand among firms. This volatility in demand raises the inter-firm mobility among workers, increases transaction costs, and disrupts the continuity of returns to human capital. The costs of adapting to these shifts in demand are reduced by OLMs because they are designed to quickly allocate labor as project demand shifts from one firm to another or when multiple skills and occupations must be used in quick succession. Because skills are well understood within OLMs, either through informal social networks or certification and licensure, the quality of workers' skills is well known within occupational labor pools (Jones et al., 1997). Thus, good matches are easier to determine in advance of hiring, and the transferability of skills allows mismatches to be easily corrected through quits, terminations, and replacement hiring. Examples of such transaction mechanisms are union hiring halls in the construction trades and the networks of senior personnel in film-making that work with entertainment unions to assemble crews who work together on a semi-regular basis and move from project to project.

These efficiencies in education, training, and job matching provided by OLMs are further enhanced by the way in which the costs and benefits of investments in occupational skills are allocated. Because OLM skills are largely transferable among firms, human capital theory tells us that workers, rather than firms, will be responsible for their own skill investments and the workers will receive the returns on their investment. Worker-driven human-capital investment relieves employers of training costs, and well-functioning job-matching arrangements help to ensure that workers will be appropriately compensated for their investments.

4.3.4   Institutions for Coordinating Project-based Production

The nexus of craft-like MOSs, OLMs, and occupational training and certification institutions is often identified with networks of small, flexible, and specialized firms such as those highlighted by Piore and Sabel (1984). But in practice it can be found in a much wider range of firm sizes and multi-firm networks, each with its own mechanisms for achieving quick and efficient project-based production. For large firms, particularly those that also engage in mass production, these mechanisms are mainly concerned with aligning internal business practices with project-based production methods. This entails the flattening of management hierarchies so as to be compatible with MOSs (Osterman, 2000, 2006) and the development of technological and organizational protocols for harmonizing quick-response sourcing with traditional procurement arrangements (Abernathy et al., 1999; Doeringer et al., 2003).

For smaller firms, however, the coordination of this nexus is often accomplished by external 'lead' organizations that serve as project entrepreneurs by regularly initiating projects with various partners (Ferriani et al., 2009; Manning, 2010). Project entrepreneurs often build so-called 'project networks' of strategically coordinated and long-term relationships with both contractors and service providers that they recruit for particular types of projects (Starkey et al., 2000; Windeler and Sydow, 2001; Manning, 2005, 2010). Project networks are activated for particular projects, yet they are sustained beyond particular collaborations. They are often highly coordinated social infrastructures, based within OLMs, because they provide longer-term employment and career opportunities by stringing together a series of short-term projects.

For example, in film production, some directors and script writers typically prefer to work for particular producers who serve as project entrepreneurs and project network coordinators. Other examples include general contractors in construction who build up long-term project-based relations with key clients and suppliers (Eccles, 1981); system integrators in complex product and system development (Hobday, 2000); researchers in project-based research networks (Manning, 2010); consulting firms, government agencies in regional and international development fields (Berggren et al., 2001; Manning and von Hagen, 2010); and clothing 'jobbers' in New York City who purchase materials, organize contracted production, and serve as an intermediary between small producers and large buyers.

'Collective' organizations – unions and professional associations, industry associations, and government agencies – may also serve as coordination intermediaries (Rychen and Zimmermann, 2008; Foster et al., 2013). Such coordination responsibilities include skill development, job matching, and certification arrangements, and assistance in organizing research and development activities, developing industry-wide policies, and setting product and employment standards. In the Massachusetts film industry, for example, a specialized government agency was established to promote contacts among out-of-town film producers, a variety of local suppliers of movie-related goods and services, and the local schools and trade unions that represent sources of skilled labor employed in movie production.

4.3.5 Agglomeration Economies and the Economic Geography of Project-based Production

Project-based production benefits from access to regional repositories of knowledge about products and technologies (Grabher, 2004). Formal occupational knowledge is often kept up to date through close contacts among workers and local education and training institutions. Tacit knowledge is kept current as workers gain experience with different project-based products within their current firms and as they rotate among related local firms (Song et al., 2003). Knowledge about the design and manufacture of one-of-a-kind products and about new materials and technologies relevant to prototype production is often shared because research institutions and project-based industries often draw workers from the same local labor pools. Because project-based production often involves changes in designs and specifications during the production process, proximity to customers is a further type of location externality for facilitating knowledge exchanges between suppliers and their clients.

Firms engaged in project-based production can also collectively augment regional agglomeration externalities. Traditional externalities can be reinforced when firms choose 'open' organizational architectures and cultures that encourage knowledge sharing, rather than those that are 'closed' (Saxenian, 1996), and by establishing collaborative sourcing relationships in place of arm's-length contracting (Piore and Sable, 1984; Abernathy et al., 1999; Doeringer et al., 2003). Other externalities can be created through fundamental changes in market design and the development of new market institutions. Historical examples of such changes are the development of apprenticeship training programs and the facilitation of labor mobility by nineteenth-century craft-based unions (Ulman, 1955; Jacoby, 1991) and the impact of local unions and employer associations on the economic regulation of industries such as apparel and machining (Teper, 1937; Slichter et al., 1960; Carpenter, 1972).

4.3.6 The Project-based Production Model: From Concept to Evidence

In the following sections, we provide evidence from two case studies in support of the proposition that the combination of project-based production and project-based regional externalities is a viable paradigm for the future of US manufacturing. The first case, women's wear manufacturing in the New York City garment district, traces a project-based industry from its original roots in craft-based production and traditional agglomeration economies through its growth period as a project-based supplier to mass markets using network governance practices developed by employer associations and trade unions, to its recent conversion back to project-based production coordinated by jobbers and developing new sources of agglomeration economies.

The second case involves an information industry, movie and television production, that has long been a model of project-based production with MOSs and OLMs. This industry has evolved from a vertically integrated production model based within large internal labor markets, to a disintegrated production model that combines a small group of firms providing financing and overall direction for a complex set of production networks that are responsible for specific projects at production locations that are increasingly dispersed around the world. By closely examining the progress of this industry in establishing a production cluster in Massachusetts, we are able to observe the dynamics of an established industry interacting with an 'infant' district.

4.4   CASE STUDY I: WOMEN'S WEAR MANUFACTURING, GARMENT DISTRICT EXTERNALITIES AND THE PRODUCT LIFE CYCLE[1]

Apparel, with its seasonal cycle for fashionable products, is a quintessential project-based industry. It is also one of the oldest and most labor-intensive industries in the United States and was once one of the largest US industries, employing over one million workers as late as 1982. By 2009, however, imports had displaced most domestic production and fewer than 133,000 workers remained in the industry. This dramatic decline in domestic production led to substantial downsizing among the firms that survive and to an increasing concentration of the industry in the two largest US garment districts, New York and Los Angeles (Rice, 2008), both of which are well endowed with local agglomeration economies that continue to support the industry that remains.

4.4.1   Industry Structure

The industry has always had a competitive structure and been dominated by small and medium-sized firms. The average establishment size in 2009 was 17 employees, down from 60 in the early 1980s, and only 0.8 percent of establishments employ 250 or more workers. The more-fashionable women's and girls' sector is the largest US product specialization, accounting for 44 percent of total industry employment (2009), and it consists almost entirely of project-based production where designs and styles change seasonally, batches are relatively small, and product life cycles occur within a season or less.

Apparel production in New York City was originally carried out in fully integrated artisan shops that acquired fabric and were staffed by skilled tailors who could make patterns, cut fabric, and assemble entire garments. By the 1880s, however, production was more standardized and began to be decentralized to less-skilled sewing contractors. Women's wear manufacturers further extended contracting chains by delegating the organization of production to 'jobbers' who acquired fabric and coordinated garment assembly. By the 1920s, the modern-day structure of the industry was in place in New York City, with jobbers and their contractors serving much of the market for women's wear while 'manufacturers' specialized in design, marketing, and other commercial activities.

4.4.2   Occupational Employment Systems and Occupational Labor Markets

Employment in the apparel industry has always been structured by occupation and the occupational employment systems of apparel firms parallel the sequence of skills used in production. Designers conceive new products, pattern makers translate the designs into templates to guide the cutting of fabric into the components for garments of different sizes and shapes, and cutters cut the fabric. Garments are then assembled by sewing machine operators, different finishes and trimmings may be applied to assembled clothing, and the final garments are pressed and prepared for shipment.

Artisan shops originally hired craft tailors, apprentices, and helpers from a variety of local labor pools, but by the 1880s, foreign-trained immigrants were becoming the primary source of skilled sewing labor for the artisan shops and of semi-skilled sewing workers for the expanding sector of apparel contractors. Sewing eventually became almost entirely a semi-skilled industrial occupation, cutting and pattern making remained separate skilled occupations,[2] and designing became a recognized occupation with its own training programs at the turn of the century. Semi-skilled production workers constitute almost two-thirds of current employment in cut-and-sew apparel manufacturing (2010) with sewing occupations accounting for 70 percent of all production workers, followed by cutters (7 percent) and pattern makers (4 percent). Designers represent about 3 percent of total apparel industry employment.

Occupational structures also shaped the structure of union organization and bargaining. Between the late 1880s and early 1900s, apparel workers began to form unions in response to the greater use of low-wage contractors for sewing work, the downward pressure on wages from immigration, and the growth of sweatshop working conditions. The skilled tailors and cutters employed in the cloak and coat sector, New York's largest and most-skilled craft at the time, were the driving force behind these early unionization efforts (Levine, 1969, pp. 92–8) and a group of craft-based local unions formed the International Ladies' Garment Workers' Union (ILGWU) in 1900. As the industry moved from artisanal to industrial production, however, the ILGWU became primarily a union of sewing machine operators employed by contractors, although skilled cutters retained separate local unions and remained an important source of union power.

4.4.3 Development of District Externalities in New York City: The Pre-union Era

Local garment districts have long been characteristic of women's wear production. Short product life cycles and volatile and uncertain consumer demand place a premium on quick and flexible supply chains that can draw upon a variety of agglomeration economies – large pools of designers and manufacturing labor, ready access to suppliers of fabrics and trims, and proximity to retail and wholesale buyers that can closely monitor the fashion preferences of their customer base. Early in its history, immigration provided New York City with large pools of skilled and unskilled labor that served both craft and industrial modes of production. Its strengths in fashion design gave the district an advantage in setting fashion trends; the size of its apparel manufacturing sector encouraged fabric and other suppliers to locate nearby; and its dominance of national markets attracted national buyers to the district.[3]

4.4.4 Pools of Labor

The important labor pools for artisan apparel manufacturing were workers with the craft skills of cutting and tailoring and the know-how to capture the hang and drape of the fabric anticipated in clothing designs. The major source of skilled labor in the post-Civil War period was recent German immigrants as well as second-generation Americans who had learned tailoring skills. As the industry grew and diversified in the 1880s to the

1900s, it was able to draw upon a large wave of immigrants from Eastern Europe, many of whom had tailoring skills or other apparel industry experience (Levine, 1969, Ch. III). The sheer number of immigrants arriving in New York during that period – 89,097 between 1882 and 1887, 48,000 a year from 1887 to 1900, and 107,347 in 1902 – also helped to keep wages for apparel workers low (Pope, 1905 [1970], Part II, Ch. I).

As the demand for ready-made women's wear increased, however, manufacturers began to contract production to smaller and more specialized firms that were being opened largely by immigrant entrepreneurs and staffed by semi-skilled immigrant workers (Levine, 1969, Ch. III; Waldinger, 1986). Low overheads, relatively inexpensive labor, and the willingness of immigrants to work hard and accept intermittent jobs allowed these small contracting shops to successfully compete with the larger and more-established manufacturers that employed skilled labor, and the contractors' share of output continued to grow throughout the late nineteenth and early twentieth centuries (Pope, 1905 [1970], pp. 62–5).

4.4.5   Proximity to Suppliers

At the turn of the century, New York's emerging apparel manufacturing drew upon suppliers that had been serving skilled tailors, seamstresses, and small artisan tailoring shops. With the growth of demand for fashionable women's wear, the industry began its relocation to a new and diversified fashion cluster in a 35-block area in mid-town Manhattan that included manufacturers, showrooms, and contractors. This new manufacturing and sales district also attracted a variety of specialized suppliers – fabric and clothing wholesalers, button shops, pattern makers, cutting shops, sample makers, embroiderers, dyeing and finishing firms, and equipment mechanics – that had the commercial skills needed to supply the increasing variety products required by highly differentiated women's wear fashion production.

4.4.6   Proximity to Buyers

New York was the first garment district to serve a national market. Larger New York City manufacturers initially hired salesmen to visit buyers, while smaller manufacturers sold through wholesalers who served small retailers. As national markets and large retailers grew in importance, and as styles, fabrics, and grades of clothing began to proliferate, New York City manufacturers and jobbers began to operate showrooms for buyers who were traveling to New York in advance of each season to view the full range of products available in the district. By 1919, New York City was an established location for buyers and the need for traveling salesmen was virtually eliminated (Levine, 1969, pp. 413–15).

4.4.7   Pools of Fashion and Design Knowledge

New York has been at the forefront of fashion and product innovation since the early nineteenth century when its seamstresses and tailors benefited from the flow of ideas about fashion trends in Europe brought back by affluent tourists or copied from clothing imported from France and England (Green, 1997, pp. 112–14). New York's first fashion specialization was in tailored women's wear products in the 1880s, but its demand for design ideas expanded rapidly as the district added specializations in shirtwaists in the early 1900s and then dresses, which became New York's largest specialization in the 1920s with 125,000 different dress styles being produced in New York by 1939 (Hochman, 1941).

New York began to develop its own sources of design in the early twentieth century. New York-based Vogue Magazine switched from featuring articles on cultural topics of broad interest to a focus on fashion and design beginning in 1909; the *Women's Wear Daily* trade newspaper was founded in 1910; and district-wide fashion shows became an important public venue for showcasing fashion ideas beginning in 1943.

A training infrastructure for producing fashion emerged in 1904 when the New York School of Art (which later became the Parsons School of Art and Design) launched a specialized fashion design program to serve the market for theatrical costumes. By the boom period of the New York City garment industry in the 1920s, the Parsons School had become a general school for fashion and design with links to the European fashion industry and a pioneering fashion program in Paris. The 1920s was also the beginning of a long period of intense product differentiation (National Retail Dry Goods Association, 1936), which further increased the demand for trained designers and led to the founding of a second fashion design school, the Fashion Institute of Technology, in 1936.

4.4.8 The Union Era: Collective Bargaining and 'Created' District Advantage

Increased immigration and the growth of immigrant contractors in the late nineteenth century led to intensely competitive labor and product markets, excess production capacity, falling wages, and the growth of sweatshop conditions (Teper, 1937, pp. 13–14; Levine, 1969, pp. 403–7, 409). Wages of factory-based sewing machine operators in 1906, for example, were 49 percent higher in Chicago than in New York, 34 percent higher in Boston, and 23 percent higher in Baltimore, with only Philadelphia coming close to New York's wage level (Segal, 1960, p. 94).

Continued immigration intensified competition, low wages, growing economies of scale, and strong agglomeration economies contributed to industry growth by holding down production costs, allowing the New York City garment industry to gain a 64.5 percent share of national apparel markets by 1899 (Levine, 1969). But falling wages, volatile employment, and poor working conditions (ibid., pp. 168–73) also led to spontaneous strikes and labor violence. Labor conflict became a negative externality for the entire district by encouraging buyers and suppliers to shift orders to other districts with less labor unrest.

The inefficiencies of strikes became an even more serious concern as garment workers began to form trade unions in the 1880s. By the 1890s, New York garment unions were becoming more prevalent and their bargaining tactics became more militant with demonstrations, marches, and mass picketing. New York's largest craft workers' union, the United Brotherhood of Cloak Makers' Union No. 1 of New York and Vicinity, convened a national convention in 1900 of 'all workers in the trade' to establish a nation-wide, craft-based union for skilled workers in the women's clothing industry (ibid., pp. 102–3), and the craft-oriented American Federation of Labor issued a charter to the ILGWU shortly thereafter (ibid., p. 103).

Employer opposition to unions intensified as union militancy increased. Workers who joined unions were discharged, lockouts were used more frequently when union workers went on strike, and larger strikes and demonstrations often led to arrests and sometimes prison terms for strikers.

The union strategy for overcoming employer opposition was to rely on even larger 'general' strikes to force employers to the bargaining table. The 1909 'Uprising of the 20,000' (in support of shirtwaist and dress workers) and the 1910 'Great Revolt' (involving about 60,000 strikers in support of cloak and suit workers), along with pressure from civic leaders and government officials, forced employers to recognize the ILGWU and to turn to their industry associations to represent them in negotiating collective bargaining agreements.

4.4.9   Collective Bargaining as a Positive District Externality

The early labor contracts contained traditional labor benefits of wage increases, improved working conditions, and greater employment security for union members. However, the 1910 cloak and coat agreement (known as the 'Protocol of Peace') also included provisions that affected market structure and district efficiency. This contract provided for arbitration procedures to prevent the disruption of production by strikes over both worker grievances and future contract negotiations, and it stabilized the employment of craft workers in inside shops by limiting the amount of contracted production (ibid., pp. 194, 196–8; Carpenter, 1972, ch. 2). This combination of economic benefits for workers, limitations on competition from contractors, and the efficiencies of reducing strikes and stabilizing employment among manufacturers was subsequently replicated in agreements covering New York City's other major product specializations in 1913, and the scope of district-wide market regulation through collective bargaining was substantially broadened in subsequent contract negotiations. As the New York City industry moved toward a more industrial and less craft-based production model, jobbers replaced manufacturers as the key contracting organizations (particularly in the dress sector where styles were proliferating) and union regulation adapted to this change by making jobbers the focal point of collective bargaining.

During this period, the unions envisioned a major restructuring of the industry to reduce excess capacity, stabilize employment, and 'remove' wages and working conditions from competition (Levine, 1969, pp. 422–4). Limits were placed on the number of contractors each jobber could employ in order to control excess capacity; contracting relationships were made more permanent by designating the specific contractors assigned to each jobber; contract prices were required to cover fixed as well as variable costs in order to reduce turnover among contractors; jobbers were obliged to share work equitably among their contractors; and the peaceful settlement of labor disputes was strengthened by establishing full-time paid positions for the chairmen of arbitration procedures. To reduce competition from outside the district, equal prices were to be paid for comparable contracted work regardless of whether it was performed by New York contractors or elsewhere, penalties were levied against runaway shops leaving the district, and the union had a contractual obligation to organize competing employers outside the New York City district. These regulations governing competition remained part of the union's compact with employers in New York City throughout much of the twentieth century (Teper, 1937, pp. 19–20, 28; Carpenter, 1972, pp. 115–38, 326–66, 488–9).

While such monopolistic restraints on trade are normally considered to be inefficient, many of these practices had positive efficiency consequences for the district when compared with the inefficiencies of cut-throat competition and strikes. Compulsory arbitration, for example, helped to reduce the disruptions from labor strife, controlling excess capacity improved resource allocation, price fixing reduced uncertainty, and minimum size-of-firm requirements helped to eliminate marginal firms and to ensure that surviving firms could achieve a minimum efficient scale of production. In addition, the ILGWU directly contributed to district efficiency by encouraging mechanization and the adoption of efficient work practices by providing training and industrial engineering services to help unionized firms improve their production systems and work organization (Disher, 1947).

Efficiency effects also flowed from the pairing of jobbers with specific contractors, and from the preferences granted to these dedicated contractors in the awarding of contracts and in the equitable sharing of work at uniform contract prices. Continuing relationships between jobbers and contractors provided new opportunities for investments in relationship-specific knowledge that improved both the productivity of contractors and the efficiency of contracting relationships. Jobbers could learn the strengths and weaknesses of their dedicated contractors and train them to be more efficient, contractors could learn about their jobbers' products and expected quality standards, and stronger channels of communication between jobbers and contractors could help jobbers to secure orders and improve profits. These stable contracting relationships applied primarily to the 'core' group of experienced contractors in New York City who worked mostly for one jobber and had a regular flow of orders, in contrast to the remaining group of 'peripheral' contractors who had highly competitive, arm's-length market relationships with multiple jobbers.

The ILGWU was reported to represent over 90 percent of women's wear employment in the district during this period (Levine, 1969, p.424) and was the major enforcer of these agreements by using strikes and boycotts against firms that violated their contractual obligations. By the end of the 1920s, a transition from cut-throat competition to market governance through collective bargaining was well underway and unionized New York employers had come to realize that regulation through collective bargaining generated both monopoly rents and efficiency gains that could be profitably shared with their unions.

While collective bargaining was never able to fully control market entry, it presumably slowed the outflow of New York City production to other districts and helped to preserve the agglomeration economies of the district. But there were also more lasting efficiency consequences that flowed from the creation of more permanent relationships between jobbers and their core contractors. Both parties were better able to invest in relationship-specific human capital, and the obligation of jobbers to share work fairly among contractors and at a common price led to the development of embedded obligations of reciprocity between jobbers and contractors.

4.4.10 The Product Cycle and the Decline of the New York Garment District

Industrial production emerged as the norm in the district during the 1920s, based on a three-tier contracting chain of specialized manufacturers, jobbers, and contractors coupled with union regulation of labor and product markets. The district developed a manufacturing model that combined the flexibility of small-scale craft production with the efficiencies of specialized supply chains and of scale economies from the division of labor. Jobbers specialized in securing materials, organizing production by contractors, and marketing clothing to retailers. Contractors specialized in fast, flexible, and low-cost sewing and final assembly. The presence of the jobber–contractor system allowed larger manufacturers to abandon production and to concentrate instead on building their scope economies of design, brand development, and marketing, while using jobbers and contractors to capture scale economies of manufacturing and provide quick and flexible supplies of many different products. Small manufacturers, with the flexibility to switch quickly from one product to another, served high-end market niches by designing and producing smaller orders of high-quality products relatively quickly.

The ILGWU in New York went through a corresponding change during this period. Its bargaining strength was originally derived from skilled workers with strong ethnic and religious ties that fostered union solidarity. As the industry came to rely more heavily on mass production methods, skilled craft workers continued to represent a hard-to-replace skill and often retained their own union locals, but the union member-ship was shifting from manufacturers to contractors and from skilled to less-skilled jobs and the ILGWU became a predominantly industrial union after the 1920s.

The 1920s also marked the peak of New York City's dominance of apparel produc-tion. While it continued to grow thereafter, its market share began to decline. The slowing of immigration during the 1920s and 1930s, and during the Second World War, weakened the district's labor cost advantage and strengthened the trend for production to decentralize toward districts in the south and west where land and labor costs were lower. Fashion preferences were also shifting away from New York City's traditional specializations in dresses and tailored women's wear toward more-casual blouses, skirts, and trousers. Many of these more-casual products could be produced more-efficiently in large factories using large-scale mass production methods rather than by the smaller-scale and more-flexible production networks prevalent in New York. The decentraliza-tion of production and the growing number of large manufacturers also made it easier for suppliers to sell directly to retailers instead of going through jobbers and buyers in New York City. These developments combined to gradually weaken union regulation in New York City.

The Great Depression of the 1930s further challenged the union-regulated system of market protection and efficiency promotion in New York City as employers sought to cut costs and prices in the face of sharply reduced demand for clothing and as union strength was eroded by membership losses. The passage in 1933 of the National Industrial Recovery Act (NRA) gave union regulation a brief respite by incorporating much of the regulatory structure of the district's collective bargaining agreements into the NRA industry codes (Carpenter, 1972, chs 16–18). However, with the demise of the NRA in 1935, the apparel industry in New York largely returned to the earlier system of private regulation through collective bargaining. By the end of the Second World War, New York's market share had fallen to 54 percent.

While the full extent of the import penetration that would occur later in the century was not anticipated in the 1950s, New York was clearly experiencing a transition from a high-growth to a mature and declining district (Helfgott, 1959, pp. 68–93; Vernon, 1966).

It had been losing men's wear production and less fashionable and more standardized women's wear products since the 1920s, and neither its strong district externalities nor the regulation of market entry through collective bargaining was able to stem the shift of mass production to regions in the south and west where wages were lower, unions weaker, and scale economies were more readily available.

The changing composition of output was also redefining New York's district advantages. New York continued to be successful in the design and development of new products and in small-batch manufacturing. A large study of the district in the mid-1950s concluded that New York was increasingly a district of smaller firms producing the most rapidly changing apparel products that had the least stable and predictable demand (Vernon, 1960, ch. 5). Its emerging district advantages were in producing more-fashionable products that required somewhat different agglomeration economies from those that contributed to large-scale production – labor pools of relatively skilled occupations (fashion design, pattern making, broadly skilled sewing machine operators), proximity to suppliers of relatively small quantities of diverse fabrics and trims, and easy access to higher-end retailers and branded manufacturers. In this sense, the district was already embarking on a return to its smaller-scale craft roots.

In the intervening years since the mid-1950s, production of more-standardized and more-casual clothing continued to be transferred to lower-cost production centers in the United States and then to offshore suppliers in the late 1960s.[4] As employment and output fell, New York City retained design, supply chain management, and marketing activities. The apparel manufacturing sector continued to serve smaller and more unpredictable market niches, although these niche markets included lower-end as well as fashion products. Skilled labor pools remained important as the New York district downsized, but mostly in pre-production activities (such as pattern making and grading), supply chain logistics, buying and selling occupations, and in sewing operations where workers needed to be broadly skilled in order to perform a wider range of high-quality tasks on each garment and to be able to switch quickly from one product to another. Proximity to suppliers and buyers continued to be important, and the pool of suppliers learned to quickly provide a broad range of fabrics and trims in relatively small quantities.

Declining output weakened the regulatory power of collective bargaining as union membership fell. The ILGWU represented less than half the apparel employees in the district by the 1980s and only 30–40 percent in the 1990s (derived from Levitan, 1998, quoted in Milkman, 2006 p. 88).

4.4.11   A Disappearing District in New York during the Second Non-union Era?

By 2000, the New York City industry had been downsizing for over four decades and the decline showed no signs of slowing. Employment in women's wear (Manufacturers, NAICS 31523 and Contractors, NAICS 315212) in New York City declined by 68.9 percent between 2000 and 2009 (see Table 4.1), with the greatest decline among contractors (71.9 percent). Nevertheless, New York continues to employ a relatively large number of workers in women's wear (13,532 in 2009).

New York also lost 58.2 percent of its women's wear manufacturers and 57.2 percent of its women's wear contractors – a slower rate of decline than in employment during this

Table 4.1 New York City's women's wear industry (2000–2009)

Year	2000	2001	2002	2003	2004	2005	2006	2007	2008	2009
Women & girls' cut-&-sew manufacturers in New York City – NAICS 31523										
Employment	16,791	14,532	12,557	10,900	10,573	7,928	8,496	6,783	6,388	6,018
Number of firms	945	806	720	594	539	343	420	322	316	355
Establishment size	17.8	18.0	17.4	18.4	19.6	23.1	20.2	21.1	20.2	17.0
Average earnings	$47,873	$53,560	$58,722	$64,766	$70,859	$83,400	$76,712	$94,375	$94,458	$88,769
Year	2000	2001	2002	2003	2004	2005	2006	2007	2008	2009
Women & girls cut-&-sew contractors in New York City – NAICS 315212										
Employment	26,702	21,094	9,332	14,482	14,440	12,456	11,302	6,208	9,478	7,514
Number of firms	1,588	1,447	668	1,133	1,005	970	856	456	747	680
Establishment size	16.8	14.6	14.0	12.8	14.4	12.8	13.2	13.6	12.7	11.1
Average earnings	$14,391	$14,917	$18,512	$15,912	$16,548	$18,968	$20,651	$28,293	$24,814	$25,031
Year	2000	2001	2002	2003	2004	2005	2006	2007	2008	2009
Total employment	43,493	35,626	21,889	25,382	25,013	20,384	19,798	12,991	15,866	13,532
Total firms	2,533	2,253	1,388	1,727	1,544	1,313	1,276	778	1,063	1,035

period. By 2009, it had only 355 manufacturers and 680 contractors. The average size of manufacturers in New York remained relatively stable at between 17 and 18 employees throughout the decade, but contractors fell in size from an average of 16 employees in 2000 to 11 employees by 2009.[5]

4.4.12   Market Re-design and 'Created' Agglomeration Economies in New York[6]

As the international product cycle continued to take its toll on New York City's garment industry, the weakened system of union regulation began to be replaced by two types of non-union regimes. Some jobbers abandoned considerations of trust and loyalty in favor of competitive contracting with the lowest bidder, while others opted to retain the strong ties with their core contractors that had been established under union regulation by continuing to maintain stable contracting relationships by sharing available orders among these contractors.

'Locked-in' contracting relationships meant that jobbers and contractors could continue relationship-specific investments in skills and knowledge without fear of losing the returns on these investments if their contractors worked for competing jobbers. Preferential contracting has helped core contractors to survive as demand declined and contractors have reciprocated by helping their jobbers to win more orders by maintaining quality standards, adhering to tight delivery schedules, and advising jobbers on how manufacturing costs could be reduced.[7]

4.4.13   Excess Capacity and the Efficiency Contracting Model

As demand for domestic production declined, however, jobbers who keep their core contractors in business by sharing orders have also created excess capacity among their contractors, which has further intensified the incentives for these contractors to increase their effort and productivity. During our interviews in 2003, jobbers frequently spoke about declining business, their obligation to support their core contractors, and their reluctance to drop contractors from this core group. The resulting excess capacity from retaining more contractors than were needed as demand declined was evident from the idle machinery and empty production lines we observed when visiting manufacturers and contractors. Our survey data also documented an average capacity utilization rate of 37 percent, far less than the national average utilization rates for women's wear contractors of 66 percent at that time.[8]

The contractors we interviewed recognized that this excess contracting capacity put them at risk of having to close if the industry continued to decline and they appeared to be making 'end-game' price and cost responses.[9] They lowered prices, absorbed the costs of changes in orders, accepted faster production schedules, and were 'on call' day and night to consult (often face to face) with their jobbers in the hope that they and their jobbers could remain in business for a little longer. Contractors also transmitted these cost-control and productivity pressures to their employees by asking them to accept lower wages, production speedups, and sometimes deteriorating working conditions in exchange for a commitment to sharing available work so as to retain as many of their employees as possible.

This result, however, is different from traditional sweatshop relationships in that these practices arise within a framework of reciprocal obligations somewhat similar to those established under union regulation. Jobbers allocate orders among core contractors in a paternalistic way that seems to place contractor survival ahead of jobbers' concern for profits and for the standard efficiencies associated with having a smaller number of contractors working at full capacity. Contractors, in turn, are even more willing to reciprocate by increasing their obligations to help their jobbers by accommodating their cost and production needs. Because there are trade-offs between the efficiencies of operating at full capacity and the effort incentives provided by excess capacity, jobbers can maximize the profits from such 'efficiency contracting' by choosing the optimal rate of excess capacity that balances the marginal efficiency losses of underutilized contractor capacity against the marginal efficiency gains from lower prices and higher contractor effort.

4.4.14   Measuring the Impact of Efficiency Contracting

The introduction of efficiency contracting practices did not slow the decline of the New York City garment district as measured by employment, but employment change is not necessarily the appropriate performance measure for practices that were intended to raise the productivity of jobbers and contractors in the district. Unfortunately, district-level measures of productivity are not available, but data on real value added per employee can be calculated for the aggregate cut-and-sew apparel industry (NAICS 3152) at the state level and is a reasonable indicator of productivity change in the New York City garment district.[10] By this measure, labor productivity in New York City jumped by 65 percent between 2000 and 2006 when efficiency contracting practices were being implemented. Productivity declined thereafter, but by 2009 it still remained 12 percent above its level in 2000.

4.4.15   Some Comparisons with Los Angeles

While the 2000–2006 productivity gain in New York is very large, it is difficult to interpret because of the possible productivity effects of marginal firms leaving the industry during this period and the lack of controls for other influences on labor productivity. One approach for sharpening this interpretation is to compare New York City with its most similar district, Los Angeles, again using state-level data on changes in real value-added per employee.

Los Angeles represents a good comparison because it is the only other major women's wear district in the United States. Its firms use similar sewing technologies to those in New York City, it draws upon a similar immigrant workforce, and, although it is known for its casual and sportswear designs, its product specializations largely overlap with those in New York (Doeringer, 2012).[11]

Many of the remaining differences between the two districts point to Los Angeles having higher labor productivity than New York. Manufacturers are 2.6 times larger (44 employees per establishment in Los Angeles compared to 17 in New York in 2009) and contractors are 14 percent larger (12.5 in Los Angeles compared to 11 in New York), suggesting greater economies of scale in labor utilization in Los Angeles.

There are also indications that Los Angeles has larger district agglomeration economies than New York. Urban size is often used as a measure of traditional agglomeration economies (Ellison et al., 2010) and Los Angeles, with about three times the women's wear employment of New York, has the larger aggregate labor pool for both manufacturers and contractors. This size advantage is also evident in more-detailed data for apparel production occupations (US Department of Labor, 2011, various occupations). The labor pool in Los Angeles for sewing machine operators is 2.1 times larger than in New York, 3.7 times larger for cutters, and 68 percent larger for patternmakers.

However, the most important difference for interpreting productivity change in New York City is in the production regimes of the two districts. Unlike New York City, Los Angeles deliberately rejected union regulation as a source of efficiency in favor of promoting intensely competitive product and labor markets. Apart from a handful of craft unions in the early decades of the twentieth century and some organizing by the ILGWU in the 1930s and during the Second World War, the apparel employers in the Los Angeles district have successfully resisted unions and other forms of labor market regulation.[12]

During the 2000s when New York was implementing its new system of jobber regulation and efficiency contracting, Los Angeles continued to follow its traditional practice of relying on arm's-length market competition between manufacturers and contractors to motivate efficiency.[13] As a result, benchmarking the trends in New York's labor productivity during the 2000s against those in Los Angeles also represents a comparison between competing modes of contracting relationships.

Comparing the trend in the real value added per employee for New York and California reveals both striking similarities and remarkable differences (Figure 4.1). New York and California experienced similar overall trends in productivity – rising from 2000 to 2006 and then falling through 2009 – suggesting that the same broad

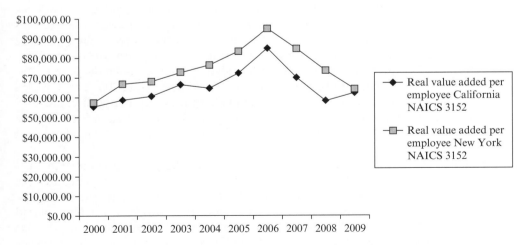

Figure 4.1   Real value added per employee: cut-and-sew manufacturers and contractors NAICS 3152

economic forces were affecting productivity in both districts.[14] However, New York had a productivity advantage over California averaging over 13 percent for 2000–09. This advantage was about 3.3 percent at the beginning of the decade and it increased to a high of 26.4 percent in 2008 before falling back to about 3 percent at the end of the decade. This productivity advantage is consistent with our thesis that the efficiency contracting system being adopted in New York City can explain a significant component of the growth in labor productivity during this period when compared to productivity trends in the Los Angeles district that was operating under a highly competitive market regime.

4.4.16   Higher- and Lower-road District Development

Recent assessments of the strengths and weaknesses of the two districts conducted by local industry experts have mapped out optimistic scenarios for the future of their districts and comparing their development strategies provides additional insights for understanding the interactions between the project-based women's wear apparel industry and its district advantages (California Fashion Association, 2011; Community Redevelopment Agency (Los Angeles), 2011; Municipal Arts Society of New York, 2011). Both scenarios reflect similar development strategies in that they propose moving toward serving niche fashion markets by drawing upon local designers and a production capacity that emphasizes smaller-scale projects and quick and flexible production. While having quick and flexible supply chains has, in one form or another, been the conventional wisdom for apparel industry survival since the 1990s (Abernathy et al., 1999; Berg et al., 2000), what is new in these proposals is a strategy that links supply chain reforms with specific product specializations and district-specific externalities.

The New York City study recommends that the district concentrate on higher-fashion products, which in general involve more design content, higher-quality fabrics, smaller production batches, and more craft-like skills than casual fashion products. New York already has established specializations in higher-fashion lingerie, dresses, and women's suits and coats and appears to be poised to increase its presence in these markets (Municipal Art Society of New York, 2011; Williams and Currid-Halkett, 2011; Doeringer, 2012). For example, New York has about 2.6 times as many designers as Los Angeles (US Department of Labor, 2011). Our field research in 2002 also revealed a large stockpiled capacity among apparel suppliers to move up the fashion ladder.[15] These high levels of unutilized capacity for fashion production are an indicator of the ability of the New York district to shift production toward more fashionable market niches.

By comparison, the Los Angeles studies recommended that the district move to 'fast-fashion' production. Fast-fashion products are attuned to the most recent, and often the most transitory, fashion trends and their market consists largely of teenagers and young women who want stylish apparel at a reasonable price that can be affordably replaced as fashions change. Fast-fashion products have a very short life cycle and new products are introduced throughout the season to maintain consumer interest and to replace popular products as soon as inventories are depleted. Fast-fashion products are design intensive in the sense that designs must be developed continuously and in large numbers throughout the year. New designs are quickly market tested and those that show promise are produced in larger quantities and rushed to market.

By aligning themselves on different sides of the 'fashion divide' between high-quality, well-designed and more expensive products and lower-quality and less-expensive fast-fashion products, New York and Los Angeles are acknowledging the subtle differences in their district externalities. The focus in New York is on fashion products where quality is more important than price and that require skilled design and manufacturing labor as well as fast and flexible supply chains. While New York can design and produce lower-end products quickly, and in large quantities as needed, the comparative advantage of the district lies in more fashionable products. It has pools of higher-end design talent and core manufacturing labor with experience in the production of fashion products that require greater skill, better quality of sewing, and greater care in the handling of costly fabrics than do fast fashion products, and its core jobber–contractor networks encourage the development of the kinds of manufacturing skills, tacit production knowledge, and problem-solving capacity that are essential for fashion products.

Differentiating their products by level of fashion and their districts by different types of buyers, suppliers, labor pools, and supply chain organization will place the New York and Los Angeles districts on different trajectories for the future. Both will benefit from having project-based production capacities that can serve smaller niche markets, but only New York is returning to its original artisanal occupational systems and specialized contracting networks where it can tap the district's externalities of fashion designs, workforce skills, and embedded efficiency relationships between jobbers and contractors. In contrast, the Los Angeles district will likely pursue a more industrial model based on advantages of speed, price, and the incentives of arm's-length competition.

4.5   CASE STUDY II: THE MOTION PICTURE, TELEVISION AND VIDEO INDUSTRY: DEVELOPING A CLUSTER IN MASSACHUSETTS[16]

The film and television industry is viewed by some economists (Vogel, 2007, pp. 71–2) as a model for the emerging network economy because of its reliance on project-based production systems (see also Jones, 1996; DeFillippi and Arthur, 1998; Starkey et al., 2000; Windeler and Sydow, 2001). There are two NAICS codes for the production side of the film and television industry, NAICS 51211 (motion picture and video production), which captures the technical workers who produce films and television shows, and NAICS 51219 (post-production and other), which captures technical activities, such as editing, titling, and special effects that occur after filming has taken place. Movie production was once the main specialization of the industry, but has been declining as television has become the major market for movies and videos, and because Canada has gained an increasing share of feature film production (Christopherson et al., 2006).

US production has long been concentrated in two locations, Los Angeles and New York City, with Los Angeles being the dominant location. The share of production by type of product and location varies considerably from year to year, but California accounted for over half (54.5 percent) of all employment in 2010, compared to 20.5

percent for New York. Television is now the largest specialization in both Los Angeles and New York City, followed by feature films and then commercials (ibid.). The remaining 25 percent of employment is apportioned among the rest of the United States, with the 10 largest states (excluding California and New York) accounting for around 44 percent of this employment.

4.5.1   Producing Films and Television Shows

No two films or television shows will be produced in exactly the same way by exactly the same people. Rather, each film or television program is a unique creative project that is assembled by teams of freelance employees and service organizations that shift from project to project. There are also important differences in the ways that different kinds of products in this industry are made. Despite all these variations, we can identify some general stages of film and television production that help to explain the industrial and occupational structure of this industry.

Perhaps the most important aspect of film and television production is the fact that it is an industry organized by contracts among relatively independent freelance employees who assemble on an 'as-needed' basis for each project. In practice, this means that each stage of production requires the assembly of a unique set of inputs of labor, financial, and material resources that are governed by a combination of short-term contracts and dense social networks among members of craft-based occupations. These inputs are assembled in stages related to the degree of completion of each project that are coordinated by a complex set of organizations and key personnel.

As Caves (2000) points out, film production typically begins with the acquisition of the rights to a story or other intellectual property. This intellectual property then becomes the content around which projects are developed and project teams are assembled. Because commercial motion picture and television projects often involve substantial upfront costs and subsequent revenue streams are uncertain, the first stage of production typically involves fundraising and the negotiation of terms under which this financing will take place (such as assignment of rights and future income streams).

Once financing is obtained, a project moves into a pre-production phase when the key members of the production team (director and star actors, supporting cast, and leaders of production crews) are secured. This stage also involves the selection of production locations and processes (for example, whether shooting is to be done on a soundstage or on location), the development of budgets, script refinement, and other technical decisions.

As projects move from pre-production to production, high initial costs are incurred as teams of technical and creative people are put to work in a studio or on location. The large number of employees involved in film production and the fact that they are typically governed by labor guidelines that increase costs if there are delays, means that projects at this stage are particularly vulnerable to cost overruns and other risk factors.

The final stage in making a film is post-production. In this stage, raw footage is edited into a final narrative, music is selected or recorded, special effects and titles are added, and the final product is assembled for distribution.

4.5.2   Industry Structure

The film and television industry has traditionally been associated with a highly concentrated, oligopolistic structure, and the motion picture industry in particular has been dominated by a few major Hollywood studios (Storper, 1989; Currah, 2007). Although film production is at its core a project-based industry, for the first half of its history these projects were managed by a small number of vertically integrated studios that controlled almost all aspects of film production, distribution, and exhibition. Indeed, until the early 1950s, the Hollywood studio system relied on long-term contracts and large, vertically integrated production, distribution, and exhibition systems. Several events led to a dramatic shift in this system, beginning in the 1940s, leading to an increased reliance on short-term contracts among complex networks of freelance employees and small film service companies (see Caves, 2000, pp. 87–102 for an excellent overview of this process).

Because it produces 'artistic' products, film and television production faces all of the traditional problems associated with creative industries including demand uncertainty, excess supply of creative inputs, skewed distributions of wages and profits, and vertically differentiated labor pools (Caves, 2000). One of the primary functions of project-based mechanisms such as MOSs, OLMs, and agglomeration economies is to mitigate the problems associated with project-based production in creative industries. Because film and television production is both contract driven and involves a high degree of uncertainty and unique combinations of inputs, this is a setting in which governance problems are likely to arise. In the absence of organizational structures, social networks help to coordinate and govern these transactions (Jones et al., 1997).

For example, vertically differentiated occupational labor markets, such as distinctions between A list versus B list personnel, help reduce uncertainties about the future performance of workers. Social networks among freelance employees organized in OLMs allow these industries to assemble complex creative products because they help decision makers identify and assemble appropriate teams and help these teams coordinate by providing role clarity and governance functions (ibid.; Foster et al., 2011). These network structures are typically coordinated by film producers and production firms (Starkey et al., 2000; Windeler and Sydow, 2001; Sydow and Staber, 2002; Manning, 2005), and these structures get reproduced on a project-by-project basis, which allows project participants to pursue project-based careers (Jones, 1996) and become members of core project teams or preferred partner pools (Manning, 2010; Manning and Sydow, 2011). In other words, instead of moving up career ladders within a single organization, employees in this sector move up inter-organizational career ladders made up of individual projects that provide valuable experience and reputation.

During the Second World War, movie stars began to form their own production companies (Caves, 2000, p. 92). The studios accommodated this move and ended the long-term contracts that had bound actors to specific studios. During the same period, the US Department of Justice began a series of anti-trust cases against the film industry due to its domination of theatrical exhibition. In 1948, this litigation culminated in a court order forcing the industry to divest its theatrical exhibition businesses. Thereafter, studios were less focused on producing high-volume (and lower-quality) films to fill their many theaters and began to focus on producing a smaller number of higher-quality products.

The nearly simultaneous arrival of television, which provided direct competition for moviegoing audiences, also contributed to this shift toward a smaller number of higher-quality, more-creative products (ibid., p. 94). These trends began the use of short-term contracts among freelance employees and small service organizations that continues to this day.

Although the financing and distribution of films and television shows that it is still controlled by six major Hollywood studios (Currah, 2007; Vogel, 2007), the actual production of these creative products now takes places through a highly decentralized series of interlocking networks of freelance labor pools and small, specialized service organizations that are assembled on a project-by-project basis.

4.5.3   Labor Market Structure

Motion picture and television projects draw upon loosely coupled networks – sometimes called 'project networks' – for their labor, services, and materials. These networks coalesce temporarily around specific productions and shift from production to production (for example, Windeler and Sydow, 2001; Manning, 2005; Manning and Sydow, 2011).

An understanding of the occupational categories in the film and television industry and how they combine in different types of productions is critical for understanding the industrial and regional dynamics of this industry. Occupations in this industry are divided into two broad categories: 'above-the-line' creative personnel and 'below-the-line' production employees. In each of the occupations within these categories, relatively senior people assemble crews who work together on a semi-regular basis and move from project to project. For example, a director of photography will regularly use the same first cameraperson who may in turn have a preferred list of second camera operators and other crew members. These crews may be based within a single region, or they may take assignments that are being filmed on location in other regions.

4.5.4   Above-the-line Employees

Above-the-line occupations include writers, directors, actors, producers, and the like. While this category contains the small number of highly paid employees such as star actors and directors, the majority of actors and creative workers are paid standard industry wages.

Unions have historically been relatively strong in the industry, particularly in feature film and dramatic television production, and above-the-line employees are organized through their own unions and trade groups (for example, the Screen Actors' Guild (SAG), the American Federation of Television and Radio Artists (AFTRA), the Writers' Guild of America, and the Directors' Guild of America). There are also many freelance employees, most of whom are also members of the union (Caves, 2000). These occupation-based unions reinforce and support the occupational structure of the labor markets within the industry.

Innovations in compensation systems developed by the above-the-line unions in conjunction with the producer's multi-employer bargaining association (Alliance of Motion Picture and Television Producers – AMPTP) have made the unions indispensable to both their members and their employers (Paul and Kleingartner, 1994). In brief, a three-tier system of compensation has been adopted that involves base minimum pay (allowing neophytes to gain experience and employers to evaluate them cheaply), individual personal service contracts (which allow highly talented stars to negotiate for additional forms of compensation such as higher salaries, a percentage of the profits, deferred compensation, or sequential employment guarantees), and residual payments. The last are payments to artists for the subsequent use of films in secondary markets such as videocassettes, DVDs, and pay per view cable TV. These union compensation arrangements have allowed the industry and its creative workforce to adapt more easily to changes in products and technologies (ibid.), and even to foreign competition (Frommer, 2003).

4.5.5   Below-the-line Employees

The employees who handle the cameras, lighting, carpentry, transportation, electrical work, and other technical aspects of film production are in the 'below-the-line' occupations. While smaller and independent productions sometimes rely on non-unionized employees, large studio productions almost always hire their technical (below-the-line) employees from one of two international unions, the International Alliance of Theatrical Stage Employees (IATSE) and the International Brotherhood of Teamsters (IBT). Of these two unions, IATSE has a much larger proportion of employees on a typical film or TV set.

IATSE is the primary union representing film, television, and theatrical employees in set construction and dressing, lighting, special effects, rigging, props, camera, sound, wardrobe, make-up, and hairstyling and includes occupations such as carpenters, electricians (gaffers), riggers (grips), camera operators, costume, hair and make-up artists, and other trades that do the technical work required to produce a film or TV show. Between 1967 and 2000, there was a 63 percent growth in members with 90–95 percent of film production in the US using IATSE members (ibid.), and our Massachusetts interviews report that this growth has continued through the 2000s.

The IBT represents the much smaller number of transportation employees that drive the trucks and other equipment used in film productions. Because it also represents transportation employees in larger local industries, film transportation workers represent a relatively small segment of total Teamster membership.

4.5.6   Technological Change and the Decentralization of US Production

The geographical concentration of the industry in Los Angeles and New York City is largely due to the agglomeration effects of local institutions such as film academies, talent agencies, and film producers that play an important role in tying creative communities as well as technical service providers to particular regions through the building and maintaining of webs of regionally embedded, professional and personal relationships (Jones, 1996; DeFillippi and Arthur, 1998; Hirsch, 2000; Lampel et al., 2000; Windeler and Sydow, 2001; Sydow and Staber, 2002; Grabher, 2004).

Increasingly, however, this production is taking place in locations outside of the traditional clusters of Hollywood and New York (USDOC, 2001) and similar trends are occurring in television production (for example, Starkey et al., 2000; Windeler and

Sydow, 2001). During the 1990s, with the development of digitalization, the production of films was no longer restricted to a particular geographical location (USDOC, 2001; Klowden, et al., 2010). Dailies (the film shot on a particular day) can now instantly be sent electronically anywhere for review and editing in time for the next day's shoot. Even post-production film work can now be conducted anywhere in the world, reducing the geographical clustering advantages of the traditional film centers.

4.5.7　Industry Subsidies and the Decentralization of Production

By the late 1990s, other states and other countries began to offer incentive programs designed to lure film and television productions away from traditional centers of production to new locations such as Georgia, Louisiana, Massachusetts, Illinois, Pennsylvania, and New Mexico and to countries such as Canada and Australia. The number of movies either wholly or partially filmed in California fell from 272 in 2000 to 160 in 2008 (ibid.). According to a recent newspaper report (Verrier, 2010), shooting days in Los Angeles were down 19 percent between 2008 and 2009. Studies have documented similar declines in production in New York (Christopherson et al., 2006).

The growth of film and television tax credit programs in the United States that began in the early 2000s was a competitive response to programs that appeared somewhat earlier in Canada. In 1997, the Canadian government implemented the Production Services Tax Credit program which provided a refundable tax credit for 16 percent of the labor costs paid to Canadian residents during the making of qualified productions. With subsequent programs developed by individual provinces, producers could generate total tax credits of between 37 and 70 percent of qualified labor and non-wage spending on film and television productions. When combined with the relative strength of the US dollar in the late 1990s, these programs lured large numbers of US film productions to Canada (InterVISTAS, 2005).

From its inception, the Canadian program attracted the attention of industry representatives in the United States and generated heated debates about the impact of so-called 'runaway productions' (for example, productions leaving for Canada) on the US film and television industry (Monitor Company, 1999; USDOC, 2001; Neil Craig Associates, 2004; Christopheron and Rightor, 2010). Recognizing the success of the Canadian programs and responding to industry lobbying efforts about the potential loss of an iconic American industry, states in the US began offering similar programs in the early 2000s, thereby joining Canada and an increasing list of international locations in competing for film and television projects.

The first regional tax-incentive program in the United States was implemented in Oklahoma in 2001. Termed the 'Compete with Canada Act', it provided a cash rebate for 15 percent of Oklahoma-sourced production expenses for productions over $1 million. By 2010, at least 40 states (including California and New York) had implemented some kind of film and television industry incentive program. As these programs proliferated, so have debates about whether they are successful and how to measure their impacts (Christoperherson et al., 2006; McMillen et al., 2008; Popp and Peach, 2008; Miller and Abdulkadri, 2009).

Table 4.2 shows the total annual employment in NAICS 5121 (Motion Picture and Video Production) in the top 12 states as of 2001. Examining these data reveals several

Table 4.2 *Average annual employment in top 12 states, 2001–2010: NAICS 51211 (motion picture and video production)*

States	2001	2002	2003	2004	2005	2006	2007	2008	2009	2010	% Change 2001–10
CA	85,913	108,104	104,905	122,773	114,290	113,465	113,399	117,282	105,120	107,659	25.31
NY	38,940	33,839	29,470	28,546	30,881	31,121	31,089	32,810	32,484	40,518	4.05
FL	5,604	5,576	4,636	4,228	4,700	4,462	4,693	4,691	3,936	3,502	(37.51)
IL	3,396	2,889	2,584	2,477	2,640	2,594	2,577	2,667	2,411	2,307	(32.07)
TX	3,292	3,218	3,330	2,730	3,074	2,982	3,084	2,831	2,591	2,698	(18.04)
UT	2,643	2,478	2,364	1,904	2,142	1,817	1,281	1,356	1,203	1,118	(57.70)
NJ	2,262	2,185	2,042	2,410	2,715	2,852	2,842	2,629	3,259	3,145	39.04
GA	2,195	2,638	2,038	1,936	1,976	1,834	1,867	1,935	2,604	2,486	13.26
PA	1,885	1,766	1,773	1,741	2,026	1,957	2,162	2,598	3,354	2,809	49.02
MA	1,753	1,471	1,285	1,187	1,124	1,295	1,299	2,440	2,672	2,164	23.45
OH	1,745	1,425	1,118	992	866	887	825	874	798	802	(54.04)
MN	1,623	1,231	1,219	1,160	1,148	1,068	1,080	1,131	1,010	916	(43.56)

trends. First, it is clear that while California and New York still have the vast majority of film and television jobs in the country, there have been some major changes in employment trends in these two centers and a handful of potential regional clusters have begun to emerge. For example, employment in California increased by 25 percent between 2001 and 2010, but only by 4 percent in New York (Table 4.2). The next four states with the highest employment in 2001 (Florida, Illinois, Texas, and Utah) all experienced double-digit net job loss over the period, while the next four states experienced significant employment gains. The last two states, Ohio and Minnesota, also experienced significant employment losses.

All of these states have incentive programs that presumably contributed to employment growth, but the majority of the states experienced job losses, and when we compare these employment trends with the timing of incentive programs, it is clear that incentives are not the only factor driving employment. States with no incentive programs until late in the period (such as California) had significant employment growth (25 percent) while other states with older programs such as Illinois (2003) and Florida (2004) experienced net job losses. In Massachusetts, film industry employment had been on the decline until 2006 when the state implemented a 25 percent tax incentive program, but there was nearly a two-year lag between the implementation of this program and job growth in 2008.

Among this group of states, New Jersey, Pennsylvania, Georgia, and Massachusetts seem likely candidates for becoming future regional industry clusters of film, television, and video production by virtue of their sustained employment levels and long-term growth. As we shall show below, Massachusetts provides a useful laboratory for exploring this hypothesis.

4.5.8 The Development of a Motion Picture and Television Cluster in Massachusetts

The Massachusetts film and television industry was on the decline in the 1990s, with total employment falling by a third between 1990 and 2005. It rebounded gradually thereafter and turned in a respectable growth rate of 23 percent between 2001 and 2010. According to data from both the Motion Picture Association of America (2009) and the QCEW, Massachusetts had captured a little over 1 percent of the total national spending on motion pictures and television productions in 2010. About half of this spending was for wages, almost 15 percent for location fees, around 3 percent for set construction, and the rest spread around a number of uncategorized expenses (Pitter, 2011). Throughout our analysis we shall focus on the two major sectors of the motion picture and video industry (NAICS 51211 and NAICS 51219).

4.5.9   Aggregate Employment Trends

Movie production in Massachusetts outperformed the national industry over the decade of the 2000s with an overall growth in employment of 23.4 percent compared to 14.2 percent for the United States. This growth was helped by industry incentives as employment in 2010 increased to 2,164 from 1,124 in 2005 just before the implementation of the state incentive program in 2006, an almost 93 percent increase compared to a 4 percent increase nationwide during this same period. However, Massachusetts employment fared less well in the post-production sector with a decline of 15.5 percent over the entire decade compared to a national decline of 6.2 percent.

Employment in the post-production sector (NAICS 51219), however, tells a particularly interesting story that may be related to its linkages with studio films. After growing rapidly from 371 employees in 2005 to over 800 in 2008, employment in this sector dropped to 236 in 2009 and 196 in 2010 (Table 4.3). The period of substantial growth in the middle of the decade coincided with a flow of studio-based films being produced in Massachusetts, which allowed local companies to build connections with studios and organizations in Hollywood and New York. Interviews with industry representatives in 2009 suggested that this growth also included the hiring of large numbers of new employees, which may explain the drop in annual average salaries as new entrants are often paid lower wages and work fewer hours than veteran employees.

The data reported in Table 4.3, however, underestimate aggregate employment in the industry. The QCEW (Quarterly Census of Employment and Wages) does not include freelance employees, who are a large proportion of the workforce in this industry and there are also undercounts of employment in small firms that are not part of the unemployment insurance system. The motion picture and television production industry is dominated by small firms with 78 percent of the Massachusetts establishments being in the 1–4 size class and another 12 percent in the 5–9 employee category (there is only one firm employing over 100 workers) and the post-production sector is similarly dominated by very small firms (US Census Bureau, 2008).[17]

The data in Table 4.3 also show that the number of establishments has declined, even as employment has grown during this decade. Interviews with industry representatives suggest that this may be due to the widespread use of freelance labor in this sector, which is often supplied through local film service companies. Because both motion picture production and the sector of independent artists tend to pay the highest wages, the changes in the mix between local and 'imported' labor could contribute to the high fluctuations in reported earnings.

Table 4.3 Average annual establishments, employment and wages in Massachusetts, 1998–2010

Average annual establishments	1998	1999	2000	2001	2002	2003	2004	2005	2006	2007	2008	2009	2010
Motion picture & video production (51211)	319	316	326	311	308	293	297	297	272	273	298	287	295
Post-production & other (51219)	34	31	35	36	33	30	30	32	28	30	31	32	29
Annual average employment													
Motion picture & video production (51211)	1,736	1,621	1,836	1,753	1,471	1,285	1,187	1,124	1,295	1,299	2,439	2,672	2,164
Post-production & other (51219)	371	301	351	282	379	230	318	371	247	803	840	236	196
Annual average wages													
Motion picture & video production (51211)	42,840	45,453	50,103	50,700	48,624	51,370	54,415	57,695	60,527	60,598	61,225	53,051	41,033
Post-production & other (51219)	31,648	39,477	46,471	49,301	30,932	49,953	35,728	34,953	51,986	18,086	19,437	63,904	72,144

Source: Bureau of Labor Statistics, Quarterly Census of Employment and Wages.

131

4.5.10   Monthly Employment Variation

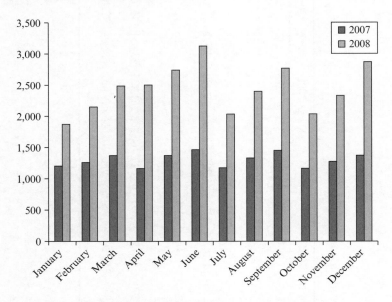

Source: Bureau of Labor Statistics, Quarterly Census of Employment and Wages.

Figure 4.2   Massachusetts monthly employment in NAICS 51211: motion picture and video production

Employment in both motion picture and video production and post-production jobs also experiences large fluctuations from month to month (Figures 4.2 and 4.3). When average annual employment in motion picture and television production rose by 88 percent (from 1,299 to 2,439 employees) between 2007 and 2008, minimum monthly levels of employment only rose by 61 percent, while the monthly maximum employment more than doubled (from 1,462 to 3,126). Fluctuations in monthly employment were even more dramatic in the post-production sector, ranging from 230 to 1,505 in 2007 and 314 to 2,480 in 2008. The trends in peak-to-peak employment provide a rough measure of trends in the level of core employment in the Massachusetts industry.

These short-term employment dynamics can also help to explain the significant drop in wages in post-production in 2007 and 2008, as our interviews reported that a large number of temporary employees were hired at relatively low wages by large film productions in Massachusetts. Another factor in the earnings variability is the growth of the local non-fiction television and post-production sector that has been hiring large numbers of relatively lower-paid new entrants, many of whom are local college graduates who are seeking experience in local television production.

4.5.11   The Effects of Project Mix

Employment trends are also affected by the type of projects coming to Massachusetts and data from the most recent analysis of the Massachusetts film and television indus-

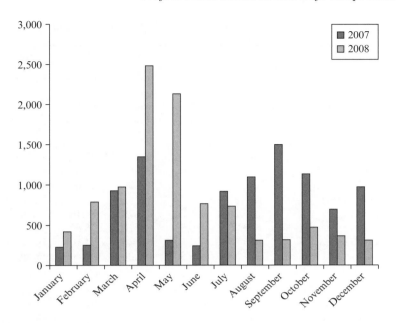

Source: Bureau of Labor Statistics, Quarterly Census of Employment and Wages.

Figure 4.3   *Massachusetts monthly employment in NAICS 51219: post-production and other*

try conducted by the Massachusetts Department of Revenue (Pitter, 2011) allow us to examine the effects of project mix on the industry in Massachusetts between 2006 and 2010 (Table 4.4). Because these data come directly from applications for the state tax credit (and because almost all commercial productions apply for the credit), they provide the most accurate picture of this industry available.

Table 4.4 shows that the total number of productions peaked in 2008 and then dropped precipitously in 2009 and again in 2010 with feature films showing the greatest volatility. A feature film shooting in Massachusetts might employ hundreds of people for weeks at a time and spend tens of millions of dollars on various combinations of highly paid out-of-state employees (typically star actors), local and out-of-state below-the-line employees, and service firms. As a result, these projects can have a disproportionate impact on local cluster development through both wage and non-wage spending patterns. Television commercials, by comparison, might have a local production budget of $250,000 and employ a handful of actors and crew paid at standard union (or industry) wages. During most of the 2006–10 period covered by Table 4.4, project spending was divided roughly one-third/two-thirds between Massachusetts and non-Massachusetts expenditures. However, when feature film production dropped in 2009 and 2010, not only did total spending fall rapidly, but the proportion of total industry spending on local employees and establishments increased from 33 to 63 percent.

Table 4.4   Film and television production and spending in Massachusetts, 2006–2010

Category of spending	2006	2007	2008	2009	2010	2006–10
Number of productions	95	122	159	97	83	556
Feature films	7	14	20	13	6	60
Commercials/advertising	45	53	86	51	51	286
Television series	26	29	28	21	14	118
Documentaries/other	17	26	25	12	12	92
Wages ($)	43.50	111.10	304.90	203.60	29.10	692.20
Wages $1 million & over	*	*	133.60	82.00	*	264.90
Wages under $1 million	*	*	171.30	121.60	*	427.30
Non-wage spending ($)						
Set construction	1.20	4.70	23.70	19.10	1.50	50.20
Location fees	9.30	10.50	42.10	36.60	8.40	107.00
Unclassified/other	30.80	30.10	109.40	74.10	19.30	263.70
Total	84.80	156.50	480.20	333.40	58.30	1,113
Of which spent on:						
MA resident/business ($)	29.90	46.60	153.00	108.40	36.70	374.60
Non-MA resident/business ($)	54.90	109.90	327.20	224.90	21.60	738.50
MA resident/busines (%)	35	30	32	33	63	34
Non-MA resident/business (%)	65	70	68	67	37	66

Note: * Data not available.

Source: Massachusetts Department of Revenue.

4.5.12   Labor Unions and OLMs in Massachusetts

The national film and television industry is heavily unionized and feature films and television productions are made under contract with the major film and television unions. Smaller independent films and documentaries, commercials, and non-fiction television productions, however, are more likely to be non-union.

There are four international labor organizations that represent crew and cast employed on motion picture productions in Massachusetts: IATSE, SAG, AFTRA, and the IBT. These international unions maintain local chapters that cover their members while they are working in Massachusetts. These locals serve numerous functions including administrating the complex labor agreements that cover their members, tracking and administering member benefits, helping to match employees with appropriate jobs, and ensuring that there are enough properly trained local members to staff future productions.

Most large motion picture and television productions in Massachusetts are made by companies that have signed national agreements with IATSE or agreements with IATSE Local 481 specifically. IATSE-represented employees make up a large proportion (up to 75 percent) of the crew on film and television productions and its members constitute a disproportionate share of the experienced core workforce in the Massachusetts industry. A large fraction of these workers are members of Local 481 (http://www.iatse481.com), which represents the studio mechanic crafts in the New England states (Massachusetts, Rhode Island, New Hampshire, Vermont, Maine).[18]

Local 481's membership has grown dramatically in recent years, as film and television production has grown in Massachusetts. Local 481's Massachusetts's membership has more than doubled, increasing from 237 in 2005 to 585 in 2008 and there have been similar rates of membership growth in other Massachusetts IATSE locals. Pension fund data show that total annual wages earned in Massachusetts by Local 481 members increased 10-fold over the same period, from approximately $3 million in 2005 to $30 million in 2008, which is a further indicator of increased continuity of employment of the core below-the-line workforce.

Local 481's membership has also increased in quality during this period of growth. Over the past few years, many Local 481 members have advanced from junior roles to become heads of departments (on a particular project), a progression that now provides them with increased responsibilities and higher wages. Experienced members of other IATSE locals, formerly based in Los Angeles or New York City, who had family ties here or who had attended universities in Massachusetts, have also moved back to the Commonwealth to work on productions.

This development is important for several reasons. First, it has enhanced the ability of Massachusetts to support large productions with less need to import key workers from out of state. For example, on a recent Hollywood feature film almost all of the departments represented by IATSE members were staffed locally from department heads down. One veteran of the local industry noted that the Commonwealth's crew base could now support 4–5 feature films at once, which was not the case two years ago; this is a remarkable increase in the capacity of this shared labor pool. Because of the structure of OLMs in film and television production, the development of local department heads is particularly important. Like general contractors in the construction industry, key employees select crews made up of people they are familiar with and trust. Because these people are more likely to be sourced locally, the localization of these key positions is a critical factor in workforce development in these sectors.

IATSE representatives report that some of these new members have migrated from related construction trades that have been experiencing significant employment contraction during the recession. There are numerous instances of carpenters who had been laid off or were underemployed in the construction industry transitioning to the motion picture industry, working steadily, and then joining Local 481. This is of particular note because it suggests that these sectors are able to absorb and rapidly retrain employees with similar skills from different occupations. It also points to the similarity of the technical aspects of film production to traditional crafts such as construction. Some of these professions are so closely related that the definitions for the official government occupational codes for electricians (7-2111) and riggers (49-9096) list their corresponding film industry occupation titles (gaffers and grips) as 'alternative occupation titles.'

SAG and AFTRA both represent performers who appear in television shows and commercials, while SAG alone represents performers who appear in motion pictures. Since motion picture production accounted for most of the recent increase in production in Massachusetts, recent workforce developments in the local branch of SAG are especially relevant to understanding the impact of these projects on the local workforce. The Boston branch of SAG grew by almost 30 percent between 2005 and 2008, with membership topping 2,100 by the end of 2008.[19] There was a 58 percent increase in the total wage bill for feature films and television programming in 2008, as compared to 2005.[20] The total spent on television commercials by members of SAG's Boston branch remained roughly constant between 2005 and 2008.

Although film and television employees represent a small proportion of Teamsters' Local 25's total membership of 11,500 employees, this group has also been growing rapidly. Prior to 2006, there were only 30 Teamsters employed in this industry, but by 2009 there were over 200. In addition to the growth in total employment, there has been a growth in the total hours worked by these employees. As in the case of IATSE members, some of these new workers have come from other local transportation industries that have experienced recent contraction.

4.5.13   OLMs and Agglomeration Economies

Even with the significant growth in both the number and skill of local film production employees, there are still some crafts with too few employees who are experienced enough to staff key positions. In mid-2008, a local assistant director/location manager reported that some crew lacked experience working on large productions and expressed the need for more local senior crew in positions such as costume and production design, special effects, directors of photography, digital image technicians, hair, and make-up. Other things being equal, film and television productions prefer to use a local crew because it saves the transportation and housing costs associated with importing talent. Because these key positions tend to hire people they have worked with before, as the Massachusetts crew base gains more experience and connections with out-of-state producers, we may find that the proportion of work on large films going to local crew will increase. This is a classic agglomeration economy one would expect to evolve from these OLMs.

The development of local crews who have a reputation for working together on certain types of projects is a key aspect of externalities developed in craft-like markets. Reputations and previous contacts become very important as a sorting mechanism for high-quality labor and also as a barrier for new less-experienced crews. Crews enhance their reputations and skill sets by working on different projects over time, and workers have an incentive to essentially engage in their own cross-training in order to enhance their attractiveness to potential project employers.

Film and television productions are material intensive and often require rapid service from local vendors. Therefore, the development of a cadre of experienced local service providers (such as in Los Angeles) is also important to servicing such a project-based industry. Often these vendors must rely on other sources of demand to survive the mercurial nature of film production schedules, but as film activity becomes more common they can shift more of their focus to this sector if it proves more lucrative.

4.5.14   Film Production Specializations

Motion picture and video production is divided into a variety of specializations – feature films, television films and series, documentaries, student films, and music videos. Feature films are further divided between studio productions and independent productions and between high- and low-budget films. Low-budget films typically have much lower cast costs and a correspondingly higher percentage of costs devoted to below-the-line labor (Christopherson et al., 2006).

Feature films comprised only 10.8 percent of the productions in Massachusetts during the 2006–10 period (see Table 4.4), but feature films have by far the biggest economic impact on the region because of their size and cost. Commercials and advertising represent the majority of the productions during this period (51.4 percent), but create less value and employment per unit than other types of projects. Television series represent 21.2 percent of the region's projects, while documentaries constitute 16.5 percent. The last two specializations, but particularly documentaries, are most reflective of the region's central specializations. They rely on the same OLMs and utilize the same MOSs as feature films, and their activities more fully illustrate the nature of the overall film production cluster in Massachusetts. Interviews with industry participants and analysis of archival data helped us identify recent developments in these sectors.

4.5.15   Television Production

Compared to feature films, television productions (especially commercials and non-fiction programs) typically use a much smaller proportion of above-the-line talent. The television production sector in Massachusetts comprises at least three different subsectors. Dramatic and scripted television begins with the production of a pilot episode. Not all pilots become long-running television shows. However, even shows that are picked up and air for a single season generate consistent employment for as many as one hundred cast and crew members. The 1980s television show, 'Spencer for Hire', generated long-term jobs for many local television production employees. However, because scripted television is typically produced in a studio, Massachusetts currently lacks a critical resource for the growth of this sector. Respondents argued that without a studio, scripted television shows may continue to use Massachusetts as a backdrop for exterior shots (as the long-running show 'Boston Legal' did), but would find it difficult to produce a full show in the Commonwealth.

Non-fiction cable television production is currently the fastest-growing and most-profitable part of the television industry. This is driven by the fact that cable networks (as opposed to broadcast networks) can generate revenue from both advertising and carrier subscription fees. Moreover, as compared to scripted television, non-fiction television has lower production costs. Respondents report that there is significant room for international growth in this sector. Industry representatives suggest that Massachusetts has the potential to be the nation's third-largest center for non-fiction television production. There are several factors that give Massachusetts a strategic advantage in this area. First, the labor pool contains experienced documentary producers, videographers, and sound recordists as well as a large pool of students who represent the potential for expanding this local labor pool. Only Los Angeles and New York City graduate more film/TV/video students annually than Massachusetts, and many of these students are currently finding jobs in the rapidly growing local non-fiction television subsector.

Second, entry into the market for non-fiction television products is relatively easier than for feature movie production. In particular, non-fiction TV has many openings for production assistants, assistant editors, and researchers. These jobs also last longer than feature film jobs because the complete production cycle of one hour of prime-time, non-fiction cable TV lasts between six and seven months, and career progression (such as to becoming an associate producer or producer) is also more rapid than in feature film production.

Massachusetts has two particular advantages that may contribute to the growth of this sector. First, it is home to the public television station WGBH, which has long been recognized as a national center for non-fiction television production. In addition, the state is home to one of the national leaders (Avid Technologies) in video editing equipment as well as to a rapidly growing digital gaming industry. The combined presence of Avid Technologies, small special effects software developers, digital gaming companies, and leading research labs in artificial intelligence and emerging media (especially at MIT) represent a powerful set of potential synergies.

The commercial and advertising sector is also starting to grow in the state. A majority of the television commercials produced in Massachusetts are made by a small handful of firms that reported that their overall business has remained stable between 2005 and 2008, a period when production of commercials in the US as a whole has been on the decline. One advertising company reported that 70 percent of its commercials were produced in the Commonwealth in 2008 compared to only 40 percent in 2005. However, Boston advertising agencies and large Massachusetts-based advertisers (for example, Fidelity, New Balance, Gillette, and Rebok) have still tended to use out-of-town production companies for most of their commercials. A local industry group, the Massachusetts Production Coalition, has recently undertaken an aggressive campaign to encourage Massachusetts-based advertisers, such as TJX, to shoot their commercials in the Commonwealth.

4.5.16   Documentaries and Narrative Producers

Documentary filmmaking has long been a distinctive strength of Massachusetts. Many of the pioneers of 16-millimeter documentary filmmaking were based here, and WGBH's role as the flagship PBS station has allowed the Commonwealth to establish and maintain a leadership position in both series and long-form television documentaries. Documentaries are often made using grants and other donations, and independent filmmakers rely on fiscal sponsors who provide the 501C3 (that is, not-for-profit) status needed to qualify for major grants. While there are many fiscal sponsors in the Commonwealth, three of them in particular work with a large number of local productions and assist filmmakers in researching, applying for, and administering grants. Together, these organizations supported approximately 150 projects in 2009. The overall number of active projects reported by the fiscal sponsorships organizations has not increased significantly since 2005, and our interviews with sponsors and filmmakers indicated that it was becoming increasingly difficult to raise money from major foundations. Funding in Massachusetts appears to have been relatively flat since 2005. The filmmakers interviewed reported that they typically shoot outside of state, while more often doing their post-production in-state.

While it is impossible to determine precisely how many independent documentary producers are working in the state, interviews with independent filmmakers and union representatives suggest that they are likely to outnumber independent narrative producers, a smaller but not insignificant group of local filmmakers. It appears that Massachusetts has the crew base and infrastructure to support a significant increase in independent narrative film production, but the funding for such projects remains unclear. Independent narrative films are either self-financed or financed by private investors, in contrast to the grants and donations typically used in documentary production. Investors are typically attracted to a narrative project if they believe that the project will be financially successful and they will receive a return on their investment. Self-financing is more common, and most independent filmmakers rely on other income sources to finance their independent films. These filmmakers also often work in film-related sectors including industrial, educational, and cable television production.

Because independent narrative filmmakers do not typically have fiscal sponsors, it was not possible to get the same broad view of narrative production over the past five years as was possible with documentary production. However, the number of low-budget feature films shot under SAG agreement in Massachusetts has doubled in recent years, rising from 18 in 2005 to 37 in 2008. The number of student films shot under SAG agreement more than doubled, going from 16 in 2005 to 41 in 2008. Although these kinds of projects do not make a large economic impact in the short term, they are important for developing young talent. In particular, young directors who achieve early success in Massachusetts may choose to shoot some or all of their future projects in the Commonwealth. Indeed, successful local actors such as Ben Affleck have recently returned to the Commonwealth to produce films here.

4.5.17 Additional Externalities

Boston is a major cultural and creative center with active performance groups and a concentration of cultural knowledge at its numerous universities and museums. It has a wide range of visually important filming locales and large pools of expertise in various film and television-related areas and it appears to have advantages in labor costs over Los Angeles and New York City, particularly in below-the-line occupations.

Academic-based education programs
Boston is an important center for students studying the production of film, television and other media. The Massachusetts College of Art and Design, Emerson College, Boston University, Fitchburg State, Curry College, and Bentley University all have film and television programs, some of which are important feeder schools for Los Angeles and New York City television and film companies. Boston University alone has over 1,000 students enrolled in Communications and Film and Television programs, and in 2009 graduated almost 300 students from these programs. Many other local schools also have drama, film, and television courses and generate many young local employees seeking jobs.

Until recently, graduates of these programs typically faced the choice of leaving Massachusetts or giving up on a career in the film industry. School officials associated with these programs and other industry representatives report that alumni who had left for Los Angeles and New York City have recently returned to Boston as more employment opportunities have opened up in the film industry here. Moreover, as noted above, local production companies are employing an increasing number of these students as interns and providing career advancement opportunities for Massachusetts college graduates. In addition to providing a local workforce for the industry, these programs also provide part-time employment for the many senior members of the local film and television industry, which helps maintain a local labor pool of skilled workers during a decline in film projects. Industry representatives described these educational resources as a unique strategic advantage for Massachusetts.

Career opportunities for local graduates seem to be particularly promising in non-fiction television production where there are numerous examples of local university programs providing both interns and new entrants (for example, production assistants, assistant editors, and researchers) for local television and post-production companies. Moreover, the jobs in this specialization tend to last longer than those in feature films, because the production cycle is longer.

Availability of service vendors and suppliers

A recent promising development for the film cluster in Massachusetts is that local vendors, such as those supplying electrical products, for large film productions have been expanding their offerings and several national firms have opened Massachusetts offices. Similarly, the recent merger of two local equipment rental firms (Rule and Boston Camera) has created a Massachusetts-based firm that possesses the scale to serve large studio productions. A national catering firm, Hat Trick, has also opened an office in Massachusetts, filling a significant gap in the local industry's capabilities and suggesting that key service firms see the location as promising. In addition, Media Services, one of a small number of national payroll companies that serves the motion picture industry, acquired CrewStar, a Massachusetts-based payroll firm. These trends suggest that there is a growing core of local film and television service firms emerging in the Commonwealth.

Labor costs

In addition to the advantages of abundant labor pools and flexible OLMs, Massachusetts appears to have a labor cost advantage over major production centers in six major production and post-production occupations for which comparable data are available (Table 4.5). The (unweighted) average wage for these occupations in the Los Angeles

Table 4.5   Wages in film-related occupations by metropolitan area, 2010 ($)

Occupation	Boston wage	New York City wage	Los Angeles wage
Multi-media artist and animators	29.14	32.73	36.98
Actors	26.20	27.35	40.01
Producers and directors	34.12*	55.14	66.66
Writers and authors	31.34	43.98	48.10
Film and video editors	30.59	32.89	44.74
Camera operators	33.96	21.55	32.16

Note: * Massachusetts wage.

Source: US Department of Labor, Occupational Employment Survey.

area is 48 percent higher than in Boston and 18 percent higher in the New York area.[21] The only occupation where Boston is more expensive is for camera operators, who receive lower pay in both New York and Los Angeles.

Intermediaries and linkages between Massachusetts and Hollywood
One of the most important questions about the emergence of regional clusters in project-based industries is whether, and how, they connect to more-established clusters and the role local organizations play in connecting highly mobile projects with local labor networks and other resources. Local universities, movie industry unions, and government agencies can all play an important role in forging such links. Universities offer temporary employment for some industry employees such as lecturers, and also produce the labor for internships, temporary jobs, and more-permanent occupations in the industry. The unions have helped connect local graduates with careers in the industry and have worked with the state to expand training opportunities.

Our research also revealed the important role that was played by the Massachusetts Film Office (MFO) in the development of the local film and television industry and in connecting this local industry to highly mobile national productions. Originally opened in the mid-1970s, it was not until 1979 that the MFO began receiving significant state funding for the purpose of marketing Massachusetts as a location to national film and television productions. From the outset, its primary activities involved nurturing ties with creative talent outside the state, soliciting specific productions, and assisting them with location scouting and connecting them with other local resources such as the free use of public facilities for locations. Political support for the MFO waned in the 2000s and the MFO was dormant between 2002 and its reopening in 2007, following the passage of a new Massachusetts tax incentive program in 2005. While it is impossible to determine how much of this employment was driven by the marketing activities of the film office as opposed to the tax incentive, the activities of the MFO illustrate the kind of network building that can be done to link local networks of labor and other resources with national and international producers of film projects.

4.5.18   Discussion

Massachusetts has experienced an uneven decade in its attempts to expand a motion picture and television production cluster within its borders. The state has little prospect of becoming a full-service region like Los Angeles and New York, but it has the ingredients for becoming one of a handful of 'satellite' production concentrations that can compete for a growing share of below-the-line jobs for major feature films that need Massachusetts as a shooting locale. Except for 'A-level' actors and directors, it has ample capacity and what appear to be wage advantages in its labor pools to compete for low- and medium-budget motion picture and television production and post-production work. There are signs of a growing core of experienced production crews and vendors with sufficient reputation to be substituted for 'imported labor and suppliers' and it has a first-class cultural and academic infrastructure that can provide expertise, part-time talent, and a flow of talented students to act, write, and support a variety of television products, independent films, and commercial videos. In addition, its union–management relations are relatively free of conflict and it has sufficient tax incentives to level the financial playing field among other states aspiring to compete for 'satellite' cluster status. It also has an 'A-level' producer of documentary films in its local NPR television affiliate. What it mainly lacks is the studio and sound-stage capacity for large-scale motion picture and made-for-television films, and reliable sources of financing for independent narrative films.

4.6   LESSONS FROM THE LITERATURE AND CASE STUDIES

Project-based production covers a wide range of manufacturing and service firms that participate in the production of one-of-a-kind or small-batch products. The production process for such products is uncertain because product development and production activities are intertwined. One example is 'first-of-a-kind' prototype projects where the manufacturing and testing of the product often reveal design and development flaws that lead to project modifications and changing project specifications. Similar issues of production uncertainty and product modification arise more generally in project industries that produce highly differentiated products with frequently changing designs, as illustrated by the case studies of fashion apparel and motion pictures where products often evolve from initial conception to final product.

Production uncertainty, interactions between production and design, rapidly changing product designs, and quick turnaround times require labor that is both broadly skilled and quickly able to identify and help resolve problems. Typically projects require workers with such skills to be able to work collaboratively in teams. Because the skills needed to produce projects are also subject to change as projects evolve, employment within the life of a single project team is fluid and the teams often change from project to project. As a result, project-based production often draws upon complex and 'loose' networks of workers, contractors, and service vendors.

Project production is typically organized by a lead firm that recruits project teams and coordinates networks of specialized contractors – a general contractor in the construction industry; a jobber or a retailer in the apparel industry; or the producer in the case of motion pictures. Lead firms retain a 'core' of experienced employees that perform these functions (and often participate in the production team as well) and they often draw upon a relatively stable 'core' of contractors.

Project-based production is often time sensitive because production delays result in lost markets or substantial increases in production costs. For example, prototype products are the preliminary step in a costly process of developing new products and opening new markets; samples are essential for securing orders in industries such as apparel where demand is seasonal and lead time to market is short; and failure to maintain production schedules for motion pictures can result in extra payments to above-the-line talent and below-the-line production crews who are idled by delays.

The intermittent and often time-sensitive demand in project-based firms and industries coupled with the need for broadly trained and experienced labor pools and networks of reliable vendors and suppliers explain why project-based production is often concentrated in particular 'districts' or regions that provide agglomeration economies tailored to support project-related activities. These districts provide an infrastructure for attracting and reinforcing clusters of project-based firms. Regional occupational labor markets in these districts complement the general skills and occupational structures of project-based production and the presence of such production allows them to retain the core of experienced workers and suppliers that is necessary to sustain it. Successful project-based districts also contain a variety of organizations – education and training institutions, professional and trade associations, and various government agencies and labor market intermediaries – that contribute to pools of knowledge through research, skill development, and the formation of network linkages. Silicon Valley, biopharmaceutical and life-sciences clusters around university research centers in Boston, San Francisco, and Raleigh-Durham, and the dominance of New York and Los Angeles in both apparel and motion picture and television production are common examples.

Whether or not the project-based model can help to revive the US manufacturing sector rests in part on the ability of regions to help develop the externalities to facilitate such production. The logic for advanced economies having a comparative advantage in project-based production is that such production requires the kind of human capital that is relatively more available in advanced economies than in those that are developing; that for some products the barriers of distance and transportation costs make time-sensitive production less vulnerable to import competition; and that the factor endowments, management capacity, and economic externalities present in developing countries lie more generally in mass production, rather than in smaller-scale niche markets. According to this logic, it is not surprising that the production of prototypes in advanced technology sectors or the small-scale production of replacement parts for older technologies should continue to be produced in the United States, and that a number of project-based firms have competed successfully in global markets. What is more controversial is whether the United States can be competitive in project-based production in medium- to low-technology industries and for products with somewhat larger global markets.

Our case studies provide evidence that this may be possible by illustrating the labor force structures and intermediary institutions that can help make project-based industries successful. The case studies also provide clues on how local economic development policies can help provide the labor networks and institutions required for project-based industries to flourish. Establishing a well-educated workforce with flexible skills and abilities to work in teams is certainly a key component. In addition, helping to facilitate the development of networks among firms either through government institutions such as the MFO, or through unions as in the case of apparel, can also assist project-based industries in meeting their production needs.

The case studies also illustrate how clusters of project-based industries can create their own externalities to aid in their growth and/or survival. The apparel industry illustrates the vulnerability of low-technology, labor-intensive industries to competition from low-cost countries. However, the New York district has survived more than eight decades of decline, first as a project-based industry using highly skilled and flexible labor and a pool of knowledge about fashion design to compete successfully against other US garment districts with low labor costs. The district remained project based as it grew, but it moved toward a network production model where lead firms (first manufacturers and then jobbers) coordinated specialized contractors to produce a wide variety of short-cycle products. This networking model eventually became the basis for mass production of fashion products, but as New York's labor costs increased relative to other districts, it was the more standardized and mass produced products that left the district while the more fashionable products with innovative designs and smaller production batches remained.

However, the longevity of the New York district depended as much on its ability to create new sources of district externalities as on its traditional externalities of knowledge of fashion and fashion design and the availability of skilled labor and flexible production methods needed for higher-end fashion products. The regulatory practices under collective bargaining initially helped to foster the production knowledge and problem-solving capacity of the district's core workforce and contracting networks, and these externalities have been preserved as jobbers have assumed responsibility for regulating contracting relationships, with the decline in collective bargaining.

Now that the combination of competition from imports and from Los Angeles has stripped away almost all of New York's relatively standardized and medium-to-large-scale production, the district is left with the most time-sensitive products and the smallest market niches, many of which are at the higher end of the fashion scale. Having evolved from its startup phase as an artisanal craft industry serving a regional market for customized fashion products, through its industrial period of contracting networks operating at different levels of fashion and scale of production and serving national markets with a myriad of differentiated fashion products, and then through decades of maturity and decline, the district is now returning to its roots in craft-like production using core contracting networks and drawing upon both traditional and created externalities.

The motion picture and television industry in Massachusetts presents a different perspective on the interaction between project-based production and regional agglomeration economies. In this industry, it is Los Angeles, and to some degree New York City, that represent the production regions with well-established externalities. Massachusetts is one of several regions seeking to establish its own production cluster. At one level, Massachusetts is trying to attract production in standard ways by offering distinctive venues for feature films and television series, lower wages for some production occupations, and tax incentives that lower production costs. However, Massachusetts also has the advantages of a nationally recognized niche in documentary production, a pool of independent film producers, a ready labor force graduating from local universities with well-rated motion picture and television schools or programs, and a union and government climate that can provide important externalities by serving as intermediaries for building local production capacity and providing linkages to motion picture and television producers in New York and Los Angeles.

While Massachusetts is unlikely to rival Los Angeles and New York in their pools of creative talent, well-trained below-the-line workers and vendors, and access to private and foundation financing for motion picture and television production, it is apparent that changes in industry structure and technology and the widespread availability of production subsidies are lessening the importance of the traditional agglomeration economies that have traditionally kept production in these districts. In the last decade, Massachusetts has gained considerable experience from having a number of feature films and television series filmed all or in part in the state and it is beginning to develop the kinds of core crews that are valued by outside producers and central to the success of its local documentary and independent producers. At the same time, national vendors and suppliers to the film and television industry have begun to trickle into the state; younger writers and directors who had been working in Los Angeles and New York are returning to Massachusetts, and filming of commercials has been growing in the state. Collectively these developments suggest that Massachusetts is assembling an infrastructure that could support a diverse portfolio of motion picture and television businesses sufficient to establish the state as a viable satellite cluster for the industry.

NOTES

1. Research support for this case study was provided by the National Science Foundation under Grant No. 0328635, the Fiscal Policy Institute, the Alfred P. Sloan Foundation, the International Labour Organization, and the Harvard University Center for Textile and Apparel Research. Sarah Crean and Seth Myers made the major contribution to the field research in New York City. We are grateful for comments from co-researchers on this case-study project – Sarah Crean, Bruno Courault, Lynn Oxborrow, Paolo Crestanello, and Daniela Bigarelli – and valuable research assistance provided by Brad Rice and Aparna Garn. The research has also benefited from comments by Frederick Abernathy, John T. Dunlop, Janice Hammond, David Weil, May Chen, Edgar Romney, and Mark Levinson as well as participants in seminars at the Federal Reserve Bank of Boston, the Garment Industry Development Corporation, MIT, American University, and the International Labour Organization's 'Decent Work Forum'.
2. The exception is in the few remaining large-scale firms where pattern making and cutting are largely automated and where electronic and programming skills have replaced traditional craft skills.
3. Los Angeles, originally a regional district serving West Coast markets, was later able to replicate many of these district externalities and began to compete with New York in sportswear and in other somewhat standardized products that it could manufacture at a relatively lower cost. New York City and Los Angeles are now the nation's largest garment districts and together account for 90 percent of all US women's wear employment.
4. Offshore sourcing was accelerated by a series of trade liberalization policies – the Caribbean Basin Initiative (1985), NAFTA (1994), and the more general reductions in apparel tariffs and quotas from 1994 to 2005 under the Uruguay Round of GATT negotiations.
5. A third way of measuring decline is through data on output. While data on women's wear output are not available at the district level, there are state-level data on value added for the cut-and-sew apparel sector (NAICS 3152). Because New York City accounts for a large fraction of apparel production in New York State, trends in statewide data provide a reasonable approximation of those at the district level. During the decade of the 2000s, New York's cut-and-sew apparel industry experienced a fall of 76.2 percent in its real value added. The magnitude of the statewide decline in real value added is somewhat larger than the corresponding change in employment.
6. This section is based on field research in New York City that was conducted in 2003 by Sarah Crean and Seth Myers under the auspices of the Fiscal Policy Institute, with Peter Doeringer participating in some of the interviews and data analysis. Survey data were collected during a series of in-depth interviews with a representative sample of 34 apparel firms in the New York City garment district in 2003. The project also had access to a counterpart survey in 2003 of 116 unionized apparel contractors in New York City, provided by the UNITE trade union. These surveys were supplemented by additional interviews with UNITE officials, large branded manufacturers, retailers, and industry associations. Doeringer has conducted more recent data analysis and follow-up discussions with industry experts.
7. These embedded obligations led to a distinction between the 'core' and 'peripheral' contractors in terms of productivity, earnings, and continuity of work, as noted by Uzzi (1996, 1997) and Palpacuer (2002) in their earlier studies of the New York City garment district in the 1980s and 1990s. Uzzi also documented the higher survival rates of core contractors relative to those in the peripheral sector of the New York district.
8. Capacity utilization in 2003 was also substantially below capacity utilization rates reported among apparel contractors in Manhattan during the Depression (Teper, 1937, p. 20).
9. The effects of falling demand and excess capacity are well described by simple economic theories of the firm. Fewer orders from jobbers and rising excess capacity caused contractors to reduce prices and raise productivity to avoid reaching their shut-down point where minimum average variable costs were no longer covered by marginal revenues. See, for example, Waldman and Jensen (2001) for a discussion of 'shut-down' conduct under perfect and monopolistic competition (pp. 30–33, 44–6).
10. Because Los Angeles County accounted for 92 percent of all shipments of cut-and-sew apparel manufacturing in California in 2009 and the corresponding share of New York State shipments accounted for by

New York City was 88 percent, statewide data provide a reasonable approximation of those at the district level.

11. New York specializes more heavily in women's tailored suits and coats while Los Angeles specializes more in women's blouses and shirts. But the largest specializations in both districts overlap and there is no a priori reason to believe that value-added per worker is higher for fashion products that require more time to produce than for more casual apparel products that have a lower labor content per garment.

12. Los Angeles also has a long history of ignoring minimum wages, overtime regulations, and health and safety standards in a climate of relatively lax enforcement of labor standards (Light, 2006; Bonacich and Appelbaum, 2002; Doeringer, 2012).

13. The major exception is among the small number of relatively large manufacturers of higher-end apparel using expensive fabric that tend to have continuing relationships with their contractors.

14. The most likely explanation for this fall in labor productivity is a combination of increased excess capacity caused by the steep declines in output after 2006 and the loss of scale and scope economies as the number of larger manufacturers fell in both districts.

15. The survey found that over 80 percent of the suppliers in the sample that were producing budget products could produce 'better' quality products, half could supply bridge and designer-quality products, and one could even do *haute couture* collections. Although the skills needed to move to higher-fashion products increase at each level of fashion, two-thirds or more of the suppliers were capable of producing at least one higher level of fashion and half were capable of moving up two levels or more on the fashion ladder.

16. Research support for this study was provided by a grant from the President's Creative Economy Initiatives Fund at the University Massachusetts. We are also grateful for the input provided by many industry representatives, organizations, agencies and individuals who commented on earlier versions of our work, and for the early introduction to the industry provided by Robert Laubacher.

17. This corresponds to national numbers where 81 percent employ 1–4 and 10 percent 5–9.

18. The 16 crafts represented by Local 481 are Art Department Coordinators, Construction, Costume/Wardrobe, Craft Services, Electric/Set, Lighting, Greens, Grip, Locations, Medical/First Aid, Properties, Set Dressing, Sound, Special Effects, Teleprompter Operators, and Video Assist.

19. SAG's reported membership is as large as the total workforce listed in the QCEW data in Table 4.3. This is largely due to the fact that SAG membership at any time will be larger than the total number of people currently employed on projects and that freelance employees are not included in the QCEW data.

20. SAG data reporting practices prevent the release of gross wages earned by local branches and only data trends are included in this report.

21. These numbers must be interpreted with caution. Some of the wage-cost differences could reflect the different mix of skills used in the different regions within the same occupation. The higher wage costs in New York City and Los Angeles could be a function of the higher proportion of workers with advanced skills in these occupations.

REFERENCES

Abernathy, F., J.T. Dunlop, J.H. Hammond and D. Weil (1999), *A Stitch in Time*, New York: Oxford University Press.

Amin, A. and N. Thrift (eds) (1994), *Globalization, Institutions and Regional Development in Europe*, Oxford: Oxford University Press.

Asheim, B.T. and A. Mariussen (2003), 'Introduction – why study temporary organizations?', in B.T. Asheim and A. Mariussen (eds), *Innovations, Regions and Projects: Studies in New Forms of Knowledge Governance*, Stockholm: Nordregio, pp. 7–11.

Atack, J. and P. Passell (1994), *A New Economic View of American History from Colonial Times to 1940*, New York: W.W. Norton.

Baker, W.E. and R.R. Faulkner (1991), 'Role as resource in the Hollywood film industry', *American Journal of Sociology*, **97** (2), 279–309.

Bechky, B.A. (2006), 'Gaffers, gofers, and grips: role-based coordination in temporary organizations', *Organization Science*, **17**, 3–21.

Berg, P., E. Appelbaum, T. Bailey and A.L. Kalleberg (2000), 'Modular production: improving performance in the apparel industry', in C. Ichniowksi et al. (eds), *The American Workplace*, Cambridge: Cambridge University Press.

Berggren, C., J. Söderlund, and C. Anderson (2001), 'Clients, contractors, and consultants: the consequences of organizational fragmentation in contemporary project environments', *Project Management Journal*, **32** (3), 39–48.

Bigarelli D. (2000), 'L'habillement en Italie: PME et systèmes régionaux de production', in B. Courault and P. Trouve (eds), *Les Dynamiques des PME: Approches Internationales*, Paris: Presses Universitaires de France, pp. 229–50.

Bigarelli, D. and P. Crestanello (2004), 'Features and changes in the Italian apparel industry', mimeo, Istituto Poster, Vicenza, Italy, June.

Bonacich, E. and R. Appelbaum (2000), *Behind the Label: Inequality in the Los Angeles Apparel Industry*, Berkeley and Los Angeles, CA: University of California Press.

Brusco, S. (1982), 'The Emilian model: productive decentralisation and social integration', *Cambridge Journal of Economics*, **6** (2), 167–84.

Burt, R.S. (2004), 'Structural holes and good ideas', *American Journal of Sociology*, **110** (2), 349–99.

California Fashion Association (2011), 'The Los Angeles area fashion industry profile', November.

Carpenter, J.T. (1972), *Competition and Collective Bargaining in the Needle Trades, 1910–1967*, Ithaca, NY: New York State School of Industrial and Labor Relations, Cornell University Press.

Caves, R.E. (2000), *Creative Industries: Contracts between Art and Commerce*, Cambridge, MA: Harvard University Press.

Chandler, A.D., Jr (1962), *Strategy and Structure: Chapters in the History of the American Industrial Enterprise*, Cambridge, MA: MIT Press.

Chinitz, B. (1961), 'Contrasts in agglomeration: New York and Pittsburgh', *American Economic Review*, **51**, 279–89.

Christopherson, S., M. Figueroa, L.S. Gray, J. Parrott, D. Richardson and N. Rightor (2006), *New York's Big Picture: Assessing New York's Position in Film, Television and Commercial Production*, Ithaca, NY: Cornell University Press.

Christopherson, S. and N. Rightor (2010), 'The creative economy as "big business": evaluating state strategies to lure film makers', *Journal of Planning Education and Research*, **29** (3), 336–52.

Christopherson, S. and M. Storper (1989), 'The effects of flexible specialization on industrial politics and the labor market: the motion picture industry', *Industrial and Labor Relations Review*, **42** (3), April, 331–47.

Cicmil, S. and D. Hodgson (2006), 'Making projects critical: an introduction', in D. Hodgson and S. Cicmil (eds), *Making Projects Critical*, Basingstoke: Palgrave Macmillan, pp. 1–25.

Community Redevelopment Agency (Los Angeles) (2011), 'Market analysis of the Los Angeles fashion district', draft mimeo, August.

Copeland, C. (2010), 'Employee tenure trend lines, 1983–2010', *EBRI Notes*, **31** (12), December, 120–22.

Courault, B. and P.B. Doeringer (2008), 'From hierarchical districts to collaborative networks: the transformation of the French apparel industry', *Socioeconomic Review*, **6** (2), April, 261–82.

Currah, A. (2007), 'Hollywood, the internet and the world: a geography of disruptive innovation', *Industry and Innovation*, **14** (4), September, 359–84.

Davies, A. and T. Brady (2000), 'Organizational capabilities and learning in complex product systems: towards repeatable solutions', *Research Policy*, **29**, 931–53.

DeFillippi, R.J. and M.B. Arthur (1998), 'Paradox in project-based enterprise: the case of film-making', *California Management Review*, **40** (2), 1–15.

Dicken, P. (2011), *Global Shift: Mapping the Changing Contours of the World Economy*, 6th edn, New York: Guilford Press.

Disher, M.L. (1947), *American Factory Production of Women's Clothing*, London: Devereaux.

Doeringer, P.B. (2012), 'Fashion clusters and market re-design in the 21st century: contracting networks, performance incentives, and garment district advantage in New York and Los Angeles', Boston University Department of Economics Working Paper, March 22.

Doeringer, P.B. and S. Crean (2006), *Socioeconomic Review*, **4** (3), 353–77.

Doeringer, P.B., C. Evans-Klock and D. Terkla (2002), *Start-Up Factories: High Performance Management, Job Quality, and Regional Advantage*, Oxford: Oxford University Press and Kalamazoo, MI: W.E. Upjohn Institute for Employment Research.

Doeringer, P.B., E. Lorenz and D.G. Terkla (2003), 'The adoption and diffusion of high-performance management: lessons from Japanese multinationals in the West', *Cambridge Journal of Economics*, **27**, 265–86.

Doeringer, P.B. and D.G. Terkla (1995), 'Business strategies and cross-industry clusters', *Economic Development Quarterly*, **9** (3), August, 225–37.

Eccles, R.G. (1981), 'The quasi-firm in the construction industry', *Journal of Economic Behavior and Organization*, **2** (4), 335–57.

Ellison G., E.L. Glaeser and W.R. Kerr (2010), 'What causes industry agglomeration? Evidence from coagglomeration patterns', *American Economic Review*, **100** (3), June, 1195–213.

Feldman, M.P. and J.L. Francis (2004), 'Homegrown solutions: fostering cluster formation', *Economic Development Quarterly*, **18**, 127–37.

Ferriani, S., G. Cattani and C. Baden-Fuller (2009), 'The relational antecedents of project-entrepreneurship: network centrality, team composition and project performance', *Research Policy*, **38**, 1545–58.

Feser, E., H. Renski and H. Goldstein (2008), 'Clusters and economic development outcomes: an analysis of the link between clustering and industry growth', *Economic Development Quarterly*, **22** (4), November, 324–44.

Foster, P., S.P. Borgatti and C. Jones (2011), 'The contingent value of embeddedness: gatekeeper search in a local cultural market', *Poetics*, **39** (4), 247–65.

Foster, P., S. Manning and D. Terkla (2013), 'The rise of Hollywood East: regional film offices as intermediaries in film and television production clusters', working paper, UMB College of Management, University of Massachusetts Boston, MA.

Frommer, G. (2003), 'Hooray for . . . Toronto? Hollywood, collective bargaining, and extraterritorial union rules in an era of globalization', *University of Pennsylvania Journal of Labor and Employment Law*, **6** (1), 56–118.

Galbraith, J.R. (1971), 'Matrix organization designs: how to combine functional and project forms', *Business Horizons*, **14** (1), 29–40.

Gann, D.M. and A.J. Salter (2000), 'Innovation in project-based, service-enhanced firms: the construction of complex products and systems', *Research Policy*, **29** (7/8), 955–72.

Giarratani, F., G. Gruver and R. Jackson (2007), 'Clusters, agglomeration and economic development potential: empirical evidence based on the advent of slab casting by U.S. steel minimills', *Economic Development Quarterly*, **21** (2), May, 148–64.

Grabher, G. (2002a), 'Cool projects, boring institutions: temporary collaboration in social context', *Regional Studies*, **36** (3), 205–14.

Grabher, G. (2002b), 'The project ecology of advertising: tasks, talents and teams', *Regional Studies*, **36** (3), 245–62.

Grabher, G. (2004), 'Architectures of project-based learning: creating and sedimenting knowledge in project ecologies', *Organization Studies*, **25** (9), 1491–514.

Green, Nancy L. (1997), *Ready-to-Wear and Ready-to-Work: A Century of Industry and Immigrants in Paris and New York*, Durham, NC: Duke University Press.

Hagedoorn, J., A.N. Link and N.S. Vonortas (2000), 'Research partnerships', *Research Policy*, **29** (4/5), 567–86.

Haunschild, A. (2003), 'Managing employment relationships in flexible labour markets: the case of German repertory theatres', *Human Relations*, **56** (8), 899–929.

Helfgott, R.B. (1959), 'Women's and children's apparel', in M. Hall (ed.), *Made in New York*, Cambridge, MA: Harvard University Press, pp. 19–134.

Hill, E.W. and J.F. Brennan (2000), 'A methodology for identifying the drivers of industrial clusters: the foundation of regional competitive advantage', *Economic Development Quarterly*, **14** (1), February, 65–96.

Hirsch, P.M. (2000), 'Cultural industries revisited', *Organization Science*, **11** (3), 356–61.

Hobday, M. (2000), 'The project-based organisation: an ideal form for managing complex products and systems?', *Research Policy*, **20** (7/8), 871–93.

Hochman, J. (1941), *Industry Planning through Collective Bargaining*, New York: International Ladies Garment Workers Union.

InterVISTAS (2005), 'Film and Television Industry Review', British Columbia Ministry of Economic Development, October.

Jackson, R. (1984), *The Formation of Craft Labor Markets*, Orlando, FL: Academic Press.

Jacoby, D. (1991), 'The transformation of industrial apprenticeship in the United States', *Journal of Economic History*, **51** (4), December, 887–910.

Jones, C. (1996), 'Careers in project networks: the case of the film industry', in M.B. Arthur and D.M. Rousseau (eds), *The Boundaryless Career: a New Principle for a New Organizational Era*, New York: Oxford University Press, pp. 58–75.

Jones, C., W.S. Hesterley and S.P. Borgatti, (1997), 'A general theory of network governance: exchange conditions and social mechanisms', *Academy of Management Review*, **22** (4), 911–45.

Klowden, K., A. Chatterjee and C. Hynek (2010), 'Film flight: lost production and its economic impact on California', Milken Institute, Santa Monica, CA, July.

Lampel, J., T. Lant and J. Shamsie (2000), 'Balancing act: learning from organizing practices in cultural industries', *Organization Science*, **11** (3), 263–9.

Lash, S. and A. Wittel (2002), 'Shifting new media: from content to consultancy, from heterarchy to hierarchy', *Environment and Planning A*, **34** (11), 1985–2002.

Levine, L. (1969), *The Women's Garment Workers*, New York: Arno & the New York Times.

Levitan, M. (1998), 'Opportunity at work: the New York City Garment Industry', Community Service Society of New York, New York, mimeo.

Light, I. (2006), *Deflecting Immigration*, New York: Russell Sage Foundation.

Lundequist, P. and D. Power (2002), 'Putting Porter into practice? Practices of regional cluster building: evidence from Sweden', *European Planning Studies*, **10** (6), 685–704.

Lundin, R.A. and C. Midler (eds) (1998), *Projects as Arenas for Renewal and Learning Processes*, Norwell, MA: Kluwer Academic.

Lundin, R.A. and A. Söderholm (1995), 'A theory of the temporary organization', *Scandinavian Journal of Management*, **11** (4), 437–55.

Manning, S. (2005), 'Managing project networks as dynamic organizational forms: learning from the TV movie industry', *International Journal of Project Management*, **23** (5), 410–14.

Manning, S. (2008), 'Embedding projects in multiple contexts – a structuration perspective', *International Journal of Project Management*, **26** (1), 30–37.

Manning, S. (2010), 'The strategic formation of project networks: a relational practice perspective', *Human Relations*, **63** (4), 551–73.

Manning, S. and J. Sydow (2011), 'Projects, paths, and practices: sustaining and leveraging project-based relationships', *Industrial and Corporate Change*, **20** (5), 1369–402.

Manning, S. and O. von Hagen (2010), 'Linking local experiments to global standards: how project networks promote global institution-building', *Scandinavian Journal of Management*, **26** (4), 398–416.

Marshall, A. (1890), *Principles of Economics*, Macmillan: London.

Martin, R. and P. Sunley (2003), 'Deconstructing clusters: chaotic concept or policy panacea', *Journal of Economic Geography*, **3**, 5–35.

McMillen, S., K. Parr and T. Helming (2008), 'The Economic and Fiscal Impacts of Connecticut's Film Tax Credit', Department of Economic and Community Development, Hartford, CT.

Meyerson, D., K.E. Weick and R.M. Kramer (1996), 'Swift trust and temporary groups', in R.M. Kramer and T.R. Tyler (eds), *Trust in Organizations*, Thousand Oaks, CA: Sage, pp. 166–95.

Midler, C. (1995), '"Projectification" of the firm: the Renault case', *Scandinavian Journal of Management*, **11** (4), 363–75.

Miller, S.R. and A. Abdulkadri (2009), 'The Economic Impact of Michigan's Motion Picture Production Industry and the Michigan Motion Picture Production Credit', Center for Economic Analysis, Michigan State University.

Milkman, R. (2006), *L.A. Story: Immigrant Workers and the Future of the U.S. Labor Movement*, New York: Russell Sage Foundation.

Mintzberg, H. and A. McHugh (1985), 'Strategy formation in an adhocracy', *Administrative Science Quarterly*, **30**, 160–97.

Monitor Company (1999), 'U.S. Runaway Film and Television Production Study Report', Directors' Guild of America/Screen Actors' Guild.

Montana, J.P. and B. Nenide (2008), 'The evolution of regional industry clusters and their implications for sustainable economic development', *Economic Development Quarterly*, **22** (4), November, 290–302.

Motion Picture Association of America (2009), *The Economic Impact of the Motion Picture & Television Industry on the United States*, Washington, DC: Motion Picture Association of America.

Motoyama, Y (2008), 'What was new about the cluster theory? What could it answer and what could it not answer', *Economic Development Quarterly*, **22** (4), November, 353–63.

Municipal Art Society of New York (2011), 'Fashioning the future: NYC's garment district', October.

National Retail Dry Goods Association (1936), *Twenty-five Years of Retailing, 1911–1936*, New York: National Retail Dry Goods Association.

Neil Craig Associates (2004), *International Film and Television Production in Canada: Setting the Record Straight about U.S. 'Runaway' Production*, Toronto: Neil Craig Associates.

Newcombe, R. (1996), 'Empowering the construction project team', *International Journal of Project Management*, **14** (2), 75–80.

Newlands, D. (2003), 'Competition and cooperation in industrial clusters: the implications for public policy', *European Planning Studies*, **11** (5), July, 521–32.

Osterman, P. (2000), 'Work reorganization in an era of restructuring: trends in diffusion and effects on employee welfare', *Industrial and Labor Relations Review*, **53** (2), January, 179–96.

Osterman, P. (2006), 'The wage effects of high performance work organization in manufacturing', *Industrial and Labor Relations Review*, **59** (2), January, 187–204.

Palpacuer, F. (2002), 'Subcontracting networks in the New York garment industry: changing characteristics in a global era', in G. Gereffi et al. (eds), *Free Trade and Uneven Development*, Philadelphia, PA: Temple University Press, pp. 53–73.

Paul, A. and A. Kleingartner (1994), 'Flexible production and the transformation of industrial relations in the motion picture and television industry', *Industrial and Labor Relations Review*, **47** (4), July, 663–78.

Piore, M.J. and C.F. Sabel (1984), *The Second Industrial Divide: Possibilities for Prosperity*, New York: Basic Books.

Pitsis, T.S., S.R. Clegg, M. Marosszeky and T. Rura-Polley (2003), 'Constructing the Olympic dream: a future perfect strategy of project management', *Organization Science*, **14** (5), 574–90.

Pitter, A. (2011), 'A Report on the Massachusetts Film Industry Tax Incentives', Department of Revenue, Commonwealth of Massachusetts, November.

PMI (2000), *A Guide to the Project Management body of Knowledge* (PMBOK guide), Newtown Square, PA: Project Management Institute.

Pope, J.E. (1905 [1970]), *The Clothing Industry in New York*, New York: Burt Franklin.

Popp, A.V. and J. Peach (2008), 'The Film Industry in New Mexico and the Provision of Tax Incentives', Arrowhead Center, Office of Policy Analysis, Las Cruces, NM.

Porter, M. (1994), 'The role of location in competition', *Journal of the Economics of Business*, **1** (1), 35–9.

Reid, N. B.W. Smith and M.C. Carroll (2008), 'Cluster regions: a social network perspective', *Economic Development Quarterly*, **22** (4), November, 345–52.

Rice, J. Bradford (2008), 'The labor market effects of long-term contracts, imports and offshoring', PhD dissertation, Boston University, Boston, MA, available through Google ebooks.

Rychen, F. and J.B. Zimmermann (2008), 'Clusters in the global knowledge-based economy: knowledge gatekeepers, and temporary proximity', *Regional Studies*, **42** (6), 767–76.

Sahlin-Andersson, K. and A. Söderholm (eds) (2002), *Beyond Project Management: New Perspectives on the Temporary–Permanent Dilemma*, Malmö: Liber.

Saxenian, A. (1996), 'Beyond boundaries: open labor markets and learning in Silicon Valley', in M.B. Arthur and D.M. Rousseau (eds), *The Boundaryless Career: A New Employment Principle for a New Organizational Era*, New York: Oxford University Press, pp. 23–39.

Segal, N. (1960), *Wages in the Metropolis*, Cambridge, MA: Harvard University Press.

Shenhar, A.J. (2001), 'Contingent management in temporary, dynamic organizations: the comparative analysis of projects', *Journal of High Technology Management Research*, **12** (2), 239–71.

Shenhar, A.J. and D. Dvir (1996), 'Toward a typological theory of project management', *Research Policy*, **25** (4), 607–32.

Slichter, S.H., J.J. Healy and E.R. Livernash (1960), *The Impact of Collective Bargaining on Management*, Washington, DC: Brookings Institution.

Söderlund, J. (2000), 'Temporary organizing – characteristics and control forms', in R.A. Lundin and F. Hartman (eds), *Projects as Business Constituents and Guiding Motives*, Boston, MA: Kluwer Academic Publishers, pp. 61–74.

Song, J., P. Almeida and G. Wu (2003), 'Learning-by-hiring: when is mobility more likely to facilitate interfirm knowledge transfer?', *Management Science*, **49** (4), 351–65.

Starkey, K., C. Barnatt and S. Tempest (2000), 'Beyond networks and hierarchies: latent organizations in the U.K. television industry', *Organization Science*, **11** (3), 299–305.

Stinchcombe, A.L. (1959), 'Bureaucratic and craft administration of production: a comparative study', *Administrative Science Quarterly*, **4** (2), 168–87.

Storper, M. (1989), 'The transition to flexible specialisation in the US film industry: external economies, the division of labour, and the crossing of industrial divides', *Cambridge Journal of Economics*, **13** (2), 273–305.

Sydow, J. and U. Staber (2002), 'The institutional embeddedness of project networks: the case of content production in German television', *Regional Studies*, **36** (3), 223–35.

Teper, L. (1937), *The Women's Garment Industry: An Economic Analysis*, New York, International Ladyies', Garment Workers' Union.

Tolbert, P.S. (1996), 'Occupations, organizations, and boundaryless careers', in M.B. Arthur and D.M. Rousseau (eds), *The Boundaryless Career: A New Employment Principle for a New Organizational Era*, New York: Oxford University Press, pp. 331–49.

Ulman, L. (1955), *The Rise of the National Union: The Development and Significance of Its Structure, Governing Institutions, and Economic Policies*, Cambridge, MA: Harvard University Press.

US Census Bureau (2008), 'County Business Patterns', Boston, MA.

US Department of Commerce (USDOC) (2001), 'The migration of U.S. film and television production', United States Department of Commerce, Washington, DC, January.

US Department of Labor (2011), 'Occupational Employment and Wages', Bureau of Labor Statistics, Occupational Employment Statistics, May.

Uzzi, B. (1996), 'The sources and consequences of embeddedness for the economic performance of organizations: the network effect', *American Sociological Review*, **61** (4), August, 674–98.

Uzzi, B. (1997), 'Social structure and competition in interfirm networks: the paradox of embeddedness', *Administrative Science Quarterly*, **42** (1), March, 35–67.

Uzzi, B. (2004), 'Collaboration and creativity: the small world problem', *American Journal of Sociology*, **111** (2), 447–504.

Vernon, R. (1960), *Metropolis 1985*, Cambridge, MA: Harvard University Press.

Vernon, R. (1966), 'International investment and international trade in the product life cycle', *Quarterly Journal of Economics*, **80** (2), 190–207.

Verrier, R. (2010), 'Company town: L.A. location filming declines 19% in 2009 from previous year', *Los Angeles Times*, 3.

Vogel, H. (2007), *Entertainment Industry Economics*, Cambridge: Cambridge University Press.

Waldinger, R. (1986), *Through the Eye of the Needle: Immigrants and Enterprise in New York's Garment Trades*, New York: New York University Press.

Waldman, D.E. and E. Jensen (2001), *Industrial Organization*, 2nd edn, New York: Addison Wesley.

Whitley, R. (2006), 'Project-based firms: new organizational form or variations on a theme?', *Industrial and Corporate Change*, **15** (1), 77–99.

Williams, S. and E. Currid-Halkett (2011), 'The emergence of Los Angeles as a fashion hub: a comparative spatial analysis of the New York and Los Angeles fashion industries', *Urban Studies*, **48** (14), November, 3043–66.

Windeler, A. and J. Sydow (2001), 'Project networks and changing industry practices – collaborative content production in the German television industry', *Organization Studies*, **22** (6), 1035–60.

5 Innovation, industry evolution and cross-sectoral skill transfer in the video game industry: a three-country study

Yuko Aoyama and Hiro Izushi

5.1 INTRODUCTION

In this chapter, we explore the creation of industry-specific skills as a complex process that juxtaposes social and economic forces in particular contexts. Research on cultural industries in economic geography suggests the role of agglomerations and clusters (Pratt, 1997a, 1997b; Power, 2002; Bathelt and Boggs, 2003; Power and Scott, 2004) in shaping specialized labor markets and developing a social division of labor within them (Storper and Christopherson, 1987; Christopherson and Storper, 1989; Scott, 1996, 1997; Coe, 2000). Unlike traditional views of industry evolution which focus on the company as their principal unit of analysis, literature in economic geography acknowledges that the presence of communities of practice (Wenger, 1998), which arise from shared obligations and commitments to a particular practice, is of equal significance linking individual careers and corporate developments with industry evolution (Arthur et al., 2001). Such communities are often found in spatial clusters of related firms. Networks of individuals and firms linked through both business relations and social ties are seen to have a major role in determining an industry's evolution and competitiveness. As institutions shaping such networks are deeply ingrained in each society and vary across countries, industry evolution is a process embedded in a specific context. This is suggested by sector-based studies such as multimedia (Scott, 1995; Preston and Kerr, 2001) and film (Jones, 2001) as well as the 'varieties of capitalism' approaches of institutional theorists (Hall and Soskice, 2001). Yet their primary focus is either on the intra-industry mobilization of resources or on the interactions with external socioeconomic environments. As a result, we remain largely uninformed of the conditions and mechanisms through which the transfer and fusion of skills take place from old to new industries.

Before an industry becomes a recognized sector of activities, in which the necessary skills are identified, and a formalized job description is developed, its attraction of a labor force relies on a variety of social networks, such as hobby clubs, meetings at shops, trade shows, and conventions, meetings between alumni of groundbreaking firms in existing industries, and contacts of an emerging industry's pioneering entrepreneurs. While economic incentives such as high wages and growth prospects undoubtedly play a role, the social acceptance and legitimacy of an emerging industry among existing industries with potentially relevant skills, as well as the socio-cultural cohesiveness between them, facilitates the transfer of skills, affecting entrepreneurial motivation and skills aspirations.

This is because the co-presence of existing industries within the country and their relative strengths affect the degree to which skills are drawn from the old to the new industry. The social and economic status attached to pioneering entrepreneurs/firms in the emerging industry in turn exerts a powerful influence upon its ability to draw skills from the existing sectors. Furthermore, the socio-cultural cohesiveness between old and new industries also lowers the barrier to skill transfers. If either of these conditions is lacking, an emerging industry may be faced with the difficulty of drawing on other sectors, which forces it to rely on an internal accumulation of human capital. Once the new industrial sector is established, a specialized labor market emerges in part through formal education programs designed to specially cater to the skill requirements of the new industry. Linkages to existing institutions (for example, universities, government agencies) are either newly formed or reorganized both at the firm and the industry levels (for example, through trade associations). This whole process gives rise to different patterns of the cross-sectoral fusion of creative talent in the same industry in different countries. The different trajectories of skill formation also in part shape competitiveness of the emerging sector.

First, we shall discuss issues of industry evolution and explore the literature on evolutionary and institutional approaches, and conclude that few studies analyze the transfer and fusion of skills from existing industries at the birth of a new industry. To demonstrate the important role of socio-cultural factors in industrial evolution, we take the case of the video game industry in three countries and assess how cross-sectoral links with existing industries shaped their evolutionary paths in three different contexts. Finally, we analyze the role of technology in shaping the cross-sectoral skills transfer as well as their changing competitive position. We argue that the process of cross-sectoral skill transfer in a newly emerging industry is shaped by socioeconomic as well as socio-cultural cohesiveness between the existing and the emerging industries. Concurrent peaks and the social legitimacy of existing industries also influence the flow of skills between the old and new industries. Also, the patterns of skill transfers depend on national contexts, varying from one country to another, and on the particular state of technology which determines relevant creative skills for the new industry. The interplay of economic, social, and technological factors in turn develops a particular techno-industrial path dependence, thereby affecting a country's competitive position globally.

5.2 INTERPRETING INDUSTRY EVOLUTION

The question of what determines the forms of organization in an economic sector has been dealt with in various ways, ranging from transaction cost explanations (Coase, 1937; Williamson, 1975), socio-institutional foundations (Piore and Sabel, 1984), and embeddedness (Granovetter, 1985). Nelson and Winter (1982) advocated an evolutionary approach, in which path dependency is observed through a developmental trajectory of technologies. Osborn and Hagerdoorn (1997) suggested a pluralistic approach that allows for a better understanding of the complexity in organizational behavior. According to the Schumpeterian evolutionary approach, three processes drive changes in an economic system, namely, varieties in products, firms, and organizations, their replication, and their selection (Nelson, 1995; Metcalfe, 1998; Malerba, 2002). These three processes are stylized in the industry life-cycle model (Utterback and Abernathy, 1975; Abernathy and Utterback, 1978; Utterback, 1994; Klepper, 1996), although empirical evidence suggests that there are both wide cross-sectoral variations in industry evolution as well as incompatibilities with the model's prediction (Malerba and Orsenigo, 1996; McGahan, 2000). The questions of how a new system emerges, and how the old and the new are linked, therefore remain unanswered by the Schumpeterian approach (Malerba and Orsenigo, 1996; Malerba, 2002).

A new industry does not emerge *de nouveau* (Jones, 2001, p. 914). It has to draw skills and knowledge from pre-existing industries or otherwise create them on its own. Whereas firms build on their existing competencies in their evolution (Teece, 1988), countries tend to innovate and create new products in sectors/technologies which are close to their existing strengths (Dosi et al., 1990; Archibugi and Pianta, 1992; McKelvey, 1997). In this sense, the formation of a new industry involves two contradictory but equally essential aspects of innovation: continuity with existing elements combined with radical change (Lundvall et al., 2002). Yet, what remains unanswered is how processes of 'integration and fusion of previously separated knowledge and technologies' (Malerba, 2002, p. 259) occur, and which factors shape such processes, particularly at the onset of a new industry. Alternatively, the institutional approach analyzes the role of formal as well as informal institutions in economic growth (Saxenian, 1994; Gertler, 1995, 2004; Amin, 1999), and provides insights into the causes of variety in economic growth at the regional, national, and cross-national levels. Institutions understood as norms, routines, habits, and conventions, as well as laws and standards, to a great extent influence how people relate to each other and learn knowledge (Storper and Salais, 1996; Lundvall et al., 2002).

However, once an industry matures, it becomes increasingly difficult to successfully enter a new industry life cycle. Many incumbent firms experience difficulties in adjusting their technical strengths and strategies to these developments (Tushman and Anderson, 1986; Henderson and Clark, 1990). Firms typically build their capabilities cumulatively around a particular trajectory. In part this is due to the inability of decision makers to consider the universe of options available to them, which means that firms tend to look to their own previous development decisions for guidance. As a result, firms concentrate their innovative efforts in areas of prior knowledge accumulation, aimed at providing consistent investments in personnel, intellectual property, inter-organizational relations, and tacit organizational knowledge (Stuart and Podolny, 1996). Thus, industry life cycles, combined with the presence of strong user communities, can lock firms in to an existing evolutionary path of products and deter them from embarking on a new cycle in the market for consumer goods. Moreover, active user communities can act as a pressure group (Olson, 1965), also exerting an influence upon the direction firms take with their innovation strategies. Just as firms in a mature industry show the same tendency, user communities tend to come to consist of individuals with similar mindsets, dispelling outsiders with different ideas.

5.3   INDUSTRY EVOLUTIONS AND INTER-SECTORAL SKILL TRANSFER

In this section, we shall briefly trace the developmental trajectory of the video game industry. It reveals a process in which pre-existing sectors play a crucial role in the emergence of a new industry, by supplying creative and skills resources. Co-presence facilitates the transfer of skills from an existing industry to a newly emerging one, but in some circumstances this transfer is predicated upon socio-cultural proximity between the two sectors.

5.3.1 Japan

Japan's video game industry drew its creative as well as technical resources initially from the toy industry. Nintendo (founded 1889) began experimenting with electronic toy products, which were still widely ignored by the mainstream toy industry. Formerly a producer of toys and playing-cards and located in the ancient capital of Kyoto, Nintendo is quite distinct from the conventional portrayal of typical Japanese firms that have become global, which typically constitute large conglomerate (*keiretsu*) firms with manager–CEOs and headquarters in Tokyo. In contrast, Nintendo continues to be a privately held company, retaining strong owner–entrepreneur-CEOs, and which has long experimented with product innovations, not all of which have seen commercial successes (for example, 'instant rice' to counter instant ramen noodles in the 1970s).

Nintendo took a particular interest in acquiring a knowledge of electronics and produced shooting games that used optical sensors. To develop in-house technical skills, in 1964 Nintendo began to hire experienced electronics hardware engineers who came from well-known consumer electronics firms, and conducted joint R&D with Sharp and Mitsubishi Electric, based in the adjacent cities of Osaka and Kobe. One of their experiments resulted in a license in Japan to produce a Magnavox video game system that offered a variation of *Pong* in 1975. Those engineers who were initially hired to develop baseball pitching machines and toy transceivers were subsequently reassigned to develop arcade games. Nintendo's first fully fledged home video game in 1983, Famicom, was in fact a latecomer in the home video game market behind Tommy and Bandai, Japan's major toy companies. Nintendo's eventual success over competitors is attributed to price competitiveness, its ability to deliver original mega-hit software such as *Super Mario Brothers* (1985), and its initial alliances with best-selling arcade video games. Although Japan's powerful electronics hardware industry had an aversion to valuing the role of software, Nintendo actively nurtured talent in software development both in-house as well as through third-party publishers. By 1990, Nintendo was a household name in Japan and the United States, as well as in Europe.

Nintendo's success in developing software content that appealed to the audience came from the crucial hiring of Shigeru Miyamoto, a Kyoto native and Nintendo's chief game developer and the creator of *Donkey Kong* and *Super Mario Brothers*. Miyamoto began his interest in *manga* in junior high school, and led the cartoonist club at school. After studying industrial design at Kanazawa College of Art, he was hired by Nintendo and was assigned to develop an arcade game for the US market in 1980. Realizing that the objective of the then popular *Space Invaders* and *Pac-Man* was simply to erase objects from the screen, he decided to create a game with a story, just as in cartoons/animation films. *Donkey Kong* is built upon a detailed *manga*-like character with an elaborate story that resembles those from animation films (Aida and Ohgaki, 1997). Miyamoto developed the lead character of *Donkey Kong* to be a blue-collar, construction worker who kept a gorilla as a pet and had a pretty girlfriend. The same lead character was employed again, appearing as Mario in *Super Mario Brothers*.

Miyamoto is credited for incorporating human and animal characters and stories with a strong influence of *manga* (comic art). Cartoons and animation films have a pervasive influence upon Japan's culture and society, far greater than those in the United States or Europe. At the turn of the millennium, Japan's comic book market was roughly 17 times the size of the US market today, and *manga* comprise over one-third of all books or magazines sold in Japan. The subjects covered by comic books range from romance to education, humor, sports, adventure, sex and violence, and include how-to *manga* (for example, cooking, finance), *manga*-fied classics, and socio-political satires. Comic books gave rise to both animated films and TV series in the 1960s and the 1970s, further reinforcing the strength of *manga* as an integral part of popular culture in Japan.

The core of the cartoon and animated film industry has always been located in Tokyo, largely due to the highly centralized publishing and broadcasting businesses, which are closely associated with central government functions in Japan. Also, Japan's most famous post-war cartoonist, the late Osamu Tezuka (1926–89), was based in Tokyo's Itabashi district. *Manga* owes its distinctive style to Tezuka (Bendazzi, 1994; *The Economist*, 1995). Influenced by Hollywood films at a young age, Tezuka revolutionized *manga* by incorporating the techniques used in films, such as close-ups, fadeouts, and varying camera angles. He has been influential in introducing new formats as well as content, developing *manga* from a previously dominant short strip humor to one involving long and complex stories. He also succeeded in weaving in serious issues, such as religion, race, war, and social justice without leaving the boundaries of entertainment. Throughout his more than 40-year career, Tezuka drew over 150,000 pages, with a record 250 million copies of sales by the mid-1980s. Tezuka was also the pioneer in producing an animation TV series in 1963, with his *manga* hit 'Astro Boy'. When Tezuka died in 1989, Japan's influential daily *Asahi Shimbun* carried an editorial that stated among many reasons for the popularity of *manga* in the country, the most important factor was that 'Japan had Osamu Tezuka'. With the quality of his works as well as his credentials as a medical doctor, Tezuka was the most influential person in raising the status of *manga* in Japan to the level of literary works.

In addition, the importance of *manga* in Japan's popular culture meant that cartoonists enjoyed a high social status; they are regarded as celebrities with recognition that at least equals popular novelists. Japan's comic artists typically possess the copyright of their own series, and therefore enjoy a greater control over their products than American serial comic book artists (Reinmoeller, 1999). Regarded as artist-entrepreneurs, the high social status associated with Japan's cartoonists is in part a reflection of their economic status. Almost every educational institution from elementary schools to universities has student-run cartoonist clubs as part of extra-curricular activities. Comic books gave rise to animation films and TV series, further reinforcing the strength of *manga* as an integral part of popular culture in Japan. Animation films and TV programs today account for a significant portion of Japan's market for films and broadcasting.

In the 1950s and 1960s, Tezuka acted as the center of a cluster, spawning a number of artists who later become Japan's notable cartoonists/animators. Tokiwa House, the apartment house where Tezuka lived in the early 1950s, became known as the mecca of *manga* and attracted Hiroshi Fujimoto and Motoo Abiko, known for the cartoon and animation character *Doraemon* and Shotaro Ishinomori, known for *Cyborg 009* and *Japan, Inc.*, among other artists. Tezuka also founded an animation film studio, Mushi

Production, in 1961, spinning off a number of studios, one of which is Sunrise Inc. (f. 1972) where Yoshiyuki Tomino created the TV animation film franchise *Mobile Suit Gundam*. Before the foundation of Mushi Production, Tezuka also had connections with another animation film studio Toei Animation which is known for being a springboard for Hayao Miyazaki, who later produced *Princess Mononoke*,[1] the second best-selling film in all of Japan's film industry. Thus, almost all professional cartoonists and many animation film directors today have been influenced by Tezuka in one form or another. As a result, the area that surrounds Tezuka's former studio Mushi Production, and the commuter train stations along Seibu lines in Tokyo's northeast became the hub of the cartoon/animation studios in Tokyo (Hanzawa, 2004, 2009).

The sharing of artistic talent between cartoon/animation films and video games in Japan has led to a number of common features that can be observed between the two forms of art. Many in the video game industry refer to their interest in cartoon/animation films as being the primary motivating factor for pursuing their current occupation. Skills transfer from *manga* to animation films was clearly one of the consequences. The core of game software production involves scenario writing and drawing, and cartoon and animation films provided the necessary skills and expertise for character production and graphic design. The higher incomes offered by the video game industry encouraged the migration of skilled designers and illustrators from the cartoon and animation industry. In the animation industry, the hierarchical structure with a series of small subcontractors tends to suppress wages, and project-based fees often reduce hourly wages. The video game industry employed workers at higher wages, and this even led to labor shortages in the animation industry.

Video games have since become far more complex and elaborate, however. Role-playing games, in which players can choose and assume a character and typically go on an adventure or a treasure hunt, enjoy broad popularity in Japan and often feature characters from *manga* and animation films. This also suggests that drawing techniques and character design are directly transferred from *manga* or animation film industries. Furthermore, the three media – video games, cartoons, and animation films – are increasingly linked to one another through joint marketing to boost their mutual sales. For example, several popular classics in animated films have been adapted for video games. These games include video clips from the originals and use the same voice actors to capture those grown-ups who used to watch the originals. Yet the best-known example of the integration of the three media is the success of Pokémon, which was first developed as a video game for Nintendo's Game Boy. Shortly after its largely unnoticed debut in 1996, the character began appearing in monthly *manga* magazines for children. This ignited its popularity, resulting in a TV animation program series in 1997, followed by a couple of blockbuster films. The Pokémon phenomenon was reinforced by the character's appearance in a variety of media, facilitating the growth of the market for video games.

Japan's video game industry is therefore linked to a historically embedded foundation of creative skills based on vibrant cartoons and animation films in various ways (Aoyama and Izushi, 2003). The presence of a competitive consumer electronics industry in Japan created a foundation for the necessary technical labor pool, and as it became socially accepted, the growing comic and animation industries served as a foundation for game creators and designers. These foundations, combined by the timely entry of platform developers such as Nintendo and Sony, played an important catalytic role in the emergence of the video game industry, and resulted in a vertically disintegrated industrial complex with hardware manufacturers as well as a plethora of small game software developers. The sharing of creative resources in Japan was in part possible due to the contemporaneous and overlapping development of *manga*, animation films, and the video game industries.

5.3.2   United States

It is well known that the video game industry had its origins in the United States (for example, Sheff, 1993; Kent, 2001; Kline et al., 2003). The industry emerged with close ties with the country's budding computer industry in the 1950s and 1960s, and drew creative talent from its computer hardware industry emerging from MIT and environs, and later, Silicon Valley. The first video game, *Space War*, was developed in the early 1960s at MIT's laboratory by Stephen Russell and others using DEC's then new interactive mainframe computer, PDP-1. DEC was a MIT spinoff, headed by Ken Olsen, a former engineer of MIT's Lincoln Laboratory. MIT generated spinoffs that served as foundations of the video game industry, such as the General Computer Corporation (f. 1981, hardware subcontractor which grew along with Atari) and software publisher Infocom (f. 1979) (later acquired by video game software firm Activision).

Nolan Bushnell, the founder of Atari (f. 1972), is known as the first entrepreneur who successfully commercialized video games. Bushnell played *Space War* at the University of Utah's computer laboratory, before moving to Silicon Valley and developing a simplified version of a computer game that did not require a fully fledged computer. Undoubtedly Atari benefited from the nation's top labor market in electronics hardware and software in Silicon Valley. According to Kent (2001), Atari recruited by simply advertising the new Video Computer Systems (VCS) division in local newspapers. The video game industry grew to a $200 million business in 1978 and to $1 billion in 1981, in which Atari accounted for half of the revenue.

Beginning in the mid-1970s, the growth potential of video games attracted a wide and rather incoherent array of entrants, ranging from new startups run by game developers to old established firms from traditional industries. The latter included those specializing in toys (Mattel, Parker Brothers), arcade games (Midway, Bally), home swimming pools (Coleco), films and broadcasting (Warner Communications, which acquired Atari), and electronics and semiconductors (Magnavox, National Semiconductor, Fairchild, General Instrument). The rush of startups in video and computer games around 1980 in Silicon Valley was a phenomenon akin to the dot.com boom of the late 1990s. However, the industry faced a quick downturn during 1982/83, known as the infamous 'video game crash', and the rapidly growing yet infant video game industry faced a sudden market collapse. Analysts blame the oversupply of game software, along with the dwindling quality, which turned away consumers and incurred significant losses to retailers and wholesalers. By 1984, Mattel and Coleco withdrew from the business, and Atari lost many of their top talents to spinoffs and competitors.

Throughout its prominence and demise, however, Atari played an important role as a seedbed for entrepreneurship in the video game industry. Spinoffs from Atari accelerated after Bushnell was replaced by Ray Kassar, formerly a textile industry executive sent in by Warner, who had little knowledge of technology, programming, games, or the West Coast culture. Atari spinoffs include the first independent (third-party) software publisher in game history, Activision (f. 1979), which in turn produced other spinoffs such as Accolade (f. 1984), Acclaim (f. 1987), and Absolute (f. circa 1987). Atari spinoffs also include Imagic (f. 1979), which was the second third-party publisher after Activision, Learning Company (f. circa 1981), Arcadia Corporation (f. 1981, and which subsequently changed its name to Starpath), as well as the hardware manufacturer, Amiga (f. 1982). In addition to spinoffs, Atari created a cadre of video game professionals in and around Silicon Valley. As Sheff (1993) noted, 'there were Atari alums in high-level spots at Electronic Arts, Lucasfilm and LucasArts, Apple, Microsoft, and a number of other companies' (p. 140).

Another firm that played a seedbed role for the US video game industry was Apple Computer. This was in part because of the personal ties between Steve Jobs and Atari (Steve was a former Atari employee), and in part due to the contemporaneous evolution between video games and personal computing in Silicon Valley. When multiple video game consoles competed for market share in the late 1970s, Apple was one of the potential platforms for digital media including video games. Electronic Arts (f. 1982), the top video game publisher in the United States today, was founded by Trip Hawkins, who was a Harvard graduate, a Stanford MBA, and also the 68th employee of Apple Computer. Electronic Arts (EA) subsequently produced a number of spinoffs and firms with personal ties with Hawkins, including Westwood (f. circa 1980), Dynamix (f. 1984) which was later purchased by Sierra On-Line (f. 1979, now part of Vivendi Universal), and Strategic Simulations, Inc. (SSI) (f. 1979).

Since its infancy in the US, the video game industry offered employment opportunities for artists and programmers who prefer to work outside their mainstream environment. Japan's software publishers today also showcase their work environment as being casual and informal, creativity oriented and divorced from the strict hierarchy of firms in traditional industries.

Thus, an examination of core talent in the early video game industry reveals that the industry evolved along with the personal computing industry, with its roots in the 'creative computing' tradition nurtured through the interface between computing and arcade games. There was a degree of cultural coherence between Atari and Apple, both of which attracted highly qualified engineers in Silicon Valley who, unlike the computer hardware-oriented industry, were not interested in associating themselves with either large firms or military contracts. The US video game industry therefore offered creative yet alternative opportunities for engineers and programmers, many of whom had been trained in close association with the country's defense interests under the cold-war regime. Bushnell was quoted as saying, 'we provided a place for creative people to be part of something completely new. These were people who wanted to create something intellectually stimulating and fun. They wanted to put their talent into making games, not bombs' (Sheff, 1993, p. 140; see also Sheff, and Eddy 1999). Active spinoffs from Atari and Apple therefore meant a geographical shift of the video game industry from Greater Boston to Silicon Valley along with the rest of the computer industry.

In the case of the US there is little evidence linking the transfer of creative skills from comic books and animation films to the video game industry. This may be due to the combined consequence of historical and geographical contexts. While comic books were an important part of national culture in the early twentieth century, the industry was largely overshadowed by TV cartoon programs by the time the video game industry emerged. Comic art originally evolved along with the newspaper industry and was centered in New York City, first in the form of editorial cartoons and later comic strips (Gordon, 1998). William Randolph Hearst, the publisher of the *New York Journal* and the *San Francisco Examiner*, used comic strips as a tool to attract advertisement revenue, once it became apparent that its regular use increased circulation. Subsequently, comic book publishers emerged in New York City in the 1930s. *Detective Comics*, published in 1937, was one of the first genre-based comic books and was filled with mysteries and detective stories. By 1943, 95 percent of American children were reading comic books (Pustz, 1999). However, the publication of Frederic Wertham's *Seduction of the Innocent* sparked controversies over comic books, and the subsequent creation of the Comics Code Authority in response to an examination by the Senate Subcommittee of Juvenile Delinquency led to widespread concern over the role of comic art as a societal vice. The number of comic book titles declined from 630 in 1952 to 250 in 1956, and circulation almost halved (ibid.), leading many publishers to leave the industry or be forced into bankruptcy. Most US comic book publishers today earn more profit from licensing characters than selling comic books (ibid.). Marvel, a New York-based comic book publisher since 1939, for example, has transformed itself as a 'character-based entertainment company', and has sold licenses to video game firms to use Marvel Comics characters. The US comic book market today is a mere 6 percent of the size of its Japanese counterpart.

The US animation film industry also preceded the video game industry decades earlier. Like comic books, New York City was the center of the animation film industry until the 1930s. The phenomenal success of Walt Disney caused a migration of talent to Burbank, California, leading to the relocation of the industry from the East Coast to the West Coast. Disney's move to California was serendipitous, motivated in part by a business failure in Kansas City, and also by the presence of a family member, his elder brother Roy, who became his lifelong business partner (Allan, 1999). Nonetheless, the origins of Disney's core talent were the synergetic outcomes between the comic art nurtured in the US East Coast and the animation film techniques that originated and centered in Europe until the First World War. Many of Disney's founding members, known as the 'Nine Old Men', studied in New York, Chicago, and Europe.

In spite of the powerful presence of comic books, animated films, and video games, the three sectors did not follow the same process of synergy in the United States as they did in Japan. While Japan's comic book publishing peaked as recently as in the mid-1990s, in the case of the US, the influence of comic books and animation films in popular culture peaked in the immediate post-war period and had already waned by the time video games emerged (Bendazzi, 1994; Wright, 2001). In contrast to the mainstream acceptance of comic books and animation films as forms of entertainment for children and adults alike in Japan, in the US and the UK, comic books had become locked in a 'ghetto location' in the cultural scene by the 1980s (King and Krzywinska, 2002, p. 21). This deprived the US and the UK of the development of a large reserve army of artistic talent that contributed to the growth of the video game industry in Japan.

As is clear, few historical links are found between comic books and animation films on the one hand and video games on the other. One documented piece of evidence of the interaction between the animation film and video game industries before the 'video game crash' is what is described as an 'unconventional move' by Don Bluth, a Disney inner-circle animator to Cinematronics, one of the oldest arcade firms, which resulted in the release of *Dragon's Lair* in 1983. Rather, more transfers of talent are observed between the video games and film industries. Film producer George Lucas collaborated with Atari to launch a game firm, LucasArts (f. 1982) in Marin County, just north of San Francisco. There are also numerous adoptions of film titles by video games in the US, including Atari's *Superman* (1979), *Raiders of the Lost Ark* (1982), and *E.T. the Extra-Terrestrial* (1982) for its console systems as well as Bally Midway's *Tron* (1982), Atari's *Star Wars* (1983) and *Indiana Jones and the Temple of Doom* (1985) in an arcade game format. Some even argue that an unsuccessful joint project between Atari and filmmaker Steven Spielberg amplified the Atari fiasco. Driven by deadlines and delivery times suited for film release but unrealistic for video game development, the video game version of *E.T. the Extra-Terrestrial* allegedly did not meet the expectations of consumers.

5.3.3   United Kingdom

Similar to the US case, the video game industry in the UK originated in computing. British mathematicians have been attributed as pioneers in conceptualizing computing and software. Among them was Alan Turing who wrote about the application of computers to games in 1953 in an article entitled 'Digital computers applied to games' (Turing, 1953). In the 1970s, UK books (for example, Bell, 1972) and computer magazine articles began featuring algorithms and 'how to' guides in building simple electronic versions of traditional card and board games (Wolf and Perron, 2003, pp. 2–3). However, this long tradition did not put the UK video game industry ahead of its US counterpart. The UK video game industry began with clones of Atari's *Pong* introduced in the UK market in 1975 and trailed behind their US and Japanese counterparts, having no prominent international firms until the 1990s. Unlike the US video game industry, few early UK game software developers had academic qualifications or any links to the then fledgling personal computer industry. Instead, the UK video game industry was founded on the accumulation of skills among 'bedroom coders' in the 1980s, which in turn led to its subsequent take-off in the early 1990s. The term 'bedroom coders' refers to a whole generation of self-trained programmers, mostly teenagers who were still in school, and who were programming and running businesses out of their bedrooms. Bedroom coders started to thrive in the early 1980s when games were still relatively simple and platforms were unsophisticated. The rise of bedroom coders was ignited by a new generation of cheap programmable home computers that became widely available, primarily led by Sinclair products (ZX80, ZX81, and ZX Spectrum) with fierce competition from Commodore VIC-20 and C64, as well as the Atari ST and Commodore's Amiga machines (Burnham, 2001, pp. 292–3). Although these computers were designed and marketed as general-purpose machines, they served as platforms to develop and play video games. Six to seven thousand titles were estimated to be produced for the Sinclair ZX Spectrum, and more than 10,000 titles for the Commodore 64 worldwide (Parkinson and Kitts, 2001, p. 370).

Most contemporary UK video game firms emerged out of this cadre of freethinking, independent programmers who subsequently helped the emergence of professional programmers. They range from current major video game developer firms such as Codemasters (f. 1986) and Rare (f. 1982 as Ultimate, acquired by Microsoft in 2002) to small studios such as Interactive Studio (f. 1991, although active since circa 1981, renamed Blitz Games in 1999), Optimus Software (f. 1988, active since circa 1981, renamed Atomic Planet in 2000), and Sensible Software (f. 1986, acquired by Codemasters in 1999).

Codemasters is in many ways a typical example of firms that grew out of the bedroom coder tradition. Brothers Richard and David Darling began as teenagers operating 'Galactic Software', a mail order business, from their bedrooms. They advertised their games in computer magazines, and also worked as contract programmers for Mastertronic (f. 1983), a specialist distributor of budget video games. In the first 15 months of the partnership with Mastertronic, nearly 750,000 copies of games written by the Darlings were sold, netting them £85,000, which they used as the initial capital to formally establish their own firm in 1986. In less than a year, Codemasters had a string of top 10 titles to its name. One of their early games, *BMX Simulator*, a motorbike racing game released in 1987, went on to become one of the world's best-selling games. Mastertronic, another major firm in the early foundation of the UK video game industry, however, is an anomaly as it was founded as a distributor and never employed in-house programmers, with the exception of debuggers and testers. Nonetheless, the firm played a pivotal role in coordinating small software houses and a large pool of bedroom coders and freelance authors, and distributed games developed by early game developers such as Codemasters and Mr. Chip Software.

Bedroom coders were loosely connected by networks of various channels. Video game enthusiasts developed informal social networks through chance encounters at local software stores, exchanging information on how to win games and sharing programming codes. Computer magazines, such as *C&VG* (f. 1981), *Sinclair User* (f. 1982), *Your Spectrum* (f. 1983), *Computer Gamer* (f. 1984), and *Input* (f. 1984), also facilitated bedroom coders to develop contacts, advertise games, and exchange machine codes. Trade shows and conventions provided another venue of information exchange between amateur programmers and professional developers. Codemasters's first encounter with brothers Philip and Andrew Oliver, both hobby programmers, was at the European Computer Trade Show. The Oliver brothers subsequently became regulars at Codemasters and wrote games for them before founding Interactive Studio in 1991. Another duo, brothers Darren and Jason Falcus, also started out as contract programmers for Codemasters before establishing Optimus Software. The cohort of bedroom coders nurtured in the 1980s became the springboard of the industry's rapid growth in the 1990s, writing games for Japanese consoles such as Famicom and PlayStation.

Bedroom coders gradually disappeared from the scene along with the advancement of hardware and software technologies in the 1990s. The entry of Nintendo and Sega consoles into the UK market, both in 1987, and an increasing US interest in the UK market, meant that bedroom coders faced competition from the increasingly large-scale and formal operations of Japanese and US firms. The introduction of Sony's PlayStation in 1995, along with Sony's purchase of the highly respected UK game developer and publisher Psygnosis (now Sony Interactive) had a decisive impact. The first batch of PlayStation games boasted high-quality titles such as *Destruction Derby* and *WipeOut* (Hayes and Dinsey, 1995, p. 137). With its advanced technology and the need to purchase expensive development tools, video game software development increasingly required capital and a team of developers, and therefore could no longer be coded by lone pro-grammers. The skills accumulation of self-trained teenage programmers was replaced by the foundation of courses on video game design and programming by higher/further education institutions as well as the entry of graduates into the industry from relevant academic subjects such as computer science and mathematics. Along with the gradual decline of the influence of bedroom coders, the UK video game industry has increasingly been concentrated in the country's core regions. Of those 30 game developers, publishers and distributors that are members of the Entertainment and Leisure Software Publishers Association (the UK's leading video games trading body) today, 26 firms (86.7 percent) are located in London and South East England.

The growth of the UK video game market in the early 1990s also coincided with its increasing integration into that of the US market. Lucrative US markets attracted UK firms, while the US firms were drawn by the programming skills of the UK firms sup-ported by a pool of thousands of bedroom coders and code-breakers. Acclaim (US), for example, entered the UK market through a merger with Optimus Software founded by the Falcus brothers. Optimus in turn partnered with Iguana Entertainment (US) in 1993 to gain a foothold in the US market, which led to the development of *NBA JAM*, and subsequently merged with Iguana UK. The sale of Iguana USA to New York-based Acclaim Entertainment in 1995 resulted in Iguana UK becoming one of Acclaim's internal development team. Subsequently, the Falcus brothers left to establish another startup, now called Atomic Planet Entertainment (f. 2000).

Similar to the US case, little evidence connects the comics and animated film industries to the emergence of the video game industry in the UK. A lack of contemporaneous evo-lution of the comic book industry deprived it of the ability to influence game developers, whereas the elite status of animators deterred their collaboration with the video game industry in its infancy. In the UK, the first comic boom began in 1890 with the publica-tion of *Comic Cuts* by Alfred Harmsworth, setting the style of comic drawing by the turn of the twentieth century. Comics had been established as quality entertainment aimed at children by 1930, followed by the publication of three formula-breaking comic maga-zines, *Dandy* (f. 1937), *Beano* (f. 1938), and *Magic* (f. 1939). The post-Second World War boom came with publication of the magazine *Eagle* (f. 1950) and British original comic books such as *Marvelman* (f. 1954). Subsequently, however, the UK comic industry experienced a gradual decline with circulations shrinking from the quarter- and half-million mark in the booming 1950s (Gifford, 1985). Furthermore, with their readership largely confined to children up to 14 years of age, comics have never achieved in the British cultural scene a mainstream status enjoyed by their counterparts in Japan and the United States.

While comic art has never been fully accepted as an art form, the UK animated film industry has been highly acclaimed. Its international recognition as an art form, however, contributed to isolating its talent from the then obscure, subculture-status video game industry during the video game industry's infancy. The UK animated film industry dates back to 1900 with the founding of the production firm Vitagraph by an Englishman, Stuart Blackton, in the United States. Studying the techniques used in Blackton's short film *Humorous Phases of Funny Faces* (1906), Walter Booth made the first British animated film, *The Hand of the Artist* (1906), which was followed by the first British full-length feature work, *The Story of the Flag* (1927), and the first British color animated film, *Old Sam* (1936), both of which were produced by Anson Dyer (Gifford, 1987). With creators such as John Halas and Joy Batchelor (*Animal Farm*, 1954) and George Dunning (*The Yellow Submarine*, 1968), the UK became the centre of animation in Europe by the 1960s. Its work received acclaim from critics and industry insiders including a number of Academy Awards (for example, Bob Godrey's *Great* in 1976, Nick Park's *Creature Comforts* in 1991 and *The Wrong Trousers* in 1994, and Daniel Grieaves's *Manipulation* in 1992). However, the industry tends to cater to the educated public of film festivals and elite TV stations (Bendazzi, 1994, p. 275) with a weakness in the production of long-form television series for family and children's viewing. The elite status of animators in the UK cultural scene and the lack of socio-cultural cohesiveness between them and bedroom coders further hampered their active involvement in the video game industry in its early phase. For instance, in spite of the accumulation of skills in computer animation at Halas & Batchelor (f. 1940), as evidenced by such titles as *What is a Computer* (1969), *Contact* (1974), *Autobahn* (1979), and *Dilemma* (1981) (ibid., p. 154), no evidence points to the transfer of skills from animation to video games. Only since the early 1990s have we observed some animation studios undertaking contract work for video game developers (PACT, 2002), once the video game industry established socioeconomic legitimacy in the country. This also coincides with the stagnant period of the UK animated film industry that faced increasing competition from firms in North America, Japan, France, and Spain.

5.4   SYNCHRONIZING TECHNOLOGICAL EVOLUTION WITH INDUSTRY EVOLUTION

As the preceding section showed, the cumulative nature of industry evolution often reinforces distinctiveness in industry formation and evolution. While compatibility between skills and product development changes over the course of industry evolution, we contend that technological progress shapes which existing industries contribute creative skills to emerging industries, and in turn influences the competitive positions of the emerging industry. Dominant skills in an industrial sector and the phases of technological progress intervene with industrial evolution in a complex manner. In the early days of the industry, Atari established the four key elements that made the video game of today a unique medium – an algorithm; player activity; interface; and graphics (Wolf and Perron, 2003, p. 14) – and also developed home video game consoles. Video games were transformed into a viable commercial venture, as the venue of game playing shifted from university labs to bars and arcades, and eventually, to the home. Concurrently, the objective of game development shifted first from satisfying a group of technology-savvy hobbyists to the general public, and second to console-based home system users who, unlike with arcade games that were designed to last for no longer than a few minutes, expected to entertain themselves longer to justify the cost of their purchase (Atari 2600 video game console was about US$200 and a game cartridge $25). The longer durations expected for home-based console games made storylines ever more important (Robinett, 2003), which in turn led to the use of character-based player-surrogates. From the typical early games, which were relatively simple with players controlling either tools (for example, paddles) or vehicles (for example, spaceships, planes, cars, tanks), developers began designing identifiable player surrogates such as human figures and animals (Wolf, 2003, pp. 50–52). Atari's *Adventure* (1979) for the 2600 console, for example, created a new genre of action-adventure games, notable for their much longer playing time (Robinett, 2003).

These shifts in markets and objectives in game playing altered the demand for creative talent. Game development in the early stages was done by a programmer taking on the entire task, from writing a storyline, to designing characters, as well as programming (ibid.). However, the US video game industry with its origins in computer programming was not well positioned to develop artistic skills capable of creating elaborate stories and characters. Developers sought to compensate for this weakness by licensing characters from films without much success, as evidenced by failures such as Atari's *Raiders of the Lost Ark* (1982) and *E.T. The Extra-Terrestrial* (1982). Moreover, the limited capacity of microprocessors and storage media at that time permitted only rudimentary characters drawn in a small number of pixels, often differentiated only by color, failing to replicate the characters from which they were licensed. Such a failure of the synergy between video games and licensed characters contributed to the quick maturing and saturation of consumer interests, and the subsequent US market crash.

Following the Atari fiasco in 1983, Nintendo achieved almost a monopoly in Japan, and played a major role in reviving the US home video game market as well as laying the foundation for the UK market's revival in the early 1990s. A number of software developers emerged as their licensees, first in Japan (for example, Namco, Capcom, Square), and then elsewhere (for example, Electronic Arts and Acclaim in the US, and Virgin Interactive and Ocean in the UK). The emergence of the Japanese video game industry can in part be explained by their effectiveness in developing storylines and characters via sourcing artistic talent from the comics and animated films industries. It is no accident that the first cartoon-like characters with names and identities of their own were designed in Japan, that is, *Pac-Man* (1980) and *Donkey Kong* (1981). As we have seen, the first division of labor between game designers and programmers also took place in Japan, with the best known being the role of Shigeru Miyamoto, the pioneer game designer of Nintendo, whose assignment was confined to developing storylines and characters (Sheff, 1993). Here technological limitations worked to their advantage; characters from comic books and animation films proved to be far more suitable to video games than their more realistic counterparts from films (Wolf, 2003, p. 52). Early cases of licensed characters in Japan include Taito's arcade game *Lupin III* (1980), which was based on the popular Japanese comics and animated film series (Burnham, 2001, p. 340).

The introduction of CD-ROM in computer games and console systems in the early 1990s once again changed the industry dynamics. Although a laser disc-based high-volume storage medium had existed since the early 1980s, the technology did not mature until the introduction of the CD-ROM in 1992. This medium allowed exponential growth in storage capacity, which in turn led to the incorporation of more detailed graphics and full-motion video clips (Burnham, 2001, p. 360; Wolf and Perron, 2003, pp. 6, 22). North American specialist graphic chip manufacturers, *n*VIDIA (f. 1993) and ATI Technologies (f. 1985), emerged in the video game industry, and a breakthrough in software technology, the 3D engine, appeared in the early 1990s. The early games using a 3D game engine – *Howertank One* and *Catacombs 3D* (both id Software, 1991) and *Wolfenstein 3D* (id Software, 1992) – were quickly followed by a series of 3D blockbuster games such as *Doom* (id Software, 1993), *Quake* (id Software, 1997), and *Tomb Raider* (Eidos, 1996), all of which were developed in the US or the UK (Lahti, 2003, pp. 160–61). These games were characterized by a more realistic graphic representation and simulation of the physical world. Furthermore, a realistic graphic representation became an important marketing tool, as both consumers and developers began judging the quality of games on it. Game developers in particular began judging programmers' achievement and status based on graphic details and game complexity (Wolf, 2003). The surging costs of development meant a greater dependence on licensed characters from films and other entertainment sectors as a means to control these costs and increase their chances of becoming top-selling games.

The technological progress that allowed detailed graphic representation also prompted the US and UK video game industries to begin exploiting creative talent more aggressively from their film industries. This trend is most evident in the US video game industry, where substantial technological expertise in special effects already existed within the film industry. Video games began borrowing from films certain forms of plotting or point-of-view structures, and films in return increasingly adopted game software tools to create special effects (Bolter and Grusin, 1999; King and Krzywinska, 2002). For example, video games include 'cut-scenes' or pre-rendered video clips, which are often used to establish the initial setting and background storyline, while some Hollywood studios began diversifying into the video game market through the licensing and sharing of storylines and characters such as the Bond franchise (King and Krzywinska, 2002). Sports games are also being developed in collaboration with professional teams, as evidenced by *FIFA* (Electronic Arts) and *Championship Manager* (Eidos) which simulate the management of professional football leagues.

The strengths of the Japanese video game industry became gradually undermined as new technologies removed some of the earlier constraints. Instead, large US and UK publishers (such as Electronic Arts, Acclaim, and Eidos) consistently began producing best-selling games that emphasize realistic graphics. The current trend suggests that the industry's center of gravity is moving back to the US with the UK also gaining some prominence, exclusively in software, which has emerged as an increasingly important source of revenues for the industry. These new video games combine technologies developed in North America with major entertainments in the countries.

Finally, once an industry matures, it poses new challenges for the firms to maintain and reward creativity in order to ensure further expansion. In such a context, user innovation is considered highly promising as it mirrors user preferences, and therefore minimizes the cost of capturing demand and reduces product development risks. Some even argue that user-led innovation helps avoid lock-ins and 'inside-the-box' thinking, with an assumption that firms and users have distinctive product ideas. Industries and products that have a following, such as a group of hobbyists previously organized or disorganized, are the most likely sources of active user-led innovation today. However, user-led innovation also involves the danger of crowd-led lock-in processes, particularly when an industry matures in which users as well as producers become entrenched with existing products. The case of Nintendo's Wii stands out as an anomaly among major console manufacturers/publishers in that it avoided hardcore gamers in an attempt to create new or expand existing markets. Instead of following industry trends toward faster, more realistic graphics, Nintendo focused on innovation in other features including a user-friendly man–machine interface. Nintendo's Wii development team deliberately avoided involvement of user communities, thereby preventing users and gaming communities from influencing their corporate strategy. As a result, Nintendo's Wii and DS widened the industry's then stagnant market base to non-gamers and casual gamers, rejecting 'the conventional wisdom that video games are the domain of testosterone-driven gadget freaks who zone out for hours while conquering computer-generated foes' (*International Herald Tribune*, 2007).[2] Nintendo was fully aware of the danger that staying close with communities of enthusiastic users might have locked the firm in to the trajectory that had already dominated the industry. The concept of Wii would have been unimaginable if Nintendo had chosen to involve hardcore gamers in its product development.

Just as in any innovation, user-led innovation emerges not only from a technology-specific environment, but also from a culturally specific context of industries. On the one hand, the internet has allowed the development of online user groups that connect communities around the world. On the other, users and markets are still bounded by language and culture, and while activities that transgress these boundaries are on the rise (for example, 'Fan Subs'), the origins of cultural products are still strongly demarcated. Whereas hardcore gamers are uniformly more influential than casual gamers in every market and therefore also constitute a stronger voice, those in Japan have been particularly significant in size and scope. They are closely linked to producers, with a blurring of boundaries between the professionals and amateurs; they are nurtured and maintained via alumni networks of vocational schools and colleges; and they have much stronger legitimacy as a well-acknowledged and dominant segment of subculture in Japan. The particularly powerful voice of the hardcore gamers in Japan may have prompted Nintendo to push further toward a radical new path.

5.5   CONCLUSION

What emerges from this research on the origins and the evolution of the video game industry is a hypothesis on the interplay of economic, social, and technological factors that influence the process of cross-sectoral skill transfer. The skill formation is embedded in specific social contexts and shapes the trajectory of industry evolution in a manner unique to each country. Japan's video game industry evolved through corporate sponsorships in arcade games, toys, and consumer electronics industries, and drew skills from the comic book and animation film sectors, both of which were contemporary growth industries and which were accepted as mainstream entertainments. In contrast, in the United States, the video game industry has its origin in computer games at university laboratories and evolved to arcade games with links to the then fledgling, entrepreneurial personal computer industry. The industry developed with few links to the comic book or animation films industries, sectors that had reached their peak decades earlier. Similarly, the video game industry in the UK had few links to comics and animated films, in part due to the lack of any concurrent evolution and in part due to the elitist culture of the animation industry. The informal nature of 'bedroom coders' with few links to risk capital may have played a role in delaying the take-off of the UK video game industry.

Therefore, the creation of industry-specific skills out of the cross-sectoral fusion of creative talent in the formation of a new industry is a combination of market conditions, social legitimacy, cultural cohesiveness, and the state of technologies. While economic incentives such as high wages and growth prospects undoubtedly play a role, they do not always lead to a cross-sectoral fusion of skills. Not only does the evolution of existing industries affect how and from where the emerging industry draws its skills, but also socioeconomic status attached to pioneering entrepreneurs/firms in an emerging industry in turn influences its capacity to draw skills from other sectors. The socio-cultural cohesiveness between old and new industries further lowers the sectoral barriers for skill transfers.

Furthermore, the state of technologies can also influence the cross-sectoral compatibility of skills. The ascendance of the Japanese video game industry in the late 1980s coincided with the relatively limited power of microprocessors and the small capacity of storage media at the time, and overcame the limitations by mobilizing creative talent in comic books and animated films. Technological change gradually eroded their advantages, however, as the technological expertise of the US and UK video game industries in manipulating more powerful microprocessors and larger-capacity storage media helped them regain their competitive strengths, combined with the creative talent from a contents industry that is more cohesive to it.

Finally, an industry life-cycle approach may offer insights into the effectiveness of user involvement. In the case of the Japanese video game industry, user involvement played a positive role in the initial stages of the industry evolution, whereas it may actually work to lead an industry into a lock-in once the market is no longer at the initial development stage. The case of Nintendo's Wii console offers a cautionary tale for placing a blind faith in the positive aspects of user and user–community involvement. User involvement is a double-edged sword that firms must scrutinize before adopting the voice of existing users, even in an industry such as the video game industry, as it can contribute to a lock-in process.

NOTES

1. A popular animation film, *Princess Mononoke* (1997) earned ¥11.3 billion, and in Japan is second only to James Cameron's *Titanic* which earned ¥16 billion in Japan (Dentsu Soken, 2001).
2. The expansion of the market to non-gamers and casual gamers had a significant impact in Japan. The Japanese market for home video games, which had continued to decline since 1997, reversed the trend in 2005 thanks to the release of the DS, and recorded an all-time high of shipments for two years in a row in 2006 and 2007 due to the continued success of the DS and the release of the Wii (*Mainichi jp.* 2007).

REFERENCES

Abernathy, W. and J. Utterback (1978), 'Patterns of industrial innovation', *Technology Review*, **80** (June/July), 41–7.
Aida, Y. and A. Ohgaki (1997), *Shin Denshi Rikkoku*, Tokyo: Nihon Hoso Shuppan Kyokai.
Allan, R. (1999), *Walt Disney and Europe*, Bloomington, IN: Indiana University Press.
Amin, A. (1999), 'An institutional perspective on regional economic development', *International Journal of Urban and Regional Research*, **23** (2), 365–78.
Aoyama, Y. and H. Izushi (2003), 'Hardware gimmick or cultural innovation? Technological, cultural, and social foundations of the Japanese video game industry', *Research Policy*, **32** (3), 423–44.

Archibugi, D. and M. Pianta (1992), *The Technological Specialization of Advanced Countries*, Dordrecht: Kluwer.

Arthur, M., R. Defillippi and V. Lindsay (2001), 'Careers, communities, and industry evolution: links to complexity theory', *International Journal of Innovation Management*, **5** (2), 239–55.

Bathelt, H. and J. Boggs (2003), 'Toward a reconceptualization of regional development paths: is Leipzig's media cluster a continuation of or a rupture with the past?', *Economic Geography*, **79** (3), 265–93.

Bell, A. (1972), *Games Playing with Computers*, London: Allen & Unwin.

Bendazzi, G. (1994), *Cartoons: One Hundred Years of Cinema Animation*, London: John Libbey.

Bolter, J. and R. Grusin (1999), *Remediation: Understanding New Media*, Cambridge, MA: MIT Press.

Burnham, V. (2001), *Supercade*, Cambridge, MA: MIT Press.

Christopherson, S. and M. Storper (1989), 'The effects of flexible specialization on industrial politics and the labor market: the motion picture industry', *Industrial and Labor Relations Review*, **42** (3), 331–47.

Coase, R. (1937), 'The nature of the firm', *Economica*, **4**, 386–405.

Coe, N. (2000), 'On location: American capital and the local labour market in the Vancouver film industry', *International Journal of Urban and Regional Research*, **24** (1), 79–95.

Dentsu Soken (2001), *Joho Media Hakusho 2001*, Tokyo: Dentsu.

Dosi, G., K. Pavitt and L. Soete (1990), *The Economics of Technical Change and International Trade*, Hemel Hempstead: Harvester Wheatsheaf.

Economist, The (1995), 'Eclectic: Japanese manga', 16 December, 116–18.

Gertler, M. (1995), '"Being there": proximity, organization, and culture in the development and adoption of advanced manufacturing technologies', *Economic Geography*, **71** (1), 1–26.

Gertler, M. (2004), *Manufacturing Culture*, New York: Oxford University Press.

Gifford, D. (1985), *The Complete Catalogue of British Comics*, Exeter: Webb & Bower.

Gifford, D. (1987), *British Animated Films, 1895–1985*, Jefferson, NC: McFarland & Company.

Gordon, I. (1998), *Comic Strips and Consumer Culture, 1890–1945*, Washington, DC: Smithsonian Institution Press.

Granovetter, M. (1985), 'Economic action and social structure: the problem of embeddedness', *American Journal of Sociology*, **91**, 480–510.

Hall, P. and D. Soskice (2001), *Varieties of Capitalism*, Oxford: Oxford University Press.

Hanzawa, S. (2004), 'The Japanese animation and home video game industries: locational patterns, labor markets, and inter-firm relationships', *Japanese Journal of Human Geography*, **56**, 29–44.

Hanzawa, S. (2009), 'Location of the games industry restructuring and the animation industry', in H. Matsubara (ed.), *Industrial Location Adjustments in Economic Geography*, Tokyo: Hara Shobo, pp. 229–43.

Hayes, M. and S. Dinsey (1995), *Games War*, London: Bowerdean.

Henderson, R.M. and K.B. Clark (1990), 'Architectural innovation: the reconfiguration of existing product technologies and the failure of established firms', *Administrative Science Quarterly*, **35** (1), 9–30.

International Herald Tribune (2007), 'Surprising experts, game players go for the Wii workout', 1 February.

Jones, C. (2001), 'Co-evolution of entrepreneurial careers, institutional rules and competitive dynamics in American film, 1895–1920', *Organization Studies*, **22** (6), 911–44.

Kent, S. (2001), *The Ultimate History of Video Games*, Roseville, CA: Prima Lifestyles.

King, G. and T. Krzywinska (2002), 'Introduction: cinema/videogames/interfaces', in G. King and T. Krzywinska (eds), *Screenplay*, London: Wallflower Press, pp. 1–32.

Klepper, S. (1996), 'Entry, exit, growth, and innovation over the product cycle', *American Economic Review*, **86** (3), 562–83.

Kline, S., N. Dyer-Witheford and G. de Peuter (2003), *Digital Play*, Montreal: McGill-Queen's University Press.

Lahti, M. (2003), 'As we become machines: corporealized pleasures in video games', in M. Wolf and B. Perron (eds), *The Video Game Theory Reader*, New York: Routledge, pp. 157–70.

Lundvall, B.-Å., B. Johnson, E. Andersen and B. Dalum (2002), 'National systems of production, innovation and competence building', *Research Policy*, **31** (2), 213–31.

Mainichijp (2007), 'Hohmu bideo geimuki: nobi ga tomaranu, geimu shijou hanbaigaku 2nen renzoku saikou', 29 December, available at: http://mainichi.jp/select/biz/news/20071229ddm008020029000c.html (accessed June 1, 2010).

Malerba, F. (2002), 'Sectoral systems of innovation and production', *Research Policy*, **31** (2), 247–64.

Malerba, F. and L. Orsenigo (1996), 'The dynamics and evolution of industries', *Industrial and Corporate Change*, **5** (1), 51–87.

McGahan, A. (2000), 'How industries evolve', *Business Strategy Review*, **11** (3), 1–16.

McKelvey, M. (1997), 'Using evolutionary theory to define systems of innovation', in C. Edquist (ed.), *Systems of Innovation*, London: Pinter, pp. 200–222.

Metcalfe, S. (1998), *Evolutionary Economics and Creative Destruction*, London: Routledge.

Nelson, R. (1995), 'Recent evolutionary theorizing about economic change', *Journal of Economic Literature*, **33** (1), 48–90.

Nelson, R. and S. Winter (1982), *An Evolutionary Theory of Economic Change*, Cambridge, MA: Belknap.

Olson, M.J. (1965), *The Logic of Collective Action: Public Goods and the Theory of Groups*, Cambridge, MA: Harvard University Press.

Osborn, R. and J. Hagerdoorn (1997), 'The institutionalization and evolutionary dynamics of interorganisational alliances and networks', *Academy of Management Journal*, **40** (2), 261–78.

Parkinson, E. and M. Kitts (2001), *The Essential Guide to Videogames*, London: Carlton Books.

Piore, M.J. and C.F. Sabel (1984), *The Second Industrial Divide: Possibilities for Prosperity*, New York: Basic Books.

Power, D. (2002), '"Cultural industries" in Sweden: an assessment of their place in the Swedish economy', *Economic Geography*, **78** (2), 103–28.

Power, D. and A. Scott (2004), *Cultural Industries and the Production of Culture*, London: Routledge.

Pratt, A. (1997a), 'Guest editorial – Production values: from cultural industries to the governance of culture', *Environment and Planning A*, **29** (11), 1911–17.

Pratt, A. (1997b), 'The cultural industries production system: a case study of employment change in Britain 1984–91', *Environment and Planning A*, **29** (11), 1953–74.

Preston, P. and A. Kerr (2001), 'Digital media, nation-states and local cultures: the case of multimedia "content" production', *Media, Culture & Society*, **23** (1), 109–31.

Producers' Alliance for Cinema and Television (PACT) (2002), 'Mouse or superhero: the UK animation production sector', available at: http://www.pact.co.uk/uploads/file_bank/ 364.pdf (accessed June 1, 2010).

Pustz, M. (1999), *Comic Book Culture*, Jackson, MS: University Press of Mississippi.

Reinmoeller, P. (1999), 'Nihon no kontentsu no kokusaika', in M. Shimaguchi, H. Takeuchi, H. Katahira and J. Ishii (eds), *Seihin kaihatsu kakushin*, Tokyo: Yuhikaku, pp. 388–414.

Robinett, W. (2003), 'Foreword', in M. Wolf and B. Perron (eds), *The Video Game Theory Reader*, New York: Routledge, pp. vii–xix.

Saxenian, A. (1994), *Regional Advantage*, Cambridge, MA: Harvard University Press.

Scott, A. (1995), 'From Silicon Valley to Hollywood: growth and development of the multimedia industry in California', Working Paper 13, Lewis Center for Regional Policy Studies, University of California, Los Angeles.

Scott, A. (1996), 'The craft, fashion, and cultural-products industries of Los Angeles: competitive dynamics and policy dilemmas in a multisectoral image-producing complex', *Annals of the Association of American Geographers*, **86** (2), 306–23.

Scott, A. (1997), 'The cultural economy of cities', *International Journal of Urban and Regional Research*, **21** (2), 323–39.

Sheff, D. (1993), *Game Over*, New York: Random House.

Sheff, D. and A. Eddy (1999), *Game Over: Press Start to Continue*, New York: Vintage Books.

Storper, M. and S. Christopherson (1987), 'Flexible specialization and regional industrial agglomerations: the case of the U.S. motion picture industry', *Annals of the Association of American Geographers*, **77** (1), 104–17.

Storper, M. and R. Salais (1996), *Worlds of Production*, Cambridge, MA: Harvard University Press.

Stuart, T.E. and J.M. Podolny (1996), 'Local search and the evolution of technological capabilities', *Strategic Management Journal*, **17** (Summer Special Issue), 21–38.

Teece, D. (1988), 'Technological change and the nature of the firm', in G. Dosi, C. Freeman, R. Nelson, G. Silverberg and L. Soete (eds), *Technical Change and Economic Theory*, London: Pinter, pp. 256–81.

Turing, A. (1953), 'Digital computers applied to games', in B. Bowden (ed.), *Faster Than Thought*, London: Pitman, pp. 286–310.

Tushman, M.L. and P. Anderson (1986), 'Technological discontinuities and organizational environments', *Administrative Science Quarterly*, **31** (3), 439–65.

Utterback, J. (1994), *Mastering the Dynamics of Innovation*, Boston, MA: Harvard Business School Press.

Utterback, J. and W. Abernathy (1975), 'A dynamic model of process and product innovation', *Omega*, **3** (6), 639–56.

Wenger, E. (1998), *Communities of Practice*, Cambridge: Cambridge University Press.

Williamson, O.E. (1975), *Markets and Hierarchies: Analysis and Antitrust Implications*, New York: Free Press.

Wolf, M. (2003), 'Abstraction in the video game', in Wolf and Perron (eds), pp. 47–65.

Wolf, M. and B. Perron (eds) (2003), *The Video Game Theory Reader*, New York: Routledge.

Wright, B. (2001), *Comic Book Nation*, Baltimore, MD: Johns Hopkins University Press.

6 Spatial divisions of labor: how key worker profiles vary for the same industry in different regions

*Ann Markusen and Anne Gadwa Nicodemus**

6.1 INTRODUCTION

Since the 1950s, regional scientists have been interested in the industrial structure of regional economies and the location decision making of firms and their establishments grouped as industries. In North America and elsewhere, as responsibility for economic development has been devolved onto state/provincial and local governments, researchers and policy makers have developed analytical and decision-making tools to identify key industries and nurture, attract, and retain firms within them. In this chapter, we challenge the narrowness of this industrial focus by exploring the semi-autonomous role of regional labor force formation in regional economic development.

First, we review how the spatial division of labor theories, which have been around for several decades, suggest that the occupational structure of an industry in core regions, where management and innovation reside, may differ substantially from the occupational structure of the same industry in other regions. We challenge the notion that only industry managers make important decisions about the location of productive activity, positing that workers also choose where to live and work in a calculus where the firm or industry presence and job offers form only one of several decision criteria. Our basic contention is that an adequate understanding of the spatial differentiation of industries and their activities requires occupational as well as industrial intelligence.

Using occupations as a counterpart to industries, we investigate the extent to which industries in metropolitan regions share similar occupational profiles. We report the results of two exercises on the occupational variation of industry employment across regions, one using employer-based data sources for all industries and occupations among a limited set of California metropolitan areas (metros), and one using worker-based data sources for the cultural industries and the occupation of artists for a subset of large US metros. While industries with routinized production processes often do possess occupational structures at the metro level similar to those at state and national levels, this is not the case for the more innovative industries such as high-tech, business services, and the information and creative sectors.

To explore the location calculus of workers as important agents in regional economy building, we test several propositions about the interrelationship between artists as a key occupational group and cultural industries across our metro set. We suggest that in occupations with high rates of self-employment, such as artists, factors other than employers' job offers or a cultural industry presence may shape workers' location choices among metros.

Our findings have important implications for industry researchers and economic development policy. Regions aspiring to sectoral specializations must also understand the extent to which activities in their region fit into a larger regional and global division of labor. Analyses of occupational structures of existing and target industries can inform public investment choices. If the formation of distinctive economic sectors consists of semi-autonomous decision making by workers and managers, an effective economic development strategy must take into account the location calculus of both sets of agents.

6.2   THEORIES OF INDUSTRIAL AND LABOR FORCE FORMATION AT THE REGIONAL LEVEL

No one ever 'sees' a regional economy. Instead, we have mental maps based on conceptual categories that implicitly treat certain decision makers as key to economic development (Markusen and Schrock, 2008b). The two most common typologies used to depict regional economies group jobs by industry and by occupation (Harrington, 1999). However, the industrial conception of a regional economy is older and much more heavily used, a genealogy we have explored elsewhere (Barbour and Markusen, 2007).

The seminal case for using occupations in addition to industries in regional analysis was made by Thompson and Thompson (1985, 1987). They argued that important insights could be had by looking at what workers do (occupations, defined by skills) rather than simply what they make (industries, defined by product output). Few scholars picked up on the idea until the late 1990s, when several efforts made unique contributions independently. Florida (2002) argued that skilled workers are attracted to certain urban amenities and that their presence, in turn, drives high-tech location. Feser (2003) argued that input–output relationships were not the only or most productive way to group related industries into clusters, and used a skills-based dataset to do so. In a subsequent paper (Renski et al., 2007), he and his colleagues showed that grouping industries by labor content rather than value chains produced very different configurations. Markusen (2004) articulated a series of causal hypotheses about why and how occupational structures are increasingly diverging across and within industries. In subsequent work, Markusen and Schrock (2006) showed that certain occupational groups are highly skewed across US metropolitan regions and that such skewness has increased over two decades. Koo (2005) applied occupational analysis to regional economic structure, while Beyers (2007) explored an occupational approach to clustering producer services activities.

Very little work, however, has been devoted to understanding the intersection between industry and occupational approaches, either theoretically, as a way of understanding location decision making, or empirically, by understanding how the two taxonomies vary in their sorting of regional economic activity. In this chapter, we attempt both.

6.3   DOES THE OCCUPATIONAL STRUCTURE OF AN INDUSTRY VARY ACROSS REGIONS?

If occupational structures of industries are invariant across regions, then researchers and policy makers need not conduct independent analyses by occupation to plan for firm expansions or relocations or to forecast future labor demand, though occupational intelligence would still be useful in understanding firm location preferences. There are good theoretical arguments that occupational composition will vary spatially, which are best articulated in the well-developed analyses of the interregional division of labor and commodity chains (Frobel et al., 1979; Massey, 1984; Markusen, 1985; Gereffi and Korzeniewicz, 1994; Saxenian, 1994). For many mature industries (steel, textiles, chemicals) at certain spatial scales (for example, within the US), industries' structures of employment by occupation do not differ much across regions. But our research finds important variations in key industries.

In a study of 11 California metros in the 1990s, we found that occupational structures in information technology (IT) industries and business services varied markedly among the metros and from the national norm (Barbour and Markusen, 2007). In this exercise, we estimated what the 1997 occupational employment by industry by metro would have been if industries' occupational structure mirrored that at the national level. We used the Industry-Occupation Matrix data from the State of California's Economic Development Department, which is available at the county level aggregated up to the metro level, and the Bureau of Labor Statistics (BLS) National Historical Industry-Occupation Matrix Time Series (NTS), 1983–1998, for 93 occupations and 181 industry categories. Overall, we found that using national occupation by industry averages closely predicted overall occupational employment, with only 5 percent of employment, or about 585,000 jobs, across the 11 metro set not accurately projected.

But for industries of great interest to economic developers, the high-tech and innovative sectors, this method was a poor predictor of occupational structure. In the IT and business services (the latter including computer and data processing), the employment levels for many occupations were severely underestimated (Table 6.1). In the IT sectors, more than one-third of natural scientists were underpredicted in the San Francisco and Oakland metros, and more than one-third of engineers were missed in San Jose.[1] The ranks of service and precision workers were overestimated in this industry in the Bay Area region, often by quite large increments. In business services, engineering and computing workers were also underestimated by a third or more, while service workers were overestimated. In San Jose, the actual totals of clerical and sales workers in business services were seriously overestimated, while precision workers – people doing prototypes and advanced manufacturing – were underestimated.

Metro differentials in innovative industries' occupational structures can also be viewed by comparing how certain occupations are over- or underestimated in each region, given national norms (Table 6.2). Across all industries in each metro, computer and IT professionals' ranks were underestimated by 32, 38, and 33 percent in San Francisco, San Jose and Oakland, respectively, while they were overestimated by 25 percent in Los Angeles. Overestimates were nearly as large for selected engineers and natural scientists for the same three metros. These discrepancies often involved a large number of jobs. These three occupations alone accounted for 29,000 of the underestimated jobs in San Jose and 15,000 of the overestimated high-tech jobs in Los Angeles. For policy makers concerned with the quality of jobs associated with target industries and with the availability of existing workforce skills for newly recruited firms, these findings suggest that independent intelligence on the occupational structures of regional industries is highly desirable, especially in high-tech and business service sectors.

Table 6.1   *Share of occupational employment unexplained by industry structure in*
            information technology and business services, California metropolitan areas,
            1997

	San Francisco	San Jose	Oakland	Los Angeles	Orange County	San Diego
Information technology industries, excluding computer and data processing services						
Managerial/professional workers	10	21	15	12	5	8
Computer/IT professionals	−11	21	15	11	−6	17
Selected engineers	4	36	19	3	7	−3
Natural scientists	48	12	35	7	19	6
Sales and related workers	3	−8	27	−22	24	−47
Clerical and administrative support	−18	−4	−2	8	11	−13
Service workers	−45	−43	−29	9	−24	−36
Precision workers	−21	−29	−8	−8	8	−16
Manual workers	−25	−34	−41	−25	−20	−1
Total employment	35,532	214,907	50,089	153,605	87,690	74,513
Business services, including computer and data processing services						
Managerial/professional workers	35	38	28	−8	2	17
Computer/IT professionals	39	57	40	−51	1	9
Selected engineers	43	61	34	−167	−35	52
Natural scientists	−30	−89	55	−32	−8	14
Sales and related workers	7	−44	−18	16	−33	−19
Clerical and administrative support	−3	−33	−14	−6	20	4
Service workers	−42	−56	−48	6	−5	−5
Precision workers	−118	28	−45	1	0	−18
Manual workers	−68	−15	14	1	−30	−28
Total employment	111,411	128,230	93,027	353,245	123,314	90,357

Sources: Barbour and Markusen (2007). Data from California Employment Development Department,
Industry–Occupation Matrix, and Bureau of Labor Statistics, National Historical Industry–Occupation
Matrix Time Series, 1983–1998.

6.4   DISAGGREGATING: DO THE OCCUPATIONAL STRUCTURES OF INDUSTRIES STILL VARY ACROSS REGIONS?

A skeptic might argue that this lack of fit may be due to overly aggregated occupational
groupings; that separating, say, civil engineers from electrical or industrial or aeronautical engineers might result in better fits between industries and occupations. Can the
finding of a considerable spatial division of labor within the same industry in different
regions be replicated with more detailed occupational groupings? In this section, we
explore this question.

The exercise just described used employer-based data for three-digit industries for

Table 6.2   High-tech-related occupations in six California metropolitan areas, 1997

	San Francisco	San Jose	Oakland	Los Angeles	Orange County	San Diego
Computer/IT professionals						
Location quotient	2.0	3.3	1.7	0.9	1.3	1.3
Employment share unexplained by industry (%)	32	38	33	−25	2	11
# Jobs unexplained by industry	8,961	18,348	8,448	−13,433	572	2,277
Selected engineers						
Location quotient	1.2	4.6	1.7	0.9	1.5	1.7
Employment share unexplained by industry (%)	10	37	28	−6	10	21
# Jobs unexplained by industry	623	9,888	2,755	−1,383	1,104	2,274
Natural scientists						
Location quotient	1.8	1.7	1.9	0.8	0.9	1.8
Employment share unexplained by industry (%)	33	18	37	−12	−4	3
# Jobs unexplained by industry	1,504	756	1,872	−1,023	−125	142

Sources: Barbour and Markusen (2007). Data from California Employment Development Department, Industry–Occupation Matrix, and Bureau of Labor Statistics, National Historical Industry–Occupation Matrix Time Series, 1983–1998.

large metros within one state. Differences in state-level industry-by-occupational data-sets make it difficult to replicate this experiment at the national scale, where we might expect more variation. For a second exercise, we chose artists as a subset of cultural workers and four subdisciplines – musicians, writers, and visual and performing artists – investigating their distributions within a set of cultural industries nationally and how these vary among a set of large US metros. We use a strict definition of artists, not including related cultural workers such as designers and architects. Social scientists generally agree that artists are core cultural workers (for example, Wassall and Alper, 1985; Heilbrun, 1987), and their rates of self-employment are much higher (Markusen and Schrock, 2006). In 2000, there were about 843,000 employed (including self-employed) artists in the US, accounting for about 0.6 percent of the workforce (Markusen et al., 2008, Table 3).[2]

6.4.1   Census Data and Metro Sets

For occupation, industry, and metro analyses, we use Census of Population 2000 data drawn from the Public Use Micro-data Sample (PUMS), a 5 percent sample that permits disaggregation by occupation and industry down to the county level and below (see Markusen and Schrock, 2008a, for a user-friendly discussion of data quality and statistical reliability issues in using the PUMS dataset for spatial analysis). The Census PUMS dataset is underexplored for investigating industry and occupational employment patterns at various geographical scales.[3] It records data on the basis of where people live rather than where they work (which is not a problem at a metro-scale analysis), and it includes self-employed workers who are not included in employer-based datasets.[4] In addition to self-employed and miscoding problems, BLS and Census employment totals will also differ because employer-based sources count every job, so that moonlighting workers will be counted twice while Census sources include only the primary occupation of respondents.

We created a set of 22 primary metropolitan statistical areas (PMSAs) to scrutinize. We first selected 18 of the 30 largest metro areas in the US. They include metros with high overrepresentation of artists (Los Angeles, New York, San Francisco, Seattle), others which are close to the national average (Chicago, Kansas City) and others with a low representation of artists (Houston, Detroit, Cleveland, San Jose). We eliminated from the largest metro set several that are contiguous to larger PMSAs (Baltimore, Nassau/Suffolk, Newark, Orange County, Riverside/San Bernardino) and several stand-alone metros with an average or below-average artistic presence (Dallas, Phoenix, Pittsburgh, St. Louis, Tampa/St. Petersburg) (Markusen and Schrock, 2006), and added several smaller metros with known outstanding pools of artists in one or more disciplines: Albuquerque, Austin, New Orleans, Santa Fe. For the correlation analysis below, we expanded the set to 30 metros. Artistic concentrations, denoted by location quotients, for all 30 metros are arrayed in Table 6.3. In this section, we explore the extent to which these differentials appear to be explained by the presence of cultural industries in each region.

We use the Census rather than employer-based data to chart artists' spatial and industrial distributions because self-employment levels among artists are very high, many times the national rate of 8 percent (Table 6.4). Employer surveys such as those relied upon in the California study do not include the self-employed. A comparison of employer-based with Census estimates of artists' employment confirms serious under-estimation of artists' ranks when using the former. The ranks of writers, for instance, are underestimated by more than sixfold for metros such as Los Angeles, Houston, Riverside/San Bernardino and Portland (Table 6.5). Even in cities where writers' formal employment rates are high – such as Minneapolis with its large educational publishing industry, Washington with its huge public sector and public interest organizations, and Kansas City with Hallmark Cards – writers' ranks are underestimated by nearly 2 to 1 or more. These differentials are particularly remarkable since the Census asks only for primary occupation (and thus misses the 15 percent of the writers identified in the CPS as self-employed as a secondary occupation) while employer-based data sources will count a dual-job person twice.

6.4.2 Defining Cultural Industries

We defined a set of cultural industries at the national level, based both on qualitative knowledge and on cultural content as revealed by occupational concentrations. We ranked all 3-digit industries at the national level by the absolute numbers of artists that they employ and the shares of their workforce accounted for by artists. We chose to include those industries ($N = 20$) that employ more than 6,000 artists, a set that accounts for 84 percent of the nation's employed artists (Table 6.6).[5] This cut-off ensures that we have enough artists in each industry at the national level to be confident of the estimates.

Table 6.3 *Location quotients for employed and self-employed artists by metro area, 2000*

	All artists	Visual artists	Performing artists	Musicians composers	Writers
Los Angeles	2.98	2.13	5.47	2.15	2.73
Santa Fe	2.92	4.27	0.83	1.16	4.20
New York City/Bergen	2.58	2.01	3.73	2.03	3.00
Nashville	1.97	1.14	1.63	5.16	1.01
San Francisco/Oakland	1.86	1.83	1.86	1.23	2.52
Seattle	1.37	1.52	1.16	1.17	1.50
Washington, DC	1.36	0.97	1.54	1.02	2.31
Austin	1.30	1.19	0.89	1.48	1.87
Boston	1.30	1.03	1.24	1.25	2.01
Albuquerque	1.24	1.64	0.96	0.87	1.08
San Diego	1.23	1.34	0.95	1.37	1.16
Minneapolis/St. Paul	1.19	1.11	1.13	1.28	1.33
Las Vegas	1.16	0.83	1.94	1.51	0.60
Miami	1.15	1.02	1.49	1.40	0.80
Portland, OR	1.12	1.02	1.12	0.95	1.51
Atlanta	1.10	1.11	1.06	1.24	0.98
Chicago	1.06	1.14	0.84	0.92	1.28
Dallas	1.00	1.10	1.08	0.95	0.74
United States	*1.00*	*1.00*	*1.00*	*1.00*	*1.00*
Philadelphia	0.98	1.03	0.91	0.97	0.95
Phoenix	0.96	1.10	0.70	1.04	0.88
Kansas City	0.94	1.22	0.59	0.84	0.82
Tampa	0.92	0.91	0.84	1.19	0.75
Denver	0.91	0.81	1.09	0.87	0.98
New Orleans	0.91	0.95	0.69	1.43	0.57
San Jose	0.86	0.95	0.75	0.67	0.95
Cleveland/Akron	0.83	0.84	0.64	1.04	0.80
Pittsburgh	0.77	0.73	0.63	1.00	0.79
Detroit	0.76	0.83	0.62	0.81	0.73
Houston	0.76	0.75	0.65	1.00	0.67
St. Louis	0.74	0.82	0.52	0.87	0.68

Source: Authors' computations from 2000 Census of Population data from Ruggles et al. (2004).

But industries are not of equal size. Huge numbers of artists in a large industry may not account for a very large share of that industry's employment. The industries in this set vary from those with very high shares of artists in their employment ranks, especially compared to the national norm of 0.65 percent, to those with several that are below the national average: other recreation, restaurants, K-12 schools and computer systems design (Table 6.6). However, because some of these industries are significant employers of particular disciplines (restaurants for musicians, management, scientific consulting services for writers), we chose not to eliminate them in the first instance. We also looked at smaller industries to see if there were any with very large shares of

Table 6.4   Self-employment trends, artistic occupations, 2002

Occupational title	Total employment	Self-employed	% Self-employed	Primary job	Secondary job
Visual artists	307,254	155,159	50	129,109	26,050
Performing artists	176,463	42,724	24	38,174	4,550
Musicians	215,425	83,121	39	56,770	26,351
Writers	138,980	94,377	68	80,509	13,868
Total, arts occupations	838,122	375,381	45	304,562	70,819
Designers	531,921	168,806	32	132,827	35,979
Architects	136,378	29,678	22	23,809	5,869
Total, all occupations	144,013,600	11,451,600	8	9,926,000	1,525,600

Source: Markusen and Schrock (2006). Data from Bureau of Labor Statistics, National Industry–Occupation Employment Matrix (http://www.bls.gov/emp/empoils.htm).

artists in their workforce. However, since we did not find any additional industries where artists comprised more than 3 percent of employment, we chose to leave them out.

Our use of artistic occupations to identify cultural industries is analogous to the use of scientific and engineering occupations in defining high-tech industries (Markusen et al., 1986). It is interesting to compare this method with other conceptual and impressionistic definitions (Pratt, 1997, 2004; Hesmondhalgh, 2002; Power, 2002). Our set shares some core industries with other empirical accounts: performing arts, media, motion pictures and video, sound recording, advertising, publishing and printing. It also includes a number of industries that are not generally considered as cultural industries: other professional, scientific and technical services; religious organizations; specialized design services; colleges and universities, and elementary/secondary schools; toys, amusements and sporting goods manufacturing; drinking places and restaurants; management, scientific and technical consulting; civic, social and advocacy organizations; and computer systems and design. Our definition does not include peripheral cultural industries that are connected through inter-industry relationships, which is a common practice in cultural industry impact studies (Beyers et al., 2004; DeNatale and Wassall, 2007). Elsewhere, we debate the theoretical rationales and empirical problems posed by sectors such as religion, fashion, education, sports and even auto manufacturing in defining cultural industries (Markusen et al., 2008).

6.4.3   Does a Cultural Industry Presence Explain Artist Distributions among Metros?

Spatial occupation by industry patterns can be studied either by mapping occupations in regions onto industries or by starting with cultural industries and exploring their occupational structures among regions. We previously investigated the metro distribution of artistic occupations among industries and found large differentials (Table 6.7). For instance, the motion picture/video industry accounts for 20 percent of visual artists in Los Angeles compared with just 3 percent in the US as a whole, and the advertising industry accounts for three times as large a share of visual artists in Chicago as it does

Table 6.5 *Writers' employment estimates, worker vs. employer sources, 2000*

Metropolitan area	Self-employed	Census/OES	Employment	
			Census	OES
Los Angeles, CA	57	6.1	12,970	2,110
Houston, TX	57	7.3	1,524	210
Portland, OR-WA	57	7.5	1,647	220
Riverside-San Bernardino, CA	56	7.3	951	130
San Francisco-Oakland, CA	55	5.8	6,260	1,075
New York, NY-NJ	54	3.8	16,443	4,350
Miami, FL	52	2.6	906	350
Denver, CO	51	3.1	1,235	400
Orange County, CA	51	5.8	1,498	260
Phoenix, AZ	51	5.6	1,520	270
Philadelphia, PA-NJ	51	5.0	2,687	540
Seattle, WA	50	4.2	2,208	530
Chicago, IL	49	4.2	5,893	1,410
Nassau-Suffolk, NY	47	5.8	1,341	230
St. Louis, MO-IL	47	3.4	1,022	300
Atlanta, GA	47	2.0	2,389	1,180
San Diego, CA	47	6.3	1,763	280
Tampa-St. Petersburg, FL	46	3.8	996	260
Detroit, MI	43	2.6	1,792	690
Pittsburgh, PA	42	4.3	988	230
Boston, MA-NH	42	3.8	4,207	1,120
San Jose, CA	40	2.6	972	370
Newark, NJ	39	4.0	1,425	360
Minneapolis-St. Paul, MN	36	1.8	2,494	1,360
Dallas, TX	35	3.1	1,489	480
Washington, DC-MD-VA-WV	35	2.3	6,877	3,000
Cleveland, OH	34	2.1	948	460
Baltimore, MD	30	1.7	1,361	810
Kansas City, MO-KS	22	2.7	847	310
United States	*47*	*3.8*	*158,116*	*41,410*

Sources: Markusen and Schrock (2006). Data from Census 2000 5% PUMS dataset, Integrated Public Use Microdata Sample, Minnesota Population Center, University of Minnesota; US Bureau of Labor Statistics, Occupational Employment Statistics.

nationally. We can speculate that these patterns can be explained in large part by the differing incidence of cultural industries among regions.

In this current exercise, we use an industrial rather than an occupational entry point, since our project compares the occupational composition of the same set of industries across all metros. For the set of broadly defined cultural industries, we computed the differential between the actual numbers and shares of artists in each metro compared with what they would have been if these shares mirrored the national shares for each industry, summing up for all cultural industries:

Table 6.6 *Distribution of artists by discipline in cutural industries, United States, 2000*

Industry	Total	Visual artists	Performing artists	Musicians and composers	Writers	Artists as % industry
Independent artists, performing arts, spectator sports	259,066	92,256	40,005	69,998	56,807	45.3
Other professional, scientific and technical services	64,536	63,383	395	44	714	22.8
Radio and television broadcasting and cable	61,263	7,152	49,230	1,172	3,709	10.4
Motion pictures and video industries	55,403	8,987	40,364	1,255	4,797	17.9
Religious organizations	55,362	595	797	53,037	933	5.6
Advertising and related services	36,048	18,523	4,284	155	13,086	6.6
Publishing, except newspapers and software	23,545	9,192	865	223	13,265	5.6
Specialized design services	22,785	21,843	369	0	573	8.4
Newspaper publishers	21,240	11,588	103	76	9,473	4.2
Colleges and universities, including junior colleges	20,268	4,785	7,230	2,421	5,832	0.7
Toys, amusement, and sporting goods manufacturing	12,685	12,404	169	0	112	9.4
Drinking places, alcoholic beverages	11,284	56	8,258	2,970	0	5.1
Other amusement, gambling, and recreation industries	9,846	2,249	4,984	2,120	493	0.7
Printing and related support activities	8,547	8,034	148	80	285	1.0
Sound recording industries	7,700	540	2,305	4,571	284	20.0
Management, scientific and technical consulting services	7,170	1,841	605	90	4,634	0.7
Restaurants and other food services	7,111	432	935	5,215	529	0.1
Civic, social, advocacy, grantmaking organizations	6,992	473	1,327	817	4,375	1.1
Elementary and secondary schools	6,571	940	1,516	2,389	1,726	0.1
Computer systems design and related services	6,147	3,046	988	78	2,035	0.5
Artists, all industries	837,862	340,561	185,413	155,593	156,295	0.6

Source: Authors' computations from 2000 Census of Population data from Ruggles et al. (2004).

Table 6.7 Employed artists, top industries, Los Angeles, Chicago, Boston Metro, USA, 2000

	% of occupational employment			
	Boston	Chicago	Los Angeles	USA
Visual artists				
Independent artists, performing arts, spectator sports	25.5	17.9	24.0	27.1
Other professional, scientific and technical services	20.1	19.1	13.9	19.6
Specialized design services	11.7	7.3	6.1	6.0
Advertising services	4.9	16.0	4.2	5.1
Newspaper publishers	4.5			3.9
Motion pictures and video industries			19.6	2.7
Management, scientific, technical consulting services		3.0		0.4
Performing artists				
Radio and television broadcasting and cable	41.5	19.1	15.6	27.5
Independent artists, performing arts, spectator sports	14.5	24.2	22.5	21.3
Motion pictures and video industries	11.4	20.4	48.7	20.0
Colleges and universities, including junior colleges	6.2			4.6
Advertising services	5.2	9.6	1.3	3.2
Employment services			3.5	0.7
Computer systems design services		2.7		0.4
Musicians and composers				
Independent artists, performing arts, spectator sports	51.2	46.5	64.9	46.8
Religious organizations	28.7	31.9	9.8	32.5
Restaurants and other food services	3.0	4.4	3.8	3.2
Sound recording industries		2.9	7.2	2.7
Elementary and secondary schools	2.6	2.3		1.6
Colleges and universities, including junior colleges	3.4			0.9
Motion pictures and video industries			2.7	0.9
Writers and authors				
Independent artists, performing arts, spectator sports	23.6	30.9	45.3	35.8
Advertising services	12.1	15.5	4.1	9.5
Publishing, except newspapers and software	14.0	11.1	6.1	7.9
Newspaper publishers		3.5		7.5
Colleges and universities, including junior colleges	6.8			3.6
Motion pictures and video industries			20.0	3.1
Radio and television broadcasting and cable			6.6	3.0
Management, scientific, technical consulting services	8.6			2.3
Civic, social, advocacy organizations, grantmaking		4.2		1.9

Source: Markusen et al. (2008), using 2000 Census data from Ruggles et al. (2004).

$$S_i\left[(E_{oir}) - (E_{oi}/E_i)(E_{ir})\right]$$

where:

  o: occupation (artist; or musician, and so on);
  r: region (metro);
  i: cultural industry; and
  E: employment.

The largest underestimates of artists occur for the huge, cultural industry-rich metros of New York and Los Angeles (Table 6.8). For each metro area, about 14,000 more artists are employed (and self-employed) in the cultural industries than would be predicted by assuming national shares for each industry. (As we demonstrate below, self-employed artists may state, or be assigned by a Census professional to, an industry in which they work.) In contrast, artists' ranks are overestimated by nearly 1,500 or more in the metros of Detroit, Denver, and Chicago.

Are these differentials large? For some metros, the answer is yes. For nine of the 22 metros in the set, the over- or underestimation of artistic occupations from national industry shares exceeds 10 percent. Santa Fe's 30 percent artist undercount is the great-

Table 6.8   Artist by industry deviations from national norms, selected US metros, 2000

Metro	All artists	Differential/total employment (%)
New York City/Bergen	14,155	18.7
Los Angeles	13,927	18.3
San Francisco/Oakland	3,675	14.9
Boston	1,948	13.3
Austin	460	8.8
Albuquerque	444	16.8
Santa Fe	417	29.9
Atlanta	40	0.3
Seattle	−66	−0.6
Washington, DC	−73	0.0
Portland, OR	−165	−2.5
New Orleans	−222	−7.0
Minneapolis/St. Paul	−283	−2.4
Miami	−363	−5.4
Kansas City	−388	−7.5
San Jose	−446	−9.5
Cleveland/Akron	−570	−7.6
Philadelphia	−690	−4.6
Houston	−872	−9.4
Chicago	−1,475	−5.6
Denver	−1,723	−28.0
Detroit	−1,768	−17.7

Source: Authors' computations from 2000 Census of Population data from Ruggles et al. (2004).

est in percentage terms, while Denver's overcount is close at 28 percent. For only six metros are the national share estimates less than 5 percent; Atlanta, Seattle, Portland, Washington, DC, Minneapolis/St. Paul, and Philadelphia. For these metros, artistic populations closely reflect the presence of cultural industries, although the direction of causation is not established.

Disaggregating by artistic discipline, the gap in actual versus estimated artists' shares by industry is even larger in many cases, revealing an important disciplinary spatial division of labor within cultural industries across space (Table 6.9). Visual artists in Santa Fe and Albuquerque's cultural industries are underestimated by 49 and 38 percent, respectively, underscoring the pre-eminence of these New Mexico metros as visual arts centers, but overestimated in Washington, DC (30 percent) and Denver (35 percent). Performing artists in the New York and Los Angeles cultural industries are underestimated by 43 and 32 percent, respectively, while they are overestimated by 43 percent in New Orleans and 88 percent in Santa Fe. Musicians' ranks are underestimated by 29 percent in both Austin and Boston, but overestimated in Albuquerque and Santa Fe by 30 and 82 percent, respectively. Writers' presence in cultural industries is undercounted by 47 percent in Santa Fe using the national shares technique and overestimated by more than 30 percent in both Kansas City and Miami, and by 57 percent in New Orleans.

Table 6.9   Artistic discipline counts by industry, deviation from national norms, selected US metros, 2000

Metros	Visual	%	Performing	%	Musicians	%	Writers	%
New York City/Bergen	−212	−1	10,389	43	661	6	3,317	20
Los Angeles	243	1	9,850	32	619	6	3,215	25
Boston	−529	−11	552	18	751	29	1,174	28
San Francisco/Oakland	1,164	12	974	18	−64	−2	1,600	26
Washington, DC	−1,860	−30	495	9.2	227	7.5	1,065	16
Miami	−363	−15	203	11	69	4	−271	−31
Albuquerque	532	37	16	4	−103	−30	0	0
Austin	−30	−2	−163	−21	−319	29	333	24
Denver	−772	−35	−384	−24	−254	−23	−312	−25
Cleveland/Akron	−99	−3	−353	−28	93	5	−210	−12
Kansas City	263	10	−260	−36	−134	−16	−257	−30
Detroit	−807	−18	−651	−36	−65	−3	−245	−14
New Orleans	34	3	−228	−43	180	20	−208	−57
Santa Fe	404	49	−78	−88	−85	−82	176	47

Source: Authors' computations from 2000 Census of Population data from Ruggles et al. (2004).

These are sizable differences. Summing over the 10 metros where they were underestimated, more than 11,000 writers would have been unaccounted for had their presence been estimated by national industry by occupation composition. Summing over the nine metros where performing artists were similarly underestimated, almost 23,000 would be missing. In 13 of the metros, more than half of the set, the numbers of artists in at least one discipline would be under- or overestimated by more than 25 percent. However, if we disaggregated the industry set to look more closely at component industries, we might find a closer fit. We intend to do this in a further exercise, breaking out motion pictures, sound recording and several other industries. (Our work so far suggests that the various cultural industries do not cluster together in any systematic way across space.)

These patterns reflect overall artistic specializations across metros (Table 6.3). Our results suggest that cultural industries alone, even with a residual 'independent, performing arts and sports' category included, do not explain the full extent of these differentials. For instance, cultural industries in the Twin Cities of Minneapolis-St. Paul employ writers at 7 percent below the national norm for the cultural industries which are present. Yet writers are heavily overrepresented in the Twin Cities. Thus their ranks include many artists working for other industries in the region.

We conducted a sensitivity analysis on the choice of cultural industries by eliminating the large industries in our set with a below-national-average share of artists: restaurants and other food services, computer systems design and related services, and elementary and secondary schools. We found almost no difference in over- and underestimates of artists' presence by doing so. This suggests that a more restricted set of cultural industries can reasonably be used as a proxy for the presence of artist-employing industries in regions.

We also eliminated the industry category 'independent artists, performing arts, spectator sport and related' from the exercise. This 'industry' accounts for 31 percent of all artists working in the 20 cultural industries nationally, so its exclusion might be expected to influence the size of over- and underestimates. If this industry group reflects the same compositional variation as other industries, then the numbers should simply be moderated. We found this to be the case for many of the metros. Eliminating this industry resulted in national norm-generated estimates of metro artists which are closer to actual Census estimates, and often substantially so, though in some metros, an underestimate became an overestimate or vice versa (Table 6.10). Underestimates fell most in absolute terms for New York, Los Angeles, and San Francisco/Oakland, but their unaccounted-for artists remained high (all more than 10 percent). Overestimates shrank the most for Detroit and Chicago. For two metros, however, Washington, DC and Seattle, norm-generated overestimates were larger than when the independent/performing arts industry was included. This reveals that self-employed and performing artists are overrepresented in those two cities and help compensate for the lower incidence in the other cultural industries. Overall, the elimination of this large industry indeed moderated the absolute and relative mis-estimates, but they still range from a 16 percent underestimation in the case of Los Angeles to a 23 percent overestimation in the case of Denver. Thus our finding that artists' employment by industry varies substantially among metros, stands without the 'independent/performing arts' industry.

From this exercise, we conclude that the industry encompassing self-employed and performing artists is best treated as a separate phenomenon, chiefly due to its inclusion of self-employed artists who do not identify as being associated with any industry. Using a set of cultural industries that excludes this potpourri 'industry' will not change the overall findings a great deal, especially in a multivariate analysis of the determinants of artists' locations by metro areas. It is regrettable that performing arts establishments

Table 6.10   Without independent artists/performing arts, selected metros, 2000

Metro employment deviation from national industry average (#)	All artists	w/o indep	Differential/total employment	w/o indep
Los Angeles	13,927	11,897	0.18	0.16
New York City/Bergen	14,155	10,272	0.19	0.14
San Francisco/Oakland	3,675	2,715	0.15	0.11
Boston	1,948	1,439	0.13	0.10
Albuquerque	444	273	0.17	0.10
Cleveland/Akron	−570	242	−0.08	0.03
Miami	−363	146	−0.05	0.02
Santa Fe	417	141	0.30	0.10
Kansas City	−388	109	−0.08	0.02
Portland, OR	−165	48	−0.03	0.01
Austin	460	−39	0.09	−0.01
New Orleans	−222	−155	−0.07	−0.05
Minneapolis/St. Paul	−283	−191	−0.02	−0.02
Houston	−872	−225	−0.09	−0.02
Atlanta	40	−247	0.00	−0.02
San Jose	−446	−433	−0.10	−0.09
Seattle	−66	−519	−0.01	−0.05
Washington, DC	−73	−593	0.00	−0.03
Philadelphia	−690	−607	−0.05	−0.04
Chicago	−1,475	−701	−0.06	−0.03
Detroit	−1,768	−743	−0.18	−0.07
Denver	−1,723	−1,388	−0.28	−0.23

Source: Authors' computations from 2000 Census of Population data from Ruggles et al. (2004).

are included in this same industry. However, since the Census also records the self-employment status of respondents, we can use this to estimate the size of those working for the performing arts and treat the rest as being truly independent.

6.4.4   Self-employment Status and Industry Orientation

Being self-employed does not mean that members of an occupation are not oriented toward a particular industry. From work on the film (Scott, 2005) and performing arts (Beyers and GMA, 1999) sectors, we know that many artists regularly work on contract, a relationship which is typical of the project organization of work in some cultural industries. Relying on interview data, the Beyers study found that only 14 percent of people working in the Seattle dance, theater, and music establishments are full-time employees, while another 39 percent are part-timers, and 47 percent are not counted as employees at all, but work on a contractual or student internship basis. Scott's (2005) work reveals the project-based relationships in the motion picture and television industries of Los Angeles, so we cannot assume that artists' presence in a region is unrelated to the presence of cultural industries solely on the basis of their being self-employed. On the other hand, many artists may be attracted to a cultural industry-rich locale simply in order to enjoy the cultural offerings or for reasons which are unrelated to culture, such as environmental and recreational opportunities.

Is it possible to explore the extent to which self-employed people are oriented toward particular industries? The Census offers us an opportunity to probe this, because it asks people to identify whether they are self-employed, as opposed to working for a for-profit, non-profit, public, or household employer, and it also asks them to identify the industry in which they work. Many self-employed artists report, or are assigned to, an industry affiliation, as we show for selected metros in Table 6.11. In Kansas City, for instance, many self-employed artists are attached to the 'other professional, scientific' industry (largely photographers), and to the printing and publishing industry, reflecting the presence of Hallmark Cards. More artists working in this metro are identified as self-employed than on a salary. Similarly, in the Los Angeles metro area, high shares of artists who are associated with the specialized design industry are self-employed. Seattle's independent/performing arts 'industry' includes higher shares of self-employed artists than in either Kansas City or Los Angeles, evidence which

Table 6.11   Artists by selected industry, metro: shares self-employed

		Wage, salary	Self-employed	% Self-employed
Kansas City, MO-KS	TOTAL	3,823	1,338	26
Independent artists, performing arts, spectator sports		425	530	55
Other professional, scientific, technical services		298	168	36
Radio and television broadcasting and cable		369	45	11
Printing and related support activities		372	44	11
Publishing, except newspapers and software		309	22	7
Elementary and secondary schools		18	22	55
Religious organizations		516	0	0
Los Angeles-Long Beach, CA	TOTAL	46,031	30,059	40
Independent artists, performing arts, spectator sports		8,587	16,132	65
Motion pictures and video industries		16,265	1,790	27
Other professional, scientific and technical services		1,335	1,790	57
Advertising and related services		1,235	623	34
Specialized design services		626	1,008	62
Publishing, except newspapers and software		761	642	46
Sound recording industries		745	482	39
Seattle-Everett, WA	TOTAL	6,240	4,601	42
Independent artists, performing arts, spectator sports		1,021	2,990	75
Other professional, scientific and technical services		335	331	50
Specialized design services		76	208	73
Motion pictures and video industries		250	122	33
Publishing, except newspapers and software		151	110	42
Sound recording industries		64	96	60
Management, scientific, technical consulting services		35	69	66

Source: Authors' computations from 2000 Census of Population data from Ruggles et al. (2004).

supports the Beyers interview data. This evidence underscores the failure of employer-based data sources to capture large numbers of people working off-salary in cultural industries.

These data permit us to unpack the independent/performing arts/sports industry and distinguish people who are self-employed from those that are employed. So for instance, in Kansas City, 530 artists reported being self-employed and unaffiliated with any other industry (though they could be affiliated with the performing arts), with 425 of these reporting wage and salary employment, presumably in the performing arts and not sports. We have thus confirmed that many self-employed artists are working chiefly in one industry and are captured this way by the Census in ways that are not possible with other databases.

6.5   REGIONAL DEVELOPMENT IMPLICATIONS

If the occupational composition of key industries is relatively similar across regions, then the case for a parallel investigation of occupational formation and industry location is not strong. If, however, as we have shown in two different exercises, the spatial division of labor within innovative industries varies across space, both regional analysis and economic development policy should take this into account.

In terms of regional research, this means investigating the relative size and significance of various occupations in the region (and *vis-à-vis* other regions), including how these occupations serve otherwise disparate industries. If, as we have yet to demonstrate, the behavior of those who create human capital (workers themselves, their households, and training institutions) is semi-autonomous from decisions made by industry managers, then their location calculus should be taken into account. There is circumstantial evidence that artists as a particular case are semi-autonomous. They exhibit relatively high rates of migration among states and regions, and although this is also the case with other high-tech occupations, artists' self-employment rates are at least three times higher than the latter, supporting the hypothesis of a relative independence from particular job offers (Table 6.12).

Since economic development tools are often designed to incentivize behavior, a more effective regional development strategy would allocate resources across a larger portfolio of investments. These should include inducements to firms to locate, expand and retain jobs, but also policies to shape human capital formation and skilled labor recruitment and retention.

Table 6.12   Occupational self-employment, localization and regional migration, 1995–2000

Occupational group (SOC Major)	% moving across:		% Self-employment	Localization coefficient
	States	Divisions		
Life, Physical, and Social Science	17.8	13.5	8.7	17.3
Computer and Mathematical	16.3	11.8	5.0	16.2
Arts, Design, Entertainment, Sports, Media	15.4	11.5	24.9	13.2
Architecture and Engineering	13.6	10.0	5.9	12.6
Community and Social Services	12.0	8.5	5.9	12.6
Business and Financial Operations	11.8	8.5	2.0	6.9
Management	11.5	8.4	17.9	4.9
Healthcare Practitioners and Technical	11.2	8.3	9.2	6.7
Legal	10.9	7.7	26.4	11.9
Food Preparation and Serving	10.7	7.9	2.4	5.6
Education, Training, and Library	10.2	7.5	2.4	4.4
Sales and Related	10.1	7.2	13.3	2.9
Personal Care and Service	9.4	6.9	29.8	5.5
Installation, Maintenance, and Repair	9.3	6.9	9.6	6.0
Office and Administrative Support	8.8	6.4	2.7	2.1
Protective Service	8.6	6.5	0.8	10.1
Healthcare Support	7.9	5.7	4.8	11.5
Transportation and Material Moving	7.9	5.8	6.1	6.1
Construction and Extraction	7.8	5.7	19.8	7.7
Building and Grounds Cleaning, Maintenance	6.8	5.0	14.5	6.7
Production	6.6	4.8	4.1	13.0
Farming, Fishing, and Forestry	6.5	4.4	7.4	24.6
Total, all occupations	*9.9*	*7.3*	*9.4*	*6.6*

Source: Authors' calculations. Data from Census 2000 5% PUMS dataset, Integrated Public Use Microdata Sample, Minnesota Population Center, University of Minnesota. Data include the self-employed. Percentages are total in labor force, domestic migration on Census Divisions (9): New England, Mid-Atlantic, E North Central, W North Central, South Atlantic, E South Central, W South Central, Mountain, Pacific.

NOTES

*   Our thanks to the National Science Foundation, Program in Geography and Regional Science, Grant No. 0136988, 2002–4, and the Public Policy Institute of California Fellowship, 2002, for support for the occupational analysis upon which this chapter draws, to the Humphrey Institute of Public Affairs for research and staff assistance, and to the Sloan Foundation for a travel grant through the Industry Studies Association to present this work at the 2008 meetings. We would like to thank the members of the interdisciplinary Innovation Seminar at Korea University for the opportunity to present a preliminary version of these ideas and findings in October 2008.
1.   'Selected engineers' include chemical engineers, civil engineers, electrical and electronics engineers, and mechanical engineers. This group comprises the vast majority of engineers. Due to data limitations, aeronautical and astronautical engineers, industrial engineers, metallurgists, mining, and petroleum engineers are excluded. 'Computer/information technology professionals' include computer engineers, systems analysts, database administrators, computer support specialists, computer programmers, computer programmer aides, programmers (numerical, tool, and process control), and all other computer scientists. 'Natural scientists' include agricultural and food scientists, biological scientists, conservation scientists and forest-

ers, medical scientists, all other life scientists, geologists, geophysicists, and oceanographers, physicists and astronomers, chemists, atmospheric scientists, and all other physical scientists.

2. Related cultural workers not included account for another 1.2 percent, or 1.5 million, of employed and self-employed workers in the US. Among designers, the largest subgroups are industrial and graphic designers.

3. Unlike Bureau of Labor Statistics (BLS) employer-based industry and occupational data used for most state and federal employment analysis, these data are based on individuals' responses to the special long form of the US Census, administered by the Census Bureau. Responses are allocated mechanically and by trained government employees to SOC occupational and NAICS industry categories.

4. Although BLS estimates self-employment at higher levels of spatial aggregation from the Current Population Survey, the CPS is too small to permit metro-specific adjustments.

5. Our cut-off was chosen on the basis of a careful look at the activities of those industries below and above the line. The three 3-digit industries that employ 5,000 to 6,000 artists, for instance, are miscellaneous retail stores; sporting goods, camera, hobby and toy stores; and other information services. These industries seem unlikely to be on artists' radar screens as significant employers.

REFERENCES

Barbour, Elisa and Ann Markusen (2007), 'Regional occupational and industrial structure: does the one imply the other?', *International Regional Science Review*, **30** (1): 1–19.

Beyers, William (2007), 'Occupational structure in industries in the United States: defining clusters and the regional distribution of selected clusters', Working Paper, Department of Geography, University of Washington, Seattle, December.

Beyers, William, Anne Bonds, Andrew Wenzl and Paul Sommers (2004), 'The Economic Impact of Seattle's Music Industry', Office of Economic Development, City of Seattle, WA.

Beyers, William and GMA Research Corporation (1999), *An Economic Impact Study of Arts and Cultural Organizations in King County: 1997*, Bellevue, WA: GMA Research Corporation.

DeNatale, Doug and Greg Wassall (2007), *The Creative Economy: A New Definition*. Boston, MA: New England Foundation for the Arts.

Feser, Edward (2003), 'What regions do rather than make: a proposed set of knowledge-based occupation clusters', *Urban Studies*, **40** (10): 1937–58.

Florida, Richard (2002), *The Rise of the Creative Class*, New York: Basic Books.

Frobel, Folker, Jurgen Heinrichs and Otto Kreye (1979), *The New International Division of Labor*, Cambridge: Cambridge University Press.

Gereffi, Gary and Miguel Korzeniewicz (eds) (1994), *Commodity Chains and Global Capitalism*, Westport, CT: Greenwood Press.

Harrington, James W. (1999), 'Categories as constraints: geographic research on services', Working Paper, Department of Geography, University of Washington, Seattle.

Heilbrun, James (1987), 'Growth and geographic distribution of the arts in the U.S', in Douglas Shaw, William Hendon and C. Richard Waits (eds), *Artists and Cultural Consumers*, Akron, OH: Association for Cultural Economics, pp. 24–35.

Hesmondhalgh, David (2002), *The Cultural Industries*, London: Sage.

Koo, Jun (2005), 'How to analyze the regional economy with occupation data', *Economic Development Quarterly*, **19** (4): 356–72.

Markusen, Ann (1985), *Profit Cycles, Oligopoly and Regional Development*, Cambridge, MA: MIT Press.

Markusen, Ann (2004), 'Targeting occupations in regional and community economic development', *Journal of the American Planning Association*, **70** (3): 253–68.

Markusen, Ann, Peter Hall and Amy Glasmeier (1986), *High Tech America: The What, How, Where and Why of the Sunrise Industries*, Boston, MA and London: Allen & Unwin.

Markusen, Ann and Greg Schrock (2006), 'The artistic dividend: urban artistic specialization and economic development implications', *Urban Studies*, **43** (10): 1661–86.

Markusen, Ann and Greg Schrock (2008a), *Leveraging Investments in Creativity* (LINC) *Artist Data User Guide*, Minneapolis, MN: Project on Regional and Industrial Economics, April.

Markusen, Ann and Greg Schrock (2008b), '*The distinctive city*', unpublished manuscript.

Markusen, Ann, Greg Wassall, Doug DeNatale and Randy Cohen (2008), 'Defining the creative economy: industry and occupational approaches', *Economic Development Quarterly*, **22** (1): 24–45.

Massey, Doreen (1984), *Spatial Divisions of Labor: Social Structures and the Geography of Production*, New York: Methuen.

Power, Dominic (2002), '"Cultural industries" in Sweden: an assessment of their place in the Swedish economy', *Economic Geography*, **78** (2): 103–27.

Pratt, Andy (1997), 'The cultural industries production system: a case study of employment change in Britain, 1984–91', *Environmental and Planning A*, **29**: 1953–74.

Pratt, Andy (2004), 'Mapping the cultural industries: regionalization; the example of South East England', In Dominic Power and Allen Scott (eds), *Cultural Industries and the Production of Culture*, New York: Routledge, pp. 19–36.

Renski, Henry, Jun Koo and Edward Feser (2007), 'Differences in labor versus value chain industry clusters: an empirical investigation', *Growth and Change*, **38** (3): 364–95.

Ruggles, S., M. Sobek, T. Alexander, C.A. Fitch, R. Goeken, P.K. Hall, M. King and C. Ronnander (2004), Integrated Public Use Microdata Series: Version 3.0, Minnesota Population Center, University of Minnesota, MN.

Saxenian, Annalee (1994), *Regional Advantage: Culture and Competition in Silicon Valley and Route 128*, Cambridge, MA: Harvard University Press.

Scott, Allen (2005), *On Hollywood: The Place, The Industry*, Princeton, NJ: Princeton University Press.

Thompson, Wilbur and Philip Thompson (1985), 'From industries to occupations: rethinking local economic development', *Economic Development Commentary*, **9**: 12–18.

Thompson, Wilbur and Philip Thompson (1987), 'National industries and local occupational strengths: the cross-hairs of targeting', *Urban Studies*, **24**: 547–60.

Wassall, Gregory and Neil Alper (1985), 'Occupational characteristics of artists: a statistical analysis', *Journal of Cultural Economics*, **9** (1): 13–34.

7   Museums in the neighborhood: the local economic impact of museums
Stephen Sheppard

7.1   INTRODUCTION*

While there is no official census of museums in the United States, the American Association of Museums estimates that there are approximately 17,500 museums[1] across the country. To put this in perspective, the number of museums in the United States is almost exactly equal to the number (17,619) of public high schools[2] (public schools that offer a curriculum for the 12th grade) in the country.

Like public high schools, museums serve a variety of missions that include education as a central component. Like public high schools, museums are extremely diverse, ranging from small local institutions that serve a neighborhood or a modest group of patrons numbering a few hundred, to large, well-funded organizations that serve hundreds of thousands of people each year. Like public high schools, there are museums that emphasize the arts, museums that emphasize science and technology, as well as many general-interest museums.

It is true that far fewer museums are funded by the local public sector. It is also true that restricting attention to the set of persons who attend each type of institution, the average time spent per year within the institution is much greater for schools than for museums so that the impact on each participating individual is likely to be greater for schools. On the other hand, museums are called upon to complement schools and play an increasing role in the provision of a specialized curriculum, particularly in arts education where many smaller communities may rely heavily on local museums.

Despite the arguably important role in providing educational services, and generally affecting the quality of life in communities, museums have received very little attention from economists. The EconLit bibliographic database yields 58,046 references to research on schools, with 425 references to schools and houses and 145 that address in some way the impact of schools on house prices. In this sense, economists seem intent on developing a better understanding of the impacts of schools on the communities and neighborhoods where they operate. The situation is much different for museums. EconLit identifies only 550 references to research on museums, and only 11 of these have anything to do with housing. The number of research papers that address museums and house prices is zero. It seems reasonable to say that economists have developed (or at least published) almost nothing that directly evaluates or measures the impact of museums on the attractiveness of the neighborhoods where they are located.

This is surprising since many authors appear to assume that analysis of the impact of museums (or the arts, more generally) on house prices is something that, while difficult or even problematic, occurs with some frequency. Thus Frey (1997) notes that the values attributed to a cultural object can also be derived from the higher rents, house and land prices that people are prepared to pay. Similarly (though more critically) McCarthy et al. (2004) assert that methods used in studies include hedonic approaches that estimate how proximity to the arts affects housing values (an indicator of the desirability of the arts to the population). While some of these analyses might be prepared and circulate as private consultants' reports, there appear to be none (or very few) that have appeared in the published economics literature. While the works referred to discuss analysis of impacts on house prices as a technique for evaluating the impacts of culture, they do not cite actual studies that carry this out.

One of the very few published papers to attempt an empirical examination of the impact of some aspect of culture on house prices is Florida and Mellander (2010). This study does not use the presence or expansion of a specific cultural amenity, but rather considers the ability of the 'Bohemian-Gay index' to explain cross-sectional variation in overall house prices for 331 US metropolitan regions in 2000. While the study is commendable for at least undertaking the analysis (rather than assuming that it *could* be done), there are a variety of problems with the evidence presented. The study focuses upon the relative explanatory power of the index without considering the potential endogeneity between the house prices and the value of the index. A more satisfactory approach would be to focus on a specific cultural amenity, and to estimate whether an increase in the availability of that amenity is associated with an increase in house prices. Even such an analysis of differences would not fully address the endogeneity problem, but it would present a more convincing evaluation of the relationship between culture and house prices.

There are several studies that pursue an alternative type of hedonic analysis looking at the impacts of culture, museums, libraries, etc. on wages. In this approach, the cultural organization is conceived of as making the community more attractive so that the local supply of labor is large and workers accept a reduction in wages in order to remain living in the community. Thus Clark and Kahn (1988) estimate the impact of cultural amenities on wages and find evidence that museums, along with several other cultural amenities, are associated with lower wages. In contrast, however, Schmidt and Courant (2006) find that neither museums nor several other measures of cultural activity have a significant impact on wages.

There are two problems with looking for the localized impact of museums through analysis of wage determination in labor markets. The first is that for all but the largest museums, the impact of the institution on the labor market may be modest and difficult to detect. While a museum may have a significant impact on a neighborhood or portion of a city, attracting residents to the neighborhood, providing educational services, helping to build social capital for the groups who reside in that part of the community, it may not affect a large enough portion of the total labor force to perturb wages in a way that can be reliably detected in noisy data.

The second problem with this approach is that it may not be what we would expect to observe given our theoretical understanding of the impacts of quality of life or non-market goods and services and how they affect property and labor markets. Consider the following observations motivated by the approach of Rosen (1979) and Roback (1982) and applied by many analysts since. Initially in a given community the households can all achieve a welfare level of V. There are several price vectors consistent with this welfare level. Higher rents or property values must in general be offset by higher wages.

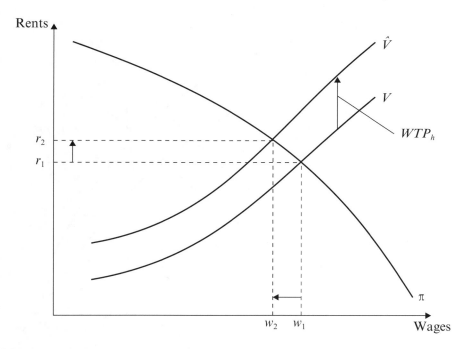

Figure 7.1   Museum impacts on households

Similarly, firms in the community must realize a given rate of profit in equilibrium (zero profit in competitive equilibrium, for example). Again several prices are consistent with this. Higher costs for space, or rents, must be compensated for by lower costs for labor, or wages. For the community there is only a single pair of prices (w,r) that is consistent with both equilibrium for households and equilibrium for firms.

Now suppose that a museum opens that provides non-market services for the households. This might be true if the museum is available free of charge, but even if the museum charges an admission fee its operation as a not-for-profit enterprise and its provision of educational opportunities for children might generate a variety of public benefits that increase the welfare of households in the neighborhood of the museum. This shifts the household welfare line up to $\hat{V}$ as indicated in Figure 7.1, with the vertical shift indicating the additional amount each household is willing to pay because of the new (or expanded) museum. This results in a new equilibrium (w_2, r_2) with higher land values and lower wage rates. While economists have perhaps been negligent in their analysis of the impact on property values, at least this suggests that the impact on wage rates could possibly be a reasonable alternative approach. There is a difficulty with this argument, however. It assumes that the museum has no impact on firm profitability. Many economists have argued, however, that such impacts are indeed possible. For example, Florida (2002) argues that culturally rich cities and neighborhoods attract creative workers that help ensure the success of enterprises located there. Lucas (1988) argues and Rauch (1993) estimates that an increase in the education level of an urban area increases the marginal productivity of all factors of production, not only labor. If museums play a

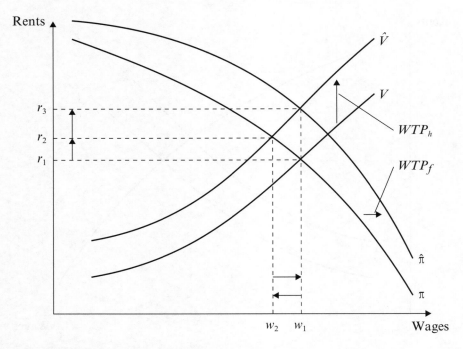

Figure 7.2   Museum impacts on households and firms

role in providing educational services to residents then it is not difficult to imagine that a strong museum sector could have an impact on firm profitability.

A new or expanded museum might then generate an impact as illustrated in Figure 7.2. Here the museum generates two effects. As before, it provides an external public benefit to households who are now willing to pay higher rents and accept lower wages in order to reside in what they see as a more attractive neighborhood. Furthermore, firms are now able (and willing) to pay higher wages, higher property rents, or both and still achieve the constant profit level π. This puts upward pressure on both property values and wages. As a result, if the museum has an impact on both firm profitability (through producing or attracting a more skilled labor force) and on household welfare (by providing entertainment, social capital, and education) then there is an unambiguous impact on property values (they increase) but an ambiguous impact on wage rates. They may either increase or decrease depending on elasticity of substitution in consumption between housing and leisure, in production between labor and space, and the impacts on household utility and firm profitability of the new or expanded museum. This indicates that if economists want to evaluate the neighborhood impact of museums (and if they accept the Rosen–Roback framework as reasonable) then the preferred approach would be via analysis of the property market.

In this chapter, we undertake such an analysis by focusing on four communities where new museums have been established or an existing museum was expanded significantly. For each city we collect data on property transactions including prices and structure characteristics including location, spanning a time period that includes transactions before and after the museum opened or expanded. Using these data we endeavor to answer the question: do museums appear to have a beneficial impact on their neighborhood? If so, how large is this impact, and how far does it extend? Finally, we consider some implications of our findings for the financial sustainability of museums and the role that such institutions might play as part of a set of policies intended to promote community development.

The next section provides brief descriptions of the four communities and museums that are the focus of this chapter. Section 7.3 describes the data collected and presents some simple descriptive statistics. Section 7.4 presents and discusses the estimates, and Section 7.5 concludes.

7.2 CASE STUDY COMMUNITIES

We have chosen four cities that present a range of population sizes and some variation in economic circumstances, although each city has been subject to a process of industrial decline and loss of employment in manufacturing that had played the central role in their local economies. This process of decline has proceeded at differing speeds in each city over the past 25 to 75 years.

7.2.1 Kenosha, Wisconsin

Kenosha is located in the southeastern corner of Wisconsin and while it is a free-standing city it is part of the larger Chicago CMSA (consolidated metropolitan statisitical area). It is 50 miles from Chicago and had an estimated 2006 population of 96,240. Kenosha was birthplace, in 1916, of Nash motors and the former location of large manufacturing facilities for Nash and its eventual successor, American Motors. These facilities were subsequently absorbed and operated by Renault for a brief period before being purchased by Chrysler in 1987, closed and demolished in 1989. Kenosha's largest employer now is Abbot Laboratories. The lakefront site of the old automobile assembly plants has been extensively redeveloped with housing, a park and walking paths, and is the location of the new Kenosha Public Museum, which opened in 2000. While our analysis focuses on the impacts of this opening, further developments are taking place. A new Civil War Museum was completed and fully opened in 2008.

7.2.2 Toledo, Ohio

Located at the western edge of Lake Erie and bordering Michigan on the north, Toledo is the fourth-largest city in Ohio, and has a current population of just over 700,000 persons in the metro area. Automobile manufacturing and automobile parts manufacturing have been important industries in Toledo. The Willys-Overland Corporation was headquartered in Toledo until 1953. The Jeep vehicles that originated with Willys were made in Toledo beginning in 1941 and continue to be manufactured in the city. Glass and glass product manufacturing have also been an important component of the local economy and firms such as Owens-Corning, Owens-Illinois and Libbey Glass all had their origins in Toledo. The largest employer now is the University of Toledo. The Toledo Museum of Art was founded by Edward Libbey (founder of Libbey Glass) in 1901 and moved to its present location in 1912. In part because of its historical connection to the Libbey family, the museum has an extensive collection of glass objects. A major capital campaign raised funds for the design and construction of a new glass pavilion that opened across the street from the existing museum to display the glass collection, provide classes and demonstrations of art glass production and to present new works of art in glass. The new glass pavilion opened in 2006.

7.2.3   Beacon, New York

Beacon is located on the east bank of the Hudson River about 60 miles north of Manhattan and 30 miles south of Poughkeepsie. It is across the river from Newburgh, New York. The 2000 census identified the population of Beacon as 13,808 and current estimates suggest a population in 2008 of about 16,000. The city was an important manufacturing center in the colonial period. In the nineteenth century it was a major center of hat-making in the US. Despite river, rail, and interstate highway transport access, Beacon experienced industrial decline and closures throughout the last three decades of the twentieth century, so that by the late 1990s nearly 80 percent of Beacon's factory and commercial spaces were vacant.

The Dia Art Foundation is based in New York City. It was founded in 1974 and has one of the world's premier collections of art from the 1960s and 1970s. Dia purchased a former factory owned by Nabisco in Beacon, and renovated the space as a museum to present significant portions of the Foundation's collection. The Dia:Beacon Riggio Galleries museum opened in 2003.

7.2.4   North Adams, Massachusetts

North Adams is located near the northwest corner of Massachusetts about 90 miles from Boston. First settled in the mid-eighteenth century, it was officially incorporated in 1878 as it grew in response to the opening of the Hoosac Tunnel that provided rail travel under the Hoosac range linking the Hudson River watershed in western Massachusetts with the Connecticut River watershed of central Massachusetts as well as the greater Boston area. The Hoosac tunnel was the second-longest transportation tunnel in the world when it was completed, and remains the longest rail or auto tunnel in the eastern United States. The improved transportation made North Adams an important manufacturing and mill town in the late nineteenth and early twentieth centuries. The population of North Adams peaked at nearly 30,000 in 1900 and declined every decade of the twentieth century. The 2000 population was 14,681 and is estimated to be approximately 15,000 in 2008.

North Adams was home to a diverse range of industries including shoe manufacture, iron works, manufacture of mill machinery, and cloth printing. The Arnold Print Works prospered in North Adams, producing printed cloth for the Union Army during the civil war and continuing until it failed during the 1930s. In 1942 the site was purchased by Sprague Electric, which operated at the site manufacturing electronic components and high-tech equipment for the military and space program as well as commercial customers. At its peak Sprague employed over 4,000, but the firm lost business, faced protracted labor disputes, and eventually closed in 1985.

After several years of continued decline in North Adams, a group of Williams College faculty and the director of the Williams College Museum of Art expressed interest in obtaining closed factory space in North Adams to be used for the display of large-scale art works. At the same time, a small number of working artists began to acquire warehouse space in the city to use for studio and live–work space. The city government of North Adams eventually joined with these groups to seek state funding for environmental site remediation and construction of a museum of contemporary art to be located in the campus of buildings that had previously been the Arnold Print Works and Sprague Electric Company. Through a combination of private fundraising and provision of $25 million of support from the state government, the Massachusetts Museum of Contemporary Art (MASS MoCA) was opened in May 1999. The museum is one of the largest spaces for display of contemporary art in the world. It maintains no permanent collection but instead commissions new works from artists. The works are displayed for periods ranging from six months to two years and then become the property of the artists. The museum attracts approximately 110,000 visitors per year to North Adams.

7.3   DATA

The central data on individual house sales including price, date of sale, address or geographical location, and other structure and lot characteristics were obtained directly from local property tax assessors' offices. The advantage of using these data (over alternative sources such as Multiple Listing Service (MLS) data collected by real estate agents or data sources such as the American Housing Survey: AHS) is that they contain the property address so that the exact location can be determined, they include all property transactions, and they are available at modest or zero cost under open public records laws. Note that while in some communities the assessors' data do not include all recorded deed transactions, the communities we study do include all transactions. We do not use assessors' estimates of structure value but instead use the agreed transaction price, and we use only those transactions that are coded as or appear to be arm's-length transactions (excluding, for example, transactions whose price is $1 or $100).

There are some disadvantages to using these data. Unlike AHS data, we do not have exactly the same set of structure and lot characteristics in each community. There is less uniformity across assessors' offices concerning the accuracy of data entry, correction of errors, or incorporation of new information when structures are modified or new features added. Unlike MLS data we have no information about the time on the market or other indicators of the nature of the bargaining process from which the observed transaction price has emerged. There is less uniformity in coding the data concerning such features as condition of structure or style or type of structure so that it is not clear how comparable a particular quality rating is in each city or whether each office would agree on the style label to apply to a home. For the most important features such as price, date of sale, location, lotsize, total living area, and age of structure, however, there is general agreement on measurement and the comprehensive coverage of the data we have obtained seems more important than the difficulties associated with use of the information.

Tables 7.1 and 7.2 present descriptive statistics for the samples used for estimation of impacts in Toledo, Kenosha, Beacon, and North Adams. For the most part these are

Table 7.1 Descriptive statistics for Toledo and Kenosha

	Toledo				Kenosha			
	μ	σ	Min	Max	μ	σ	Min	Max
Real price	103,590	102,336	7,277	7,210,962	90,307	43,221	7,388	977,403
Sq ft living area	1,545.03	738.01	0	12,874	1,422.09	519.14	324	10,661
Rooms/bedrooms	6.31	1.78	0	23	3.06	0.86	1	9
Lotsize	11,280.84	37,137.96	0	3,288,562	0.17	0.10	0.02	3.23
Distance to CBD	8,426.99	4,282.65	527.68	17,999.34	3.55	1.90	0.18	11.13
Real price of gasoline	0.87	0.14	0.68	1.49	0.94	0.20	0.68	1.49
Sold after museum	0.04	0.19	0	1	0.47	0.50	0	1
Distance to museum (pre)	7,231.90	4,055.14	0	19,842.24	2.15	2.41	0	11.80
Distance to museum (post)	273.30	1,544.32	0	19,507.75	1.90	2.47	0	10.93
Distance to museum	7,505.20	3,856.96	197.23	19,842.24	4.05	1.94	0.45	11.80
Age at sale	54.73	30.52	1	182	46.70	30.29	1	170
Year built	1916.06	239.43	0	2005	1952.87	29.92	1837	2006
Baths	1.50	0.70	0	9	1.57	0.62	0	11
Pct Black	13.43	21.07	0.06	95.94				
Pct Hispanic	4.53	4.12	0.70	37.26				
Fireplaces								
Observations	137,657				18,458			
Other indicator variables	Four classes of height of structure				Three classes of height of structure			
	Seven classes of type of exterior wall covering				Sixteen classes of house style			
	Four classes of type of garage				Five classes of proximity to lake shore			
	Eight classes of land use type				Four classes of land use			
	Five classes of quality of construction				Presence of central air conditioning			
					Absence of garage			

Table 7.2 Descriptive statistics for Beacon and North Adams

	Beacon				North Adams			
	μ	σ	Min	Max	μ	σ	Min	Max
Real price	1,092	548	124	6,926	61,120	48,904	6,525	1,344,847
Sq ft living area	1,600.51	671.71	528	5,644	1,915.72	932.88	532	6,891
Rooms/bedrooms	2.91	1.03	1	9	8.18	3.89	0	27
Lotsize	21,727.66	214,547.00	435.60	9,291,348.00	33,707.90	497,290.30	1,197.9	1.74E+07
Distance to CBD	2,136.09	1,565.87	21.40	5,764.58				
Real price of gasoline	0.84	0.10	0.68	1.02	0.82	0.07	0.68	1.11
Sold after museum	0.22	0.41	0	1	0.46	0.50	0	1
Distance to museum (pre)	682.82	626.55	1	1,960.91	290.60	379.64	1	1,536.02
Distance to museum (post)	196.52	450.16	1	1,959.93	227.18	345.82	1	1,647.27
Distance to museum	878.35	573.12	38.19	1,960.91	516.78	364.15	51.82	1,647.27
Age at sale	50.50	40.66	1	279	85.53	38.83	1	241
Year built	1950.61	40.88	1720	2004	1912.04	38.39	1760	2003
Baths	2.11	0.96	0	12	1.76	0.96	0	8
Pct Black								
Pct Hispanic								
Fireplaces					0.24	0.52	0	4
Observations		2,322				1,240		
Other indicator variables	Five classes of height of structure				Three classes of style for multi-family dwellings			
	Three classes of types of exterior wall covering				Six classes of condition of structure			
	Eleven classes of house style				Nine classes of type of heating in house			
	Nine classes of local government jurisdiction				Four classes of types of fuel used for heating			
	Three classes of types of fuel used for heating				Presence of central air conditioning			
	Located within Beacon school district							

self-explanatory but a few remarks are in order. Toledo and Kenosha are much larger cities than Beacon or North Adams, and the samples are correspondingly larger. This will have an impact on the precision with which impacts in each city can be measured, with smaller samples generally offering less precise estimates. It should also be noted that the larger cities have more staff in their assessors' offices, and this permits greater specialization in data cleanup and presentation. Toledo, for example, makes their entire database with GIS viewer available on DVD for a very modest cost.

All house prices are adjusted relative to the house price index available from the US Federal Housing Finance Agency (FHFA). Toledo has an index calculated for the metro area. There is an FHFA index for Kenosha County and Lake County used for Kenosha. Beacon is part of the Poughkeepsie–Newburgh metro area and the index for this area is used for Beacon. North Adams is part of the Pittsfield MSA (metropolitan statistical area) and the FHFA index for Pittsfield is used to adjust North Adams prices.

7.4   ESTIMATION

Our approach to estimating the hedonic model, including the impact of the opening or expansion of the museum, is similar in each city. For each city we estimate a hedonic model of the form:

$$\ln\left(\frac{P}{i}\right) = \beta_0 + \sum_i \beta_i \cdot \ln(x_i) + \sum_j \delta_j \cdot x_j + \beta_m \cdot \delta_{post} + \beta_{pre} \cdot \ln(d_{pre}) + \beta_{post} \cdot \ln(d_{post}) \quad (7.1)$$

(hedonic for other characteristics)   (determines the impact of the museum)

where:

P	=	sales price of the property
i	=	house price index for local housing market
β_0	=	constant
β_i	=	parameter for quantifiable characteristic
x_i	=	quantifiable charateristic
δ_j	=	parameter for dichotomous characteristic
x_j	=	dichotomous charateristic
β_m	=	impact of museum for properties adjacent to museum
δ_{post}	=	1 if sale occurs after museum built or expanded, 0 otherwise
β_{pre}	=	impact of distance from museum location prior to museum
d_{pre}	=	distance from museum if sale occurs before museum built, 1 otherwise
β_{post}	=	impact of distance from museum location after museum built and
d_{post}	=	distance from museum for sales after museum built, 1 otherwise.

The β and δ variables are all parameters to be estimated. The variables x_i measure the property characteristics that are quantifiable, such as total living area, number of rooms, and age. The variables x_j refer to dichotomous indicators of structure characteristics. The variable d_{pre} refers to the distance from the museum, with the actual distance set to 1

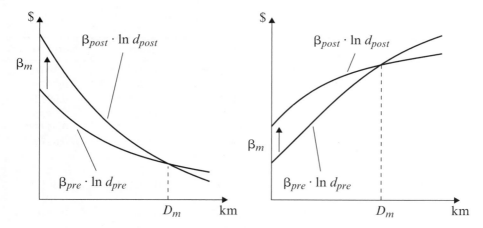

Figure 7.3   Estimating the impact of museums on neighborhoods

(the logarithm of which is zero) for properties that sold after the museum was opened. Similarly, the variable d_{post} is the actual distance from the museum for properties that sold after the museum opened, and 1 for those that sold before the opening.

The last three terms of equation (7.1) are of central importance in measuring the localized impact of museums in the neighborhood. Figure 7.3 illustrates. In both panels there are two lines, indicating the impact on house prices as we consider properties that are more distant from the location of the museum. In each case the line that is lower at distance zero is the relationship that holds before the museum opens, estimated by $\beta_{pre} \cdot \ln d_{pre}$ and the upper line represents the relationship that holds after the museum opens, estimated by $\beta_{post} \cdot \ln d_{post}$. The vertical distance between the lines at the vertical axis intercept is determined by the value of β_m, and represents the impact on house prices for properties that are adjacent to the museum location.

In the left panel we see a situation in which house values tend to decline as we move away from the location of the museum. In the figure this is true both before and after the museum opens, and could represent a situation where the neighborhood that will eventually be the location of the museum was relatively attractive by comparison with other locations in the city before the museum opens. Opening the museum makes it even more attractive.

In the right panel is illustrated an example where in general house prices increase for properties more distant from the museum location. Again, this is true both prior to and after the opening of the museum. This might be true when the museum is located in a neighborhood that is troubled in other ways and those disadvantages are not fully compensated by the presence of the museum.

In both panels the two curves intersect at distance D_m. This indicates the maximum extent of positive influence on house prices. It may well happen that the entire urban area is contained within the area that is positively affected. Alternatively, the distance D_m may identify a location within the urban area.

Table 7.3 presents the estimates for selected parameters of the hedonic price functions obtained using data from each of the four cities. The table does not report parameter

Table 7.3   Estimated parameters of hedonic price functions

Variable	Toledo	Kenosha	Beacon	North Adams
Total living area	0.6581***	0.5345***	0.3972***	0.3901***
	0.009	*0.015*	*0.040*	*0.077*
Rooms/bedrooms	−0.1444***	0.0084	0.1186***	−0.0922
	0.012	*0.012*	*0.032*	*0.093*
Lotsize	0.0719***	0.0140	0.1099***	0.0549**
	0.004	*0.009*	*0.017*	*0.023*
Distance to CBD	0.2236***	−0.0568**	0.0321	
	0.008	*0.027*	*0.017*	
Price of gasoline	1.0225***	0.1609***	0.2029**	0.3419*
	0.011	*0.014*	*0.081*	*0.182*
Museum change	0.3801***	0.2349***	0.5088***	0.2140
	0.111	*0.015*	*0.130*	*0.275*
Pre-museum distance	−0.0342***	0.3778***	0.0025	0.0896***
	0.008	*0.033*	*0.019*	*0.034*
Post-museum distance	−0.0721***	0.1819***	−0.0552**	0.0499
	0.014	*0.032*	*0.023*	*0.035*
Age	0.7465***	0.3498***	0.0750**	0.2336***
	0.004	*0.010*	*0.031*	*0.044*
Year built	44.9644***	22.7775***	6.8601***	10.8657***
	0.301	*0.747*	*1.611*	*1.656*
Baths	0.2841***	0.0839***	−0.0346	0.0174
	0.007	*0.010*	*0.029*	*0.058*
Extent of impact	22.7 km	3.3 km	6.7 km	0.72 km
Observations	134,501	17,818	2,301	1,232
R^2	0.602	0.452	0.529	0.336
Root MSE	0.529	0.314	0.355	0.494

Notes:
Standard errors printed in italics.
* Significant at 0.1, **Significant at 0.05; *** Significant at 0.01.

estimates for the various dichotomous indicators of structure characteristics. These vary somewhat from city to city and are not central to the argument and questions addressed here. The logarithmic structure of the estimated hedonic implies that for all variables except the 'museum change' variable (β_m), the estimated parameters can be interpreted as elasticities of real house price with respect to the characteristic. The museum change variable can be interpreted as the percentage change in house price for a structure located adjacent to the new or expanded museum that is attributable to the museum's opening.

With reference to Figure 7.3, Toledo fits the model of the image in the left-hand panel, Kenosha and North Adams are similar to the situation illustrated in the right-hand panel, and Beacon is intermediate with house values increasing with distance from the museum before the museum is built and decreasing afterwards.

Most of the estimated parameters are of the expected signs. The museum change effect is not statistically significant in North Adams. This may be due to the noisy conditions in the local housing market, the small sample size, or simply because the museum has had less impact on properties in the city. Anecdotal evidence, consisting of the high level of redevelopment in the area near the museum, suggests otherwise. This remains an area for further study.

One thing we can say is that it is in fact possible to estimate the impact on property values that appears to be associated with the opening or expansion of a museum. For properties nearest the museum, values appear to increase between 20 and 50 percent. This effect tapers off as we move away from the museum.

These estimated impacts are consistent with the predictions of the Rosen–Roback framework discussed above. Museums in the neighborhood are important sources of public benefits. This improvement in the quality of life generates a move to a new equilibrium in which property values are increased. This may be due both to the benefits realized by households, and to benefits realized by firms through availability of a more productive, educated, or creative workforce.

7.5   IMPLICATIONS AND CONCLUSION

The first implication of this analysis is that museums do appear to be having a positive impact on the quality of life in neighborhoods. This is the most reasonable interpretation of the associated increase in property values. This observation may, in turn, be raised by museums as an argument for public support of the institution. If they are generating these rents for the community, it seems only reasonable to facilitate their capture of a portion of the rents in order that they be sustained and made economically viable.

There are a variety of mechanisms that might be used to achieve this. If property tax structures permit, an estimate of the increase in value of properties could be incorporated into tax assessments and a portion of the gain taxed away in support of the museum. The few tax-supported museums in the US (such as the St. Louis Art Museum) could be viewed in this way. Even in situations where property taxes cannot be used in this way, an estimate of the gain could be used either as an argument made privately to the homeowners to solicit donations or to the local government to make revenues available from some other source.

Finally, it must be acknowledged that while economists might view these results with interest, many museums will view them with mixed feelings at best and alarm at worst. The interpretation will be that as generators of higher property values, they themselves are partly to blame for what they see as gentrification of their neighborhoods.

What can be noted from the analysis presented above is that museums are clearly producing something valuable for their neighborhoods. This is not a problem, it is desirable. Whenever something valuable is produced, there will be competitive processes that arise between consumers who seek access to it. The challenge is to design mechanisms that help make equitable sharing of these benefits more certain. This may involve making provisions for affordable housing in the neighborhoods, or encouraging museums to pursue other types of outreach to less accessible neighborhoods. The creation of the valuable improvement in the quality of life is desirable. The economic and political challenge is to share the benefits.

NOTES

*   Support from the Institute of Museum and Library Services and the Ford Foundation is gratefully acknowledged. Errors and omissions are the responsibility of the author.
1.   To qualify as a museum, the organization must maintain and present a group of objects, must employ some person in a curatorial role, and must be open to the public at least 120 days per year.
2.   National Center for Educational Statistics, Core of Common Data.

REFERENCES

Clark, D.E. and Kahn, J.R. (1988), 'The social benefits of urban cultural amenities', *Journal of Regional Science*, **28** (3), 363–77.

Florida, R. (2002), *The Rise of the Creative Class*, New York: Basic Books.

Florida, R. and Mellander, C. (2010), 'There goes the metro: how and why bohemians, artists and gays affect regional housing values', *Journal of Economic Geography*, **10** (2), 167–88.

Frey, B. (1997), 'Evaluating cultural property', *International Journal of Cultural Property*, **6**, 231–46.

Lucas, Robert E. (1988), 'On the mechanics of economic development', *Journal of Monetary Economics*, **22** (1), 3–42.

McCarthy, K.F., Ondaatje, E.H., Zakaras, L. and Brooks, A. (2004), *Gifts of the Muse: Reframing the Debate About the Benefits of the Arts*, Santa Monica, CA: Rand Corporation.

Rauch, J.E. (1993), 'Productivity gains from geographic concentration of human capital: evidence from the cities', *Journal of Urban Economics*, **34** (3), 380–400.

Roback, J. (1982), 'Wages, rents, and the quality of life', *Journal of Political Economy*, **90** (6), 1257–78.

Rosen, S. (1979), 'Wages-based indexes of urban quality of life', in P. Mieszkowski and M. Straszheim (eds), *Current Issues in Urban Economics*, Baltimore, MD: Johns Hopkins University Press, pp. 74–104.

Schmidt, L. and Courant, P.N. (2006), 'Sometimes close is good enough: the value of nearby environmental amenities', *Journal of Regional Science*, **46** (5), 931–51.

PART III

HIGH-TECHNOLOGY SECTORS

8 Spinoff regions: entrepreneurial emergence and regional development in second-tier high-technology regions – observations from the Oregon and Idaho electronics sectors
Heike Mayer

8.1 INTRODUCTION

There has been a great bias in economic geography and industry studies toward studying pioneering high-tech regions such as Silicon Valley. As a result, smaller regions that have managed to establish entrepreneurial and innovative high-tech clusters have often been overlooked. Yet, these so-called 'second-tier' high-tech regions have also been successful in growing and fostering concentrations of specialized high-tech firms (Mayer, 2009, 2011). Moreover, these regions might be able to shed light on one of the most important questions in economic geography and industry studies: how do clusters of knowledge-based industries emerge? Second-tier high-tech regions might be ideal cases to examine this question. Unlike Silicon Valley, they do not have certain prerequisites of high-tech growth such as a world-class research university and large amounts of venture capital. Instead, these high-tech regions have bootstrapped their economies through extensive spinoff processes. In this chapter, I argue that it is exactly these spinoff processes that can help us understand the emergence of second-tier high-tech regions and more specifically clusters in general.

A focus on spinoff regions will help us address a lack of understanding about cluster formation and the processes by which spatial concentrations of knowledge-based industries come into existence. In recent years, scholars have started to examine the genesis of clusters and they are paying particular attention to the role of entrepreneurship (Braunerhjelm and Feldmann, 2006). Economic geographers and industry studies scholars are starting to develop concepts and theories about the genesis and formation of clusters.

This chapter presents case studies of two second-tier high-tech regions in the United States. I illustrate how the high-tech economies of Portland (Oregon) and Boise (Idaho) evolved in the post-war period. Portland and Boise represent so-called 'spinoff regions' and the case studies highlight how a few major high-tech firms helped catalyze an entrepreneurial spinoff process that resulted in the formation of dynamic cluster economies. I shall advance four premises. The first is that second-tier high-technology regions have emerged in the shadow of pioneer regions such as Silicon Valley. Even though they are smaller in size, and often lack world-class universities or large amounts of venture capital, second-tier high-tech regions need to be taken seriously. They have become part of a global economy and represent 'nodes' of specialized economic activity. The second premise refers to the role of firms. Firms and not universities drive the growth of second-tier high-technology economies. Firms can play the role of 'surrogate universities' if they have certain characteristics (Mayer, 2005b). They contribute to regional entrepreneurship and innovation. This leads to the third premise which describes firms as heterogeneous regional actors. The fourth premise is that the nature and extent of firm-building activities determines the entrepreneurial dynamics of a second-tier high-tech region. In other words, the types of firms, their evolution, their interactions with other economic actors, and so on determine the ways in which these firms act as incubators for spinoffs.

Second-tier high-tech regions manage to grow and evolve primarily through spinoff processes and we can also call them 'spinoff regions'. A spinoff region can be defined as an area of dynamic new firm formation, which in turn leads to cluster development. Spinoff regions grow a specialized set of industries through entrepreneurial activities. It is through the spinoff process that skills, capabilities, and capacities are transferred but also converted by entrepreneurial individuals who carry routines and institutions learned in their previous experiences. Martin (2010) called these processes 'layering and conversion' and argues that regional economic development paths are created and changed through entrepreneurship. Spinoff regions develop agglomeration economies only after they have rooted a critical mass of entrepreneurial firms.

The remainder of this chapter proceeds as follows. First, in an effort to explain cluster emergence I juxtapose two competing explanations (Section 8.2). I argue that regional emergence has to be explained through the analysis of spinoff activities. I then focus on the influence of firm building on entrepreneurship (Section 8.3). To ground these theoretical considerations, I then present two case studies of second-tier high-tech regions that emerged due to spinoff processes (Section 8.4). In Section 8.5, I reflect on the role of entrepreneurship as a bridging concept between economic geography and industry studies. Section 8.6 concludes.

8.2   CLUSTER EMERGENCE: TWO COMPETING EXPLANATIONS

In general, there are two competing explanations as to how high-tech regions evolve. On the one hand, many scholars argue that clusters grow because of agglomeration economies. As such, agglomeration fosters entrepreneurship. On the other hand, other scholars perceive agglomerations to grow because of spinoff processes, whereby entrepreneurship fosters agglomerations.

Regarding the first approach, and directly linking clusters to entrepreneurship, Porter argues that 'new business ideas will tend to bubble up within clusters because of the concentration of firms, ideas, skills, technology, and needs there. Once an idea is perceived, the barriers to entry and growth are lower at cluster locations' (Porter, 2000, p. 269). This perspective assumes that agglomeration economies provide cost advantages that reside outside the firm and thus yield efficiencies stemming from labor market pooling, knowledge spillovers, networks, physical proximity to other firms such as suppliers and customers, and so on. These agglomeration economies are seen to give rise to entrepreneurial opportunities. The perspective, however, implies that a certain level of economic activity has to be present for a cluster to emerge. Yet, it is unclear how agglomeration economies evolve in the first place and what factors spur their emergence. Indeed, many scholars have criticized this perspective for being rather imprecise, especially regarding the dynamic aspects of cluster formation and growth (Martin and Sunley, 2003; Lorenzen, 2005).

Yet, this perspective is prominent in the literature, particularly in studies of flexibly specialized industrial districts and in explanations of how high-tech regions such as Silicon Valley emerge. While many of the studies in this tradition are not very specific about the origins of these districts, they seem to assume that the flexibly specialized district makes it easier for new firms to start. Firms are able to enter the district's firm networks due to lower entry barriers, and spinoffs are therefore more prominent in those regions that exhibit these types of flexibly specialized organization patterns. In this view, new firms originate from a specific regional context that pre-exists before entrepreneurial processes start to take root. Clusters foster entrepreneurial processes because new firms are able to do business with other cluster firms, role models are present, an existing entrepreneurial culture lowers the perceived risks associated with starting a firm, and clusters provide the necessary specialized support infrastructure from which startup firms can benefit. The most prominent assessment of a high-tech region from this perspective is the work that has been done on Silicon Valley. Saxenian (1985, 1994a, 1994b), for example, argues that the entrepreneurial success of Silicon Valley (compared with Boston's Route 128) is due to the region's ability to facilitate experimentation, risk taking, learning, and networking. Others echo these notions and point to a set of constituents of the Silicon Valley ecosystem that enabled entrepreneurial development such as the presence of universities and research institutes, venture capital, a support infrastructure, an entrepreneurial spirit, lead users, and a talent pool (Bahrami and Evans, 1995; Smilor et al., 2007).

Trying to explain the emergence of clusters from the perspective of agglomeration economies is limiting not only because of the lack of precision in trying to assess what factors and dynamics have triggered the development of clusters but also – and more importantly – because the perspective does not incorporate an explanation why regions that do not possess agglomeration economies in the first place do indeed develop clusters (or alternatively do not). The second-tier high-tech regions discussed in this chapter are a case in point; here, specialized high-tech clusters evolved despite the lack of agglomeration economies.

The competing explanation highlights the role of spinoff processes in the creation of agglomeration economies (Klepper, 2001b, 2009). In this view, existing firms or other types of organization are the source of entrepreneurship because they play the role of incubators. Employees exploit opportunities and create new ventures. The spinoff process is often path dependent (Martin and Sunley, 2006) reflecting local processes and dynamics such as those experienced and learned by the founder preceding his or her entry into entrepreneurship. Actors involved in spinoffs – parent firms, entrepreneurs – shape institutions, rules, and routines in the region through the spinoff process. Often, entrepreneurs engage in building the local cluster because they become investors themselves or they engage in networking and mentoring activities (Feldman et al., 2005). This engagement facilitates the formation of a cluster, but it does so after a critical mass of firms is established. This competing perspective seems to be clearer about cause and effect in the emergence of high-tech regions and allows analysts to avoid the notion of fuzzy concepts in the analysis of regional economies (Markusen, 1999).

The spinoff perspective is used to explain the evolution and spatial concentration of certain industries. It is argued that a new industry emerges because of the presence of certain firms that function as incubators for spinoffs. The nature of these incubating firms determines the performance and success of the spinoffs because founders inherit and exploit skills acquired at their previous employer (Klepper, 2001a). The previous employers are conceptualized as parent firms. Studies by Klepper et al. (Klepper and Sleeper, 2005; Klepper, 2001b, 2009) and Boschma et al. (Boschma and Weterings, 2005; Boschma and Wenting, 2007) present empirical evidence for the importance of spinoff processes in the evolution of industries. In short these studies have shown that industries evolve through spinoff processes and that founders transfer inherited institutions and routines to their new ventures. The nature of the parent firm is important because better-performing parents (that is, market leaders) beget better-performing spinoffs. Spinoffs tend to operate in related industries because their founders have gained experience in these industries through the parent firms. Survival of spinoffs is determined by the success of the inherited capacities. As a result, regions that are able to root emerging industries are those that have had more successful parent firms which in turn have had spinoffs that were able to survive competition.

This perspective has three shortcomings. First, the geographical perspective is underdeveloped. The studies focus on the role of spinoff processes in the evolution of industries and not necessarily on the evolution of regional clusters. Proponents of this perspective take on an implicit view of geography as they argue that the spinoff process is a local phenomenon. They contend that founders have location inertia and that the spinoff is typically established where the founders live and work (Stam, 2007). Second, the spinoff argument assumes that agglomeration economies do not influence the evolution of clusters and that agglomeration economies develop as a result of the spinoff process. It might be the case, however, that spinoff processes and agglomeration economies influence each other at different stages of the evolution of the cluster and the evolution of the spinoff. Third, even though the studies assume firm heterogeneity when they argue that the nature of the firms determines the fitness of the spinoffs, they do not pay sufficient attention to the nature of firm-building processes and how they may influence the evolution of an industry and a cluster. This chapter attempts to make a contribution to these three shortcomings.

8.3   LINKING FIRM BUILDING AND ENTREPRENEURSHIP

If we want to analyze the emergence of second-tier high-tech regions, we need to pay attention to the role of the firm and the nature of firm building. Economic geography and industry studies have been characterized by a relative absence of a theory of the firm (Maskell, 2001; Taylor and Oinas, 2006) and an even deeper theoretical gap exists for the role of the firm as it relates to its role in entrepreneurship (Taylor, 2006). We do not have a clear understanding about what types of firms encourage or inhibit the emergence of high-tech clusters through spinoff processes. Also missing is a good theoretical understanding about the role of the firm as an incubator of startups. Yet, as reviewed above, entrepreneurs play a critical role in the emergence and growth of clusters and it is important to understand where they come from and how their previous experiences shape cluster evolution. To develop a general understanding, I shall draw on an emerging literature in economic geography on the theory of the firm. I shall connect this literature with another emerging field, namely the ecology of entrepreneurship.

Maskell (2001) and Taylor (2006) review a set of theories of the firm that are relevant to entrepreneurship and regional development. The first theory is the resource-based theory, which was developed by Penrose in the late 1950s (Penrose, 1959). The theory focuses on the internal conditions, structures, and resources of the firm. In contrast to dominant spatial paradigms in economic geography such as industrial districts, industry clusters or new industrial spaces, the resource-based view of the firm embraces the notion of firm heterogeneity. Firms are different, especially in terms of their resource endowment. Firms can have excess resources that are not used internally but may be exploited by employees who would like to start firms. Here the resource-based view of the firm connects with the knowledge spillover theory of entrepreneurship (Audretsch and Lehmann, 2005). One strand of the resource-based theory sees people – employees – as the essential knowledge resources of the firm (Kogut and Zander, 2003). The second theory is the behavioral theory of the firm, which was developed by Cyert and March in the early 1960s (Cyert and March, 1963). This perspectives focuses on the decision-making process in the firm and the role of conflict, search, and learning. The firm's decision making involves different parties (that is, stockholders, employees, suppliers, customers, and so on). Decisions at a firm may influence startup activity (that is, the ways in which a firm interacts with startups and provides them with business opportunities, how decisions influence employees who might want to start a business, and so on). The third theory is the evolutionary theory of the firm, which was developed by Nelson and Winter in the early 1980s (Nelson and Winter, 1982). Like Penrose's view, this theory sees the firm as having competencies and resources. The way in which they implement these resources, however, changes depending on their environment. The theory focuses on three important elements of firm behavior and context: routines, search, and the selection environment. The three theories add to our understanding of the firm, but they fall short in terms of understanding the spatial implications of the ways in which the firm arranges and develops its resources, its decision-making process, and its evolution. Moreover, the theories do not incorporate an explanation of how existing firms spawn new companies or how startup firms evolve and what are the spatial implications of these entrepreneurial events. Taylor (2006) also laments the failure of the theories to incorporate entrepreneurship. They do, however, develop a good perspective of the firm-building process.

The theories of the firm allow us to understand the key characteristics of corporations. As mentioned earlier, firms play an important role as incubators of startups. Considering the firm–entrepreneur nexus, we need to outline a theory of entrepreneurship and connect it with ideas of firm building as they emerge from the theory of the firm. Here organizational ecology theories provide a useful perspective and we can focus on theories of the ecology of entrepreneurship (Carroll and Khessina, 2005). The field of organizational ecology studies the various populations of organizations and focuses on how they change over time. The field highlights the need to understand background conditions and how they determine organizational founding. Scholars of entrepreneurship have unfortunately mostly ignored this field (ibid.) and so have economic geographers. The ways in which firms are organized, how they are structured, their products, their business and innovation models, what kind of culture they develop, and so on shape regional development and, in particular, regional entrepreneurship (Glasmeier, 1988). We therefore need to pay attention to how these firm characteristics influence startup activity and how firm heterogeneity influences entrepreneurship, which has a direct impact on the spatial context.

Firm-building characteristics at established firms in a region influence entrepreneurship. As Cooper notes:

> [A]ny established firm is a potential incubator organization, employing and influencing potential entrepreneurs who may 'spin off' to establish their own firms. Regional entrepreneurship is closely related to the established firms or incubator organizations located in that same region. New firms are typically founded by entrepreneurs who are already employed in organizations in the same geographic area: (Cooper, 1971, p. 18)

Thus we need to pay attention to the internal dynamics of the incubator organization and how they influence entrepreneurship.

The behavioral theory of the firm assumes that the firm goes through a decision-making process that involves various partners. These decisions lead to corporate changes that can be positive or negative. Corporate change, in turn, facilitates entrepreneurship because it creates critical moments in time at which established firms show a higher rate of spinoff than at other times (Mitton, 1990; Klepper, 2001a; Neck et al., 2004). Corporate changes can be positive or negative. The growth of a firm constitutes a positive change, while layoffs or restructuring may constitute negative change. Positive corporate change influences entrepreneurship in more indirect ways: more successful firms attract more capable employees, which in turn can be more capable entrepreneurs (Klepper, 2001b). Growing firms learn and change their existing routines, better routines lead to better-performing firms, which in turn can lead to better-performing startups (Klepper, 2001a).

Cooper (1971) notes that if the incubator is in a rapidly growing industry, then it offers opportunities for small firms with good ideas. Growth may also encourage entrepreneurship because of its symbolic value such as the indication for a growing demand for the sector's products or services (Romanelli and Schoonhoven, 2001). Negative corporate changes facilitate entrepreneurship because they can act as push factors, meaning that employees may leave if changes at their firm impact them in negative ways. Corporations undergoing crises show higher rates of spinoff (Cooper, 1985). Crises such as mergers and acquisitions, a change in corporate leadership, or slow growth facilitate entrepreneurship because these impact employees (Brittain and Freeman, 1986). Slow growth, for example, blocks career mobility and this may encourage the entrepreneurially minded employee to leave. New corporate executives often bring new ideas which may not be popular with key employees. Mergers and acquisitions may lead to restructuring and layoffs, which can directly affect those interested in entrepreneurship. In combination these corporate changes facilitate disagreement among employees which is seen as a motivating entrepreneurial factor (Klepper and Thompson, 2005). Frustration can be a powerful entrepreneurial force (Cooper, 1971; Bhide, 2000; Benneworth, 2004).

Corporate linkages and connections to markets also impact the character and extent to which firms influence entrepreneurship in a region. If firms engage in supplier or subcontracting relationships with other firms within the region, then these linkages can provide important business opportunities for startups (Glasmeier, 1988), especially where large and dominant firms produce backward and forward linkages (Bresnahan et al., 2001). Spinoffs may start out with contracts with their parent firms or with customers and thus they do not have to go out and create new markets (Glasmeier, 1988). New firms can also become subcontractors that the lead firms in a region can draw on (Tappi, 2005). In addition, the position and connections of an incubator firm to its market is important. Firms that are leaders in their markets show a higher spinoff rate (Klepper, 2001b). They may provide entrepreneurs with important contacts and connections to potential partners, subcontractors, and suppliers. These firms can channel important knowledge and industry-specific information to the region and to the potential startups (Tappi, 2005). Spinoffs most often exploit similar niches and markets as their parents' (Cooper, 1971; Bhide, 2000; Klepper and Sleeper, 2005).

The type of product and business lines that incubator organization is involved in also influences startup activity. Firms with more-varied products and with products that show more variation have more startups. The spinoff rates are also higher in industries that are in the early stage of the product life cycle (Klepper, 1996). This may indicate the levels of experimentation within a firm and the degree to which the firm produces new ideas and knowledge that can then be exploited by potential entrepreneurs. Spinoffs are also more likely if a firm's products are based on attributes rather than price, and they are less likely for firms that specialize in standardized products and are heavily focused on production and execution (Glasmeier, 1988). Firms with more-varied products also show more startup activity because they have a richer learning environment than firms that are focused on a single product (Klepper, 2001a). Yet, if the firm's focus is too scattered and its energies are channeled in too many directions, then innovations may not be commercialized in-house because corporate leadership might miss them (Chesbrough, 2002; Mayer, 2005a).

Closely related to the types of products a firm produces is the nature of the production process. As mentioned earlier, high-tech regions are often described as flexibly specialized industrial districts. In those types of regions, firms gain a competitive advantage by subcontracting with other firms and specializing in niche areas within a larger production process. Flexibly specialized firms may have more startups because they may offer business opportunities for entrepreneurs. In contrast, firms characterized by vertical integration and/or mass production may show limited rates of startups because they have fewer connections to the local economy (Glasmeier, 1988).

Innovation is another key determinant of spinoff activity. Generally, more-innovative firms have more spinoffs (Klepper, 2001a). But the nature of the innovation process could influence entrepreneurship in different ways. Firms that focus mainly on product innovation may invest more in ideas and knowledge, which in turn may not all be exploited in-house. In contrast, firms focused on process innovations may not display such a great variation in products and show a greater focus on improving the production process. Radical innovation or competence destroying innovations at a firm may be exploited by startups because the incubator firm may not recognize the opportunity (Christensen, 1997).

Corporate policies and the culture at the firm influence startup activity. Firms that foster an environment in which employees can develop their skills, particularly managerial and sector-specific skills, may have more and better startups than those that do not have such a focus. Similarly, firms that encourage entrepreneurial behavior – either internally which is known as 'intrapreneurship' or externally through funding, and so on – may have more startups. Firms also need to develop highly skilled labor and have human resources in place that give employees a chance to hone not only their technical skills, but also their managerial and entrepreneurial skills. In the high-tech sector, for example, the 'engineer-manager' combines these two critically important skills (Bresnahan and Gambardella, 2004). Firms that allow employees to leave once a startup fails may also have more startups than other firms. The knowledge spillover theory of entrepreneurship predicts that entrepreneurial activity is higher in the context of high knowledge investments (Audretsch and Lehmann, 2005). Thus, if the incubator firm is focused on innovation, it invests in ideas and knowledge and fosters the talent of its employees. The organization structure of a firm can also influence entrepreneurship. If the incubator organization is organized as a series of small businesses, then it can contribute to more spinoffs (Cooper, 1971) because smaller firms provide more useful lessons to employees about how to manage a startup. Also, startups are social products (Staber, 2005) and they tend to emulate their parents. Thus the incubator organization leaves an important imprint on the firm (Aldrich and Martinez, 2001; West and Simard, 2006).

The knowledge-based theory of the firm emphasizes the importance of human capital, in other words the employees of a firm who can also be potential entrepreneurs. Firms with superior labor spawn more spinoffs (Klepper, 2001a) and those firms that are good at recruiting ambitious and capable people will function as fertile incubators (Cooper, 1971). Entrepreneurs tend to enter industries in which they have some kind of experience (Cooper, 1985; Sorenson and Audia, 2000). The firm has to have the right mix of labor and develop technical as well as managerial talent. High-level employees tend to become the founders of startups and the leading firms in an industry tend to have superior managerial employees and will therefore have more and better startups (Klepper, 2009). In addition, these types of employees tend to develop a broad background and contacts that may help with starting a company (Cooper, 1971). If the firm hosts only technical workers or technicians, it will have fewer startups and therefore will not function as an incubator in the region (Glasmeier, 1988).

The extent to which the firm's ideas and knowledge are embedded in physical or human capital influences the degree to which it can function as an incubator organization. Firms with richer, broader, and more transferrable assets tend to spawn more spinoffs than those with fixed assets (Klepper, 2001a). Klepper further argues that the easier it is to access a firm's know-how, the lower the barriers are for startups to commercialize ideas and knowledge. Firm know-how that is embodied in physical assets is harder to access. Thus, the types of assets a firm develops determine the rate of spinoff activity. Some of these are also summarized in the following quote:

> A firm with the following characteristics probably would be a very good incubator. It would be in a rapidly growing industry which offered opportunities for the well-managed small firm with good ideas; it would be a small firm or would be organized as a series of 'small businesses;' it would be good at recruiting ambitious, capable people; and it would periodically be afflicted with internal crises sufficient to frustrate many of its professional employees and lead them to believe that opportunities were being missed and that '*even I could manage the business better.*' This, incidentally, is a fairly good definition of many of the firms which have been established in the Palo Alto area in the past ten years: (Cooper, 1971, p. 25, original emphasis).

8.4 SECOND-TIER HIGH-TECH REGIONS

Portland and Boise can be considered as emerging second-tier high-tech regions. Their high-tech economies are smaller, yet the location quotients demonstrate high levels of industry concentration (see Table 8.1). Second-tier high-tech regions evolved despite the absence of a set of prerequisites often deemed necessary to grow a high-tech economy. They generally do not host a world-class research university such as Stanford or MIT, nor do they attract large amounts of venture capital. Second-tier high-tech regions specialize in certain subsectors of the high-tech economy and take advantage of the presence of leading high-tech firms. Often they got their initial start through the growth of one or two home-grown high-tech firms and/or through the attraction of branch facilities. In many cases, second-tier high-tech regions benefited from a shift of economic activity away from successful high-tech centers such as Silicon Valley. Silicon Valley firms started to look for alternative, often cheaper locations as they expanded in the 1960s and 1970s. At the time, the Valley already faced diseconomies such as high land costs, a lack of skilled labor, and a competitive market for talent. Firms responded by setting up branch plants in smaller metropolitan areas within easy reach of their headquarters. Portland and Boise, for example, can be reached from Silicon Valley by a 2-hour flight and Silicon Valley firms looked at these locations favorably. Glasmeier notes that the exodus of firms from regions such as Silicon Valley 'created a number of independent technical centres outside the core regions of high tech development' (Glasmeier, 1988, p. 290).

Emerging second-tier high-tech regions represent fast-growing medium-sized metropolitan areas that are often the 'envy of many other places' (Markusen et al., 1999, p. 3). Their emergence as high-tech locations is often the result of industrial restructuring and economic transformation. Specifically they have grown vibrant economies because they host leading firms that have become incubators for startup firms. As such they can also be called 'spinoff regions'.

Table 8.1   Comparing high-tech employment in pioneer and emerging high-tech regions

		High-tech employment		LQ for high-tech (2005)
		2005	1998	
Pioneer high-tech regions	Washington–Arlington–Alexandria, DC–VA–MD–WV	306,271	249,830	2.64
	Los Angeles–Long Beach–Santa Ana, CA	302,194	362,754	1.17
	Boston–Cambridge–Quincy, MA–NH	218,392	239,164	1.96
	San Jose–Sunnyvale–Santa Clara, CA	197,253	262,286	4.64
	Seattle–Tacoma–Bellevue, WA	162,713	95,154	2.31
Emerging high-tech regions	Portland–Vancouver–Beaverton, OR–WA	58,646	64,776	1.35
	Boise City–Nampa, ID	18,969	22,222	1.76

Source: County Business Patterns.

Table 8.2   Comparing Oregon and Idaho

	Portland–Vancouver–Beaverton, OR–WA	Boise City–Nampa, ID
High-tech economy		
High-tech employment (2005)	58,646	18,969
High-tech establishments (2005)	5,614	1,335
% high-tech employment share (2005)	7	9
% high-tech location quotient (2005)	1.35	1.76
R&D employment share (2005)	75.8	5.8
Entrepreneurship		
Average number of high-tech firm births (1998–2000)	24	23
% self–employment (2005)	14.6	18.7
VC deals (per 1,000, 2000–05)	6.2	1.0
SBIR grants (per 1000 people, 2000–05)	5.5	0.3

Note: VC = venture capital; SBIR = small business innovation research.

Sources: County Business Patterns; US Small Business Administration; Census.

Portland is the largest city in the state of Oregon, which sits between the states of California to the south and Washington to the north. In 2005, about 5,614 high-tech firms employed 58,646 people. The region is often referred to as the 'Silicon Forest', a label that was given to the region by a local entrepreneur in the 1980s. The region specializes in semiconductor manufacturing, computers, instruments, and software development. These sectors comprise the core of the Silicon Forest and the most prominent firms that are represented in the region are Intel, Tektronix, Electro Scientific Industries, and Hewlett-Packard.

Boise is the largest city in the state of Idaho, which is often considered part of the Pacific Northwest. Boise is part of Idaho's Treasure Valley, which is located in the southwest corner of the state. Over the last three decades, the metropolitan area has seen tremendous growth: from 1970 to today, the metropolitan area has grown fivefold from 115,000 to about 532,000 residents (Blanchard, 2005). The region's high-tech economy builds on two firms, Micron Technology and Hewlett-Packard, and many small firms.

Table 8.2 illustrates the connection between regional structure, firm building characteristics and entrepreneurship. As we see in the table, total high-tech employment in the region is 18,969 and there are about 1,335 high-tech firms. Hewlett-Packard employs about 3,350 people and Micron Technology employs about 10,000.

8.4.1   Case Study 1: Portland, Oregon

The first case study examines the evolution of Portland's Silicon Forest. The discussion will focus on the role of Tektronix and Intel, the two leading firms in the region, in spurring entrepreneurship. Portland's history of high-tech development goes back to the 1930s when the Forest Service Radio Laboratory (FSRL), located in Portland from 1933 to 1951, pioneered the development and use of lower power, lightweight, shortwave wireless radio sets (Gray, 1982). The innovation provided a way for forest rangers and firefighters to communicate in the rugged, forested terrains of the Pacific Northwest. The Lab contracted with local firms and was also the nucleus of the local chapter of the Institute of Radio Engineers (IRE), which functioned as a meeting place for local radio enthusiasts including one of the founders of Tektronix (Lee, 1986). These early developments established a culture of experimentation and innovation in high-tech and honed the skills of local entrepreneurs.

Tektronix was founded in 1946 and quickly grew into the world's leading manufacturer of oscilloscopes, test and measurement instruments that have become critical tools to view and measure electronic signals. Tektronix is widely credited with commercializing the first oscilloscope that incorporated a so-called 'triggered sweep circuit', an innovation that allowed users to pick up and display high-speed electronic events without delays or interruptions. Tektronix expanded from 109 employees in 1950 to 23,890 employees in 1980, of which about 15,000 were based in Portland. Besides Tektronix, the Silicon Forest hosted only a handful other high-tech firms and by 1976, Silicon Forest employment had grown to about 17,378. In 1976 Intel established its first branch plant facility outside of Silicon Valley in a suburban community in the Portland metropolitan region to manufacture semiconductor memory chips. In 1978 and in 1980, respectively, Wacker Siltronic, a German-based silicon wafer manufacturer, and Hewlett-Packard established manufacturing facilities in the Silicon Forest. The in-migration of high-tech firms – particularly Japanese-owned firms such as Epson, NEC, and Sharp – followed. The region's high-tech industry grew in the absence of a world-class research university. Instead, Tektronix and Intel functioned as so-called 'surrogate universities' because they attracted and developed talent, fostered innovation, and functioned as incubators of startup firms (Mayer, 2005b). The Silicon Forest got its initial start by fostering the growth of two leading companies, but it evolved and emerged as a second-tier high-tech region because of entrepreneurship and startup activity. By 2008, for example, 91 companies could trace their genealogical roots directly to Tektronix and at least an additional 53 companies can be considered among the second-, third- and fourth-generation startups linked to Tektronix. Intel's Portland branch plant has seen 64 startups that were founded by former Intel employees. These startups in turn have had 34 companies in subsequent generations. Why have these firms functioned as incubators? What attributes of Tektronix and Intel facilitated or hindered entrepreneurship?

Firm building and entrepreneurship in the Silicon Forest
Tektronix is a home-grown corporation that was founded by a team of entrepreneurs, who after they returned from military duty during the Second World War wanted to stay in the Portland area. Working with wartime surplus parts, Tektronix developed its first commercially successful oscilloscope which went into production in 1947. The instrument was an instant success especially among other high-tech firms, laboratories, and with the military: it was small and portable, enclosed in a well-designed metal case, and above all capable of making accurate measurements. Throughout the next decades Tektronix set standards for test and measurement instruments, and the firm became a world leader as developer and manufacturer of oscilloscopes. Net sales rose from $1.2 million in 1950 to more than $31 million in 1959 (Lee, 1986). To satisfy its own high standards of quality, Tektronix produced many critical components such

as the cathode ray tubes or transformers in-house. As a result, Tektronix evolved as a vertically integrated company with a diverse portfolio of in-house manufacturing, research and development (R&D) competencies. Commercial success also helped Tektronix to diversify into many different product areas such as color printers, and video and networking equipment. Market leadership allowed Tektronix to invest heavily in R&D. In addition, a culture that valued R&D and innovation encouraged the pursuit of new ideas. One former Tektronix employee recalls that often a conversation with company executives over a cup of coffee was sufficient to gain approval of a new project. Other employees remember Tektronix as a 'great finishing school'. The result of Tektronix's liberal policy toward research was the development of many different areas of competence and expertise as well as a reputation for cutting-edge work. In 1972, Tek Labs was established as an in-house R&D organization to conduct research in areas as diverse as integrated circuits, solid-state devices, cathode ray tubes, and software programming. The Labs represent a fine example of America's pioneering industrial research laboratories such as Bell Labs and Xerox PARC. In its heyday the Labs employed more than 400 researchers who were allowed to freely experiment very much like in an academic setting and contribute to the knowledge base of the emerging electronics industry.

Tektronix also had a reputation for attracting and developing a strong talent base. One Tektronix engineer emphasized that Tektronix served as a magnet for the best and the brightest:

> Most of the people that came to Tektronix in the early days were highly motivated to learn the latest technology. And we attracted some of the very best and brightest people from around the world in the early days because they wanted to be at you know the center of technology development at least the way they saw it at the time. So, people came here because they were already very good and they came here because they wanted to learn.

Tektronix provided an extensive in-house education program, which filled a critical gap in the Portland region. Inside Tektronix, an open, informal, and egalitarian culture was pivotal in promoting the transfer of knowledge between the firm's groups and divisions. As a result of diversification inside the firm, Tektronix senior-level engineers often had the opportunity to become managers of business units. These engineers were able to rotate into management positions and learn critical skills that they could later use in their entrepreneurial ventures.

Tektronix experienced significant corporate restructuring starting in the 1980s. In response to increasing market pressures from US and Japanese competitors, Tektronix began to restructure by divesting business units, laying off staff, and refocusing its product lines, and through the integration of R&D into product areas by eliminating Tek Labs. During this time, Tektronix went from more than 24,000 people employed worldwide in 1981 to about 4,500 employees worldwide and fewer than 2,800 employees in Portland in 2007. In addition, Tektronix's local ownership came to an end in 2007 when Danaher Corporation of Washington, DC acquired the Portland firm.

Restructuring efforts at Tektronix especially affected R&D efforts; Tek Labs were set up separately from other corporate units which contributed to its inability to turn innovation into products. One R&D manager recalls the closing of the Labs in the late 1990s:

At about 1995, the decision was made that our laboratories were too far removed from our product development. Good technology was being developed there but we were not getting it into products . . . we basically abandoned Tek Labs. And the people were moved into the businesses they were most closely aligned to.

Some technologies developed at Tek Labs spilled over to the region in the form of startup companies. TriQuint Semiconductors, a startup firm founded in 1985, commercialized research on gallium arsenide semiconductors and technological advances in color projectors were commercialized by the startup Planar Systems.

The restructuring at Tektronix unleashed entrepreneurial dynamics in the region. While Tektronix spawned 17 firms until the 1970s, more than 72 firms were spawned from the 1980s onward. These startup firms invigorated the Silicon Forest during a time when its major employer – Tektronix – downsized. Several factors seemed to have been responsible for this flurry in startup activity. In 1984 Tektronix formed the Tektronix Development Corporation (TDC) as an internal venture capital group. TDC was set up to invest in startups that commercialized technologies which Tektronix had failed to take advantage of. Corporate restructuring also created a great deal of employee frustration and dissatisfaction which led to engineers voting with their feet and leaving the company.

Tektronix created important spillovers that contributed to regional high-tech growth. Corporate growth until the 1980s attracted and created a pool of skilled and talented workers. Wide-ranging corporate education offerings were developed not only to respond to Tektronix's internal needs but also to compensate for the absence of an adequate higher education system. Once corporate restructuring in the form of layoffs and divestitures took effect, a very skilled workforce was available to other high-tech firms and to startups. Tektronix's failure to commercialize technology developed in its labs resulted in spillovers in the form of entrepreneurial ventures that contributed to the region's specialization in high-tech subsectors such as display technology, semiconductor, test and measurement instruments, and printers.

As Tektronix declined, Intel began to develop and flourish in the Silicon Forest. Intel established its first branch operation outside of California in Portland, Oregon in 1976. The branch facility was set up to manufacture semiconductor memory chips, a product that at the time was not yet overtaken by Japanese semiconductor manufacturers. Subsequently, US firms exited the semiconductor memory production market (Leachman and Leachman, 2004). The only exception was Micron Technology in Boise, which will be discussed later in this chapter. In 1974, an Intel facility manager in Santa Clara checked alternative locations for corporate expansion. According to him, one of the main requirements was that the new site had to be relatively close to Santa Clara and could be reached by a 1.5- to 2-hour plane trip. After drawing the 2-hour radius on the map, Portland showed up within the circle as a potential location for the new branch facility. Soon after the manager's visit to Portland, Intel decided to buy a 30-acre site in one of the western suburbs and started to manufacture in 1976. Intel's initial location decision incorporated orthodox corporate considerations: 'There was no concern about having a major university . . . we only wanted quality workers and availability of water and power because it was a production site', the facility manager who became the first Intel Oregon manager explained. Intel management also thought that Oregon was a more viable location for attracting and retaining labor since Silicon Valley already had a high rate of labor mobility.

Intel's expansion outside of Silicon Valley took place at a time when there was an explosion of demand for integrated circuits. After Intel exited the memory business, Intel's Oregon facilities were transformed into a manufacturing and R&D site for integrated circuit semiconductors. One Intel Oregon manager recalls, 'Oregon kind of grew from being a manufacturing-only site to being a manufacturing and R&D site. And that is actually unique in the Intel system. There is no other location at which they have both manufacturing and R&D'. This evolution was facilitated by the relocation of several engineering groups. One of these groups, led by a native of the Pacific Northwest, moved from Silicon Valley to Portland and was charged with developing a microprocessor (the so-called 'iAPX432'). The processor proved to be a commercial failure, but the relocation of the team set the groundwork for Intel's most successful chip, the Pentium processor, which was subsequently developed by a team of engineers at Intel's Silicon Forest campus in the early 1990s.

Unlike Tektronix, Intel never set up a separate in-house R&D laboratory. Intel aims to closely link innovation and manufacturing so as not to lose time between the development of new products and their market introduction. Intel operates so-called 'process development fabrication facilities', in which engineers develop new chips along with the necessary process for mass production. Most of this type of development work is done in Intel's Portland facilities. For example, Intel's D1D fabrication work was completed in 2003 and is the site for the development of the 65 and 45 nanometer chips, and the facility is expected to develop new chip generations until 2013. In 2009, Intel announced that it will invest approximately $1.5 billion as part of its push to develop 32 nanometer chips. Many of the chips' codenames reflect the engineers' geographical roots in Oregon. Names such as Klamath, Cascades, Tualatin, Willamette, and Nehalem, remind us of geographical landmarks in the Pacific Northwest and indicate how rooted Intel's R&D is in Oregon. From 1990 to 1999, for example, Intel inventors registered more than twice as many parents in Oregon as engineers at Intel's Silicon Valley headquarters (684 versus 298).

Compared to Tektronix, Intel has not gone through an extensive corporate restructuring and as a result the degree to which Intel has functioned as an incubator for startups has been lower. Given the importance and the size of Intel's Oregon facilities (today Intel Oregon is the largest Intel site in the world with 15,000 employees), the firm has not spawned as many startups as Tektronix. Various factors are responsible for Intel's limited contributions to regional entrepreneurship. Intel's employee stock ownership programs and generous stock options may function like 'golden handcuffs' and deter employees from venturing out on their own. Internal entrepreneurship programs – also known as 'intrapreneurship' – try to capture any knowledge spillovers before employees decide to leave and start their own firm. Even though Intel operates the world's largest venture capital group (Intel Capital) and key personnel are located in Oregon, the fund has not impacted the region. Investments are made worldwide to capture ideas and innovations relevant for the corporation as a whole. In addition, Intel is widely known for its rigorous strategic focus. This in turn may limit the range of ideas employees are working on. Intel, however, influenced the evolution of the Silicon Forest primarily through the development of a cluster of interrelated firms. Intel attracted specialized suppliers and subcontractors, and its relocation to Oregon signaled to its competitors that the region was a viable place to locate semiconductor manufacturing operations.

8.4.2   Case Study 2: Boise, Idaho

As we saw in Tables 8.1 and 8.2, Boise's high-tech economy is small but highly specialized as evidenced by a high-tech location quotient of 1.76. With about 10,000 employees locally, Micron Technology is the largest high-tech employer in the region. Hewlett-Packard is the second-largest high-tech employer in Boise with about 3,340 employees locally. Started locally in Boise in 1981, Micron Technology specializes in semiconductor production and produces memory and image sensor chips. Most US semiconductor firms ceased to produce semiconductor memory chips. Other semiconductor firms such as ZiLOG, Cypress Semiconductors, Marvell Semiconductors Applied Materials, Avago, and Inapac have branch facilities in Boise. There are also a few semiconductor startup firms such as American Semiconductor and Ovonyx (co-founded by one of the entrepreneurs who started Micron Technology). Other local startup companies include the semiconductor equipment makers Anestel Corporation and JST Manufacturing. Most other firms specialize in information technology services, internet services, networking, and electronic products that integrate hardware and software (especially embedded software, and firmware). Many of the firms in these industry segments are spinoffs from Hewlett-Packard or provide contracting services to HP (that is, Extended Systems, TenXsys, Treetop Tech, Stratus Global Partners, and so on), who relocated several divisions to Boise in 1973. Since HP started in Boise in 1973 and Micron was founded in 1981, the region has developed a critical mass of business support services and a small, but active local angel and venture capital community. The region's higher education infrastructure and policy support system has improved significantly, but is nowhere near the level and quality of more prominent high-tech regions.

Firm building: Hewlett-Packard and Micron Technology
Even though Hewlett-Packard's presence in Boise is that of a branch facility, 32 companies were started by former HP employees. An additional 19 firms were started by employees of HP startups. In contrast only seven firms were started by former employees of Micron Technology. Micron started 11 subsidiaries and divisions. Micron PC, a subsidiary of Micron Technology, saw 10 startups that in turn spawned five companies as children and grandchildren of Micron PC. To understand the difference in the firms' influence on startup activity, we have to review each firm's corporate evolution in the Boise region.

In 1973, HP selected Boise as a location for the manufacturing of line printers and magnetic tape drives. The formation of the Boise Division followed a well-established organizational tradition at HP. In 1958 the company introduced the division structure to manage its growing size. According to this principle, any group within HP becomes an independent unit when it grows to 1,500 people. The resulting independent organization functions like a small business. From its beginning in 1973, the Boise Division acted like an independent business unit. Boise was selected over Salt Lake City not only because it was within a 2-hour plane flight from its headquarters in Palo Alto, but also because of quality of life. The general manager responsible for selecting Boise said that 'if there was one primary item attracting us to this city, it would have to be the livability of Boise and the fact that people here wanted us' (Guerber, 1973). He also mentioned other location advantages such as an excellent air connection with other major cities and an adequate supply of power. The lack of a world-class research university, however, did not deter HP from locating in the region. In 1977, HP managed to attract 200 employees to Boise and the company hired an additional 800 employees locally. That year, HP issued the first line printer solely designed in Boise. In 1976, HP added a new division in Boise, the Disc Storage Unit. This started a period of memory production at the facility. And in 1981, the Boise division started to manufacture laser printers. Today, HP's operations solely focus on laser printers and it hosts four units working on color, monochrome, multi-function printers, and connectivity-related functions.

Since locating in Boise, HP has gone through various corporate changes. In 1999, it spun off the test and measurement business and created Agilent Technologies. The HP Boise operation was affected because the local semiconductor production facilities became those of Agilent Technologies (later sold to Marvell Technology Group). In 1998, Jabil acquired the manufacturing assets of HP, which included the printed circuit assembly for the LaserJet printer in Boise. Changes in products and technology created other important implications for the Boise facility. When HP introduced the laser printer, manufacturing of the line impact printer went overseas (first to Japan and then to China). In addition, the partnership with Canon, which produced the engine for the laser printer, allowed the Boise operation to focus mainly on R&D in printer performance, embedded software, connectivity, and marketing. Driven by a question to make the printer cheaper, smaller, faster, and quieter (product innovations), HP's Boise facilities primarily focused on R&D and marketing. As a result, HP's labor force changed from one dominated by mechanical engineers to software engineers and marketing professionals.

Micron Technology is a semiconductor company that specializes in the production of computer memory chips including DRAM, SDRAM, flash memory, and CMOS image sensing chips. All its competitors are foreign and mostly manufacture in low-cost countries such as Taiwan and China. The firm was founded in 1978 by four Idaho natives. Most of them had worked for Mostek Corporation in Dallas, Texas, and for a brief time at Inmos, a British-financed competitor of Mostek. Three of the Micron founders developed an integrated circuit for Inmos. However, legal challenges from Mostek created an unpleasant work environment and they left Inmos to start their own firm. They were able to obtain initial financing from three Idaho-based angel investors including J.R. Simplot, Idaho's most prominent potato farmer. A local bank in their hometown also provided financing early on. With this support, they were able to set up a manufacturing facility in Boise.

During the 1980s, Micron Technology was able to carve out a niche in the semiconductor market primarily because it could produce more reliable and smaller chips than its competitors. As a result, Micron cut production costs and prices. But the firm has always been subject to the cyclical nature of its industry; during the mid-1980s, prices plummeted and Micron had to lay off half of its workforce and stop production lines. Micron's fortunes reversed in the early 1990s when semiconductor prices rose, revenues for Micron increased and the company initiated an expansion phase. In 1995, Micron announced that it would build a manufacturing facility in nearby Lehi, Utah. It also added facilities overseas. As prices fell again in early 1996, Micron suspended the construction of the Utah branch plant and mothballed the facility until it opened in 2006 to manufacturer NAND flash memory in collaboration with Intel.

In the early 1990s, Micron Technology began to diversify into other industry segments, most prominently the personal computer market. All new divisions started operating in Boise. In 1991, Micron entered the personal computer market and created Edge Technology which later would become known as Micron Computer or Micron PC. Micron later acquired ZEOS International and merged it with Micron Custom Manufacturing and Micron Computer to form Micron Electronics. The formation of Micron Electronics was the most important diversification. In recent years, Micron began to operate production facilities in other countries facilitated through the acquisition of Texas Instruments' DRAM fabs, including a recent expansion in China. Boise, however, remains the company's most important R&D and production site.

Micron is in a market that is dominated by a drive toward lower prices. As a so-called 'commodity memory chip producer', Micron closely integrates production and design within the same manufacturing facility. Innovations are mostly made to the production process. Even though so-called 'fabless chip design firms' emerged, the production and the design of commodity memory devices stayed within IDM (integrated device manufacturer) firms such as Micron Technology. As Leachman and Leachman (2004, p. 224) note:

> [F]or such high-volume commodity products, it is essential to strive for the lowest possible manufacturing cost. This requires the development and refinement of a fabrication process technology optimized for the specific product. The number of process steps must be reduced wherever and whenever possible, certain process machines may need to be dedicated and tuned to perform specific process steps, and frequent relatively small modifications of the process technology enabling smaller design rules ('shrinks') likely will be advantageous.

As a result, Micron Technology's innovation environment may be characterized as one driven by considerations to decrease costs, retain control over each step in the design and manufacturing process, high-volume manufacturing, and less of a concern for the customer. This stands in contrast to the nature and type of products that HP produces and markets from its Boise operations.

There are major differences in the ways in which Micron Technology and Hewlett-Packard contributed to entrepreneurial firm formation in Boise. Both firms have gone through significant corporate changes involving restructuring, layoffs, and diversification. These 'critical events' influence entrepreneurial firm formation because they may turn employees into nascent entrepreneurs. In addition to corporate changes, the nature and type of product a high-tech firm produces can also play an important role in determining the extent to which an organization can play a role as an incubator for entrepreneurship. HP's technologies and products are characterized by a higher degree of customization and they were less sensitive to prize variation. In addition, the product was highly targeted toward the consumer as the end customer. In contrast, Micron Technology's products – memory chips – are commodities that are highly sensitive to price variations. Micron's focus on lowering prices and increasing efficiencies in the production process may not have allowed for much creativity to occur on the shop floor. Micron's main activities are in product assembly with a strong focus on process improvement and innovation (how can we make more chips at a lower price?). Its customers are other high-tech firms and not the end consumer. Thus, the technical nature of production at Micron is more focused on the execution/production phase rather than the conception phase. This contrasts with HP which is more focused on the conception phase and product development. Opportunities for backward and forward linkages do exist for both firms. However, more firms indicated that they have developed backward linkages (supplier) with HP than with Micron. This may also give rise to entrepreneurial opportunities as many ventures utilize their parent firms as customers.

Both firms occupy prominent positions in their respective markets. Micron Technology is one of a few memory chip producers in the United States and Hewlett-Packard is a leader in laser printer production and development. Such prominent market positions may explain why Boise has not been able to develop similarly sized competitors. HP and Micron may crowd out smaller firms. In addition, high entry barriers in both industry segments prevent many small firms from entering the same market. From an entrepreneurial learning perspective, the interviews indicated that entrepreneurs learn critical skills both in terms of technology and markets at their parent firm and they are able to exploit market connections as well as connections to global production networks.

Corporate policies play an important role in encouraging or hindering entrepreneurial activities. Interviews indicated a sharp contrast between HP and Micron. HP was often labeled as a 'great place to work', 'very supportive environment', 'cutting edge', and 'innovative'. Many mentioned that HP provided an open door to employees who left to start a business or work for another firm and wanted to come back. This 'welcome mat' offered employees the chance to take entrepreneurial risks knowing that they would have a fallback. In some cases, entrepreneurs were able to work part-time for HP while they were developing their business. HP also allowed employees to work with so-called 'lab stock', electronic supplies that could be used by employees in their spare time, and some utilized HP equipment and tools to build prototypes of their venture's products and technologies. Qualitative insights into Micron's culture yield a different picture. Interviewees noted that Micron was 'secretive', 'frugal', not very diversified in terms of its products ('Micron is just a chip manufacturer') and many had a sense that the firm was not well connected to the local business community. This confirms other research on the global semiconductor industry that has shown that this type of high-tech industry does not exhibit the stylized notions of industrial clustering (McCann and Arita, 2006).

Both Micron and HP attracted world-class talent to the Boise region. R&D, marketing and management professionals were attracted to Boise because of the region's high quality of life. Startup companies that emerged over time were able to draw on this pool of talent. Interviewees noted that it was easy to recruit talent and that they often used personal networks. As a result, the ways in which these two firms have organized themselves and the differences between them explain some of the variation in entrepreneurial dynamics.

8.5   REFLECTION

The case studies explored in this chapter illustrate how second-tier high-tech regions can emerge through endogenous spinoff processes. The cases, however, also illustrate that the nature of the firm influences the degree to which it can function as an incubator of startups. A firm's corporate evolution, the degree to which it allows startups to engage in business activities, the nature of the product and production process, its innovation model, and corporate policies toward human resources and entrepreneurship all influence startup dynamics. Examining why certain types of firms are more fertile than others when it comes to spawning startups, allows for a much more nuanced perspective of firm building and its links to entrepreneurship. Previous studies of entrepreneurial high-tech regions such as Silicon Valley or Boston's Route 128 have not paid enough attention to firm-level dynamics.

Much of the literature on entrepreneurial high-tech regions assumes that certain factors have to exist that encourage startup activity. On top of the list is an adequate supply of venture capital to finance startups. Other ingredients that are often mentioned are the presence of a risk-taking and entrepreneurial culture and the location of a major world-class university. Startup activity in a region, however, seems to emerge from existing firms and may not depend on the presence of these ingredients. In fact, an entrepreneurial culture may be formed *after* a critical mass of startup firms has emerged and is not necessarily an a priori necessity.

The cases explored here illustrate how certain firms seem to be more encouraging of spinoff activity than others. Corporate changes – especially as they relate to corporate adjustment to changing global markets in the form of restructuring, layoffs, and so on – influence startup activity. Corporate restructuring from vertical integration to disintegration created business opportunities for startups. In the case of Tektronix, layoffs and divestitures functioned as motivating forces for employees to start their own firms. The parent firm's industry leadership ensured the creation of a critical mass of skilled labor, in the form of both technical and managerial skills. Firms with products that are focused on customer needs rather than price had more startups than those focused on commodity markets. Table 8.3 illustrates the various ways in which fertile parent firms differ from those less fertile.

8.6   CONCLUSIONS

The case studies of second-tier high-tech regions reviewed here illustrate some important insights into the ways in which agglomerations of knowledge-based economic activity emerge. Common to these types of regions is the role of large, dominant, innovative, and often market-leading firms. These firms shape the regional environment through spinoffs (they function as incubators and become parents of new ventures), they attract and develop labor, they exert political power and shape the region's business environment, they provide business opportunities for other firms, they can implant their resources in a region, and through their market relationships they link to other regions. Moreover, corporate changes and evolution play an important role in the development of the local economy. Negative corporate events such as acquisitions, layoffs and restructuring can have positive impacts on the local economy. In all these activities the organizational structure and corporate strategies of these firms play a significant role, and economic geographers and industry studies scholars need to pay attention to these firm-specific aspects. In other words, firm-building dynamics are intimately connected

Table 8.3 Comparing parent firms

	Fertile parent firms		Less fertile parent firms	
	Tektronix	Hewlett-Packard	Intel	Micron Technology
Industry	Measurement Instruments	Consumer Electronics	Semiconductor	Semiconductor
Corporate changes	Disintegration Restructuring Refocus on core products	Transformation from manufacturing to R&D and marketing	Continued corporate expansion inside the region; focus on process development	Corporate expansion mainly outside of region
Linkages	Disintegration facilitated entrepreneurial opportunities	Disintegration facilitated contracting opportunities	Expansion induced clustering	Did not induce clustering
Connections to markets	Industry leader Strong market connections	Industry leader Strong market connections	Intermediary supplier	Intermediary supplier
Product type	Customized for industry use	Customized for end consumers	Standardized commodity	Standardized commodity 'Just making chips'
Nature of production	Move toward integration of R&D and manufacturing	Move away from manufacturing to prototyping, design, marketing	Vertically integrated Mass production	Vertically integrated Mass production
Innovation	Product innovation Tek Labs	Product innovation Break with 'NIH'* syndrome	Manufacturing process innovation	Manufacturing process innovation
Corporate policies & culture	Similar to HP Way Strong culture of talent development "Welcome mat" for entrepreneurs Divisionalization	HP Way Strong culture of talent development 'Welcome mat' for entrepreneurs Divisionalization into independent business units	Intrapreneurship Corporate stock options limit spinoff activity	'Secretive' 'Frugal' Limited divisionalization (Micron PC)
Capital assets	Tek Labs ceased to exist thereby limiting research capacity	Change in human resources toward software & marketing	Physical assets dominate Strong IP assets	Physical assets dominate Strong IP assets
Labor	Engineer	Engineer manager	Engineer production	Technical production

Note: *Not invented here.

to the ways in which clusters evolve and whether a region is able to grow as a spinoff region or not.

The intention of this chapter was to examine the role of firm-building processes in the evolution of a high-tech region. I connected firm-building mechanisms with entrepreneurship and illustrated the ways in which corporations function as fertile or less fertile incubators for spinoffs. Firm-building dynamics are inherently local processes and affect a region through their influence on spinoffs. Spinoffs in turn help create a local cluster and entrepreneurs shape agglomeration economies. The case studies illustrate these dynamics and provide evidence for Klepper's argument about the role of spinoffs in the formation of new industries.

REFERENCES

Aldrich, H. and Martinez, M.A. (2001), 'Many are called, but few are chosen: an evolutionary perspective for the study of entrepreneurship', *Entrepreneurship Theory and Practice*, **25** (4), 41–56.

Audretsch, D. and Lehmann, E. (2005), 'Does the knowledge spillover theory of entrepreneurship hold for regions?', *Research Policy*, **34**, 1191–202.

Bahrami, H. and Evans, S. (1995), 'Flexible re-cycling and high-technology entrepreneurship', *California Management Review*, **37** (3), 62–89.

Benneworth, P. (2004), 'In what sense "regional development?": entrepreneurship, underdevelopment and strong tradition in the periphery', *Entrepreneurship and Regional Development*, **16**, 439–58.

Bhide, A. (2000), *The Origin and Evolution of New Businesses*, Oxford and New York: Oxford University Press.

Blanchard, C. (2005), 'This urban Idaho', *Idaho Issues Online*, available at: http://www.boisestate.edu/history/issuesonline/spring2006_issues/5f_numbers_06spr.html# (accessed November, 4, 2007).

Boschma, R.A. and Wenting, R. (2007), 'The spatial evolution of the British automobile industry: does location matter?', *Industrial and Corporate Change*, **16** (2), 213–38.

Boschma, R.A. and Weterings, A.B.R. (2005), 'The effect of regional differences on the performance of software firms in the Netherlands', *Journal of Economic Geography*, **5**, 567–88.

Braunerhjelm, P. and Feldmann, M. (2006), *Cluster Genesis: Technology-based Industrial Development*, Oxford: Oxford University Press.

Bresnahan, T. and Gambardella, A. (2004), *Building High-Tech Clusters: Silicon Valley and Beyond*, Cambridge: Cambridge University Press.

Bresnahan, T., Gambardella, A. and Saxenian, A. (2001), '"Old economy" inputs for "new economy" outcomes: cluster formation in the new Silicon Valleys', *Industrial and Corporate Change*, **10** (4), 835–60.

Brittain, J. and Freeman, J. (1986), 'Entrepreneurship in the semiconductor industry', unpublished manuscript, University of California at Berkeley.

Carroll, G.R. and Khessina, O.M. (2005), 'The ecology of entrepreneurship', in S.A. Alvarez, R. Agarwal and O. Sorenson (eds), *Handbook of Entrepreneurship Research: Disciplinary Perspectives*, Heidelberg: Springer, (pp. 167–200).

Chesbrough, H. (2002), 'Graceful exits and missed opportunities: Xerox's management of its technology spin-off organizations', *Business History Review*, **76** (4), 803–37.

Christensen, C. (1997), *The Innovator's Dilemma: When New Technologies Cause Great Firms to Fail*, Boston, MA: Harvard Business School Press.

Cooper, A. (1971), *The Founding of Technologically-based Firms*, Milwaukee, WI: Center for Venture Management.

Cooper, A. (1985), 'The role of incubator organizations in founding growth-oriented firms', *Journal of Business Venturing*, **1**, 75–86.

Cyert, R.M. and March, J.G. (1963), *A Behavioral Theory of the Firm*, Englewood Cliffs, NJ: Prentice-Hall.

Feldman, M., Francis, J. and Bercovitz, J. (2005), 'Creating a cluster while building a firm: entrepreneurs and the formation of industrial clusters', *Regional Studies*, **39** (1), 129–41.

Glasmeier, A. (1988), 'Factors governing the development of high tech industry agglomerations: a tale of three cities', *Regional Studies*, **22**, 287–301.

Gray, G.C. (1982), *Radio for the Fireline: A History of Electronic Communication in the Forest Service 1905–1975*, Washington, DC: US Department of Agriculture, Forest Service.

Guerber, S. (1973), 'Question of why Hewlett-Packard chose Boise gets nebulous reply', *The Idaho Statesman*, June 14.

Klepper, S. (1996), 'Entry, exit, growth, and innovation over the product life cycle', *American Economic Review*, 86 (3), 562–83.

Klepper, S. (2001a), 'Employee startups in high-tech industries', *Industrial and Corporate Change*, 10 (3), 639–73.

Klepper, S. (2001b), 'The evolution of the U.S. automobile industry and Detroit as its capital', available at: http://www.druid.dk/conferences/winter2002/gallery/klepper.pdf (accessed November 11, 2008).

Klepper, S. (2009), 'Silicon Valley, a chip off the old Detroit bloc', in Z. Acs, D. Audretsch and R. Strom (eds), *Entrepreneurship, Growth and Public Policy*, Cambridge: Cambridge University Press, pp. 79–116.

Klepper, S. and Sleeper, S. (2005), 'Entry by spinoffs', *Management Science*, 51 (8), 1291–306.

Klepper, S. and Thompson, P. (2005), 'Spinoff entry in high-tech industries: motives and consequences', available at: http://www.fiu.edu/~economic/wp2005/05-03.pdf (accessed January 29, 2009).

Kogut, B. and Zander, U. (2003), 'Knowledge of the firm and the evolutionary theory of the multinational corporation', *Journal of International Business Studies*, 34, 516–29.

Leachman, R. and Leachman, C. (2004), 'Globalization of semiconductors: do real men have fabs, or virtual fabs?', in M. Kenney and R. Florida (eds), *Locating Global Advantage: Industry Dynamics in the International Economy*, Stanford, CA: Stanford University Press, pp. 203–31.

Lee, M.M. (1986), *Winning with People: The First 40 Years of Tektronix*, Portland, OR: Tektronix, Inc.

Lorenzen, M. (2005), 'Why do clusters change?', *European Urban and Regional Studies*, 12 (3), 203–8.

Markusen, A. (1999), 'Fuzzy concepts, scanty evidence, policy distance: the case for rigour and policy relevance in critical regional studies', *Regional Studies*, 33 (9), 868–84.

Markusen, A.R., Lee, Y.-S. and DiGiovanna, S. (1999), *Second Tier Cities: Rapid Growth beyond the Metropolis*, Vol. 3, Minneapolis, MN: University of Minnesota Press.

Martin, R. (2010), 'Roepke Lecture in Economic Geography – Rethinking regional path dependence: beyond lock-in to evolution', *Economic Geography*, 86 (1), 1–27.

Martin, R. and Sunley, P. (2003), 'Deconstructing clusters: chaotic concept or policy panacea?', *Journal of Economic Geography*, 3, 5–35.

Martin, R. and Sunley, P. (2006), 'Path dependence and regional economic evolution', *Journal of Economic Geography*, 6, 395–437.

Maskell, P. (2001), 'The firm in economic geography', *Economic Geography*, 77 (4), 329–44.

Mayer, H. (2005a), 'Planting high technology seeds: Tektronix role in the creation of Portland's Silicon Forest', *Oregon Historical Quarterly*, 106 (4), 568–93.

Mayer, H. (2005b), 'Taking root in the Silicon Forest: the role of high technology firms as surrogate universities in Portland, Oregon', *Journal of the American Planning Association*, 71 (3), 318–33.

Mayer, H. (2009), *Bootstrapping High-tech: Evidence from Three Emerging High Technology Metropolitan Areas*, Washington, DC: Brookings Institution.

Mayer, H. (2011), *Entrepreneurship and Innovation in Second Tier Regions*, Cheltenham, UK and Northampton, MA, USA: Edward Elgar Publishing.

McCann, P. and Arita, T. (2006), 'Clusters and regional development: some cautionary observations from the semiconductor industry', *Information Economics and Policy*, 18, 157–80.

Mitton, D. (1990), 'Bring on the clones: a longitudinal study of the proliferation, development, and growth of the biotech industry in San Diego', in N.C. Churchill, W.D. Bygrave, J.A. Hornaday, D.F. Muzuka, K.H. Vespter and W.E. Wetzel Jr (eds) *Frontiers of Entrepreneurship Research*, Conference Proceedings, Babson College, Wellesley, MA, pp. 344–58.

Neck, H., Meyer, D.G., Cohen, B. and Corbett, A. (2004), 'An entrepreneurial system view of new venture creation', *Journal of Small Business Management*, 42 (2), 190–208.

Nelson, R. and Winter, S. (1982), *An Evolutionary Theory of Economic Change*, Cambridge, MA: Harvard University Press.

Penrose, E.T. (1959), *The Theory of the Growth of the Firm*, New York: Wiley.

Porter, M. (2000), 'Locations, clusters, and company strategy', in G.L. Clark, M. Feldmann and M.S. Gertler (eds), *The Oxford Handbook of Economic Geography*, Oxford: Oxford University Press, pp. 253–74.

Romanelli, E. and Schoonhoven, C.B. (2001), 'The local origins of new firms', in C.B. Schoonhoven and E. Romanelli (eds), *The Entrepreneurship Dynamic: Origins of Entrepreneurship and the Evolution of Industries*, Stanford, CA: Stanford University, Press, pp. 40–67.

Saxenian, A. (1985), 'The genesis of Silicon Valley', in P. Hall and A. Markusen (eds), *Silicon Landscapes*, Boston, MA: Allen & Unwin, pp. 20–34.

Saxenian, A. (1994a), 'Lessons from Silicon Valley', *Technology Review*, 97, 42–51.

Saxenian, A. (1994b), *Regional Advantage: Culture and Competition in Silicon Valley and Route 128*, Cambridge, MA: Harvard University Press.

Smilor, R., O'Donnell, N., Stein, G. and Welborn, R. (2007), 'The research university and the development of high-technology centers in the United States', *Economic Development Quarterly*, **21** (3), 203–22.

Sorenson, O. and Audia, P.G. (2000), 'The social structure of entrepreneurial activity: geographic concentration of footwear production in the United States, 1940–1989', *American Journal of Sociology*, **106** (2), 424–61.

Staber, U. (2005), 'Entrepreneurship as a source of path dependency', in G. Fuchs and P. Shapira (eds), *Rethinking Regional Innovation and Change: Path Dependency or Regional Breakthrough*, New York: Springer, pp. 107–26.

Stam, E. (2007), 'Why butterflies don't leave: locational behavior of entrepreneurial firms', *Economic Geography*, **83** (1), 27–50.

Tappi, D. (2005), 'Clusters, adaption and extroversion: a cognitive and entrepreneurial analysis of the Marche music cluster', *European Urban and Regional Studies*, **12** (3), 289–307.

Taylor, M. (2006), 'Fragments and gaps: exploring the theory of the firm', in M. Taylor and P. Oinas (eds), pp. 3–31.

Taylor, M. and Oinas, P. (2006), *Understanding the Firm: Spatial and Organizational Dimensions*, Oxford and New York: Oxford University Press.

West, J. and Simard, C. (2006), 'Balancing intrapreneurial innovation vs. entrepreneurial spinoffs during periods of technological ferment', Paper presented at the Babson College Entrepreneurship Research Conference, Bloomington, IN, June 8–10.

9 Location, control and firm innovation: the case of the mobile handset industry
*Ram Mudambi**

9.1 INTRODUCTION

The first industrial revolution that began in eighteenth-century England was based on technological innovations that produced a wide range of machinery and the factory system. This revolution replaced expensive uniqueness of craft manufacture and locally specialized agriculture industry with the cheap standardization of mass production (Crafts, 1985). Through the twentieth century the basic human desire for individual identity and uniqueness has inexorably chipped away at the basic mass production model, initially creating larger margins for firms implementing differentiation strategies (Porter, 1985). This process has recently accelerated to a torrent whereby 'mass customization' and 'mass personalization' (Kotha, 1995; Tseng et al., 2010) are rapidly consigning mass production to the pages of economic history.

The first industrial revolution marked a dramatic and discontinuous upward shift in the value of commercial knowledge. For the next two centuries the bulk of this knowledge was embodied in tangible assets. Over the last several decades the world economy has been witnessing what can only be described as another revolution in terms of the nature of value creation. The source of value has been shifting from tangible to intangible assets at an accelerating pace. For all the G7 economies put together, intangible assets have been estimated to constitute about 30 percent of the stock of all long-term assets (IMF, 2006).[1] This shift is occurring through the emergence of technologies and institutions that have made it increasingly cost effective to separate intangible assets from their associated tangible assets.

The returns to intangible assets can appear in the form of legally defensible rents as in the case of patents, copyrights, and brands (Lev, 2001).[2] However, they can also appear in the form of superior returns generated by inimitable organizational structures and inter-organizational relationships (Kogut and Zander, 1993; Augier and Teece, 2006). A key aspect of intangible assets is the overwhelming importance of human creativity (Howkins, 2001; Florida, 2002). In all cases, the firm controlling an intangible asset is able to generate higher returns, *ceteris paribus*, than a competing firm that does not control the asset.

Intangible assets have also been called 'intellectual assets' (Lev, 2001), a terminology that is more helpful since it makes clear that all these assets are based on various forms of commercial knowledge. The role of commercial knowledge in value generation has long been recognized (Hayek, 1945), especially in creative industries. Value creation in these industries is almost entirely based on intellectual content in the form of texts, music, media, and so on (Caves, 2000; Scott, 2000). Traditionally, creative industries have also been characterized by very strong cluster effects (Florida, 2002; Maskell and Lorenzen,

2004). The economic geography literature has developed fine-grained analyses of location, regional specialization, and clustering in knowledge-intensive industries, focusing especially on urbanization, the power of cities and the consequent rise of regional disparities (Amin and Thrift, 2005; Lorenzen, 2004; Scott and Storper, 2003).

However, the geographical dispersion of value creation has recently begun to play an increasingly important role in the analysis of creative industries (Cantwell and Santangelo, 1999). National systems of innovation (NSIs) provide 'the location-specific supply base of technological and knowledge externalities that firms draw upon for their competitiveness' (Amin and Cohendet, 2004: 88) and NSIs vary dramatically in terms of their comparative strengths and weaknesses (Lundvall, 2007). Thus, firms can enhance their competitive advantage by dispersing their creative endeavors, tapping into multiple centers of excellence and coordinating knowledge across geographical space (Lorenzen, 2004). For example, Canon U.S. Life Sciences Inc. is networked into the US NSI, specifically into the life sciences cluster along the eastern seaboard, thousands of miles away from its home-based R&D headquarters in Japan (Uchida, 2008).

This example illustrates that understanding the effects of this dispersion on the creation and use of intellectual assets requires relating them to the optimizing decisions made by the individual business firm. The relevant decisions focus on the firm's value chain that is composed of the 'technologically and economically distinct activities that it performs to do business' (Porter and Millar, 1985: 151). Addressing these questions requires analyzing the value chain along two dimensions: control and location.

Activities within the firm's value chain can be broadly grouped into three categories: the upstream (input) end, the downstream (output or market) end and the middle. Activities at the upstream end generally comprise design, basic and applied research, and the commercialization of creative endeavors. Activities at the downstream end typically comprise marketing, advertising and brand management, and after-sales services. Activities in the middle comprise manufacturing, standardized service delivery, and other repetitive processes in which commercialized prototypes are implemented on a mass scale.

How should the firm control the various parts of the value chain and where should it locate them? More specifically, the research questions addressed in this chapter are: to what extent should the firm implement vertical integration and geographical dispersion with respect to its value chain activities? These location and control choices are presented in a simplified manner in Table 9.1. The answers to these fundamental questions with regard to firm organization and activity location are crucial: they will determine the global geography of economic activity in general and creative activity in particular during the coming decades.

Table 9.1   Strategic choice: location and control

		Geographical location strategy	
		Concentrated	Dispersed
Control strategy	Vertical integration	1. Onshore in-house	3. Captive offshore
	Specialization	2. Onshore outsourced	4. Offshore outsource

There is a voluminous literature in international business examining the organization of the firm across national borders (Buckley and Casson, 1976; Dunning, 1993). The economic geography literature has dealt exhaustively with questions regarding the location of economic activity, in both the regional and international contexts (Fujita et al., 1999; Dicken, 2003). However, the interface between these two literatures is surprisingly thin (McCann and Mudambi, 2005). This chapter draws on both literatures in an attempt to incorporate both the firm and location perspectives on value creation in creative industries. This analysis enables us to highlight both the macro (country level) and the micro (firm level) implications of the ongoing process of globalization.[3]

At the macro level, the value chains of individual firms interweave through complex relationships and complementarities to form the 'value constellations' of creative industries (Normann and Ramírez, 1993). These are becoming locationally disaggregated as discrete parts of firm value chains are coalescing in different country locations. Under the current location pattern, high value-added activities are largely performed in advanced market economies, with low value-added activities performed in emerging market economies.[4] However, this pattern is under pressure from three separate processes. Firms from emerging market economies are striving to develop competencies in high value-added activities ('catch-up'). Firms from advanced market economies are stripping out standardized parts of their high value-added activities and cutting costs by relocating these in emerging market economies ('spillover'). This spillover process is reinforced by obsolescence that is creating pressures for the relocation of 'sunset' industries to emerging market economies. Rapid innovation, so far largely in advanced market economies, is spawning entirely new value constellations ('industry creation').

Examining global creative industries at the firm level, distinct trends are emerging. Two divergent strategies can be discerned with regard to the control of the value chain. A vertical integration strategy emphasizes taking advantage of 'linkage economies' whereby controlling multiple value chain activities enhances the efficiency and effectiveness of each one of them. In contrast, a specialization strategy focuses on identifying and controlling the creative heart of the value chain, while outsourcing all other activities. However, along the location dimension, a common pattern of geographical dispersion appears to be developing. Firms are increasingly implementing strategies to take advantage of the comparative advantages of locations. This results in a wider geographical dispersion of firms' activities, with direct implications for the future of creative industries' global value constellations.

The chapter is organized as follows. A theoretical framework for the analysis of the economic organization of knowledge-intensive industries is developed in Section 9.2. The theory is illustrated within the context of a case study of the global mobile handset industry in Section 9.3. Implications of the theory and research propositions are presented in Section 9.4. The final section includes.

9.2   CONTROL, LOCATION AND ECONOMIC ORGANIZATION IN CREATIVE INDUSTRIES

There is no well-accepted definition of knowledge-intensive industries (Malecki, 1984). The OECD definition of 'high-technology' industries is limited to manufacturing (see

OECD, 1996). More importantly, for the purposes of the chapter, we are interested in knowledge-intensive activities, not knowledge-intensive firms. We specify that high knowledge activities are creative and specialized, whereas low knowledge activities are repetitious and standardized (Nelson and Winter, 1982). In other words, the difference between high and low knowledge activities is based on a 'fundamental difference between a focus on new products and a primary concern with low-cost, standardized production' (Malecki, 1984: 264). This definition underpins the conceptualization of knowledge used in the chapter as related to 'new concept development' and 'marketing': the two ends of the firm's value chain. Thus, the R&D activities of a textile manufacturer are included, while the repetitious printing and binding activities of a book publisher are not.

The macro data indicating the rapidly rising share of intangible assets in major economies implies that creative and knowledge-intensive industries account for an increasing share of value created. Creating and capturing value from knowledge assets is therefore becoming a cornerstone of firm strategy (Teece, 1998). We argue that our understanding of the strategic aspects of creating and capturing value from knowledge can be enhanced by placing them within the context of the firm's value chain (Porter and Millar, 1985: 150), that is, a conceptualization of value creation, identifying the value added by each activity. The value chain should *not* be read as an intertemporal sequence going from inputs to outputs. It is quite possible that sources of value at the 'market' or right end may be created before sources of value at the 'input' or left end. For instance, market research efforts may occur first or jointly with product or service design, with prototyping and production occurring later.

Successfully extracting and capturing value in creative industries depends on two crucial strategic nexuses: the control and location of value chain activities. In other words, for a firm to be successful in creating and capturing value from knowledge it is essential that it makes optimal decisions within these two domains.

9.2.1   Organization and Control: Coasian Approaches to the Firm

Optimal decisions regarding the governance of the firm's value chain emerge from the application of transaction cost analysis. Traditionally transaction costs have been defined as the costs of using the market mechanism (Coase, 1937; Williamson, 1975). Since this definition means that almost anything can be explained as a suitably defined transaction cost (Williamson, 1979), the subsequent literature has specified transaction costs to be those associated with coordinating and policing market transactions (Ricketts, 2002). It readily follows that whenever firms obtain significant benefits from vertical integration, the costs of using market transactions to perform these activities is relatively high and outsourcing is unattractive.

The firm simultaneously disaggregates the value chain and selects the activities over which to maintain control. Coasian analysis implies that the firm should retain control over the activities or operations where it can create and appropriate the most value. Conversely, operations where it can create and appropriate less value should be implemented through market transactions. In a seminal application, Buckley and Casson (1976) applied this reasoning to the geographical context, providing a theoretical rationale for the existence and organization of multinational enterprises (MNEs).

Technological advances, especially in the areas of information and communication have made it possible to disaggregate the firm's business processes into progressively finer slices. Firms are able to specialize in increasingly narrow niches, which need not even be contiguous in the value chain. This makes it crucial for the firm to identify the process activities over which it has competitive advantage, since these are the basis of the firm's core competencies (Hamel and Prahalad, 1990) and enable it to generate rents.

Along with the rising importance of intangibles, this process of value chain disaggregation and geographical dispersion is a complementary 'megatrend'. This development has led to the accelerating shift in firms' focus from goods and services to *activities* or tasks. Value chain activities are the units of analysis over which firms exercise their control (make or buy) and location (offshoring) decisions. This underpins the reality that a good as simple as a T-shirt is the product of a complex global value chain (GVC), encompassing cotton production in the US, cutting and assembly in China and recycling/reuse in Africa (Rivoli, 2009). Comparing today's GVC to Adam Smith's pin factory, we notice dramatic changes along two dimensions. In Smith's description, the 18 activities that were required to produce a pin were all undertaken in a single firm (vertical integration) in a single location (geographical concentration). In a GVC, the pin firm would retain just the most knowledge intensive of the 18 activities in-house and outsource all the others. It would also locate each activity (either directly or through supplier choice) in the most efficient global location. While the output may remain the same, the entire architecture of the firm that controls its production has been altered beyond recognition.

For some firms, the logic of transaction cost analysis pushes them toward exercising high control over and concentrating resources on specific activities while having a strong tendency to outsource others (Calantone and Stanko, 2007). Other firms tend to exercise greater control over the entire value chain, with much less outsourcing, though bounded rationality arguments – decreasing returns to management in the words of Coase (1937) – imply that such control cannot be extended indefinitely. In the terminology of industrial organization, these strategies correspond to greater and lesser degrees of vertical integration and focus on the strategic choice between cells 1 and 2 in Table 9.1.[5]

A critical research question that arises in this context pertains to the observation that competing firms within the same industry often implement widely differing levels of vertical integration. For example, in the US auto industry GM typically implemented the highest degree of vertical integration, followed by Ford and Chrysler (including its successor, DaimlerChrysler).[6] Through its ownership of Denso, Toyota has maintained an even higher level of vertical integration than GM (Conybeare, 2003). These differences have been observed over long periods of time and have not historically been related to differences in firm performance (Mudambi and Helper, 1998; Rubenstein, 2001). The persistence of these differences along with the lack of a systematic link to firm performance suggests that they are not disequilibrium phenomena.

A direct implication of these observations is that transaction costs have significant firm- in addition to industry-level components. The study of technology in neoclassical economics has tended to focus on the industry level of analysis. The industrial organization literature has developed sophisticated analyses explaining why and how industries differ from each other in terms of the extent of vertical integration. However, it is the firm-level components which cause firms within a single industry to differ from each other in terms of the control of their value chain activities. We argue that these firm-level transaction costs are not easily captured using standard tools of neoclassical economics.

Technologies largely determine economies of scale, scope, and experience and these are generally common across leading-edge firms in most industries (Mansfield, 1985; Pavitt, 1998). This implies that these economies cannot be the source of firm-level transaction costs; they cannot be used to explain systematic and persistent differences in the extent of vertical integration among these leading firms (Mudambi, 2008).

A particularly important aspect of value chain organization concerns not its constituent activities *per se*, but the linkage between them. Economies of scale, scope, and experience relate to the technologies associated with individual activities, that is, they are properties of individual production functions and are directly determined by technology. However, firms may also realize economies simply because they control multiple activities in the value chain. Design activities may become more efficient due to control of manufacturing, since information may flow more readily between units within a single firm. These economies may be defined as 'linkage economies'. Linkage economies arise from linkages between the production functions associated with *different* activities. See the appendix in Mudambi (2008) for details.

Hirschman (1968, 1977) was one of the first to note that linkages in the value chain of inputs and outputs create benefits beyond the direct gains from trade. Within his generalized analysis of linkages, his conceptualization of 'technological linkages' is the most relevant for the purposes of this chapter. Technological 'linkages can be expected to be rather weak if the required input comes from an industry whose process and technique is totally unfamiliar . . . The linkage dynamic may thus be held back by the difficulties of making a technological leap' (Hirschman, 1977: 77). This idea translates quite readily to an input–output interface at the level of the individual firm. Some firms will have the competencies to devise better routines to stimulate cross-activity coordination, learning, and innovation. Such firms enjoy high levels of linkage economies. Vertical integration is attractive for such firms since it results in falling costs and improved quality for both inputs and outputs. Other firms will find that controlling a wide range of activities detracts from their focus on each one. Such firms have low linkage economies or may even suffer from linkage diseconomies. Specialization is attractive for such firms and they have lower costs and superior quality by focusing on a narrow spectrum of activities while buying inputs from the market.

High linkage economies mean that controlling multiple activities in the value chain improves the efficiency and effectiveness of each one of them. Linkage economies are likely to be based on firm-specific routines and procedures (Zollo and Winter, 2002). These routines often vary across firms even when the underlying technologies being implemented are common (Rosenberg, 1982: 257). Linkage economies are likely to arise from the transfer of knowledge from one activity to another within the firm; the intra-firm context is expected to be particularly efficient when transfers involve highly tacit knowledge and skills (Nelson and Winter, 1982; Cantwell and Santangelo, 1999; Maskell and Malmberg, 1999). Further, different firms within the same industry have been shown to implement different knowledge management strategies (McMillan et al., 2000). Thus, linkage economies are an important knowledge-based means of explaining different levels of vertical integration within an industry.[7]

It is beyond the scope of the present chapter to explore the sources of linkage economies in detail. However, a few conjectures may be offered. A firm that is able to minimize knowledge 'stickiness' (Szulanski, 1996) may enjoy high levels of linkage economies, since it is able to stimulate intra-firm knowledge transfer. Such transfers are likely to occur over activity boundaries, for example, between production engineering and marketing, suggesting that an effective boundary-spanning function may be a key resource in this context (Mudambi and Swift, 2009).

9.2.2   Location: Value Added and the Value Chain

Mechanization and standardization have reduced the costs of manufacturing and logistics processes. Processes supporting mass customization (Kotha, 1995) have become widely available and subject to rapid imitation. This in turn has reduced the scope for the use of such processes to generate the differentiation required to support value creation. It is difficult for firms to extract high value added from either tangible products or standardized services (Maskell and Malmberg, 1999). Firms are finding that value added is becoming increasingly concentrated at the upstream and downstream ends of the value chain (Mudambi, 2007, 2008). Activities at both ends of the value chain are intensive in their application of knowledge and creativity.

Activities at the left or 'input' end are supported by R&D knowledge (basic and applied research and design), while activities at the right or 'output' end are supported by marketing knowledge (marketing, advertising and brand management, sales and after-sales service). The pattern of value added along the value chain may therefore be represented by the 'smiling curve' (Everatt et al., 1999) or the 'smile of value creation' as depicted in Figure 9.1 (Mudambi, 2007, 2008). Firms combine the comparative advantages of geo-

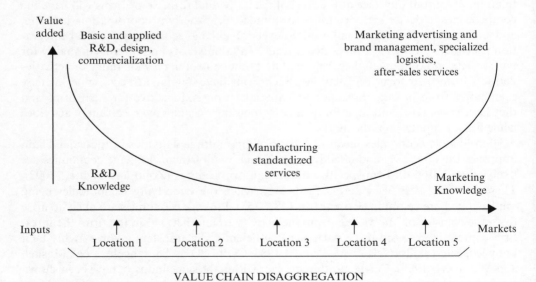

Source: Mudambi (2008).

Figure 9.1   The smile of value creation

graphical locations with their own resources and competencies to maximize their competitive advantage (McCann and Mudambi, 2005; Mudambi and Venzin, 2010). The classic international diversification question focuses on evaluating the comparative advantage of different geographical locations against the costs of geographically dispersed operations, that is, the strategic choices between cells 1 and 3 or between cells 2 and 4 in Table 9.1.

The geographical realities associated with the smile of value creation are that the activities at the ends of the overall value constellation are largely located in advanced market economies, while those in the middle of the value chain are moving (or have moved) to emerging market economies (Gereffi, 1999; Smakman, 2003; Pyndt and Pedersen, 2006).[8] Trade across national borders is increasingly in terms of value chain activities (so-called 'tasks') rather than complete goods or services (see, for example, Smakman, 2003: 17; Pyndt and Pedersen, 2006: 14). These realities emerge naturally from the application of the classic product cycle model (Vernon, 1966), at a point in time, to industry value constellations.

Examples of the 'smile of value creation' are ubiquitous. In the athletic shoe industry, the locational disaggregation of Nike's value chain has been in place for decades. Research, design and marketing are located in advanced market economies, intermediate manufacture and assembly in emerging market economies and basic component manufacture in low-cost locations (Yoffie, 1991). Nike concentrates on design and marketing, while outsourcing and closely coordinating production through a hierarchical offshore network of low-cost suppliers. Nike controls and owns the core intangible asset, the brand. The value of this intangible asset is crucially dependent on the highly creative design and marketing activities that Nike controls at the two ends of the value chain. Nike has been particularly successful at decoupling the tangible from the intangible aspects of its business, both in space and in time. However, a similar pattern of locational disaggregation may be seen in the operations of firms in many other industries. In the auto industry, the value chains underlying GM's Pontiac Le Mans and Ford's Fiesta incorporate design and marketing in advanced market economies and assembly in emerging market economies (Cao, 2002). In the pop music industry, 'artistic' and 'humdrum' activities are often locationally disaggregated, with the former driven by creativity and the latter by cost (Maskell and Lorenzen, 2004). In the film industry, Vang and Chaminade (2007) report that the Toronto cluster services the creative center in Hollywood by specializing in 'humdrum' activities.

This analysis provides the rationale for the enormous efforts by some technologically leading firms to break their final products or services into separable self-contained elements or modules (Kotabe et al., 2007). Increasing modularization allows the firm to amplify its focus on narrower activities within the value chain associated with the highest value added, an approach which may be called 'fine slicing'. In tandem, it allows the firm to outsource other activities (associated with lower value added) more cheaply and efficiently (Ernst and Lim, 2002).

The firms to which these lower value-added activities are outsourced view them as stepping stones in the course of moving into higher value-added activities. This is what underlies the enormous efforts of firms from emerging markets to develop R&D and marketing capabilities (Everatt et al., 1999; Smakman, 2003). These efforts often generate negative cashflow in the short run as resources are withdrawn from low margin contract manufacturing and assembly or standardized service delivery and transferred to R&D

and marketing where the firm has little experience. However, many emerging market firms view these short-run losses as investments in developing crucial competencies.

9.2.3   Location: Dynamic Analysis of the Value Constellation

Firm strategy
Over time, a firm's dynamic competencies are based on linking the two ends of the 'smile' so that marketing knowledge is used to calibrate and focus R&D-based knowledge creation (Leenders and Wierenga, 2002; Winter, 2003). At the firm level, such an integration of marketing with design and R&D underpins the ability to sustain the competitive advantage by a constant process of market-led innovation.

Improving process technology depresses the middle of the smile and pulls up the ends, making the smile more intense. The middle of the smile is driven down by increased efficiency in the operation of standardized processes that are not, however, rare, inimitable or organizationally embedded (Maskell and Malmberg, 1999). The ends of the smile are pulled upwards by increased personalization and customization in design and delivery. These competencies are based on R&D and market knowledge and skills that are rare, highly tacit, inimitable, and unique to each organization (Wernerfelt, 1984). Such resources often reside within the firm's human capital that then becomes a crucial source of value creation (Amit and Schoemaker, 1993).

Economy-wide processes
As noted above, firms controlling various activities within the value chain have differing incentives. Their responses to these incentives generate processes that change economy-wide patterns of economic activity. These processes may be broadly grouped into three categories that may be labeled 'catch-up', 'spillover', and 'industry creation' (see Figure 9.2).

Firms controlling activities in the middle of the value chain have strong incentives to acquire the resources and competencies that will enable them to control higher value-added activities. Thus, firms from emerging market economies such as China, India, Brazil, and Mexico are moving to develop their own brands and marketing expertise in advanced economies to increase their control over the downstream end of the value chain. Locating their R&D and marketing operations in advanced market economies also enables them to increase their absorptive capacity (Zahra and George, 2002; Phelps, 2008). They are attempting to develop capabilities to 'catch up' with rivals based in advanced market economies.

Firms that control the ends of the value chain, mostly from advanced market economies, are faced with an increasingly competitive landscape, including aggressive new entrants from emerging market economies intent on catching up. They have strong incentives to increase the efficiency and effectiveness of the high value-added activities that they control. Modularization enables these firms to strip out standardized activities from both the upstream R&D and downstream marketing activities that can then be relocated to emerging market economies. Thus, as firms such as GE, Microsoft, and IBM locate R&D sites in India they improve the cost efficiency of their overall R&D operations (Mudambi, 2011). The high value-added local activities of such MNEs create knowledge spillovers into emerging market economies.

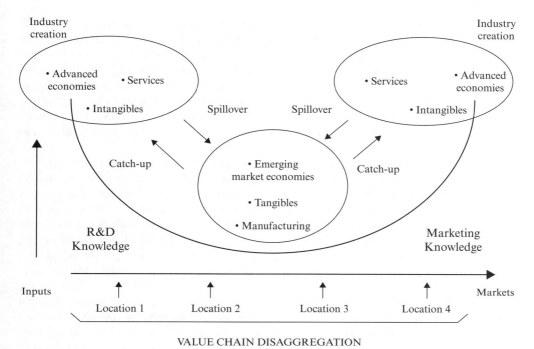

Figure 9.2   The smile – dynamic analysis

The two processes can act in concert when MNE subsidiaries established with the objective of controlling costs through implementing low-level tasks, evolve over time to compete for more advanced mandates within the firm. This process of subsidiary evolution is well documented (Cantwell and Mudambi, 2005). GE's John F. Welch Technology Center (JFWTC) located in Bangalore, India, may be considered a case in point (Ernst and Dubiel, 2009).

Finally, the ends of the 'smile' are not static. Innovation at these two ends is the essence of Schumpeterian entrepreneurship (Schumpeter, 1934). New industries emerge from basic and applied R&D at the upstream end (for example, biotech, nanotech) and through marketing and distribution innovations at the downstream end (for example, e-tailing, online auctions). At the moment, this process is overwhelmingly concentrated in advanced market economies. The process of 'industry creation' is the manifestation of Schumpeter's gale of creative destruction. It accelerates obsolescence in advanced market economies and pressures some sunset industries to relocate to emerging market economies.

9.3   AN ILLUSTRATION: THE MOBILE HANDSET INDUSTRY

The mobile handset industry provides a particularly useful setting to illustrate both the micro and macro aspects of the theory developed in this chapter.[9] Mobile handsets are the product of the successful convergence of technology and design aimed at fitting into cultural and lifestyle niches. They are rapidly morphing from 'technological objects' into key 'social objects'. Firms in the industry strive to provide mobility to a range of desired functionalities, ranging from simple internet access through audio and video entertainment to social networking. As with personal computers, consumers want mobile devices to serve as platforms to run a wide range of work and leisure applications supplied by creative industries. In this role, the mobile handset industry provides the consumer interface that creative industries use to deliver content such as text, audio, video, and application services.

Perhaps more importantly, mobile devices are argued to be the linchpin of the next techno-cultural shift, following personal computing in the 1980s and the internet in the 1990s (Rheingold, 2002). Super-efficient mobile communications (cellular phones, personal digital assistants, wireless-paging, and internet-access devices) allow people to connect with anyone, anywhere, anytime. Mobile devices make possible the new convergence of pop culture, cutting-edge technology, and social activism. The cultural impact of these devices comes not from the technology itself, but from how people adapt to it and ultimately use it to transform themselves, their communities, and their institutions.

The industry has global importance with sales exceeding $100 billion and volume growth of 29 percent in 2004 (Maheshwari, 2005). However, revenue growth in 2004 was more modest at 18 percent, reflecting the increasing intensity of competition along the lines discussed above. Markets in emerging economies such as India and China are expanding rapidly as the penetration rate of mobile devices rises, while markets in most advanced market economies have matured. In all markets, consumers are becoming more design conscious and resistant to standardized offerings. Over the 1991–2003 period, the industry has coalesced around a core set of product features in both voice and data communications, reflecting the emergence of a dominant design (Koski and Kretschmer, 2007).

Analyzing the industry's value chain reveals the 'smile of value creation'. As illustrated in Figure 9.3, high value-added activities appear at the ends of the value chain. Firms from emerging market economies such as Huawei of China that began as electronics manufacturing service companies, supplying private label products to firms from advanced market economies, are building marketing competencies to develop and support their own brands (Figure 9.4). At the moment such firms compete on the basis of low cost. However, their brands are becoming more valuable. This puts pressure on manufacturers in advanced market economies such as Nokia, Motorola, Apple, and Ericsson to continually innovate to maintain their high levels of value added. These established players' innovations are increasingly design driven, recognizing the highly variegated needs of individual markets. All these firms' design strategies are aimed at buttressing and enhancing the value of their brands.

Firms from recently developed countries such as Korea find themselves pushed to differentiate themselves from their emerging market competitors. For example, Samsung has accelerated its R&D efforts to minimize its dependency by developing its own chipsets. In addition to efforts in manufacturing, it is implementing a design-driven strategy with design centers in London and Milan in Europe, Tokyo in Japan, and Silicon Valley in the US.

Thus, we observe a convergence in the location strategies of all firms in the industry.

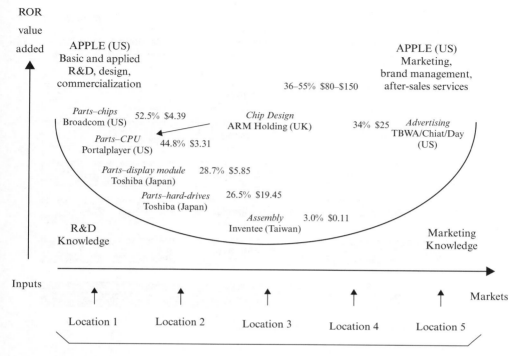

ROR
value
added

APPLE (US)
Basic and applied
R&D, design,
commercialization

APPLE (US)
Marketing,
brand management,
after-sales services

36–55% $80–$150

Parts–chips 52.5% $4.39
Broadcom (US)

Chip Design
ARM Holding (UK)

34% $25 *Advertising*
TBWA/Chiat/Day
(US)

Parts–CPU 44.8% $3.31
Portalplayer (US)

Parts–display module 28.7% $5.85
Toshiba (Japan)

Parts–hard-drives 26.5% $19.45
Toshiba (Japan)

Assembly 3.0% $0.11
Inventee (Taiwan)

R&D
Knowledge

Marketing
Knowledge

Inputs

Location 1   Location 2   Location 3   Location 4   Location 5

Markets

Source: Adapted from Linden et al. (2007).

Figure 9.3   Value chain disaggregation (March 2006)

Firms from advanced market economies, those from emerging market economies and
those from recently developed countries are all conforming to the 'smile of value creation'. In the short run, these strategies increase the concentration of high value-added
activities in advanced market economies. However, local demands in emerging market
economies are already imposing demands on the design capabilities of firms from
advanced market economies. Nokia Design, a unit comprising 250 people worldwide,
has implemented design projects in locations as diverse as Uganda and India. The unit
involves psychologists, industrial designers, materials experts, and anthropologists, and
leverages human-behavioral research to deliver location-focused product design.

9.3.1   Differences in Firm Strategy and Organization

Along with the convergence in location strategies, we observe a divergence in control
strategies. Nokia and Samsung remain highly vertically integrated, while Apple,
Motorola, and Ericsson have largely outsourced the middle of the value chain. Both
strategies are responses to the same pressures being exerted by mobile service providers
such as Vodafone and AT&T. As service providers face tougher market competition,
they are increasingly using the unique software and features (different menus, features,
branding, languages, and so on.) built into the devices they offer to generate competitive

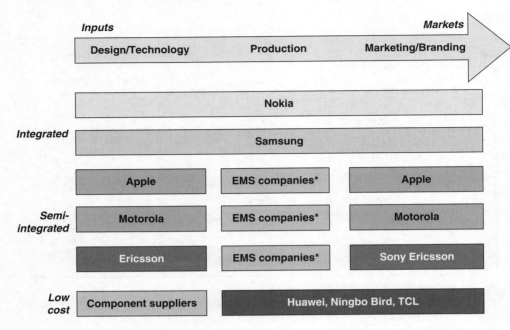

Note: *Electronics Manufacturing Service companies.

Source: Gartner Dataquest, HSBC, BCG.

Figure 9.4 Competitors in the mobile handset industry

advantage. They want software to be installed by manufacturers before the handsets leave the factory. Further, they want the handsets to be capable of supporting an increasingly wide range of application software.

Mobile handset manufacturers have responded and oriented production into two distinct processes. In the first, they build the internal components of the handset, the so-called 'engine'. These are generic devices that can be customized to take on different jobs. In the second process, the raw engines are customized to the requirements of different service providers and markets. Vertically integrated manufacturers retain control over both processes, while so-called 'semi-integrated' players retain design and customization while outsourcing actual manufacture. This organizational divergence may be explored by comparing Nokia on the one hand with Apple on the other.

Nokia is an engineering-driven company with a focus on manufacturing excellence. In 2006, it shipped more than 300 million units: twice as many handsets as it did just four years earlier. To do so, it handled more than 100 billion parts in its 10 factories scattered around the world. (See Nokia annual reports). These plants are located in advanced as well as in emerging market economies. The challenges of handling such huge volumes are enormous, but over the past 15 years Nokia has turned high-tech manufacturing and logistics into one of its core competencies.

Nokia's control of manufacturing enables it to execute the second process of customization extremely rapidly, transforming raw engines into hundreds of thousands of built-to-order phones in a matter of days. The need to control this complex process with the highest precision and quality is why Nokia has never chosen to outsource its manufacturing.[10] Indeed, Nokia sees its manufacturing expertise as a key means of enhancing its design skills. Reciprocally, its huge volume and customization requirements put pressure on its design capabilities. In short, Nokia is a firm with high levels of linkage economies.

Apple, on the other hand, is a company that focuses on the intangible aspects of its product offering. From its earliest days, it recognized that style and ease of use are as important as substance in terms of developing a brand. This strategic approach implies that it is crucial to control the fundamental building blocks that support the brand, that is, design and marketing. On the other hand, manufacturing is less important for such a firm.

In the mobile handset industry, Apple's well-known iPhone provides an apt illustration of the implementation of its strategy (Figure 9.3). Apple controls R&D-intensive activities at the upstream end of the value chain and marketing-intensive activities associated with brand management at the downstream end. However, more manufacturing and applications-oriented activities in the middle of the value chain are outsourced. These activities are more strongly connected to the tangible aspects of the iPhone and less linked to the intangible aspects. Like Nike, Apple has decoupled the tangible and intangible aspects of its business.

Reinforcing its strategy to appropriate value from intangibles, Apple runs iTunes, an online service that delivers audio, video, and gaming content. While the iTunes service is only marginally profitable in its own right, it is a powerful complementary asset that supports Apple's iPod and iPhone sales (Carr, 2004). The ability of Apple's products to run device-neutral content such as MP3 audio and Mpg video, along with the incompatibility of iTunes with competitors' hardware products, establishes a powerful competitive advantage in the crucial link between the device and creative content. Users of Apple's devices face large switching costs since their portfolio of music from iTunes will not work on a rival device.

Apple's focus on the core intangibles within the value proposition has enabled it to take advantage of huge network externalities. It has carved out its own iPod- and iPhone-related community which has been buttressed by the general acceptance of 'podcasts' (a technology that aggregates audio content into easily downloadable files) by a wide variety of content producers (McFedries, 2005). As complementary products compatible with iPods and iPhones appear in cars, clubs, airlines, and commercial establishments to service this community, the so-called 'iWorld subculture' expands and Apple benefits.

Apple's outsourcing pattern conforms to the 'smile of value creation', whereby higher value-added activities are located in the UK and Germany and controlled by firms such as ARM Holdings (chip design) and Balda AG (touchscreens). Marketing support activities at the downstream end are located in the US and controlled by firms such as TBWA/Chiat/Day. Repetitious manufacturing and assembly is undertaken in Taiwan by firms such as Inventec and Hon Hai Precision Industry. Relatively complex items such as chips are manufactured to design specifications by Samsung in Korea and NXP Semiconductor in the Netherlands. Recent estimates presented in Figure 9.3 demonstrate the huge advantages Apple derives from being the orchestrator of the iPhone GVC.

It is important to recognize that the subassemblies subsumed within complex products like the iPhone may themselves be subjected to similar analysis. Thus, there may be a 'smile' underlying the value chain of Balda's touchscreens. 'Smiles of value creation' may be nested one inside the other, like Russian dolls.

The differences between the vertical integration strategy of Nokia and the specialization strategy of Apple illustrate some fundamental differences in the approaches to generating knowledge, innovation, and value in creative industries. The stark differences between the two appear in their approaches to the nexus of control. Apple implements a very high degree of outsourcing, while Nokia is highly vertically integrated. We have argued that one of the key drivers of this difference is the extent of linkage economies. Linkage economies may therefore be seen as an aspect of 'organizational architecture' on the basis of which firms differ in terms of their ability to replicate the intimacy of local networks over long distances (Amin and Cohendet, 2005).

Nokia's manufacturing generates significant economies in its (upstream) design and (downstream) marketing activities and vice versa. This creates strong incentives to choose a hierarchical approach to firm organization, since the marginal value product of investments in manufacturing is relatively high. Apple, on the other hand, has relatively strong brand intangibles. These provide strong incentives to outsource manufacturing, since the marginal value product of investments in manufacturing is relatively low. Conversely, Apple has strong incentives to reinforce its brand as the center of a loyal community by investing in complementary corporate assets such as iTunes.

While both Nokia and Apple have geographically dispersed value chain activities, their strategic decisions regarding control affect their location patterns. Nokia maintains manufacturing facilities in Salo, Finland, as well as Germany and the UK, in addition to facilities in emerging market economies such as China, India, Brazil, and Mexico. The location of Apple's outsourced manufacturing is determined more flexibly, since it can simply choose the best partner or supplier for the components that it designs.

Finally, Apple's R&D is focused on specific activities in the value chain. It does not need to spend its R&D budget on activities that are outsourced. Thus, it is able to piggyback and profit from the R&D expenditures of its suppliers. Nokia is obliged to spread its R&D budget over the entire value chain. The two different control strategies therefore have direct implications with regard to innovation performance. Apple's focused R&D has produced significantly better financial performance in recent years. Apple's R&D/sales ratio was 3.8 percent in 2005, compared to Nokia's 11 percent. However, Apple outperformed Nokia on a wide range of measures of financial performance over the 2001–05 period, reflecting a greater leverage of its R&D spending.[11]

9.4   DISCUSSION

The large and growing share of intangibles in wealthy economies underscores the importance of knowledge-intensive and creative industries as the engines of wealth generation, now and into the future. Definitions of what does and what does not constitute a creative industry vary widely and are rapidly overtaken by events. What is clear is that technology and culture are increasingly interlinked and difficult to disconnect. Technology and the resulting tools and devices strongly influence the nature, form, and social context of popular culture. In turn, devices such as the iPod have become inseparable parts of popular culture (McFedries, 2005).

It is also clear that knowledge-based assets are becoming the most important source of value. Strategies to control these assets and their output of content, whether in the form of a design, a video, or a software application, are now the key to firm-level value appropriation. The success or failure of such strategies depends crucially on the firm's ability to span the techno-cultural divide. Apple's relatively successful use of iTunes (Carr, 2004) stands in contrast with the attempts of Hollywood studios to resist technology and create a '"closed" sphere of innovation on a global scale' (Currah, 2007: 362). The results of resistance to technological advances can also be seen in the recorded music industry, where record labels continue to push digital music CDs despite plummeting sales (Bockstedt et al., 2006).

9.4.1   Innovation

The current study presents a theoretical analysis of the future of creative processes over geographical space. The evidence presented is based on a case study: it is illustrative and suggestive, but does not provide any conclusive results. Its objective is to highlight and delineate the research questions that should be addressed in more in-depth empirical research.

The implications of this analysis for businesses appear along the two basic nexuses of location and control. There appears to be strong evidence that strategies along the location nexus will lead firms in creative industries to geographically disperse their value chain activities. The evidence here is impossible to ignore (Smakman, 2003; Pyndt and Pedersen, 2006). The continual dispersion of design, R&D and other creative activities by ever smaller firms is moving hand in hand with the emergence of increasingly specialized niche business activities, many of which are strongly anchored in geographical space (Calderini and Scellato, 2005).

However, it appears that two fundamentally different strategies are emerging in terms of how the value chain is controlled. One strategy is based on maintaining high control over both tangible and intangible aspects of the firm's value proposition. Such a strategy is likely to appeal to firms that have relatively strong competencies in repetitive or 'humdrum' activities (Caves, 2000) as well as the ability to link these competencies to the high value-added upstream and downstream activities within the value chain. In other words, such firms have strong *linkage economies* whereby their repetitive activities become more efficient and their creative activities become more effective through common ownership. The successful value propositions that emerge from such firms are likely to deliver excellence based on a deep understanding of current market expectations.

Greater vertical integration based on linkage economies should enhance a firm's advantage in delivering excellence to an existing customer base. Further, a greater extent of vertical integration is likely to be associated with a tendency to favor incremental innovation. Vertical integration also implies that intra-firm coordination of value chain activities is a crucial source of competitive advantage, while modularization is relatively less important. The firm tends to be better at in-house cross-functional integration.

The implication of the above argument is that the vertical integration strategy involves being attuned to and closely following current market demands. It follows that this strategy requires the firm to continually improve the quality and lower the cost of individual activities, while 'the underlying core design concepts, and the links between them, remain the same' (Henderson and Clark, 1990: 12). This may be formally stated as follows:

Proposition 1: Firms with strong linkage economies excel at incremental innovation.

An alternative strategy is based on focusing on the activities in the value chain that require the highest levels of commercial creativity and generate the highest levels of value added. Such a strategy is likely to appeal to firms that have relatively stronger competencies at the ends of the value chain in design and marketing. Specialized firms that outsource their repetitive activities to focused suppliers (that therefore do not enjoy linkage economies) may not be able to match the costs of their vertically integrated rivals. This disadvantage implies that for specialized firms to survive and excel, they must look beyond the expectations of the existing market by developing entirely new value propositions. The specialization strategy involves predicting where the market is going and leading it.

A successful specialized strategy also requires the implementation of modularization. For instance, in the case of manufacturing, individual technologies must be compartmentalized, developed as modular sub-assemblies and contracted to specialist suppliers as illustrated by the example of the iPhone (Figure 9.3). Activities in the value chain must be decoupled from each other. Coordination across organizational boundaries and orchestration of the entire network is particularly important to the success of modularization. Firms implementing a specialized strategy are likely to develop more sophisticated external networks as in the case of the US motion picture industry (Scott, 2005).

Firms that implement specialized strategies often create, and maintain competitive advantage by reconfiguring existing core technologies in novel ways that is, through 'architectural innovation' (Henderson and Clark, 1990).[12] Architectural innovation falls between incremental innovation, where vertically integrated firms are likely to have an edge and radical innovation where considerations of uncertainty are so acute that it is difficult to fund within the firm. Firms with specialized strategies implementing successful architectural innovation make 'modest changes to the existing technology . . . that have quite dramatic competitive consequences' (ibid.: 10). In short, successful architectural innovation requires developing and controlling system design by, for example, black-boxing proprietary intellectual assets. These arguments may be stated formally as follows:

Proposition 2: Firms with specialization strategies excel at architectural innovation.

The specialization strategy is based on two imperatives. The first is the focus on value-creating ideation and high knowledge activities that are retained in-house. The second is the cost-driven outsourcing of standardized activities, typically to local firms in emerging market economies. It is likely that the strategy of specialization will generate greater flexibility, at the firm and geographical levels (Graf and Mudambi, 2005; Mudambi and Venzin, 2010). Outsourced activities can be rapidly transferred to competing vendors in alternative locations. Along with this flexibility comes high R&D leverage; the firm's innovative efforts are concentrated on very specific activities in the value chain, but it captures a large share of the value added from the entire GVC. However, a critical research question concerns whether firms implementing a specialized strategy will lose the key complementary knowledge assets associated with standardized activities and become technologically hollow over time (Kotabe and Mudambi, 2009).[13]

With a vertical integration strategy, the need for modularization and black-boxing is considerably lower. It is more resilient in institutional contexts with weak intellectual property rights, since it transfers less knowledge to its supplier network (Gertler, 2003). However, its R&D spending has lower leverage, since it is spread over a wider repository of activities and competencies. Further, its high-linkage economies are valuable during periods of stable growth, but the associated inflexibility becomes a burden when technology trajectories change.

Nokia prospered for over a decade as mobile handsets evolved along a stable path defined by the primary functionality of the phone. The theory propounded here implies that its success during this period can be attributed to its distinctive competencies in incremental innovation that were advanced by its strategy of vertical integration. However, there is considerable evidence that these competencies do not support innovative responses to discontinuous change (Dunlap-Hinkler et al., 2010) and the company found itself in difficulties when it tried to respond to the industry disruption caused by the introduction of the smartphone.

On the other hand, as documented above, Apple has focused on architectural innovation from the very birth of the company. These competencies were developed through its strategy of specialization and enabled it to survive and thrive, as its disruptive innovative successes (the Apple Mac, the iPod, the iPhone, the iPad) have more than paid for its failures (the Newton, the Pippin, the TAM). The specialization strategy yields both operational and innovative flexibility, implying that it is likely to be dominated in periods of stable growth, but yield superior results when the competitive environment is very volatile.

9.4.2   Communities

More and more discontinuous change is occurring through interplays between the two ends of the value chain. The boundary between arts and commerce is becoming increasingly blurred (Caves, 2000). Entrepreneurial firms are recognizing that technology platforms such as social media can enrich their interface with their customers or audiences. Established firms are recognizing that their brands, suitably managed, can be leveraged to become the hubs of virtual communities, enhancing their presence in the popular culture.

This discussion leads to some conjectures. Specialized firms are heavily dependent on their brand and image intangibles. It is becoming recognized that brands are associated with a deep-seated human desire to 'belong' (Fournier, 1998). Such firms' success is likely to be heavily influenced by their success in building vibrant communities around their value propositions. The value proposition consists of a 'hard' center (the product) encased in a 'soft' shell (services). However, in an increasingly networked economy, the success of the value proposition is likely to depend on the vitality of the community that embraces it. Interpersonal interaction either in virtual space (for example, online groups, social media) or in actual contact, reinforce such a value proposition.

In contrast, vertically integrated firms are more likely to depend on the excellence of the 'hard' center of their value proposition, that is, the more tangible aspects. Repeated individual use and the associated personal satisfaction reinforce such a value proposition. This argument may be stated formally as follows:

Proposition 3:   Firms with specialization strategies are better at building and capturing value from the virtual communities associated with their products.

9.5   CONCLUDING REMARKS

This chapter made a series of important points. First, the creation of value is increasingly stemming from intangibles. Second, GVCs are becoming disaggregated and spatially dispersed. Third, two primary firm strategies can be discerned with respect to the GVC – a vertical integration strategy whereby the firm tries to maintain control over the value chain within the firm and a specialization strategy, whereby the firm focuses on narrow, high value-added activities. Finally, as the business environment becomes more volatile and the global economy becomes increasingly networked, specialized firms are more likely to survive and thrive.

Ironically, the extent to which firms and locations can benefit from the entrepreneurial value propositions that they create depends on the extent to which the key creative and knowledge assets are embedded within organizational and geographical boundaries, and therefore resistant to imitation by rivals in competing locations (Maskell and Malmberg, 1999). Success in this dynamic environment depends on not only creating value, but also appropriating it.

NOTES

*   This chapter draws heavily on my 2008 paper 'Location, control and innovation in knowledge-intensive industries', *Journal of Economic Geography*, **8** (5): 699–725.

1.   The percentage of market valuation of the S&P 500 US firms related to intangible assets increased from 38 percent in 1982 to 62 percent in 1991 (Blair and Wallman, 2001) and to about 85 percent by 2001 (Nakamura, 2003). By 2004, annual investment in intangibles in the US economy was conservatively estimated at over 8 percent of GDP or about $1 trillion (Hofmann, 2005, citing unpublished data from Nakamura). In these estimates, about a third of the $1 trillion in intangibles is software; one-third is intellectual property, such as patents and copyrights; and one-third is advertising and marketing.

2.   Intangible assets are intangible in the sense that they cannot be valued with certainty or precision. However, they are assets in that they generate a stream of future returns. Lev (2001: 5) defines an intangible asset as 'a claim to future benefits that does not have a physical or financial (a stock or a bond) embodiment'.

3.   For the purposes of this chapter, we adopt the relatively narrow definition of globalization as 'the shift towards a more integrated and interdependent world economy . . . including the globalization of markets and the globalization of production' (Hill, 2008: 6). This is in contrast to those who define globalization as a broader phenomenon that transcends economic development and includes political, technological, and cultural dimensions, owing in large part to the rise of 'instantaneous electronic communication' (Giddens, 2003).

4.   For the purposes of this chapter, the advanced market economies may be taken to be the Triad economies

of North America, Western Europe, and Japan, also including Oceania. Emerging market economies range from the large BRIC economies (Brazil, Russia, India, and China) to many smaller economies in Asia, transition economies of Central and Eastern Europe and some economies in South America (BIS, 2007).

5. Attempts at developing internal hybrids by introducing market forces within the firm have been dogged by severe problems. It is very difficult for managers to make credible commitments to workers that they will consistently allow internal market forces to work. Hence the motivational benefits of internal markets are seldom realized and almost never sustained. See, for example, Foss (2003).

6. In the 1990s, GM controlled the production of about two-thirds of the parts that went into its cars, while Ford controlled about half and Chrysler a third (Rubenstein, 2001).

7. Spulber (1989) defines economies of sequence, a concept that is related to linkage economies. Economies of sequence arise when 'cost gains (are) achieved by combining a sequence of production stages' (Spulber, 1989: 113). These economies affect the firm's technology, as defined within the neoclassical paradigm; a logical implication is that if two firms have access to the same technology, they are able to enjoy the same economies of sequence. In other words, they are not meant to explain firm-level differences.

8. Smakman (2003) presents consistent evidence of this trend for the Singapore garment industry. Pyndt and Pedersen (2006) present compelling and in-depth evidence for Denmark at both the firm and industry levels.

9. This case study was developed using secondary sources. Industry studies, consulting reports, company annual reports, and web sources were used.

10. It does use contractors for a small number of handsets, mainly older models that do not require customization or rapid delivery.

11. These data were drawn from Apple and Nokia annual reports and other public sources. Financial performance was measured in terms of sales growth, gross margin percentage, gross profit growth, operating margin percentage, operating income growth, total shareholder returns, and market capitalization growth. However, using Nokia's larger total sales, its brand was judged to be considerably more valuable than Apple's in 2005 and 2006 by the marketing consulting company, Interbrand.

12. In the formative years of the personal computer industry in the late 1970s and early 1980s, Apple implemented a specialized strategy, focusing on a novel system architecture made up of relatively modest (and outsourced) component technologies (Christensen, 1997). This control of system design and outsourcing of modular components persists in the iPhone as seen in Figure 9.3.

13. Examples abound of firms that transferred technology to outsourcers in emerging market economies only to be eventually surpassed and supplanted by their former suppliers. In 1981, Schwinn Bicycle Company of Chicago transferred equipment and technology to Giant Bicycles of Taiwan and outsourced millions of bicycles for the US market. Over time Giant drove its former mentor into bankruptcy and today is the dominant firm in the industry (Witte, 2004).

REFERENCES

Amin, A. and Cohendet, P. (2004), *Architectures of Knowledge: Firms, Capabilities and Communities*, Oxford: Oxford University Press.

Amin, A. and Cohendet, P. (2005), 'Geographies of knowledge formation in firms', *Industry and Innovation*, **12** (4): 465–86.

Amin, A. and Thrift, N. (2005), 'Citizens of the world', *Harvard International Review*, **27** (3): 14–17.

Amit, R. and Schoemaker, P.J.H. (1993), 'Strategic assets and organizational rent', *Strategic Management Journal*, **14** (1): 33–46.

Augier, M. and Teece, D.J. (2006), 'Understanding complex organization: the role of know-how, internal structure and human behavior in the evolution of capabilities', *Industrial and Corporate Change*, **15** (2): 395–416.

Bank for International Settlements (BIS) (2007), *Bank for International Settlements 77th Annual Report*, Basel: BIS.

Blair, M.M. and Wallman, S.M.H. (2001), *Unseen Wealth: The Value of Corporate Intangible Assets*, Washington, DC: Brookings Institution Press.

Bockstedt, J.C., Kauffman, R.J. and Riggins, F.J. (2006), 'The move to artist-led on-line music distribution: a theory-based assessment and prospects for structural changes in the digital music market', *International Journal of Electronic Commerce*, **10** (3): 7–38.

Buckley, P.J. and Casson, M.C. (1976), *The Future of Multinational Enterprise*, London: Macmillan.

Calantone, R.J. and Stanko, M.A. (2007), 'Drivers of outsourced innovation: an exploratory study', *Journal of Product Innovation Management*, **24** (3): 230–41.

Calderini, M. and Scellato, G. (2005), 'Academic research, technological specialization and the innovation performance in European regions: an empirical analysis in the wireless sector', *Industrial and Corporate Change*, **14** (2): 279–305.

Cantwell, J.A. and Mudambi, R. (2005), 'MNE competence-creating subsidiary mandates', *Strategic Management Journal*, **26** (12): 1109–28.

Cantwell, J.A. and Santangelo, G.D. (1999), 'The frontier of international technology networks: sourcing abroad the most highly tacit capabilities', *Information Economics and Policy*, **11** (1): 101–23.

Cao, L. (2002), 'Corporate and product identity in the postnational economy: rethinking U.S. trade laws', *California Law Review*, **90** (2): 401–84.

Carr, N. (2004), 'The corrosion of IT advantage: strategy makes a comeback', *Journal of Business Strategy*, **25** (5): 10–15.

Caves, R. (2000), *Creative Industries: Contracts between Art and Commerce*, Cambridge, MA: Harvard University Press.

Christensen, C. (1997), *The Innovator's Dilemma: When New Technologies Cause Great Firms to Fail*, Boston, MA: Harvard Business School Press.

Coase, R.H. (1937), 'The nature of the firm', *Economica*, New Series, **4** (16): 386–405.

Conybeare, J.A.C. (2003), *Merging Traffic: The Consolidation of the International Automotive Industry*, Oxford: Rowman & Littlefield.

Crafts, N.F.R. (1985), *British Economic Growth during the Industrial Revolution*, Oxford: Clarendon.

Currah, A. (2007), 'Hollywood, the internet and the world: a geography of disruptive innovation', *Industry and Innovation*, **14** (4): 359–84.

Dicken, P. (2003), *Global Shift: Reshaping the Global Economic Map in the 21st Century*, Thousand Oaks, CA: Sage.

Dunlap-Hinkler, D., Kotabe, M. and Mudambi, R. (2010), 'A story of breakthrough vs. incremental innovation: corporate entrepreneurship in the global pharmaceutical industry', *Strategic Entrepreneurship Journal*, **4** (2): 106–27.

Dunning, J.H. (1993), *Multinational Enterprises and the Global Economy*, Reading MA: Addison-Wesley.

Ernst, D. and Lim, L. (2002), 'Global production networks, knowledge diffusion and local capability formation', *Research Policy*, **31**: 1417–29.

Ernst, H. and Dubiel, A. (2009), 'How to build and manage a global R&D center: the case of GE in India', European Case Clearing House Case #309-039-1.

Everatt, D., Tsai, T. and Cheng, B. (1999), 'The Acer Group's China manufacturing decision', Version A. Ivey Case Series #9A99M009, Richard Ivey School of Business, University of Western Ontario.

Florida, R. (2002), *The Rise of the Creative Class: And How It's Transforming Work, Leisure, Community and Everyday Life*, New York: Basic Books.

Foss, N.J. (2003), 'Selective intervention and internal hybrids: interpreting and learning from the rise and decline of the Oticon spaghetti organization', *Organization Science*, **14** (3): 331–49.

Fournier, S. (1998), 'Consumers and their brands: developing relationship theory in consumer research', *Journal of Consumer Research*, **24** (4): 343–53.

Fujita, M., Krugman, P.R. and Venables, A.J. (1999), *The Spatial Economy: Cities, Regions and International Trade*, Boston, MA: MIT Press.

Gereffi, G. (1999), 'International trade and industrial upgrading in the apparel commodity chain', *Journal of International Economics*, **48** (1): 37–70.

Gertler, M. (2003), 'Tacit knowledge and the economic geography of context, or the undefinable tacitness of being (there)', *Journal of Economic Geography*, **3** (1): 75–99.

Giddens, A. (2003), *Runaway World: How Globalization Is Re-Shaping Our Lives*, London: Taylor & Francis.

Graf, M. and Mudambi, S. (2005), 'The outsourcing of IT-enabled business processes: a conceptual model of the location decision', *Journal of International Management*, **11** (2): 253–68.

Hamel, G. and Prahalad, C.K. (1990), 'The core competence of the corporation', *Harvard Business Review*, **68** (3): 79–93.

Hayek, F.A. (1945), 'The use of knowledge in society', *American Economic Review*, **35** (4): 519–30.

Henderson, R.M. and Clark, K.B. (1990), 'Architectural innovation: the reconfiguration of existing product technologies and the failure of established firms', *Administrative Science Quarterly*, **35** (1): 9–30.

Hill, C.W.L. (2008), *International Business*, 7th rev edn, New York: McGraw-Hill.

Hirschman, A.O. (1968), 'The political economy of import-substituting industrialization in Latin America', *Quarterly Journal of Economics*, **82** (1): 1–32.

Hirschman, A.O. (1977), 'A generalized linkage approach to economic development with special reference to staples', *Economic Development and Cultural Change*, **25** (Supplement): 67–97.

Hofmann, J. (2005), 'Value intangibles', *Current Issues*, Deutsche Bank Research, October 19.

Howkins, J. (2001), *The Creative Economy: How People Make Money from Ideas*, London: Allen Lane, Penguin Press.

International Monetary Fund (IMF) (2006), *World Economic Outlook: Globalization and Inflation*, Washington, DC: IMF April.

Kogut, B. and Zander, U. (1993), 'Knowledge of the firm and the evolutionary theory of the multinational corporation', *Journal of International Business Studies*, **24** (4): 625–45.

Koski, H. and Kretschmer, T. (2007), 'Innovation and dominant design in mobile telephony', *Industry and Innovation*, **14** (3): 305–24.

Kotabe, M. and Mudambi, R. (2009), 'Global sourcing: opportunities and challenges', *Journal of International Management*, **15** (2): 121–5.

Kotabe, M., Parente, R. and Murray, J. (2007), 'Antecedents and outcomes of modular production in the Brazilian automobile industry: a grounded theory approach', *Journal of International Business Studies*, **38** (1): 84–106.

Kotha, S. (1995), 'Mass customization: implementing the emerging paradigm for competitive advantage', *Strategic Management Journal*, **16** (5): 21–42.

Leenders, M. and Wierenga, B. (2002), 'The effectiveness of different mechanisms for integrating marketing and R&D', *Journal of Product Innovation Management*, **19** (4): 305–17.

Lev, B. (2001), *Intangibles: Management, Measurement and Reporting*, Washington, DC: Brookings Institution Press.

Linden, G., Kraemer, K. and Dedrick, J. (2007), 'Who captures value in global innovation system?', Personal computing Industry Centre, University of California, Irvine, June.

Lorenzen, M. (2004), 'Knowledge and geography', *Industry and Innovation*, **12** (4): 399–407.

Lundvall, B-Å. (2007), 'National Innovation Systems: analytical concept and development tool', *Industry and Innovation*, **14** (1): 95–119.

Maheshwari, S. (2005), *The Mobile Handset Industry Asia, 2004–2009*, Washington, DC: Research Connect Inc.

Malecki, E.J. (1984), 'High technology and local economic development', *Journal of the American Planning Association*, **50** (3): 262–9.

Mansfield, E. (1985), 'How rapidly does new industrial technology leak out?', *Journal of Industrial Economics*, **34** (2): 217–23.

Maskell, P. and Lorenzen, M. (2004), 'The cluster as market organization', *Urban Studies*, **41** (5–6): 991–1009.

Maskell, P. and Malmberg, A. (1999), 'Localised learning and industrial competitiveness', *Cambridge Journal of Economics*, **23**: 167–86.

McCann, P. and Mudambi, R. (2005), 'Analytical differences in the economics of geography: the case of the multinational firm', *Environment and Planning A*, **37** (10): 1857–76.

McFedries, P. (2005), 'The iPod people', *IEEE Spectrum*, **42** (2): 76.

McMillan, G.S., Hamilton, R.D. III and Deeds, D.L. (2000), 'Firm management of scientific information: an empirical update', *R&D Management*, **30** (2): 177–82.

Mudambi, R. (2007), 'Offshoring: economic geography and the multinational firm', *Journal of International Business Studies*, **38** (1): 206.

Mudambi, R. (2008), 'Location, control and innovation in knowledge-intensive industries', *Journal of Economic Geography*, **8** (5): 699–725.

Mudambi, R. (2011), 'Hierarchy, coordination and innovation in the multinational enterprise', *Global Strategy Journal*, **1** (3–4): 317–23.

Mudambi, R. and Helper, S. (1998), 'The 'close but adversarial' model of supplier relations in the U.S. auto industry', *Strategic Management Journal*, **19** (8): 775–92.

Mudambi, R. and Swift, T. (2009), 'Professional guilds, tension and knowledge management', *Research Policy*, **38** (5): 736–45.

Mudambi, R. and Venzin, M. (2010), 'The strategic nexus of offshoring and outsourcing decisions', *Journal of Management Studies*, **47** (8): 1510–33.

Nakamura, L. (2003), 'A trillion dollars a year in intangible investment and the New Economy', in J.R.M. Hand and B. Lev (eds), *Intangible Assets: Values, Measures and Risks*, Oxford: Oxford University Press, pp. 19–47.

Nelson, R.R. and Winter, S.G. (1982), *An Evolutionary Theory of Economic Change*, Boston, MA: Belknap Press of Harvard University Press.

Normann, R. and Ramírez, R. (1993), 'From value chain to value constellation: designing interactive strategy', *Harvard Business Review*, **71** (4): 65–77.

Organisation for Economic Co-operation and Development (OECD) (1996), *Technology, Productivity and Job Creation*, Paris: OECD.

Pavitt, K. (1998), 'Technologies, products and organization in the innovating firm: what Adam Smith tells us and Joseph Schumpeter doesn't', *Industry and Corporate Change*, **7** (3): 433–52.

Phelps, N.A. (2008), 'Cluster or capture? Manufacturing foreign direct investment, external economies and agglomeration', *Regional Studies*, **42** (4): 457–73.

Porter, M. (1985), *Competitive Advantage*, New York: Free Press.

Porter, M. and Millar, V.E. (1985), 'How information gives you competitive advantage', *Harvard Business Review*, **63** (4): 149–60.

Pyndt, J. and Pedersen, T. (2006), *Managing Global Offshoring Strategies: A Case Approach*, Copenhagen: Copenhagen Business School Press.

Rheingold, H. (2002), *Smart Mobs, the Next Social Revolution: Transforming Cultures and Communities in the Age of Instant Access*, New York: Basic Books.

Ricketts, M.J. (2002), *The Economics of Business Enterprise*, Cheltenham, UK and Northampton, MA, USA: Edward Elgar.

Rivoli, O. (2009), *The Travels of a T-shirt in the Global Economy*. 2nd edn, New York: Wiley.

Rosenberg, R. (1982), *Inside the Black Box: Technology and Economics*, Cambridge: Cambridge University Press.

Rubenstein, J.M. (2001), *Making and Selling Cars: Innovation and Change in the U.S. Automotive Industry*, Baltimore, MD: Johns Hopkins University Press.

Schumpeter, J.A. (1934), *The Theory of Economic Development*, Cambridge, MA: Harvard University Press (originally published in German in 1911; reprinted by Transaction Publishers, New Brunswick, NJ in 1997).

Scott, A.J. (2000), *The Cultural Economy of Cities*, London: Sage.

Scott, A.J. (2005), *On Hollywood: The Place, the Industry*, Princeton, NJ: Princeton University Press.

Scott, A.J. and Storper, M. (2003), 'Regions, globalization, development', *Regional Studies*, **37** (6–7): 579–93.

Smakman, F. (2003), *Local Industry in Global Networks: Changing Competiveness, Corporate Strategies and Pathways of Development in Singapore and Malaysia's Garment Industry*, PhD dissertation, Utrecht University, The Netherlands: Rozenberg.

Spulber, D.F. (1989), *Regulation and Markets*, Boston, MA: MIT Press.

Szulanski, G. (1996), 'Exploring internal stickiness: impediments to the transfer of best practices within the firm', *Strategic Management Journal*, **17**: 27–43.

Teece, D.J. (1998), 'Capturing value from knowledge assets: the New Economy, markets for know-how and intangible assets', *California Management Review*, **40** (3): 55–79.

Tseng, M.M., Jiao, R.J. and Wang, C. (2010), 'Design for mass personalization', *CIRP Annals – Manufacturing Technology*, **59** (1): 175–8.

Uchida, T. (2008), 'Location strategy for Life Sciences R&D on the US Eastern Seabord', Presentation to the Canon Strategy Conference, Tokyo, March 8.

Vang, J. and Chaminade, C. (2007), 'Global–local linkages, spillovers and cultural clusters: theoretical and empirical insights from an exploratory study of Toronto's film cluster', *Industry and Innovation*, **14** (4): 401–20.

Vernon, R. (1966), 'International investment and international trade in the product cycle', *Quarterly Journal of Economics*, **80** (2): 190–207.

Wernerfelt, B. (1984), 'A resource-based view of the firm', *Strategic Management Journal*, **5** (2): 171–80.

Williamson, O.E. (1975), *Markets and Hierarchies: Analysis and Antitrust Implications, a Study in the Economics of Internal Organization*, New York: Free Press.

Williamson, O.E. (1979), 'Transaction-cost economics: the governance of contractual relations', *Journal of Law and Economics*, **22** (2): 233–61.

Winter, S. (2003), 'Understanding dynamic capabilities', *Strategic Management Journal*, **24** (10): 991–5.

Witte, G. (2004), 'A rough ride for Schwinn Bicycle', *The Washington Post*, A01, December 3.

Yoffie, D. (1991), Nike (A), Harvard Business School Case #391238.

Zahra, S.A. and George, G. (2002), 'Absorptive capacity: a review, reconceptualization and extension', *Academy of Management Review*, **27** (2): 185–203.

Zollo, M. and Winter, S.G. (2002), 'Deliberate learning and the evolution of dynamic capabilities', *Organization Science*, **13** (3): 339–51.

10 How has information technology use shaped the geography of economic activity?
Chris Forman

10.1 INTRODUCTION

It is widely believed that the diffusion of the commercial internet has led to a reduction in communication costs that has the potential to reshape the geographical variance in economic activity. One line of reasoning that has received particular attention speculates that lower communication costs disproportionately benefit economic actors in low density, economically isolated locations by enabling them to plug into economic activity in other locations. Such models lead to the conclusion that the diffusion of information technology (IT) will lead to a convergence of economic activity across locations. This view has been espoused in books such as Cairncross's (1997) *The Death of Distance* and Friedman's (2005) *The World is Flat*.

However, both recent theoretical models and a variety of empirical evidence have argued that the link between IT diffusion and economic activity is more nuanced. For example, IT investments in business often require complementary inputs that are disproportionately found in cities, and may benefit from traditional Marshallian externalities. Second, most communication is local, so if IT-enabled communication channels complement existing channels, then IT-enabled channels may reinforce existing communication links and patterns of economic activity. Further, IT-enabled communication channels are less rich than other channels such as face-to-face communication, and so may be less effective at conveying certain kinds of 'tacit' knowledge; as a result, regular face-to-face interactions may be required even when IT-enabled communication is used. As a result, the diffusion of IT may lead to an increasing concentration or 'divergence' of economic activity in large cities, or more nuanced patterns of activity.

While IT use has had the potential to reshape geographical variance in economic activity for some time, lower communication costs enabled by internet technology have resulted in increasing interest in this question, leading to rapid growth in this research area over the past 10 years. Research in this area has examined this question from a variety of perspectives: for example, an analysis of how the diffusion of IT influences employment and wage growth across regions; how IT reshapes the geography of innovation; how new IT-enabled distribution channels influence consumer behavior; and the extent to which IT has facilitated the globalization of goods and services, to name just a few.

Why is a review of research on this question appropriate for a Handbook of Industry Studies and Economic Geography? As will be shown, the impact of IT on the geographical variance in economic activity will often depend upon the market and firms and institutions in which IT use is embedded; the type of IT (in particular the need for complementary inputs); and the nature of economic transaction. In short, the institutional details of the settings in the studies we review will frequently play an important role in shaping their outcomes. As a result, industry studies work has played and will continue to play an important role in research in this area.

The goal of this chapter is not to review the entire literature in this area, but to distill several common themes. Section 10.2 begins with a brief review of theoretical models. Next, we discuss several perspectives from empirical research, including geography and IT adoption (Section 10.3); IT and convergence/divergence in economic growth (Section 10.4); IT and the geography of innovation (Section 10.5); the implications of IT-enabled retail and wholesale channels (Section 10.6); and implications for research on IT and globalization, an important but still under-researched topic (Section 10.7). Section 10.8 concludes.

10.2   THEORETICAL MODELS OF THE IMPLICATIONS OF IT USE

The implications of IT use for cities and regional economic activity depend crucially on whether IT-enabled and other communications channels are complements or substitutes. The 'death of distance' model of IT and communication that is highlighted in books such as Friedman's *The World is Flat* argues that face-to-face and electronically enabled communication (such as email, videoconferencing, and chat rooms) are substitutes for one another. Improving quality and declining costs for the electronic channel will cause agents to shift out of other channels and into the electronically enabled one. One implication of these types of models is that cities, which traditionally enjoy lower costs of face-to-face communication, will become less important.

One implicit assumption of the most basic version of these types of models is that the costs of using the electronically enabled channel will fall for all types of communication equally. Such models do not highlight the comparative advantage that one channel may enjoy over others in certain types of communication. There are good reasons to believe that such assumptions may be inaccurate. A long line of literature, starting with Polanyi (1966) but continuing on in diverse fields such as urban economics and regional studies (for example, Moss, 1998; Leamer and Storper, 2001; Storper and Venables, 2004) and communications (for example, Daft and Lengel, 1984; Daft et al., 1987) has shown the unique advantages that face-to-face interaction has over other forms of communication, particularly in communicating certain kinds of tacit or 'sticky' knowledge (for example, von Hippel, 1994). For example, while IT may be an effective means of coordinating ongoing projects and collaborations, it may be less effective as a means of establishing new partnerships or collaborative relationships (for example, Gaspar and Glaeser, 1998; Charlot and Duranton, 2006; Glaeser and Ponzetto, 2007).

Allowing for heterogeneity in the ability of IT-enabled communications to substitute for face-to-face contact will have important implications for how lower communication costs for IT will impact on cities and more broadly on regional economic outcomes. While IT-enabled communications may substitute for some face-to-face interactions, it may increase the demand for face-to-face interactions that cannot easily be performed electronically (Gaspar and Glaeser, 1998). This can make cities even more appealing, particularly for industries or activities where ideas are complex and difficult to communicate electronically.

Since the relationship between IT-enabled and other communications media may differ systematically across industries, the implications of IT use for local outcomes may vary by industry as well (for example, Glaeser and Ponzetto, 2007). For example, lower communication costs may enable some industries such as manufacturing to move out of cities and into the hinterland. However, innovative ideas-producing industries that involve frequent exchange of complex knowledge will continue to rely on face-to-face interactions in cities (ibid.), and such industries will continue to be agglomerated. Such industry-level variance has been used to explain the resurgence of cities with high concentrations of innovative industries such as New York and San Francisco, and for the decline of traditional manufacturing centers such as Detroit and Cleveland (ibid.).

Declines in communication costs can affect not only geographical variance in the location of industries, but also functional areas (Duranton and Puga, 2005). The costs of performing headquarters and support functions have historically been lower in cities due to the propensity of such functions to outsource business services (Aarland et al., 2007). The concentration of business service providers such as legal, accounting, and advertising in large cities makes the costs of outsourcing lower in such locations (Ono, 2007; Davis and Henderson, 2008). However, there may exist Marshallian externalities or other efficiencies in locating production activities outside of big cities where the concentration of intermediate suppliers may be strong and where operating costs may be lower. While this implies that there may be advantages to locating production and support activities in different locations, coordination costs may act to keep firms integrated. However, as IT-enabled communication costs fall so may the costs of managing multiple firm locations, so that we may observe both an increasing number of multi-unit organizations and a specialization of cities by functional area. In particular, one equilibrium outcome of such a process will be headquarters activities concentrated in a small number of large cities while production locates in smaller cities with lower operating costs (Duranton and Puga, 2005).

10.3 EMPIRICAL EVIDENCE ON IT ADOPTION

Empirical investigation of the impact of IT diffusion on cities has proceeded in one of two ways. One approach has been to explore geographical variance in the adoption of IT that reduces communication costs. This approach relies on revealed preferences; under the probit or 'rank' model of adoption (for example, David, 1969; Karshenas and Stoneman, 1993), firms and individuals will adopt when net benefits are positive, so we can recover geographical variance in the net benefits to IT investment by examining adoption patterns. The other approach examines the implications of IT investment for local growth in employment, wages, and establishments. In this section we examine the empirical evidence on IT adoption and in the next turn to the implications of IT use for local economic growth.

10.3.1　IT Adoption among Firms

For concreteness, the discussion in this section will be motivated by the framework used in Forman et al. (2005). Drawing on the probit or 'rank' model of adoption, they argue that an establishment i will adopt internet-enabled technology by time t if:

$$NB(x_i, z_i, t) = B(x_i, z_i, t) - C(x_i, z_i, t) > 0,$$

where NB are the net benefits to adoption, B are the gross benefits of adoption, and C is the cost of adoption. They allow the variable x_i to capture location-specific characteristics that may influence the costs and benefits of adoption; for example, local population size, the number of other adopters, or other variables such as local labor market characteristics or the supply of services firms. z_i captures other establishment or industry characteristics that may influence the value of adoption, and t represents time. Individuals adopt when net benefits are positive and when the net benefits at time t exceed any other time t'. Thus, the adoption decision reveals establishments with high and low valuations from use.

One insight of Forman et al. is that the costs and gross benefits of technology adoption may vary significantly across geographical locations, often in quite different ways. For example, the highest-value users of internet technology may reside in rural areas and small cities, because of the potential for the internet to reduce the costs of economic isolation. However, the costs of adoption may also be highest in such regions. In particular, the costs of IT inputs such as broadband service may be higher because of weaker competition, while more importantly there is also likely to be weaker supply of key complementary inputs such as skilled labor or third-party services firms that may aid in implementation. They find that the net benefits of adoption in 2000 are decreasing in location size for basic internet technologies which they term 'participation'. In short, such technologies reduce the costs of economic isolation and so their gross benefits are highest in rural areas. Further, because their implementation is straightforward, their adoption costs do not vary much across locations. In contrast, they find that the net benefits of adoption are increasing in location size for advanced technologies – which they term 'enhancement' – that require extensive adaptation and co-invention (Bresnahan and Greenstein 1996) to be used successfully. This will be particularly true for small, single-establishment firms that are unable to rely on IT skills and other complementary inputs that may reside elsewhere in the organization and which rely on external markets to facilitate implementation of new IT (Forman et al., 2008). Thus, like the theory models mentioned above, these adoption studies find that the net benefits of new IT are frequently higher in urban areas, although the mechanism underpinning this finding is quite different from that of theory work. In particular, these studies focus on lower adoption costs in urban areas rather than higher (gross) benefits.

Firm-level data on IT adoption is difficult to acquire and a lack of data has constrained research in this area. However, several authors have demonstrated that adoption of internet technology is increasing in location size using data on domain name registrations (for example, Moss and Townsend, 1997; Kolko, 2000). Domain name registrations are a useful measure of internet investment because they are based on the business location of the registration rather than that of the internet service provider

(ISP), although they are limited in that a firm can have internet investment without a domain name. Further, domain names will usually be available only at the firm level, so it is difficult to use them to identify the effects of geography among multi-establishment firms.[1] Still, they are more widely available than other measures of internet investment, and are a useful complement to other research in this area. Work on domain name registrations has also supported the hypothesis that the net benefits of adoption are increasing in location size.

Several authors have explored the micro foundations of why adoption costs may be declining in location size. For example, Arora and Forman (2007) and Ono (2007) have demonstrated that the supply of third-party outsourcing firms that are used in IT implementations are increasing in location size, and that the use of such firms is greater in large urban areas. Since outsourcing firms frequently play a key role in the implementation of frontier IT, such variance in local outsourcing supply is likely to influence adoption costs. Further, a rich literature has demonstrated variance in the supply of broadband providers and ISPs across locations (for example, Downes and Greenstein, 2002; Prieger, 2003; Flamm, 2005; Zook, 2005). Such variance may influence the costs of technical inputs such as broadband service and, more broadly, internet connectivity. However, they are less likely to be a significant influence on more advanced margins of investment such as Forman et al.'s (2005) enhancement, where differences in implementation and co-invention costs (rather than local internet service costs) are more likely to shape the geography of adoption.

10.3.2 IT Adoption for Individuals

A variety of studies have shown variance in the extent of individual internet adoption across urban and rural (and small city) regions (for example, Hindman, 2000; Wellman et al., 2001; Mills and Whitacre, 2003; Agarwal et al., 2009;). Much like firm-level work, this research has found that much of the urban–rural variance is due to other factors that may be correlated with location, such as income, age, and education (for example, Hindman, 2000; Mills and Whitacre, 2003).

However, even after controlling for these demographic factors, some studies have demonstrated that location characteristics may play an independent role on adoption. One reason is again differences in the local supply of internet service. Due to low fixed costs of entry, dial-up ISPs quickly entered most small geographical markets relatively soon after the commercialization of the internet, providing access at competitive rates in all but the smallest markets (Downes and Greenstein, 2002). In contrast, due to differing economics of deployment, differences in the supply of broadband providers have persisted (Prieger, 2003; Flamm, 2005; Zook, 2005). Since markets for internet service are local, such differences in local supply are likely to influence the costs of internet adoption.

Another way that location can influence the speed of internet adoption is through local spillovers, which exist when the likelihood of adoption is increasing in the penetration among other users. Even when researchers are able to identify that local spillovers exist, they are frequently unable to recover the theoretical mechanism generating these spillovers. For example, two common mechanisms often cited are that spillovers result from direct communication externalities related to use of email or the internet, or that they arise from decreasing learning costs, as when potential adopters can query neighbors about potential concerns or problems.

Several recent papers have sought to demonstrate that spillovers have shaped the adoption of internet technology among individuals. For example, Agarwal et al. (2009) have shown that adoption is correlated among users in the same metropolitan statistical area (MSA), using instrumental variable estimates to address endogeneity concerns about endogenous group formation and correlated preferences (for example, Manski, 1993). Their results support the existence of network effects, particularly among those located in regions with high housing density and those within a dense network of social interactions. Agarwal et al.'s approach builds upon earlier work by Goolsbee and Klenow (2002) who find evidence that spillovers influenced the adoption of personal computers; they show that these spillovers are tied to use of the internet, which provides evidence of network effects in adoption. Goldfarb (2006) also provides evidence that local spillovers influenced individual adoption of the internet. He shows that the impact of prior university attendance on internet use is much higher for people who attended university in the mid-1990s than for others. This is not true of other computing technologies such as word processing. Universities may have taught students to use the internet, suggesting a social network effect. Alternatively, network externalities may be the driving factor: students may have an extra benefit from using the internet because they know more people online.

These studies provide evidence of local correlation in behavior. Though the exact behavioral mechanism cannot be identified, they are suggestive that adoption rates may be higher in urban areas where learning spillovers and network externalities may be higher. However, they do not provide any direct evidence addressing the questions posed in the theoretical models described in Section 10.2; that is, they do not provide any evidence on whether IT-enabled communications are a complement or substitute for face-to-face interactions. One paper that does is Wellman et al. (2001). They show that internet technology is used to maintain social ties among friends, and that the frequent use of email is associated with frequent face-to-face and telephone interactions; that is, face-to-face and electronic communications are complementary. Using data on workplace communications in France, Charlot and Duranton (2006) also show that different communication channels are complementary, although they find no evidence that face-to-face communications are more common in cities. Their explanation for this latter finding is that while the number of communication partners is likely to be larger in cities – facilitating more face-to-face interactions – the cost of face-to-face interactions is likely to be higher as well (due to higher transportation costs within cities).

10.4   IT INVESTMENT AND LOCAL ECONOMIC OUTCOMES

Research on IT investment and local economic outcomes has shed light on whether the diffusion of IT has contributed to convergence or divergence. One view is that the diffusion of IT (particularly, internet technology) will lead to employment growth and wage gains in regions that have low population and are economically isolated; that is, by lowering communication costs, IT contributes most to economic growth in regions that are not well off. An alternative view is that IT will lead to divergence; that is, that it will disproportionately benefit regions that have large cities with populations that are highly skilled and who already have high incomes. We review the evidence for both view-points below. Research in this area is relatively recent and still evolving; only recently has enough time elapsed to permit accurate measurement of the implications of internet investment. On balance, more evidence points to divergence, although more work needs to be done in this important area.

10.4.1 Divergence

A key theme of research in this area is that IT investment will have heterogeneous impacts on the productivity of firms and on the demand for labor, and that this heterogeneity will in turn influence how IT investment influences local economic outcomes. First, the returns to IT investment may be greater in large cities due to Marshallian externalities. Moreover, a long literature on skill-biased technical change has suggested that IT investment and skilled labor are complementary: IT investment will shift out the demand for skilled labor but has the potential to either complement or substitute unskilled labor (for example, Katz and Autor, 1999; Autor et al., 2003). Further, the productivity benefits of IT investment have been shown to be systematically higher for a subset of 'IT-intensive' industries that have typically had long-lived IT capital investments (for example, Stiroh, 2002; Jorgenson et al., 2005).[2] Both skilled labor and IT-intensive industries are heterogeneously distributed across locations, and are disproportionately concentrated in cities. As a result, firms' response to new IT will be likely be non-uniform across regions, leading to divergence.

Forman et al. (2010) examine the association between investment in advanced internet technology and local wage growth across 2,743 counties in the US. They find that on average the impact of advanced internet investment on local wages is small and on employment is non-existent. However, advanced internet investment does have a statistically and economically strong effect on both wages and employment in regions that are already doing well – regions with large populations and with high concentrations of skilled labor, IT-intensive firms, and high incomes. Thus, advanced internet investment contributes to divergence.

Other papers have examined the connection between local skills, technology adoption, and wage growth. Beaudry et al. (2006) examine the labor market implications of local PC adoption over a longer time period than do Forman et al. (2010). They show that cities that are endowed with relatively cheap and abundant skilled labor will adopt PCs more rapidly than other cities, and show that the returns to skill are highest in cities that adopt PCs intensively. Kolko (2002) examines employment growth across industry locations. He shows that IT-intensive industries converge more slowly than other industries; however, the reason is that these industries intensively use skilled labor inputs and have been growing very rapidly, both factors which tend to affect the rate of convergence. Kolko finds that once these factors are controlled for, IT-intensive industries converge more rapidly than others.[3]

10.4.2 Convergence

Available evidence on convergence is more sparse. One example is Kolko (2007), who studies the co-agglomeration of service industries to understand the micro foundations of Marshallian externalities. Kolko finds that IT investment contributes to co-agglomeration of industries at the zip code level among industries that trade with one another but decreases co-agglomeration among trading industries at the state level. That is, industries that trade with one another are more likely to collocate within the same zip code if IT use is high, but less likely to collocate in the same state if IT use is high. One potential interpretation of this result is that IT reduces the costs of transporting service outputs over long distances.

10.5   IT AND INNOVATION

Lower communication costs enabled through IT can influence the productivity of scientists as well as shape the localization of innovation. This line of research is important for several reasons. First, understanding what influences the productivity of individual scientists is inherently important for firms and science policy. Further, researchers have long observed that innovative activity is localized (for example, Jaffe et al., 1993), and there is an important public policy question about the extent to which recent declines in communication costs can enable more geographically dispersed innovation (for example, Macher and Mowery, 2008). Last, scientific research collaborations leave a tangible record about the existence of communication and collaboration among researchers. Thus, in contrast to other areas we review, research in this area allows for a more direct examination of how individual economic agents interact and so allow for a more nuanced study of the relationship between IT-enabled and other communication channels.

Most research in this area has examined how IT investments have influenced research productivity and collaboration patterns in academe. Researchers in this area have generally pursued one of two research strategies: time-series analyses of trends in collaboration patterns among academic scientists, or an examination of how institution-level investments in IT (such as acquiring a domain name or adopting BITNET, a predecessor to the internet) influence the productivity of academic scientists. Interestingly, these different approaches have provided very different results about how IT investments have led to changes in the productivity of researchers and the geography of their collaborations.

As noted above, several authors have examined time-series trends in research collaborations and attribute their results, at least in part, to the effects of IT-enabled communications. Such research generally finds that co-authorship has risen over time across a wide variety of fields (Hammermesh and Oster, 2002; Jones et al., 2008), and co-authorship has increasingly spanned metropolitan areas (Hammermesh and Oster, 2002) and university boundaries (Jones et al., 2008).

However, while research in this area has found that co-authorship has increased, it has also found that the trend has been increasingly toward segmentation or 'balkanization' of research collaborations. For example, research in this area has found that the incidence of collaboration among different tiers of universities has decreased. That is, multi-university collaborations are increasingly within rather than across tiers (ibid.). Further, some researchers have found that, at least within economics, collaborations are increasingly within subfields rather than across fields (Rosenblat and Mobius, 2004). This latter finding is consistent with theoretical work from Rosenblat and Mobius (ibid.)

as well as Van Alstyne and Brynjolfsson (2005) about the effects of IT on social collaborations. Both argue that if agents have preferences to collaborate with those with similar preferences and if IT lowers the costs of collaborating across distance, than the diffusion of new IT will lead to a 'balkanization' of communities and that within-group separation may increase even while the costs of distant collaborations decline. We note, however, that this research remains at a relatively early stage of development and that much more needs to be done to examine how IT use influences social relationships, currently a very active area of research. Some authors (for example, McAfee, 2009) have argued that new Web 2.0 tools such as wikis and blogs will facilitate the formation of weak ties (Granovetter, 1973) in organizations, and will facilitate knowledge sharing among heterogeneous groups.

Another research strategy in this area has examined how university adoption of electronic networks has influenced researcher productivity and collaborations. As suggested above, the results of these studies differ from those of the time-series work. For example, one important paper by Agrawal and Goldfarb (2008) examines how BITNET adoption influences the likelihood of collaboration among engineering scientists in universities. In contrast to the time-series results discussed above, they find that BITNET disproportionately increased collaboration between top- and middle-tier universities, particularly among those that were collocated. They argue that this result may reflect gains from trade, perhaps through the increased use of underutilized research equipment or increased specialization. Research on life scientists has also shown that investments in IT are associated with an increase in researcher productivity (Winkler et al., 2009; Ding et al., 2010), and disproportionately aids researchers in lower-tier institutions (Winkler et al., 2009) and female scientists (Ding et al., 2010).

In short, research in this area provides ambiguous predictions about the relationship between the diffusion of IT and the localization of academic research. This heterogeneity in results may reflect not only differences in research design but also differences in setting. The research settings above included scientists from economics (Hammermesh and Oster, 2002; Rosenblatt and Mobius, 2004), life sciences (Winkler et al., 2009; Ding et al., 2010), engineering (Agrawal and Goldfarb, 2008), and other disciplines (Jones et al., 2008). As Walsh and Bayma (1996) note, the value of IT-enabled communication tools and how they are used will likely vary significantly by research field. For example, they find that fields that use tightly coupled but geographically dispersed work groups (such as particle physics) use IT-enabled communications more than those that utilize relatively autonomous research groups (such as experimental biology). Additional fieldwork such as that of Walsh and Bayma (1996) will help us to better understand differences in the use of IT-enabled communication channels across fields, and engender a better understanding of how IT use will influence the geography of innovation and research.

10.6 RETAIL PURCHASES AND TRADE

IT-enabled communications have the potential to disproportionately benefit economically isolated consumers through electronic commerce. As has been noted elsewhere, electronic commerce (e-commerce) can benefit consumers through lower prices (surveyed in Baye et al. 2006), lower search costs (Brynjolfsson et al., 2003), and better convenience (for example, Sinai and Waldfogel, 2004; Forman et al., 2009). These benefits are likely to be particularly salient in small markets, where the number of retailers is likely to be low and where consumers with idiosyncratic or minority preferences are likely to be particularly underserved (for example, Waldfogel, 1993; George and Waldfogel, 2003;).

As noted above, by connecting to the internet consumers in isolated locations can gain access to content not easily available to them in the offline world. However, as Sinai and Waldfogel (2004) note, much online content is local (that is, news, directories, education, entertainment) and the extent of this local content will be greatest for large cities. Studying data from 2000, Sinai and Waldfogel find a positive relationship between local population and the likelihood of a household connection. However, they find that once they control for the extent of local content then the relationship between population size and internet adoption flips; increases in population are associated with a decline in the likelihood of an internet connection. Further, they find that an individual's online spending is increasing in the distance to the nearest store, providing further evidence that the internet and e-commerce substitute for offline offerings.

Several papers have probed in further detail how consumers substitute between local offline offerings and the online channel. These papers are motivated in part by the work of Balasubramanian (1998), who modeled consumer channel choice in commodity markets as a trade-off between the fixed disutility costs of buying online (such as shipping time or the inability to physically view the product) and the lower search and transportation costs of buying online (in addition to the price differences between the two channels). These papers have shown that, all else equal, as the number of local stores increases, that consumers will shift out of the online channel for products offered in offline stores, and that the magnitude of these behavioral shifts are significant (Brynjolfsson et al., 2009; Chiou, 2009; Forman et al., 2009). However, one advantage of the online channel is the selection it offers, online retailers have the potential to offer a much greater product selection than what can be carried by any physical store (Brynjolfsson et al., 2003; Anderson, 2006). As a result, consumer propensity to purchase such 'niche' or 'long tail' productions online is insensitive to local offline supply (Brynjolfsson et al., 2009; Forman et al., 2009).

In short, buyers can use the online channel to substitute for the disadvantages of a poor location. However, by lowering search costs, e-commerce can improve offline options as well if information about offline products is offered online. This can lead either (or both) lower average prices and less price dispersion. For example, Overby and Forman (2009) show that increasing use of e-commerce in wholesale car auctions led to price convergence across geographically dispersed auction sites; buyers increasingly shifted from using high-price to low-price auction sites because they could more easily observe prices in other locations. Goldmanis et al. (2009) show that competition from the online channels shifted the market structure of offline industries such as travel agencies, bookstores, and new car dealers. Through lower search costs, growth in consumer use of the internet is tied to the exit of smaller (and presumably high-cost) establishments but has little effect on the number of large establishments.

While growing evidence shows that consumers use the internet to lower the costs of economic isolation, there also remains significant evidence that location significantly shapes how consumers behave online. Consumers are more likely to visit websites that are hosted by firms geographically proximate to them. One reason is that a lot of online content is local (Sinai and Waldfogel, 2004); further, consumer tastes vary significantly across regions (for example, Jank and Kannan, 2005). As a result, consumers may self-select into websites that tailor to their preferences, and this is particularly true for taste-dependent digital products such as music and games (Blum and Goldfarb, 2006). Consumers have also shown a preference to trade with others who are geographically proximate to them. Again, this is in part because many products are heavily taste dependent, especially products that are consumed almost entire locally such as theater seats or sports memorabilia (Hortacsu et al., 2009). However, there are other reasons. First, shipping times and transport costs vary with distance (Ellison and Ellison, 2008; Overby and Forman, 2009), particularly for big-ticket items such as automobiles (ibid.). Further, consumers must pay sales taxes for e-commerce items purchased from retailers with a physical presence in the same state (Goolsbee, 2000; Ellison and Ellison, 2008); this may influence where online retailers locate their operations (Avery et al., 2008). Last, consumers may purchase from local sellers when seller reputation is low and geographical proximity offers the possibility of product returns (Hortacsu et al., 2009). Thus, while e-commerce improves buyer options, consumers retain a preference for consuming local products and content.

10.7 FRICTIONS FROM MOVING IT-ENABLED WORK OFFSHORE

This chapter has thus far focused on the impact of IT on the geographical variance in economic activity across the US. This approach has been guided by two constraints. First, the focus of this chapter has been primarily on empirical testing of theoretical work, and both data constraints and empirical identification strategies drive the researcher to focus on single-country identification strategies. Further, much of the work we have reviewed aims to understand the impact of IT on cities. However, a central concern of business leaders, policy makers, and academics has been the extent to which IT has facilitated the globalization of economic activity. In this section we turn to this question.

A wealth of anecdotal evidence has been used to argue that IT investments, by reducing coordination costs, have facilitated the globalization of economic activity (for example, Friedman, 2005). Further, a mounting body of empirical evidence has documented the increasing globalization of service work (for example, Arora et al., 2001, 2009; OECD, 2006). While none of this work measures the impact of IT *per se*, it is widely believed that IT has been an enabler for the globalization of service work that we see in the data. However, systematic evidence on the link between IT investment and globalization is relatively rare. One exception is the work of Freund and Weinhold (2002, 2004), who examine the association between IT investment and trade in goods and services. Freund and Weinhold (2002) find that a 10 percent increase in web hosts is related to a 1.7 percentage point increase in services export growth between 1995 and 1999 and a 1.1 percentage point increase in services import growth, while Freund and Weinhold (2004) find that a similar 10 percent increase in web hosts is associated with a 0.2 percentage point climb in goods exports over the same period. Freund and Weinhold (2002, 2004) argue that the internet will have a greater impact on trade volume in services since many services can now be transported costlessly.

Despite this evidence, there remain significant barriers to increasing globalization. For example, Ghemawat (2001, 2007) describes in his CAGE framework four frictions to global expansion – cultural distance, administrative distance, geographical distance, and economic distance. While each of these factors is important, in the remaining pages we focus on the one friction which is most salient to the question of interest in this chapter: how IT influences the margin between what can and cannot be traded.

Blinder (2006) and others have argued that what can be traded has been steadily increasing over time. While traditionally any good that can be shipped and placed in a box has been considered tradable, as Blinder (p. 118) notes, what IT has changed are the sets of services that can be delivered at a distance:

> The critical divide in the future may instead be between those types of work that are easily deliverable through a wire (or via wireless connections) with little or no diminution in quality and those that are not. And this unconventional divide does not correspond well to traditional distinctions between jobs that require high levels of education and jobs that do not.

As Blinder notes, it is clear that some services work can never be done at a distance – hairdressers need hair to cut and janitors cannot be in another continent to do their job. However, there are a number of occupations at the margin, and recent work has attempted to identify which kinds of work presently represent tradable services or soon will.

Several approaches have been used by researchers to identify this question. Jensen and Kletzer (2005) develop an approach where they use the geographical concentration of an industry within the US to identify whether or not it is likely to be tradable. Using this method, they find that a significant share of employment in services is in tradable service industries and occupations, and that workers in such industries have higher skills and wages. They further find that displacement rates in tradable service industries are higher than in other industries.

Arora and Forman (2007) similarly use geographical variance in observed economic behavior to infer the extent of tradability of service activities. Studying the IT services industry, they examine the sensitivity of IT services demand to local supply. Their logic is that if some elements of IT services must be supplied locally, then suppliers must be located near customers and demand for that service will be sensitive to changes in local supply. In contrast, for nontradable services, local demand will be invariant to local supply. They find that some service activities such as system design are very sensitive to local supply, while others such as hosting services are not. They argue that their results reflect differences in the nature of client–service provider communication across these services. As has been noted elsewhere in this chapter, the transmission of certain types of information, in particular that which is equivocal, uncertain, or complex, is often poorly suited for IT-enabled communications.

An alternative approach to identifying tradable work is pursued by Mithas and Whitaker (2007), who identify tradable services by looking directly at the work involved. They examine 140 service occupations from the 1990 Standard Occupational Classification (SOC) codes, and use a content analysis to measure the codifiability, standardizability, and modularizability of each occupation. They find that these three characteristics and the information intensity of the occupation are positively correlated with tradability. In short, research in this area demonstrates that many occupations remain nontradable. Further, there remains some ambiguity about the extent to which high- or low-skill occupations are more tradable. Thus, while a large body of evidence has pointed to complementarity between IT investment and the demand for high-skilled labor (for example, Katz and Autor, 1999), as noted by Blinder (2006) the implications of IT-enabled globalization may not impact on labor demand along traditional high/low-skill lines. For example, Autor et al. (2003) and Levy and Murnane (2005) argue that work that involves more heuristic information processing and more interpersonal contact is less easily digitized. While these work characteristics may be correlated with occupational skill, they will be so imperfectly.

The research above uses large-sample or aggregate data to determine what kinds of work produce tradable outputs. Other papers have used case-study evidence to shed light on the same question. For example, Aron and Liu (2005) examine services offshoring and study what factors contribute to perceived process complexity in services-consuming countries such as the United States and the United Kingdom versus those in service providing countries such as India and Singapore. They find that in services-consuming countries, managers rated analytically or computationally demanding processes as the most complex, while managers in provider countries said the most complex processes involved contextual interpretation and implicit rules. Work that was considered 'subjective, context-dependent, and implicitly understood' (ibid., p.379) was viewed as more process complex by provider countries, and more difficult to transfer. This evidence is consistent with the evidence mentioned elsewhere in this chapter, of the challenges of transferring 'tacit' information over long distances using IT-enabled communication channels.

Similar challenges have affected the globalization of innovative activity. One particular issue here is the need for user innovation and input as part of the innovation process (for example, Rosenberg, 1963). As an example, such user activity is particularly important for the development of business software that is often bundled with a set of business rules and assumptions about business processes that must be integrated with an existing business organization, its activities and its processes. Several authors have argued that user needs have high information transfer costs and represent 'sticky' local information (von Hippel, 1998). Such costs increase over distance, so that innovative activity is difficult to undertake away from users (Bhide, 2008). In the case of business software where lead users (at least at present) continue to be concentrated in North America, this suggests that business software innovation will continue to be concentrated within the US (Arora et al., 2009).

In short, while there is little doubt that IT has aided globalization, there are limitations. More work is needed to understand how these can be overcome.

10.8   CONCLUSIONS

This chapter has reviewed recent research on how IT investments influence the geographical variance in economic activity. Reflecting the diversity of research on the topic, a large number of areas have been reviewed, including IT adoption, convergence/divergence of wages and employment, the geography and organization of innovation, trade and consumer behavior, and the globalization of work. This review has demonstrated that the relationship between IT investments and geographical activity are complex. In particular, the review showed that there are many cases where IT investments may lead to an increasing propensity to concentrate economic activity in cities. In cities where IT investment costs are lower because of lower input costs, the productivity benefits of IT investment may remain higher because of persistent Marshallian externalities, and most communication therefore remains local. More broadly, we discussed how there remain many types of communication and information transfer for which IT-enabled channels remain poorly suited. This fact also influences the extent to which some work can be performed away from the point of final demand, or 'offshore'.

The approach taken here has been to survey empirical work that has used economics, and in particular urban economics, as its primary lens. Though the scope of the chapter has been broad, it has focused on several key themes that have shaped the relationship between IT investment and the geography of economic activity, rather than to aim for a comprehensive review that covers all work in the area.[4]

We have also attempted to highlight areas for future research where appropriate. One theme common throughout this chapter has been the often contradictory results across research using different settings and methodologies. The sometimes disparate nature of findings, and lack of consensus in some research areas, reflects the still-new and evolving nature of work in this area. It is also important to note that many important issues, such as telecommuting, were not discussed because they are so new that a large body of work has yet to be formed. An implication of this is that many of the issues discussed here remain fertile ground for future research.

NOTES

1. Perhaps most significantly, they are likely to be biased toward finding investment in large cities, since registrations will likely occur in corporate headquarters that are disproportionately found in the largest cities (for example, Aarland et al., 2007).
2. Note that the productivity benefits of IT investments among IT-intensive firms have been found to be particularly strong in large cities (for example, Henderson, 2003).
3. Several papers have also investigated the relationship between local broadband availability and local economic outcomes (for example,; Gillett et al., 2006; Crandall et al., 2007; Van Gaasbeck et al., 2007; Kolko, 2010). These have consistently found a positive average relationship between the local broadband availability and local employment growth. However, as Kolko (2010) notes, in the majority of these studies, causality has been an issue–it is difficult to identify empirically whether broadband provision leads to employment growth or whether regions with high employment growth have more broadband providers. Further, none of these studies examines heterogeneity in outcomes in region; in particular whether broadband availability disproportionately benefits large or small cities or urban or rural regions.
4. For a more comprehensive undertaking that addresses these questions from a slightly different perspective, see Malecki and Moriset (2008).

REFERENCES

Aarland, Kristin, James C. Davis, J. Vernon Henderson and Yukako Ono (2007), 'Spatial organization of firms: the decision to split production and administration', *RAND Journal of Economics*, **38** (2): 480–94.

Agarwal, Ritu, Animesh Animesh and Kislaya Prasad (2009), 'Social interactions and the "digital divide": explaining variations in internet use', *Information Systems Research*, **20** (2): 277–94.

Agrawal, Ajay and Avi Goldfarb (2008), 'Restructuring research: communication costs and the democratization of university innovation', *American Economic Review*, **98** (4): 1578–90.

Anderson, Chris (2006), *The Long Tail: Why the Future of Business is Selling Less of More*, New York: Hyperion.

Aron, Ravi and Ying Liu (2005), 'Determinants of operational risk in global sourcing of financial services: evidence from field research', *Brookings Trade Forum*: 373–98.

Arora, A., V.S. Arunachalam, V.S. Asundi and R. Fernandes, (2001), 'The Indian software services industry', *Research Policy*, **30** (8): 1267–87.

Arora, Ashish and Chris Forman (2007), 'Proximity and information technology outsourcing: how local are IT services markets', *Journal of Management Information Systems*, **24** (2): 73–102.

Arora, Ashish, Chris Forman and Jiwoong Yoon (2009), 'Software', in Jeffrey T. Macher and David C. Mowery (eds), *Innovation in Global Industries: U.S. Firms Competing in a New World*, Washington, DC: National Academies Press, pp. 53–100.

Autor, David, Frank Levy and Richard J. Murnane (2003), 'The skill content of recent technological change: an empirical exploration', *Quarterly Journal of Economics*, **118** (4): 1279–334.

Avery, Jill, Mary Caravella, John Deighton and Thomas J. Steenburgh (2008), 'Adding bricks to clicks: the effects of store openings on sales through direct channels', Working Paper, Harvard Business School, Cambridge, MA.

Balasubramanian, S. (1998), 'Mail versus mall: a strategic analysis of competition between direct marketers and conventional retailers', *Marketing Science*, **17**: 181–95.

Beaudry, Paul, Mark Doms and Ethan Lewis (2006), 'Endogenous skill bias in technology adoption: city-level evidence from the IT revolution', Working Paper 06-24, Federal Reserve Bank of San Francisco.

Bhide, Amar (2008), *The Venturesome Economy: How Innovation Sustains Prosperity in a More Connected World*, Princeton, NJ: Princeton University Press.

Blinder, Alan S. (2006), 'Offshoring: the next industrial revolution?', *Foreign Affairs*, **85** (2): 113–28.

Blum, Bernardo and Avi Goldfarb (2006), 'Does the internet defy the law of gravity?', *Journal of International Economics*, **70**: 384–405.

Bresnahan, Timothy and Shane Greenstein (1996), 'Technical progress in computing and in the uses of computers', *Brookings Papers on Economic Activity: Microeconomics*: 1–78.

Brynjolfsson, Erik, Yu Hu and Mohammad S. Rahman (2009), 'Battle of the retail channels: how product selection and geography drive cross-channel competition', *Management Science*, **55** (11): 1755–65.

Brynjolfsson, E., Y. Hu and M. Smith (2003), 'Consumer surplus in the digital economy: estimating the value of increased product variety', *Management Science*, **49**: 1580–96.

Cairncross, F. (1997), *The Death of Distance*, Cambridge, MA: Harvard University Press.

Charlot, Sylvie and Gilles Duranton (2006), 'Cities and workplace communication: some quantitative French evidence', *Urban Studies*, **43** (8): 1365–94.

Chiou, Lesley (2009), 'Empirical analysis of competition between wal-mart and other retail channels', *Journal of Economics and Management Strategy*, **18** (2): 285–322.

Crandall, Robert, William Lehr and Robert Litan, (2007), 'The effects of Broadband deployment on output and employment: a cross-sectional analysis of U.S. data', Issues in Economic Policy Discussion Paper No. 6, Brookings Institution, Washington, DC.

Daft, R.L. and R.H. Lengel (1984), 'Information richness: a new approach to managerial information processing and organizational design', in B. Staw and L. Cummings (eds), *Research in Organizational Behavior*, Greenwich CT: JAI Press, pp. 191–233.

Daft, R.L., R.H. Lengel and L.K. Trevino (1987), 'Message equivocality, media selection, and manager performance: implications for information systems', *MIS Quarterly*, **11** (3): 354–66.

David, Paul A. (1969), 'A contribution to the theory of diffusion', Memorandum No. 71, Stanford Center for Research in Economic Growth, Stanford, CA.

Davis, James C. and J. Vernon Henderson (2008), 'The agglomeration of headquarters', *Regional Science and Urban Economics*, **38** (5): 445–60.

Ding, Waverly W., Sharon G. Levin, Paula E. Stephan and Anne E. Winkler (2010), 'The impact of information technology on academic scientists' productivity and collaboration patterns', Working Paper, Haas School of Business, University of California, Berkeley, CA.

Downes, Tom and Shane Greenstein (2002), 'Universal access and local internet markets in the U.S.', *Research Policy*, **31** (7): 1035–52.

Duranton, Gilles and Diego Puga (2005), 'From sectoral to functional urban specialization', *Journal of Urban Economics*, **57**: 343–70.

Ellison, Glenn and Sara Fisher Ellison (2008), 'Tax sensitivity and home state preferences in internet purchasing', Working Paper, Massachusetts Institute of Technology, Cambridge, MA.

Flamm, Kenneth (2005), 'The role of economics, demographics, and state policy in broadband availability', Working Paper, University of Texas, Austin, TX.

Forman, Chris, Anindya Ghose and Avi Goldfarb (2009), 'Competition between local and electronic markets: how the benefit of buying online depends on where you live', *Management Science*, **55** (1): 47–57.

Forman, Chris, Avi Goldfarb and Shane Greenstein (2005), 'How did location affect the adoption of the commercial internet? Global village vs. urban density', *Journal of Urban Economics*, **58** (3): 389–420.

Forman, Chris, Avi Goldfarb and Shane Greenstein (2008), 'Understanding the inputs into innovation: do cities substitute for internal firm resources?', *Journal of Economics and Management Strategy*, **17** (2): 295–316.

Forman, Chris, Avi Goldfarb and Shane Greenstein (2010), 'The internet and local wages: convergence or divergence?', Working Paper, College of Management, Georgia Institute of Technology, Atlanta, GA.

Freund, Caroline and Diana Weinhold (2002), 'The internet and international trade in services', *American Economic Review*, **92** (2): 236–40.

Freund, Caroline and Diana Weinhold (2004), 'The effect of the internet on international trade', *Journal of International Economics*, **62**: 171–89.

Friedman, Thomas (2005), *The World Is Flat: A Brief History of the Twenty-First Century*, New York: Farrar, Straus, & Giroux.

Gaspar, J. and E.L. Glaeser (1998), 'Information technology and the future of cities', *Journal of Urban Economics*, **43**: 136–56.

George, Lisa and Joel Waldfogel (2003), 'Who affects whom in daily newspaper markets?', *Journal of Political Economy*, **111** (4): 765–84.

Ghemawat, Pankaj (2001), 'Distance still matters,' *Harvard Business Review*, Reprint R0108K.

Ghemawat, Pankaj (2007), *Redefining Global Strategy: Cross Borders in a World Where Differences Still Matter*, Boston, MA: Harvard Business School Press.

Gillett, Sharon, William Lehr, Carlos Osorio and Marvin Sirbu (2006), 'Measuring the economic impact of broadband deployment', US Department of Commerce, Economic Development Administration, Washington, DC.

Glaeser, E.L. and Giacomo A.M. Ponzetto (2007), 'Did the death of distance hurt Detroit and help New York?', NBER Working Paper 13710, National Bureau of Economic Research, Cambridge, MA.

Goldfarb, Avi (2006), 'The (teaching) role of universities in the diffusion of the internet', *International Journal of Industrial Organization*, **24** (2): 203–25.

Goldmanis, Maris, Ali Hortacsu, Chad Syverson and Onsol Emre (2009), 'E-commerce and the market structure of retail industries', *Economic Journal*, **119** (October): 1–32.

Goolsbee, Austan (2000), 'In a world without borders: the impact of taxes on internet commerce', *Quarterly Journal of Economics*, **115** (2): 561–76.

Goolsbee, Austan and Peter J. Klenow (2002), 'Evidence on learning and network externalities in the diffusion of home computers', *Journal of Law and Economics*, **45** (2): 317–43.

Granovetter, M. (1973), 'The strength of weak ties', *American Journal of Sociology*, **78** (6): 1360–80.

Hammermesh, Daniel S. and Sharon M. Oster (2002), 'Tools or toys? The impact of high technology on scholarly productivity', *Economic Inquiry*, **40** (4): 539–55.

Henderson, J. Vernon (2003), 'Marshall's scale economies', *Journal of Urban Economics*, **53**: 1–28.

Hindman, D.B. (2000), 'The urban–rural digital divide', *Journalism and Mass Communication Quarterly*, **77** (3): 549–60.

Hortacsu, Ali, F. Asis Martinez-Jerez and Jason Douglas (2009), 'The geography of trade in online transactions: evidence from eBay and MercadoLibre', *American Economic Journal: Microeconomics*, **1** (1): 53–74.

Jaffe, A., M. Trajtenberg and R. Henderson (1993), 'Geographic localization of knowledge spillovers as evidenced by patent citations', *Quarterly Journal of Economics*, **108** (3): 577–98.

Jank, Wolfgang and P.K. Kannan, (2005), 'Understanding geographic markets of online firms using spatial models of customer choice', *Marketing Science*, **24**: 623–34.

Jensen, J. Bradford and Lori G. Kletzer (2005), 'Tradable services: understanding the scope and impact of services offshoring', *Brookings Trade Forum: 2005*: 75–133.

Jones, Benjamin F., Stefan Wuchty and Brian Uzzi (2008), 'Multi-university research teams: shifting impact, geography, and stratification of science', *Science*, **322**: 1259–62.

Jorgenson, Dale, Mun S. Ho and Kevin Stiroh (2005), *Productivity Volume 3: Information Technology and the American Growth Resurgence*, Cambridge, MA: MIT Press.

Karshenas, Massoud and Paul L. Stoneman (1993), 'Rank, stock, order, and epidemic effects in the diffusion of new process technologies: an empirical model', *RAND Journal of Economics*, **24** (4): 503–28.

Katz, Lawrence F. and David H. Autor (1999), 'Changes in the wage structure and earnings inequality', in Orley Ashenfelter and David Card (eds), *Handbook of Labor Economics, Volume 3A*, London: Elsevier, pp. 1463–558.

Kolko, Jed (2000), 'The death of cities? The death of distance? Evidence from the geography of commercial internet usage', in I. Vogelsang and B.M. Compaine (eds), *The Internet Upheaval*, Cambridge, MA: MIT Press, pp. 73–98.

Kolko, Jed (2002), 'Silicon mountains, silicon molehills: geographic concentration and convergence of internet industries in the US', *Information Economics and Policy*, **14**: 211–32.

Kolko, Jed (2007), 'Agglomeration and co-agglomeration of services industries', MPRA Paper 3362, University Library of Munich.

Kolko, Jed (2010), 'Does broadband boost local economic development?', Working Paper, Public Policy Institute of California, San Fransisco, CA.

Leamer, E.E. and M. Storper (2001), 'The economic geography of the internet age', *Journal of International Business Studies*, **32** (4): 641–65.

Levy, Frank and Richard J. Murnane (2005), *The New Division of Labor: How Computers are Creating the Next Job Market*, Princeton, NJ: Princeton University Press.

Macher, J. and D. Mowery (2008), *Innovation in Global Industries: U.S. Firms Competing in a New World*, Washington, DC: National Academies Press.

Malecki, Edward J. and Bruno Moriset (2008), *The Digital Economy: Business Organization, Production Processes and Regional Developments*, Abingdon, UK: Routledge.

Manski, Charles F. (1993), 'Identification of endogenous social effects: the reflection problem', *Review of Economic Studies*, **60** (3): 531–42.

March, James G. and Herbert A. Simon (1958), *Organizations*, New York: Wiley.

McAfee, Andrew 2009, *Enterprise 2.0: New Collaborative Tools for Your Organization's Toughest Challenges*, Boston, MA: Harvard Business School Press.

Mills, B.F. and B.E. Whitacre (2003), 'Understanding the non-metropolitan–metropolitan digital divide', *Growth and Change*, **34** (2): 219–43.

Mithas, Sunil and Jonathan Whitaker (2007), 'Is the world flat or spiky? Information intensity, skills, and global service disaggregation', *Information Systems Research*, **18** (3): 237–59.

Moss, M.L. (1998), 'Technology and cities', *Cityscape: A Journal of Policy Development and Research*, **3** (1): 107–27.

Moss, M.L. and A.M. Townsend (1997), 'Tracking the net: using domain names to measure the growth of the internet in U.S. cities', *Journal of Urban Technology*, **4**: 47–60.

Ono, Yukako (2007), 'Market thickness and outsourcing services', *Regional Science and Urban Economics*, **37** (2): 220–38.

Organisation for Economic Co-operation Development (OECD) (2006), *OECD Information Technology Outlook 2006*, Paris: OECD.

Overby, Eric and Chris Forman (2009), 'The market is flat (or is it?): the effect of electronic trading on buyer reach, geographic transaction activity, and geographic price variance and levels', Working Paper, College of Management, Georgia Institute of Technology, Atlanta, GA.

Polanyi, M. (1966), *The Tacit Dimension*, New York: Doubleday.

Prieger, James E. (2003), 'The supply side of the digital divide: is there equal availability in the broadband internet access market?', *Economic Inquiry*, **41** (2): 346–63.

Rosenberg, Nathan (1963), 'Technological change in the machine tool industry, 1840–1910', *Journal of Economic History*, **23**: 414–43.

Rosenblat, T. and M. Mobius (2004), 'Getting closer or drifting apart', *Quarterly Journal of Economics*, **119** (3): 971–1009.

Sinai, Todd and Joel Waldfogel (2004), 'Geography and the internet: is the internet a substitute or complement for cities?', *Journal of Urban Economics*, **56** (1): 1–24.

Stiroh, Kevin J. (2002), 'Information technology and the U.S. productivity revival: what do the industry data say?', *American Economic Review*, **92** (5): 1559–76.

Storper, M. and A.J. Venables (2004), 'Buzz: face-to-face contact and the urban economy', *Journal of Economic Geography*, **4** (4): 351–70.

Van Alstyne, Marshall and Erik Brynjolfsson (2005), 'Global village or cyber Balkans? modeling and measuring the integration of electronic communities', *Management Science*, **51** (6): 851–68.

Van Gassbeck, Kristen, Stephen Perez, Ryan Sharp, Helen Schaubmeyer, Angela Owens and Lindsay Cox

(2007), 'Economic Effects of Increased Broadband Usage in California', Summary Report, Sacramento Regional Research Institute, Sacromento, CA.

von Hippel, Eric (1994), '"Sticky information" and the locus of problem solving: implications for innovation', *Management Science*, **40** (4): 429–39.

von Hippel, Eric (1998), 'Economics of product development by users: the impact of "sticky" local information', *Management Science*, **44** (5): 629–44.

Waldfogel, Joel (1993), 'Preference externalities: an empirical study of who benefits whom in differentiated-product markets', *RAND Journal of Economics*, **34** (3): 557–68.

Walsh, John P. and Todd Bayma (1996), 'Computer networks and scientific work', *Social Studies of Science*, **26** (3): 661–703.

Wellman, B., A.Q. Haase, J. Witte and K. Hampton (2001), 'Does the internet increase, decrease, or supplement social capital? Social networks, participation, and community commitment', *American Behavioral Scientist*, **45** (3): 437–56.

Winkler, Anne E., Sharon G. Levin and Paula E. Stephan (2009), 'The diffusion of IT in higher education: publishing productivity of academic life scientists', Working Paper, University of Missouri-St. Louis, St. Louis, MO.

Zook, Matthew A. (2005), *The Geography of the Internet Industry: Venture Capital, Dot-coms, and Local Knowledge*, Oxford: Blackwell.

11 R&D, knowledge, economic growth and the transatlantic productivity gap
Raquel Ortega-Argilés

11.1 INTRODUCTION TO THE LINKAGES BETWEEN R&D, KNOWLEDGE AND PRODUCTIVITY

This chapter reviews the available evidence regarding the role and relationship between research and development (R&D) and the performance of firms, sectors and industries, and nations. The broad range of evidence regarding these links is examined, and particular emphasis is placed on the role of new and general-purpose technological change. The chapter then proceeds to frame these discussions in the context of the issues arising from the emergence of the transatlantic productivity gap during the 1990s, a productivity gap which challenged much of the orthodox thinking regarding these relationships.

11.2 THE R&D PRODUCTIVITY LINK AND RETURNS TO R&D

In the last decades the literature of economic performance has stressed the importance of R&D from a national- to a micro-level perspective, and increasingly also at a geographical or regional perspective. The role of technology in productivity was originally prompted by the productivity slowdown noted in much of the industrialized world in the 1970s (Griliches, 1985, 1986). As research into the role of technological change in economic growth indicated that technological change is one of the key explanatory factors in productivity growth (Solow, 1957), the decline in productivity led to concerns that the level of technological change was diminishing. The work of Griliches (1979) started a blossoming empirical literature devoted to investigating the relationship between R&D and productivity at the firm and sectoral levels. This in turn led to increased efforts to assess the importance of R&D expenditure, along with other indicators of technology, in influencing both the level of productivity and changes in productivity for different countries and different periods. Many of the ensuing studies examined the determinants of productivity at an aggregate country level, or by industry, although some research took the firm as the unit of analysis (Lichtenberg and Siegel, 1991; Hall and Mairesse, 1995; Wakelin, 2001). The main conclusion arising from this literature is the beneficial effect on economic performance, measured by a set of different indicators of conducting investments in R&D. The general results of the analyses show that investments in R&D have associated *learning-by-doing* effects and greater benefits when they are *complemented* with other types of investments such as infrastructures, information and communication technology (ICT), or human or physical capital. The literature also emphasizes the important role of *spillover* and *externality* effects associated with these types of investments.

Among the most commonly used indicators in the growth accounting literature that capture the performance of countries, industries and firms are GDP; GDP growth; and productivity measures (TFP, total factor productivity;[1] MFP, multifactor productivity;[2] labour productivity[3] and capital deepening[4]). In the case of firm outputs using output prices, other types of more sophisticated output variables such as nominal output measures or real output measures have been constructed.[5] Industrial R&D is the activity in which R&D employees use their skills to create new products, processes and services. R&D encompasses different types of activities that can occur in any order and across multiple organizations: *basic research* is aimed purely at the creation of new knowledge; *applied research* is work that is expected to have a practical but not a commercial outcome. 'Development' is when the technologies behind a product or service are integrated and honed towards commercial application. The boundaries between different types of R&D are difficult to identify and have not yet been explicitly captured by the empirical literature. Concerning the common indicators used to capture the effort on R&D, the literature has used accounts for private and public R&D. Regarding firm R&D, several indicators have captured the different aspects of R&D investments such as R&D employment, R&D intensity and R&D stock, among others, that will be discussed in more detail in the following sections.

The literature in the subject has shown that the effects of R&D differ significantly depending on the levels of analysis (macro – country, meso – region or industry and micro – firm) and within the levels of analysis (between countries, industries and types of firms). In the following sections the main stylized facts from the literature on the R&D productivity link will be drawn, the conclusions from the literature will be classified according to the following levels of analysis: national, industry and individual levels, and then we shall consider a specific geographical case which has generated widespread interest, namely the transatlantic productivity divergence.

11.2.1   At the National Level

There is a rich literature aimed at understanding the causes of certain countries' economic success and the main drivers in their economic growth accounting (Solow, 1957; Maddison, 1982; Denison, 1985; Abramovitz, 1989; Grossman and Helpman, 1991). Neoclassical growth models concluded that economic growth is the result of a set of returns obtained by a combination of physical capital inputs (buildings, equipment, and machinery), labour and knowledge in the production process in the short run. Because of the diminishing returns to capital, long-run growth is exogenously determined by the saving rate (Harrod–Domar model), knowledge accumulation, or the rate of technical progress (Solow model). However, the savings rate and rate of technological progress remain unexplained. Evidence shows that more than 65 per cent of productivity growth variance is due to its dependence on gross domestic expenditure on R&D expressed as a percentage of GDP (GERD) and that the range of GERD between 2.3 and 2.6 per cent maximizes the long-run impact on productivity growth (Coccia, 2009). As the literature points out, R&D is directly linked with the development level of the nations and this feature explains the high concentration of R&D in a few developed countries.

The OECD countries had a particularly large share of world R&D in the 1970s, 1980s and 1990s, with Germany, Japan and the US accounting for higher R&D shares in the OECD. However, in very recent years R&D has increased sharply in several countries outside the OECD, notably China and India (Sveikauskas, 2007).

New R&D-based growth theory (Romer, 1990; Grossman and Helpman, 1991; Aghion and Howitt, 1992) introduces endogenous technological change (as a function of the level of human capital) and incorporates imperfect markets and R&D into previous growth models. The first generation of these models consider the assumption of constant returns to technological knowledge and predict that the long-run growth rate of an economy increases in the level of R&D inputs and thus larger economies should grow at a higher rate (Grossman and Helpman, 1991). The engine for growth can be as simple as a constant return-to-scale production function, or more complicated set-ups with the presence of spillover effects, or multiproduct production by increasing the number of produced goods or increasing the quality of existent products.

The main conclusions derived from the different R&D theories is that R&D and technological knowledge appear to be one of the main drivers of the economic progress of a nation. The fully endogenous 'Schumpeterian' approaches (Aghion and Howitt, 1998; Dinopolous and Thompson, 1998; Peretto, 1998; Howitt, 1999; Peretto and Smulders, 2002; Zachariadis, 2003, 2004) suggest that R&D intensity is the proper empirical measure for the R&D input of the innovation function in the context of endogenous growth. The models build on the notion that the proliferation of product varieties reduces the effectiveness of R&D aimed at quality improvements, by the spreading of the R&D effort over a number of different sectors. The innovation activity, measured as the generation of product and process innovations, is directly influenced by the intensity and the quality of R&D (R&D expenditures, researchers – headcounts or hours worked – and perceptions of the quality of science and research institutions). The new theoretical underpinnings from endogenous growth theory argue that economic output is supposed to be positively correlated with the flow of new products, including both radical and incremental innovations.[6]

More recently, other new R&D-based growth theories have appeared, among them the semi-endogenous growth approach where diminishing returns to the stock of knowledge of R&D are incorporated into previous R&D-based models (Jones, 1995, 2002; Kortum, 1997; Segerstrom, 1998). In the semi-endogenous growth approach, technology complexity needs to be supported by growth in R&D labour (measured as high-skilled workers such as the number of scientists and engineers engaged in R&D, R&D labour growth rates, or educational attainment) in order to maintain the rates of TFP growth. Jones (2002) finds that about 80 per cent of the US economic growth in the second half of the twentieth century was due to temporary factors such as increases in educational attainment and research intensity.

In parallel, other authors developed the new R&D-based Schumpeterian endogenous growth models which maintain the constant returns to technological knowledge assumption. The 'neo-Schumpeterian' approach has as one of its main contributions the role of technology as an important source for growth. Thus, this approach has introduced technological asymmetries between countries as a crucial aspect to explain trade, specialization, forging ahead, catching-up and falling behind. The models incorporate the assumption that as an economy grows, the proliferation of product varieties reduces the effectiveness of R&D aimed at quality improvements, by causing it to be spread over a large number of different sectors. As a result, to ensure sustained TFP growth, R&D has to increase over time to counteract the increasing range of products that lower the productivity effect of R&D activity. The theory is consistent with the observed coexistence of stationary TFP growth and growing R&D labour. Therefore R&D leads simultaneously to an increase in GDP and in the use of factors. Zachariadis (2003) finds direct evidence that R&D expenditures as a fraction of GDP, one variant of the product-proliferation-adjusted R&D input that should drive productivity growth according to Schumpeterian theory, is indeed what drives productivity growth in US industry. On the other hand, Schumpeterian growth theory criticizes semi-endogenous growth theory, arguing that there is no reason to believe that long-run TFP growth is governed exclusively by population growth (among many others, Aghion and Howitt, 1998; Dinopoulos and Thompson, 1998; Peretto and Smulders, 2002; Zachariadis, 2003; Ha and Howitt, 2007).

Regarding other determinants that affect productivity in addition to R&D at the level of the country, the literature has found: infrastructure, ICTs, education attainment and human capital, market development and institutional context. In recent years other new drivers of productivity growth have been identified including business quality, managerial ability or entrepreneurial culture, and societal disparities. The literature has also developed several theories of endogenous growth relating productivity gains to trade and international relationships (Nelson and Winter, 1982; Grossman and Helpman, 1991; Coe and Helpman, 1995). Some of them have found that cross-country R&D spillovers are an important source of productivity growth (Grossman and Helpman, 1991). To illustrate this point some authors have introduced situations of trade availability, where the final output of a country is produced by the use of intermediate inputs that are accessible via trade arrangements, allowing for the capturing of the role of foreign knowledge spillovers (Coe et al., 1997). R&D affects output by increasing the number, or improving the quality, of available intermediates. In the absence of trade the country's output is determined only by its own accumulation of R&D. The ability of a country to take advantage of technology developed abroad has been defined as 'absorptive capacity'. The absorptive capacity of nations is clearly influenced by the quantity and quality of their R&D investments (Jones and Williams, 1998; Griffith et al., 2004), the availability of human capital (Benhabib and Spiegel, 1994; Eaton and Kortum, 1996; Engelbrecht, 1997; Xu and Wang, 2000) and, by the absorption barriers related to costs determined by their institutions (Parente and Prescott, 1994, 1999, 2003). In general, countries with less-regulated goods and labour markets tend to have a higher absorption capacity.

The literature has also found evidence regarding complementarities between determinants, for instance trade matters, in addition to technology. Countries with less-regulated markets in services and labour tend to be characterized by a relatively higher absorptive capacity. Countries which were more open (especially to the technological leader) caught up faster. Markets that face monopoly positions tend to have a lower absorptive capacity (Nelson and Phelps, 2002). The quality and quantity of different types of infrastructures (for example, ports, airports, railroads and information technology (IT), such as broadband development) have an important role as a benchmark and engine of economies because they can act in facilitating the knowledge exchange between the players of an economy. Infrastructures facilitate the production and exchange of ideas, services and goods, and feed into the innovation system through increased productivity and efficiency, lowering transaction costs and increasing the accessibility to markets. Together with infrastructures, the role of energy (electricity output; electricity consumption; renewables used) is essential in an economy. Finally, and with regard to infrastructures, the role of information, communication and telecommunications infrastructures is a driving force for the competitiveness and productivity of nations. Several studies have shown that characteristics such as fixed telephone lines per inhabitant, mobile cellular telephone subscription, international internet bandwidth per internet user, and households with a computer or with internet access, explain a relatively important part of the economic growth of nations.

The level and standards of the educational system and human capital formation have an important effect on the innovation capacity and the economic growth of nations. Among others, the literature has used sets of indicators aiming at capturing achievements in elementary and secondary education levels, education expenditure and school-life expectancy. Additionally the literature has also used the quality of education measured through the results to the OECD Programme for International Student Assessment (PISA), which examines 15-year-old students' performances in reading, mathematics and science, and the pupil–teacher ratio. The results show that countries which have invested more in schooling tend to absorb new technologies more quickly than countries endowed with less education. The results stress the crucial role played by higher education in capturing the priority given to the sectors traditionally associated with innovation (science and engineering) and the mobility of tertiary students which has an effect on the skill levels necessary to innovation. Higher education appears crucial for economies to move up the value chain beyond simple production processes and products. Other researchers have found that technical change has a direct influence on the skill level of the labour force (Machin and van Reenen, 1998, for a set of OECD countries).

With respect to the role of markets, the market regulatory level has influenced greatly the differences in productivity among nations (Parente and Prescott, 1999; Nicoletti and Scarpetta, 2003). Among others, the services and labour markets have had a direct effect on the level of development. With regard to the financial markets, factors such as credit availability, venture capital and start-up finance, and the degree to which collateral and bankruptcy laws facilitate lending by protecting the rights of borrowers and lenders as well as the rules and practices affecting the coverage and scope and accessibility to credit information, are all found to be important. The literature has concluded that the more competitive economies have a higher absorptive capacity. Other factors such as the international geographical extent of the market in which firms operate (internationalization and export activity) together with the role of multinationals have also clearly influenced the business sector and national growth.

Furthermore, trade can stimulate faster innovation or learning through a number of routes. Imports from the technological leader will provide new knowledge embodied in the most technologically advanced new machines. Greater openness through lower tariffs can increase product market competition and force firms to adopt best practices in order to survive; alternatively, trade with the less developed nations may push developed countries into defensive innovation. The seminal contribution to the literature on the role of trade in the diffusion of international knowledge spillovers and their subsequent effect in the country productivity across 22 developed nations was developed by Coe and Helpman (1995). The authors constructed a 'stock of knowledge' by the weighted sum of trade partners' cumulative R&D spending for each developed country and then measured access to this by weighting these stocks by some measure of the volume or share of bilateral import share. The results show that both domestic and foreign knowledge stocks are important sources of productivity growth. Using this approach, evidence of knowledge spillovers on trading partners' rates of TFP or GDP growth have been found among developed countries and from developed to developing countries, suggesting that foreign direct knowledge spillovers from the northern to the southern countries are relevant (Coe et al., 1997). Using the same approach, Lumenga-Neso et al. (2005) found that countries that do not trade with each other directly also experience R&D trade-related spillovers that have an effect on their productivity similar to that experienced by direct trade. The authors conclude that exposure to trade is not necessarily relevant in the transmission of knowledge and technology. Similarly, however, there appears to be only a limited role for trade in stimulating new innovations; primarily, trade seems to be a way to facilitate the adoption of best practices rather than stimulating firms to come up with new ideas. By increasing the communication between countries, they can encourage a more efficient employment of domestic resources through the cross-border learning of production methods, product design, organizational structures and market conditions.

With regard to the institutional environment, based on the political environment (quality of public and civil services, policy formulation and implementation or perceptions of trust), the institutional settings related to the costs of implementing new technologies are important (Parente and Prescott, 1999, 2003). In the majority of cases these institutions in the economic growth literature have been associated with national levels, but they may have regional identities as well. Policy formulation is more related to the perception of the ability of governments to formulate and implement policies that promote the development of the private sector (property rights, court, policy) and reduce the level of the rigidity of labour and business regulations (administrative burdens) or taxation. Government intervention has also played a fundamental role in industrialization and specialization patterns in many economies (production of domestic markets, or export orientation) and therefore has a subsequent effect on their productivity. In particular, government support to human capital formation, its role in industrial development, in scientific and educational systems, and in innovation and technology systems, is often seen to be crucial.

Finally, the characteristics of the business environment and their level of sophistication concerning innovation activities are important issues in the economic growth of nations. Among many others, research confirms the importance of factors related to the quality of the workers and to the scientific background (knowledge-intensive worker) and the efforts of the firm to increase the technological level of the workers to match the new skills needed to adapt to new technologies (firms offering formal training). The literature also pays attention to the innovation linkages that can be generated by the private–public partnerships (university–industry collaborations) or by the economies of scales of industry specialization (state of cluster development), the quantity of joint ventures and co-patenting activities with other non-resident firms.

11.2.2 At the Industry Level

Having examined the R&D implications at the aggregate growth level together with additional economic growth determinants, this sub section will be devoted to analysing the role of R&D in growth accounting at the individual industry levels. Industry-level analyses allow us to shed further light on issues that macro-level analyses may fail to capture, such as the different effects of specific policies – including product market regulations and trade restrictions – on industry performance, and the disparities in the effect of R&D on productivity under different levels of technological requirements, knowledge intensity or production and commercialization of services. Likewise, differences in growth patterns at the industry level may also point to variations in the extent to which countries are benefiting from broader economic changes, or from the potential offered by new technologies. Technological change has enabled rapid productivity growth in the IT-producing and, most recently in the IT-using industries, but there are considerable variations in the degree to which countries can benefit from these technological opportunities. The literature stresses the fact that R&D contributes to explaining potential cross-sectional differences in sectoral productivity levels. Thus, Hall (1996) reports a range of elasticities around 0.10 to 0.15, while Griliches (1995) reports an estimated elasticity of output with respect to R&D capital of between 0.06 and 0.10. When focusing on particular industries (see Table 11.1), the R&D elasticities vary with respect to the analysis conducted (cross-sectional) or (time-series) and the quality of the sample. High-technology sectors show a higher R&D elasticity than studies with a mixture of manufacturing sectors.

The literature on productivity at the industry level is vast. The analyses of the comparability of industries can be classified into two groups: one group analyses aggregate trends of productivity growth in sectors (for example, Timmer et al., 2010) and the other analyses micro data to draw conclusions on industry comparison (for example Ortega-Argilés et al., 2011c). The first set of studies compared the productivity records of manufacturing sectors (see Table 11.2) given that the services accounts were still not very complete, among other problems of accountability of R&D in the service sectors (Griliches and Lichtenberg, 1984a, 1984b; Gallouj and Savona, 2010). However, the intensity of the R&D–productivity relationship may vary widely across different industrial sectors. Indeed, technological opportunities and appropriability conditions are so different across sectors (see Freeman, 1982; Pavitt, 1984; Winter, 1984; Aghion and Howitt, 1996; Dosi, 1997; Greenhalgh et al., 2001; Malerba, 2004) as to suggest the possibility of substantial differences in the specific sectoral R&D–productivity links.

The most recent literature at the level of the industry shows the importance of R&D on the performance of a set of R&D-intensive or technologically driven industries. Examples of this type of study can be found in Cameron (2005), who analyses the impact of human capital and R&D on the productivity gap between 11 Japanese and US industries during the 1963–89 period. Añón-Higón (2007) uses an error correction model (ECM) framework to distinguish the short- and long-run impact of R&D capital for the case of eight UK manufacturing industries over the 1970–97 period. Brandt (2007) analyses 23 manufacturing industries for a group of OECD countries (Canada, France, Germany, Italy, Japan and the US) for the 1980–98 period. His results show that the impact of R&D on productivity growth appears significant only in R&D industries.

Table 11.1 Cross-sectional and time-series estimates of research elasticity (firm-level European and US studies)

Work	R&D elasticity cross section		R&D elasticity time series		Sample country, # firms, sector or industry, cross-sectional year, (period)
	R&D elasticity	Details of specification	R&D elasticity	Details of specification	
Minasian (1969)	0.26	Total estimate	0.08	Within estimates	US, 17 firms, chemicals, (1984–57)
Griliches (1980)	0.07	Industry dummies	0.08	Average growth rates, industry dummies	US, 883 manufacturing firms, 1963, (1957–65)
Link (1981)			2.31	Average TFP growth, private basic research over net sales Industry dummies	US, 51 large manufacturing firms, (1973–78)
Link et al. (1982)			0.0312–0.538	TFP, R&D expend. over net sales	US, 97 manufacturing firms, (1975–79)
Schankerman (1981)	0.10	Total estimate			US, 110 firms, chemicals and Oil, 1963
	0.16	Corrected data			
Griliches and Mairesse (1983)	0.05	Total estimate	0.02	Average growth rate	US and France, 343+185 manufacturing firms, (1973–78)
Griliches and Mairesse (1984)	0.18	Total estimate	0.09	Within estimates with labour	US, 133 manufacturing firms, (1966–77)
			0.16	Within estimates	US, 77 firms, scientific sectors, (1966–77)
Cuneo and Mairesse (1984)	0.20	Total estimate corrected data	0.11	Within estimates, corrected data	France, 182 manufacturing firms, (1972–77)
			0.05	Within estimates with labour	
	0.21	Total estimate corrected data			France, 98 firms, scientific sectors, (1972–77)
	0.11	Total estimate			
Mairesse and Cuneo (1985)	0.18	Corrected data	0.02	Growth between extreme years	France, 390 chemicals, (1974–79)
	0.16	Corrected data			France, 296 firms, scientific sectors, (1974–79)
	0.10	Corrected data industry dummies and skill vars.			

Study					Data
Griliches (1986)	0.11 0.09	POLS* corrected labour variable	Average growth rate industry dummies	0.12	US, 652 manufacturing firms, (1966–77)
Jaffe (1986)	0.20	Profits, total estimate	Profit growth between extreme years	0.10	US, 491 manufacturing firms, 1972; US, 491 manufacturing firms, 1977
Lichtenberg and Siegel (1991)			TFP	0.35	US, 432 manufacturing firms, (1973–79)
Hall (1993)			Production function	0.02–0.04	US, 2,000 manufacturing firms, (1973–85); US, 1,200 manufacturing firms, (1964–90)
Hall and Mairesse (1995)			OLS FE FD	0.18–0.25 0.05–0.07 0.02–0.16	France, 197 manufacturing firms, (1980–87)
Adams and Jaffe (1996)			Output elasticity TFP elasticity Output elasticity	0.01–0.03 0.06–0.08 0.06–0.10	US, 1,400 chemical plants, (1974–88)
Klette (1996)	0.014	TFP, R&D by firms in line of business that plant belong to			US, 80 manufacturing firms, (1974–88)
Klette and Johansen (1998)			D log TFP Plant level R&D 1st yr. diff. Plant level R&D 3rd yr. diff.	0.007 0.014	Norway, 804 manufacturing plants (1989–90); Norway, 804 manufacturing plants (1980–92)
Capron and Cincera (1998)			Overall sample, log Output (sales)	0.13–0.33	World, 625 manufacturing firms, (1987–94)
Crépon et al. (1998)	0.12	VA, production function			France, 6,145 manufacturing firms, 1990
Harhoff (1998)			OLS FE BE, FE High-tech	0.13 0.09 0.014 0.04–0.1	Germany, 443 manufacturing firms, (1979–89)
Los and Verspagen (2000)					US, 680 manufacturing firms, (1974–93)
Mairesse et al. (2001)			Lagged Current	0.05 0.09	US and France, 482 US and 486 French firms, (1982–93)
Branstetter (2001)				0.37	US, 209 firms, (1983–89)

279

Table 11.1 (continued)

Work	R&D elasticity cross section		R&D elasticity time series		Sample country, # firms, sector or industry, cross-sectional year, (period)
	R&D elasticity	Details of specification	R&D elasticity	Details of specification	
Greenhalgh and Longland (2002)			0.04	FE (full sample)	UK, 740 production firms, including non-R&D firms, (1986–95)
			0.02	FE (non-high-tech)	
			0.07	FE (high-tech)	
Ballot et al. (2002)			0.10	OLS	Sweden, 200 firms, (1987–93)
			0.15	GMMSYS	
			0.05		France, 100 manufacturing firms, (1987–93)
			0.02		Sweden, 200 manufacturing firms, (1987–93)
Bond et al. (2002)			0.04	OLS	UK, 230 large manufacturing firms, (1987–96)
			0.06	GMMSYS	
			0.09	OLS	Germany, 205 manufacturing firms, (1987–96)
			0.08	GMMSYS	
O'Mahony and Vecchi (2002)			0.11		US, 2,925 firms, (1988–97)
Medda et al. (2003)			0.03	Treatment effects	Italy, 1,008 manufacturing firms, (1992–95)
			0.02		Italy, 689 manufacturing firms, (1992–95)
Bond et al. (2003)			0.08 (n. s.)	FE	Germany, 234 large manufacturing firms (1987–96)
			0.06	GMMSYS	UK, 239 manufacturing firms (1987–96)
Griffith et al. (2004)			0.03	OLS	UK,188 listed manufacturing firms, (1990–2000)
			0.03	GMMSYS	
Poldahl (2004)			0.01	GMMSYS	Sweden, manufacturing firms (1990–2000)

Mairesse et al. (2005)	POLS*		0.043			France, 488 manufacturing, firms, 2000
			0.028			France, 351 manufacturing, firms, 2000
Bond et al. (2005)				0.08	Dynamic production function	Germany, 234 manufacturing firms, (1988–96)
				0.05	GMM-SYS	UK, 239 manufacturing firms, (1988–96)
Bloom et al. (2005a)			n.s.			US, 736 firms, (1981–2001)
Cassidy et al. (2005)	Output			0.05		Ireland, 1,383 manufacturing firms, (1999–2000)
Graversen and Mark (2005)				0.02–0.01		Denmark, 2228 firms, (1991–2001)
Griffith et al. (2006)				0.03	OLS	UK, 188 listed manufacturing firms, (1990–2000)
				0.01–0.02	GMM-SYS	
				0.01	Olley-Pakes	
Rogers (2009)	POLS*	Manufacturing	0.12–0.16			UK, 719 manufacturing and non-manufacturing firms, (1989–2000)
		Non-manufacturing	0.12–0.23			
	IV*	Manufacturing	0.12–0.15			
		Non-manufacturing	0.12–0.22			
Ortega-Argilés et al. (2011a)	POLS*	Whole	0.10	0.10	RE	EU, 532 manufacturing and services firms, (2000–05)
		High-tech	0.17	0.14		
		Medium-tech	0.115	0.13		
		Low-tech	0.03	0.05		
Ortega-Argilés et al. (2011b and 2011c)	POLS**	Whole	0.21	0.09	FE	US and EU, 1,809 manufacturing and services, (1990–2008)
		US	0.23	0.10		
		EU	0.15	0.06		
		Manufacturing	0.23	0.08	FE	US, 914 manufacturing and 256 service firms, (1990–2008)
		Services	0.22	0.12		
		Manufacturing	0.15	0.05	FE	EU, 469 manufacturing and 170 service firms, (1990–2008)
		Services	0.14	0.09		

Note: (n.s.) non-significant value, * with sector and time dummies, ** with sector, country and time dummies.

Table 11.2   Returns to firm R&D (European and US firm-level data studies)

Work	R&D effect		Sample country, # firms, sector or industry, cross-sectional year, (period)
	R&D return	Details of specification	
Minasian (1962)	0.25	Total productivity Value added	US, 18 firms, chemicals, (1947–57)
Mansfield (1980)	0.27	Total productivity Value added	US, 16 firms, chemicals and petroleum, (1960–76)
Link (1981)	–0.00	Total productivity	US, 174 firms, (1971–76)
	0.07	Value added	US, 33 firms, chemicals, (1971–76)
	0.05		US, 34 firms, machinery, (1971–76)
	0.15		US, 19 firms, transport equipment, (1971–76)
Link (1983)	0.06	Total productivity Sales	US, 302 firms, (1975–79)
Griliches and Mairesse (1983)	0.28 0.12	Sales Sales Industry dummies	US and France, 343 + 185 firms, (1973–78)
Clark and Griliches (1984)	0.18 0.20	Sales Industry dummies Total productivity Sales Industry dummies	US, 924 business units, (1971–80)
Bernstein and Nadiri (1988)	0.07	TFP	US, 48 manufacturing firms, (1965–1978)
Fecher (1989)	0.04	Total productivity Sales Industry dummies	Belgium, 292 firms, (1981–83)
Lichtenberg and Siegel (1989)	0.13	Total productivity Sales Industry dummies	US, 5,240 firms, (1972–85)
Griliches and Mairesse (1990)	0.41 0.27 0.25	Sales Sales Industry dummies Sales Industry dummies Free returns	US, 525 firms, (1973–80)
Bernstein and Nadiri (1991)	0.09–0.20	Output	US, 35 firms, (1959–66)
Lichtenberg and Siegel (1991)	0.29	TFP on R&D intensity	US, 2,000 manufacturing business units, (1973-1985)
Klette (1994)	0.10	Growth rates on R&D intensity	Norway, 200 plants, (1978–85)
Hall (1993)	0.22	Sales	US, 1,200 manufacturing firms, (1964–90)

Table 11.2 (continued)

Work	R&D effect		Sample country, # firms, sector or industry, cross-sectional year, (period)
	R&D return	Details of specification	
Hall and Mairesse (1995)	0.08–0.23	Value added per employee	France, 197 manufacturing firms, (1980–87)
Harhoff (1998)	0.66 (overall) 0.77 (high-tech) 0.38 (non-high-tech)	Sales	Germany, 443 manufacturing firms, (1979–89)
Wakelin (2001)	0.27 (full sample) 0.26 (innovators)	Sales	UK, 170 quoted firms Innovators belong to SPRU survey, 1988–96/1988–92 (for the R&D var.)
Bond et al. (2002)	0.38 (UK sample) 0.19 (n.s.) (German sample)	Output	UK, 239 manufacturing firms (1987–96) Germany, 234 large manufacturing firms, (1987–96)
Griffith et al. (2004)	0.16 (mean firm)	Value added	UK, 188 manufacturing firms, (1990–2000)
Rogers (2009)	0.40–0.58 (manufacturing) 0.53–1.08 (non-manufacturing)	Output	UK, 719 manufacturing and non-manufacturing firms, (1989–2000)
Ortega-Argilés (2011c)	0.35 (overall)	Value added	EU, 532 manufacturing and service firms, (2000–05)

Note: (n.s.) non-significant value.

Finally, Sterlacchini and Venturini (2011) using data for 12 manufacturing industries over the 1980–2006 period develop a comparative analysis of the effect of R&D and productivity in high-tech industry firms for the cases of Italy and Spain. Their results show that Spanish high-tech industries have presented higher elasticities of R&D than their Italian counterparts since the mid-1990s.

In terms of the role of R&D in high-versus low-tech sectors, a controversial hypothesis put forward in the current debate is the alleged advantage of low-tech compared with high-tech sectors in achieving productivity gains from R&D investments. The argument here is that catching-up low-tech sectors are investing less in R&D but benefit from a 'late-comer advantage', while high-tech sectors should be affected by a sort of 'decreasing returns' effect (see Marsili, 2001; Mairesse and Mohnen, 2005; Von Tunzelmann and Acha, 2005). If such were the case, we would expect a weaker relationship between R&D and productivity growth in high-tech sectors in comparison with their low-tech counterparts. However, this hypothesis is strikingly in contrast with the available empirical evidence. Indeed, previous sectoral studies clearly suggest a greater impact of R&D investment on productivity in the high-tech sectors than in the low-tech ones.

Examples for the European or American case here are Griliches and Mairesse (1982) and Cuneo and Mairesse (1983), who performed two companion studies using micro-level data, while making a distinction between firms belonging to science-related sectors and firms belonging to other sectors. They found that the impact of R&D on productivity for scientific firms (elasticity equal to 0.20) was significantly greater than for other firms (0.10). In the same vein, Verspagen (1995) tested the impact of R&D expenditures using OECD sectoral-level data on value added, employment, capital expenditures and R&D in a standard production function framework. The author singled out three macro sectors: high-tech, medium-tech and low-tech, according to the OECD classification (Hatzichronoglou, 1997). The major finding of his study was that the impact of R&D was significant and positive only in high-tech sectors, while for medium- and low-tech sectors no significant effects could be found.

Using the methodology set up by Hall and Mairesse (1995), Harhoff (1998) studied the R&D/productivity link on the basis of a slightly unbalanced panel of 443 German manufacturing firms over the 1977–89 period, and found a significant impact ranging from a minimum of 0.068 to a maximum of 0.137, according to the different specifications and the different econometric estimators adopted. The effect of R&D capital was considerably higher for high-tech firms than for the other groups of enterprises. In particular, for the high-tech firms the R&D elasticity always turned out to be highly significant and ranging from 0.125 and 0.176, while for the remaining firms the R&D elasticity was either not significant (although positive) or lower (ranging from 0.090 to 0.096), according to the different estimation techniques.

Similarly, Los and Verspagen (2000), following the works of Cuneo and Mairesse (1984), Griliches and Mairesse (1984) and Hall and Mairesse (1995) estimated the impact of technology spillovers on productivity for a sample of US manufacturing firms between 1977 and 1991. The authors split the total sample into high-, medium- and low-tech subsamples following the OECD classification. Their results are in line with Cuneo and Mairesse (1984) and Griliches and Mairesse (1984), in that there exists a lower elasticity of physical capital in the case of the 'within' model, apparent in all three different technological-level sector groups. The 'own R&D' elasticities are positive and significant for the total group and for the high-tech group, for both the 'within' and 'between' (10 per cent for high-tech) models. For the other subsamples the authors did not find any significant effect of the R&D input. The authors attribute this result partly to the potential-double counting effect.

More recently, Wakelin (2001) applied a Cobb–Douglas production function where productivity was regressed on R&D expenditures, capital and labour using panel data (170 UK quoted firms during the 1988–92 period). She found that R&D expenditures had a positive and significant role in influencing a firm's productivity growth. However, in firms belonging to sectors defined as 'net users of innovations', R&D activities had a significantly larger impact on productivity.

Rincon and Vecchi (2003) also used a Cobb–Douglas framework in dealing with panel micro data extracted from the Compustat database over the 1991–2001 period. They found that R&D-reporting firms were more productive than their non-R&D-reporting counterparts throughout the entire period. However, the positive impact of R&D expenditures was statistically significant both in manufacturing and services in the US, but only in manufacturing in the three main European countries (Germany, France and the UK). Their estimated significant elasticities ranged from 0.15 to 0.20.

Finally, other examples are the works at the European level by Ortega-Argilés et al. (2010, 2011c), who looked at the top EU R&D investors, using an unbalanced longitudinal database consisting of 577 large European companies over the 2000–05 period, extracted from the UK-DTI Scoreboards. The authors found that the R&D-productivity coefficient was significantly different across sectors. In particular, the coefficient increased monotonically, moving from the low-to the medium–high- and high-tech sectors, ranging from a minimum of 0.03/0.05 to a maximum of 0.14/0.17. This outcome has been interpreted as evidence that firms in high-tech sectors are still far ahead in terms of the impact on productivity of their R&D investments, at least as regards top European R&D investors.

On the whole, the available sectoral empirical studies using different datasets across different countries suggest a greater impact of R&D investments on firm productivity in the high-tech sectors than in the low-tech ones.

11.2.3   Technology Transfer within and between Sectors: Services versus Manufacturing

In terms of industry comparisons, Griliches (1992) and Solow (1992) in their introduction to a special journal issue on productivity in the service sector, reached the conclusion that, after all, service and goods-producing sectors are not that different in that productivity analysis raises similar difficulties in both sectors. Several papers investigate the differences between service and manufacturing industries regarding the R&D–productivity link. O'Mahony and Vecchi (2009) used company accounts data for five countries (US, UK, Japan, France and Germany) to analyse the relationship between intangible assets and productivity. In order to capture the differences in knowledge-intensive and innovative activities between and within sectors, they integrated the company data with industry information on tangible and intangible investments. The results provide evidence of higher productivity in R&D- and skill-intensive industries, and a higher R&D elasticity in non-manufacturing firms (0.251) than in manufacturing firms (0.170). Their results are similar to the results obtained by Ortega-Argilés et al. (2011a), who found the rather surprising result of higher returns to R&D investments in the service sectors. They argue that this is partly due to the composition of the service firms' samples, where the majority of the firms belonged to R&D-intensive service sectors, such as business and professional services.

Services play a growing role in economic activity, accounting for around 70 per cent of GDP in OECD countries. It is also widely acknowledged that the service sector can be innovative and that service innovation – which occurs throughout the economy – can be a key source of growth for firms, sectors and nations in the context of intensified global competition and the economic crisis. Even though service innovation plays an increasing role, mainstream policies which affect these activities have been developed from a mainly technological or manufacturing perspective, which tends to neglect the specificities of this type of innovation. Likewise, the underlying policy rationale is often based on indicators which are still biased towards R&D, technological innovation and manufacturing. With limited quantitative evidence on service innovation, existing R&D and innovation policy has paid little attention to this type of innovation. The formulation and implementation of policies aimed at promoting service innovations face significant challenges, as obstacles are difficult to identify and a broader evidence base is needed to inform discussions on how to design new (or improve existing) policy instruments.

Rather than service versus manufacturing sectors, a large number of studies have focused on comparing different sets of industries by the technological component of their production (high-, medium- and low-tech sectors) or by their knowledge content (knowledge-intensive versus non-knowledge-intensive or traditional industries). In terms of the relationship between manufacturing and services, quantitative measures of innovation (for example, R&D expenditure) suggest that service firms are less innovative than product-producing firms, thereby potentially failing to capture all of the innovation efforts (Gallouj and Djellal, 2010). However, many highly innovative service firms have not only obtained competitive advantages but also disrupted their competitors as a result of 'radically innovating' their services (for example, Ryanair, Amazon and so on). The analysis of R&D in services is extremely difficult, among other reasons, due to the lack of recognition and awareness of R&D within service businesses; the existing fragmentation of the service industries; the more open nature of R&D in these particular industries (for example, 'outward' *vis-à-vis* 'inward' facing, Howells and Tether, 2004); the fact that service activities appear to be blurring with other activities and functions (for example, consultancy and design) both internally and externally to the business (co-generation between user and producer); and the boundary of where R&D undertaken is often very unclear.

In recent years, however, a relatively large number of papers have focused on the productivity accounts of IT and non-IT sectors and on the productivity accounts of IT-producing and-using sectors. This is because of their important role in explaining productivity gaps between the most important countries (Timmer et al., 2010) or between innovators and non-innovators, and because of the important role of innovations in transferring the returns from R&D to productivity (Wakelin, 2001). In recent years new studies have also emerged that try to capture differences in the R&D productivity link between manufacturing and service sectors. As an illustration of these changes, Figure 11.1 shows how the contribution by the industries to the productivity growth in the US has changed over the last decades; what stands out is the change in the contribution of IT-related industries. In particular, the emphasis has shifted from IT-producing to IT-using sectors, which suggests that the technology transfer relationship between sectors and between production factors and different sources of growth is itself evolving.

Following on from this idea, some studies pointed to the need to differentiate between increases in the productivity growth of one factor (output per worker) because of high levels of input such as labour or capital, or high levels of technical efficiency (TFP). For example, Griffith et al. (2004) measured the potential of technology transfer by the distance between each economy's level of productivity in a particular industry and the level in the technological frontier in that industry ('technology gap') in a panel of industries across 12 OECD countries. They treated the highest level of productivity in a particular industry as the frontier. Therefore in each industry, they calculated an economy's level of productivity relative to the productivity leader. The greater the distance between the economy's level of productivity and that in the leading economy, the greater the potential for technology transfer. These techniques have also been used to calculate

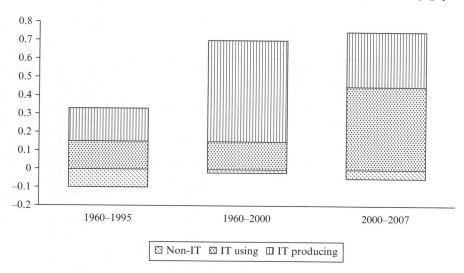

Source: Based on the presentation by Jorgenson et al. (2012) at: http://post.economics.harvard.edu/faculty/
jorgenson/.

Figure 11.1 Industry contribution to productivity growth (Domar weighted productivity)

the productivity growth differentials, and to compare the relative levels of outputs to the relative levels of factor inputs (hours worked or hours worked adjusted by the skill composition of the labour force), where factor inputs are weighted appropriately. The authors found a role for R&D investment in stimulating both innovation and technology transfer; the greater the potential for technologies to be transferred through R&D the higher the rates of productivity growth. This provides support to the idea that there is an important second role for R&D in enabling agents to understand and assimilate existing technologies. It suggests that studies which focus on the innovative role of R&D investment alone may well underestimate the 'true' rate of return to R&D in countries that are not technological leaders.

11.2.4 Private versus Social Returns to Industry R&D

Following this line of argument, the productivity of private inputs in research varies as a function of the aggregate knowledge which is outside the control of any individual firm. Caballero and Jaffe (1993) postulate that it takes time for additional knowledge to diffuse sufficiently to be of use to other inventors, and this tends to limit the ability of very recent knowledge in generating new knowledge. On the other hand, old knowledge eventually is made obsolete by the emergence of newer and superior knowledge. They call this phenomenon 'knowledge' or 'technological obsolescence', and distinguish it from the obsolescence in value represented by creative destruction. In other words, new ideas have two distinct effects on the current stock of ideas: they make the products represented by those ideas less valuable (creative destruction or value obsolescence), and they also make the knowledge represented by those ideas less relevant in the production of new knowledge (knowledge or technological obsolescence). The strength of

Table 11.3   Evidence on the rate of return to private R&D (OECD, European and US studies)

Author (year)	Private return	Social return	Country (level of analysis)
Terleckyj (1974)	0.29	0.48–0.78	US (industry)
Mansfield (1977)	0.25 (median)	0.56 (median)	US (industry)
Sveikauskas (1981)	0.7–0.25	0.50	US (industry)
Griliches and Lichtenberg (1984a, 1984b)	0.11–0.31	0.50–0.90	US (industry)
Scherer (1982, 1984)	0.29–0.43	0.64–1.47	US (industry)
Bernstein and Nadiri (1988)	0.10–0.27	0.11–1.11	US (industry)
Sterlacchini (1989)	0.12–0.20	0.19–0.20	UK (industry)
Bernstein and Nadiri (1991)	0.15–0.28	0.20–1.10	US (industry)
Nadiri (1993)	0.20–0.30	0.50	US (industry)
Wolff and Nadiri (1993)	0.11 (manufacturing) 0.19 (overall)	0.27 (manufacturing) 0.47 (overall)	US (industry)
Wolff (1997)	0.10–0.125	0.53	US (industry)
Bernstein (1996)	0.16	0.64	US (industry)
Van Meijl (1997a, 1997b)	0.13–0.17	0.11–0.13	France (industry)
Bernstein (1998)	0.164	0.28–1.67	US (industry)
	0.128	0.19–1.45	Canada (industry)
Bernstein and Mohnen (1998)	0.44	0.47	US (industry)
	0.47	0.00	Japan (industry)
Hubert and Pain (2001)	0.029	0.032	UK (industry)
Luintel and Khan (2004)	0.42	1.32	OECD (industry)
Griffith et al. (2004)	0.47–0.67	0.57–1.05	OECD (industry, country)
Añón-Higón (2007)		0.942 (inter-industry)	UK (Manufacturing industries)
Park (2004)	0.44–0.85	1.19 (median) 0.57 (US)	OECD, East Asia (manufacturing and non-manufacturing industries)

Note: The results can vary in the weighting scheme (patent, innovations, simple external sector-specific R&D stock or inter-industry flows).

Source: Extension of Fraumeni and Okubo (2005).

knowledge spillovers, and hence the growth of the economy, will depend on the parameters of the processes of knowledge diffusion and knowledge obsolescence.

With regard to the contribution of R&D to the industrial productivity growth, Table 11.3 (an amplification of the table in Fraumeni and Okubo, 2005) presents a selected group of studies to determine the private and social rate of returns to privately funded R&D. These estimates suggest that the social returns to R&D are higher (typically 2–4 times) than the private rates of return to R&D and highlight the role of knowledge externalities.

By examining industry data, analysts are able to include spillovers between the different firms within an industry, and the evidence suggests that there are important differences between firm and industry returns to R&D. As Griliches (1979) remarks, firm knowledge leaks out fairly rapidly, so firm R&D depreciates rapidly. On the other hand, much of this knowledge is gained by other firms, so social returns depreciate more slowly than firm returns. Similarly, there is a greater lag before social returns take effect, and social returns are substantially greater than private returns. Consequently, many of the central features of R&D stocks are noticeably different in industry data compared to firm data. If satellite accounts for R&D are to include the economic impact of spillovers, the key channel through which R&D affects productivity and output growth, national income accountants will have to move beyond asset effects to examine spillovers, using alternative values to measure central concepts such as depreciation, lags and the rate of return.

Considerable evidence describes the leakages of R&D from firms to the broader industry. Mansfield (1985) showed that information about new technology leaks out to rival firms within a year or two. Caballero and Jaffe (1993), using market value and patent data on 567 large US firms for the 1965–81 period, similarly find rapid leakages. Jaffe (1986) found the pool of nearby research affected technological progress (the number of patents) more strongly than it affects private returns (the profits or market value of firms). Nelson's (1988) argument that R&D reflects the presence of collateral technological opportunities applies with particular force at the industry level, where major differences in technological possibilities are most visible. For example, no one would reasonably expect productivity growth to become as rapid in lumber as it is in computers if R&D intensity in lumber were raised to the levels typical for computers. Yet, that is what the usual cross-industry regressions assume. Nelson recommended that the returns to research should therefore be determined not from regressions across firms or industries, but instead from the careful study of the returns to individual innovations.

The interest in different innovation contexts – service environments as opposed to the well-studied product environments – is gradually increasing (Drejer, 2004). The stringent environmental regulations induce more R&D and promote further productivity in certain industries. As we shall see shortly, in recent years, economists have begun to pay far more attention to the idea that new technology requires very substantial complementary investments.

11.2.5 At the Firm Level

On the whole, the existing economic literature has found robust evidence of a positive and significant impact of R&D on productivity at the firm level. The consensus about the existence of a positive and significant impact of R&D on productivity stands on different studies using different proxies for productivity according to the data available: labour productivity measured as the ratio between value added and employment; labour productivity as the ratio between value added and hours worked; TFP; Solow's residual; and so on (see, for instance, Lichtenberg and Siegel, 1991; Hall and Mairesse 1995; Janz et al., 2004; Klette and Kortum, 2004; Lööf and Heshmati, 2006; Rogers, 2009; Ortega-Argilés et al., 2011c). In this literature, the estimated overall elasticity of productivity with respect to R&D is positive, statistically significant and with a magnitude – depending on the data and the adopted econometric methodology – ranging from 0.05 to 0.25 (see Tables 11.1–3 for a summary of studies focusing on the R&D, innovation and productivity linkages, and for more comprehensive surveys at the firm level, see Mairesse and Sassenou, 1991; Griliches 1995, 2000; Mairesse and Mohnen, 2001). Hence, the legacy of the previous microeconometric literature is clear in indicating the role of R&D in enhancing productivity at the firm level.

Considering the relationships between the characteristics of firms and R&D performance, Klette and Kortum (2004) presented a list of stylized facts on the relationship between firm size, R&D effort, productivity and growth. Among others, the authors found that there is a positive relationship between R&D activity and the level of productivity across firms, whereas the longitudinal relationship between firm-level differences in R&D and productivity growth is typically insignificant. The literature discusses the role of patents as an intermediate step for capturing the returns to R&D in productivity gains. Klette and Kortum (2004) found that the relationship between R&D and patents varies between the cross-sectional dimension (being constant) and in the longitudinal dimension (being negative).

The empirical literature on the subject has devoted increased attention to the problems associated with the measurement of firm-specific R&D activities. Hall and Mairesse (1995), among others, have shown the importance for firm performance of developing R&D in a continuous manner, because of the hysteresis of developing complex investments and the diminishing risk and costs associated with them. Additionally, several authors have stressed the positive role that persistent R&D plays in business performance. However, the authors have also made us aware of the differences in the results associated with the choice of the depreciation rate of R&D investments. Another additional problem associated with the R&D measurement is related to the potential double counting of R&D expenditures in capital and labour accounts. The problem of double counting originally raised by Schankerman (1981), argues that the double counting of labour and physical capital employed in R&D would yield negatively biased estimated elasticities with respect to R&D. Some authors found evidence supporting this hypothesis (Cuneo and Mairesse, 1984; Hall and Mairesse, 1995) while others find no evidence that would affect the results significantly (Verspagen, 1995).

Mairesse and Sassenou (1991) surveyed 18 econometric studies at the firm level in the United States, France and Japan between 1969 and 1988 to document the estimated variation of the contribution of R&D to firm productivity. Among their conclusions, the authors observed improvements in the studies due to the increase in the quality of the accessible data; however, they found that more improvements in the data were needed in particular in the measurement of output, input prices and quantities. The authors mentioned the important aspect of accounting for the history in R&D investments because of the possibility of better capturing the diversity of the situations of individual firms during their lifetime, and overcoming the differences associated with cross-section and panel data studies in the returns of R&D to firm productivity.

More recently, Mairesse and Mohnen (2003) provide a review of the empirical firm-level studies finding that, for the US data up to the mid-1980s, the rate of return on private R&D is between 13 and 25 per cent. Griffith (2000) references other studies and states that the private rates of return tend to be between 10 and 15 per cent and that elasticity estimates are around 0.07. Griffith et al. (2004) calculate a value of 16 per cent for the mean firm in their sample. Meanwhile, although the Bond et al. (2002) paper does not report rates of return explicitly, it does claim that the UK firms' rate of return must be higher than that for German firms (since elasticity estimates are similar, while UK firms have lower R&D intensities). The only direct study on rates of return (Wakelin, 2001) estimates it to be around 27 per cent. The UK studies find R&D elasticities of between 0.02 and 0.07, although some of these differences may stem from calculating R&D stocks in different ways. Crespi et al. (2008) found knowledge spillovers associated with flows from competitors, suppliers and plants that belong to the same group.

In general, the estimates for the elasticity tend to be higher from cross-sectional estimates and lower from within or difference estimations. This is consistent with the idea that, given the presence of measurement error, the coefficients are biased downwards more in 'within' or first-difference estimations.

11.3　THE US–EU PRODUCTIVITY GAP

The productivity performance of an economy is a result of the ability of firms, sectors and activities to generate employment and the contribution of this employment to productivity in general. By the early 1990s the European economy had almost caught up with the US economy according to various productivity indices, but since then a significant transatlantic productivity gap has emerged at precisely the time when the creation of the Single Market meant that the EU was embarking on its most fundamental period of deregulation and integration. Why this gap emerged at precisely the time when it would be least expected, provides some important insights and lessons into the role of R&D, and the role played by knowledge more generally, within the economy. In particular, it suggests that there are important differences in these mechanisms between the US and the EU, but the reasons for this are as yet not clear-cut and important debates have emerged. Disparities in productivity associated with the performance of particular sectors of activity in the economy due to differences in the number of firms or employees in them are known as the 'structural effect', whereas disparities in productivity due to the performance of individuals in the economy are known as the 'intrinsic effect'. Yet, the contribution to the disparities of these two effects, and the interactions between these effects, is not entirely clear, and such issues also need to be considered in the light of other possible factors that might have influenced the EU–US productivity divergence.

There is widespread evidence to suggest that in comparison with the EU economy, the US economy is still characterized by higher levels of investments in ICTs, which represent today's most important general-purpose technologies. These differences in ICT investments, and the so-called 'New Economy' effect such investments induce, are argued by many commentators to be one of the main underlying explanations behind the transatlantic productivity gap (Jorgenson and Stiroh, 1999; Oliner and Sichel, 2000; Stiroh, 2002a, 2002b; van Ark et al., 2002, 2003; O'Mahony and van Ark, 2003; Bloom et al., 2007; Rogerson, 2008). The argument broadly is that the US firms were in the vanguard of the New Economy sectors such as the ICT-producing and nanotechnology sectors, and these firms gave the US a distinct productivity advantage as the New Economy effect grew in momentum, However, the evidence also suggests that other ICT-using sectors such as retailing, and many other manufacturing and service industries also played a very important role in the transatlantic productivity gap.

In terms of medium- and long-run historical analyses, the productivity performance of Europe *vis-à-vis* the US during the latter decades of the twentieth century and the first decade of the twenty-first century has been examined by, among others, van Ark (2002), Erken (2004), Gordon (2004a, 2004b), McGuckin and van Ark (2004), Jorgenson et al. (2008), van Ark et al. (2008), McMorrow et al. (2010), Timmer et al. (2010) and Uppenberg (2011). The broad picture which emerges from this body of work is that the European private sector was falling behind from 1870 to 1950, experienced a catch-up after 1950 and by 1995 had almost entirely closed the productivity gap, and then fell behind again after 1995.

Almost all of the available evidence now points to the emerging disparities in the growth patterns of both economies as being associated with the endogenous development in investment rates (in different input factors) and the adoption of technical change (Ortega-Argilés, 2012). In the mid-1990s, the US economy experienced a boost in the productivity of ICT-producing industries and a capital-deepening effect from investments in ICTs in different sectors of the economy. US ICT-using industries, and principally those in market services, exhibited increased productivity, after a certain delay due to the required reorganizations necessary for adopting these new technologies. In Europe, however, a continuous lag in the adoption of ICTs stalled such a productivity shift, leading to a widening productivity gap. Over the decade between the mid-1990s and the mid-2000s, the GDP growth gap between the EU and the US was almost entirely driven by differences in TFP associated with the widespread restructuring related to the adoption of new ICT technologies across a diverse range of sectors (Jorgenson et al., 2008; van Ark et al., 2008; McMorrow et al., 2010). These differences in TFP are associated with differences in the quality and levels of ICT capital deepening during the early 1990s, an effect which appears to play a less prominent role as a source of productivity growth after 2000.

A slightly different approach was adopted by Bourlès and Cette (2007) who considered the productivity trends in the US and other industrialized countries in terms of hourly labour productivity. For the 2000–04 period, US structural productivity slowed down and its trend growth (about 2 per cent a year) was between that which was typical in the second half of the 1990s (2.6 per cent) and what was observed during the 1980–95 period (1.6 per cent). There is no such slowdown for overall observed productivity, however, because it was offset by the effects of decreases in the employment rate and average working time. Therefore, since 2000, US productivity gains seem to have been structurally less significant than those which were evident during the second half of the 1990s. However, from the early or mid-1990s, depending on which country is considered, both observed and structural productivity declined in all countries relative to the US, apart from Norway and Sweden. This relative deterioration was attributable not only to the acceleration in productivity in the US but also to the even greater slowdown in productivity in almost all the other countries. The very high levels of observed productivity in some European countries in recent years compared with the US appear to be largely attributable to a lower number of hours worked and lower employment rates, and as such have not led to an overall concomitant positive impact on aggregate productivity. In the 1990s, average annual labour productivity growth in the market economy accelerated from 1.9 per cent (1973–95) to 2.9 per cent (1995–2006) in the US, while in the EU it fell from 2.5 to 1.5 per cent. Timmer et al. (2010) argue that this slowdown in EU labour productivity was connected *in the short run* with labour restructuring issues in several

European economies during this period (Blanchard, 2004; Dew-Becker and Gordon, 2008).

The various explanations offered for the overall transatlantic productivity gap include: the lower quality of EU human capital (Gu et al., 2002; Inklaar et al., 2003), the rigidity of the European labour markets (Gordon and Dew-Becker, 2005; Gomez-Salvador et al., 2006), delays in the speed of diffusion and implementation of ICTs or general-purpose technologies in the EU (Caselli and Wilson, 2004; Wilson, 2009; Jorgenson, 2011), the higher importance of new managerial practices and organizational investments in US companies (Gu and Wang, 2004; Bloom et al., 2005a, 2005b; Crespi et al., 2007, 2008), and the disparities of the contribution of service sectors to both economies (Inklaar et al., 2003). However, the fact that structural hourly productivity levels are still higher in the United States than elsewhere shows that the US is indeed setting the technical frontier in terms of productive efficiency, and that other countries to varying degrees are lagging behind.

11.3.1   Intra-EU Productivity Variations

During the period in which the productivity gap emerged, however, some European countries such as Ireland, Finland and Sweden, appeared to perform as well as the US in terms of productivity. This implies that in some cases the overall aggregate EU underperformance hid the positive performance of some European countries as a consequence of the aggregation procedure. Many EU countries achieved higher MFP growth rates than the US over the 1990s, including Ireland, Finland, Sweden, Denmark, Norway, Canada and Austria. Some, but not all of these countries surpass the US in PC use per household and or in the share of ICT expenditure. What differs most between Europe and the US is the low level of PC adoption and ICT expenditure in the 'olive belt' ranging from Portugal and Spain in the west to Italy and Greece in the east? The result is that the heterogeneity between EU countries is more pronounced than the differences between the overall EU and the US (Gordon, 2004b; Gordon and Dew-Becker, 2005; Timmer et al., 2010). Overall, while Europe is lagging behind the US, within Europe the R&D–productivity link is clearly characterized by increasing returns in R&D-intensive regions. The results also show the high returns in labour productivity of internal investments in physical capital, in the case of low-R&D-intensive manufacturing sectors. As such, the specialization patterns of the EU economies and the geographical characteristics of the EU regional locations are some of the main explanations of the gap in productivity and R&D both between Europe and the US and also within Europe.

For advanced OECD countries the patterns of convergence across sectors have differed since 1970, and while productivity in market services appeared to converge, this convergence was not found in manufacturing industries (Bernard and Jones, 1996; Cameron, 2005; Inklaar and Timmer 2009; Brakman et al., 2011). Taken as a whole, there is no generally applicable common trend or pattern providing a clear-cut explanation of international or interregional differences in productivity growth, because it depends on the capital intensity, the scale and scope of operations, the technological and innovation capacity and the degree of deregulation. However, while much of the observed productivity gap is very robust to measurement issues, it is also clear that adjusting labour productivity measures for transatlantic differences in the hours worked does close a very large portion of the gap.

11.4   CONCLUSIONS

R&D leads to undoubted gains in productivity over time. However, the actual magnitude of the R&D–productivity link depends on the nature of the R&D, the sector of the R&D, the nature of the firm, and the national and regional structural features. These principles are consistent across almost all contexts. However, the observation of a widening transatlantic productivity gap led to a widespread reconsideration of the nature, and determining characteristics, of these possible mechanisms. The various sectoral analyses outlined here support the general argument that ICT producers and also ICT users such as market services and retail, were the industries that most accounted for the differences between the US and the EU in terms of productivity gains from the mid-1990s onwards. During the 1980s and early 1990s, the ICT-producing sectors were in the vanguard of the transatlantic productivity gap. However, after 1995 it was the differences in performance of the ICT-using sectors, the New Economy effect, that accounted for most of the transatlantic productivity gap (Timmer et al., 2010). Although the ICT-intensive industries in Europe did perform better than Europe's non-ICT industries, their performance as a whole was still below that of their US counterparts. As such, the various explanations offered for the EU underperformance point to the need for wider structural reforms to many aspects of Europe's economy, including the removal of barriers to entrepreneurship and labour market restructuring (Ortega-Argilés, 2012), in order to spur and facilitate the wider dissemination of newly emerging knowledge and technologies across sectors and regions.

NOTES

1. 'Total factor productivity' is defined as the change in output after taking account of growth in physical capital and changes in the quantity and quality of labour input.
2. 'Multifactor productivity' represents the residual portion of output growth that cannot be explained by changes in labour and capital. MFP growth is labour productivity growth minus the effect on productivity of change in the capital–labour ratio. MFP growth in the long run is explained by factors such as technological progress, rising education standards and changes in the socioeconomic environment. In some of the literature MFP is referred to as TFP.
3. 'Labour productivity' is defined as 'real' (constant price) output divided by labour inputs (measured in terms of persons or hours).
4. 'Capital deepening' measures the increase in the value of capital per worker. As capital deepening is measured in volume terms, it also captures the effect of falling ICT prices on labour productivity growth.
5. Mairesse and Jaumandreu (2005) checked the potential underestimation problems due to the non-accessibility to information of output prices. They found no evidence of a significant difference in the estimation of the revenue function (with nominal prices) with the use of a proper production function (with real output measures).
6. Process innovation increases the global productivity of factors, thus increasing the product supply and reducing the unit production cost and therefore price. Product innovation increases efficiency per volume unit and increases demand for units of efficiency. For that reason an increasing number of countries have introduced fiscal incentives and subsidies for R&D that may increase the innovative activity of firms but they may also alter the strategic interactions between firms that determine market shares.

REFERENCES

Abramovitz, M. (1989), *Thinking about Growth*, Cambridge: Cambridge University Press.

Adams, J.D. and A.B. Jaffe (1996), 'Bounding the effects of R&D: an investigation using matched establishment–firm data', *RAND Journal of Economics*, **27** (4), 700–721.

Aghion, P. and P. Howitt (1992), 'A model of growth through creative destruction', *Econometrica*, **60** (2), 323–51.

Aghion, P. and P. Howitt (1996), 'The observational implications of Schumpeterian growth theory', *Empirical Economics*, **21** (1), 13–25.

Aghion, P. and P. Howitt (1998), *Endogenous Growth Theory*, Cambridge, MA: MIT Press.

Añón-Higón, D. (2007), 'The impact of R&D spillovers on UK manufacturing TFP: a dynamic panel approach', *Research Policy*, **36** (7), 949–63.

Ballot, G., F. Fakhfakh and E. Taymaz (2002), 'Who benefits from training and R&D: the firm or the workers? A study on panels of French and Swedish Firms', Working Paper in Economics 02/01, Economics Research Center (ERC), Middle East Technical University, Ankara, Turkey, June.

Benhabib, J.I. and M.M. Spiegel (1994), 'The role of human capital in economic development: evidence from aggregate cross-country data', *Journal of Monetary Economics*, **34**, 143–73.

Bernard, A.B. and C.I. Jones (1996), 'Comparing apples to oranges: productivity convergence and measurement across industries and countries', *American Economic Review*, **86** (5), 1216–38.

Bernstein, J.I. (1996), 'International R&D spillovers between industries in Canada and the United States', *Canadian Journal of Economics*, **29**, Special issue, 463–7.

Bernstein, J.I. (1998), 'Factor intensities, rates of return, and international spillovers: the case of Canadian and U.S. industries', *Annales d'Économie et de Statistique*, **49–50**, 541–64.

Bernstein, J.I. and P. Mohnen (1998), 'International R&D spillovers between U.S. and Japanese R&D intensive sectors', *Journal of International Economics*, **44**, 315–38.

Bernstein, J.I. and M.I. Nadiri (1988), 'Interindustry spillovers, rates of return, and production in high-tech industries', *American Economic Review*, **78**, 429–34.

Bernstein, J.I. and M.I. Nadiri (1991), 'Product demand, cost of production, spillovers, and the social rate of return to R&D', NBER Working Paper 3625, Cambridge, MA.

Blanchard, O. (2004), 'The economic future of Europe', *Journal of Economic Perspectives*, **8**, 3–26.

Bloom, N., S. Dorgan, J. Dowdy, J. van Reenen and T. Rippin (2005a), 'Management practices across firms and nations', Mimeo, Centre for Economic Performance, London School of Economics.

Bloom, N., R. Sadun and J. van Reenen (2005b), 'It ain't what you do, it's the way that you do I.T.: testing explanations of productivity growth using US affiliates', Mimeo, Centre for Economic Performance, London School of Economics.

Bloom, N., R. Sadun and J. van Reenen (2007), 'Nobody does IT better', *CEPR Policy Insight*, **7**, June.

Bond, S., J.A. Elston, J. Mairesse and B. Mulkay (2003), 'Financial factors and investment in Belgium, France, Germany, and the United Kingdom: a comparison using company panel data', *Review of Economics and Statistics*, **85** (1), February, 153–65.

Bond, S., D. Harhoff and J. van Reenen (2002), 'Corporate R&D and productivity in Germany and the United Kingdom', CEP (Centre for Economic Performance) Discussion Paper, London School of Economics and Political Science.

Bond, S., D. Harhoff and J. Van Reenen (2005), 'Investment, R&D and financial constraints in Britain and Germany', *Annales d'Économie et de Statistique*, **79–80**, 433–60.

Bound, J., C. Cummins, Z. Griliches, B.H. Hall and A. Jaffe (1984), 'Who does R&D and who patents?', in Griliches (ed.), R&D, Patents and Productivity, Chicago, IL: University Chicago Press, pp. 393–416.

Bourlès, R. and G. Cette (2007), 'Trends in "structural" productivity levels in the major industrialized countries', *Economic Letters*, **95**, 151–6.

Brakman, S., R. Inklaar and C. Van Marrewijk (2011), 'Structural change in OECD comparative advantage', *Journal of International Trade and Economic Development*, October, 1–22.

Brandt, N. (2007), 'Mark-ups, economies of scale and the role of knowledge spillovers in OECD industries', *European Economic Review*, **51**, 1708–32.

Branstetter, L.G. (2001), 'Are knowledge spillovers international or intranational in scope? Microeconometric evidence from the U.S. and Japan', *Journal of International Economics*, **53** (1), 53–79.

Caballero, R. and A. Jaffe (1993), 'How high are the giant's shoulders: an empirical assessment of knowledge spillovers and creative destruction in a model of economic growth', *NBER Macroeconomics Annual*, **8**, 15–73.

Cameron, G. (2005), 'The sun also rises: productivity convergence between Japan and the USA', *Journal of Economic Growth*, **10**, 387–408.

Capron, H. and M. Cincera (1998), 'Assessing the R&D determinants and productivity of worldwide manufacturing firms', *Annales d'Économie et de Statistiques*, **49–50**, 565–87.

Caselli, F. and D.J. Wilson (2004), 'Importing technology', *Journal of Monetary Economics*, **51** (1), 1–32.
Cassidy, M., H. Görg and E. Strobl (2005), 'Knowledge accumulation and productivity: evidence from plant level data for Ireland', *Scottish Journal of Political Economy*, **52** (3), 344–58.
Clark, K.B. and Z. Griliches (1984), 'Productivity growth and R&D at the business level: results from the PIMS database', in Griliches (ed.), *R&D, Patents and Productivity*, Chicago, IL: University Chicago Press, pp. 393–416.
Coccia, M. (2009), 'What is the optimal rate of R&D investment to maximize productivity growth?', *Technological Forecasting and Social Change*, **76** (3), 433–46.
Coe, D.T. and E. Helpman (1995), 'International R&D spillovers', *European Economic Review*, **39**, 859–87.
Coe, D.T., E. Helpman and A.W. Hoffmaister (1997), 'North–South R&D spillovers', *Economic Journal*, **107**, 134–50.
Crépon, B., E. Duguet and J. Mairesse (1998), 'Research, innovation, and productivity: an econometric analysis at the firm level', *Economics of Innovation and New Technology*, **7**, 115–56.
Crespi, G., C. Criscuolo, J. Haskel and M. Slaughter (2008), 'Productivity growth, knowledge flows and spillovers', NBER Working Paper 13959, Cambridge, MA.
Crespi, G., J.E. Haskel and J. Haskel (2007), 'Information technology, organizational change and productivity', CEPR Discussion Paper 6105, London.
Cuneo, P. and J. Mairesse (1983), 'Productivity and R&D at the firm level in French manufacturing', NBER Working Paper 1068, Cambridge, MA.
Cuneo, P. and J. Mairesse (1984), 'Productivity and R&D at the firm level in French Manufacturing', in NBER, *R&D, Patents, and Productivity*, Cambridge, MA: National Bureau of Economic Research pp. 375–92.
Denison, F. (1985), *Trends in American Economic Growth 1929–1982*, Washington, DC: Brookings Institution.
Dew-Becker, I. and R.J. Gordon (2008), 'The role of labor market changes in the slowdown of European productivity growth', NBER Working Paper 13840, National Bureau of Economic Research, Cambridge, MA.
Dinopoulos, E. and P. Thompson (1998), 'Schumpeterian growth without scale effects', *Journal of Economic Growth*, **3** (4), 313–35.
Dosi, G. (1997), 'Opportunities, incentives and the collective patterns of technological change', *Economic Journal*, **107**, 1530–47.
Drejer, I. (2004), 'Identifying innovation in surveys of services: a Schumpeterian perspective', *Research Policy*, **33** (3), 551–62.
Eaton, J. and S. Kortum (1996), 'Measuring technology diffusion and the international source of growth', *Eastern Economic Journal*, **22**, 401–10.
Engelbrecht, H.J. (1997), 'International R&D spillovers, human capital and productivity in OECD economies: an empirical investigation', *European Economic Review*, **41**, 1479–88.
Erken, H. (2004), 'An international comparison of productivity performance: the case of Netherlands', in G.M.M Gelauff, S.E.P. Klomp and T.J.A Roelandt (eds), *Fostering Productivity, Patterns, Determinants and Policy Implications*, London: Elsevier, pp. 9–28.
Fecher, F. (1989), 'Effets directs et indirects de la R-D sur la productivité: une analyse de l'industrie manufacturière Belge', *Cahiers Économiques de Bruxelles*, **128**, 459–83.
Fraumeni, B. and S. Okubo (2005), 'R&D in the national income and product accounts: a first look at its effect on GNP', in C. Corrado, J. Haltiwanger and D. Sichel (eds), *Measuring Capital in the New Economy*, NBER, Chicago, IL: University Chicago Press, pp. 275–316.
Freeman, C. (1982), *The Economics of Industrial Innovation*, London: Pinter.
Gallouj, F. and F. Djellal (eds) (2010), *The Handbook of Innovation and Services*, Cheltenham, UK and Northampton, MA, USA: Edward Elgar.
Gallouj, F. and M. Savona (2010), 'Towards a theory of innovation in services: a state of the art', in: Gallouj and F. Djellal (eds), pp. 27–48.
Gomez-Salvador, R., A. Musso, M. Stocker and J. Turunen (2006), 'Labour productivity developments in the euro area', European Central Bank Occasional Paper 53, Frankfurt am Main.
Gordon, R.J. (2004a), 'Five puzzles in the behavior of productivity, investment and innovation', NBER Working Paper 10660, National Bureau of Economic Research, Cambridge, MA.
Gordon, R.J. (2004b), 'Why was Europe left at the station when America's productivity locomotive departed?', NBER Working Paper 10661, National Bureau of Economic Research, Cambridge, MA.
Gordon, R.J. and I. Dew-Becker (2005), 'Why did Europe's productivity catch-up sputter out? A tale of tigers and tortoises', Federal Reserve Bank of San Francisco, Proceedings.
Graversen, E.K. and M. Mark (2005), 'The effect of R&D capital on firm productivity', Danish Centre for Studies in Research and Research Policy Working Paper 2005/3, Aarhus University.
Greenhalgh, C. and M. Longland (2002), 'Running to stand still? Intellectual property and value added in innovating firms', Oxford Intellectual Property Research Centre Working Paper Series, 1, October.
Greenhalgh, C., M. Longland and D. Bosworth (2001), 'Technology activity and employment in a panel of UK firms', *Scottish Journal of Political Economy*, **48**, 260–282.

Griffith, R. (2000), 'How important is business R&D for economic growth and should the government subsidise it?', Institute for Fiscal Studies, Briefing Note 12, London.

Griffith, R., R. Harrison and J. van Reenen (2006), 'How special is the special relationship? Using the impact of U.S. R&D spillovers on U.K. firms as a test of technology sourcing', *American Economic Review*, **96** (5), 1859–75.

Griffith, R., S. Redding and J. Van Reenen (2004), 'Mapping the two faces of R&D: productivity growth in a panel of OECD countries', *Review of Economics and Statistics*, **22** (4), 445–56.

Griliches, Z. (1979), 'Issues in assessing the contribution of research and development to productivity growth', *Bell Journal of Economics*, **10**, 92–116.

Griliches, Z. (1980), 'R&D and the productivity slowdown', *American Economic Review*, **70** (2), May, 343–8.

Griliches, Z. (1985), 'Productivity, R&D, and basic research at the firm level in the 1970s', NBER Working Paper 1547, Cambridge, MA.

Griliches, Z. (1986), 'Productivity, R&D, and basic research at the firm level in the 1970's', *American Economic Review*, **76** (1), 141–54.

Griliches, Z. (1992), 'The search for R&D spillovers', *Scandinavian Journal of Economics*, **94** (0), S29–47, Supplement.

Griliches, Z. (1995), 'R&D and productivity: econometric results and measurement issues', in P. Stoneman (ed.), *Handbook of the Economics of Innovation and Technological Change*, Oxford: Blackwell, pp. 52–89.

Griliches, Z. (2000), *R&D, Education, and Productivity*, Cambridge, MA: Harvard University Press.

Griliches, Z. and F.R. Lichtenberg (1984a), 'Interindustry technology flows and productivity growth: a reexamination', *Review of Economics and Statistics*, **66**, 324–9.

Griliches, Z. and F.R. Lichtenberg (1984b), 'R&D and productivity growth at the industry level: is there still a relationship?', in Griliches (ed.), *R&D, Patents and Productivity*, Chicago, IL: University Chicago Press, pp. 406–502.

Griliches, Z. and J. Mairesse (1982), 'Comparing productivity growth: an exploration of French and US industrial and firm data', NBER Working Paper 961, Cambridge, MA.

Griliches, Z. and J. Mairesse (1983), 'Comparing productivity growth: an exploration of French and US industrial and firm data', *European Economic Review*, **21** (1–2), 89–119.

Griliches, Z. and J. Mairesse (1984), 'Productivity and R&D at the firm level', in Griliches (ed.), *R&D, Patents and Productivity*, Chicago, IL: University Chicago Press, pp. 339–374.

Griliches, Z. and J. Mairesse (1990), 'R&D and productivity growth: comparing Japanese and US Manufacturing firms', in C. Hulten (ed.), *Productivity Growth in Japan and the United States*, Chicago, IL: University Chicago Press, pp. 317–48.

Grossman, G. and E. Helpman (1991), *Innovation and Growth in the Global Economy*, Cambridge, MA and London, UK: MIT Press.

Gu, W., M. Kaci, J.P. Maynard and M.A. Sillamaa (2002), 'The Changing Composition of the Canadian Workforce and its impact on productivity growth', in J.R. Baldwin and T.M. Harchaoui (eds), *Productivity Growth in Canada*, Ottawa: Statistics Canada, pp. 69–75.

Gu, W. and W. Wang (2004), 'Information technology and productivity growth: evidence from Canadian industries', *in Economic Growth in Canada and the United States in the Information Age*, Industry Canada Research Monograph Series, Industry Canada Research Publications Program, Ottawa, pp. 51–81.

Ha, J. and P. Howitt (2007), 'Accounting for trends in productivity and R&D: a Schumpeterian critique of semi-endogenous growth theory', *Journal of Money, Credit and Banking*, **39** (4), 733–74.

Hall, B.H. (1993), 'Industrial research during the 1980s: did the rate of return fall?', *Brookings Papers on Economic Activity*, Micro (2), 289–344.

Hall, B.H. (1996), 'The private and social returns to research and development', in B.L.R. Smith and C. Barfields (eds), *Technology, R&D, and the Economy*, Washington, DC: Brookings and American Enterprise Institute, pp. 289–331.

Hall, B.H. and J. Mairesse (1995), 'Exploring the relationship between R&D and productivity in French manufacturing firms', *Journal of Econometrics*, **65** (1), 263–93.

Harhoff, D. (1998), 'R&D and productivity in German manufacturing firms', *Economics of Innovation and New Technology*, **6**, 29–49.

Hatzichronoglou, T. (1997), *Revision of the High-technology Sector and Product Classification*, Paris: OECD.

Howells, J. and B.S. Tether (2004), 'Innovation in Services: Issues as Stake and Trends', Report for European Commission, DG Enterprise and Industry, Contract INNO-Studies 2001: Lot 3 (ENTRC/2001).

Howitt, P. (1999), 'Steady endogenous growth with population and R&D inputs growing', *Journal of Political Economy*, **107**, 715–30.

Hubert, F. and N. Pain (2001), 'Inward investment and technical progress in the United Kingdom manufacturing sector', *Scottish Journal of Political Economy*, **48** (2), May, 134–47.

Inklaar, R., M. O'Mahony and M. Timmer (2003), 'ICT and Europe's productivity performance industry-level growth account comparisons with the United States', Groningen Growth and Development Centre Research Memorandum GD-68, Groningen, The Netherlands.

Inklaar, R. and M.P. Timmer (2009), 'Productivity convergence across industries and countries: the importance of theory-based measurement', Groningen Growth and Development Centre Research Memorandum GD-109, Groningen, The Netherlands.

Jaffe, A.B. (1986), 'Technological opportunity and spillovers of R&D: evidence from firms' patents, profits and market value', *American Economic Review*, **76** (5), 984–1001.

Janz, N., H. Lööf and B. Peters (2004), 'Firm level innovation and productivity – is there a common story across countries?', *Problems and Perspectives in Management*, **2**, 1–22.

Jones, C.I. (1995), 'R&D-based models of economic growth', *Journal of Political Economy*, **103** (4), August, 759–84.

Jones, C.I. (2002), 'Sources of U.S. economic growth in a world of ideas', *American Economic Review*, **92**, 220–39.

Jones, C.I. and J.C. Williams (1998), 'Measuring the social return to R&D', *Quarterly Journal of Economics*, **113** (4), 1119–35.

Jorgenson, D.W. (2011), 'Innovation and productivity growth', *American Journal of Agricultural Economics*, **93** (2), 276–96.

Jorgenson, D.W., M.S. Ho and J.D. Samuels (2012), 'Information technology and U.S. productivity, growth: evidence from a prototype industry production account, in M. Mas and R. Stehrer (eds), *Industrial Productivity in Europe: Growth and Crisis*, Cheltenham, UK and Northampton, MA, USA Edward Elgar, pp. 35–64.

Jorgenson, D.W., M.S. Ho and K.J. Stiroh (2008), 'A retrospective look at the U.S. productivity growth resurgence', *Journal of Economic Perspectives*, **22** (1), 3–24.

Jorgenson, D.W. and K.J. Stiroh (1999), 'Information technology and growth', *American Economic Review Essays and Proceedings*, **89** (2), 109–15.

Klette, T.J. (1994), 'R&D Spillovers and performance among, heterogeneous firms: an empirical study using micro data, Statistic Norway Research Department Working Paper 133.

Klette, T.J. (1996), 'R&D, scope economies and plant performance', *RAND Journal of Economics*, **27** (3), 502–22.

Klette, T.J. and F. Johansen (1998), 'Accumulation of R&D capital and dynamic firm performance: a not-so-fixed effect model', *Annales d'Économie et de Statistique*, **49–50**, 389–419.

Klette, J. and S. Kortum (2004), 'Innovating firms and aggregate innovation', *Journal of Political Economy*, **112**, 986–1018.

Kortum, S. (1997), 'Research, patenting and technological change' *Econometrica*, **65** (6), 1389–419.

Lichtenberg, F.R. and D. Siegel (1989), 'The effect of control changes on the productivity of U.S. manufacturing plants', *Journal of Applied Corporate Finance*, **2** (2), 60–67.

Lichtenberg, F.R. and D. Siegel (1991), 'The impact of R&D investment on productivity: new evidence using linked R&D–LRD data', *Economic Inquiry*, **29** (2), 203–29.

Link, A.N. (1981), 'Basic research and productivity increase in manufacturing: additional evidence', *American Economic Review*, **71** (5), December, 1111–12.

Link, A.N. (1982), 'Productivity growth, environmental regulations and the composition of R&D', Bell Journal of Economics, The RAND Corporation, **13** (12), 548–54.

Link, A.N. (1983), 'Inter-firm technology flows and productivity growth', *Economic Letters*, **11**, 179–84.

Lööf, H. and A. Heshmati (2006), 'On the relation between innovation and performance: a sensitivity analysis', *Economics of Innovation and New Technology*, **15**, 317–44.

Los, B. and B. Verspagen (2000), 'R&D spillovers and productivity: evidence from US manufacturing micro-data', *Empirical Economics*, **25**, 127–48.

Luintel, K.B. and M. Khan (2004), 'Are international R&D Spillovers costly for the United States?', *Review of Economics and Statistics*, **86** (4), 896–910.

Lumenga-Neso, O., M. Olarreaga and M. Schiff (2005), 'On "indirect" trade related R&D spillovers', *European Economic Review*, **49** (7), 1785–98.

Machin, S. and J. van Reenen (1998), 'Technology and changes in skill structure: evidence from seven OECD countries', *Quarterly Journal of Economics*, **93** (4), 1215–44.

Maddison, A. (1982), *Phases of Capitalist Development*, Oxford: Oxford University Press.

Mairesse, J. and P. Cuneo (1985), 'Recherche-développement et performances des entreprises: une étude économétrique sur données individuelles', *Revue Économique, Programme National Persée*, **36** (5), 1001–42.

Mairesse, J., B.H. Hall and B. Mulkay (2001), 'Investissement des entreprises et contraintes financières en France et aux États-Unis', *Économie et Statistique, Programme National Persée*, **341** (1), 67–84.

Mairesse, J. and J. Jaumandreu (2005), 'Panel-data estimates of the production function and the revenue function: what difference does it make?', *Scandinavian Journal of Economics*, **107** (4), 651–72.

Mairesse, J. and P. Mohnen (2001), 'To be or not to be innovative: an exercise in measurement', NBER Working Paper 8644, Cambridge, MA.

Mairesse, J. and P. Mohnen (2003), 'R&D and productivity: a reexamination in light of the innovation surveys', Paper Presented at the DRUID Summer Conference on Creating, Sharing and Transferring Knowledge, Copenhagen, 12–14 June.

Mairesse, J. and P. Mohnen (2005), 'The importance of R&D for innovation: a reassessment using French survey data', *Journal of Technology Transfer*, **30**, 183–97.

Mairesse, J., P. Mohnen and E. Kremp (2005), 'The importance of R&D and innovation for productivity: a reexamination in light of the 2000 French innovation survey', *Annales d'Économie et Statistique*, **79–80**, 489–529.

Mairesse, J. and M. Sassenou (1991), 'R&D and productivity: a survey of econometric studies at the firm level', NBER Working Paper 3666, Cambridge, MA.

Malerba, F. (ed.) (2004), *Sectoral Systems of Innovation*, Cambridge: Cambridge University Press.

Mansfield, E. (1977), 'Social and private rates of return from industrial innovations', *Quarterly Journal of Economics*, **91** (2) 221–40.

Mansfield, E. (1980), 'Basic research and productivity increase in manufacturing', *American Economic Review*, **70** (3), 863–73.

Mansfield, E. (1985), 'How rapidly does new industrial technology leak out?', *Journal of Industrial Economics*, **34** (2), 217–23.

Marsili, O. (2001), *The Anatomy and Evolution of Industries*, Cheltenham, UK and Northampton, MA, USA: Edward Elgar.

McGuckin, R.H. and B. van Ark (2004), *Performance 2003, Productivity, Employment and Income in the World's Economies*, New York: The Conference Board, March.

McMorrow, K., W. Roeger and A. Turrini (2010), 'Determinants of TFP growth: a close look at industries driving the EU–US TFP gap', *Structural Change and Economic Dynamics*, **21**, 165–80.

Medda, G., C. Piga and D.S. Siegel (2003), 'On the relationship between R&D and productivity: a treatment effect analysis', Fondazione Eni Enrico Mattei Nota di Lavoro, 34-2003, Milan.

Minasian, J.R. (1962), 'The economics of research and development', in R. Nelson (ed.), *The Rate and Direction of Inventive Activity: Economic and Social Factors*, Cambridge, MA: National Bureau of Economic Research, pp. 93–142.

Minasian, J.R. (1969), 'Research and development, production functions and rates of return', *American Economic Review*, **59** (2), March, 80–85.

Nadiri, M.I. (1993), 'Innovation and technological spillovers', NBER Working Paper 4423, Cambridge, MA.

Nelson, R.R. (1988), 'Modelling the connections in the cross-section between technical progress' and R&D intensity', *RAND Journal of Economics*, **19**, 478–85.

Nelson, R.R. and E. Phelps (2002), 'Investment in humans, technological diffusion and economic growth', *American Economic Review*, **56**, 69–75.

Nelson, R.R. and S.G. Winter (1982), *An Evolutionary Theory of Economic Change*, Cambridge, MA: Harvard University Press.

Nicoletti, G. and S. Scarpetta (2003), 'Regulation, productivity and growth', *Economic Policy*, **36**, 11–72.

O'Mahony, M. and B. van Ark (eds) (2003), *EU Productivity and Competitiveness: An Industry Perspective: Can Europe Resume the Catching-up Process?*, Luxembourg: European Commission.

O'Mahony, M. and M. Vecchi (2002), 'Do intangible investments affect companies' productivity performance?', Employment Prospects in the Knowledge Economy (EPKE) Working Paper 05. Previously published as 'Tangible and intangible investment and economic performance: evidence from company accounts', in *Competitiveness and the Value of Intangible Assets*, Cheltenham, UK and Northampton, MA, USA: Edward Elgar (2000), pp. 199–227.

O'Mahony, M. and M. Vecchi (2009), 'R&D, knowledge spillovers and company productivity performance', *Research Policy*, **38** (1), February, 35–44.

Oliner, S. and D. Sichel (2000), 'The resurgence of growth in the late 1990s: is information technology the story?', *Journal of Economic Perspectives*, **14**, 3–22.

Ortega-Argilés, R. (2012), 'The transatlantic productivity gap: a survey of the main causes', *Journal of Economic Surveys*, **26** (3), 395–419.

Ortega-Argilés, R., M. Piva, L. Potters and M. Vivarelli (2010), 'Is corporate R&D investment in high-tech sectors more effective? Some guidelines for European Research Policy', *Contemporary Economic Policy*, **28** (3), July, 353–65.

Ortega-Argilés, R., M.C. Piva and M. Vivarelli (2011a), 'Productivity gains from R&D investment: are high-tech sectors still ahead?', IZA Discussion Papers 5975, Institute for the Study of Labor (IZA), Bonn.

Ortega-Argilés, R., M.C. Piva and M. Vivarelli (2011b), 'Productivity gains from R&D investment: are high-tech sectors still ahead?', IZA Discussion Paper 5975, Institute for the Study of Labor (IZA), Bonn.

Ortega-Argilés, R., L. Potters and M. Vivarelli (2011c), 'R&D and productivity: testing sectoral peculiarities using micro data', *Empirical Economics*, **41** (3), 817–39.

Parente, S.L. and E. Prescott (1994), 'Barriers to technology adoption and development', *Journal of Political Economy*, **102**, 298–321.

Parente, S.L. and E. Prescott (1999), 'Monopoly rights: a barrier to riches', *American Economic Review*, **89**, 1216–33.

Parente, S.L. and E. Prescott (2003), *Barriers to Riches*, Cambridge, MA: MIT Press.

Park, J. (2004), 'International and intersectoral R&D spillovers in the OECD and East Asian economies', *Economic Inquiry*, **42** (4), 739–57.

Pavitt, K. (1984), 'Sectoral patterns of technical change: towards a taxonomy and a theory', *Research Policy*, **13**, 343–73.

Peretto, P. (1998), 'Technological change and population growth', *Journal of Economic Growth*, **3** (4), 283–311.

Peretto, P. and S. Smulders (2002), 'Technological distance, growth and scale effects', *Economic Journal*, **112** (481), 603–24.

Poldahl, A. (2004), 'Domestic vs international spillovers: evidence from Swedish firm level data', FIEF *Working Paper* 200, Stockholm.

Rincon, A. and M. Vecchi (2003), 'Productivity performance at the company level', in O'Mahony and van Ark (eds), pp. 169–208.

Rogers, M. (2009), 'R&D and productivity in the UK: evidence from firm-level data in the 1990s', *Empirica*, **37** (3), 329–59.

Rogerson, R. (2008), 'Structural transformation and the deterioration of European labor market outcomes', *Journal of Political Economy*, **116** (2), 235–59.

Romer, P. (1990), 'Endogenous technological change', *Journal of Political Economy*, **98** (5), S71–S102.

Schankerman, M. (1981), 'The effects of double-counting and expensing on the measured returns to R&D', *Review of Economics and Statistics*, **63** (3), 454–8.

Scherer, F.M. (1982), 'Inter-industry technology flows in the US', *Research Policy*, **11**, 227–45.

Scherer, F.M. (1984), 'Using linked patents and R&D data to measure interindustry technology flows', in Z. Griliches (ed.), *R&D, Patents, and Productivity*, Chicago, IL: University of Chicago Press, pp. 287–343.

Segerstrom, P.S. (1998), 'Endogenous growth without scale effects', *American Economic Review*, **84** (1), 1290–310.

Solow, R.M. (1957), 'A contribution to the theory of economic growth', *Quarterly Journal of Economics*, **70**, 65–94.

Solow, R.M. (1992), 'Proceedings of a Symposium on Productivity Concepts and Measurement Problems: Welfare, Quality and Productivity in the Service Industries, Uppsala, May 1991: Introduction', *Scandinavian Journal of Economics*, **94**, S5–7, Supplement.

Sterlacchini, A. (1989), 'R&D, innovations and total factor productivity growth in British manufacturing', *Applied Economics*, **21**, 1549–62.

Sterlacchini, A. and F. Venturini (2011), 'R&D and productivity in high-tech manufacturing: a comparison between Italy and Spain', MPRA Paper 30048, University Library of Munich.

Stiroh, K.J. (2002a), 'Information technology and the US productivity revival: what do the industry data say?', *American Economic Review*, **92**, 1559–76.

Stiroh, K.J. (2002b), 'Reassessing the role of IT in the production function: a meta-analysis', Working document, Federal Reserve Bank of New York.

Sveikauskas, L. (1981), 'Technological inputs and multifactor productivity growth', *Review of Economics and Statistics*, **63**, 275–82.

Sveikauskas, L. (2007), 'R&D and productivity growth: a review of the literature', US Bureau of Labor Statistics Working Paper 408, Washington, DC.

Terleckyj, N.E. (1974), *Effects of R&D on the Productivity Growth of Industries: An Exploratory Study*, Washington, DC: National Planning Association.

Timmer, M.P., R. Inklaar, M. O'Mahony and B. van Ark (2010) *Economic Growth in Europe: A Comparative Industry Perspective*, Cambridge: Cambridge University Press.

Uppenberg, K. (2011), 'Economic growth in the US and the EU: a sectoral decomposition', *EIB Papers*, **16** (1), 18–52.

Van Ark, B. (2002), 'Measuring the New Economy: an international comparative perspective', *Review of Income and Wealth*, **48** (1), 1–14.

Van Ark, B., R. Inklaar and R.H. McGuckin (2002), 'Changing gear: productivity, ICT, and services in Europe and the United States', mimeo University of Groningen, Groningen and The Conference Board, New York.

Van Ark, B. R. Inklaar and R.H. McGuckin (2003), 'ICT and productivity in Europe and the United States: where do the differences come from?', CESifo Group, *CESifo Economic Studies*, **49** (3), 295–318; doi:10.1093/cesifo/49.3.295.

Van Ark, B., M. O'Mahony and M.P. Timmer (2008), 'The productivity gap between Europe and the United States: trends and causes', *Journal of Economic Perspectives*, **22**, 25–44.

Van Meijl, H. (1997a), 'Measuring intersectoral spillovers: French evidence', *Economic Systems Research*, **9** (1), 25–46.

Van Meijl, H. (1997b), 'Measuring the impact of direct and indirect R&D on the productivity growth of industries: using the Yale Technology Concordance', *Economic Systems Research*, **9** (2), 205–11.

Verspagen, B. (1995), 'R&D and productivity: a broad cross-section cross-country look', *Journal of Productivity Analysis*, **6**, 117–35.

Von Tunzelmann, N. and V. Acha (2005), 'Innovation in "low-tech" industries', in J. Fagerberg, D.C. Mowery and R.R. Nelson (eds), *The Oxford Handbook of Innovation*, New York: Oxford University Press, pp. 407–432.

Wakelin, K. (2001), 'Productivity growth and R&D expenditure in UK manufacturing firms', *Research Policy*, **30** (7), 1079–90.

Wilson, D.J. (2009), 'IT and beyond: the contribution of heterogeneous capital to productivity', *Journal of Business and Economic Statistics*, **27** (1), 52–70.

Winter, S.G. (1984), 'Schumpeterian competition in alternative technological regimes', *Journal of Economic Behavior and Organization*, **5** (3–4), 287–320.

Wolff, E.N. (1997), 'Spillovers, linkages and technological change', *Economic Systems Research*, **9** (1), 9–23.

Wolff, E.N. and M.I. Nadiri (1993), 'Spillover effects, linkage structure, and research and development', *Structural Change and Economic Dynamics*, **4** (2), 315–31.

Xu, B. and J. Wang (2000), 'Trade, FDI and international technology diffusion', *Journal of Economic Integration*, **15** (4), 585–601.

Zachariadis, M. (2003), 'R&D, innovation, and technological progress: a test of the Schumpeterian framework without scale effects', *Canadian Journal of Economics*, **36** (3), 566–86.

Zachariadis, M. (2004), 'R&D-induced growth in the OECD?', *Review of Development Economics*, **8** (3), 423–39.

PART IV

RESOURCE-BASED SECTORS

12 The changing structure of the global agribusiness sector

*Ruth Rama and Catalina Martínez**

12.1 INTRODUCTION

Following their review of the International Business (IB) literature, Griffith et al. (2008) argue that one of the most important themes to emerge from such analyses concerns international corporate processes and the differences which are apparent among various industrial sectors. Using data from the United Nations Conference on Trade and Development (UNCTAD), Senauer and Venturini (2005) show that the distribution of foreign direct investment (FDI)[1] is geographically uneven and varies by industry. Thus, the geography of multinational enterprises (MNEs) requires studies which take sectoral specificities into consideration.

This chapter analyses the changing structure of the global agribusiness sector and some of the theories surrounding it, in an attempt to understand the evolution of its geographical patterns. The agribusiness sector comprises segments such as agriculture, food and beverage processing, R&D, retailing and restaurants. We examine the entire sector, with the exception of retailing and restaurants, although these are also mentioned briefly.

Agriculture accounted for 31 per cent of total world employment (40 per cent in developing economies) in 2002–06, and the food and beverage processing industry (hereafter, the F&B industry) for 23 million jobs worldwide and 15 per cent of industrial value added (UNCTAD, 2009). According to data for 2002 provided by the United Nations Industrial Development Organization (UNIDO) and the CIAA,[2] the European Union (EU) was responsible for 24 per cent of world F&B production, the United States for 21 per cent and Japan for 10 per cent; other important producer countries are China (4 per cent), Brazil (2 per cent) and Canada (2 per cent) (Ayadi et al., 2006).

MNEs play an important role in these substantial industries. All over the world, the F&B industry is dominated by small and medium-sized enterprises (SMEs), although the 100 largest MNEs in this industry accounted for approximately 27 per cent of the world's production of processed foods and beverages and 14 per cent of employment in 2002. Furthermore, they also influenced agricultural production worldwide through FDI, and contract farming and purchases in arm's-length markets (Oman et al., 1989; Echánove and Steffen, 2005; Ayadi et al., 2006; UNCTAD, 2009). Such companies accounted for 41 per cent of F&B production and 26 per cent of sectoral employment in the 10 most important producer countries, which are usually the home countries of the companies (Ayadi et al., 2006). F&B MNEs are also key players in the worldwide technological development of the food chain, including technology employed in agriculture, F&B processing and auxiliary industries (for example, food packaging) (Christensen et al., 1996; von Tunzelmann, 1998). The world's 100 largest food and drink MNEs (hereafter the Top 100) supply approximately 50 per cent of the patentable inventions which are usable in this sector and in auxiliary industries worldwide (Patel and Pavitt, 1991; Alfranca et al., 2002). In 2007, the share of foreign affiliates in R&D in food, beverages and tobacco was over 40 per cent of the national total in the industries of countries such as Germany, Portugal, Sweden, the United Kingdom and, especially, several Eastern European countries which had recently joined the EU.[3]

As stated above, our intention is to analyse changes in the geographical patterns of the agribusiness sector in the light of some of the theories aimed at explaining the location of F&B MNEs, their foreign affiliates and their R&D activities. We employ case studies, econometric analyses, patent statistics and other statistical data, and review theories from a variety of disciplines, such as IB, international management (IM), the economics of technological change and economic geography.

Section 12.2 provides an overview of FDI in the agribusiness sector and discusses the information sources employed in the present chapter. Section 12.3 attempts to identify new patterns in the geographical origin of capital in the agribusiness sector.[4] Section 12.4 is concerned with the spatial patterns of the agribusiness sector. Section 12.5 focuses on the internationalization of the R&D activities of F&B MNEs. Each section provides a review of the literature and empirical evidence. Finally, Section 12.6 offers our conclusions.

12.2   OVERVIEW OF FDI IN THE AGRIBUSINESS SECTOR

This section provides an overview of FDI in the agribusiness sector and discusses the information sources employed in this chapter.

12.2.1   Recent Evolution

Between 1989–91 and 2005–07, outward FDI flows doubled in agriculture, hunting, forestry and fishing and quadrupled in food, beverage and tobacco manufacturing (see Table 12.1, below), due to a range of new circumstances and policy measures such as the liberalization of capital and trade, the formation or the enlargement of trading blocs (for example, the EU), the adoption of the market system in erstwhile state-managed economies (or in some of their regions, as in China) and increasing per capita gross domestic product (GDP) in the emerging economies. The F&B industry is considered to be a non-cyclical sector, a 'refuge' industry in times of crisis, attracting institutional investors (for example, pension funds), especially in the US and, to a lesser extent, in Europe. This new configuration of shareholders has apparently been accompanied by demands for relentless rhythms of growth and the achievement of global goals by F&B companies, which have often contributed to weakening their embeddedness in specific regions of the world by promoting their worldwide expansion instead (Caswell, 1987; Muller and Van Tulder, 2005; Palpacuer and Tozanli, 2008). We now turn to the sources of information available for the study of the global geography of the agribusiness sector.

12.2.2   Data Sources

At sector level, data regarding FDI and MNE activity is frequently patchy; this paucity has often restricted attempts to map MNE activity by sector. While there are some exceptions (see, for instance, Gabel and Bruner, 2003), these contain little information regarding agri-food MNEs.

We combine several data sources in order to understand the geographical patterns of such companies. We employ data on FDI investment[5] flows and stock, although as no comprehensive international statistics are available at the sectoral level, this information needs to be complemented by other sources.

Thus, to specifically analyse the geography of F&B MNEs, we use an upstream measure, that is, data concerning the location of the affiliates[6] of the world's 100 largest F&B MNEs. The distribution of affiliates is one of the proxies proposed by the OECD (2004) to construct MNE-related globalization indicators. While a minor rebalancing of a company's sales portfolio or mere currency appreciation/depreciation may erroneously suggest substantial changes in its geographical patterns (Osegowitsch and Sammartino, 2008), the analysis of affiliate location provides a measurement which is less subject to short-term changes.

To analyse the location of affiliates we use the AGRODATA database, which despite having been underexploited in studies published in English, contains the most comprehensive information available on the activities and location of the affiliates of the world's 100 largest F&B MNEs (Appendix 12A.1). F&B MNEs included in the database must have at least one food processing plant outside the home country and agri-food sales of at least US$1 billion per year. The database includes world-renowned firms (for example, Nestlé, Unilever and Ajinomoto) from the five continents. The companies selected are active in a variety of industries, such as meat processing, dairy products, canned specialities, spirits and so on. While all are food or beverage processors, a number of them also engage in agricultural production and the production of non-food items.

Admittedly, data on the distribution of affiliates may also have certain drawbacks, as the control of the parent company over its affiliates may vary in such an international industry. However, the nature of affiliates is relatively homogeneous in AGRODATA, in which each parent company controls, on average, 70 per cent or more of the share capital in 90 per cent of its affiliates. Nevertheless, the identification of the loci selected by F&B MNEs to perform their innovative activities poses specific methodological difficulties, which are tackled in Section 12.5.

12.3   SOURCES FOR AGRI-FOOD FDI: AGRI-FOOD COMPANIES AND THEIR HOME COUNTRIES

12.3.1   Competitive Advantages and International Expansion

The eclectic paradigm of international production provides a framework for explaining the foreign production of firms (for an extended version of the eclectic paradigm, see Dunning, 1993). The eclectic (or OLI) paradigm maintains that firms may have competitive advantages related to three crucial variables: ownership, location and internalization. These competitive advantages, in turn, explain the extent of foreign affiliates and other assets owned and controlled by companies.

Ownership (O) advantages of enterprises of one nationality over those of another include property rights, innovative capacity, marketing systems, human capital and so on. New knowledge is an important competitive tool for companies in general and for MNEs more specifically (Frankho, 1989). In IB theory, the internalization of knowledge production is a method which firms use to minimize the risks of involuntary spillovers of knowledge. Such risks may be quite real when new products are relatively easy to imitate, as is the case with new foodstuffs (Gallo, 1995). Internalization (I) advantages consist of the internalization of markets within the company, a strategy adopted to protect the firm from market failure or to exploit it. As described below, in this process of knowledge internalization, firms may invest abroad in various forms of R&D (we analyse this question in detail in Section 12.5).

In the IB literature, new products, new processes and new skills are ownership O-advantages of the MNE, which are often difficult to copy by rivals. Although the F&B industry is traditionally considered to be low-tech, some empirical studies suggest that F&B MNEs possessing such O-advantages are more likely to expand internationally. Analysing more than 800 international food companies, an econometric study finds that capital-intensive firms with high levels of intangible assets (for example, brand names), profitability and knowledge capital were more likely to internationalize (Wendt and Pedersen, 2006). Another econometric study shows that the fastest-growing F&B MNEs are highly internationalized, capital-intensive companies which have diversified into food-related technological activities (for example, biotechnology) (Anastassopoulos and Rama, 2005). Analysing the Top 100, Tozanli (2005) confirms the importance of other O-advantages, such as global brand names, in the expansion of firms.

As stated above, I-advantages consist of the internalization of markets within the company, a strategy adopted to protect the firm from market failure or to exploit such failure. Analysing the Top 100, Tozanli argues that I-advantages are losing importance for these very large companies. By contrast, explanations for the emergence of successful agri-food MNEs based in developing countries often underline their allegedly superior capacity to internalize markets, that is, their I-advantages. According to Burch and Goss (2005), large F&B MNEs based in Southeast Asia have been able to avoid the conflicts that in Western countries have characterized the relationships between F&B companies and retailers in recent years. In their view, companies such as CP (Thailand) and the Salim Group (Indonesia) have achieved vertical integration along the entire commodity chain in a way no Western agri-food MNE has been able to, and this strategy has been the foundation of their successful international expansion. Vertical integration along the food chain towards food processing, packaging and retailing has also been implemented by some Asian MNEs operating in the consumer goods sector, and by Brazilian F&B processors who have recently internationalized (Azevedo et al., 2004; Sim, 2007; Pozzobon, 2008). In the case of Asian conglomerates, another I-advantage may be their capacity to internalize financial markets (Buckley et al., 2007). According to these authors, Asian conglomerates may operate an inefficient internal capital market which can subsidize FDI. Market imperfections, they argue, may become O-advantages for firms based in emerging markets.

What factors explain the predominance of some countries as home locations for MNEs? L-advantages, which may help to determine the home or host countries of MNEs, include resource endowment, international transport and communication costs, investment incentives and disincentives, barriers to trade, R&D, and the institutional framework. We now briefly discuss three potential L-advantages of F&B MNEs: their technological environment, their institutional environment and their natural resource endowment.

Theories dealing with national systems of innovation emphasize the importance of space in learning processes, arguing that companies are more likely to seek new technology in the home country. The user and producer theory (Andersen and Lundvall, 1988; Lundvall, 1988) was developed in Denmark, an important exporter of agri-food goods and, as will be seen below, of agri-food equity capital. Language, common culture and geographical proximity, this theory claims, facilitate links between companies, industries and universities, thereby positively affecting R&D cooperation and product upgrading. Andersen and Lundvall argue that the longstanding competitiveness of Danish food firms in international markets is associated with strong Danish positions in related technological areas, such as food processing machinery. In other small industrialized countries besides Denmark, they claim, the specialization of the engineering sector also reflects the national history of agriculture and food processing. Another study tested whether F&B MNEs performing well internationally (as measured by global margins and the return on capital employed, ROCE) come from home countries which enjoy support from innovative food and food-related industries (for example, food processing machinery), as measured by patent counts (Rama, 1999). It found that successful newcomer and smaller F&B MNEs were likely to originate from such innovative national backgrounds. However, an R&D-intensive national environment is apparently less important to large F&B MNEs and incumbents (the capacity of large F&B MNEs to obtain technology worldwide is analysed in Section 12.5). Thus, the O-advantages of some companies with regard to new technology may be combined with the L-advantages of home countries which have R&D-intensive sectoral systems of innovation.

As indicated earlier, the institutions of the home country may also feature among the L-advantages influencing the emergence and development of native MNEs. Sim (2007) argues that while the so-called 'Western' theories of the MNE have neglected the role played by the state, some Asian governments have actually promoted the internationalization of native firms and sometimes even influenced their direction. Two empirical studies analyse the role played by governments in the internationalization of agribusiness in Australia and Southeast Asia, and New Zealand (Burch and Goss, 2005; Pritchard, 2005). Government stimuli may have contributed to the expansion of agribusiness companies, especially those based in developing countries which lack sufficient natural resources (for example, China) (Buckley et al., 2007; UNCTAD, 2009). However, the Japanese government has also encouraged (for instance, through insurance guarantee schemes) outward FDI to developing Asian countries, in order to ensure the supply of raw materials for Japanese industry (Dunning, 1993). The previous discussion suggests that government support (an L-advantage) may have played some role in the current resurgence of resource-seeking investment in this sector.

By contrast, the role played by structural reform and its effects upon the availability of cheap agricultural products is still a matter of debate. One study claims that such reforms have helped Latin American economies to incubate native MNEs, including the largest F&B MNEs based in the region (Cuervo-Cazurra, 2008). Seven out of 20 very large *multilatinas* (MNEs based in Latin America) analysed by the authors operate in the food chain: two examples are Bimbo (Mexico) and Sadia (Brazil). All but one became international after 1979, and this was no coincidence because by that year the previous import-substitution model had ended and structural reforms were implemented by Latin American governments. Under pressure from the collapse of the previous model and the debt crisis of 1982, the *multilatinas* (including agri-food MNEs) restructured their finances, developed new technologies and faced the challenge to diversify geographically in order to reduce risk.

However, in their study of Thailand, Burch and Goss (2005) show that CP, the most important native agri-food MNE, internationalized a decade ahead of the liberalization policies. Moreover, Pritchard (2005) questions the possibilities for the successful internationalization of agri-food firms based in small, open economies. He claims that since the 1980s, some have viewed the pioneering liberalization of the agri-food trade in Australia and New Zealand as the first step towards the emergence of powerful F&B MNEs based in the two countries. In his opinion, however, the agri-food export competitiveness of these companies can make them the target of takeovers from foreign firms, as an alternative to internationalization through FDI. Other studies would appear to confirm that the availability of natural resources may both attract foreign F&B MNEs (Makki et al., 2004) and promote, in the later stages of development of well-endowed countries, the emergence of native F&B MNEs (CEPAL, 1982; Schvarzer, 1989; Azevedo et al., 2004; Farina and Viegas, 2005; Gutman et al., 2006).

Paradoxically, good soil and climate conditions in the home country may restrict the international expansion of native F&B companies through FDI and instead encourage exports of agri-food products. Studies in economic geography underline the importance of a 'geography of quality' with regard to certain foods and beverages (Mansfield, 2003). Consumers often associate the high quality of particular products to specific sites in the world. The 'country of origin effect' (so-called in management literature) may limit the internationalization of F&B firms, especially wine producers; for example, there is only one Champagne region in the world and this name is protected by EU regulations (Filippaios and Rama, 2008). Producers of some high-quality products tend to serve foreign markets through exports rather than through FDI, and this may be one explanation for the limited expansion through FDI of F&B firms based in certain European countries, such as Portugal (da Silva Lopes, 2005).

One of the issues still hotly debated in the IB literature is why firms based in certain countries internationalize while firms based in others do not. As this subsection shows, L-advantages provide some of the answers, although an integrated theory has also been proposed. This maintains that there is an investment development path (IDP) by which some countries gradually reach a stage of development which allows their companies to go international (Dunning and Narula, 1996). However, Burch and Goss (2005) argue that the stages of development proposed by the model imply a degree of uniformity which is not apparent, at least in the food and fibre sector. They claim that in developing countries, a highly sophisticated and productive food processing sector may be established on the basis of very different ownership and organizational forms such as peasant farming, plantations, cooperatives, collective ownership and so on.

We turn now to the empirical evidence for source countries in the global agribusiness sector.

12.3.2   Changes in the Origin of Capital

Most FDI originates in developed countries and the agribusiness sector is no exception. In clear confirmation of this, Table 12.1 shows outward FDI flows between 1989–91 and 2005–07 for both developed and developing countries. We argue, however, that the composition of outward FDI in this sector changed substantially between the two periods. Since no comprehensive data on the geographical origin of agri-food capital is available, we employ complementary sources to analyse this question.

First, the share of developed countries in such outward FDI flows fell between 1989–91 and 2005–07. The reduction in their share was moderate (from 98 to 95 per cent of the total) in the food, beverage and tobacco industry, but was substantial (from 91 per cent of the total to only 52 per cent) in agriculture, hunting, forestry and fishing (hereafter, agriculture and related industries), owing to the dynamic expansion of FDI flows originating in developing countries.

In 2007, 12 of the world's 25 largest agriculture-based and plantation MNEs were based in developing countries (UNCTAD, 2009), coinciding with the divestment from land of many Triad-based MNEs since the early 1980s, due to the nationalization of plantations and the migration of such companies to more rewarding business lines (for example, agricultural technology and food processing)[7] (Oman et al., 1989). Other Triad-based agri-food MNEs have preferred to outsource production to local networks of suppliers of agricultural products (for example, milk, fruit and vegetables), and thus their geographical links in foreign countries are difficult to trace and measure, although they have been illustrated by case studies since the 1970s (Echánove and Steffen, 2005; UNCTAD, 2009). Some authors describe such arrangements as new forms of international investment (rather than of FDI), since MNEs which outsource agricultural production are often involved in financial, organizational and technological aspects of local agricultural production, but not in land ownership (Oman et al., 1989). To summarize, as UNCTAD (2009) makes clear, after a long period of little FDI involvement in agriculture, a recovery may be underway, but coming today from developing rather than from developed source countries. As stated earlier, government support (L-advantages) may have played some role in the current resurgence of resource-seeking investment in this sector.

Second, changes have also occurred in the geography of source countries within the F&B processing subsector. As Tozanli (2005, p. 22) states, the world ranking of the Top 100 'shows the supremacy of the Triad, even though the composition within the Triad has changed'. During 1978–2000, according to her study, 88 per cent of the Top 100 companies were Triad based, and this figure remained stable throughout. As she notes, however, changes within the Triad are apparent, and especially the emergence of very large Japanese companies, which increased their share from only 9 to 20 per cent of the Top 100 during the 1978–2000 period. According to Tozanli, in the 1970s and 1980s such companies internationalized partly in reaction to changes in international trade regulations, such as the 1974 Law of the Sea; a good example, she claims, are the new Japanese

Table 12.1 Estimated worldwide outward FDI flows, by sector and industry, 1989–1991 and 2005–2007 (in millions of dollars)

Sector/Industry	1989–1991			2005–2007			
	Developed Countries	Developing economies	World	Developed Countries	Developing economies	Southeast Europe and CIS	World
Total	217,637	6,142	223,779	1,332,782	140,901	270	1,473,953
Primary	9,869	291	10,160	133,672	12,392	879	146,943
Agriculture, hunting, forestry and fishing	467	45	512	599	495	49	1,143
Manufacturing	80,050	3,494	83,543	335,135	24,414	98	359,647
Food, beverages and tobacco	12,233	253	12,486	45,723	2,617	-12	48,327
Services	110,661	2,021	112,682	755,164	98,438	-618	852,985
Private buying and selling of property	497	–	497	3,370	–	–	3,370
Unspecified	16,561	336	16,897	105,441	5,657	-89	111,008

Notes:
The world total was extrapolated on the basis of data covering 27 countries in 1989–91 and 50 countries in 2005–07, or the latest three-year period average available. They account for over 90% of world outward FDI flows in the periods 1989–91 and 2005–07. Only countries for which data for the three main sectors were available were included. The distribution share of each industry of these countries was applied to estimate the world total in each sector and industry. As a result, the sum of the sectors for each group of economies is different from the totals shown in Annex Table B.1. in UNCTAD (2009). Approval data were used for Taiwan Province of China. In the case of Japan, the actual data were estimated by applying the implementation ratio of realized FDI to approved FDI to the latter: 75% in 1989–91. The world total in 1989–91 includes the countries of Southeast Europe and the CIS, although data by sector and industry are not available for that region.
* A considerable share of investment in business activities is in Hong Kong (China), Which accounted for 87% of developing economies and 12% of the world total during 2005–07. Hong Kong (China) data include investment holding companies.

Source: UNCTAD.

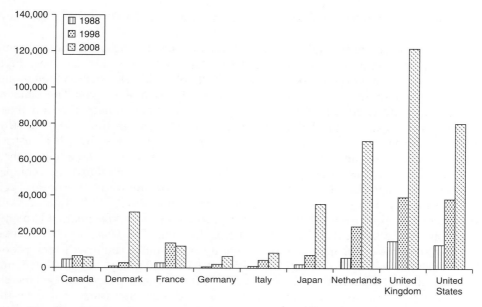

Source: Authors' elaboration, based on OECD statistics on globalization, http://stats.oecd.org/index.aspx, as of February 2010.

Figure 12.1 Outward FDI positions in the food, beverage and tobacco industry, 1988–2008 (in millions of US dollars)

fishing affiliates located in Latin America (as will be seen below, other reasons may also exist).

Showing the outward FDI position of several OECD countries in 1988, 1998 and 2008, Figure 12.1 corroborates and extends the information provided by analysis of the Top 100. Denmark and Japan, which displayed relatively low rates in 1988, quickly increased their FDI positions in F&B in the following 20 years. The UK became the most important source country for FDI in this industry, overtaking the US. Within the Triad, the growth rates of outward FDI in this industry differed according to the origin of capital. In 1988–2008, the outward FDI position (stock) of the US multiplied by six, that of the UK and Italy by eight each and that of the Netherlands (the most dynamic source country) by 12-fold, while the position of Canada, for instance, increased by only 1.5 times, despite it having been a traditional exporter of F&B equity capital (hereafter, F&B capital)[8] (Rugman, 1987).

Another cause of changes within the Triad was the emergence of new exporters of F&B capital: Spain (US$4.8 billion); Austria (US$2.3 billion); Finland (US$2.3 billion) and Norway (US$2.3 billion) are some examples (2008 data for outward FDI positions in the F&B industry).[9] F&B MNEs such as Grupo Ebro and SOS (both Spanish), Fazer (Finnish) and Orkla (Norwegian) are now members of the Top 100 (AGRODATA, 2005). Even nations such as Iceland and some Eastern European countries (Slovakia, the Czech Republic and, especially, Poland), which had never been reported as exporters of F&B capital, currently display some small outward F&B FDI. All in all, the

IDP theory appears to be supported by the recent evolution of FDI in the agribusiness sector.

O-advantages may partly explain why the share of countries such as Japan and some small European countries in outward F&B FDI has risen so quickly. Japanese F&B companies are now important producers of new technology in fields such as food inputs and ingredients (additives, vitamins and so on), and biotechnology (von Tunzelmann, 1998), and their R&D affiliates form a larger part of their total affiliates than any other F&B MNEs (Filippaios et al., 2009). Some Dutch and Danish agri-food companies (for example, Numico, Danisco) have successfully penetrated new fast-growth industries such as nutraceuticals, aquaculture and fish feed, a strategy some authors link to their dynamic international expansion (Tozanli, 2005). Finally, there are four Dutch companies (including Anglo-Dutch Unilever) among the 10 most innovative European F&B MNEs, as measured by patent counts (Martínez and Rama, 2012). As Section 12.5 will show, major European F&B MNEs have selected countries such as Denmark, Germany, France, the Netherlands, the UK and the US as locations for their innovative activities; these are some of the most important and dynamic source countries for agri-food FDI. As summarized by Tozanli (p. 26), within the Top 100 group, 'the most dynamic and innovative MNEs won over those that placed their competitive advantages merely on raw material procurement'. According to the previous discussion, therefore, the O-advantages of firms and the L-advantages of some home countries regarding the presence of centres of agri-food technological excellence may be possible explanations for the emergence of several new source countries for FDI in this sector or the outstanding dynamism of others.

As we have underlined, data sources must often be complemented. For 1988–2008, the OECD provides no information on the outward F&B FDI positions of Australia and New Zealand, although some analyses emphasize the activities of very large F&B MNEs based in these countries during this period (Pritchard, 2005; Tozanli, 2005). For example, Fonterra, a large New Zealand producer of dairy products, is now one of the Top 100; the availability of cheap agricultural products and government support (that is, L-advantages offered by the home country) appear to have positively influenced its internationalization (Pritchard, 2005).

In addition to the emergence of new source countries in Europe and Oceania, developing nations in Africa, Asia and Latin America have also become home to their own F&B MNEs. As Table 12.1 shows, the share of developing countries in outward FDI flows in food, beverage and tobacco manufacturing rose from 2 to 5 per cent of the total between 1989–91 and 2005–07. Empirical studies report the presence of F&B MNEs based in emerging economies, such as Brazil, Indonesia, Mexico, Thailand and so on (Burch and Goss, 2005; ECLAC, 2005). Some examples are the Charoen Pokphand Group (CP) (Thailand), or the *multilatinas* operating in various beverage markets of the Americas, which have received little attention from academics. As Burch and Goss note, most current literature characterizes the model of globalization as a process instigated by the dynamism of large corporations based in the Triad, a view which fails to consider MNEs based in less developed countries. Even less research, they claim, has been devoted to the role of agri-food MNEs based in developing countries, in spite of their significant regional and even global activity (as defined below). As the discussion above suggests, L-advantages (related to the availability of natural resources and the institutional background of the respective home country) and I-advantages (sometimes related to the exploitation of market failure) may have contributed to the internationalization and dynamism of agri-food MNEs based in developing countries.

To summarize, changes in the geographical origin of agri-food FDI have been evident from the late 1970s to the present decade. In agriculture, there has been a resurgence of FDI outflows, driven principally by companies based in developing countries. In the F&B industry, important changes have taken place within the Triad, although Triad-based MNEs are still dominant. Outside the Triad, new source countries for capital have emerged in both the developed and the developing worlds.

12.4 GEOGRAPHICAL PATTERNS OF AGRI-FOOD COMPANIES

We now examine the theories which attempt to explain the location of agri-food firms and their route to international expansion, and begin by reviewing studies which explore the determinants of FDI in F&B processing. According to the literature, such firms prefer countries with a large internal market, a high GDP per capita, a large urban population, high levels of protection for food and beverages and easy availability of cheap inputs and raw materials, while membership of a trade bloc is a plus (Ayadi et al., 2006; Gopinath et al., 1999; Pick and Worth, 2005; Rama and Wilkinson, 2008).

12.4.1 The Location of Food and Beverage MNEs

One econometric study finds that US MNEs in the processed food sector are not especially interested in countries with low wage rates (Makki et al., 2004). Analysing the Top 100, another study also observes that large F&B firms are chiefly attracted by high-income countries with a strong demand for high value-added foods and drinks, rather than by countries which can provide cheap labour (Ayadi et al., 2006). Using data from the World Bank for 2002, these authors note that 73 per cent of the nearly 8,000 affiliates of the Top 100 were located in countries with an average GDP per capita of over US$9,075. However, they observe that some affluent countries (such as Bahrain, Kuwait or Saudi Arabia) have not attracted such companies because of their low levels of industrialization and, especially, their small population. By contrast, they argue, less affluent countries such as Brazil, China, South Africa, Turkey or Egypt, have become poles of attraction for such firms as a result of their large urban populations. Their study suggests that in emerging economies urban dwellers now tend to follow international patterns of food consumption. Various studies have predicted that the agribusiness sector would expand to developing countries in order to take advantage of the natural resources available, low salaries and cheap agricultural goods (Constance and Heffernan, 1993). However, Dunning (1993) argues, in opposition, that natural resources such as land have become less important for MNEs. In general, the studies reviewed here provide only some general indications regarding the geography of agri-food MNEs.

Several theories have attempted to explain the path companies take to internationalization and, subsequently, the location of MNEs. We briefly examine two such theories and various empirical studies which have tested them, using data for specifically agri-food companies. The Uppsala school of thought maintains that the sequence of penetration of different foreign markets proceeds according to their cultural similarity with the home country of the MNE (Johanson and Vahlne, 1977; Shenkar, 2001). According to theories of international production, the more dissimilar the home and the host country are in terms of tastes, values, ethics and so on, the more difficult it will be for MNEs to operate and to respond to local demand (Goerzen and Beamish, 2003).

Cultural factors may be especially important with regard to food and drink consumption (Selvanathan and Selvanathan, 2006). Ning and Reed (1995), who investigated the location determinants of US FDI in food and related products from 1983 to 1989, find that US firms tend to invest in either English-speaking or European countries, due to their cultural similarities. In 1999, the sales of US F&B MNE affiliates in the UK, Germany and the Netherlands accounted for more than half their sales in Europe, which may reflect the effects of these countries' cultural similarities with the US (Pick and Worth, 2005).

Cultural questions may have also facilitated the recent internationalization of some F&B firms based in developing countries, such as the small F&B MNEs located in North Africa which have expanded into regional markets (Bachta and Ghersi, 2004) and the small Taiwanese and Korean F&B MNEs which now cater to the demands of Asian minorities in Latin America. Similarly, some producers of typical Mexican foods have been able to penetrate the US market and tap into the demands of Mexican immigrants (ECLAC, 2005). These examples suggest the potential importance of subnational ethnic markets in the development of some F&B MNEs. This aspect has been underexplored by the Uppsala school of thought, which has focused on the country level, but may well be important today, given the current dimension of migration flows.

Is the expansion of F&B MNEs regional or global? Recent research supports the contention that most MNEs actually operate on a regional basis within the Triad (Kozul-Wright and Rowthorn, 1998; Rugman and Verbeke, 2002, 2004; Rugman, 2005a).

A study testing Rugman and Verbeke's (2004) regionalization theory with empirical data for the international food industry finds that although F&B MNEs seem at first sight good candidates to become global companies,[10] only a few pursue a truly global strategy (Filippaios and Rama, 2008). MNEs operating in this sector prefer regional to global strategies. The main reason for this, the authors argue, is that food consumption is still largely culturally bound, and therefore companies find it difficult to employ their firm-specific assets across regions and cultures. Using a database comprising approximately 7,000 affiliates, the study analyses the geographical pattern of the world's largest F&B MNEs in the 1996–2000 period; the macro regions analysed are Africa, Asia, the EU, Latin America, North America, the Rest of Europe and the Rest of the World. The authors find only nine global firms with 20 per cent or more of their affiliates in at least three regions each but less than 50 per cent in any of these regions; 23 companies followed a bi-regional strategy, with at least 20 per cent of their affiliates in each of two regions, but less than 50 per cent in either of them; and 49 firms followed a home-region strategy, with the home region hosting at least 50 per cent of their affiliates. F&B MNEs which adopt a global strategy are likely to be very large, and thus F&B MNEs smaller than those analysed in the study are likely to pursue a home-region or bi-regional strategy.

The study also finds a significantly higher proportion of global firms among the F&B MNEs based in non-EU Western European countries than in the total sample, a result attributable to the presence in this group of Nestlé and Novartis, two very large companies based in a small country (Switzerland). F&B MNEs based in the EU follow either a bi-regional or a home-region strategy (the EU and North America or the EU and Latin America) but there are no global firms among them. The study shows a significantly higher proportion of home-region-oriented firms among F&B MNEs based in Japan than in the total sample (we return to this question below). Nevertheless, it concludes that while global strategy at the company level is likely to be a myth (Rugman, 2005b), globalization at the industry level is not. Most of the regionally oriented F&B MNEs locate a part, however small, of their affiliates in extra-regional locations. Another empirical study gives similar results for retailing, another important segment of the food chain; large MNEs in this subsector also prefer regional to global strategies (Rugman and Girod, 2003).

Tozanli (2005) argues that, in the F&B European industry, large plants with a continental structure currently supply different national markets simultaneously while remaining in constant touch with retailers' demands. The study also shows that, between 1987 and 2002, 78 per cent of plant closures related to the Top 100 took place in Western Europe. In our opinion, the current centralization of production may stimulate European firms to choose home-region strategies because this new form of organization provides them with scale economies. As noted by McCann and Mudambi (2004), the internal organization of companies is likely to be associated with specific geographical patterns.

Finally, a further study argues that the geographical orientation (global or regional) of F&B MNEs is associated with the shareholder configuration and the product mix of the company. Examining selected European food chains (milk, sugar, cereals and meat) from a global value chain (GVC) perspective, Palpacuer and Tozanli (2008) investigate the international scope of 22 leading firms' activities, distinguishing two major strategies. Global strategies, they argue, are characterized by homogeneous market approaches (that is, firms sell the same portfolio of products in their macro region and elsewhere) and by the search for economies of scale across the world's macro regions (for example, Africa, North America, Western Europe). By contrast, a second group of leading firms concentrate their operations within the home region.

This piece of research finds that all the global firms with homogeneous business activities in their home regions and elsewhere operate in the downstream segment of food chains and use agri-food processed products (for example, sugar) to manufacture their own products for the end market; a downstream chain position, large size, a strong presence of institutional shareholders and US origin are key characteristics of the global segment of European food chains. By contrast, they also find that smaller size, family or farmer ownership (cooperatives), capital of European origin and different chain positions (that is, upstream or downstream) are statistically associated with regional strategies. In our view, this result is coherent with Muller and Van Tulder (2005), who maintain that firms tend to be more nationally or regionally embedded when stakeholders such as cooperatives and local suppliers, rather than institutional investors, have a large say in company governance. Palpacuer and Tozanli (2008) appear to confirm, for the food industry, that company organization and its geographical pattern are likely to be associated (McCann and Mudambi, 2004).

Palpacuer and Tozanli conclude that although global corporations have become dominant among European GVCs, locally embedded firms focusing on country-specific production are still of great importance. Nevertheless, they argue, the reform of the Common Agricultural Policy (CAP) which took place at the start of the 2000s is likely to stimulate global sourcing, especially for non-perishable items (for example, milk powder). EU liberalization policies are likely to contribute, in their opinion, to a dislocation of upstream production from European nations to other countries (for example, Brazil, New Zealand and Australia) and to a downstream-driven globalization of European food chains. We turn now to empirical evidence of changes in the geography of the global agribusiness sector.

12.4.2   Host Countries

Table 12.2 displays the changes in inward stocks of FDI by sector in 1990 and 2007. Throughout this period, developing economies were the most important areas for investment in agriculture and related industries, accounting for 57 per cent of total stock in this sector. However, after China (by far the most important host country), the largest shares of such investment went to two developed nations, the US and Canada (Table 12.3). Moreover, in 2007, various socialist and transition countries (in descending order of importance, China, Vietnam,[11] the Russian Federation, Ukraine and some Eastern European countries) accounted for more than one-third of inward FDI stock in agriculture and related industries. Their increasing importance as recipients of inward stock, particularly after 1989 (Chobanova, 2009) has certainly involved a major transformation of the geographical pattern of FDI in agriculture and related industries.

Table 12.4 provides evidence of this predominance of developing countries, which accounted for 90 per cent of inward FDI flows in agriculture and related industries in 2005–07. Although comprehensive statistical information on the geographical distribution of investment by home country is not available, a review of the literature (for example, UNCTAD, 2009; FAO, 2012) and the comparison of Tables 12.1 and 12.4 suggest that currently a large share of total FDI in agriculture and related industries is South–South investment. It is often intra-regional investment, as shown by studies on Latin America.[12]

Information on the distribution of agricultural[13] affiliates of the Top 100 by macro region completes the information provided in Tables 12.3 and 12.4. All such affiliates are F&B processors but, as described earlier, some also engage in the activities indicated in note 11. In 1981, according to AGRODATA, the most important locations for these affiliates were, in descending order, North America (the US and Canada) (35 per cent of the total number of agricultural affiliates), the EU (at that time the EEC) (25 per cent) and Africa (20 per cent). By 2000, the geography of these specialized affiliates had changed dramatically. While it is true that most were still located in North America (33 per cent) and the EU (31 per cent), Africa's share had fallen to only 1 per cent of the total and that of Asia had increased from 4 to 16 per cent; moreover, a number of these affiliates (3 per cent) were located in non-EU nations in Central and Eastern Europe for the first time.[14] In African agriculture and related primary industries, the Top 100 may have been replaced by investors based in developing countries (such as Saudi Arabia or China, that is, from nations which lack agricultural resources) and by European retailers who operate through contract farming rather than FDI (UNCTAD, 2009).

The empirical evidence suggests that the prediction of Dunning (1993), namely that

Table 12.2   Estimated worldwide inward FDI stock, by sector and industry, 1990 and 2007 (in millions of US dollars)

Sector/Industry	1990			2007			
	Developed countries	Developing economies	World	Developed countries	Developing economies	Southeast Europe and CIS	World
Total	1,579,483	362,632	1,942,116	11,583,162	3,816,510	297,204	15,696,876
Primary	151,505	30,349	181,854	863,657	240,791	67,988	1,172,436
Agriculture, hunting, forestry and fishing	3,466	4,571	8,036	11,830	17,997	2,182	32,010
Manufacturing	640,572	158,026	798,598	3,251,613	916,814	77,407	4,245,834
Food, beverages and tobacco	69,940	10,401	80,341	390,734	46,919	12,378	450,030
Services	78,457	169,243	947,701	7,300,508	2,586,293	133,682	10,020,483
Private buying and selling of property	–	–	–	6,043	–	–	6,043
Unspecified	8,949	5,014	13,963	161,341	72,612	18,126	252,079

Notes:
The world total was extrapolated on the basis of data covering 54 countries in 1990 and 92 countries in 2007, or the latest year available. They account for over four-fifths of world inward FDI flows in 1990 and 2007. Only countries for which data for the three main sectors were available were included. The distribution share of each industry of these countries was applied to estimate the world total in each sector and industry. As a result, the sum of the sectors for each group of economies is different from the totals shown in Annex Table B.2. in UNCTAD (2009). In the case of some countries where only approval data were available, the actual data were estimated by applying the implementation ratio of realized FDI to approved FDI to the latter (56% in 1994 for Japan, 10% in 1990 and 7% in 1999 for Lao People's Democratic Republic, 84% in 2007 for Malaysia, 44% in 2002 for Mongolia, 39% in 1990 and 35% in 2007 for Myanmar, 41% in 1990 and 35% in 1999 for Nepal, 62% in 1995 for Sri Lanka, 73% in 1990 and 52% in 2007 for Taiwan Province of China). The world total in 1990 includes the countries of Southeast Europe and the CIS, although data by sector and industtry are not available for that region.
* A considerable share of investment in business activities is in Hong Kong (China), which accounted for 88% of developing economies and 40% of the world total in 2007. Hong Kong (China) data include investment holding companies.

Source: UNCTAD.

Table 12.3   Inward FDI stock/flows in agriculture, forestry and fishing, various years (in millions of US dollars and percentages)

Host region/economy	Millions of dollars				Percentage share in total			
	Flows		Stock		Flows		Stock	
	2002–2004	2005–2007	2002[b]	2007[c]	2002–2004	2005–2007	2002[b]	2007[c]
World	2,286.9	3,327.8	18,969.5	32,010.0	0.4	0.2	0.3	0.2
Developed economies	156.5	38.9	6,694.7	11,830.3	0.0	0.0	0.1	0.1
Europe								
Czech Republic	27.8	29.0	20.3	196.5	0.5	0.3	0.1	0.2
France	25.4	61.5	351.3	616.4	0.1	0.1	0.1	0.1
Germany	5.6	–6.7	194.0	225.2	0.0	–0.0	0.1	0.0
Hungary	26.6	13.6	387.3	493.9	0.8	0.2	1.1	0.5
Italy	83.0	28.6	264.3	624.3	0.5	0.1	0.2	0.2
Netherlands	21.2	–	349.2	–	0.1	–	0.1	–
Poland	43.6	73.9	185.7	446.3	0.6	0.4	0.4	0.4
Romania	16.8	67.7	108.2	412.8	0.3	0.7	0.9	0.7
United Kingdom	–2.0	84.7	243.4	490.8	–0.0	0.0	0.0	0.0
Other developed countries								
Australia	54.4	–74.7	642.6	624.2	0.3	–0.8	0.5	0.2
Canada	–	–	662.2	1,497.8	–	–	0.3	0.3
United States	–195.7	31.0	1,997.0	2,561.0	–0.2	0.0	0.2	0.1
Developing economies	2,040.8	2,980.0	11,978.2	17,997.1	1.1	0.2	0.8	0.5
Africa								
United Republic of Tanzania	40.5	40.5	210.7	252.4	9.4	9.4	6.2	6.7
Latin America and the Caribbean								
Brazil	153.3	420.9	392.0	383.6	0.9	1.6	0.6	0.4
Chile	4.8	49.5	789.6	949.7	0.2	2.3	1.5	1.5
Peru	1.5	51.0	51.1	208.6	0.5	8.7	0.4	1.3
Asia and Oceania								
China	1,047.7	747.0	4,120.3[d]	6,156.2[d]	1.9	1.0	1.9	1.9
Korea, Republic of	–4.9	1.3	400.6	400.5	–0.1	0.0	0.9	0.6
Vietnam	61.9	51.4	1,753.1	–	4.4	3.0	6.7	–
Southeast Europe and CIS	89.5	308.9	296.5	2,182.5	0.4	0.7	0.4	0.7
Russian Federation	7.3	187.7	87.0	953.0	0.1	1.0	0.4	0.9
Ukraine	–	57.3	113.6	557.6	–	4.0	2.1	1.9

Notes:
The world totals, as well as totals for developed economies developing economies Southeast Europe and CIS, were extrapolated from the data for countries for which detailed statistics FDI in agriculture were available. The coverage of dats available were as follows: about 100 countries for inward flows, accounting for over 90% of world inward FDI flows and around 90 countries for inward stock, accounting for over 85% of world inward stock.
a.   Including the hunting industry.
b.   Or closest year available.
c.   Or latest year available.
d.   Based on approval data.

Source: Annex A.1.4 and A.1.6 in UNCTAD (2009) and UNCTAD, FDI/TNC database.

Table 12.4 Estimated worldwide inward FDI flows, by sector and industry, 1989–1991 and 2005–2007 (in millions of US dollars)

Sector/Industry	1989–1991			2005–2007			
	Developed countries	Developing economies	World	Developed countries	Developing economies	South-East Europe and CIS	World
Total	151,998	34,551	186,549	1,060,084	367,294	43,886	1,471,264
Primary	8,998	3,860	12,858	124,046	33,639	13,205	170,891
Agriculture, hunting, forestry and fishing	–6	628	623	39	2,980	309	3,328
Manufacturing	47,769	16,081	63,849	232,141	113,850	7,192	353,183
Food, beverages and tobacco	4,790	2,361	7,151	34,051	5,079	1,415	40,545
Services	83,477	10,634	94,111	636,238	208,180	22,931	867,349
Private buying and selling of property	113	–	113	9,766	–	1	9,767
Unspecified	11,642	3,977	15,619	57,892	11,624	557	70,073

Notes:
The world total was extrapolated on the basis of data covering 70 countries in 1989–91 and 104 countries in 2005–07, or the latest three-year period average available. They account for 88 and 95% of world inward FDI flows respectively in the periods 1989–91 and 2005–07. Only countries for which data for the three main sectors were available were included. The distribution share of each industry of these countries was applied to estimate the world total in each sector and industry. As a result, the sum of the sectors for each group of economies is different from the totals shown in Annex Table B.1. in UNCTAD (2009). Approval data were used for Israel (1994 instead of 1989–91).Mangolia (1991–93 instead of 1989–91) and Mozambique (2003–05). In the case of some countries, the actual data was estimated by applying the implementation ratio of realized FDI to approved FDI to the-later: Bangladesh (2% in 1989–91), Cambodia (9% in 1994–95), China (47% in 1989–91), Indonesia(15% in 1989–91) the Islamic Republic of Iran (69% in 1993–95 and 22% in 2001–03), Japan (20% in 1989–91), Jordan (74% in 2001–03), Kenya (7% in 1992–94), the Lao People's Democratic Republic (1% in 1989–91), Myanmar (70% in 1989–91), Nepal (30% in 1989–91 and 53% 1996–98), Papua New Guinea (20% in 1993–95 and 36% in 1996–98), Solomon Islands (1% in 1994–95 and 3% in 1996), Sri Lanka (47% in 1995 and 91% in 2005–07), Taiwan Province of China (65% in 1989–91 and 50% in 2005–07), Turkey (40% in 1989–91) and Zimbabwe (23% in 1993–95).The world total in 1989–1991 includes the countries of Southeast Europe and the CIS, although data by sector and industry are not available for that region.
* A considerable share of investment in business activities is in Hong Kong (China), which accounted for 44% of developing economies and 11% of the world total during 2005–07. Hong Kong (China) data include investment holding companies.

Source: UNCTAD.

321

natural resources such as land would become less important for MNEs, may have been accurate for Triad-based agri-food MNEs but not for other agri-food MNEs. The thesis of an expansion of agricultural FDI towards developing countries (Constance and Heffernan, 1993) appears to be supported by the data, with two important caveats. First, a substantial proportion of the growing FDI in agriculture and related primary industries is currently channelled to socialist and transition countries. Second, some of the principal foreign investors appear at present to be MNEs based in developing countries (rather than Triad-based companies, as expected). Both of these circumstances were obviously difficult to foresee at the beginning of the 1990s.

The food, beverages and tobacco industry, by contrast, displays a clear predominance of developed countries, which received 87 per cent of inward FDI stock for these sectors in both 1990 and 2007 (Table 12.2). Furthermore, the evolution of FDI flows from 1989–91 to 2005–07 shows that developed countries became increasingly important (from 67 to 84 per cent of the total), despite the fact that the inward FDI flows received by developing economies and by Southeast Europe[15] and the CIS countries[16] also grew during this period (Table 12.4).

In what follows we study various countries as both exporters and importers of capital. In 2008, the most important countries (as measured by the volume of their outward FDI stocks) in the food, beverages and tobacco industry were, in descending order, the UK, the US, the Netherlands, Japan and Denmark (Figure 12.1). A comparison with Figure 12.2 shows that particular countries (that is, the US, the UK and the Netherlands) are both the most important source countries and also the most important recipients for FDI in this industry. For the food industry in 2008, Figure 12.3 shows the US position

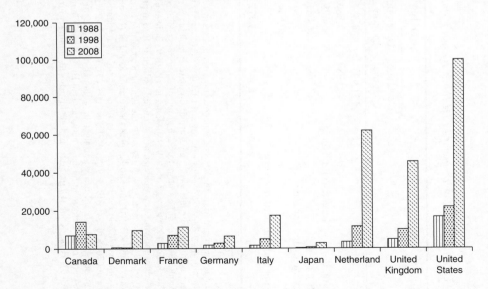

Source: Authors' elaboration, based on OECD statistics on globalization, http://stats.oecd.org/index.aspx, as of February 2010.

Figure 12.2   Inward FDI positions in the food, beverage and tobacco industry, 1988–2008 (in millions of US dollars)

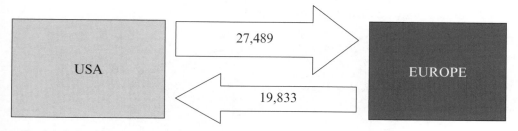

Note: Europe includes Russia. Historical cost basis.

Source: Authors' elaboration, based on the Survey of Current Business.

Figure 12.3   Direct investment position of the US in Europe and direct investment position of Europe in the US for food manufacturing, 2008 (in millions of US dollars)

(stock of FDI) in Europe and the European position in the US: there is a high level of reciprocity between the two areas, although the US stock of FDI in Europe is greater. This phenomenon is not new, as is shown also by sales data. By the mid-1990s, European firms were responsible for a majority (73 per cent) of foreign affiliates output in the US food and kindred products industry and, similarly, the majority (50 per cent) of foreign affiliate sales of US firms took place in Europe[17] (Pick and Worth, 2005).

For FDI in the food industry, the empirical evidence appears to support the hypothesis that foreign investors cluster in the same countries and, therefore, that rival firms in the same industry have a similar geographical distribution of their sales or assets (Knickerbocker, 1973). Recent developments of Knickerbocker's oligopolistic rivalry theory have been used to explain the so-called 'transatlantic reversal', that is, European FDI investment in the US (Ietto-Gillies, 2005), a clear trend in this industry. However, as described above, cultural and geographical proximity to home countries may also have contributed to these spatial patterns of food FDI.

This is suggested by the analysis of Japanese outward FDI in food, which shows evidence of a search for new markets (instead of a tendency to cluster in the same European countries and in the US). Figure 12.4 shows that in 1989–94 most Japanese FDI in this industry went to North America, Oceania and Europe; by 2000–04, however, the share of these saturated markets had declined, while those of Latin America and (especially) Asia had clearly risen. FDI data, therefore, confirm the importance of the home-region strategies of Japanese F&B MNEs, as discussed above (Section 12.3).

12.5   THE GEOGRAPHY OF CORPORATE R&D

MNEs undertake R&D and innovative activities in both their home countries and in host countries. The internationalization of R&D activities by firms (hereafter, the internationalization of R&D) has become increasingly common (OECD, 2008; UNCTAD, 2005). Firms innovate abroad for many different reasons: to adapt their products to host-country tastes; to absorb new knowledge from world centres of excellence; to

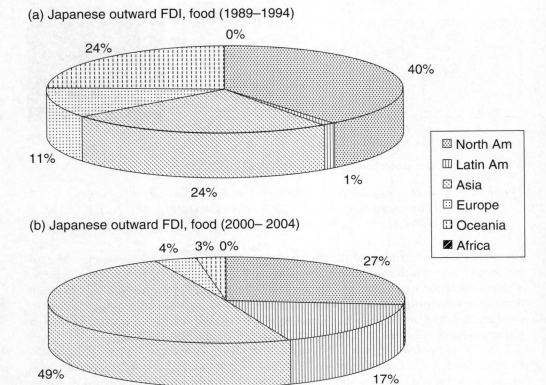

(a) Japanese outward FDI, food (1989–1994)

(b) Japanese outward FDI, food (2000– 2004)

Legend:
- ⊠ North Am
- ⊞ Latin Am
- ⊠ Asia
- ⊞ Europe
- ⊡ Oceania
- ▨ Africa

Source: Authors' elaboration, based on data from the Japanese Ministry of Finance, http://www.mof.go.jp/english/.

Figure 12.4   Japanese outward FDI in the food industry (by region)

benefit from low-cost, good-quality local R&D; and so on (Blanc and Sierra, 1999; Cantwell and Iammarino, 2000; OECD, 2005). Although such strategies are contributing to a new geography of corporate R&D, the empirical evidence available regarding this internationalization is still insufficient (Dunning, 1994; Dunning and Narula, 1996; Serapio et al., 2004), especially for mature industries such as food and beverages.

However, sectoral factors appear to strongly influence MNEs' choice of geographical location for their R&D activities (Patel and Pavitt, 1991; Cantwell and Janne, 2000), for two principal reasons. First, MNEs internationalize R&D to support international production, and geographical patterns of FDI differ by sector (Blanc and Sierra, 1999; Ietto-Gillies, 2002). Second, they also internationalize R&D to absorb new knowledge which may be not available at home; world centres of scientific and technological excellence, however, are not located in the same countries for all industries (Cantwell and Piscitello, 1999).

Apparently, F&B MNEs are especially likely to undertake their R&D activities abroad (Cantwell and Hodson, 1991; Patel, 1995; Alfranca et al., 2005), probably because it is essential for them to adapt their products to different national tastes and food safety regulations. Despite trends towards the homogenization of food and drink consumption in Western countries (Connor, 1994), differences in local tastes are significant and persistent.

12.5.1   The Literature on FDI and R&D

Some authors, described by Archibugi and Iammarino (1999) as the 'sceptics of globalisation', maintained in the 1990s that many MNEs have little interest in internationalizing their R&D activities because they prefer to invent in their home countries (Patel and Pavitt, 1991, 1995, 1997; Patel and Vega, 1999). A recent review of the literature suggests that MNEs continue to perform much of their innovative activity at home (Dunning and Lundan, 2009). However, various authors are currently calling attention to a new phenomenon, namely the alleged preference of Triad-based companies for offshoring R&D to the emerging economies (Bardhan and Jaffee, 2004; Edler, 2008).

In our view, there are several explanations for this lack of consensus. First, authors may use different types of samples for analysis. Their results concerning the geographical patterns of R&D internationalization may be influenced not only by the above-mentioned sector-specific factors but also by country-specific questions. European, US and Japanese companies have approached the internationalization of R&D differently (von Zedtwitz and Gassmann, 2002), while geographical and cultural proximity appear to influence the choice of corporate R&D location (OECD, 2008). According to some authors, the internationalization of R&D may be largely a regional process, principally involving European MNEs innovating in other European countries (Archibugi and Michie, 1995). In addition, different types of R&D projects may display different patterns of internationalization (Sachwald, 2008). Despite the specificity of results, such conclusions are sometimes generalized for all types of MNEs or for all types of R&D projects.

Second, agreement has not yet been achieved among researchers regarding important methodological issues which may affect the research results, and these issues therefore require further examination. Data regarding the internationalization of R&D are not fully comparable and research methods vary between studies (OECD, 2005). This restricts the possibility of comparing different authors' results, and requires internationalization to be approached from various angles employing a variety of indicators. Firms rarely provide information on their R&D expenditure broken down by geographical location. Empirical studies therefore often measure the innovative performance of firms using patent data, and although there are drawbacks associated with such information, the advantages of its availability and richness are widely recognized (Griliches, 1990).

A patent is a title, granted by a patent office, which gives the holder the right to exclude others from making, using, selling or distributing an invention without his/her consent (for example, through a licensing agreement). Such a right is legally enforceable in cases of infringement, and patents can be granted for inventions on products and processes. They are generally only valid for a maximum of 20 years from the date of filing and are restricted to the geographical area under the jurisdiction of the patent office where protection is sought. For instance, while patents assigned by the European Patent Office (EPO) may protect the intellectual property rights of patentees in up to 36 European countries,[18] patents assigned by the United States Patent Office (USPTO) protect these rights in the US. As will be seen below, the type of patent information employed may affect research results.

Several studies, using patent data, have tested whether F&B MNEs internationalize their R&D. Cantwell and Hodson (1991) and Patel (1995) found that between 24 and 31 per cent of the patents granted in the United States to the world's largest food and drink companies in the mid-1980s and early 1990s were attributable to research performed outside companies' home countries. However, studies of European F&B MNEs have found higher levels of R&D internationalization. The largest such companies apparently produce 83 per cent of their total patentable inventions (hereafter, inventions) abroad, while the equivalent figure for the largest US F&B MNEs is only 10 per cent (Alfranca et al., 2005; Cantwell and Janne, 2000). Criscuolo and Patel (2003) find that large EU MNEs in the food and drink industry undertake over 50 per cent of their innovative activities outside their home countries.

It must be remembered, however, that most such analyses have been based on the count of patents granted by the USPTO to companies. By contrast, a study which also investigates location indicators for all the inventors listed in patent documents, but employs both USPTO and EPO data (instead of a single source), suggests that research which only analyses USPTO information may overstate the relative dimension of corporate R&D internationalization (Martínez and Rama, 2012). This study establishes that, according to USPTO information, major European F&B MNEs produced 56 per cent of their inventions abroad in 1978–2001, a result which is in line with previous analyses. However, the examination of EPO applications for a similar time period provides more nuanced conclusions; figures using this information source indicate that such firms produced abroad only 42 per cent of their inventions. The predominance of the home country as a 'locus' for R&D activities is corroborated by the analysis of the patent families applied for by these companies. Patent families may provide information concerning inventions protected in markets other than those in Europe and the US (for example, Japan),[19] and research based only on USPTO data may therefore overestimate the patenting of European F&B MNEs abroad. In order to allow for this, the material discussed in this subsection uses both EPO applications and USPTO data as complementary sources of information, and we have also analysed the location of specialized R&D affiliates which may perform patentable and non-patentable R&D (for example, basic research). However, the studies reviewed in this subsection have rarely analysed in what parts of the world F&B MNEs choose to locate their international R&D activities, and we turn to this question now.

12.5.2   The Coordination and Management of Global R&D

This subsection examines the location of the specialized R&D affiliates of the world's 100 largest F&B MNEs. As we have just seen, different types of corporate R&D may display different geographical distributional patterns (Sachwald, 2008). This is confirmed by a previous study (Filippaios et al., 2009) which uses a similar sample to the one we use in this subsection. MNEs today divide their innovative activities among a large number of dispersed localities (we shall return to this question below). Consequently, they may risk losing technological coherence (Blanc and Sierra, 1999), and to avoid doing so may establish affiliates specializing in research-related activities and which are responsible for coordinating and directing innovation within the multinational network (Gassmann and von Zedtwitz, 1998; Gerybadze and Reger, 1999; von Zedtwitz et al., 2004). This type of R&D organization appears to have originally been implemented by MNEs operating in high-tech sectors, but it is currently being adopted by F&B MNEs, especially when these are highly internationalized or innovative (Filippaios et al., 2009). While these specialized affiliates are not necessarily located in the home country, according to Cohen et al. (2009) traditional centres of research located in the country of the parent company enjoy accumulated expertise and reputation, while foreign R&D-related affiliates have a long learning curve. The present subsection investigates where the world's 100 largest F&B MNEs choose to locate their R&D-related affiliates (hereafter R&D affiliates).

We define R&D affiliates as those which, according to the AGRODATA database (2000–02), specialize in seed production, proteins, biotechnology, engineering, industrial research laboratories, research centres and medical and veterinary services (Rama, 1996).[20] As shown by a previous study (Filippaios et al., 2009), these affiliates encompass both adaptation and 'home-base augmenting' types of R&D (Kuemmerle, 1999). The sampled companies own 368 such affiliates which, it should be emphasized, enjoy an independent status and are not merely laboratories attached to MNE production facilities. Some examples of these specialized affiliates are Nestlé Product Technology Center, Danapak R&D Center A/S (Arla Foods), Tate & Lyle Process Technology and Nutreco Aquaculture Research Center.

As shown by Figure 12.5, the world's 100 largest F&B MNEs own R&D affiliates

Note: Includes domestic and foreign affiliates.

Source: Own elaboration based on AGRODATA. Map prepared by the authors using the program Cartes & Données (www.articque.com).

Figure 12.5   *R&D affiliates of the world's 100 largest food and beverage MNEs (2000–2002)*

in five continents. They have been attracted by the emerging economies, such as Brazil or China, but also (although to a lesser extent), by less developed nations, such as the Ivory Coast. Nevertheless, in 2000–02, major F&B MNEs preferred to locate most such affiliates in Europe, Japan and the US.

A comparison with a previous study based on similar data (Rama, 1996) suggests, however, that the 100 largest F&B MNEs decentralized the control and management of R&D to a certain degree during the period from 1988 to 2000–02. The proportion of R&D affiliates located within the EU (the EEC, in 1988) fell from 50 to 43 per cent of the total number. Furthermore, within Europe, companies may have redistributed these affiliates. The proportion of R&D affiliates positioned in France, the UK and the Netherlands fell, respectively, from 16 to 8 per cent, from 14 to 6 per cent and from 7 to 5 per cent of the world total during the period examined. At the same time the share of those located in the Czech Republic, Poland, Romania and Slovakia (that is, in new member states of the EU27) rose from 0 to 13 per cent, underlining the importance of intra-European R&D investment in this industry, as most of these new R&D affiliates belong to Western European F&B MNEs. The share of R&D affiliates located in the US rose slightly, from 20 to 21 per cent of the total, while that of those operating in other developed countries[21] increased from 17 to 20 per cent, probably as a consequence of the emergence of new source countries, such as Norway, for FDI in this industry (see Section 12.3). Finally, the proportion of R&D affiliates located in developing countries rose from 13 to 15 per cent of the total in this period. Overall, the share of some traditional locations (for example, the US, the UK, France and the Netherlands) increased only slightly or even fell, while that of new locations (other developed countries, Eastern Europe and some developing countries) rose.

To summarize, F&B MNEs are likely to retain within the Triad those tasks which involve the coordination and management of global R&D, although a trend towards some degree of geographical decentralization is noticeable when we compare 1988 with 2000–02.

F&B MNEs may produce their inventions both in the R&D affiliates analysed in this subsection and in laboratories attached to production centres. Such companies' inventions may also be the result of research performed outside the MNE, through R&D collaboration or subcontracting agreements with other public or private institutions. We analyse below the spatial pattern of the generation of inventions in the largest European F&B MNEs, as reported in patent documents.

12.5.3   The Geography of Patented Inventions

Large European MNEs play a substantial role with regard to innovations employed worldwide by the food and drink sector and auxiliary industries (Christensen et al., 1996; von Tunzelmann, 1998). As early as the 1970s there was a noticeable trend towards the international sourcing of technology by such firms (OECD, 1979). This subsection examines, from the late 1970s to the present decade, the changing geography of the innovative activities[22] of 59 major European F&B MNEs whose parent companies are based in 11. EU countries and Switzerland and which have a total of 8,432 affiliates (Appendix 12A.2).

We analyse the 8,626 EPO applications filed by the sampled firms and their affiliates in 1978–2005 and the 3,650 USPTO granted patents they applied for in 1978–2001. As Europe and the US are the two major markets for European F&B MNEs (Filippaios and Rama, 2008), these two types of patents are likely to protect the most important inventions produced by such companies, and we therefore employ USPTO and EPO data as complementary sources of information. We observe a relatively long time period, to ensure that we capture as many innovations as possible in the mature and conservative F&B industry, where consumer tastes tend to change slowly (Galizzi and Venturini, 2008).

According to the OECD (2005), the country where the inventor is located provides an indication of where the technology has been produced. Contained in patent documents, information on the inventor's country of residence enables us to analyse important changes in the geography of corporate R&D. In what follows, therefore, we study the locations preferred by the sampled companies for their innovative activities, as proxied by the stated location of inventors,[23] to calculate the share of each country in the total innovative activities of the MNEs in the sample.

First, we focus on EPO applications. Between 1978–89 and 1990–2005 the sampled companies increased their aggregate number of EPO applications from 1,848 to 6,776 and the number of countries involved in the production of their patentable inventions from 25 to 51 (home countries included). Figure 12.6 shows in darker tones the most popular countries for the production of inventions in 1978–89. According to EPO data, 41 per cent were generated in the UK. Other common locations were, in descending order of importance, the Netherlands, the US, Switzerland, Germany and France. There are two possible explanations for such preferences. First, corporate R&D tends

Legend
0
1–5
6–10
11–25
26–50
51–150
151–250
251–500
501–1000
>1000

Elaborated by Unit of GIS (CCHS-CSIC)

0   1125   2250   4500 Miles

Source: Own elaboration, based on patent data from PATSTAT September 2008 and information on affiliates from BvD Amadeus 2008 for a selection of Top Food European MNEs, taken from Agrodata 2005.

Figure 12.6   EPO application by inventor country, filling years 1978–1989

to follow, with a time lag, FDI (Blanc and Sierra, 1999). In the F&B industry, because a substantial proportion of innovation consists of small improvements and it is crucial to adapt foodstuffs to national tastes (Galizzi and Venturini, 2008), companies need to locate their laboratories close to their manufacturing facilities. The UK, which hosts 20 per cent of the F&B MNEs' foreign affiliates in our sample, the US (7.5 per cent), Germany (6.7 per cent), France (6.1 per cent) and the Netherlands (3.8 per cent) are also the most important foreign locations for the production facilities of the sampled firms (as measured by the number of their affiliates). If we consider both domestic and foreign affiliates, the share of the UK increases to 28 per cent of the total, and that of France, Germany and the Netherlands to 8, 7 and 6 per cent, respectively. These are important markets indeed for major European F&B MNEs, which strongly encourages companies to select them as locations for their innovative activities.

Another explanation for the preference for these countries is probably the quality of their environment with regard to food and food-related technology (Christensen et al., 1996). In 1969–94, according to the USPTO information analysed by these authors, the US accounted for 67 per cent of the world's patents in food, 62 per cent in food equipment, 71 per cent in agricultural machinery and 59 per cent in biotechnology,[24] while Western Europe generated 19, 23, 18 and 20 per cent, respectively.[25] These figures suggest that in choosing a suitable location to perform R&D, the European F&B MNEs in our sample may also have taken into account the specialized technological achievements of the US and Western Europe and the possibilities they offer for knowledge acquisition.

Figure 12.7 maps, in turn, the countries in which the sampled companies produced their inventions (measured once more by EPO applications) in 1990–2005. Comparison

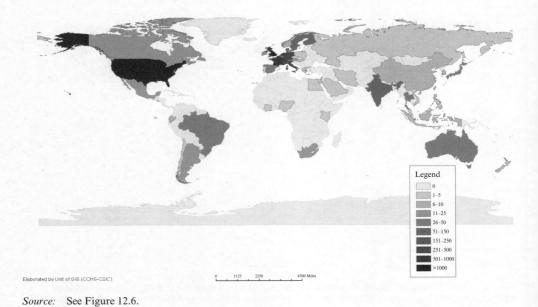

Elaborated by Unit of GIS (CCHS-CSIC)

0   1125   2250   4500 Miles

Source: See Figure 12.6.

Figure 12.7   EPO application by inventor country, filling years 1990–2005

with Figure 12.6 provides evidence of some important changes in the geography of corporate R&D between 1978–89 and 1990–2005. First, as stated earlier, top European F&B
MNEs currently perform R&D in more countries than previously. In Latin America, for
instance, in 1978–89 only Brazil and Argentina were selected to perform local innovative
activities, but in 1990–2005, such activities were extended to Chile, Ecuador, El Salvador
and, especially, Mexico. In 1990–2005, for the first time, the sampled companies engaged
in innovative activities in Eastern European nations (Hungary, Poland and the Czech
Republic), which became EU member states by the end of the period. A few large
European food and beverage MNEs had already become involved in certain business
undertakings (for example, licences) in these countries prior to 1989 (Chobanova, 2009)
but not, according to our patent data, in innovative activities.

Furthermore, major European F&B MNEs increased the proportion of R&D activities performed in emerging countries, such as (in descending order) Brazil, Thailand,
Argentina, Singapore and South Africa, although the share of such nations remained
comparatively small throughout the 1990–2005 period. According to the empirical
evidence, the F&B industry does not clearly display a shift of corporate R&D towards
emerging countries, as is the case of other industries, such as electronics (Reddy, 2000;
Bruche, 2009). In our sample, India, now of similar importance to Sweden as a location for the sampled companies' R&D (1.2 per cent of the inventions for which they
seek patent protection in Europe), is currently the most important destination for R&D
outside the Triad.

Two possible explanations can be provided for such changes. First, the internationalization of R&D may be following the internationalization of production, as suggested
by the rapid expansion of the sampled companies in developing and transition countries.
Second, the current wave of R&D internationalization may be aimed at reducing costs
by recruiting highly qualified scientists from developing nations, where salaries are lower
than in the Triad (Reddy, 2000). Finally, in 1990–2005, the group of top locations (that
is, those in which the majority of inventions are concentrated) displays some degree of
spatial decentralization. The share of inventions produced in the UK fell from 41 to 30
per cent of the total, in contrast to the increase in the relative share of other European
countries, such as (in descending order) France, Germany, Italy, Sweden, Spain and
Austria. Moreover, the US became the second preference for innovative activities, after
the UK, replacing the Netherlands, another European country. Consequently, the share
of inventions produced in the US increased, in 1978–89 and 1990–2005, from 13 to 25
per cent of the total.

As Figures 12.8 and 12.9 show, USPTO data corroborate these findings, confirm-
ing the attractiveness of the US for major European F&B MNEs. According to this
source, the US became their most important location for R&D activities; from 1978–89
to 1990–2001, its share grew from 26 to 43 per cent of the total number of such companies' inventions (as measured by their USPTO patents). These results are not surprising; as stated earlier, the US is an important market for European F&B MNEs and the
most important centre worldwide for food and food-related technology (Christensen et
al., 1996). Logically enough, the European companies in our sample are likely to use
USPTO patents chiefly to protect the inventions they produce in the US. However, the
comparison of Figures 12.6 and 12.7, on the one hand, and Figures 12.8 and 12.9, on the
other, suggests that research based exclusively on USPTO information may overestimate

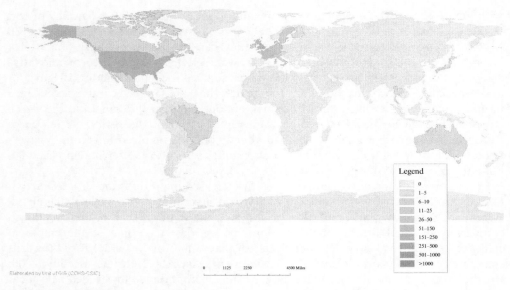

Source: See Figure 12.6.

Figure 12.8   USPTO granted patents by inventor country, filling years 1978–1989

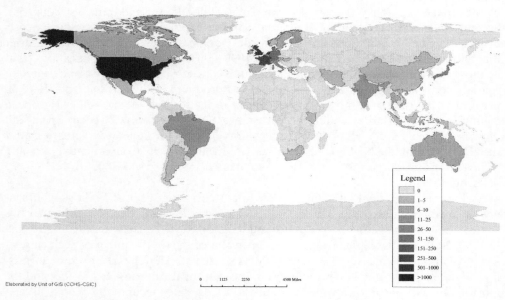

Source: See Figure 12.6.

Figure 12.9   USPTO granted patents by inventor country, filling years 1990–2001

the innovative activities of European F&B MNEs in the US. This corroborates research into European MNEs in other sectors (Criscuolo et al., 2005), indicating that European MNEs in general prefer to generate their inventions in Europe.

To summarize, the R&D activities of European F&B MNEs have become geographically more dispersed in recent years. However, in 1990–2005, such companies still preferred to spatially concentrate these activities in a handful of Western European countries and in the US. More specifically, the empirical evidence does not indicate, at least for the F&B industry, that the EU is becoming less attractive for domestic corporate R&D, as various authors argue (Bijman et al., 1997; Erken and Gilsing, 2005; Sachwald, 2008).

12.6   CONCLUSIONS

This chapter has analysed the changing structure of the global agribusiness sector in order to better understand its geographical patterns. FDI in the global agribusiness sector has increased swiftly from the end of the 1980s to the present and, as in other sectors, most such investment has come from companies based in developed countries. Although Triad-based investors are still prominent, the configuration of the source countries for equity capital has changed substantially in this sector. The share of developed countries has fallen noticeably with regard to outward FDI flows in agriculture, hunting, forestry and fishing. This trend may be the result of a variety of causes, such as divestment of land by Triad-based MNEs; their choosing of new forms of investment (other than FDI), such as the outsourcing of local agricultural production; and, most particularly, the outstanding dynamism of FDI flows originating in developing countries. Much of the outward FDI of developing countries in agriculture and related primary industries appears to consist of South–South investment, that is, FDI channelled to other developing countries.

L-advantages, such as government support, are apparently instrumental in explaining the expansion of resource-seeking MNEs based in either developing or developed countries. Second, the share of developed countries in outward FDI in food and beverages has fallen only moderately, although changes in the composition of source countries are observable, both inside and outside the Triad. The emergence of several new source countries or the special dynamism displayed by others appear to be associated with: the O-advantages of indigenous companies (technology); I-advantages, such as the vertical integration of the food chain, which is especially important for agribusiness based in developing countries; and certain L-advantages which home countries are able to offer native companies, such as R&D-intensive sectoral systems of innovation or easy access to finance. By contrast, L-advantages related to the availability of cheap natural resources or outstanding soil and climate conditions in the home country have no clear effects on the internationalization of native agribusiness, although these benefits may have played a positive role in some specific cases. The fact that successive waves of source countries have emerged in the agribusiness sector indicates support for the IDP theory, namely that nations appear to reach threshold levels of development which enable their agribusiness to become multinational.

FDI in agriculture and primary related industries goes chiefly to developing countries. However, the US and Canada are the most important host countries after China, and socialist and transition countries also play a substantial role. While the search for land may have become less important for Triad-based MNEs, as predicted by Dunning (1993), it remains a crucial strategy for MNEs based in developing countries, especially those lacking sufficient natural resources. By contrast, FDI in food and beverages goes primarily to developed countries, whose importance appears to have increased in recent years, despite the flows received by developing countries also having grown. Some reciprocity of investment is apparent, at least between the US and Europe. Moreover, some of the most important home countries are at the same time the most important host countries for FDI in this industry. Knickerbocker's (1973) oligopolistic rivalry theory and cultural proximity are probable explanations of the majority of these developments. On the other hand, Japan appears to have reduced its involvement in other developed countries, tending instead to channel its FDI to Latin America and, especially, to the rest of Asia. Increasing income levels in many of these countries and, in some cases, cultural proximity to the home country, may help to explain these trends.

The world's 100 largest F&B MNEs prefer to locate their specialized R&D units within the Triad, although certain developing nations and Eastern European countries are increasingly regarded as new locations for such activities. According to patent analysis, major European F&B MNEs tend to locate their innovative activities in an increasing number of countries. However, since most of these new locations are European nations, this trend seems to support the view that the internationalization of R&D is, for European firms, chiefly a European rather than a global phenomenon (Archibugi and Michie, 1995). The US, nevertheless, is also a very important location for the innovative activities of European food and beverage MNEs, while emerging economies, especially India, today host a part of these innovative activities. Companies are apparently attracted by those countries which host large shares of their production facilities, probably because this arrangement enables them to better adapt their products to local tastes. Asset-seeking behaviour and the search for world centres of excellence for food and food-related technology are also apparent.

NOTES

*   We wish to thank Stéphane Maraut for developing the matching algorithms used to assign patents to MNE groups. We are also grateful to Juan Fernández-Sastre for research assistance and to Selma Tozanli for help with the data. Ruth Rama gratefully acknowledges the financial support provided by the SEJ-5827 Project (Junta de Andalucía). Catalina Martínez acknowledges funding from the Spanish Ministry of Economics and Competitiveness, project CS0 2012–32844.
1. According to UNCTAD, 'FDI refers to an investment made to acquire lasting interest in enterprises operating outside of the economy of the investor. Further, in cases of FDI, the investor's purpose is to gain an effective voice in the management of the enterprise. The most important characteristic of FDI, which distinguishes it from foreign portfolio investment, is that it is undertaken with the intention of exercising control over an enterprise', http://www.unctad.org/.
2. See: http://www.ciaa.be/asp/index.asp (Confédération des Industries Agro-alimentaires).
3. OECD statistics on globalization: 'Inward activity of multinationals – share in national total', from http://stats.oecd.org/index.aspx, as of February 2010.
4. Agri-food firms include both agricultural companies (for example, plantations) and F&B processors. Firms classified as F&B companies because their main business is food and drink processing may nevertheless have some business lines related to primary production (for example, agriculture and aquaculture).
5. Flow data record the value of investments undertaken in a specific year, while stock data represent the net accumulated value resulting, at a point in time, from past flows (Ietto-Gillies, 2005).

6. An affiliate is an incorporated or unincorporated enterprise in which an investor owns a stake that permits a degree of control of the management of that enterprise (ibid.).
7. Traditionally, the Triad comprises Western Europe, the US and Japan.
8. When a company launches a foreign affiliate, the MNE is actually exporting equity capital to the foreign nation (Caves, 1996).
9. OECD statistics on globalization, http://stats.oecd.org/index.aspx, as of February 2010.
10. The Top 100 spread, on average, to 20 foreign countries in 2000–02 (AGRODATA). To put these figures into perspective, note that the average MNE spread to only 13.6 countries in 2000 (Ietto-Gillies, 2002). Country spread indicates the number of countries where a company is active through FDI. Another indicator confirms that F&B MNEs are highly internationalized: according to information provided by AGRODATA, the share of foreign affiliates to the total number of affiliates rose, in the Top 100, from 52 per cent in 1980–89, to 53 per cent in 1990–95 and to 55 per cent in 1996–2000.
11. 'Socialist countries' or 'Socialist republics' are China, Vietnam, Laos and Cuba (as of 2012). 'Transition Countries', as defined by UNCTAD, are Southeastern European countries and the CIS.
12. Land grabbing in Latin America, Canadian Journal of Development Studies/Revue Canadienne d'é tudes du development, Special Issue 33 (4), 2012.
13. Including agriculture, horticulture, animal husbandry, viticulture, pisciculture, aviculture, silviculture and fisheries (source: AGRODATA).
14. The shares of Latin America and Oceania remained relatively stable (11–10 per cent and 4–5 per cent, respectively).
15. Albania, Bosnia and Herzegovina, Croatia, Montenegro, Serbia and the FYR of Macedonia.
16. CIS (Commonwealth of Independent States): Armenia, Azerbaijan, Belarus, Georgia, Kazakhstan, Kyrgyzstan, Republic of Moldova, Russian Federation, Tajikistan, Turkmenistan, Ukraine and Uzbekistan.
17. Data from the Survey of Current Business.
18. The EPO comprised 36 member countries in 2009, including EU countries, but also non-EU members such as Switzerland, Norway and Turkey. Once a patent is granted by the EPO, it must be validated in the member countries chosen by the patentee, which usually requires the payment of a fee and the translation of the patent document into the national language. For a complete list, see http://www.epo.org/about-us/epo/member-states.html.
19. The OECD *Patent Statistics Manual* (2009) defines patent families as 'the set of patents (or applications) filed in several countries which are related to each other by one or several common priority filings'.
20. These activities correspond to the UN-ISI codes 111024, 312180, 832000 (excluding real estate, marketing and investment counselling services), 832030, 832020, 832021, 932000 and 933000 in the AGRODATA database, plus those affiliates which, included under code 832010 (management and IT services), have the term 'research' in the description of their activities.
21. Australia, Canada, Japan, New Zealand, Norway, South Korea and Switzerland.
22. We refer here to the innovative activities of the MNEs or their R&D activities, as measured by their patentable inventions. It should be borne in mind, however, that these companies may also perform R&D which in principle is not patentable, such as basic research. For an overview of differences among jurisdictions on patentable subject matter, see Martínez and Guellec (2004).
23. Following the OECD (2009) advice for analyses of the internationalization of R&D, we use the whole count of patents (as opposed to fractional counts, which assign a part of the patent to each country of residence). Some 82 per cent of all EPO applications and 87 per cent of all US patents in our sample are produced by inventors located in a single country. Therefore, in our database, the number of patents which protect inventions achieved by the collaboration of inventors located in different countries is quite small.
24. These data may, however, overestimate the level of innovativeness of US inventors, since USPTO patents are actually, for them, domestic patents. Domestic patents are usually cheaper and easier to obtain than international patents.
25. These figures include the US patents granted to all types of inventors: MNEs, one-nation firms, institutions (for example, universities) and individuals.

REFERENCES

Alfranca, O., R. Rama and N. von Tunzelmann (2002), 'A patent analysis of global food and beverage firms: the persistence of innovation', *Agribusiness: An International Journal*, **18**, 349–68.

Alfranca, O., R. Rama and N. von Tunzelmann (2005), 'Innovation in food and beverage multinationals', in Rama (ed.), *Multinational Agribusinesses*, New York and London: Haworth Press, pp. 13–500.

Anastassopoulos, G. and R. Rama (2005), 'The performance of multinational agribusinesses: effects of product and geographical diversification', in Rama (ed.), *Multinational agribusinesses*, New York and London: Haworth Press, pp. 73–113.

Andersen, E.S. and B.-Å. Lundvall (1988), 'Small national systems of innovation facing technological revolutions: an analytical framework', in C. Freeman and Lundvall (eds), *Small Countries Facing the Technological Revolution*, London and New York: Pinter, pp. 9–36.

Archibugi, A. and S. Iammarino (1999), 'The policy implications of the globalisation of innovation', *Research Policy*, **28**, 317–36.

Archibugi, D. and J. Michie (1995), 'The globalisation of technology: a new taxonomy', *Cambridge Journal of Economics*, **19**, 121–40.

Ayadi, N., J.-L. Rastoin and S. Tozanli (2006), 'Les opérations de restructuration des firmes agroalimentaires multinationales entre 1987 et 2003', Working Paper 8, Unité Mixte de Recherche MOISA, Montpellier (France), available at: http://ideas.repec.org/p/umr/wpaper/200608.html.

Azevedo, P.F., F.R. Chaddad and M.M.Q. Farina (2004), 'The food industry in Brazil and the United States: the effects of the FTAA on trade and investment', Working Paper SITI-07, Inter-American Development Bank, Buenos Aires.

Bachta, M.S. and G. Ghersi (2004), 'Restructuration des filières et stratégies de croissance des entreprises agroalimentaires dans les pays du Sud et de l'Est du bassin méditerranéen', in Bachta and Ghersi (eds), *Agriculture et alimentation en Méditerranée*, Paris: CIHEAM, IRESA, KARTHALA, pp. 111–38.

Bardhan, A.D. and D. Jaffee (2004), 'On intra-firm and multinationals: foreign outsourcing and offshoring in manufacturing', Haas School of Business, available at: http://www.brookings.edu/pge/offshoring_Bardhan.pdf (accessed May 2013).

Bijman, W.B., R. van Tulder and M. van Vliet (1997), 'Internationalisation of Dutch agribusiness and the organisation of R&D', Seminar on Globalization of the Food Industry, University of Reading, Reading.

Blanc, H. and C. Sierra (1999), 'The internationalisation of R&D by multinationals: a trade-off between external and internal proximity', *Cambridge Journal of Economics*, **23**, 187–206.

Bruche, B. (2009), 'The emergence of China and India as new competitors in MNCs' innovation networks', *Competition and Change*, **13**, 269–90.

Buckley, P.J., J. Clegg, A.R. Cross, X. Liu, H. Voss and P. Zheng (2007), 'The determinants of Chinese outward foreign direct investment', *Journal of International Business Studies*, **38**, 499–518.

Burch, D. and J. Goss (2005), 'Regionalization, globalization, and multinational agribusiness: a comparative perspective from Southeast Asia', in R. Rama (ed.), *Multinational Agribusinesses*, New York and London Haworth Press, pp. 253–82.

Cantwell, J. and C. Hodson (1991), 'Global R&D and UK competitiveness', in Mark Casson (ed.), *Global Research Strategy and International Competitiveness*, Oxford, UK and Cambridge, MA: Basil Blackwell, pp. 133–83.

Cantwell, J. and S. Iammarino (2000), 'Multinational corporations and the location of technological innovation in the UK regions', *Regional Studies*, **34**, 317–32.

Cantwell, J. and O. Janne (2000), 'Globalization of innovatory capacity: the structure of competence accumulation in European home and host countries', in F. Chesnais, G. Ietto-Gillies and R. Simonetti (eds), *European Integration and Global Corporate Strategies*, London and New York: Routledge, pp. 121–77.

Cantwell, J. and L. Piscitello (1999), 'The emergence of corporate international networks for the accumulation of dispersed technological competences', *Management International Review*, **1** (Special Issue), 123–47.

Caswell, J.A. (1987), 'Dominant forms of corporate control in the US agribusiness sector', *American Journal of Agricultural Economics*, **69**, 11–21.

Caves, R.E. (1996), *Multinational Enterprise and Economic Analysis*, Cambridge: Cambridge University Press.

CEPAL (1982), 'Sugar cane, alcohol production and the interests of transnational corporations in Brazil', E/CEPAL/R 324, United Nations Economic Commision for Latin America and the Caribbean.

Chobanova, Y. (2009), *Strategies of Multinationals in Central and Eastern Europe Innovation Systems and Embeddedness*, London: Palgrave Macmillan.

Christensen, J.L., R. Rama and N. von Tunzelmann (1996), 'Study on innovation in the European food products and beverages industry', EIMS/SPRINT, European Commission, Brussels.

Cohen, S.S., A. Di Minin, Y. Motoyama and C. Palmberg (2009), 'The persistence of home bias for important R&D in wireless telecom and automobiles', *Review of Policy Research*, **26**, 55–77.

Connor, J.M. (1994), 'North America as a precursor of changes in Western European food-purchasing patterns', *European Review of Agricultural Economics*, **21**, 1–173.

Constance, D.E. and W.D. Heffernan (1993), 'Transnational corporations and the globalization of the food system', *International Journal of Sociology of Agriculture and Food*, **1**, 43–56.

Criscuolo, P. and P. Patel (2003), 'Large firms and internationalization of R&D: "Hollowing out" of national technology capacity', paper presented at Science, Technology and Industry (SETI) workshop, Rome.

Criscuolo, P., R. Nasula and B. Verspagen (2005), 'Role of home and host country innovation systems in R&D internationalisation: a patent citation analysis', *Economics of Innovation and New Technology*, **14** (5), 417–33.

Cuervo-Cazurra, A. (2008), 'The multinationalization of developing country MNEs: the case of *multilatinas*', *Journal of International Management*, **14**, 138–54.

Da Silva Lopes, T. (2005), 'Competing with multinationals: strategies of the Portuguese alcohol industry', *Business History*, **79**, 559–85.

Dunning, J. H. (1993), *The Globalisation of Business*, London and New York: Routledge.

Dunning, J.H. (1994), 'Multinational enterprises and the globalization of innovatory capacity', *Research Policy*, **23**, 67–8.

Dunning, J.H. and S.M. Lundan (2009), 'The internationalization of corporate R&D: a review of the evidence and some policy implications for home countries', *Review of Policy Research*, **26**, 13–34.

Dunning, J. and R. Narula (1996), 'The investment development path revisited: some emerging issues', in Dunning and Narula (eds), *Foreign Direct Investment and Governments: Catalysts for Economic Restructuring*, London and New York: Routledge, pp. 1–40.

Echánove, F. and C. Steffen (2005), 'Agribusiness and farmers in Mexico: the importance of contractual relations', *The Geographical Journal*, **171**, 166–76.

ECLAC (ed.) (2005), *Trans-Latins in the Food and Beverages Industry*, Santiago de Chile: ECLAC (UN).

Edler, J. (2008), 'Creative internationalization: widening the perspectives on analysis and policy regarding international R&D activities', *Journal of Technology Transfer*, **33**, 337–52.

Erken, H. and V. Gilsing (2005), 'Relocation of R&D – a Dutch perspective', *Technovation*, **25**, 1079–92.

Farina, E. and A. Viegas (2005), 'Multinational firms in the Brazilian food industry', in R. Rama (ed.), *Multinational Agribusinesses*, New York and London: Haworth Press, pp. 283–321.

Filippaios, F., R. Pearce, M. Papanastassiou and R. Rama (2009), 'New forms of organisation and R&D internationalisation among the world's 100 largest food and beverages multinationals', *Research Policy*, **38**, 1032–43.

Filippaios, F. and R. Rama (2008), 'Globalisation or regionalistion? The strategies of the world's largest food and beverages MNEs', *European Management Journal*, **26**, 59–72.

Food and Agriculture Organization (FAO) (2012), Trends and Impact of Foreign Investment in Developing Country Agriculture: Evidence from Case Studies, Rome: Food and Agriculture Organization of the United Nations, Trade and Market Division.

Frankho, L.G. (1989), 'Global corporate competition: who's winning, who's losing, and the R&D factor as one reason why', *Strategic Management Journal*, **10**, 449–74.

Gabel, M. and H. Bruner (2003), *Global Inc. An Atlas of the Multinational Corporation*, New York: New Press.

Galizzi, G. and L. Venturini (2008), 'Nature and determinants of product innovation in a competitive environment of changing vertical relationships', in R. Rama (ed.), *Handbook of Innovation in the Food and Drink Industry*, New York and London: Taylor & Francis, pp. 51–79.

Gallo, A.E. (1995), 'Are there too many new product introductions in US food marketing?', *Journal of Food Distribution Research*, **26**, 9–13.

Gassmann, O. and M. von Zedtwitz (1998), 'Organization of industrial R&D on a global scale', *R&D Management*, **28**, 147–61.

Gerybadze, A. and G. Reger (1999), 'Globalization of R&D: recent changes in the management of innovation in transnational corporations', *Research Policy*, **28**, 251–74.

Goerzen, A. and P.W. Beamish (2003), 'Geographic scope and multinational enterprise performance', *Strategic Management Journal*, **24**, 1289–306.

Gopinath, M., D. Pick and U. Vasavada (1999), 'The economics of foreign direct investment and trade with an application to the U.S. food processing industry', *American Journal of Agricultural Economics*, **81**, 442–52.

Griffith, D.A., S.T. Cavusgil and S. Xu (2008), 'Emerging themes in international business research', *Journal of International Business Studies*, **39**, 1229–35.

Griliches, Z. (1990), 'Patent statistics as economic indicators: a survey', *Journal of Economic Literature*, **28** (4), 1661–707.

Gutman, G., R. Bisang, P. Lavarello, M. Campi and V. Robert (2006), 'Les mutations agricoles et agroalimentaires des années 90: libéralisation, changement technologique, firmes multinationales', *Région et Développement*, **23**, 215–46.

Ietto-Gillies, G. (2002), *Transnational Corporations: Fragmentation amidst Integration*, New York: Routledge.

Ietto-Gillies, G. (2005), *Transnational Corporations and International Production: Concepts, Theories and Effects*, Cheltenham, UK and Northampton, MA, USA: Edward Elgar.

Johanson, J. and J.-E. Vahlne (1977), 'The internationalization process of the firm: a model of knowledge development and increasing foreign markets commitments', *Journal of International Business Studies*, **8** (1), 23–32.

Knickerbocker, F.T. (1973), *Oligopolistic Reaction and Multinational Enterprise*, Cambridge, MA: Harvard University Press.

Kozul-Wright, R. and R. Rowthorn (1998), 'Spoilt for choice? Multinational corporations and the geography of international production', *Oxford Review of Economic Policy*, **14**, 74–92.

Kuemmerle, W. (1999), 'Foreign direct investment in industrial research in the pharmaceutical and electronics industries: results from a survey of multinational firms', *Research Policy*, **28**, 179–93.

Lundvall, B.Å. (1988), 'Innovation as an interactive process: from user–producer interaction to the national system of innovation', in G. Dosi, C. Freeman, R. Nelson, G. Silverberg and L. Soete (eds), *Technical Change and Economic Theory*, London and New York: Pinter, pp. 349–69.

Makki, S.S., A. Somwaru and C. Bolling (2004), 'Determinants of foreign direct investment in the food-processing industry: a comparative analysis of developed and developing economies', in US Department of Agriculture Economic Research Service (ed.), Washington, DC: Market and Trade Economics Division of ERS, pp. 1–8, available at: http://ageconsearch.umn.edu/bitstream/123456789/7946/1/35030060.pdf.

Mansfield, B. (2003), 'Spatializing globalization: a "geography of quality" in the seafood industry', *Economic Geography*, **79**, 1–16.

Martínez, C. and D. Guellec (2004), 'Overview of recent changes and comparison of patent regimes in the United States, Japan and Europe', Chapter 7 in *Patents, Innovation and Economic Performance. OECD Conference Proceedings*, Paris: OECD, pp.127–62.

Martínez, C., and R. Rama (2012), 'Home or next door? Patenting by European food and beverage multinationals', *Technology Analysis and Strategic Management*, **24** (7), 647–61.

McCann, P. and R. Mudambi (2004), 'The location behaviour of the multinational enterprise: some analytical issues', *Growth and Change*, **35**, 491–524.

Muller, A. and R. Van Tulder (2005), 'Exploring patterns of upstream internationalization: the role of home-region "stickiness"', ERS-2005-084-ORG, ERIM Report Series Research in Management, Rotterdam.

Ning, Y. and M.R. Reed (1995), 'Locational determinants of the US direct foreign investment in food and kindred products', *Agribusiness. An International Journal*, **11**, 77–85.

Oman, C., F. Chesnais, J. Pelzman and R. Rama (1989), *New Forms of Investment in Developing Country Industries: Mining, Petrochemicals, Automobiles, Textiles, Food*, Paris: OECD.

Organisation for Economic Co-operation and Development (OECD) (1979), *Impact of Multinational Enterprises on National Scientific and Technical Capacities*, Paris: OECD.

Organisation for Economic Co-operation and Development (OECD) (2004), *Handbook on Economic Globalisation Indicators*, Paris: OECD.

Organisation for Economic Co-operation and Development (OECD) (2005), 'Background Report. Internationalisation of R&D: Trends, Issues and Implications for S&T Policies. A Review of the Literature', OECD Forum on the Internationalisation of R&D, Brussels.

Organisation for Economic Co-operation and Development (OECD) (2008), *The Internationalization of Business R&D*, Paris: OECD.

Organisation for Economic Co-operation and Development (OECD) (2009), *Patent Statistics Manual*, Paris: OECD.

Osegowitsch, T. and A. Sammartino (2008), 'Reassessing (home-)regionalisation', *Journal of International Business Studies*, **39**, 184–96.

Palpacuer, F. and S. Tozanli (2008), 'Changing governance patterns in European food chains: the rise of a new divide between global players and regional producers', *Transnational Corporations*, **17**, 69–100.

Patel, P. (1995), 'Localised production of technology for global markets', *Cambridge Journal of Economics*, **19**, 141–53.

Patel, P. and K. Pavitt (1991), 'Large firms in the production of the world's technology: an important case of "non-globalisation"', *Journal of International Business Studies*, **22**, 1–21.

Patel, P. and K. Pavitt (1995), 'Patterns of technological activity: their measurement and interpretation', in P. Stoneman (ed.), *Handbook of the Economics of Innovation and Technological Change*, Oxford: Blackwell, pp.14–51.

Patel, P. and K. Pavitt (1997), 'The technological competencies of the world's largest firms: complex and path-dependent, but not much variety', *Research Policy*, **26**, 141–56.

Patel, P. and M. Vega (1999), 'Patterns of internationalisation of corporate technology: location vs. home country advantages', *Research Policy*, **28**, 145–55.

Pick, D. and T. Worth (2005), 'Foreign direct investment in the U.S. food and kindred products', in R. Rama (ed.), *Multinational Agribusinesses*, New York and London: Haworth Press pp.149–64.

Pozzobon, D.M. (2008), 'Explorando solucoes internacionais: O caso dos frigoríficos brasileiros', in ANPAD (ed.), *XXXI Encontro da ANPAD*, Rio de Janeiro: ANPAD, pp.1–16.

Pritchard, B. (2005), 'The internationalization paths of Australian and New Zealand food MNEs', in R. Rama (ed.), *Multinational Agribusinesses*, New York and London: Haworth Press, pp.219–52.

Rama, R. (1996), 'Les multinationales et l'innovation: localisation des activités technologiques de l'agro-alimentaire', *Économie Rurale. Paris*, **231**, 62–8.

Rama, R. (1999), 'Innovation and profitability of global food firms: testing for differences in the influence of the home base', *Environment and Planning A*, **31**, 735–51.

Rama, R. and J. Wilkinson (2008), 'Foreign direct investment and agri-food value-chains in developing countries: a review of the main issues', *Commodity Markets Review*, 2007–08, 51–66.

Reddy, P. (2000), *Globalization of R&D: Implications for Innovation Systems in Host Countries*, London and New York: Routledge.

Rugman, A.M. (1987), 'The firm specific advantages of Canadian multinationals', *Journal of International Economic Studies*, **2**, 1–14.

Rugman, A. (2005a), *The Regional Multinationals: MNEs and 'Global' Strategic Management*, Cambridge: Cambridge University Press.

Rugman, A.M. (2005b), 'A further comment on the myth of globalization', *Journal of International Management*, **11**, 441–45.

Rugman, A. and S. Girod (2003), 'Retail multinationals and globalization: the evidence is regional', *European Management Journal*, **21**, 24–37.

Rugman, A. and A. Verbeke (2002), 'The regional multinationals: the location-bound drivers of global strategy', Templeton Research Paper 2002, University of Oxford, Oxford.

Rugman, A. and A. Verbeke (2004), 'A perspective on regional and global strategies of multinational enterprises', *Journal of International Business Studies*, **35**, 3–18.

Sachwald, F. (2008), 'Location choices within global innovation networks: the case of Europe', *Journal of Technology Transfer*, **33**, 364–78.

Schvarzer, J. (1989), *Bunge & Born: Crecimiento y diversificación de un grupo económico*, Buenos Aires: CISEA.

Selvanathan, S. (2006), 'Consumption patterns of food, tobacco and beverages: a cross-country analysis', *Applied Economics*, **38**, 1567–84.

Senauer, B. and L. Venturini (2005), 'The globalization of food systems: a conceptual framework and empirical patterns', The Food Industry Center, University of Minnesota, St Paul, MN.

Serapio, M.G., H. Takabumi and D. Dalton (2004), 'Internationalization of research and development: empirical trends and theoretical perspectives', in Serapio and Takabumi (eds), *Internationalization of Research and Development and the Emergence of Global R&D Networks*, Amsterdam: Elsevier, pp. 85–112.

Shenkar, O. (2001), 'Cultural distance revisited: towards a more rigorous conceptualization and measurement of cultural differences', *Journal of International Business Studies*, **32**, 519–35.

Sim, A.B. (2007), 'Emerging Southeast Asian and Taiwanese multinational firms and their internationalization strategies', paper presented at the Oxford Business and Economics Conference, Oxford, 24–27 June.

Tozanli, S. (2005), 'The rise of global enterprises in the world's food chain', in R. Rama (ed.), *Multinational Agribusinesses*, London and New York: Haworth Press, pp. 1–72.

UNCTAD (2005), 'World Investment Report 2005. Transnational Corporations and the internationalization of R&D', United Nations, New York and Geneva.

UNCTAD (2009), 'World Investment Report 2009. Transnational Corporations, Agricultural Production and Development', United Nations, Geneva.

von Tunzelmann, G.N. (1998), 'Localized technological search and multi-technology companies', *Economics of Innovation and New Technology*, **6**, 231–55.

von Zedtwitz, M. and O. Gassmann (2002), 'Market versus technology drive in R&D internationalization: four different patterns of managing research and development', *Research Policy*, **31**, 569–88.

von Zedtwitz, M., O. Gassmann and R. Boutellier (2004), 'Organizing global R&D, challenges and dilemmas', *Journal of International Management*, **10**, 21–49.

Wendt, M. and G. Pedersen (2006), 'Foreign direct investment in the food manufacturing industry', The Food Industry Center, University of Minnesota, St Paul, MN.

APPENDIX 12A.1

The sources of AGRODATA, a database compiled by the Institut Agronomique Méditérrannéen de Montpellier (France), are Moody's Industrial Manual, the Fortune Directory of the 500 largest corporations, the 'Dossier 5.000' of the largest European corporations, Dun & Bradstreet, the annual reports of the enterprises and so on. The Top 100 are not continuing firms since some companies have dropped out of this group for a variety of reasons (for example, acquisitions by another firm) and 'new' groups have become large enough to be part of it. In English, Tozanli (2005) provide tables containing some of the data on the Top 100. In this chapter, however, we also use unpublished information. Information on the IAMM and AGRODATA (in French) is available on the following web page: http://www.iamm.fr/default.htm.

APPENDIX 12A.2

The companies analysed in this subsection are European-based multinationals included in the worldwide ranking of agro-food multinationals in the AGRODATA database (see Appendix 12A1). We combined information from this source and from other databases on corporate information and patents to obtain a global picture of their R&D facilities and patenting activities.

First, we identified all the affiliates of the selected F&B MNEs and extracted information regarding their names, locations and principal industrial sectors of activity from the Bureau van Dijk (BvD) AMADEUS database, version March 2008. Second, we matched patent counts to the company names corresponding to the F&B MNEs selected. We are aware that mergers and acquisitions and the closure of affiliates prior to the compilation of the information on affiliates may alter patent counts but, like Criscuolo et al. (2005), we feel that this methodology is acceptable for our purposes, since most multinationals apply for the majority of their patents using variations of their corporate name. We extracted information from the September 2008 EPO Worldwide Patent Statistics Database (PATSTAT) on USPTO patent grants and EPO applications filed by the F&B MNEs sampled; we obtained from Amadeus the names of all their affiliates and corresponding host countries and matched them with the names and countries of residence of EPO applicants and USPTO assignees.

References

Criscuolo, P., R. Narula, and B. Verspagen (2002), 'The relative importance of home and host innovation systems in the internationalisation of MNE R&D: a patent citation analysis', Eindhoven Centre for Innovation Studies, The Netherlands.

Tozanli, S. (2005), 'The rise of global enterprises in the world's food chain', in R. Rama (ed.), *Multinational Agribusinesses*, London and New York: Haworth Press, pp. 1–72.

13 Social capital and the development of industrial clusters: the northwest Ohio greenhouse cluster
Michael C. Carroll and Neil Reid*

13.1 INTRODUCTION

Much has been written about how social capital enhances economic activity. The literature credits social capital with reducing transaction costs, enhancing trust, and aiding knowledge diffusion. Unfortunately, most of the literature simply takes the theoretical underpinnings of social capital as given. Little attention is paid to the levels on which social capital operates, for example, individual, organizational, or regional – it is not uncommon to see social capital characteristics identified between individuals and then automatically extended to firm-to-firm interactions, for example.

This chapter examines the theoretical underpinnings of social capital as it relates to local economic development. In particular it looks at how social capital can be and has been used to facilitate the growth of an industrial cluster. The chapter is divided as follows. Section 13.2 provides a brief overview of the social capital literature and defines the concept. Section 13.3 examines the cognitive limits of individual actors and how these limits influence the optimal size and composition of a social capital network. Section 13.4 utilizes the case study of the northwest Ohio greenhouse cluster to demonstrate how the concept of social capital was used to facilitate the growth and development of that cluster. In the final section we discuss the ways in which the theoretical ideas presented in the earlier sections are relevant to the development of the greenhouse cluster.

13.2 DEFINING AND MEASURING SOCIAL CAPITAL

Social capital is one of those omnipresent topics in many current academic literatures. Many have attempted to define the concept but few have done it complete justice. The World Bank defines social capital as the institutions, relationships, and norms that shape the quality and quantity of a society's social interactions (World Bank, 2002), a definition which largely follows Putnam's (1993) original approach. Somewhat slightly shifting focus, Putnam (1995, 2000) later summarizes social capital in terms of the horizontal associations between people, to include the 'social networks and the norms of reciprocity and trustworthiness that arise from them' (Putnam, 2000, p. 67). Here, Putnam distinguished between 'bonding' and 'bridging' forms of social capital. Bonding social capital refers to the links between like-minded people and therefore reinforces homogeneity. Bridging social capital refers to the building of connections between heterogeneous groups. He argued that bridging social capital is often fragile but is likely to enhance social inclusion (Carroll and Stanfield, 2003).

More often than not, social capital is treated as a separate and distinct asset of a community. It is believed that regions that have properly invested in social capital development can expect to reap positive economic expansion (World Bank, 2002). More properly, social capital 'flows from the endowment of mutually respecting and trusting relationships, which enable a group to pursue its shared goals more effectively' (Szreter, 2000, p. 57). If the goals are economic, social capital is better viewed as an indication of the economy's embeddedness (Carroll and Stanfield, 2003). In regions that possess high levels of social capital, the economic process is enmeshed in the social fabric of the community. In other words, there is no completely separate economic sphere with a distinct set of motives and function. In global market economies this integration may not be complete. Therefore, it may be more useful to speak of the degree to which the local economy is embedded. Areas with high social capital may have a higher degree of economic embeddedness, whereby social capital becomes an enabling linkage of economic activity.

Social capital, however, is very difficult to measure. Since social capital is often unique to certain segments of the economic community, sampling strategies must be aggressive and the process is often very time-consuming. However, given the difficulty and expense, a number of projects have attempted to provide a general measure of social capital (World Bank, 2002; Grootaert et al., 2003). Most of these employ some form of questionnaire methodology. The best known of these projects include the World Bank's Social Capital Assessment Tool (SOCAT) and the Social Capital Integrated Questionnaire (SC-IQ).

In the literature, one of the links between social capital and local economic development relates to the role which social capital may play in the development of clusters and networks. Most cluster projects attempt to increase the number of linkages which each cluster participant has in the cluster (Casper and Murray, 2005; Casper, 2007). It is generally assumed that the denser the network – the larger the number of connections for the members – the better it is for the cluster, because the denser the network the greater is the probability and speed of knowledge transfers. Also, a greater density lessens the risk of network collapse if a particular key actor were to drop out.

13.3   HUMAN COGNITIVE LIMITS AND SOCIAL CAPITAL

One of the issues rarely discussed in the local or urban economic development literature, however, is that limits in human cognition may not permit the scale and types of network densities that many theories suggest might be necessary to support successful cluster development.

Human cognition is defined in terms of the dimensions of perceptions, mental concepts, memory, reasoning, decision making, information gathering, problem solving, and language acquisition (Goldstein, 2008). The reason is that the management of knowledge and human cognition are linked. Individuals use their senses to acquire information, and then use the information to create mental models. 'When confronted with a highly complex world, the mind constructs a simple mental model of reality and tries to work within that model. The model may have weaknesses, but the individual will try to behave rationally within the constraints or boundaries of that model' (Dalkir, 2005,

p. 61). Through the use of these mental models, humans process and organize information into bounded rational behavior and knowledgeable actions developing personalized mental concepts such as schema, cognitive maps, and scripts (Dalkir, 2005).

In the seminal work of Miller (1956a), cognitive limits are limited to seven plus or minus two absolute judgments. These cognitive limitations, which are specifically human-capacity limits known as 'elements', are the limitations to processing information in a short-term working memory. Miller finds that an individual can remember more items if the items are coded or 'chunked'.[1] For example, an individual recalls learned patterns, such as a recognized sequence of words or identified groups of objects from memory and past experiences. Or in group behavior, humans will more easily associate with those with similar backgrounds because they process the information less analytically. An individual's perception is also influenced by stored information in long-term memory which is brought forth to the daily working memory, thereby greatly increasing the working memory. More recent research, termed the 'psychological cognitive revolution' (Miller, 2003), emphasizes that individuals are information processors, and applied cognitive psychology and instructional design maintains that an individual's processing ability is limited, and individuals may expand and develop expertise by applying learning methods. In a complex society this is facilitated by the fact that humans create institutions to act as repositories for knowledge precisely to assist individual cognitive reasoning and social interaction processes (Anderson, 1983, 2005). The assumed link between social capital, networks, and clusters is the assumption that social capital in part plays the role of being such a repository for the network or cluster, while also in part helping to increase the repositories of knowledge within networks and clusters. At the same time, the informal institutions, rules, and norms associated with social capital may help cluster or network members to overcome their individual cognitive limitations.

13.3.1   Boundaries of Rationality, Cognitive Capacity, and Limited Membership

A difficulty with this argument, however, is that individual interactions and communication behavior within a group (such as a cluster or network) may be both limited, and also constrained by the group behavior. With every additional member to the group, a more than symmetrical increase in potential reciprocal interactions and relationships occurs (Kephart, 1950). These increased contacts and the resulting complexity of relationships may increase the cognitive load, at some point reaching the cognitive capacity limits of individuals' mental perspectives (Stiller and Dunbar, 2007) and leading to cognitive overload. In such cases, a network actor's negative understanding and communication limits thereby challenge any coherent information flow, resulting in negative social capital (Carroll and Stanfield, 2003; Burt and Ronchi, 2007).

Information overload may therefore limit cognitive information processing due to the number of elements used between sender and receiver (Miller, 1960). The factors necessary for successful individual membership behavior within collective group structures (institutions) require cognitive capacity, involving learned heuristic models, often called 'schemata'. That is, if schemata are learned, there is a need for fewer elements of working or short-term cognitive capacity (van Merrienboer and Sweller, 2005). For membership, groups may require high element characteristics for cohesiveness, density, and closed boundaries or low density, low cohesiveness, and open boundaries, and sometimes a more complex mixture of these characteristics. Understanding and developing cognitive social skills (schemata and scripts) may be the limiting factor for most individuals (Todd and Gigerenzer, 2007).

Considering the similarities and differences of individuals within a group, group efficiency improves the goal attainment of collective action because of division of labor, roles played, and collective knowledge (Kudo and Dunbar, 2001; Lehmann et al., 2007). For example, an individual's long-term experiences (sometimes called 'mental images') and various types of reciprocity allow for an individual to construct temporal relationships such as the development of trust or distrust, development of positive or negative social capital, and motivation to resist or interact with others (Dunbar, 1996, 2004). The attractiveness of a group or structured network to an individual, and the individual's choice to be a member, is dependent on the concurrence of the collective structure and the individual's goals (Napier and Gershenfeld, 1999; Oyserman, 2003). Economic cluster formation is argued to increase the potential for the number of relational contacts; at the same time, these relational contacts increase the complexity of information flow, increasing the cognitive load of individual actors. The network structure for knowledge dissemination, maintenance, and accumulation must be defined for each individual actor's choice as a member (Pinch et al., 2003).

The cognitive passage from an individual's own participation and interests to achieve her or his own goals within a group is best understood through the use of the concept called 'theory of mind'. An individual's own goals with a group lead to a group collective's goals, initiating group interaction and the resultant relationships among other groups. The interactions between individual and social cognition are best understood in the theory of mind through the concept of an individual's perceptual mentalization of others' intentions. Neural research, through the use of brain imaging, infers the mentalization of intentions (Frith and Frith, 1999, 2006). Shared attention is understood as communicative intent, or the interaction of the group's shared mentalizations for group goals (Sperber and Wilson, 1995). By associating these mentalizations (chunking) from long-term memory, individuals may interact and participate in multiple group network structures. The overcoming of possible cognitive overload is accomplished by pre-learned, individual mental representations of information as knowledge content (Saxe, 2006), and shared attention through interpersonal contacts is the best way to transplant innovative new knowledge (Rogers, 2003; Wolfe and Gertler, 2004). It is here that institutions, norms, and habits act as repositories of knowledge and representative agencies for social development, and institutionalized group structures allow for formal and informal codes of membership behavior to be subjectively accepted. Individuals obtain organizational network benefits by means of membership in large clubs, unions, or trade organizations (Olson, 1971), although the demands of keeping track of the complexity of informational processing with relationship characteristics in interpersonal contacts are still limited by individual cognitive social calculations.

Dunbar's research describes the development of individual cognitive abilities as the result of benefits of social interaction and shared cooperation within group membership, which is sometimes collaborative and cooperative, and more often than not, manipulative, to achieve an individual goal (Dunbar, 1998). Human relationships and organization structures are limited by personal levels of intentionality and memory

(Dunbar and Spoors, 1995; Hill and Dunbar, 2003; Stiller and Dunbar, 2007). An individual's cognitive limits due to the increasing complexity of group interactions, thereby restricts an individual's group network size. Given the cognitive limits of an individual's capacity, the maximum human social group size is estimated at 150. This is the maximum number of individuals one person can maintain as social possibilities for interaction, along with the elements of information for processing similarities and differences, all of which are limited by individual cognition. One the other hand, more intense relationships are supported by smaller groups of approximately 50 (Hill and Dunbar, 2003). The patterns of group size of 50 and 150 therefore profile both the constraints of human cognitive information processing capacity and the evolutionary development of human cognitive information processing capacity (Dunbar et al., 2005). The cluster and network project initiated in the greenhouse industry of northwest Ohio and described in the following section explicitly took account of these various social capital, cognitive, and individual–group interaction features, in terms of its design logic, and also its mode of network formation, membership, and goal-setting objectives.

13.4   THE NORTHWEST OHIO GREENHOUSE CLUSTER PROJECT

The northwest Ohio greenhouse cluster project began in 2003 and ended in 2011.[2] The goal of the project (funded by the US Department of Agriculture: USDA) was to help the northwest Ohio greenhouse industry enhance its economic competitiveness. As Principal Investigators on the project our role was one of overall project coordination. The industry comprises 70+ family-owned small and medium-sized enterprises (SMEs) and is in the mature stage of the industrial life cycle. The industry faced (and continues to face) some significant competitive challenges including international competition, high energy costs, and stagnant markets. After conducting an initial assessment of the industry (including a survey of growers and a SWOT analysis) the research team (led by the two authors) agreed that some of the challenges facing the industry (a) were common to many growers and (b) could best be overcome if the growers came together to address them collectively and collaboratively.

However, we knew that getting the growers to engage in collaborative initiatives (see Figure 13.1) would be challenging. The growers were fiercely independent, had little history of collaboration, were conservative in their business practices, and because they were struggling to keep their heads above water had little time or inclination to think about doing things any differently from what they had done for decades. Further, we were viewed as outsiders and did not share any social capital with the group. The group in many instances actually had negative social capital created over decades of competition.

In October 2003 we made a presentation to eight growers. Our objective was to try to get the growers to consider, and eventually participate in, collaborative projects that would help their competitiveness. The growers who attended the presentation were carefully chosen. In consultation with locally based USDA research scientists we identified and invited growers who were considered to be among the more open-minded,

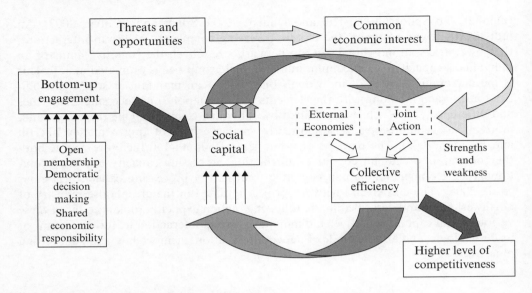

Figure 13.1   Cluster-based economic development

innovative, and forward thinking in the region. It was critical that we got these growers to explore the possibility of coming together to collectively address their industry's challenges.

In preparing our presentation we were aware of numerous studies that suggested that collaboration among competitors was more likely when an industry (and its constituent members) faced exogenous circumstances that threatened its future economic viability (Nadvi, 1999; Svendsen and Svendsen, 2000). As a result our SWOT analysis became the centerpiece of the message that we delivered to the growers. We asked the growers the following question – how do you leverage your *strengths* to take advantage of *opportunities* to overcome *weaknesses* and address *threats*?

In the presentation we documented the current status of their industry and, more importantly, painted a picture of what the future might hold if the industry continued on its current trajectory. The picture that we painted can best be described as bleak. On the other hand we offered the growers a possible pathway which, if they decided to follow it, would help them begin to address some of the competitive challenges that their industry was facing. This pathway focused on growers collectively defining their common economic interests (Figure 13.1), identifying their main challenges, and working collaboratively to address them. The growers agreed to consider this approach. Approximately six weeks later (December 2003) the group reconvened. At that meeting the growers informed us that they were willing to begin the process of working towards collaborative problem solving. In January 2004, with the support of the eight growers, we attended the annual winter conference of the Toledo Area Flower and Vegetable Growers Association (TAFVGA) and asked the broader grower community to participate in the project. With a critical mass of growers on board the next step was to staff the project. The USDA grant afforded sufficient funds to engage a full-time project manager and a half-time project champion.

Choosing the project manager and project champion were critical steps. The primary function of the project manager was to oversee the day-to-day running of the project, while the role of the project champion was to visit growers in their greenhouses, learn about the challenges they were facing, and identify opportunities for collaboration (that is, create positive social capital). Both positions required unique skill sets.

Ideally, the project manager should have experience running an SME. All of the greenhouses were SMEs and having someone running the day-to-day activities of the project who understood what it was like to run a small business would be beneficial. A project manager with experience in economic development would also be beneficial. This was, after all, an economic development initiative designed to help northwest Ohio greenhouses become more economically competitive. Excellent networking, brokering, and communication skills were also a prerequisite for the job. We knew that getting the growers to come together and collaborate would be challenging, and an individual with this skill set would be a significant advantage.

The person who was hired to fill the position of project manager was the ideal candidate. He had previously owned and operated his own laundry and dry cleaning business, had served as Commissioner of Economic Development for the City of Toledo, and brought the added bonus of having worked as a project manager on a similar University of Toledo project focused on solar energy. Due to his diverse experience this individual was very well networked within the local business, economic development, and university communities and brought with him vast experience of brokering deals in a number of different environments.

With regard to the position of project champion it was important that this individual also have excellent networking, brokering, and communication skills. However, because this person was effectively the field agent for the project and would spend much of his/her time visiting greenhouses and talking with individual owners it was critical that this also had to be someone who had experience in the industry and who was respected and trusted by the growers. The importance of having someone who was trusted was such that we decided to let the growers guide us in our choice. We, therefore, engaged the growers in the search process. The individual identified by the growers was an interesting choice. He was an agricultural extension agent for Michigan State University. The fact that the growers' preferred candidate was currently employed full-time in a neighboring state presented both opportunities and challenges. The major challenge to overcome was negotiating an agreement with Michigan State University that would allow our chosen candidate to spend two days a week helping growers in Ohio who were, in all reality, in competition with growers in Michigan. Our colleagues in Michigan were very excited about our proposed project in northwest Ohio, however, and were interested in the possibility of replicating it in southeastern Michigan if it proved to be successful. Thus having one of their extension agents participate in our project was highly attractive to them as it would provide them with inside knowledge of how the various aspects of our project were implemented. The process of choosing the project champion was the first step in enhancing the stock of social capital among the network of growers. We had anticipated that there might be disagreement among the growers as to who should fill the role of project champion and were pleasantly surprised when the growers very quickly coalesced around one individual. More likely than not this was a reflection of the esteem with which this individual was held by the growers rather than our ability to bring the

Table 13.1   Timetable of major initiatives in the northwest Ohio greenhouse project

Initiative	Date launched
Initial meeting with growers	October 2004
Project manager hired	January 2005
Project champion hired	May 2005
Branding and marketing consultants hired	August 2005
Maumee Valley Grower brand introduced	November 2005
First Maumee Valley Grower collaborative marketing campaign	March 2006
Initial discussions about natural gas purchasing program take place	March 2006
Northwest Ohio natural gas purchasing program established	October 2006
Natural gas purchasing program expanded statewide	June 2007
Natural gas purchasing program expanded into Michigan	April 2008

growers to agreement on this decision.[3] The project manager was hired in January 2005 and the project champion in May 2005.

With the project manager and the project champion in place the next step was to bring the growers together on a regular basis to identify common challenges and solutions to those challenges. We agreed, in consultation with the growers, that monthly meetings would work best and that the Toledo Botanical Gardens (a neutral site) was a meeting venue that would be acceptable to all growers. The monthly meetings would be open to all growers plus any other stakeholders (academics, local economic development officials, local elected officials, and so on) who were interested in attending. We chaired the early stakeholder meetings but worked very closely with the growers (the original eight) to establish meeting agendas. Getting growers involved early on in agenda and goal setting, establishing a culture of bottom-up engagement (Figure 13.1), and getting growers to take ownership of the process was, in our minds, critical to both the short- and long-term success of the project. The monthly stakeholder meetings became critical in building social capital. In addition to the regular business portion of the meeting, growers would inevitably remain behind afterwards and engage in conversation.

With stakeholder meetings underway it was important that we move as quickly as possible to identify and implement the first collaborative project. The growers were busy. They had little patience for meetings that achieved nothing. Hence we had to move swiftly. The first project had to have certain characteristics. First, it had to demonstrate the value of collaboration. Second, it had to have a high probability of success. Failure in the first project would result in a number of growers (perhaps all) giving up on the idea of collaboration and walking away from the project. Third, the project had to be non-threatening to growers. It could not, for example, require them to share proprietary information or invest resources in what they perceived to be a risky venture. Fourth, the project had to enhance the stock of social capital among the growers. It had to engage as many growers as possible and had to enable them to build trust and respect for one another. We were convinced that enhancing the stock of social capital in this initial project would lay the foundation for getting the growers to engage in more complex, perhaps more risky collaborative projects in the future (Figure 13.1).

After discussion the growers agreed that the first project should focus on branding and marketing of the industry. This was a project that met the four criterian identified above. In addition, it met a critical need of the industry. The industry had no brand identity in the region and the growers admitted that their individual marketing efforts were naive and non-strategic. A local branding and marketing firm was hired to assist the growers in developing a brand identity. Thus was born the Maumee Valley Growers brand (www.maumeevalleygrowers.com). The brand was launched in November 2005 and then used as the underpinnings of a comprehensive and strategic marketing campaign that included the growers participating in collaborative advertising efforts such as purchasing full-page common space in local newspapers where participating growers advertised their individual businesses. The first of many collaborative marketing efforts was set in motion in March 2006. The process of arriving at agreement on a brand identity and developing a collaborative marketing strategy brought the growers together in a completely new way, and resulted in new relationships being established and existing ones being strengthened. More importantly they were beginning to see the benefits of collaboration.

Having successfully navigated the branding and marketing initiative, the growers were ready to tackle a more complex problem – that of high energy costs. After labor costs, energy costs were the second-largest variable cost with which the growers were burdened. The majority of the greenhouses were heated by natural gas. Natural gas is purchased on the spot market with growers making individual purchasing decisions. Purchasing natural gas involves a number of decisions with the most important being when to purchase, what volume to purchase, and for what length of time to lock-in a particular purchase contract. As we engaged in discussion with growers over the process of purchasing natural gas we discovered that they were spending an inordinate amount of time researching the natural gas market, agonizing over the purchase (when, how much, and for how long), and then second-guessing themselves once the purchase was made. We also discovered that the purchasing decisions being made by growers were often suboptimal. Our solution to the natural gas challenge was to engage a locally based natural gas consultant. The consultant would advise the growers on the vagaries of the natural gas market, engage them in strategic thinking about their natural gas needs, and make one single purchase on behalf of a collective group of growers. A group purchase of natural gas would generate economies of scale that would reduce the unit cost of natural gas to individual growers. While this seemed a rather straightforward and easily understandable concept (buy in bulk and save money) the successful implementation of this program took approximately seven months. We discovered that, despite the agonizing associated with individual purchases, the growers were very reluctant to give up the autonomy that independent decision making afforded them. In a group-purchasing scenario individual growers were concerned about who would make the buying decision, particularly if the group became large and the purchasing authority was delegated to a smaller decision-making subgroup. After approximately seven months of coaxing and cajoling on the part of the project manager, a sufficient number of growers agreed to purchase natural gas collectively and Grower Energy Solutions (the program's brand identity) was born in October 2006 (http://www.maumeevalleygrowers.com/mvga_natural_gas_program. htm). The fear among those growers that they would lose decision-making autonomy was well-founded. Such was the success of the program in northwest Ohio that growers in other parts of the state asked if they could join the group. Thus the program expanded in June 2007 and an 11-member statewide advisory board was established to make buying decisions on behalf of participating growers. Further expansion of the program occurred in April 2008 when growers in the neighboring state of Michigan joined the program.

Our ability to engage growers in the natural gas purchasing program was a major victory. We felt that it represented a significant breakthrough in the willingness of the growers to step outside of their comfort zone and to engage in collaborative initiatives. The natural gas purchasing initiative was also important because it engaged both retail and wholesale growers. The branding and marketing program had primarily benefited the retail growers, that is, growers who sold directly to the general public. The wholesale growers who sell directly to large buyers (primarily big-box stores such as Home Depot and Wal-Mart) had not benefited from the branding and marketing program. They did, however, benefit from the natural gas program. Indeed, due to their larger scale of operations, the wholesale growers were critical to the success of the natural gas purchasing program as their participation allowed the group to attain greater economies of scale more quickly.

In addition to the branding, marketing, and natural gas initiatives, the growers have come together on a number of other collaborative projects. These include an electricity purchasing program (modeled after the natural gas program), a plant purchasing program, and a recycling program. The growers have also engaged in a number of collaborative projects that have benefited the community, including beautification projects throughout the city, Habitat for Humanity, and Plant Purple (a pancreatic cancer awareness program). While growers have a long tradition of giving back to their community, the scale and scope of what they are able to do collectively is much greater than individual efforts.

As researchers utilizing federal funds to assist the northwest Ohio greenhouse industry it was incumbent upon us to conduct an assessment of the success of our efforts. This we did by conducting a number of surveys of growers. The data provided by these surveys suggested that we have been successful in our efforts to build social capital within the greenhouse industry (Reid and Smith, 2012). The first indicator of success can be found in the fact that growers continue to be engaged in the monthly stakeholder meetings. Average attendance at these meetings was 15.0 in 2004 but had risen to 23.3 in 2010. The fact that the group has held together and that these meetings continue to be well attended by growers is an indication that they see value in coming together and working with one another on identifying and solving common challenges. Another indicator that we were successful in building social capital comes from a 2009 survey in which 77.8 percent of growers indicated that they had an increased level of communication with their peers as a result of participating in the project. As part of our assessment of relationship building we also conducted a social network analysis of growers and non-grower stakeholders. This analysis compared sources of advice and support for the growers in 2007 and 2009. The analysis showed that between 2007 and 2009 the growers became more dependent upon one another for advice and support and less dependent on the project manager and champion for advice and support. Not only were growers building and strengthening relationships with one another but they were also building relationships with academic and community partners. For example, results from the

2009 survey showed that 57.4 percent of the growers said that the project had enhanced their access to university researchers. As result of their participation in this project the growers also exhibited a new-found optimism about their economic future. The same 2009 survey indicated that 57.4 percent were optimistic about the future of their business. This stands in stark contrast to the 27 percent who were similarly optimistic in 2004.

USDA funding for the project ended in August 2011. This means that the two local universities (University of Toledo and Bowling Green State University) have reduced their level of engagement with the project. The growers, however, are determined to see their collaborative efforts continue. They (the Maumee Valley Growers) have hired the project manager (whose position was defunded in August 2011 when the grant ended) as their half-time executive director. The project champion position was also defunded. The individual holding that position is still working in the region as an agricultural extension educator for Ohio State University, so she is still functioning as a resource for the industry.

13.5 CONCLUSIONS

This chapter examined the role social capital plays in industrial cluster formation from the perspective of a local economic development initiative. We explained how, in the case of the northwest Ohio greenhouse cluster, the building of social capital can be used to facilitate cluster formation and how social capital can lower the transaction costs in cluster activity. Prior to our engagement with the greenhouse industry the stock of social capital had been relatively low. Through a strategic process of bringing the growers together, helping them see the benefits of collaboration, and finally getting them to engage in successful collaborative initiatives, we were able to enhance the stock of social capital within the industry. In doing so we hope that we have been able to lay the foundation for ongoing collaborations among growers and between growers and non-growers (for example, academic and community partners).

We also described how the literature on human cognitive limits sometimes conflicts with traditional cluster theory. For example, most models show how cluster density needs to be maximized but human limits may not be able to support that level of interaction. In the case of the greenhouse cluster, however, the small size of the industry meant that we did not face that issue. Despite the existence of over 70 greenhouses in the region, only a subset of this population could really be considered as active participants in the cluster. Thus we have been able to build a fairly dense network of relationships within that subset of the industry. For example, 40 growers participate in the project's most popular initiative, the natural gas purchasing program. The fact that some growers choose not to participate in cluster initiatives may be explained by Madill et al.'s (2004, p. 355) observation that small business owners do not network because of a 'lack of time, lack of growth aspirations, as well as reluctance to network arising from the entrepreneur's need for independence'.

Our discussion of social capital also highlighted the importance of trust and bonding and suggested that these develop at different speeds. One of the key roles that we played within this project was to act as a bridge between the grower and academic communities.

Evidence suggests that we were successful at filling this role; as noted above, 57.4 percent of growers felt that the cluster brought them enhanced access to university researchers. This included researchers at the University of Toledo's Plant Science Research Center as well as faculty in the social and business sciences, all of whom worked with the industry to provide information and knowledge demanded by growers. The Urban Affairs Center at the University of Toledo and the Center for Regional Development at Bowling Green State University also utilized their extensive community connections to connect the growers with community partners. The project manager and champion also played a bridging role between the growers and the local community. For example, the project manager (as a result of a previous business relationship) was able to very quickly bring a local energy consultant to the table when the growers decided to explore the possibility of cooperative natural gas purchasing.

Our discussion of social capital also suggests that cluster members of similar backgrounds develop trust and bonding social capital with other members faster than if the backgrounds were different. It takes more effort to develop bridging social capital because the mind does not have consistent experiences to help process information. Within this project a number of different communities were represented. First and foremost this project represented a major collaborative initiative between the academic (public) and industry (private) sectors. Little social capital existed between these two groups and it was a slow process to build up the stock. Academia and private industry often have different agendas, work at different rates, and have different expectations. As academics, we viewed this project as an opportunity to test some ideas and theories related to cluster development and to bring these findings to the academic community via conference presentations and peer-reviewed publications. From the growers' perspective, they were primarily interested in enhancing their industry's economic competitiveness. Despite these differing agendas, both groups were able to coalesce around the realization that satisfying both agendas was mutually beneficial. From our perspective we wanted the cluster to succeed so that we could report this success (and the processes driving it) to our peers in academia. From the growers' perspective, they realized that the academic research that we were conducting would benefit them as it would generate new knowledge that would be of value to them.

One example of mutually beneficial research was a 2009 survey of northwest Ohio residents that provided critical information to the growers about customer profiles and consumer product preferences, while at the same time contributing to applied literature in marketing geography (Reid et al., 2009). A second set of communities that were represented within this project were the retail and wholesale growers. As noted above, the branding and marketing initiative benefited, almost exclusively, the retail growers. That particular project was chosen because it was deemed to be 'low-hanging fruit' and could be executed fairly expeditiously. The disadvantage, however, was that while the wholesale growers did participate in the brand selection process, it did not engage or benefit them once the marketing campaign was executed. This made the next project, the natural gas purchasing project, critical. It would engage retail and wholesale growers in a common project and would start to build social capital among those two communities of growers.

To a large extent the northwest Ohio greenhouse project had the building up of social capital as its central strategy. It was a strategy that ultimately enabled the growers to move beyond the passive agglomeration economies to which they already had access and to engage in meaningful collaboration that would allow them to achieve economic goals that were beyond the reach of any grower individually.

NOTES

* The authors would like to thank Mark Zeller for his work on the cognitive limits section.
1. Researchers support Miller's (1956b) inquiry that information and memory may be retained by association and grouping with other mental experiences (Tulving and Craik, 2000). That is, if a set of items have been structured or associated, recall capacity is greatly increased.
2. The project 'ended' in 2012 in the sense that USDA support of the project ceased. This means that the two universities engaged in this project, the University of Toledo and Bowling Green State University, will significantly reduce their level of engagement with the project. The growers continue to meet, however, and continue to identify and implement collaborative projects.
3. The project champion retired in 2007 and was replaced by an agricultural extension agent from Ohio State University.

REFERENCES

Anderson, J.R. (1983), *The Architecture of Cognition*, Cambridge, MA: Harvard University Press.
Anderson, J.R. (2005), *Cognitive Psychology and Its Implications*, (6th edn), New York: Worth.
Burt, R.S. and Ronchi, D. (2007), 'Teaching executives to see social capital: results from a field experiment', *Social Science Research*, **36** (3), 1156–83.
Carroll, M.C. and Stanfield, J.R. (2003), 'Social capital, Karl Polanyi, and American social and institutional economics', *Journal of Economic Issues*, **37** (2), June, 397–404.
Casper, S. (2007), 'How do technology clusters emerge and become sustainable? Social network formation and inter-firm mobility within the San Diego biotechnology cluster', *Research Policy*, **36**, 438–55.
Casper, S. and Murray, F. (2005), 'Careers and clusters: analyzing the career network dynamic of biotechnology clusters', *Journal of Engineering and Technology Management*, **22**, 51–74.
Dalkir, K. (2005), *Knowledge Management in Theory and Practice*, Amsterdam: Elsevier.
Dunbar, R. (1996), *Grooming, Gossip, and the Evolution of Language*, Cambridge, MA: Harvard University Press.
Dunbar, R.I.M. (1998), 'The social brain hypothesis', *Evolutionary Anthropology*, **6**, 178–90.
Dunbar, R. (2004), *The Human Story: A New History of Mankind's Evolution*, Chatham, UK: Faber & Faber.
Dunbar, R., Barrett, L. and Lycett, J. (2005), *Evolutionary Psychology: A Beginner's Guide*, Oxford: Oneworld.
Dunbar, R.I.M. and Spoors, M. (1995), 'Social networks, support cliques and kinship', *Human Nature*, **6** (3), 273–90.
Frith, C.D. and Frith, U. (1999), 'Interacting minds: a biological basis', *Science*, **286** (5445), 1692–6.
Frith, C.D. and Frith, U. (2006), 'The neural basis of mentalizing', *Neuron*, **50**, 531–4.
Goldstein, E.B. (2008), *Cognitive Psychology: Connecting Mind, Research, and Everyday Experience*, (2nd edn), Belmont, CA: Thomson Wadsworth.
Grootaert, C., Narayan, D., Jones, V.N. and Woolcock, M. (2003), 'Measuring social capital: an integrated questionnaire,' World Bank Working Paper 18, World Bank, Washington, DC.
Hill, R.A. and Dunbar, R.I.M. (2003), 'Social network size in humans', *Human Nature*, **14** (1), 53–72.
Kephart, W.M. (1950), 'A quantitative analysis of intragroup relationships', *American Journal of Sociology*, **55** (6), 544–9.
Kudo, H. and Dunbar, R.I.M. (2001), 'Neocortex size and social network size in primates', *Animal Behaviour*, **62**, 711–22.
Lehmann, J., Korstjens, A.H. and Dunbar, R.I.M. (2007), 'Group size, grooming and social cohesion in primates', *Animal Behaviour*, **74**, 1617–29.
Madill, J.J., Haines Jr G.H. and Riding, A.L. (2004), 'Networks and linkages among firms and organizations in the Ottawa-region technology cluster', *Entrepreneurship and Regional Development*, **16**, 351–68.
Miller, G.A. (1956a), 'The magical number seven, plus or minus two: some limits on our capacity for processing information', *Psychological Review*, **63** (2), 81–97.
Miller, G.A. (1956b), 'Information and memory', *Scientific American*, **195** (2), 42–6.

Miller, G.A. (2003), 'The cognitive revolution: a historical perspective', *Trends in Cognitive Science*, **7** (3), 141–4.

Miller, J.G. (1960), 'Information input overload and psychopathology', *American Journal of Psychiatry*, **116**, 695–704.

Nadvi, K. (1999), 'Collective efficiency and the collective failure: the response of the Sialkot surgical instrument cluster to global quality pressures', *World Development*, **27** (9), 1605–16.

Napier, R.W. and Gershenfeld, M.K. (1999), *Groups: Theory and Practice*, (6th edn), Boston, MA: Houghton Mifflin.

Olson, M. (1971), *The Logic of Collective Action*, (rev. edn). Cambridge, MA: Harvard University Press.

Oyserman, D. (2003), 'Self-concept and identity', in A. Tesser and N. Schwarz (eds), *Blackwell Handbook of Social Psychology: Intraindividual Processes*, Malden, MA: Blackwell, pp. 499–517.

Pinch, S., Henry, N., Jenkins, M. and Tallman, S. (2003), 'From "industrial districts" to "knowledge clusters": a model of knowledge dissemination and competitive advantage in industrial agglomerations', *Journal of Economic Geography*, **3** (4), 373–88.

Putnam, R.D. (1993), 'The prosperous community: social capital and public life', *American Prospect*, **4**, 35–42.

Putnam, R.D. (1995), 'Bowling alone: America's declining social capital', *Journal of Democracy*, **6** (1), 65–78.

Putnam, R.D. (2000), *Bowling Alone: The Collapse and Revival of American Community*, New York: Simon & Schuster.

Reid, N. and Smith, B.W. (2012), 'Assessing the success of an industrial cluster', *International Journal of Applied Geospatial Research*, **3** (3), 21–36.

Reid, N., Smith, B.W., Haase, D., Ross, P. Mirzoyants, A. and Gatrell, J.D. (2009), 'Marketing and growing place-based clusters: the case of the northwest Ohio greenhouse industry', *Papers of the Applied Geography Conferences*, **32**, 40–46.

Rogers, E.M. (2003), *Diffusion of Innovations*, (5th edn), New York: Free Press.

Saxe, R. (2006), 'Uniquely human social cognition', *Current Opinion in Neurobiology*, **16**, 235–9.

Sperber, D. and Wilson, D. (1995), *Relevance: Communication and Cognition* (2nd edn, Malden, MA: Blackwell.

Stiller, J. and Dunbar, R.I.M. (2007), 'Perspective-taking and memory capacity predict social network size', *Social Networks*, **29**, 93–104.

Svendsen, G.L.H. and Svendsen, G.T. (2000), 'Measuring social capital: the Danish co-operative dairy movement', *Sociologia Ruralis*, **40** (1), 72–86.

Szreter, S. (2000), 'Social capital, the economy, and education in historical perspective', in S. Baron, J. Field and T. Schuller (eds), *Social Capital: Critical Perspectives*, Oxford: Oxford University Press, pp. 56–69.

Todd, P.M. and Gigerenzer, G. (2007), 'Mechanisms of ecological rationality: heuristics and environments that make us smart', in R.I.M. Dunbar and L. Barrett (eds), *The Oxford Handbook of Evolutionary Psychology*, New York: Oxford University Press, pp. 197–210.

Tulving, E. and Craik, F.I.M. (eds) (2000), *The Oxford Handbook of Memory*, New York: Oxford University Press.

van Merrienboer, J.J.G. and Sweller, J. (2005), 'Cognitive load theory and complex learning: recent developments and future directions', *Educational Psychology Review*, **17** (2), 147–78.

Wolfe, D.A. and Gertler, M. S. (2004), 'Clusters from the inside and out: local dynamics and global linkages', *Urban Studies*, **41** (5/6), 1071–93.

World Bank (2002), *Social Capital Project Report*, New York: World Bank.

14 Computational structure for linking life cycle assessment and input–output modeling: a case study on urban recycling and remanufacturing

Joyce Cooper, Randall Jackson and Nancey Green Leigh*

14.1 INTRODUCTION

Recent models of sustainable industrial system growth reflect an increased interest in changing material flows in urban and rural landscapes and populations. Within this context, the term 'changing material flows' means introducing new commodity uses and sources or ending existing ones and introducing new waste treatments into the environment or placing a moratorium on others. There are many examples that illustrate this trend, such as using field crops for biofuels production instead of food production and recycling waste materials to retain their value.

A framework for modeling and assessing the impact of material flows to advance the mutual goals of sustainable industrial, urban, and rural systems is explored here through an urban setting case study. The environmental impact and economic benefits of these flows occur at different spatial levels and scales, from the individual urban scale to international trade and the global environment. This requires developing and using models that can capture, quantify, and qualify materials and flows across these different scales in order to comprehensively assess their impacts.

Our case study investigates extracting or the 'mining' of specific products and their associated materials from metropolitan regions through new recycling and remanufacturing networks and facilities in an urban region. It then examines methods for formally modeling the economic development and environmental effects of different material flow scenarios on these regions. The concepts presented are intended to be generally applicable to a wide range of emerging and existing economic systems and situations.

14.2 MOTIVATION

Our research application highlights the role of metropolitan regions in sustainability because it is these regions that contain the most substantial and growing fraction of the population, and therefore of the material and energy flows associated with the use and disposal of products. As such, they are one of the most critical factors in the human influence on the environment. Indeed, as a recent Brookings Institution (2007, p. 4) report argues,

> Today, our nation – and our economy – is metropolitan. U.S. metropolitan areas – complex regions of interwoven cities and suburbs – are home to more than eight in ten Americans and jobs. These metros range from global economic centers like New York, Chicago, and San Francisco; to major trade hubs like Louisville, Houston, and Seattle; to smaller, highly

productive centers like Bridgeport, Durham, and Des Moines. They concentrate and strengthen the assets that drive our economic productivity, grow the skills and incomes of our workers, and contribute to our environmental sustainability. Our major metro areas reflect the face of America in a global economy where, for the first time, more than half the world's population is metropolitan.

Re-engineering the flows of material, and especially the patterns of their disposal, is critical to achieving sustainable systems within metropolitan areas as well as within other region types. The disposal of consumer and business durable goods into landfills is a growing problem, particularly in dense population regions, and especially those with limited landfill space. Disposal is not only costly in real and sustainable terms, but it is also under increasing criticism for its impact on adjacent communities and the limitations that closed landfills place upon future development (Blum, 1976; Hite et al., 2001; Katz, 2002). The European Union, which is home to many densely populated areas, has acted legislatively to reduce waste to landfill through several directives focused on promoting the recovery, reuse, and recycling of electronics and automobiles (EU 2000, 2003a, 2003b, 2003c). Japan has also adopted similar measures, and the US has enacted bans on landfilling cathode ray tubes in 17 states since November 2008 (www.e-takeback.org/docsopen/Toolkit_Legislators/state legislation/state_leg_main.htm).

Furthermore, research shows that waste diversion from landfills has significantly higher positive impacts on the economy than did disposal, resulting in more than a doubling of total sales and value added and nearly a doubling of jobs, output, and total income (Goldsman and Ogishi, 2001). This signifies that encouraging new manufacturing activity through waste diversion in distressed areas is a promising economic development strategy for promoting urban sustainability.

To estimate the material flows associated with discarded durables, it is necessary to identify their sources, the rates at which those sources will generate various products, the materials associated with them, and their most favorable processing scenarios and locations with respect to socioeconomic and environmental effects. Because of the symbiotic material flow relationships between manufacturing companies and urban regions, engineering and regional planning can make significant contributions to the development of systematic ways to plan and (re-)engineer material flow systems for sustaining growth; systems that are efficient in terms of material, energy, and land use, as well as in providing some of the components necessary for the development of social capital.

14.3   CHALLENGES OF INTERDISCIPLINARY RESEARCH

While combining the efforts of engineering and regional planning provides a useful framework for modeling regional recycling and remanufacturing processes, there are inherent challenges that stem from the different scales at which the two disciplines operate. Engineers perform life cycle assessments (LCAs) to estimate the environmental impacts of products, processes, or services through their production, usage, disposal, reuse, or remanufacturing. These assessments begin at the micro or unit (product) level; for example, estimating energy and material use and waste for a single industrial process. Regional analysts typically operate at a larger or macro spatial scale, such as a city, region, state, or nation, to conduct system-wide assessments for a regional economy. Input–output (IO) analysis, for instance, shows how the output of one industry becomes an input to other industries, illustrating the regional inter- and intra-industry dependencies between output customers and input suppliers. Both LCA and IO models have their own distinct terminologies and notations, necessitating challenging cross-learning by interdisciplinary research teams. For example, the 'technology' matrix in LCA and denoted $\mathbf{A}$ by convention is equivalent to a Leontief matrix denoted $(\mathbf{I} - \mathbf{A})$ in IO analysis, while a technology matrix in IO analysis is represented simply as $\mathbf{A}$. The greater challenge, however, stems from the need to feed information gained from the micro or LCA scale into the macro or regional IO scale to scale up the engineering data developed at the unit level to the industry level in order to make use of it in the IO model.

14.4 METHODS

In developing models and tools to shape the next generation of industrial systems for materials mined from metropolitan regions, the spatial distribution of these material resources must be integrated because the sustainable systems cannot be successfully designed if they occur in a geographical vacuum; the 'where' of a system matters, in both its ecological and its human dimension. Thus, we use Geographic Information System (GIS) tools to specifically identify where materials (in our example, waste electronics or 'e-waste') are located with the objective to mine or collect them for reuse and processing, rather than sending them for disposal in a landfill. We identify our mining sources as those associated with residences and businesses and estimate the number of e-waste units (for example, obsolete computers, monitors, or cell phones) that are yielded by households and businesses. In doing so, the yields we estimate are distinguished by the household income level on the one hand and by industry sector on the other.

14.4.1 Life Cycle Assessment

For the LCA, the estimate of the metropolitan flows of e-waste is made by the number of units (for example, the number of computer monitors or cell phones). Units are characterized by whether they are remanufactured, recycled, disposed into landfills, or removed (or leaked, in IO terms) from the region. The materials within each e-waste type are further characterized by determining the variations in the amount of materials across equipment types, makers, and equipment sizes, all dictating the type and quantities of materials managed in the remanufacturing, recycling, and landfilling processes.

14.4.2 Input–Output Analysis

Next, an extended IO model explicitly incorporates recycling industries and related commodity accounts to analyze the economic impact of e-waste recycling. In addition, our model accounts for the physical flow of e-waste and the economic value along with the subsequent transactions of e-waste within the metropolitan economic system. There is no explicit identification of a recycling industry in published IO data. Instead, the recycling activities that do exist are a part of the more aggregate waste management sector. Therefore, the industry and commodity accounts must be reorganized to identify a relevant recycling industry and commodity. Furthermore, an end-of-life electronic product has traditionally been regarded as waste void of economic value. The flow of these products is observed in physical (non-monetary) units. Increasingly, and aided by e-waste legislation, e-waste collectors, remanufacturers, and recyclers view these e-wastes as a resource. Economic value is created along the transaction of e-waste between the discarding household or business and the e-waste collectors and processors in a metro area. Thus, the economic values of e-waste in the transactions among these economic agents have to be incorporated into the IO table.

In the following pages, we assess the modeling of the recycling and remanufacturing processes within metropolitan regional economies at the micro and macro levels. We provide an example elaborating these processes at the micro level and enumerate the problems and solutions in characterizing these new industries, including integration with environmental LCA which is geared toward embedding the results in a macroeconomic modeling framework. Our objective here is to develop procedures that are general to remanufacturing processes and other recyclable materials.

14.5   BUILDING COMPLEMENTARY LCAS AND IO REGIONAL MODELS

LCA is a protocol standardized by the International Standards Organization (ISO2006a, 2006b) to assess the life-cycle impacts of energy and material use and waste by an industrial system. LCA is most frequently used to quantify environmental impacts (for example, life-cycle energy consumption, contribution to climate change, acidification, toxic impacts, land use, and so on) and includes four interrelated phases of research:

1.   *Goal and scope definition*: stating the intended application and scope of the LCA.
2.   *Inventory analysis*: compiling an inventory of material and energy use and waste as inputs and outputs of the industrial system.
3.   *Impact assessment*: evaluating the potential impacts given the inventory.
4.   *Interpretation*: explaining the results (sensitivity, uncertainty) in relation to the objectives of the study.

In LCA, the life-cycle inventory analysis describes the interaction of industrial processes, ideally extending from materials and energy acquisition (mining and agriculture) through materials processing, construction/manufacturing, technology use and maintenance, and ultimately to reuse, remanufacturing, recycling, and/or disposal. The construction of a life-cycle inventory typically starts with a single technology or a 'core' set of processes of interest. It then moves concentrically 'upstream', adding the processes needed to produce materials and energy which are in the core and beyond, and 'downstream', adding the processes which use or manage the materials and energy for the core and beyond. This concept of the 'core' set of processes is the foundation for the link to regional IO modeling.

Consider specifically our case study on the regional management of e-waste depicted

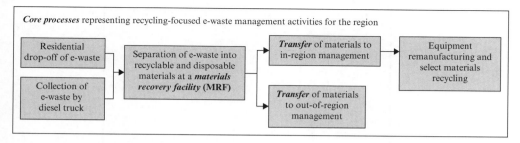

Figure 14.1   Case study core e-waste management system

in Figure 14.1. Here, we are interested in how new and existing recycling-focused e-waste management activities in our study regions might impact regional economic development and the environment. To the extent that some of the activities are already captured but masked by aggregation in IO accounts, the industry representations developed will form the basis for disaggregating existing models. Should entirely new processes be introduced into a region, the industry representations developed will be used to augment the existing accounts.

Next, Table 14.1 presents hypothetical process data for our core example and assumes that the e-waste management system is new to the region. As in a life-cycle inventory, processes are represented as columns in a matrix with process inputs as positive numbers and process outputs as negative numbers, forcing links between processes. For instance, the input to the e-waste separation process in our system is e-waste to be disassembled (coming from residential drop-offs and collected by truck) and the outputs link to both logistics (movement of materials from separation to remanufacturing/recycling or land-filling) and to processes representing materials recycling. The units of measurement for the process inputs and outputs are typical for a life-cycle inventory based on physical units such as pounds (lbs), or units of e-waste (for example, a monitor or CPU), or ton-miles for logistics (representing the weight transported times the assumed transport distance).

Here, as in any LCA, inventory inputs and outputs are designated as either 'to or from the technosphere' or 'to or from the environment'. The 'technosphere' refers to the set of industrial processes being assessed, that is, all processes within the system boundary. In the LCA of our e-waste system, this includes not only the core processes but also the upstream and downstream processes needed to complete the life cycle as depicted in Figure 14.2 (note that this example presents only a subset of what could be included). Inputs and outputs 'to or from the technosphere', such as e-waste or recyclable materials, move among industrial processes. Inputs and outputs 'to or from the environment', such as crude oil from the earth or carbon dioxide emissions into the air that enters or leaves the technosphere, are called 'environmental flows' and are accounted for in forming the life-cycle inventory results.

To solve the life-cycle inventory problem as described by Heijungs and Suh (2002), the processes in the technosphere are typically formulated into a non-singular matrix (known as the technology matrix and designated as **A**), which is inverted and then subjected to a demand vector f (representing what the entire system should ultimately

Table 14.1 Example core process data for new regional e-waste management activities

	New activity in the region						
	E-waste management	Residential drop-off of e-waste at MRF	Collection of e-waste by diesel truck	Separation of materials from e-waste at MRF	Transfer of recyclables by truck	Transfer of materials to landfill by truck	Equipment remanufacturing and materials recycling
Managed e-waste (units of e-waste)	1	0	0	0	0	0	0
E-waste dropped off at MRF by residents (ton-miles)	-0.039	1	0	0	0	0	0
collected e-waste (ton-miles)	-0.017	0	1	0	0	0	0
E-waste to be disassembled (units of e-waste)	-1	0	0	1	0	0	0
Recyclable materials to recycling (ton-miles)	0	0	0	-0.041	1	0	0
Materials to landfill (ton-miles)	0	0	0	-0.014	0	1	0
Remanufacturable equipment to remanufactured equipment/ recyclable materials to recycled materials (lb)	0	0	0	-8.3	0	0	1

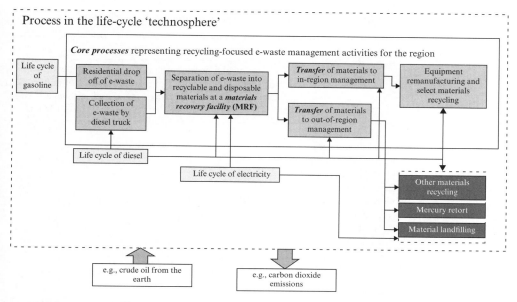

Figure 14.2   Life-cycle inventory processes

produce among the inputs and outputs) to solve for a scaling vector *s* (representing the amount of each process needed to meet the specified demand):

$$\mathbf{A}^{-1}f = s. \tag{14.1}$$

Next, *s* is used to scale the environmental flows for each process, represented as matrix **B** with columns corresponding to each process in **A** and rows representing inputs and outputs from the environment (for example, crude oil and carbon dioxide emissions):

$$\mathbf{B}s = g, \tag{14.2}$$

such that the inventory result (vector *g*) summarizes the life-cycle resource use and emissions. Hypothetical data corresponding to the set of core processes described above are presented in Table 14.2a. For the LCA, the core data presented in Table 14.1 have been repeated, the **A** matrix has been extended to include the life cycle of four commodities (landfilling and the production of gasoline, diesel, and electricity), and the **B** matrix has been added to represent example environmental flows (crude oil, select air emissions, and land use). This set-up can be used to demand, for example, any number of e-waste units to be managed in the region of interest (using various versions of *f*), allowing *g*, or the total life-cycle use of crude oil, air emissions, and land use to be estimated for a variety of scenarios.

For example, Table 14.2b reports life-cycle computations derived from Table 14.2a, whereby, given *f* demanding the management of 280,000 units of e-waste, the life-cycle

Table 14.2a   Example LCA matrices for new e-waste management activities

		New activity in the region			
		E-waste management	Residential drop-off of e-waste at MRF	Collection of e-waste by diesel truck	Separation of materials from e-waste at MRF
New Activity in A	Managed e-waste (units of e-waste)	1	0	0	0
	E-waste dropped off at MRF by residents (ton-miles)	−0.039	1	0	0
	Collected e-waste (ton-miles)	−0.017	0	1	0
	E-waste to be disassembled (units of e-waste)	−1	0	0	1
	Recyclable materials to recycling (ton-miles)	0	0	0	−0.041
	Materials to landfill (ton-miles)	0	0	0	−0.014
	Remanufacturable equipment to remanufactured equipment/recyclable materials to recycled materials (lb)	0	0	0	−8.3
Existing Industry in A	Commodity 1 – Materials to be landfilled (lb)	0	0	0	−2.8
	Commodity 2 – Gasoline (gal)	0	−0.0033	0	0
	Commodity 3 – Diesel (gal)	0	0	−0.000094	−0.00066
	Commodity 4 – Electricity (kwh)	0	0	0	−0.083
Environmental flows in B	Crude oil from the earth (lb)	0	0	0	0
	Carbon dioxide emissions to air (lb)	0	0.065	0.0021	0.015
	Methane, nitrous oxide, and HFC emissions to air (lb)	0	0.068	0.0022	0.015
	Land use (acres)	0	a lot, if you consider road and facility construction		

Note: Although all data are presented only for the purpose of developing our example, data for truck emissions and the life cycles of the production of gasoline, diesel, and electricity are based on data in the US Life Cycle Inventory Database, maintained by the US Department of Energy's National Renewable Energy Laboratory and available at http://www.nrel.gov/lci/.

			Existing Industries			
Transfer of recyclables by truck	Transfer of materials to landfill by truck	Equipment remanufacturing and materials by recycling	Materials landfilling	Life cycle of the production of gasoline	Life cycle of the production of the diesel	Life cycle of the production of electricity
0	0	0	0	0	0	0
0	0	0	0	0	0	0
0	0	0	0	0	0	0
0	0	0	0	0	0	0
1	0	0	0	0	0	0
0	1	0	0	0	0	0
0	0	1	0	0	0	0
0	0	0	1	0	0	0
0	0	0	0	1	0	0
−0.0000086	−0.0000086	−0.0013	−0.0000043	0	1	0
0	0	−0.3	0	0	0	1
0	0	0	0	−7.0	−7.9	−0.030
0.00019	0.00019	0.029	0.00010	2.6	2.9	1.6
0.00020	0.00020	0.031	0.00010	0.029	0.033	0.0034

Table 14.2b   *Life-cycle inventory computations*

f		s		g	
280,000	Managed e-waste (units of e-waste)	280,000	E-waste management	−44,000	Crude oil from the earth (lb)
0	E-waste dropped off at MRF by residents (ton-miles)	10,780	Residential drop-off of e-waste at MRF	1,100,000	Carbon dioxide emissions to air (lb)
0	Collected e-waste (ton-miles)	4,620	Collection of e-waste by diesel truck	79,000	Methane, nitrous oxide, and HFC emissions to air (lb)
0	E-waste to be disassembled (units of e-waste)	280,000	Separation of materials from e-waste at MRF	not estimated	Land use (acres)
0	Recyclable materials to recycling (ton-miles)	11,550	Transfer of recyclables by truck		
0	Materials to landfill (ton-miles)	3,850	Transfer of materials to landfill by truck		
0	Reman. equipment/recyclable materials (lb)	2,310,000	Equipment remanufacturing and materials recycling		
0	Commodity 1 – Materials to be landfilled (lb)	770,000	Materials landfilling		
0	Commodity 2 – Gasoline (gal)	36	Life cycle of the production of gasoline		
0	Commodity 3 – Diesel (gal)	3,238	Life cycle of the production of diesel		
0	Commodity 4 – Electricity (kwh)	607,698	Life cycle of the production of electricity		

inventory computations estimate that this implies the extraction of 44,000 lb of crude oil from the earth; and the emitting of 1.1 million lb of carbon dioxide into the atmosphere, along with 79,000 lb of methane, nitrous oxide, and HFCs.

Although in reality the e-waste management activities can be newly introduced or already captured in the IO accounts, we can treat them as though they were new for the purposes of quantifying the data needed to modify the IO model. To form the data for the *make-use* tables in support of our regional IO model, we identified only one modification to the LCA technology matrix $\mathbf{A}$ presented in Table 14.2a. Specifically, we note that the non-core processes in the technosphere represent existing industries whose interactions with other existing industries in the region are already captured in the regional IO model. Thus, as presented in Table 14.3a, we reformulated the portion of $\mathbf{A}$ representing the existing industries as an identity matrix (the lower right-hand portion of Table 14.3a) to eliminate double counting of the relationships between existing sectors. We denoted the new matrix as $\mathbf{A}'$. This modification can be viewed as a redefinition of the LCA system boundaries, truncating the LCA at the point at which additional activity in existing industries is triggered.

Given this, the scaling vector s' for an f' which demands the management of 280,000 units of e-waste is described in Table 14.3b, and which shows only a minute change in the diesel scaling factor from s to s', due to the minor change from $\mathbf{A}$ to $\mathbf{A}'$ in our example (only one cell of the matrix was changed, as is clearly shaded).

Finally, we use only a portion of s' to make our transition to our regional IO model. Specifically, the s' vector estimate that corresponds to 'materials recycling' represents the weight of recyclable materials 'made' in our system, the estimate that corresponds to 'materials landfilling' represents additional use of regional landfills (as the weight received by the landfill from the new activities), and the estimates that corresponds to the life cycles of gasoline, diesel, and electricity also correspond to additional energy use in the region. To make the transition to data for use in the regional make-use tables, each of these s' vector estimates is multiplied by their commensurate prices, as is shown in Table 14.4.

Thus, for example in Table 14.4, our new industry represents a new column in our regional use table, including $58,000 for landfill operations, $95 for gasoline consumption, $11,000 for diesel consumption, and $67,000 for electricity consumption. The corresponding table in the regional make table would include the production of recycled materials at $510,000. We do note, however, that our hypothetical data are based only on material and energy prices and landfill tipping fees and, therefore, are pending estimates of other business costs.

To provide a comprehensive framework for regional analysis, the activities can be further disaggregated. For example, the e-waste to disassembly (in units of e-waste); the recyclable materials to recycling (in ton-miles); the materials to landfill (in ton-miles); the recyclable materials to recycled materials (in lb); can all be split into two activities each, by adding suffixes for 'in-region' and 'out-of-region'. Further, local industry supply percentages for the materials used in the new activities can either be set to known values or estimated by regional supply percentages. Finally, the outputs of recycled materials generated can be disaggregated by material type.

Table 14.3a   Modified LCA technology matrix for use in preparing regional IO models

		New Activity in the Region			
		E-waste management	Residential drop-off of e-waste at MRF	Collection of e-waste by diesel truck	Separation of materials from e-waste at MRF
New Activity in A'	Managed e-waste (units of e-waste)	1	0	0	0
	E-waste dropped off at MRF by residents (ton-miles)	−0.039	1	0	0
	Collected e-waste (ton-miles)	−0.017	0	1	0
	E-waste to be disassembled (units of e-waste)	−1	0	0	1
	Recyclable materials to recycling (ton-miles)	0	0	0	−0.041
	Materials to landfill (ton-miles)	0	0	0	−0.014
	Remanufacturable equipment to remanufactured equipment/ recyclable materials to recycled materials (lb)	0	0	0	−8.3
Existing Industry in A'	Commodity 1 – Materials to be landfilled (lb)	0	0	0	−2.8
	Commodity 2 – Gasoline (gal)	0	−0.0033	0	0
	Commodity 3 – Diesel (gal)	0	0	−0.000094	−0.00066
	Commodity 4 – Electricity (kwh)	0	0	0	−0.083
Environmental flows in B	Crude oil from the earth (lb)	0	0	0	0
	Carbon dioxide emissions to air (lb)	0	0.065	0.0021	0.015
	Methane, nitrous oxide, and HFC emissions to air (lb)	0	0.068	0.0022	0.015
	Land use (acres)	0	a lot, if you consider road and facility construction		

				Existing Industries		
Transfer of recyclables by truck	Transfer of materials to landfill by truck	Equipment re-manufacturing and materials by recycling	Materials landfilling	Life cycle of the production of gasoline	Life cycle of the production of the diesel	Life cycle of the production of electricity
0	0	0	0	0	0	0
0	0	0	0	0	0	0
0	0	0	0	0	0	0
0	0	0	0	0	0	0
1	0	0	0	0	0	0
0	1	0	0	0	0	0
0	0	1	0	0	0	0
0	0	0	1	0	0	0
0	0	0	0	1	0	0
−0.0000086	−0.0000086	−0.0013	0	0	1	0
0	0	−0.3	0	0	0	1
0	0	0	0	−7.0	−7.9	−0.030
0.00019	0.00019	0.029	0.00000	2.6	2.9	1.6
0.00020	0.00020	0.031	0.00000	0.029	0.033	0.0034

Table 14.3b   Life-cycle inventory computations

f'		s'	
280,000	Managed e-waste (units of e-waste)	280,000	E-waste management
0	E-waste dropped off at MRF by residents (ton-miles)	10,780	Residential drop-off of e-waste at MRF
0	Collected e-waste (ton-miles)	4,620	Collection of e-waste by diesel truck
0	E-waste to be disassembled (units of e-waste)	280,000	Separation of materials from e-waste at MRF
0	Recyclable materials to recycling (ton-miles)	11,550	Transfer of recyclables by truck
0	Materials to landfill (ton-miles)	3,850	Transfer of materials to landfill by truck
0	Reman, equipment/recyclable materials (lb)	2,310,000	Equipment remanufacturing and materials recycling
0	Commodity 1 – Materials to be landfilled (lb)	770,000	Materials landfilling
0	Commodity 2 – Gasoline (gal)	36	Life cycle of the production of gasoline
0	Commodity 3 – Diesel (gal)	3,235	Life cycle of the production of diesel
0	Commodity 4 – Electricity (kwh)	608,698	Life cycle of the production of electricity

Table 14.4   Life-cycle inventory computations

S'			Price Units		Result		
. . .	. . .				*(total)*	*($/make$)*	
2,310,000	Equipment remanufacturing and materials recycling	$0.22	$/lb (as in the mass-weighted value of the recycled materials)		$510,000	$1.00	Make value as the value of recycled materials generated
770,000	Materials landfilling	$0.075	$/lb (as in a tipping fee)		$58,000	$0.11	Use value as the tipping fees
36	Life cycle of the production of gasoline	$2.66	$/gal		$95	$0.0002	Use value as consumption of gasoline
3,235	Life cycle of the production of diesel	$3.29	$/gal		$11,000	$0.02	Use value as consumption of diesel
608,698	Life cycle of the production of electricity	$0.11	$/kwh		$67,000	$0.13	Use value as consumption of electricity
						$0.27	Total use$/make$

14.6   SCENARIO CONSTRUCTION AND IMPLEMENTATION

Once the new use and make table values have been computed, the regional tables can be directly edited. In the event that the estimated values are deemed to represent entirely new additions to the economy, a new industry column augments the use table and a new industry row augments the make table. The values in the use column correspond to the commodities used by the new recycling or remanufacturing industry while the values in the new make row correspond to the regional production of commodities. In the event that the newly parameterized industry values are deemed to have been embedded in the IO accounts within an aggregate industry such as waste management, the new rows and columns still augment the make and use tables, but their values are subtracted from the original aggregate industry.

Given the IO accounts in absolute value, product inventory estimates, and product life estimates, the forecasts of the number of units to be processed as e-waste can be generated. These translate into new values for intermediate demands and supplies of inputs and outputs. A number of alternatives exist for impact model drivers. The first and most straightforward alternative is simply to allow all new outputs to enter the production system as replacements for imports. This method reflects the consideration of *avoided* life cycles in LCA (for example, a remanufactured computer monitor temporarily precludes the need to construct a new computer monitor). Post-adjustment output, employment, and income levels can be compared to pre-adjustment levels to determine impacts. However, should the total demand for the new activity output be less than total new output, a final demand entry corresponding to exports will be required to balance the accounts, a concept that would be reflected in a well-developed, consequential LCA (as in Ekvall and Andræ, 2006). Likewise, other well-founded final demand forecasts can be used.

14.7   DISCUSSION

Although the method presented here is highly generalizable, the numerous fundamental differences in systems with changing material flows will require careful attention and potentially some additional modifications to the LCA and IO models. Changes in the production mix and the use of field crops from food production to biofuel production, for example, would have global market implications if US fertilizer imports and food exports drastically change in amounts estimated by LCA. In this instance, global IO models could be used to represent the global market responses.

For an example which is specific to recycling, consider the distinct differences between the types of products being recycled, such as in the cases of the collection activity for carpet recycling versus e-waste recycling. While e-waste can be delivered by consumers to transfer points (such as retail outlets, waste transfer stations, or community collection events) or can be picked up at businesses, schools, and so on, consumers do not tend to deliver waste carpets to any central collection points or recycling facilities. These kinds of differences, in addition to differences in the types of materials and remanufacturing/recycling processes required, must be addressed explicitly when moving from one kind of recyclable product to another.

Although we have included several of the important aspects of e-waste recycling in our case study here, we have also omitted others. For the sake of brevity, for example, we did not include the reuse of e-waste and the re-entry of reused and remanufactured equipment and recycled materials into the system. In short, these additions would add to **A** not only those columns for a host of upstream and downstream processes to complete the life cycle, but also the processes representing the life cycle of new electronics as reuse and remanufacturing reduces the need to manufacture new electronics. Within this same context, the production of recycled materials theoretically avoids the need to produce similar materials from virgin feedstocks, which also was omitted from our life-cycle inventory example. Although the implications of these omissions in **A** are also expected to have implications in **A′**, we leave their investigation to future research.

NOTE

* This work was supported in part by the US National Science Foundation under Award No. 0628139 and 0628190.

REFERENCES

Blum, S.L. (1976), 'Tapping resources in municipal solid waste', *Science*, 191 (4228), February, 669–75.
Brookings Institution (2007), *Metropolitan Policy Program, MetroNation: How U.S. Metropolitan Areas Fuel American Prosperity*, Washington, DC.
Ekvall, T. and A.S.G. Andræ (2006), 'Attributional and consequential environmental assessment of the shift to lead-free solders', *International Journal of Life Cycle Assessment*, 11 (5), 344–53.
European Union (2000), 'Directive 2000/53/EC of the European Parliament and of the Council of September 18 2000 on End-Of-Life Vehicles', *Official Journal of the European Communities*, 269, 34–42, Brussels.
European Union (2003a), 'Directive 2002/96/EC of the European Parliament and of the Council of 27 January 2003 on Waste Electrical and Electronic Equipment', *Official Journal of the European Communities*, 37, 24–38.
European Union (2003b), 'Directive 2003/108/EC of the European Parliament and of the Council of 8 December 2003 Amending Directive 2002/96/EC on Waste Electrical and Electronic Equipment (WEEE)', *Official Journal of the European Communities*, 345, 106–7, Brussels.
European Union (2003c), 'Directive 2002/95/EC of the European Parliament and of the Council of 27 January 2003 on the Restriction of the Use of Certain Hazardous Substances in Electrical and Electronic Equipment', *Official Journal of the European Communities*, 37, 19–23, Brussels.
Goldman, G. and A. Ogishi (2001), 'The Economic Impact of Waste Disposal and Diversion in California: A Report to the California Integrated Waste Management Board', available at: http://are.berkeley.edu/extension/EconImpWaste.pdf (accessed August 2008).
Heijungs, R. and S. Suh (2002), 'The Computational Structure of Life Cycle Assessment', Dordrecht: Kluwer Academic.
Hite, D., W. Chern, F. Hitzhusen and A. Randall (2001), 'Property-value impacts of an environmental disamenity: the case of landfills', *Journal of Real Estate Finance and Economics*, 22 (2–3), 185–202.
International Standards Association (ISO), (2006a), '*ISO 14040:2006 Environmental management – Life cycle assessment – Principles and framework*'.
International Standards Association (ISO), (2006b), '*ISO 14044:2006 Environmental management – Life cycle assessment – Requirements and guidelines*'.
Katz, J. (2002), 'What a waste: the generation and disposal of trash imposes costs on society and the environment: should we be doing more?', *Regional Review* (Q1), 22–30, available at: http://www.bos.frb.org/economic/nerr/rr2002/q1/waste.pdf (accessed August 2008).

15 The importance of the water management sector in Dutch agriculture and the wider economy
Frank Bruinsma and Mark Bokhorst

15.1 INTRODUCTION

In the Netherlands the national government, the provinces and the district water boards are the principal water system managers. District water boards have been managing the water since the Middle Ages, and as such are the oldest democratic organizations in the country. Nevertheless, the role of these boards is not well known to the public. The district water boards are responsible for:

- the control of the water levels, via the construction and maintenance of pumping stations and sluices;
- the protection against flooding via the construction and maintenance of dikes, dunes and other dams; and
- the control of the quality of the surface water, via the construction and maintenance of wastewater purification plants.

The district water boards are not responsible for drinking water; this undertaking is the responsibility of semi-privatized utility firms.

Over the past decades the number of district water boards has fallen from 2,700 in 1940 to only 26 at present. This means that there has been a huge increase in the scale of the individual boards due to mergers. There are now more district water boards than Dutch provinces (12), but fewer than Dutch municipalities (430), but whereas district water boards are functional units, provinces and municipalities are administrative units. The borders of the district water boards correspond to the watersheds between the catchment areas of two different water systems, and due to the functional structure, the borders of the district water boards therefore do not always correspond to the administrative borders.

To get some idea of the size of the involvement of the parties, the total turnover in the water management system of the national government was about €1.4 billion in 2007 (about €300 million for flood defences, and the remainder in water management costs), whereas in the same year, the turnover of the district water boards was about €2.45 billion (€200 million for flood defences, €800 million for water quantity, and the remainder for water quality). The turnover for the provinces was about €165 million, and that for the municipalities was €1.1 billion (mainly for the local sewerage systems) (Ministry of Transport and Public Works, 2009).

Although the organizational structure originally developed rapidly from many small, local organizations towards a regional network, there is considerable political debate about the continuation of district water boards. The boards have their own taxes to provide finance for their activities, but it is often argued that they are not operating efficiently enough and that their functions should be transferred to the provinces. Not only are district water boards structured on a functional basis that does not always correspond to the administrative division of provinces; there are more arguments in favour of their continuation as distinct from provincial administration. In particular, the district water boards have developed specialized knowledge about the specific regional water management systems, and this cannot simply be transferred to the provinces without a loss of knowledge and information. Furthermore, the boards also play an important intermediary role between various different interest groups and stakeholders within their territory, including the provinces, farmer organizations, nature conservation groups and environmentalists. Finally, as we shall see below, in the near future the district water boards will be faced with new and increasing challenges which will be difficult to cope with, and which will require high levels of specialized knowledge. For the provinces, the transfer of the present water management system will be a large enough challenge to deal with.

In this chapter we shall examine three partly interrelated and new challenges which the water management sector is facing: Section 15.2 deals with the implications of climate change on safety; Section 15.3 addresses the problems that arise due to the fact that the polders are becoming brackish; and Section 15.4 focusses on the implications for the water management system of the transformation of the countryside from a production into a consumer area. The final section discusses the implications of those developments on the organization of the Dutch water management system.

15.2   SAFETY AND CLIMATE CHANGE

The Netherlands has a total of 3,500 km of primary flood defences. These consist of dikes (along rivers, lakes and seas), dunes, flood barriers, dams and weirs. They protect the Netherlands from flooding from the major rivers, from Lake IJsselmeer and Lake Markermeer, and from the sea. About 90 per cent of the primary barriers are managed by the district water boards. Several dozen kilometres are in the hands of municipal councils and provincial authorities, while the remainder is managed by the national government (Ministry of Transport and Public Works, 2004). The primary barriers protect 55 per cent of the surface area of the Netherlands and 67 per cent of the Dutch population. In addition, there are about 14,000 km of secondary barriers such as storage basin dikes, polder embankments and canal dikes, which protect the land from flooding from the inland waters.

Over time the Dutch reduced the defence line against the sea by cutting off sea arms. A good example is the Zuiderzee. The completion of the IJsselmeerdam (Afsluitdijk) in 1932 across the mouth of a brackish arm of the North Sea meant a huge reduction in the coastal defence line (see Figure 15.1). The Zuiderzee was cut off from the North Sea and became Lake IJsselmeer. In addition, Lake IJsselmeer became a 350,000 hectare freshwater lake. Draining the Wieringermeer in the 1930s and reclaiming the Flevoland polders until the 1960s, left 190,000 hectares of open water (ibid., 2004). The vital role of this freshwater lake will be discussed below.

(a) Afsluitdijk   (b) Delta Works

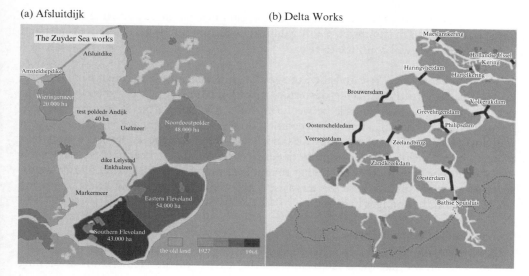

Source: www.deltawerken.com.

Figure 15.1   The closure of the Zuiderzee by the Afsluitdijk and the Delta Works

After the disastrous floods in 1953 in the Province of Zeeland, the southern part of Zuid-Holland and the western part of Brabant, in which over 1,800 people lost their lives and 15,000 hectares of land were flooded, the Delta Plan was developed. As we see in Figure 15.1, the Delta Plan provided for a series of dike reinforcements and the closure of a number of sea arms in the south of the country. In 1997 the Delta Works (Deltawerken) were completed by the Maeslant flood barrier, whereby two hollow arched doors in the Nieuwe Waterweg near Hoek van Holland (Hook of Holland) enable the entrance to Rotterdam harbour to be closed automatically when the sea level rises three metres above the average. The Delta Works programme as a whole reduced the total length of the coastal defences by almost 800 km. Because of its economic importance for the port of Antwerp, the Westerschelde is the only tidal inlet to remain open. The Delta Works were of great importance, not only from a safety point of view, but in addition, the border between fresh- and saltwater systems was moved further west, thereby improving the agricultural freshwater supply. The excess water could also be transported north in the direction of Lake IJsselmeer; we shall return to the importance of this freshwater transport issue below.

All of these historical infrastructure and planning developments must now be seen in the wider context of climate change. According to the climate change scenarios published by the Royal Netherlands Meteorological Institute (KNMI, 2006), climate change will have the following consequences for water management:

● warming will continue, producing more mild winters and hotter summers;
● winters will become wetter on average and the frequency of extreme rainfall events will also increase;

- the intensity of extreme rainfall events in summer will increase, while the number of rainy days in summer will fall. Summers will contain longer drought events; and
- the sea level will continue to rise.

The relative sea-level rise and the expected further soil subsidence must be taken into account in the already low-lying western parts of the country. In 2050, the average temperature is expected to increase between 0.9 and 2.3°C during the winter and between 0.9 and 2.8°C during the summer, depending on the various scenarios. Furthermore, in the same year, and again depending on the various scenarios, the sea level is expected to increase by between 15 and 35 cm. By the end of the twenty-first century the sea level is expected to be some 40 to 90 cm higher than it is at present (ibid.). In the following subsections we shall discuss these three issues; namely, the falling ground levels, the rising sea levels, and the changes in rainfall.

15.2.1   Falling Ground Levels

Figure 15.2 shows that the western and northern parts of the Netherlands are falling while the southeastern part is rising slightly, due to tectonic movements that are related to the formation of the Alps, and the enlargement of the Atlantic Ocean due to the melting of ice at the poles. The western and northern parts are also subsiding locally, but this is primarily related to human activities. In the past the subsidence in the river deltas was largely compensated for by the clay and sand deposited during the flooding of major rivers. However, after the dikes were built along the rivers this was no longer possible. Another cause of the local soil subsidence is the commercial extraction of peat and clay in the west of the country. This ground-soil type naturally contains a lot of groundwater, and when the water is drained off, as has been the case in the western part of the country for hundreds of years, there is subsidence. Another problem with draining peat areas is that peat oxidizes and therefore sinks when it lies above the groundwater level. Over the centuries, local soil subsidence of up to seven metres has been measured in the peat meadows of western Netherlands, although, due to improved water management, soil subsidence was limited to 50 cm in the twentieth century. The aim is to reduce any further soil subsidence to just 25 cm in the twenty-first century (Ministry of Transport and Public Works, 2004).

The greatest soil subsidence now, however, is expected in the north, due to the extraction of natural gas at a depth of about 3 km in the province of Groningen, where the ground level is expected to fall some 45 cm by the year 2050 (NAM, 2010).

15.2.2   Rising Sea Levels

It is estimated that due to climate change, the relative sea-level rise might be about one meter on the Dutch coast by the end of the twenty-first century. Not only is the sea level rising, but, as explained above, the whole coastal area of the Netherlands is subsiding as well. Together, these two developments seem quite significant. However, one has to bear in mind that the sea level has risen by about 100 metres since the last ice age ended about 11,000 years ago, and the current defence system is strong enough to protect the country from flooding. The main impact of these rising sea levels is the deeper inland

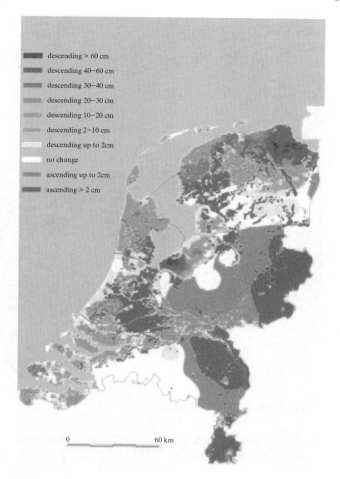

descending > 60 cm

descending 40–60 cm

descending 30–40 cm

descending 20–30 cm

descending 10–20 cm

descending 2–10 cm

descending up to 2cm

no change

ascending up to 2cm

ascending > 2 cm

0   60 km

Source: Ministry of Transport and Public Works (2004).

Figure 15.2   Changes in the ground level in the Netherlands

penetration of the saltwater by the tidal inlets, in particular the Westerschelde and the Nieuwe Waterweg.

The increasing inward land penetration of saltwater via open river mouths is controlled by several factors. First, rivers are already at sea level up to about 75 km upstream from the river mouth. Increasing sea-level rises cause a higher concentration of saltwater in the last tens of kilometres of the rivers. Second, longer periods of drought in the Rhine and Meuse catchment areas result in lower river levels, so the seawater is able to flow into the river beds. Third, in the 1960s, three weirs were constructed on the river Rhine to control the water division between the Rhine and the IJssel tributary. As a result the discharge of the Rhine has decreased, thereby allowing seawater to flow into the riverbeds. Fourth, fresh river water is used for crop irrigation in dry periods, contributing to more seawater penetration.

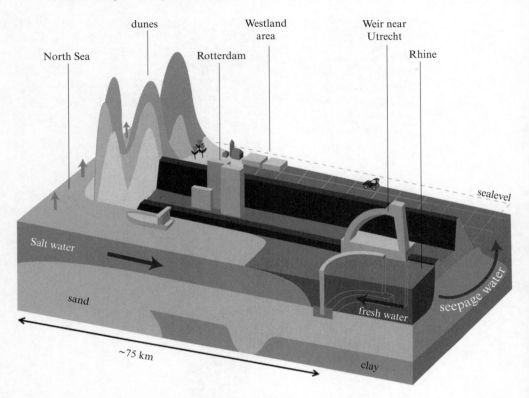

Figure 15.3　Penetration of seawater into agricultural areas

As we see in Figure 15.3, seawater penetration into the riverbeds results in the salinization of the groundwater and soil in the crop fields and grasslands which are adjacent to
the river. Such areas are situated several metres lower than the river levels, due both to
soil subsidence and also to the fact that the dikes prevented clay and sand sedimenta-
tion of the rivers. The salty river water enters the groundwater systems of the farmland,
underneath the dikes, and particularly through sandy soil. Most crops are very sensitive
to the adverse effects of salty groundwater, and mitigating the effects of the increasing
salinization of the groundwater systems is therefore a major and increasing financial
burden for Dutch agriculture. This is most notably the case for flower and bulb production, which is particularly sensitive to these changes, and which represents a major export
industry for the Netherlands.

The Delta Works in the provinces of Zuid-Holland and Zeeland and the Afsluitdijk
between Noord-Holland and Friesland were constructed in order to shorten the coastline
and to provide extra safety against flooding. As a result, the Zeeland and Zuid-Holland
estuary and the Zuiderzee (later Lake IJsselmeer) all became freshwater areas. These
new freshwater bodies reduced the saltwater inlets, but also now function as freshwater
reservoirs which can be used for different purposes.

To prevent crops from dying due to highly saline groundwater, fresh water is
flushed through the ditches in the polders to decrease the levels of salt concentra-

tion. This rinsing process requires large amounts of additional fresh water which is mainly supplied by Lake IJsselmeer. Subsequently, this extra pumping results in an even greater salinization of the groundwater in the polder. This process is explained in Section 15.3.

15.2.3   Changes in Rainfall

Climate change will affect rainfall. On the one hand, the rain is expected to fall more intensively, with individual rainfalls becoming heavier in a shorter period. On the other, there will also be longer periods without rainfall, causing serious drought problems. In this subsection these two issues will be discussed.

Intensified rainfall

More important than the risk of flooding due to rising sea levels, is the risk of flooding from the main rivers of the Rhine and the Meuse, due to the intensified periods of rainfall. After the flooding disaster in 1953 an acceptable flood-event-chance system was developed, which was based on the predictability of floods, and the levels of saltwater- or freshwater-related damage that such flooding would cause. The new dike heights were calculated on the basis of historical flood information, and the dikes were adjusted accordingly. The high water levels of 1993 and 1995 in the Meuse provided the first incentives for the adoption of another strategy. To make water challenges more manageable, a policy was pursued by the Dutch Ministry of Transport and Public Works which offers more 'room' for water (Ministry of Transport and Public Works 2000), thereby allowing the water to follow a more natural course, so as to further reduce the risks of flooding. The decision to allow more room for rivers instead of just increasing the height of the river dikes, was also based on the principle that the higher the dikes, the higher the water in the rivers, and the more serious are the consequences if a dike were to break.

By 2015 the carrying capacity of the Rhine and the Meuse must be increased to 16,000 m³/s and 3,800 m³/s, respectively. In order to achieve this, there are two types of measures which must be undertaken so as to accommodate the increased inflows of water into the two rivers: the first focuses on the enlargement of the carrying capacity of the rivers themselves; and the second concentrates on the storage of the excess rainwater within the Netherlands.

Measures of the first type include:

- the lowering of flood plains;
- the moving of dikes inland;
- the digging of additional channels along rivers ('green rivers');
- the use of retention areas (emergency flood storage areas); and
- the creation of meanders in small canalized rivers.

Measures of the second type include:

- the use of detention ponds to store excess rainwater; and
- the creation of more water recreation areas in parks and densely inhabited areas.

So-called 'green rivers' are bypasses of the main river which are used only in situations of high water levels in main rivers. Most bypasses are located near urban areas, to prevent the urban areas from flooding.

Retention areas are areas with low economic value, and which are allowed to become flooded first. They are located upstream of the river and are intended to prevent flood damage to economically valuable areas downstream, such as the urban Randstad area. The problem with retention areas is that once they have been flooded, they may completely lose their value as agricultural land, because it is unknown whether the water that flooded the area was polluted. These uncertainties affect both the current and future value of the land.

Detention ponds are areas where excess rainfall can be stored until the rivers have excess capacity again. The Netherlands contains the deltas of the Meuse and Rhine rivers, both of which carry water from their hinterlands in Belgium, Germany, France and Switzerland. The Netherlands is therefore sometimes known as the 'drain of Europe'. However, due to the increased scale of the paved areas in the hinterlands, such as, for example, in the Ruhr area, less rainwater is absorbed by the local surface area. This means that the rainwater flows much faster towards the main rivers. In addition, the water also flows faster because over time many of the river bends have been straightened. As a consequence, the carrying capacity of the rivers has to be increased in order to cope with this intensified inflow of rainwater. So in principle the Netherlands has to store this excess rainfall on its own land, and wait until the carrying capacity of the Rhine and the Meuse is large enough before draining the excess rainfall into the rivers. Detention ponds are located both in the countryside and also within urban areas. At the same time, Dutch urban areas have to cope with their own excess rainwater. Given the largely paved character of Dutch cities, this means that a large extension of the storage capacity within cities is needed. This is provided by the use of fountains, waterfalls, wadis, and also many previously filled-in canals which increasingly need to be re-excavated.

As a consequence of these various developments it is a huge task for the district water boards to cope with the different requirements. Much work will be needed on both the primary and the secondary defence systems; the primary defence system should be designed to address the first set of measures, while the secondary system should deal with the creation of detention ponds.

Periods of drought
Before discussing the issue of drought, it is important to explain the difference between water depletion and drought. In 2000, about half a million hectares of nature areas were water depleted in the Netherlands. This is about 12 per cent of the total land area. There are three causes of water depletion: 60 per cent is caused by dehydration and accelerated water drainage for agriculture; 30 per cent is due to the extraction of groundwater for drinking water, industrial water and irrigation; and the remaining 10 per cent is caused by an increase in paved surfaces, deforestation and sand extraction (Ministry of Transport and Public Works, 2004). Water depletion can be tackled by water management measures.

Drought, on the other hand, is caused by occasional water shortages. Again this can be the result of human interventions but it is also the result of climatic conditions. Unlike water depletion, drought affects not only the countryside but also water use. For instance the summer of 2003 was dry and hot in the Netherlands, as it was in the countries upstream of the major rivers. Low river levels meant that barges could not be fully loaded and power stations could not be cooled sufficiently, putting the continuity of electricity supply at risk. In polders the water levels could not be maintained and peat dikes were drying out, causing increased instability and even leading to a dike breakthrough near Wilnis, in the province of Utrecht, in that year.

Measures were taken to set priorities for the distribution of fresh water in the event of water shortages, and the reserves of fresh water in Lake IJsselmeer and the new reserves created by the Delta Works play an important role here. To cope with the problems of drought, an advisory committee (*Deltacommissie*) has advised the Minister of Transport and Public Works to increase the level of Lake IJsselmeer by 1.5 metres to create a freshwater reserve. Of course, an increase in the water level will have huge impacts for the water management system in large areas surrounding the lake. The polders will no longer be able to drain their excess rainwater into the lake, and it will be difficult to maintain the groundwater levels at levels which are acceptable for agricultural purposes. However, the freshwater reserve can be used in periods of drought: to irrigate the land; to secure the availability of cooling water for energy production; and to flush the western and northern parts of the country with fresh water so as to combat both the salinization of polders and the further inland penetration of the saltwater tongue. By the end of 2009 a draft National Waterplan was submitted to parliament, recommending a rise in the water level of Lake IJsselmeer of 30 cm. The final National Waterplan is to be approved in 2015. Obviously, it will be a huge task for the district water boards to comply with these requirements.

15.3 THE WESTERN PART OF THE COUNTRY BECOMES BRACKISH

The Netherlands has about 3,000 sea and river polders, and the drained and reclaimed lakes and ponds (*droogmakerijen*). The polders are low-lying tracts of land which are enclosed by dikes. An extensive and complex system of ditches and waterways serves to manage their groundwater level and every polder is connected to a pumping station that transports the water to a drainage outlet or pool. From there, it is pumped out to other waterways and, finally, flows into the sea (ibid.).

Polders originate from before AD 1000. Population growth in the central medieval period forced the inhabitants of the Rhine and Meuse delta area to exploit the peat moors for food supply. Therefore the naturally high groundwater table had to be lowered to one metre below the surface. As the peat bogs were above sea level, ditches could be dug to drain the water away to the sea. However, the entry of oxygen into the peat causes oxidation and a consequent lowering of the surface, such that over time the water level had to be drained to ever lower and lower levels. Sluices and dikes had to be constructed, and when these were themselves below the low-tide water level, lines of windmills were used to drain the peat areas. Now, the peat areas are about 1–2 metres below sea level. Swampy areas including shallow lakes could also be drained to arable land areas by using the same mill-pumping techniques; the transition to land reclamation by the draining of lakes can therefore be seen as a gradually developed process. The first (shallow) reclaimed lake is thought to be the Achtermeer near Alkmaar in the province of Noord-Holland, around the year 1533 (Borger, 2004).

Peat was also dug and dried and cut into turfs for household and industrial heating. Lakes up to five metres deep were thus created in the western part of the country. Over time, wave erosion during storms enlarged and united many of the lakes, turning large parts of the province of Noord-Holland into one huge lake that could merge into the Zuiderzee (the area now occupied by Lake IJsselmeer). Investments from merchants primarily associated with the Dutch East India Company (the VOC) made possible the drainage of these large and deep lakes. The drained lakes offered new arable land for food production for the nearby cities such as Amsterdam, and the first reclaimed lake was the Beemster in 1612, where 60 windmills had to be used for pumping the water. Smaller numbers of windmills were also required for continuous pumping of rain and seepage water out of the lake. In the nineteenth century the windmills were replaced by steam pumping stations and in the twentieth century by electric pumping stations.

However, new and unexpected problems arose, as the groundwater in the reclaimed lakes became more and more brackish. Long before the peat areas were reclaimed, the sea had dominated the western and northern parts of the Netherlands, leaving behind thick layers of sand and clay. These sand and clay deposits, which are still found in the coastal zones and in the deep reclaimed lakes, were saturated by seawater. Since peat growth had dominated the area for about 3,000 years, over centuries the rainwater surplus had accumulated on top of the salt water, pushing the salt water down into the sediment. The body of fresh water, including the deep reclaimed lakes, has made normal agricultural activities possible in the area. However, as we see in Figure 15.4, the continuous pumping activities in the reclaimed lakes drained away not only the rain and seepage water, but also the old water pockets that were underneath. After a few centuries of pumping, large parts of the deepest reclaimed lakes become increasingly and irreversibly brackish, due to the complete removal of 3,000-years worth of rainwater surplus in the reclaimed lakes. As noted above, the problem is that crops are not resistant to brackish water.

Lake IJsselmeer is now used to provide the freshwater supply required to rinse the brackish polders. As the duration of dry periods increases and polders become more and more brackish, more fresh water will be needed in the future. Raising the water table of Lake IJsselmeer by 1.5 metres, as suggested by the Delta Committee, means that more of this rinsing water will be made available. However, this process also increases the speed of the salinization of the groundwater itself. The extra pressure of the lake water body increases the seepage into the reclaimed lake polders, so that more pumping is necessary. As a result, more deep saltwater rises to the surface.

15.4   RURAL AREAS: FROM PRODUCTION TO CONSUMPTION AREAS

The appearance of the Dutch rural landscape has changed dramatically, due to post-war agricultural mechanization and increasing agricultural productivity. Even today the number of farms is still shrinking while their average size is increasing. Large land consolidation schemes have also changed the rural landscape; enlarged lots have been equalized and barbed wire has replaced the traditional fences and hedges.

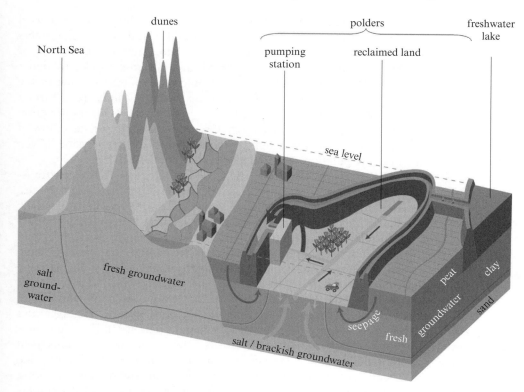

Figure 15.4   Dutch polders become brackish

The decrease in the number of farms, and increasing lot sizes and mechanization has led to a decrease in the level of labour intensity in the agricultural sector. Most of the resulting labour surplus in rural areas tried to find employment in urban areas. However, the depopulation in rural areas also led to a decrease in the level of support for all kind of services in such areas. For many services, ranging from shops to education and health care, the level of support fell below the critical threshold values and many policies have been developed to maintain the rural economies. Many new non-agricultural activities, such as architecture, arts, and financial services, were increasingly allowed to locate in former farm buildings.

Apart from changes in the agricultural sector itself, the rural areas have also been transformed by exogenous developments in society as a whole. Due to rising levels of wealth, health and welfare, the Dutch population has become increasingly mobile with more leisure time and disposable income. Between 1990 and 2010, car ownership rose from 344 to 462 cars per 1,000 inhabitants (CBS, 2010). This increased car ownership, in combination with more leisure time and disposable income, has led to a greater interest in rural areas on the part of the urban population, as areas for recreation. This has also led to an increased attention on, and interest in, cultural and historical landscapes as well as nature. The result was that, in contrast to the long-run agricultural trends of larger farm sizes, there emerged a new focus on the preservation of small-scale culturally and historically valuable landscapes, including historical farm buildings. This increased focus on rural areas also offered new business opportunities. For instance, small farmers found new sources of income, such as setting up mini-camping areas on their farm, or selling home grown produce. In addition, the increased car ownership also led to higher levels of individual mobility, thereby allowing households to choose to reside in the countryside while still working in urban areas. The pressure on dwellings (and former farms) in the countryside therefore became considerable, in particular in locations within commuting distance of the major urban areas. Finally, there was an increased inflow of retired people into the quietest and most highly valued parts of the countryside. Given the ongoing ageing of the population, this trend is likely to continue.

The result of all these post-war developments is that rural areas have been transformed from being predominantly agricultural production into multifunctional spaces, in which there is a large diversity of actors and activities (Huigen, 1996; Haartsen, 2002; Daalhuizen, 2004). Rural areas have seen a widespread shift from agricultural production towards activities related to nature and landscape preservation, recreation and tourism, as well as other non-agricultural activities and residential functions. As such, rural areas have been changing from being predominantly agricultural to increasingly becoming areas of leisure and consumption. These emerging activities, such as nature preservation and new residential land uses, have all laid spatial claims in rural areas. Furthermore, such changes in land use also have major consequences for the water management systems in rural areas. This is because these different land-use functions require different groundwater levels. Therefore, within the former water-management systems, subsystems should be developed to cope with those differing requirements, and this implies the construction of additional dams, dikes, ring canals and pumping stations.

A simple case study serves to demonstrate these issues. In the province of Drenthe, the Dutch National Forest Service (Staatsbosbeheer) is implementing a programme to preserve and restore active peat bog formation in original old moorland on the Dutch–German border. Before the deforestation and cultivation in the nineteenth century, Bourtanger Moor was approximately 3,000 km² in area, and as such it was one of the largest moors in Northern Europe. The Bourtanger Moor–Bargerveen International Nature Park is now a nature reserve on the Dutch–German border and has an area of about 140 km². As we see in Figure 15.5, the Dutch part, Bargerveen, is a Natura 2000 site, and with an area of some 2,100 hectares. It is high moorland, which means that peat grows above the groundwater level in rainwater and is thus acidic and nutrient poor. This results in high levels of biodiversity and therefore this is a highly valued nature reserve. Various types of sphagnum moss play a major role in the formation of peat. The rootless plants live off plain rainwater, absorbing it much like a sponge. A clump of sphagnum moss grows at the top and dies off at the bottom. The acidic water keeps oxygen out and prevents the remains from fully decomposing, thus forming an increasingly thicker layer of peat. It is therefore a closed self-supporting system. A high and stable water level and a nutrient-deficient environment are the prerequisites for active peat bog formation.

To achieve this situation, first, the peat bog remnants are embanked in order to retain the rain water as far as possible. Second, on the north side of the nature reserve a lower water basin is constructed in order to control the water level in the nature reserve. The water basin has to provide enough counter pressure to the high water level inside the nature reserve itself, so as to prevent a decrease of the water level in the nature reserve

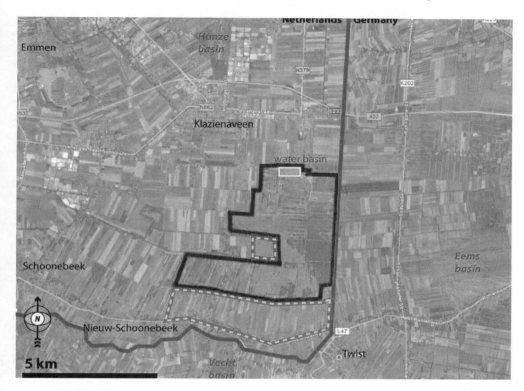

Note: The embankments of the central peat bog area are indicated in black, while the counter pressure water body is indicated in white. The dashed lines indicate future 'new nature' areas with raised water levels that will also function as counter pressure water bodies.

Figure 15.5   Overview of the situation at the Bargerveen nature reserve

area during periods of drought. This reservoir will therefore serve as a buffer against water seeping out of the reserve into the surrounding area. The basin makes it possible to regulate the water level inside the nature reserve, in order to stimulate further peat growth.

Figure 15.5 shows that the Bargerveen nature reserve is surrounded by agricultural land. In the past decades a system of more than 40 km of peat dikes was constructed in order to retain as much rainwater as possible, along with culverts and weirs to closely regulate the water level. More than 50 km of watercourses have been filled to prevent drainage (Dutch Forestry Commission, 2002). The water level within the nature reserve has been isolated as far as possible from the surrounding area and as we can see in Figure 15.6, the groundwater level in the peat has risen. New and stronger embankments have been constructed on and along the edge of the Bargerveen reserve, in order to be able to maintain high water levels in the area, without the risk of the embankment collapsing. The cost of implementing these infrastructure investments was approximately €40 million for the 1968–2005 period (Waterschap Velt en Vecht, 2008). In 2008 an additional €20 million was allocated (ibid.) for implementing the further infrastructure

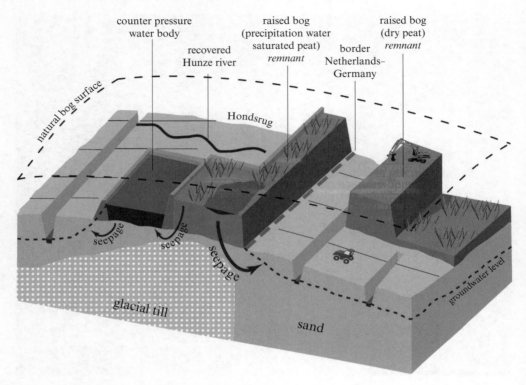

Figure 15.6   Hydrological complications of the Bargerveen nature reserve

investments required to separate both systems. In the same agreement between the District Water Board, the Ministry of Agriculture, the Province of Drenthe, and the Dutch Forestry Service, a claim from farmers' representatives was also approved. In a buffer zone of some 500 metres around the Bargerveen nature reserve, farmers will be offered a fair price for their land in these consolidation schemes. This 500-metre buffer zone, which in total amounts to about 225 hectares, will perform the function of a 'hydrological buffer' and 'new nature' zone. Due to the rising groundwater levels in this zone, it is no longer possible to farm there with heavy machinery.

To summarize, the development of a nature reserve in an agricultural area is complex. A wide range of stakeholders are involved, including farmers, different levels and arms of government, and nature preservation organizations. The land-use impacts cover a much larger area than are demarcated by the project itself, and there are also clear external effects. In particular, the value of the agricultural land falls due to the increasing ground-water levels or the increasingly unstable groundwater levels. With this simple example it becomes clear that the transformation of rural areas from predominantly agricultural production into more multifunctional spaces, places an increasing emphasis and level of responsibility on the role of the district water boards. In particular, the district water boards have to cope with the diverse requests from various actors for groundwater levels which cannot be as sharply demarcated in space as these user functions require. As such, the district water boards therefore have increasingly adopted the role of an intermediary actor who has to manage the differing spatial claims of the different user groups and all of the directly and indirectly related stakeholder interests.

15.5   CONCLUSIONS

In the near future, the Dutch water management system will have to adapt to face many new hydrological challenges. As well as climate change, these new challenges are also due to the transition of the rural areas from being predominantly agricultural into multifunctional consumption areas. In this chapter we have discussed these various challenges including: the rising sea levels; the salinization of the western part of the country; the intensified periods of heavy rainfall; the extended periods of drought; and the intensified land use functions. All these developments have major implications for the water management sector. The main threat of flooding no longer comes from the sea, but rather from the rivers during periods of heavy rainfall. Excess capacity needs to be created within the river system itself and additional retention areas must be developed in both rural and urban areas, so as to store the excess rainwater until the river system can cope with the overflow. The salinization which is due to the rising sea levels and the pumping of the polders makes fresh water a highly valuable asset. The extended periods of drought make fresh water an even more valuable commodity and the storage of large freshwater reserves indispensable. These freshwater reserves are vital not only for rinsing brackish areas so as to keep them fit for agricultural use, but also for maintaining the water levels in the river system in periods of drought, in order to ensure that inland water transport continues and enough cooling water is provided for the energy sector. The storage of large freshwater reserves, such as in Lake IJsselmeer, for example, has also led to major changes in the water management system of the adjacent areas. Instead of draining their excess water into the lake, these areas have to find an alternative solution, while at the same time having to cope with more excess water due to seepage from the lake and also greater salinization due to the increased pumping of excess water. Finally, the increased pressure on the rural landscape from agriculture, business, housing, recreation, nature and leisure, complicates the water management system when those land-use functions require different levels of groundwater.

It is therefore to be expected that the water management sector will become more complicated in the near future, due to the greater land-use pressures and the larger number of stakeholders who are involved. Formerly, district water boards were concerned only with safety and the interests of farmers regarding groundwater levels. Now, more stakeholders are laying their claims on the desks of the district water boards: the national, provincial and local governments all have to develop retention areas; planning agencies want to develop new residential areas and industrial sites; environmentalists want to develop 'typical Dutch' water landscapes; citizens and firms want to keep their feet dry; and farmers want the groundwater levels to be about one metre below the surface. The district water boards therefore have to deal with many, often rather conflicting, interests, acting as a neutral intermediary between the stakeholders involved, with the specific knowledge and expertise to come up with the most appropriate solutions. Transferring the water management system to the provincial level would mean somewhat less neutral parties becoming responsible for the water management sector. This in turn might affect the public support for the difficult decisions which need to be taken in order to adjust the water management systems appropriately. The resulting public inquiry procedures may seriously delay the planning and implementation processes that are required to cope efficiently with the new issues that confront the water management sector, as discussed in this chapter.

REFERENCES

Borger, G.J. (2004), 'De Achtermeer bij Alkmaar, de oudste droogmakerij?', *Historisch Geografisch Tijdschrift*, **2**, 37–49 (in Dutch).
CBS (2010), Statline.
Daalhuizen, F.B.C. (2004), *Nieuwe bedrijven in oude boerderijen. De keuze voor een Voormalige Boerderij als Bedrijfslocatie*, Deflt: Eburon.
Dutch Forestry Commission (2002), *Bargerveen: Management over the Next Few Years*, Dutch Forestry Commission for the Groningen-Drenthe Region, Noordwolde.
Haartsen, T. (2002), 'Platteland: boerenland, natuurterrein of beleidsveld? Een Onderzoek naar Veranderingen in Functies, Eigendom en Representaties van het Nederlandse Platteland', Faculty of Spatial Sciences, University of Groningen.
Huigen, P.P.P. (1996), 'Verliest het Platteland Zijn Streken?', Faculty of Spatial Sciences, University of Groningen.
KNMI (2006), *Klimaat in de 21e eeuw: vier scenario's voor Nederland* (Climate in the 21st century: four scenarios for the Netherlands), De Bilt: KNMI.
Ministry of Transport and Public Works (2000), *Ruimte voor de Rivier* (Room for the River), The Hague: Ministry of Transport and Public Works.
Ministry of Transport and Public Works (2004), *Water in the Netherlands*, The Hague: Ministry of Transport and Public Works.
Ministry of Transport and Public Works (2009), *National Water Plan 2009–2015*, The Hague: Ministry of Transport and Public Works.
NAM (2010), 'Bodemdaling door Aardgaswinning', Nederlandse Aardolie Maatschappij BV, Groningen.
Waterschap Velt en Vecht (2008), *Bagerveen, Natura 2000 en de Waterhuishouding*, Coevorden: Waterschap Velt en Vecht.

PART V

KNOWLEDGE- AND NETWORK-BASED ACTIVITIES

16 The geography of research and development activity in the US

*Kristy Buzard and Gerald Carlino**

16.1 INTRODUCTION

Although metropolitan areas account for less than 20 percent of the total land area in the United States, they contain almost 80 percent of the nation's population and nearly 85 percent of its jobs. In other words, the United States has, on average, 24 jobs per square mile, but metropolitan areas average about 124 jobs per square mile. According to Strange (2009), the population of six Canadian metropolitan areas (Toronto, Montreal, Vancouver, Ottawa, Calgary, and Edmonton) account for almost one-half of the national population but less than 1 percent of Canada's land area. Very similar concentration patterns are evident in data from Europe (Combes and Overman, 2004) and Asia (Fujita, et al., 2004).

This high degree of spatial concentration of people and jobs leads to congestion costs, such as increased traffic and pollution, and higher housing costs. For example, according to the Texas Transport Institute's annual Mobility Report, US drivers spent on average 4.2 billion hours in traffic delays in 2007; Los Angeles-area drivers sat the longest (70 hours per traveler), while motorists in the Wichita, Kansas, area spent only 6 hours per traveler in delays.[1] Congestion has become so severe in London that in February 2003 the city imposed a congestion fee, currently £8 a day, on all vehicles entering, leaving, driving, or parking on a public road inside the charging zone between 7:00 a.m. and 6 p.m., Monday through Friday. On January 3, 2006, Stockholm became the second European city to introduce a congestion charge. Similar fees are now in effect in Singapore, Oslo, and Rome. In the United States, New York City considered a similar plan and the city of Chicago is currently considering congestion fees for cars parked downtown. To offset these congestion costs, workers must receive higher wages, and higher wages increase firms' costs.

If congestion costs were the only effect of the spatial concentration of firms, firms could easily disperse to reduce these costs; yet they do not. This is because the negative effects of concentration make up only one side of the urban ledger. The positive effects of agglomeration economies – efficiency gains and cost savings that result from being close to suppliers, workers, customers, and even competitors – make up the other. Other things equal, firms will have little incentive to move if congestion costs are balanced by the benefits of agglomeration economies.

In this chapter, we use a new dataset on the location of almost 3,500 research and development (R&D) labs in 1998 to establish some stylized facts regarding the spatial concentration of innovative activity in the United States. We use a variant of the Ellison and Glaeser (1997) index of agglomeration developed by Guimarães et al. (2007) to examine the spatial distribution of R&D labs. To address the issue of the significance of clusters, we follow the lead of Duranton and Overman (2005) in that we are able to identify R&D clusters that are significantly different from spatial randomness. Specifically, we use the geographical location of manufacturing employment as a benchmark against which to measure significant clustering. Hence, R&D clusters are identified as 'significant' only when they contain more R&D labs than would be expected on the basis of manufacturing employment alone.

We show that while economic activity tends to be geographically concentrated, spatial concentration is even more pronounced among establishments doing basic R&D. We find, in particular, that R&D activity for most industries tends to be concentrated in the Northeast corridor, around the Great Lakes, in California's Bay Area, and in southern California.

We conjecture that more than most types of economic activity, R&D depends on a particular byproduct of agglomeration economies called 'knowledge spillovers' – the continuing exchange of ideas among individuals and firms. A high geographical concentration of R&D labs creates an environment in which ideas move quickly from person to person and from lab to lab. Locations that are dense in R&D activity encourage knowledge spillovers, thus facilitating the exchange of ideas that underlies the creation of new goods and new ways of producing existing goods. We find several pieces of evidence that support this view. We run a regression of a variant of the Guimarães et al. (2007) – hereafter GFW – index measuring the spatial concentration of R&D labs on geographical proxies for knowledge spillovers and other location-specific characteristics, and find evidence that localized knowledge spillovers are important for innovative activity. In particular, we show that a strong positive correlation exists between the geographical concentration of R&D labs and citation-weighted patent intensity (our proxy for knowledge spillovers).[2] All else equal, the index of agglomeration for R&D labs will be 15 percent greater in a county with twice the citation intensity of another county. In addition, we find evidence (although it is mixed) to support the existence of Jacobs externalities for R&D activity.

We also find evidence that human capital is highly correlated with the clustering of R&D labs. In fact, of the things we considered, by far the most powerful effect on spatial clustering of labs is generated by local human capital. Specifically, a 1 percent increase in the share of employment accounted for by professional and specialty occupations is associated with a 3.5 percent increase in the spatial concentration of R&D labs.

16.2   LITERATURE REVIEW ON KNOWLEDGE CLUSTERING

Krugman (1991) and Audretsch and Feldman (1996) developed a 'locational Gini coefficient' to answer the question of which manufacturing industries cluster geographically. A locational Gini coefficient shows how similar (or dissimilar) the location pattern of employment in a particular industry is from the location pattern of overall employment. Let s_{ij} represent location i's share of employment in industry j, and x_i represent location i's share of aggregate employment or total population. The spatial Gini coefficient for industry j is defined as:

$$G_j = \sum_i (x_i - s_{ij})^2,$$ (16.1)

where $G = 0$ indicates that employment in a given manufacturing industry is no more or less geographically concentrated than overall manufacturing employment, and $G > 0$ implies that employment in the industry is overconcentrated. Audretsch and Feldman use the United States Small Business Administration's Innovation Data Base that consists of innovations compiled from the new product announcements sections in manufacturing trade journals. They found that innovation tends to be relatively more concentrated in industries where knowledge spillovers tend to be important.

Importantly, Ellison and Glaeser (1997) – hereafter EG – have identified a potential problem with the locational Gini coefficient. They argue that if an industry consists of a small number of establishments, the locational Gini coefficient may indicate localization of the industry under consideration, even if there is no agglomeration force behind the industry's location.[3] EG have developed an alternative concentration measure that controls for an industry's organization:

$$\gamma = \frac{G_j - (1 - \Sigma_i x_i^2) H_j}{\left(1 - \Sigma_i x_i^2\right)(1 - H_j)}, \tag{16.2}$$

where H_j represents the employment Herfindahl index for industry j:

$$H_j = \Sigma_k z_{jk}^2,$$

where $(z_{jk} : k = 1, \text{L}, m_j)$ denotes the distribution of employment across m_j plants in industry j. Using Proposition 1 in EG, the numerator of (16.2) can be expressed as:

$$G_j - (1 - \Sigma_i x_i^2)[\gamma + (1 - \gamma) H_j]. \tag{16.3}$$

Let $\gamma = \gamma^{na} + \gamma^s - \gamma^{na} \gamma^s$ where γ^{na} reflects the benefits of a location's natural advantages (ports, resource endowments, and so on) and γ^s index reflects spillovers (for example, knowledge spillovers).

Consider the special case where plants are randomly distributed across locations. That is, they are influenced neither by natural advantage nor by spillover effects ($\gamma^{na} = \gamma^s = 0$). If we treat this spatial randomness case as the null hypothesis, then EG show that $(1 - \Sigma_i x_i^2) H_j$ is the expected value, $E(G_j)$, of G_j under this hypothesis. In addition, they show that $E(G_j) > (1 - \Sigma_i x_i^2) H_j$ otherwise. If G_j is taken as an estimate of $E(G_j)$ then the EG index provides a test of the null hypothesis. That is, EG compare the degree of spatial concentration of employment in an industry with what would arise if all plants in the industry were randomly distributed across locations. EG, and more recently Rosenthal and Strange (2001), find evidence of the geographical concentration of employment in many US manufacturing industries.

Duranton and Overman (2005) – hereafter DO – use plant-level data for manufacturing activity in the UK and show that the geographical concentration of manufacturing jobs is not simply an American phenomenon. Their data identify the postal codes for each manufacturing plant in the UK, allowing them to geocode the data. This is important, since DO are not bound by a fixed geographical classification (such as states, metropolitan statistical areas (MSAs), or counties) but base their approach on the actual distance between firms. Additionally, rather than using a specific index to measure geographical concentration, such as the EG index, DO take a non-parametric approach (that is, kernel density methods). Essentially, DO construct frequency distributions of the pairwise distances between plants in a given industry. When the mass of the distribution is concentrated on the left of the distribution, this represents a spatial concentration of plants in the industry. Alternatively, if the mass of the distribution is concentrated on the right of the distribution, this represents a more dispersed spatial pattern. Importantly, DO consider whether the number of plants at a given distance is *significantly* different from the number found if their locations were randomly chosen. This represents an important improvement over the rule-of-thumb approach used by EG to determine differing levels of the spatial concentration of an industry.

A study by Arzaghi and Henderson (2008) looks at the location pattern of firms in the advertising industry in Manhattan. They report that Manhattan accounts for 20 percent of total national employment in the ad industry, 24 percent of all advertising agency receipts, and 31 percent of media billings. They show that for an ad agency, knowledge spillovers and the benefits of networking with other nearby agencies are large but the benefits dissipate very quickly with distance from other ad agencies and are gone after roughly half a mile.

Holmes and Stevens (2004) take a broader approach. They use employment data for all US industries, not just manufacturing, and not for just a single industry, such as advertising. Among the 15 most concentrated industries, they find that six are in mining and seven are in manufacturing; only two industries fall outside mining and manufacturing (casino hotels, and motion picture and video distribution).

Several other studies find that knowledge spillovers dissipate rapidly with distance. See, for example, Audretsch and Feldman (1996), Keller (2002) and Arzaghi and Henderson (2008). Agrawal et al. (2008) find that every 1,000-mile increase in the distance between inventors reduces the probability of knowledge flow as measured by patent citations by about 2 percent.

Our work differs from past studies in three ways. First, rather than looking at the geographical concentration of firms engaged in the production of goods (such as manufacturing) and services (such as advertising), we consider the spatial concentration of private R&D activity.[4] Second, rather than focusing on the concentration of employment in a given industry, we look at the clustering of individual R&D labs.[5] Third, following DO, we look for geographical clusters of labs that represent statistically significant departures from spatial randomness using simulation techniques.

16.3   THE DATA AND THE MODEL

We used 1998 data on R&D labs from the *Directory of American Research and Technology* (1999) to electronically code the addresses and other information about R&D labs, data that were not previously available in a machine-readable format. Since the directory lists the complete address for each establishment, we were able to assign a geographical identifier (using geocoding techniques) to 3,446 R&D labs in the US in 1998.[6] The data on manufacturing employment at the zip code level are found in the

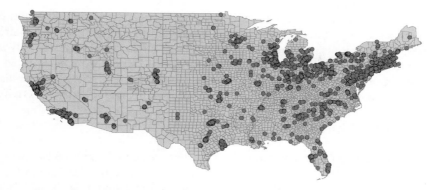

Note: Each dot represents a spatial concentration of overall R&D labs.

Figure 16.1 Location of total R&D labs

Department of Commerce's Zip Code Business Patterns 1998 data. We assigned these data to each point by assuming that manufacturing employment is uniformly distributed across points within a zip code.

16.3.1 Clustering of R&D Labs

Figure 16.1 shows a map of the spatial distribution of R&D labs that reveals a striking clustering of this activity. The dots shown on the map tend to represent concentrations of R&D labs. A prominent feature of the map is the high concentration of R&D activity in the Northeast corridor, stretching from northern Virginia to Massachusetts. There are other concentrations, such as the cluster around the Great Lakes and the concentration of labs in California's Bay Area and in southern California. But some states that account for a relatively large share of the nation's jobs account for a much smaller share of the nation's R&D labs. For example, Texas ranks second among states in terms of employment, but it ranks eighth in terms of labs. Similarly, Florida ranks fourth in employment but 13th in terms of labs.

As already noted, recent studies have shown that economic activity, especially manufacturing, also tends to be geographically clustered. However, it appears that R&D labs are more highly concentrated than establishments in general or establishments in manufacturing. There are more than 3,100 counties in the US, and all of them are engaged in some type of economic activity. All but 33 counties are engaged in some form of manufacturing activity. In contrast, only 519 of them have at least one R&D lab, and far fewer have a notable concentration of labs.

Another way to quantify relative concentrations is to compute each county's share of total R&D labs and rank counties by descending order of this share. Moving down this ranking, we compute a cumulative total for the share of R&D labs. We also construct a similar ranking for establishments in general and for manufacturing establishments in particular. The top 50 counties ranked by number of R&D labs account for 58 percent of all R&D labs, while the top 50 counties ranked by number of manufacturing establishments account for only 36 percent of all manufacturing establishments and only

32 percent of all establishments. It appears that R&D labs are more highly concentrated than economic activity in general and overall manufacturing activity in particular. This is important because it means that the concentration of R&D labs does not simply reflect the concentration of manufacturing activity. Since R&D is more concentrated than manufacturing activity, this suggests that some factors, such as knowledge spillovers, may be a more centralizing force for R&D than they are for manufacturing activity.

16.3.2   Which R&D Labs Cluster?

To answer the question of which R&D labs cluster, we shall follow the lead of GFW, who have generalized the EG index to include the case where the data are in the form of establishments (labs, in our case) rather than employment shares, as in the EG index. The GFW locational Gini, or the GFW index, is constructed as follows: let: n_{ij} = the number of labs in county i, in industry j, n_j = the total number of labs in industry j across all i counties in the US, x_i is county i's share of aggregate manufacturing employment. Let the spatial Gini based on counts be defined as:

$$G_{j,c} = \sum_i \left(\frac{n_{ij}}{n_i} - x_i \right)^2.$$ (16.4)

The adjusted spatial Gini ($\hat{G}_j$) for industry j is given by:

$$\hat{G}_j = \frac{n_j G_{j,c} - \left(1 - \sum_i x_i^2 \right)}{(n_j - 1)\left(1 - \sum_i x_i^2 \right)}.$$ (16.5)

($\hat{G}_j$) is similar to that of the EG index in equation (16.2) except that in the above index, H_j is replaced by $1/n_j$ and the spatial Gini for manufacturing employment, G_j in the EG index, is replaced by its counterpart expressed in terms of counts of labs instead of employment. The expression $(n_j - 1)(1 - \sum_i x_i^2)$ is included so that the index has the property that $\hat{G}_j = 0$ when labs are no more or no less concentrated than manufacturing employment. For our county data, $(1 - \sum x_i^2)$ takes on values close to one, 0.99593.[7]

We use the adjusted GFW index as our measure of concentration for R&D by industry. Our sample consists of 376 four-digit Standard Industrial Classification industries at the county level. We find an adjusted GFW index of 0.0457 for R&D in the average industry at the *county* level. In studying the agglomeration patterns in the manufacturing industries, Rosenthal and Strange (2001) report an average adjusted Gini coefficient (using the EG index) of 0.0193 for manufacturing in 2000 at the county level.[8] Thus, our R&D labs appear to be more spatially concentrated, on average, than is manufacturing activity. Our measure of concentration, the adjusted GFW index, has a maximum value of about one for R&D in five industries.[9] However, there are only two R&D labs in each of these industries, so it is not surprising to find a large value for the adjusted Gini index if the two firms are located in proximity to each other.[10] Table 16.1 shows the values of the adjusted GFW index for industries with 20 or more labs. The table shows that R&D

Table 16.1   *Concentration of R&D labs for selected industries*

Industry	Number of labs	Adjusted GFW index[a]
Highly concentrated industries[b]		
Oil & gas field machinery	22	0.33
Tires and tubes	14	0.12
Computer storage devices	34	0.08
Motor vehicles & car bodies	26	0.06
Electronic computers	57	0.06
Moderately concentrated industries[c]		
Semiconductors	278	0.03
Prepackaged software	359	0.03
Motor vehicle parts	134	0.03
Optical instruments and lenses	36	0.03
Radio and TV communication equipment	185	0.02
Dispersed industries[d]		
Search, detection, navigation	155	0.01
Paints, varnishes, etc.	131	0.01
Refrigeration, heating equipment	36	0.00
Printed circuit boards	64	0.00
Electronic connectors	66	0.00

Notes:
a. The adjusted GFW index for a given industry shows the sum of the squared differences of the share of employment in manufacturing from the share of labs in given industry, adjusted to account for the industrial organization of the industry under consideration.
b. R&D in an industry is highly concentrated if the adjusted Gini coefficient is at least 0.05.
c. R&D in an industry is moderately concentrated if the adjusted Gini coefficient is at least 0.02, but less than 0.05.
d. R&D in an industry is dispersed if the adjusted Gini coefficient is less than 0.02.

tends to be most concentrated in the oil and gas field machinery industry, the computer storage devices industry, and the electronic computer industry.

Our findings indicate that 256, or 68 percent, of all R&D labs have an adjusted Gini index greater than zero, suggesting that R&D labs are appreciably more concentrated than manufacturing employment. Earlier we reported that the top 50 counties ranked by number of R&D labs account for 58 percent of all R&D labs, while the top 50 counties ranked by number of manufacturing establishments account for only 36 percent of all manufacturing establishments. Thus, the concentration of labs is broadly similar when looking at the top 50 counties or the adjusted Gini index. Only 1 percent of the labs are associated with an index that is negative, indicating dispersion.

While an adjusted Gini index could have a value greater than zero, an important question is, 'Does this represent a significant departure from the average concentration of manufacturing employment?'. We performed a simulation procedure to determine what value of the adjusted GFW indices constitutes a significant departure from the concentration of manufacturing employment.[11] We find that R&D labs in 129 of the 376 industries considered (34.3 percent) are significantly more concentrated than is manufacturing employment.

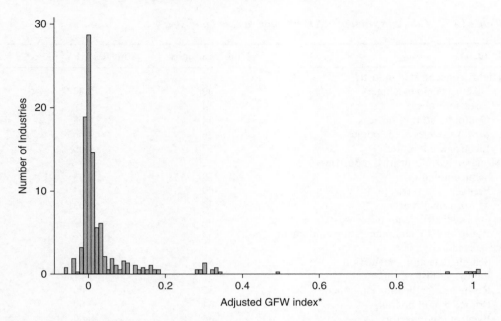

Note: The adjusted GFW index shows the sum of squared differences of the share of overall labs in a given industry, adjusted to account for industry structure.

Figure 16.2   *Histogram showing the frequency distribution of the adjusted GFW index that compares the concentration of R&D labs in a given industry with the concentration of manufacturing employment*

Figure 16.2 shows the distribution of the adjusted GFW index for R&D activity. Each bar shows the number of industries associated with a particular value for the adjusted GFW index. Following EG, we consider R&D in an industry to be highly concentrated if the adjusted Gini index is at least 0.05 and moderately concentrated if the index is at least 0.02, but less than 0.05. R&D in an industry is considered to be dispersed if the index is less than 0.01. A prominent feature of Figure 16.2 is the large number of industries falling into the range we have classified as not very concentrated (an adjusted GFW index less than 0.02). The tallest bars tend to surround an adjusted GFW index around zero. In fact, 69 percent of the industries have an adjusted GFW index below 0.02.[12] Sixty-six of the 376 industries considered have an adjusted GFW index that is at least 0.05. That is only 18 percent of all industries. In addition, these 66 highly concentrated industries account for only 6 percent of all R&D labs. If we include industries that are moderately concentrated, that is, those with an adjusted GFW index that is at least 0.02 but less than 0.05, we can add another 49 names to the list of industries that tend to be more concentrated relative to manufacturing employment. Still, these 115 concentrated industries (66 highly concentrated industries plus 49 moderately concentrated industries) account for only 31 percent of all industries and for only 29 percent of all R&D labs.

Until now, we have looked at the concentration of R&D labs relative to the con-

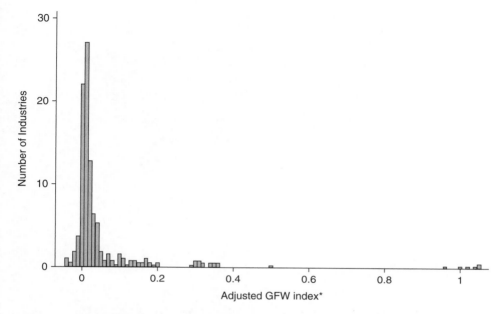

Note: The adjusted GFW index shows the sum of squared differences of the share of employment in manufacturing from the share of labs in a given industry, adjusted to account for industry structure.

Figure 16.3   *Histogram showing the frequency distribution of the adjusted GFW index that compares the concentration of R&D labs in a given industry with the concentration of overall labs*

centration of manufacturing employment. We would also like to know whether labs in a particular industry (such as pharmaceuticals) are more or less concentrated than overall R&D labs. To get this information, we recalculated the adjusted GFW index to reflect the geographical concentration of labs in individual industries relative to the overall concentration of R&D labs (as opposed to the overall concentration of manufacturing employment). The distribution of the adjusted GFW index when the benchmark is overall R&D labs (Figure 16.3) is remarkably similar to the distribution when the benchmark is overall manufacturing employment (Figure 16.2). However, there tends to be slightly more concentration of labs in individual industries compared with the location of labs in general. Thirty-six percent of the industries are at least moderately concentrated, compared with 31 percent when the benchmark is manufacturing employment. Still, the tallest bars in Figure 16.3 tend to surround an adjusted GFW index around zero, suggesting that for the majority of industries, labs at the industry level tend not to be more spatially concentrated than labs overall.

Maps of R&D activity for individual industries (for example, software, Figure 16.4; pharmaceuticals, Figure 16.5; and chemicals, Figure 16.6) confirm the findings of the locational Gini coefficient in that the location pattern of R&D activity for the majority of industries is broadly similar to the location pattern of overall R&D

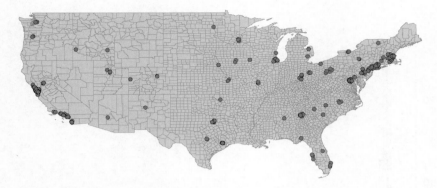

Note: Each dot represents a spatial concentration of software R&D labs.

Figure 16.4   Location of software R&D labs

Note: Each dot represents a spatial concentration of pharmaceutical R&D labs.

Figure 16.5   Location of pharmaceutical R&D labs

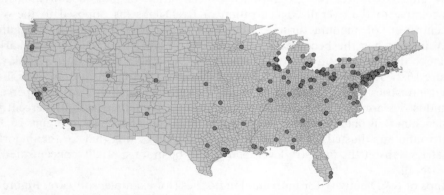

Note: Each dot represents a spatial concentration of chemistry R&D labs.

Figure 16.6   Location of chemistry R&D labs

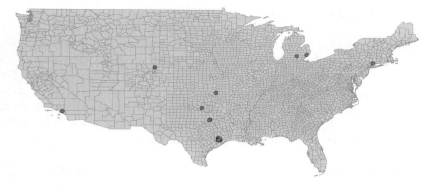

Note: Each dot represents a spatial concentration of oil and gas field machinery R&D labs.

Figure 16.7   Location of oil and gas field machinery R&D labs

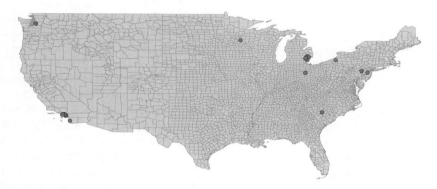

Note: Each dot represents a spatial concentration of motor vehicle and car body R&D labs.

Figure 16.8   Location of motor vehicle and car body R&D labs

activity. That is, R&D activity for most industries tends to be concentrated in the Northeast corridor, around the Great Lakes, in California's Bay Area, and in southern California.

As indicated, there are a number of exceptions to the general pattern of geographical concentration just described. One exception is R&D activity in the oil and gas field machinery industry, which tends to be concentrated in Texas, especially in the Houston area, and accounts for about 60 percent of the labs doing R&D in this industry (Figure 16.7). Another exception is the location of R&D activity in the motor vehicle and car body industry, which tends to be concentrated in Michigan, especially in the Detroit area, and which accounts for just under 40 percent of the labs doing R&D in this industry (Figure 16.8). This industry is composed of establishments primarily engaged in manufacturing motor vehicle parts and accessories.

16.4   WHY DO R&D LABS CLUSTER?

A number of theories have been advanced to explain firms' (not just R&D labs) tendency to cluster spatially. Firms may attempt to minimize transport costs by locating close to a natural resource used as an input, or to their suppliers, or to their markets. Or firms may cluster to share inputs, such as specialized workers. Finally, firms may cluster to take advantage of knowledge that 'spills over' when firms are located near one another. Among these, the sharing of inputs and especially of knowledge spillovers is likely to be most important for R&D labs when choosing a location.

16.4.1   Knowledge Spillovers

While theories of knowledge spillovers were originally developed to explain the concentration of industries in general, we think that they are particularly important to an explanation of the clustering of R&D labs. More than most industries, R&D depends on new knowledge. Often, the latest knowledge about technological developments is valuable to firms but only for a short time. Thus, it behoves firms to locate as close as possible to the sources of information. The high spatial concentration of R&D activity facilitates the exchange of ideas among firms and aids in the creation of new goods and new ways of producing existing goods.

Two types of knowledge spillovers are thought to be important in understanding the location pattern of R&D labs: MAR spillovers and Jacobs spillovers. According to the MAR theory of spillovers, the concentration of establishments (labs in our case) in the same industry in a common area helps knowledge travel among labs and their workers and facilitates innovation and growth.[13] Using data for US manufacturing, Rosenthal and Strange (2001) and Ellison et al. (2007) consider the importance of input sharing, matching, and knowledge spillovers for manufacturing firms at various levels of geographical disaggregation (state, MSA, county, and zip code levels). These studies find evidence for all three mechanisms. Importantly, Rosenthal and Strange (2001) find that the effects of knowledge spillovers on the agglomeration of manufacturing firms tend to be quite localized, influencing agglomeration only at the zip code level.[14]

Jacobs (1969) believed that knowledge spillovers are related to the diversity of industries (diversity of labs in our case) in an area, in contrast to MAR spillovers, which focus on firms in a common industry. Jacobs argued that an industrially diverse environment encourages innovation. Such environments include knowledge workers with varied backgrounds and interests, thereby facilitating the exchange of ideas among individuals with different perspectives. This exchange can lead to the development of new ideas, products, and processes. While other factors could be at work, the adjusted GFW indices appear to offer support for Jacobs's diversity view, in that R&D labs for the vast majority of industries (about two-thirds) tend to exhibit a common overlapping pattern of concentration. Feldman and Audretsch (1999) used the US Small Business Administration's Innovation Data Base and focused on innovative activity for particular industries within specific MSAs. They found less industry-specific innovation in MSAs that specialized in a given industry, a finding that also supports Jacobs's diversity thesis.

16.4.2 Other Forces for Concentration

While it is tempting to argue that the broadly similar geographical clustering of R&D labs in many different industries is suggestive of Jacobs externalities, this conjecture is simply based on a visual inspection of a map (Figure 16.1). The finding that R&D labs tend to display a common overlapping pattern of concentration suggests that Jacobs spillovers may be more important for R&D labs than MAR spillovers. Jacobs spillovers are one possible way to account for the common overlapping pattern of concentration among R&D labs, but other forces might be at work. One such source is the natural advantages an area offers to firms that locate there. The natural advantages of an area, such as climate, soil, and mineral and ore deposits, could explain the location of some R&D labs. For example, oil deposits, an essential ingredient for testing equipment, may be largely responsible for the concentration of R&D labs in the oil and gas field machinery industry (the most highly concentrated industry according to our adjusted GFW indices) in Texas, especially in the Houston area. But the draw of ore deposits seems to be industry specific and is therefore unlikely to account for the common overlapping pattern of concentration among R&D labs in many different industries. Of course, if R&D labs tend to be drawn to areas offering amenities such as pleasant weather, proximity to the ocean, and scenic views, this could explain the overlapping concentration in amenity-rich locations, such as the concentrations found in California. While local amenities might explain some of the concentrations of labs, the vast majority of R&D labs tend to be highly concentrated in the relatively low-amenity rust belt region of the country.

Another type of an area's natural advantage is its workers and its institutions, especially its universities. Universities are key players not only in creating new knowledge through the basic research produced by their faculties but also in supplying a pool of knowledge workers on which R&D depends. It is well known that Silicon Valley and the Route 128 corridor became important centers for R&D as a result of their proximities to Stanford and MIT. Saxenian (1994) describes how Stanford's support of local firms is an important reason for Silicon Valley's success. Two of Stanford's star engineering professors, John Linvill and Fred Terman, not only drew some of the best and brightest students to Stanford but also trained their students (and encouraged them) to seek careers in the semiconductor industry.

There is also evidence that an area's human capital can be an important type of natural advantage. Carlino et al. (2007) looked at the effect of a metropolitan area's human capital (the share of the adult population with at least a college education) on an area's ability to innovate (measured by patents per capita). Of the explanatory factors they considered, by far the most powerful effect on local innovation is generated by local human capital. They find that a 10 percent increase in the share of the adult population with at least a college degree is associated with an 8.6 percent increase in patents per capita. Lin (2007) finds that applications and adaptations of new work are positively correlated with an area's human capital and industrial variety.

There is also general evidence that R&D at local universities is important for firms' innovative activity. Audretsch and Feldman (1996) and Anselin et al. (1997) found evidence of localized knowledge spillovers from university R&D to commercial innovation by private firms, even after controlling for the location of industrial R&D. However,

Carlino et al. (2007) found that R&D at local universities has only modest effects on local innovative activity. They found that a 10 percent increase in R&D intensity of local universities is associated with less than a 1 percent increase in patent intensity.

16.4.3   Estimates of the Determinants of R&D Clustering

In this subsection, we consider the role of knowledge spillovers and access to skilled human capital on the spatial clustering of R&D labs. Recall that we have only one adjusted GFW index for each industry. These industry indices can, however, be used to construct an *overall* adjusted GFW index for each county. We do this by weighting each industry's adjusted GFW index by the share of the county's R&D labs accounted for by that industry. Each of the industry-weighted adjusted GFW indices for a given county are then summed to arrive at an overall adjusted GFW index for each county.

The overall adjusted GFW index for a county can be correlated with proxies for agglomeration economies. One such economy is the ability of firms in a common endeavor to share specialized inputs. Highly skilled labor is likely to be an important, if not the most important, input in the R&D process. We measure highly skilled labor using those jobs falling into the Census Bureau's classification of professional specialty occupations. This grouping includes engineers, scientists, social scientists, doctors, and other health professionals. But it also includes teachers, lawyers, artists, and athletes. This is a residency-based measure of employment in 1990. We expect a positive correlation between the GFW index and the professional specialty occupations' variable.

Two proxies are used for knowledge spillovers available to labs in the same county. Citation-weighted patents normalized by the number of workers in professional specialty occupations are one variable used to proxy for knowledge spillovers. As Rosenthal and Strange (2001) point out, one concern about using patents as an indicator of knowledge spillovers is that the value of patents is very highly skewed. Most are not worth very much, while some have values that are higher by several orders of magnitude (see, for example, Harhoff et al., 1999). Fortunately, there are ways to introduce an adjustment for quality into these counts, just as is done for journal articles, by counting the number of citations a patent receives in subsequent patents. A number of empirical studies document a strong positive correlation between these 'forward' citations and the economic value these patents contribute to the firms that own them. For example, Hall et al. (2005) show that a one-citation increase in the average number of patents in a publicly held firm's portfolio increases its market value by 3 percent. In addition, these citations present a concrete illustration of knowledge spillovers.[15] Thus, we use citation-weighted patents per worker in the professional specialty occupations in 1990 at the county level as one of our proxy variables for knowledge spillovers. In addition, we use universities' R&D in the years 1987–89 as a proxy variable for information spillovers from universities to private R&D labs. R&D performed by academic institutions is normalized by total full-time enrollment at colleges and universities in the MSA in those years.

A Herfindahl index of industrial diversity is used to address the question as to whether knowledge spillovers are largely Jacobs or largely MAR. By construction, a county is said to be more highly specialized or less diversified as the value of the diversity index increases.[16] Recall that as the value of the adjusted GFW index increases, the extent of the spatial concentration of labs in the industry also increases. A positive correlation between the overall county-adjusted GFW index and the specialization index means that as the county becomes more specialized industrially, its labs are also becoming more geographically concentrated. This is evidence favoring MAR spillovers. On the other hand, if the geographical concentration of labs tends to increase as the specialization index decreases – indicating a more industrially diverse (or less specialized) area – this negative correlation provides evidence in favor of Jacobs spillovers.

The share of employment in the manufacturing industry is included in all regressions to control for the fact that the vast majority of patents are issued to firms in the manufacturing sector. Finally, we used eight census region dummy variables to broadly control for an area's natural advantages, such as climate (New England is the excluded region in all regressions).

16.4.4   Estimates of the Determinants of Concentration of R&D Labs

The forces underlying the agglomeration of R&D labs are estimated using the following regression framework:

$$GFW_i = \beta X_i + \varepsilon_i, \tag{16.6}$$

where GFW_i is the industry-weighed adjusted GFW index based on R&D labs in 1998 for county i; X_i is a vector of county characteristics; and ε_i is the usual error term. To mitigate any bias induced by endogeneity or reverse causation, all the independent variables are lagged – none reflects economic activity after 1990. Our results are presented using robust standard errors (White corrected) to control for any heteroskedasticity.

16.4.5   Findings

The findings of the regression results are summarized in Table 16.2. Column (1) of the table summarizes the results for a robust OLS regression for all counties (approximately 3,100 counties). An important finding is that the citation-weighted patents intensity variable is positive and highly significant, indicating the importance of knowledge spillovers for R&D labs. The relationship between the county-adjusted GFW index and the citation-weighted patents intensity variable is economically significant, displaying an elasticity (evaluated at the mean) of 0.15; a 10 percent increase in citation intensity results in almost a 1.5 percent increase in the weighted adjusted GFW index.

The coefficient on the university R&D variable is positive, as expected, but not statistically significant, suggesting little information spillover from university R&D to private lab R&D. This finding is consistent with Carlino et al. (2007), who found that R&D at local universities has only modest effects on local innovative activity. Interestingly, we found a negative and highly significant correlation between the overall county-adjusted GFW index and the specialization index, evidence favoring Jacobs spillovers. The evidence from the regressions favors Jacobs spillovers and supports the intuition from our maps showing broadly similar geographical clustering of R&D labs in many different industries, also suggestive of Jacobs externalities.

By far the most powerful effect is generated by human capital (the share of the employment accounted for by professional specialty occupations). This variable is positive, highly

Table 16.2   Determinants of spatial concentration of R&D labs

	Robust OLS		
	(1) All counties	(2) All counties	(3) MSA counties
Herf. index	−0.0012	−0.0004	−0.0947
	(1.79)*	(0.79)	(2.74)***
Professional share,1990	0.4086	0.2633	0.2543
	(4.37)***	(2.88)**	(2.60)***
Citation-weighted patents, 1990	0.6294	0.5030	1.3145
	(2.28)**	(1.97)**	(1.65)*
University R&D per student, 1987–1989	0.0001	0.0001	0.0001
	(1.39)	(1.37)	(1.40)
MSA dummy		0.0129	
		(3.33)***	
No. of obs.	3108	3108	752
R^2	0.0344	0.0401	0.0469

Notes:
All regressions include census region dummy variables (New England is the excluded region) and the share of county employment in manufacturing.
*,**,*** indicates significance at the 10, 5, and 1 percent levels.

significant, and economically significant too, with an elasticity of 3.5. Finally, the coefficients on the regional dummy variables are not statistically significant, suggesting that an area's natural advantages do not influence the location decisions of private R&D labs.

Given that the vast majority of labs tend to be located in metropolitan counties, the regression summarized in Column (2) of Table 16.2 adds a dummy variable that is unity for metropolitan counties and zero otherwise. The coefficient on the metropolitan county dummy variable is positive and highly significant. With the exception of the Herfindahl index, the results after adding the metropolitan dummy variable are broadly similar to the regression without this dummy variable. Interestingly, the coefficient on the Herfindahl index is negative but no longer statistically significant. One possibility is that metropolitan counties are more industrially diverse than non-metropolitan counties and that this greater diversity is being captured by the metropolitan dummy variable. To investigate this possibility, Column (3) of Table 16.2 summarizes the results when only the 752 metropolitan counties are used in the regression. The coefficient on the Herfindahl index is now negative and highly significant.

16.4.6   Spatial Dependence

There is a very high degree of spatial inequality in the distribution of R&D labs. As Figure 16.1 shows, labs tend to be highly concentrated in the metropolitan areas of the Northeast corridor, around the Research Triangle in North Carolina, and in California's Silicon Valley. Even though the coefficients on our regional dummy variables are typically insignificant, this clustering of innovative activity suggests that there could be strong spatial dependence at a more localized level and, if so, it should be controlled for in our empirical analysis.

The conjecture, then, is that a cluster of labs in one county may be highly correlated with a cluster in nearby counties; this is especially likely for counties in the same MSA. The consequences of spatial autocorrelation are the same as those associated with serial correlation and heteroskedasticity: when the error terms across counties in our sample are correlated, OLS estimation is unbiased but inefficient. However, if the spatial correlation is due to the direct influence of neighboring counties, OLS estimation is biased and inefficient (Anselin, 1988).

The literature suggests two approaches to dealing with spatial dependence. In the first approach, spatial dependence is modeled as a spatial autoregressive process in the error term:

$$\varepsilon = \lambda W + \mu$$
$$\mu \sim N(0, \sigma^2),$$

where λ is the spatial autoregressive parameter and μ is the uncorrelated error term. W is a spatial weighting matrix where non-zero off-diagonal elements represent the strength of the potential interaction between the sth and tth counties. We use the inverse of the square of the geographical distance between counties to fill in the off-diagonal elements of W. (The spatial weights are row standardized.) The null hypothesis of no spatial error dependence is $H_0 : \lambda = 0$.

The second approach models the spatial dependence in R&D labs via a spatially 'lagged' dependent variable: $GFW = \rho WGFW + X\beta + \varepsilon$, where GFW is an $N \times 1$ vector and N is the number of locations in our study; ρ is the autoregressive parameter (a scalar); W is the $N \times N$ spatial weight matrix described above; X is an $N \times K$ matrix of other explanatory variables from before; and ε is the $N1$ random error term. The null hypothesis of no spatial lag is $H_0 : \rho = 0$.

Following Anselin and Hudak (1992), we perform three tests for spatial autocorrelated errors: Moran's I test, the Lagrange multiplier (LM) test, and a robust Lagrange multiplier test (robust LM). We also perform two tests for the spatial lag model (LM test and a robust LM test). The Moran's I test is normally distributed, while the LM tests are distributed χ^2 with k and one degree of freedom, respectively.

We estimate the OLS specifications previously reported in column (2) of Table 16.2 using these various tests for spatial dependence. The null hypothesis of zero spatial lag cannot be rejected in any specification. The results for spatial error are somewhat more ambiguous. The null hypothesis is clearly rejected according to the Moran's I test and the LM test, but not according to the robust LM test. Still, spatial lag dependence is likely to be an issue for our specifications. Given this, we re-estimate the OLS specification reported in column (2) of Table 16.2, incorporating a correction for either spatial error or spatial lag. Columns 1 and 2 of Table 16.4 present the results for the regressions that correct for spatial dependence. Note that the results after correcting for spatial error are virtually identical with the results after correcting for a spatial lag. Importantly, the evidence for knowledge spillovers is strengthened. First, as before, the correlation between citation-weighted patents per worker in the professional specialty occupations and the GFW index remains positive and highly significant. In addition, the coefficient on the

Table 16.3   Spatial dependence tests[a] (P-values)

Test for:	All counties		MSA counties	
	Spatial error	Spatial lag	Spatial error	Spatial lag
Moran's I $\lambda = 0$	0.0144		0.6330	
LM $- \lambda = 0$	0.0590		0.4908	
Robust LM $- \lambda = 0$	0.1301		0.8781	
LM $- \rho = 0$		0.025		0.5015
Robust LM $- \rho = 0$		0.054		0.9827

Note: $N = 3,108$. [a] Moran's I is based on standardized z-values that follow a normal distribution. The Lagrange multiplier (LM) tests are distributed as χ_1^2 with critical levels of 3.84 ($p = 0.05$).

Table 16.4   Correcting for spatial effects

	(1) All counties Spatial error	(2) All counties Spatial lag
Herf. index	−0.0012	−0.0012
	(0.473)	(0.468)
Professional share, 1990	0.4000	0.3950
	(5.51)***	(5.50)***
Citation weighted patents, 1990	0.6028	0.5960
	(1.72)*	(1.70)*
University R&D per student, 1987–1989	0.0001	0.0001
	(2.97)**	(2.99)**
λ	0.1306	
	(2.19)**	
ρ		0.1456
		(2.51)**
No. of obs.	3,108	3,108
R^2	0.0358	0.0369

Notes:
All regressions include census region dummy variables (New England is the excluded region) and the share of county employment in manufacturing.
*,**,*** indicates significance at the 10, 5, and 1 percent levels.

university R&D variable is now positive and significant, suggesting that R&D at local universities is important in the location decisions of private R&D labs. However, the elasticity is small at 0.04. The results are still consistent with the view that private R&D labs may be drawn to areas that have a relative abundance of highly skilled workers that the industry requires. Unfortunately, after correcting for spatial dependence, the coefficient on the Herfindahl index, while remaining negative, is no longer significant. Thus, our results regarding the importance of Jacobs spillovers for R&D labs are mixed.

Interestingly, as Table 16.3 shows, the null hypothesis of zero spatial error ($\lambda = 0$)

as well as the null hypothesis of zero spatial lag ($\rho = 0$) cannot be rejected when the sample is restricted to the 752 MSA counties. The lack of spatial dependence in the MSA sample suggests that the spatial dependence found in the sample using all 3,108 counties is largely due to spatial dependence among labs in counties within the same metropolitan area.

In sum, we find evidence for agglomeration economies in the clustering of R&D labs at the county level. The strongest evidence for agglomeration economies is found for the citation-weighted patents per worker in the professional and specialty occupations variable, a proxy for localized knowledge spillovers. The coefficient on this variable is positive and highly significant and is robust to sample size (a sample of all counties and a sample of only MSA counties) and robust to corrections for spatial dependence. The evidence for knowledge spillovers from academic R&D to private lab R&D is mixed. The coefficient on the university R&D variable is positive but not significant in either the full or the MSA sample. Interestingly, the coefficient on the academic R&D variable is positive and significant after correcting for spatial dependence. Still, the estimated magnitude of the effect of academic R&D on the clustering of private R&D labs is small. We find evidence that human capital in an area may be a draw for private R&D labs. An elasticity of 3.5 is found for the spatial concentration of labs with respect to the share of employment accounted for by professional specialty occupations. Finally, the evidence for Jacobs-style spillovers is mixed. We found evidence favorable to Jacobs in both the full sample and in the MSA sample, but this evidence is not robust to corrections for spatial dependence in the full sample.

16.5 CONCLUSION

In this chapter, we show that R&D activity for most industries tends to be concentrated in the Northeast corridor, around the Great Lakes, in California's Bay Area, and in southern California. We hypothesize that the relatively high spatial concentration of R&D activity is due to the fact that R&D depends on knowledge spillovers more than most types of business activities. We find evidence that supports this view. We run a regression of a variant of the EG index measuring the spatial concentration of private R&D labs at the county level on geographical proxies for knowledge spillovers as well as other characteristics, and find evidence that localized knowledge spillovers are important for the spatial clustering of innovative activity. In particular, we show that a strong positive correlation exists between the geographical concentration of R&D labs and citation-weighted patents per worker in professional and specialty occupations (a proxy for knowledge spillovers). All else equal, the index of agglomeration for R&D labs will be 15 percent greater in a county with twice the citations intensity of another county. In addition, we find evidence that supports the idea that Jacobs externalities are important for R&D activity, although the evidence is mixed. By far the most powerful effect is generated by human capital (the share of the employment accounted for by professional specialty occupations). This variable is positive and highly significant and it is economically significant too, with an elasticity of 3.5.

Policy makers view the success of areas such as Silicon Valley in California, the Route 128 corridor in Boston, and North Carolina's Research Triangle as a miraculous recipe for local economic development and growth. But are these examples exceptions rather than the rule? The answer appears to be no. We show that equally remarkable concentrations may be found in many other types of R&D activity, such as the concentration of R&D in the pharmaceutical industry in northern New Jersey and southeastern Pennsylvania. In this chapter, we show that many types of R&D establishments are highly concentrated geographically. However, studies by Saxenian (1994) and Duranton (2008) provide a cautionary note for policy makers who view the success of areas such as Silicon Valley as a recipe for local economic development and growth. While investing in science centers to attract R&D activity is fairly common in the US, Saxenian's study suggests that creating the right corporate culture to make the centers successful is more challenging. Duranton points out that designing cluster policy is extremely tricky, and even if policy makers get it right, often the benefits of clustering may be too small to justify the cost of bringing them about. We suggest that policy makers, instead of targeting industries, consider strategies that help to establish a good business environment and the efficient provision of locally provided public goods and services.

NOTES

*   The authors especially thank Jake Carr and Robert O'Loughlin for excellent research assistance. This chapter has benefited from comments from Robert Hunt, Leonard Nakamura, and Tony Smith. We alone are responsible for any remaining errors. The views expressed here are those of the authors and do not necessarily represent the views of the Federal Reserve Bank of Philadelphia or the Federal Reserve System.
1.   2007 Annual Urban Mobility Report, Texas Transport Institute: http://mobility.tamu.edu/ums/report/.
2.   We define citation-weighted patent intensity as citation-weighted patents that are normalized by the number of workers in professional and specialty occupations.
3.   EG use employment in the US vacuum cleaner industry to illustrate the concern. Seventy-five percent of employment in the industry is *industrially* concentrated in just four plants. Thus, using equation (16.1) to calculate a measure of spatial concentration of this industry suggests strong *spatial* concentration. But the strong spatial concentration may reflect nothing more than the fact that employment is industrially concentrated in a small number of plants.
4.   A number of other studies look at innovative output across cities, such as the study by Audretsch and Feldman (1996). What is unique about our chapter is that we look at the spatial clustering of *private* R&D activity.
5.   The study by Guimarães et al. (2007) is the only other study we are aware of that looks at spatial clustering at the establishment level. Specifically, they look at the geographical concentration of over 45,000 plants in 1999 for *concelhos* (counties) in Portugal.
6.   Our data on individual labs were limited to the top 1,000 public companies in terms of expenditure on R&D. The 1,000 labs in our dataset cover over 95 percent of all R&D performed by public companies.
7.   See GFW for details on the construction of the adjusted GFW index used in this chapter as well as a discussion of the EG index.
8.   Ellison et al. (2007) report an average adjusted Gini coefficient of 0.03 for manufacturing in 1997 at the *metropolitan area* level.
9.   They are R&D activity in hog production; the production of brooms and brushes; the production of fiber cans, tubes, and drums; the bottled and canned soft drinks and carbonated waters industry; and the rolling mill machinery and equipment industry.
10.   There is a negative relationship between the size of the adjusted GFW index and the number of labs in an industry. However, this relationship is not strong: a correlation coefficient of –0.09 that is only marginally significant (at the 10 percent level).
11.   To develop measures of statistical significance for the adjusted GFW indices, we divide our labs into six non-overlapping groups based on the number of labs in a given industry. The first group consists of industries with between two and nine labs. The second group consists of industries with 10 to 30 labs,

while the third group consists of industries with between 31 and 50 labs. The fourth group consists of industries with between 51 and 100 labs, while the fifth group consists of industries with 101 to 200 labs. The final group consists of industries composed of over 200 labs. For each group, we performed a simulation procedure to produce a probability distribution for the adjusted GFW index. In the simulation we randomly allocated labs to counties while maintaining the counties' shares of national manufacturing employment. Therefore, if a given county has a relatively high share of the nation's manufacturing jobs, the county is more likely to be randomly assigned more R&D labs, too. For each group the simulation produces a value for the adjusted GFW index. For each group, we performed 1,000 simulations and formed a probability distribution for the adjusted GFW indices. From the distribution we can calculate critical values (one positive and one negative) that allow us to say that we are 95 percent certain that any value that exceeds (falls below) the critical value indicates that labs in that grouping are significantly more concentrated (significantly more dispersed) than is the distribution of manufacturing employment.

12. Similar to our finding that the largest percentage of R&D labs is generally not more concentrated than manufacturing employment, Ellison and Glaeser's finding shows that the largest number of manufacturing industries could also be classified as not very concentrated.

13. Glaeser et al. (1992) coined the term 'MAR spillovers'. MAR spillovers are so-called because Marshall (1890) developed a theory of knowledge spillovers that was later extended by Arrow (1962) and Romer (1986) – hence, MAR.

14. Several other studies have found that knowledge spillovers dissipate rapidly with distance. See for example, the articles by Audretsch and Feldman (1996); Keller (2002); Arzaghi and Henderson (2005); and Kolko (2007). The extent to which innovations in communication technologies are rendering face-to-face contacts obsolete is not so clear. Gaspar and Glaeser (1998) argue that improvements in telecommunications technology increase the demand for all interactions. So while technology may substitute for face-to face contacts, this effect is offset by the greater desire for all kinds of interactions, including face-to-face contacts.

15. In a survey of 1,300 inventors, Jaffe et al. (2000) found that approximately half of the patent citations refer to some sort of knowledge spillovers, of which 28 percent correspond to a very substantial spillover. Jaffe et al. (1993) provide evidence that these spillovers are at least initially localized.

16. The Herfindahl index is calculated by squaring and summing the share of establishments accounted for by each industry in a given county. The squaring of industry shares means that the larger industries contribute more than proportionately to the overall value of the index. Thus, as the index increases in value for a given county, this implies that the county is more highly specialized or less diversified industrially.

REFERENCES

Agrawal, Ajay, Devesh Kapur and John McHale (2008), 'How do spatial and social proximity influence knowledge flows? Evidence from patent data', *Journal of Urban Economics*, **64**, 258–69.

Anselin, Luc (1988), *Spatial Econometrics: Methods and Models*, Boston, MA: Kluwer Academic.

Anselin, Luc and S. Hudak (1992), 'Spatial econometrics in practice: a review of software options', *Regional Science and Urban Economics*, **72**, 509–36.

Anselin, Luc, Attila Varga and Zoltan Acs (1997), 'Local geographic spillovers between university and high technology innovations', *Journal of Urban Economics*, **42**, 442–48.

Arrow, Kenneth J. (1962), 'The economics of learning by doing', *Review of Economic Studies*, **29**, 155–73.

Arzaghi, Mohammad and J. Vernon Henderson (2008), 'Networking off Madison Avenue', *Review of Economic Studies*, **75**, 1011–38.

Audretsch, David B. and Maryann P. Feldman (1996), 'R&D spillovers and the geography of innovation and production', *American Economic Review*, **86** 630–40.

Carlino, Gerald A., Satyajit Chatterjee and Robert M. Hunt (2007), 'Urban density and the rate of invention', *Journal of Urban Economics*, **61**, 389–419.

Combes, Pierre-Philippe and Henry G. Overman (2004), 'The spatial distribution of economic activities in the European Union', in J.V. Henderson and J.-F. Thisse (eds), *Handbook of Regional and Urban Economics, Vol. IV: Cities and Geography*, Amsterdam: Elsevier, pp. 2845–909.

Directory of American Research and Technology (1999), 23rd edn, New York: R.R. Bowker.

Duranton, Gilles (2008), 'California dreamin': the feeble case for cluster policies', Working Paper, University of Toronto.

Duranton, Gilles and Henry G. Overman (2005), 'Testing for localization using micro-geographic data', *Review of Economic Studies*, **72**, 1077–106.

Ellison, Glenn and Edward. L. Glaeser (1997), 'Geographic concentration in U.S. manufacturing industries: a dartboard approach', *Journal of Political Economy*, **105**, 889–927.

Ellison, Glenn, Edward L. Glaeser and William Kerr (2007), 'What causes industry agglomeration? Evidence from coagglomeration patterns', Discussion Paper 2133, Harvard Institute of Economic Research, Cambridge, MA, April.

Feldman, Maryann P. and David B. Audretsch (1999), 'Innovation in cities: science-based diversity, specialization, and localized competition', *European Economic Review*, **43**, 409–29.

Fujita, Masahisa, Tomoya Mori, J. Vernon Henderson and Yoshitsugu Kanemoto (2004), 'Spatial distribution of economic activities in Japan and China', in J.V. Henderson and J.-F. Thisse (eds), *Handbook of Regional and Urban Economics, Vol. IV: Cities and Geography*, Amsterdam: Elsevier, pp. 2911–77.

Gaspar, Jess and Edward Glaeser (1998), 'Information technology and the future of cities', *Journal of Urban Economics*, **43**, 136–56.

Glaeser, Edward, Hedi Kallal, Jose Scheinkman and Andrei Shleifer (1992), 'Growth in cities', *Journal of Political Economy*, **100**, 1126–53.

Guimarães, Paulo, Octávio Figueiredo and Douglas Woodward (2007), 'Measuring the localization of economic activity: a parametric approach', *Journal of Regional Science*, **47**, 753–44.

Hall, Bronwyn H., Adam B. Jaffe and Manuel Trajtenberg (2005), 'Market value and patent citations', *RAND Journal of Economics*, **36**, 16–38.

Harhoff, Dietmar, Francis Narin, F.M. Scherer and Katrin Vopel (1999), 'Citation frequency and the value of patented inventions', *Review of Economics and Statistics*, **81**, 511–15.

Holmes, Thomas J. and John J. Stevens (2004), 'Spatial distribution of economic activities in North America', in J.V. Henderson and J.-F. Thisse (eds), *Handbook of Regional and Urban Economics, Vol. IV: Cities and Geography*, Amsterdam: Elsevier, pp. 2797–843.

Jacobs, Jane (1969), *The Economy of Cities*, New York: Vintage Books.

Jaffe, Adam B., Manual Trajtenberg and Michael S. Fogarty (2000), 'Knowledge spillovers and patent citations: evidence from a survey of inventors', *American Economic Review*, **90**, Papers and Proceedings of the 113th Annual Meeting of the American Economic Association, pp. 215–18.

Jaffe, Adam B., M. Trajtenberg and R. Henderson (1993), 'Geographic localization of knowledge spillovers as evidenced by patent citations', *Quarterly Journal of Economics*, **108**, 577–98.

Keller, Wolfgang (2002), 'Geographic localization of international technology diffusion', *American Economic Review*, **92**, 120–42.

Kolko, Jed Public Policy Institute of California, (2007), 'Agglomeration and co-agglomeration of services industries', unpublished manuscript, April.

Krugman, Paul (1991), *Geography and Trade*, Cambridge, MA: MIT Press.

Lin, Jeffery (2007), 'Innovation, cities, and New Work', Federal Reserve Bank of Philadelphia Working Paper 07-25, October.

Marshall, Alfred (1890), *Principles of Economics*, London: Macmillan.

Romer, Paul M. (1986), 'Increasing returns and long run growth', *Journal of Political Economy*, **94**, 1002–37.

Rosenthal, Stuart and William C. Strange (2001), 'The determinants of agglomeration', *Journal of Urban Economics*, **50** 191–229.

Saxenian, AnnaLee (1994), *Regional Advantage: Culture and Competition in Silicon Valley and Route 128*, Cambridge, MA: Harvard University Press.

Strange, William C. (2009), 'Viewpoint: agglomeration research in the age of disaggregation', *Canadian Journal of Economics*, **42**, 1–27.

17 Offshore assembly and service industries in Latin America

Elsie L. Echeverri-Carroll

17.1 INTRODUCTION

Several factors have played important roles in attracting low-skilled manufacturing jobs to relatively few developing countries, mostly those with large labor markets. Mexico and Brazil, for example, are the main countries that have attracted such jobs within Latin America. Proximity to the US market and local programs to facilitate cross-border movement of intermediate goods, such as Mexico's Border Industrialization Program (which created the maquiladora[1] industry), have been crucial in this regard. In addition, history shows that two other factors have played a key role in the growth of the offshore-assembly industry in developing countries, namely technological advances that have lowered transportation costs and differences in cost of labor between developing and industrialized countries.

Reductions in transportation costs have made it economically feasible for US manufacturers to offshore portions of their production to developing countries. Glaeser and Kohlhase (2003) observe that railroad costs (in 2001 dollars) declined from more than 18 cents per ton-mile in 1890 to 2.3 cents in 2002, and that trucking costs (in 2001 dollars) fell from 38 cents a ton-mile in 1985 to 28 cents a ton-mile in 1999. They also calculate the changes in ratio of the nation's freight bill to GDP – for highways, rail, navigable waterways, and pipelines – between 1960 and 2000, finding a decline from 0.09 in 1960 to 0.06 in 2002. Most of that decrease took place between 1960 and 1990, the period when offshore assembly first took off.

Starting in the 1960s with the textile industry, and following in the 1970s with the consumer electronics industry, US companies reacted to increasing international competition by relocating labor-intensive production, mainly, in the newly industrialized countries (NICs) of Korea, Singapore, Taiwan, and Hong Kong. In the 1980s, Mexico became a major location for the labor-intensive facilities (or 'maquiladoras') of US firms after devaluation of the Mexican peso made maquiladora wages more attractive than wages in NICs (Suarez-Villa, 1984; Grunwald and Flamm, 1985; Fernandez-Kelley, 1987; Sklair, 1989; Echeverri-Carroll, 1994; Wilson, 1992).[2]

During the emergence of the offshore-assembly industry (1960–80), developing countries exhibited trade-related distortions, including import quotas, high tariffs, overvalued exchange rates, and foreign-exchange controls (World Bank, 2001). In a parallel trend, the United States protected its textile, electronics, and automobile industries, the three sectors that represented the bulk of the global-assembly industry. A key question, then, is how and why did offshore-assembly plants (that depend on easy movement of intermediate goods across international borders) flourish during this period?

The growth of global assembly happened because both developed and developing

countries implemented policies creating 'free-trade enclaves' within their highly protected markets. One of the most important policies was US tariff item 9802.00.80 (formerly item 807.00), which since 1962 permits the duty-free re-entry of US components
sent abroad for assembly. Similarly important were developing countries' special trade
provisions that allowed for the free importation of components and parts to be used in
products for export (for example, Mexico's maquiladora program or export processing
zone – EPZ). The value of imports from developing countries under item 9802.00.80
serves as a proxy to measure the size of US production-sharing during this protectionist
period (1960s, 1970s, and most of the 1980s). In contrast, data collected by developing
countries allows for the measurement of the size of the offshore-assembly industry in
each country (for example, maquiladora data in Mexico), but the data are not necessarily
comparable across countries.

One of the most significant achievements of the 1990s was the integration of many
developing countries into the World Trade Organization (WTO) and the proliferation
of free-trade agreements, such as the North American Free Trade Agreement (NAFTA)
between the United States, Mexico, and Canada, which would diminish the usage of
item 9802.00.80 and maquiladora-style programs. But, because the agreements regarding the dismantling of tariffs and nontariff barriers occurred gradually, trade flows from
developing countries under 9802.00.80 could still be used as a good indicator of US
production sharing throughout the 1990s. However, these data do not serve us well after
2000, by which time trade barriers between Mexico and the United States were mostly
eliminated, facilitating movement of goods without the use of 9802.00.80. China's entry
into the WTO in 2001 had a similar impact.

Membership in the WTO required China to eliminate or reduce practices such as high
tariffs and nontariff barriers, which distorted trade to and from China. By significantly
liberalizing trade and investment regimes and with increased access to markets of industrialized countries, China became a major player in global assembly and undermined
the cheap-labor advantages of Mexico and NICs in the process. Some US companies
assembling products in Mexico moved their operations to China, mostly those assembling textiles and small electronic products that could be transported long distances in a
cost-effective manner. These were also the maquiladoras with the lowest level of technological sophistication, competing mainly on the basis of cheap labor, and the difference
in wages between China and Mexico was large. In 2001, workers in Mexico earned an
average of US$2.96 per hour, while Chinese workers earned 72 cents per hour (Gallagher
and Zarsky, 2007, p. 134).

Computers were introduced primarily in the 1980s to improve the efficiency of workers
within the same firm, but, with the development of the internet and the Web in the 1990s,
computers rapidly became an efficient way to move data and information between firms
(Echeverri-Carroll and Ayala, 2007). This greater movement of information was made
possible by the development of electronic networks that strengthened communication
systems, including local-area networks (which link workers in the same office), wide-area
networks (which connect employees of a large organization or multiple organizations
across multiple locations), and the internet (which potentially could unite all people and
all organizations in a global communication network). These information technologies
now made it possible to trade business services that were previously untradable, giving
birth to the widespread outsourcing of services.

Service offshoring depends not only on advances in communications and transportation technologies but also on the supply of skilled personnel, and India, with its large number of low-paid information-technology (IT) workers, has captured a major share of this market. Indeed, US debates on offshoring seem almost entirely focused on the loss of software programming jobs to India (Kirkegaard, 2005). Service offshoring limits using imports under 9802.00.80 to measure the size of US production sharing since the provision measures only trade in goods, and not in services.

Given all the above, has Latin American industry, which was built on low-wage assembly jobs, lost an edge that it can never reclaim? The hypothesis here is that although the Latin American assembly of *manufactures* has lost significant ground in several low-wage sectors, the industry is finding new ways to grow and compete. Manufacturing in Latin American is maturing, leaving behind its low-wage roots. As part of the process, it is becoming more technologically sophisticated and showing rapid gains in productivity. Moreover, the region continues to have a clear advantage in the assembly of some manufacturing goods for the US market, such as automobiles and refrigerators, that are costly to transport from Asia. In addition, Latin America is becoming an important competitor in the offshoring of *services*, as the wages for IT workers in India increase. IT firms, both large and small, are emerging in Latin America, ready to supply services to foreign companies (Echeverri-Carroll, 2008). Recent media articles such as 'Offshoring takes off in Latin America' (Hall, 2009) and 'The new economics of outsourcing' (King, 2008) demonstrate that the region is garnering attention as an attractive location for service offshoring.

To probe this hypothesis, this chapter is divided as follows. Section 17.2 reviews the theory of offshoring, analyzing the ability of companies and countries to participate in global supply chains in which the many tasks required to manufacture complex industrial goods, and increasingly to provide knowledge-intensive services, are performed in several countries. Section 17.3 describes trends in outsourcing of manufacturing to Latin America. Section 17.4 analyzes outsourcing of services to Latin America, and conversely, examines how IT local-service firms there have been able to use the domestic market to build a platform for international expansion. Section 17.5 looks at the growing presence of Indian companies in the Latin American offshore-service industry. Section 17.6 presents conclusions.

17.2 THEORY OF OFFSHORING

Outsourcing is the segmentation of tasks by firms across boundary lines. Whether to integrate vertically or to outsource – the 'to make or to buy' decision – is an important topic in the theory of the firm (Williamson, 1979). To illustrate the difference between vertical integration and outsourcing more clearly, we analyze the case of the automotive industry.

Holmes (2009) presents the 1920s' Ford factory, in which the raw materials such as steel went in one end of the factory and finished automobiles came out the other, as an extreme example of vertical integration. In this case, automakers produced most of their own parts. Klier and Rubenstein (2008), however, note that today, instead of gathering thousands of individual parts and components at their assembly plants, carmakers are purchasing large modules and systems ready to be installed on the final assembly line. This arrangement explains employment in car-parts businesses being much larger than employment in final-assembly plants. In 2007, for example, employment in vehicle parts in the United States totaled 673,000, compared with 186,000 in final assembly (ibid.). In addition, many parts are produced in other countries (offshoring) by carmakers' own subsidiaries. The WTO (1998) reported that only 37 percent of the production value of an automobile is generated in the United States.

This cross-border aspect is the distinguishing feature of offshoring – that is, whether tasks are sourced from within the same economy (insourcing) or abroad (offshoring),[3] and not whether they are sourced from within the same company (vertical integration) or from domestic suppliers (outsourcing) (Van Welsum and Reif, 2006). Grossman and Helpman (2005) note that the trade literature on offshoring deals with the question of whether intermediate products and services can be outsourced abroad, while Yeats (1998) uses trade in intermediate inputs as a proxy for global production sharing.

According to trade theory, firms that decide to offshore would choose the geographical distribution of their production that minimizes costs. In this regard, the basis for global outsourcing is the location of each production stage (manufacturing or services) in the country where it can be performed at least cost (Grunwald and Flamm, 1985). This spatial disaggregation is the outcome of firms combining the comparative advantages of other geographical locations with their own resources and competencies to maximize competitiveness (McCann and Mudambi, 2005). For example, automobile firms take advantage of relative endowments of countries by locating design and marketing services where there are abundant supplies of skilled labor, as in the United States, Europe, or East Asia. On the other hand, they place assembly of unskilled-labor-intensive parts, for example, wire harnesses, mainly in low-wage countries such as Mexico and China. As this example shows, one could say that the theory of offshoring deals with the question of why firms in the 'North' decide to offshore certain parts of their production to the 'South'?[4]

Grossman and Rossi-Hansberg (2008) maintain that the nature of international trade is changing from trade in goods to trade in tasks (within both manufacturing and services), with bits of value being added in different countries. In this context, detailed information about product specifications and tasks to be performed can be conveyed electronically, and intermediate goods can now be transported more quickly and at lower cost than ever before. Grossman and Rossi-Hansberg cite the examples of radiology, copy editing, and tax preparation services where the product can be sent electronically, with no loss of time and at virtually no cost. They conclude that in the present global-production processes, firms take advantage of differences in factor costs and expertise across countries, to offshore not only manufacturing but also services.

Advances in transportation and communications have therefore made it increasingly viable to incorporate organizational advances, such as just-in-time inventory systems and virtual project teams, into the time and space separation of tasks. For example, Klier and Rubenstein (2008) report that automakers are developing long-term relationships with suppliers for the life of a specific model or longer, where parts are delivered on a just-in-time basis, often only a few minutes before they are needed. In this regard, Grossman and Helpman (2005) state that outsourcing means more than just the purchase of intermediate goods. It means finding a partner (search costs) and relationship-specific investments. Offshoring might appear to be attractive if inputs can be found more cheaply abroad, but it can also be costly if remote performance of tasks limits opportunity to monitor and coordinate workers.

Comparative advantage therefore helps to explain the division of production between countries endowed with highly educated (highly skilled) workers and those with a relatively large supply of less-educated (less-skilled) workers. The question then arises as to how firms choose among developing countries. Which 'southern' countries will have the edge in offshore assembly? More specifically, will Latin American countries, in particular, continue to have comparative advantages in global assembly and services?

Latin American countries compete with India and China, both of which have abundant skilled and unskilled labor, not to mention domestic markets with huge potential. However, countries in Latin America do enjoy certain advantages, in particular, geographical proximity to the US market, the same general time zone, and lower costs of transportation for heavy goods. These relative benefits are reflected in three trends. First, Latin America continues to export electronic components, automobile parts, and IT services in spite of the slowdown in the US economy and increased global competition. Second, a significant group of IT firms, ready to supply assembly and services to foreign clients, is emerging in the region. Third, Latin American countries are increasingly attracting Indian companies, who are eager to use Latin America as a base to offshore IT services to the US.

17.3   MEXICO LEADS LATIN AMERICA IN MANUFACTURING OUTSOURCING

Imports under HTS Chapter 98 (9802.00.80 + 9802.00.60)[5] before 2000 are good proxy statistics for US production sharing in Latin America with respect to products other than textiles and apparel articles.[6] Using Chapter 98 data, two CEPAL researchers, Ventura-Dias and Duran-Lima (2001) analyze production-sharing trends in Latin America between 1980 and 2000. They find that Mexico, with 70 percent of US imports under HTS Chapter 98 in 2000, is by far the leading location for US assemblers, followed at a large distance by Brazil. Their data show that US imports from Mexico under Chapter 98 were US$2.2 billion in 1980, whereas US imports from Brazil were US$111 million. On top of that, imports from Mexico under these provisions increased 88 percent, to US$19.4 billion in 2000, while those from Brazil declined 91 percent, to a low of US$10 million. The remaining US imports from Latin America (30 percent) under Chapter 98 in 2000 were apparel and textile imports from the Caribbean Basin countries and Colombia.

What explains the difference between Mexico and Brazil in the usage of Chapter 98? Ventura-Dias and Duran-Lima believe that it is due to the differing economic strategies the countries started in the 1980s. Mexico pursued a greater reliance on US markets, whereas Brazil looked to its domestic market and then more recently to South America. Given the large role Mexico plays in the decisions of US companies to offshore manufacturing to Latin America, the rest of this chapter deals mainly with Mexico.

17.3.1   The Maquiladora Industry

The Mexican government initiated the Border Industrialization Program (BIP) in 1965, allowing foreign and domestic enterprises to import duty free all inputs, machinery, and replacement parts needed for assembly of products to be exported. That and US provision 9802.00.80 were the building blocks of the maquiladora industry, as provision 9802.00.80 made goods imported from Mexico subject to US tariffs only on the value added, not on the inputs previously sent from the US into Mexico.[7] The maquiladora industry, however, did not take off until 1982, when devaluation of the peso made Mexican wages lower than those in NICs.

In 1975, the average hourly cost per worker was US$1.44 in Mexico and 59 cents in NICs. By 1990, according to Echeverri-Carroll (1994), hourly wages were $3.70 in NICs and only $1.64 in Mexico. This reversal brought explosive growth to the maquiladora industry. The number of plants grew from 620 in 1980 to 1,703 in 1990, then to 2,810 in 2006. Data from Mexico's Instituto Nacional de Estadística y Geografía (INEGI) show (Figure 17.1) that after 1982, maquiladora employment expanded dramatically up to the year 2000. The data also show that the industry concentrated in three sectors: textiles, automobiles, and electronics. These sectors accounted for 69 percent of the employment and 49 percent of the firms in 2006, the last year for which data are available.

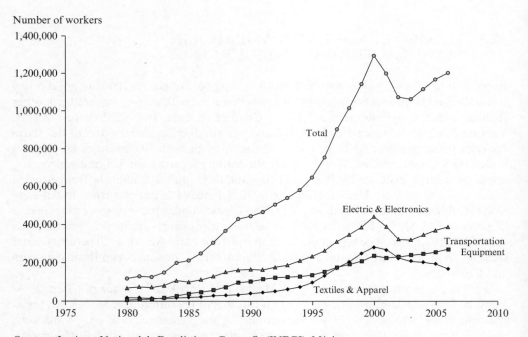

Source: Instituto Nacional de Estadística y Geografía (INEGI), México.

Figure 17.1   Employment in maquiladora industry, 1979–2006

17.3.2 Textile Maquiladoras

Between 2000 and 2006, however, employment in textile maquiladoras dropped 40 percent and 12 percent in electronics, but with an increase of 14 percent in the automobile sector. Several factors contributed to deceleration of the maquiladora industry, especially the clothing sector, during this period. The US recession impacted maquiladoras severely throughout 2001; by February 2002, the industry had shed 26.7 percent of its jobs (Cañas and Gilmer, 2009). Moreover, changes in trade policy occasioned the relocation of many textile plants to East Asian countries. Carrillo (2009) finds 48 percent of closed maquiladoras moved to East Asia.

The Multi Fibre Agreement (MFA) governed world trade in textiles and garments, imposing quotas on the amount that developing countries could export to developed countries, from 1974 until it expired January 1, 2005. In the 1990s, NAFTA gave Mexican apparel decisive advantages by reducing or eliminating many of these quotas and by allowing duty-free entry into the United States if all components (from the thread on) were of NAFTA origin. Mexico's cutting-and-sewing sector boomed as foreign companies shifted operations from around the world into Mexico, to gain access to the North American market. The number of hours worked in textile and apparel maquiladoras expanded by 22.9 percent a year between 1990 and 2000 (Cañas and Gilmer, 2009). However, after the 2000s, the sector experienced strong competition from the Caribbean Basin and China.

The CBI expanded US market access to twenty-four low-wage countries throughout the Caribbean and Central America, beginning in 1984,[8] but when NAFTA took effect in 1994, CBI countries lost their advantage until 2000, when they achieved 'NAFTA parity'. Coincidentally, China entered the WTO in 2001 and the MFA was ended in January 2005. Once Mexico lost NAFTA and MFA preferences, textile manufacturers began to move closer to Mexico City, the traditional home to the domestic apparel sector, to take advantage of the region's experienced workers and significantly lower wages (ibid.). However, employment in the Mexican apparel maquiladoras still fell from 282,755 in 2000 to 169,490 in 2006 as many plants moved to other countries. During this time, both China and the Caribbean Basin countries[9] overtook Mexico in textile and apparel exports to the United States. In light of these developments, Gruben (2004) believes that Mexico seems unlikely to be able to compete again in low-wage, low-skill markets. On the other hand, the trends in electronics and automobiles are more positive.

17.3.3 Electronics Maquiladoras

Gallagher and Zarsky (2007) identify two clusters of electronics maquiladoras in Mexico. The cluster in the state of Jalisco (mainly in the capital, Guadalajara) specializes in IT. This area emerged as the heart of Mexico's computer and telecommunications industry in the second half of the 1990s. The relative abundance of water (as opposed to Monterrey), flight connections with US high-tech cities, and programs implemented by both federal and state governments to promote the computer industry, all played a major role in its rapid growth (Echeverri-Carroll, 1999). In 1998, the *Wall Street Journal* called this region the 'Silicon Valley of the South'.

Things changed significantly after 2000 with the relocation of many plants to East

Asia. In a recent study of the maquiladora industry in Guadalajara, Gallagher and Zarsky (2007) find that maquiladoras that did not relocate are converting to contract manufacturing (CM). Hence, while flagship companies such as Hewlett-Packard (HP), IBM, Kodak, and Intel, among others, continue to have facilities in Guadalajara, they are increasingly specializing in contract manufacturing. Local CM companies, particularly Flextronics, Solectron, SCI Sanmina, and Jabil Circuit, are expanding as they assemble more and more products for original equipment manufacturers (OEMs) such as IBM, HP, or Cisco.

There is another important cluster, of audio and video maquiladoras, in what Gallagher and Zarsky call 'the border zone'.[10] Many of these firms are in Tijuana (in Baja California, on the Pacific Ocean) because they are Japanese owned and need access to Asian suppliers (Cañas and Gilmer, 2009). Indeed, the seven largest electronics maquiladoras in or around Tijuana – Hitachi, JVC, Matsushita, Sanyo, Samsung, Sony, and Sharp – are all Japanese owned. According to the state of Baja California's economic development office, maquiladoras there produced 17.5 million television sets and computer monitors in 2006 (*Twin Plant News*, April 2007). They continue to prosper because they have become more technologically sophisticated. Carrillo (2009) finds that while some plants still produce conventional television sets (18 percent of all production) and computer monitors, most have switched to manufacturing the latest in technology, that is, flat screen sets: liquid crystal display (LCD), digital light processing (DLP), and plasma.

17.3.4   Automotive Maquiladoras

In the 1980s, strong international competition (especially from Japanese companies) led General Motors, Chrysler, and Ford to open assembly facilities in Mexico (Echeverri-Carroll, 1996). Mexico's proximity to the United States made the transportation of heavy products, such as automobile components and parts, economically feasible. Then, NAFTA's greater flexibility allowed suppliers to move into nontraditional (for maquiladoras) cities such as Guanajuato, Saltillo, Hermosillo, and Aguascalientes, where the auto-assembly plants are located. Cañas and Gilmer (2009) report that these modern plants, spread across northern and central Mexico, have produced about two million autos a year since 2000.

Vehicles, along with their engines and parts, are a sector in which China is not making gains. Automobile production is bulky and thus more sensitive to transportation costs, it requires an extensive network of just-in-time suppliers, and also uses a lot of capital in combination with skilled and semiskilled labor (Anderson and Gerber, 2008). Contrary to the experience of others in the maquiladora industry (for example, textiles), automotive manufacturing in Mexico grew between 2000 and 2005. Since 2007, however, because of the US recession, even the auto assembly has suffered (Carrillo, 2009).

17.4   LATIN AMERICA'S INCREASING SHARE OF SERVICE OFFSHORING

Production sharing is no longer limited to manufacturing. It has now been extended to service industries such as insurance, banking, healthcare, and IT. Although production sharing in services does not involve the physical assembly and shipment of components or finished goods, decisions to locate processes in multiple locations are based on similar variables. In particular, the cost of labor is often the most important variable in decisions on the geographical distribution of manufacturing processes or on the contracting of services overseas. Other aspects, such as dependable transportation and telecommunications infrastructure, local tax policies, and contract enforceability, are also important (Tafoya and Watkins, 2005).

The Bureau of Economic Analysis (BEA) provides data on *unaffiliated* service transactions between US and foreign residents (cross-company trade). It also provides data on *affiliated* services transactions within multinational companies (intra-company trade), and specifically on trade between US parent companies and their foreign affiliates, as well as trade between US affiliates and their foreign-parent companies (Koncz and Flatness, 2008). This section follows the methodology of previous studies (GAO, 2004, Grossman and Rossi-Hansberg, 2006), using both affiliated and unaffiliated US imports of 'business, professional and technical services (BPT)' as a proxy for the offshoring of services by US companies.[11]

Figure 17.2 shows 2007 data on total US imports of BPT services (affiliated and unaffiliated) for selected countries. The data reveal the dominance of India in US offshoring services and the relative importance of South and Central America (as a region) in providing these services to US companies. The United States imported US$6.2 billion of

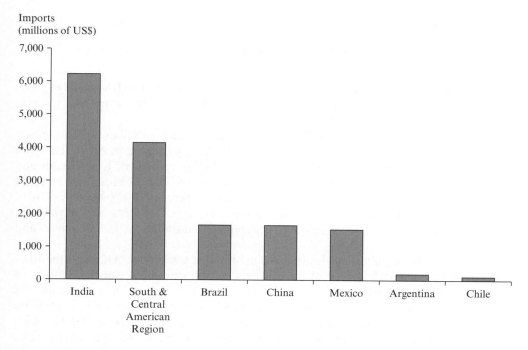

Source: BEA, *Survey of Current Business*, October 2008.

Figure 17.2   US imports of business, professional, and technical services in 2007

Imports
(millions of US$)

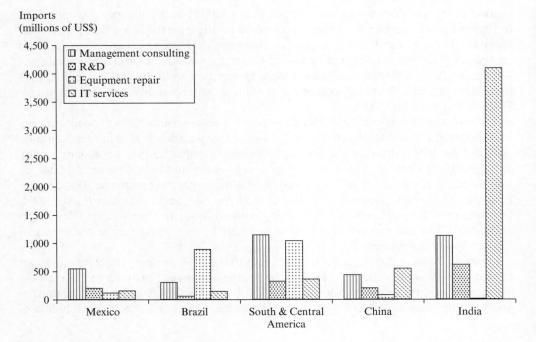

Source: BEA, *Survey of Current Business*, October 2008.

Figure 17.3   US imports of business, professional, and technical services by type, 2007

BPT services from India and US$4.1 billion from South and Central America in 2007. Mexico and Brazil (each with approximately US$1.5 billion of BPT exports to the US) were the two largest Latin American providers.

Figure 17.3 breaks down US BPT imports (affiliated and unaffiliated) from major Latin American countries, as well as from India and China, by type, in 2007. The figure reveals the offshore-service industry in India to be highly specialized in computer and information services, as they accounted for 65.4 percent of US BPT imports from India in 2007. In contrast, such services constituted only 8.4 percent of US imports of BPT services from South and Central America in the same year. The data also show Latin America dominating in the offshoring of equipment installation, maintenance, and repairs.

Before 2006, BEA published statistics for unaffiliated trade only. Although the BEA completed a benchmark survey of international services in 2006 to include affiliated trade and also to improve data accuracy (Bach, 2008), only data on unaffiliated US imports are available in a historical series. Figure 17.4 shows US service imports from unaffiliated partners in selected countries 1990–2006 and reveals the degree to which India has been closing the gap on South and Central America over the last 25 years. In 1991 the United States imported 40 times more unaffiliated services from South and Central American countries than from India; in 2006 it imported only 1.2 times more. Within Latin America, Mexico and Brazil continue to dominate the market.

Imports
(millions of US $)

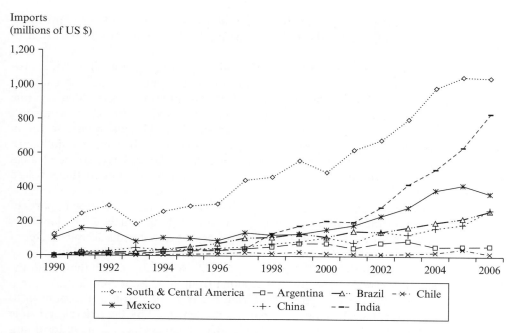

Source: BEA, *Survey of Current Business*, several issues.

*Figure 17.4   US imports of business, professional, and technical services (unaffiliated)
for selected countries, 1990–2006*

Similar time zones, an increasing supply of engineers and scientists, geographical and
cultural similarities, on top of cost advantages, still make Latin American countries
attractive BPT-outsourcing hubs for US companies. Intrafirm (affiliated) imports
account for a large share of total imports from Latin America. Of total US imports from
Mexico and the rest of Latin America in 2007, 34 and 30 percent, respectively, were
between branches of the same company (Zeile, 2003).

In the IT sector, however, it appears that US imports from the region are increasingly among unaffiliated partners, reflecting the development of a significant number
of local IT startups in Latin America that are selling their services to US companies.
For example, the Brazilian IT sector has developed world-class expertise in IT-related
banking technology.[12] Junqueira-Botelho et al. (2005) explain that local businesses
there, such as banks, responded to foreign competition resulting from liberalization of
the economy, by refocusing on their core business activities. This strategy led them to
outsource software development instead of producing in-house, and constituted a basis
for the expansion of small in-country IT firms. Using a survey of leading companies
in Brazil, Junqueira-Botelho et al. find that a majority of new IT firms are outgrowths
of existing firms. Some were established as true spinoffs, in the sense that the parent
company started and had a stake in the new firm, but the majority were separate companies created by employees of the mother firm, who saw an opportunity to create a
new business, often without support from, and sometimes even in competition with, the

parent firm. According to Junqueira-Botelho et al., these companies have plans to go international, especially within the Latin American market, as a natural extension of their domestic growth.

Politec, with 2006 revenues of US$1.5 billion, is the largest IT-service provider in Brazil, and is involved mainly with consultancy and general IT support. Other firms include CPM (2006 revenue of US$180 million), G&P (2006 revenue of US$39 million), and Serpro, a public IT-services provider to the government. Junqueira-Botelho et al. point out that the success of the IT-outsourcing sector in Brazil has been linked to the presence of domestic clients with demands similar to those of major international firms. In their view, these clients have provided local software firms opportunities for learning and skill refinement akin to those found when exporting.

Mexico is also becoming a center for offshoring services, with Monterrey in particular attracting significant investment (Business Monitor International, 2009). This city, traditionally known for its large industrial enterprises, has developed a sizable cluster of IT firms. A survey of local IT companies, conducted by researchers at the University of Texas at Austin and reported by Echeverri-Carroll (2008, 2009), reveals that, as in the Brazilian case, Monterrey's IT sector also resulted from large local companies concentrating their efforts in core competencies during the transition from protectionism to free trade. Moreover, recent IT-targeted policies implemented by the federal and state government, along with the development of high-tech business incubators in local universities (Instituto Tecnológico y de Estudios Superiores de Monterrey and Universidad Autónoma de Nuevo León), have accelerated the growth of small technology firms in the area.

Two IT companies in Monterrey, Neoris and Softek, have become the largest IT-service providers in Latin America. Softek, founded in 1982 by local engineers who left Dinamica (a large local holding company), now has more than 5,000 employees providing IT services to corporations in more than 20 countries.[13] Neoris, which started as an IT department within CEMEX (a global building-materials company), and currently an independent company partially owned by CEMEX, is the chief IT consulting and systems-integration company in Mexico (Neoris, 2009). Neoris is a multinational company with operations in the United States, Europe, Latin America, Africa, and the Middle East.

That Brazil and Mexico have developed successful IT clusters and dominate most of the offshore-service industry in Latin America is not surprising. IT services depend on an abundance of skilled workers and, as Figure 17.5 shows, Mexico and Brazil have by far the largest supply of engineers and scientists in the region.

17.5   INDIA'S PRESENCE IN SERVICE-OFFSHORING FROM LATIN AMERICA

Today elite Indian outsourcing providers have branches in Monterrey and throughout Latin America (Laszlo et al., 2008). Tata Consultancy Services (TCS) is the main Indian company operating from Latin America, employing more than 5,000 tech workers in Mexico (Guadalajara and Monterrey) and six other countries in the region while serving

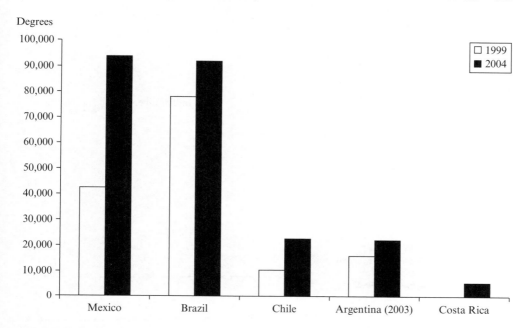

Source: National Science Board, *Science and Engineering Indicators*, 2002 and 2008.

Figure 17.5 Science and engineering degrees in 1999 and 2004 by selected countries in Latin America

customers such as General Motors, Goodyear, and Motorola. Sasken Communication and Infosys Technologies have also set up operations in Monterrey to provide consulting and back-office services (for example, accounting) for corporate clients in the United States and Latin America. Satyam also serves Latin American businesses from its center in Brazil, and Wipro has facilities in Monterrey and Curitiba, Brazil. In short, as Americans worry about high-tech work being offshored to India, India is moving into outsourcing from the USA's backyard.

Benjamin (2008) cites S. Jani Janakiraman, president of the Indian R&D firm, Mindtree, as predicting that within a decade, salaries for engineers in India will equal those of their American counterparts. Competition for technology workers in India has driven up costs, which, along with the Indian rupee's rise against the US dollar, makes Latin America more and more attractive. But perhaps the biggest motivation behind the location of Indian IT companies in Latin America is the increased demand of clients in both North and South America for the near-shore supply of services.

Compared to Latin America, India still has a much larger IT labor force and significantly lower wages. King (2008) points out that Mexico has about 500,000 IT workers and graduates an additional 65,000 each year, while Brazil has around 1 million IT workers with 100,000 graduates a year. India's numbers, though, are staggering, with more than 1.6 million IT workers and 495,000 more graduating yearly. A similar gap is seen in wages. According to King, the average salary in 2007 for IT workers was

Currency units per US$

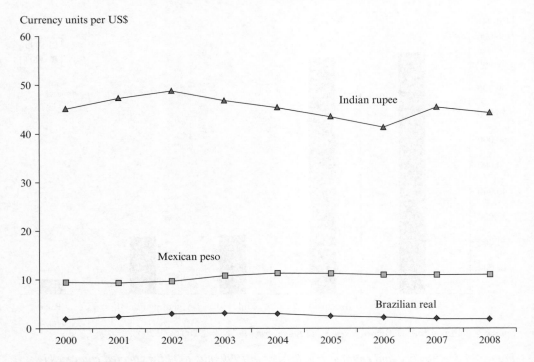

Source: Federal Reserve Board.

Figure 17.6   Average rates of exchange for India, Brazil, and Mexico, 2000–2008

US$7,779 in India, US$13,163 in Brazil and US$17,899 in Mexico. However, India's cost differential continues to erode as salaries there, over the last 10 years, have gone up by 10–20 percent annually (The Economist, 2013).

Indian's loss of competitiveness can also be explained, in part, by the appreciation of the Indian rupee against the US dollar.[14] As Figure 17.6 shows, the rupee began, in 2006, to appreciate significantly while the Mexican peso held steady against the dollar in 2003–08 and the Brazilian real dropped in value during the same period. Inflation, high attrition, sluggish global growth plus competition from East Asia and Eastern European countries have also weakened India's position (Grover, 2009). At the same time, an ongoing negative factor for far-offshore locations such as India and China, is the high cost of management and consulting. That US customers can visit and monitor operational progress on all sorts of matters, with partners in the same general time zone, makes for more effective communication and offsets, to a considerable degree, Latin America's higher labor costs.

For Indian companies, finding the right Latin American partner can entail sizable costs. To help minimize such outlays, the Monterrey Institute of Technology (Instituto Tecnológico y de Estudios Superiores de Monterrey) has created a Soft Landing Program. The program provides startup office space in the Institute's off-campus Pavilion Tec, helps companies match up with local software engineers and managers, and offers guidance in navigating Monterrey's governmental procedures (Laszlo et al., 2008).

17.6   CONCLUSIONS

Jensen and Kletzer (2008) present evidence that the number of US jobs at risk of being offshored to low-wage labor-abundant countries is 15 to 20 million, with about 40 percent of these jobs in the manufacturing sector. They do not say, however, which developing countries might benefit.

For most of the past century, Latin American countries had a comparative advantage in manufacturing stages that rely heavily on unskilled labor. Spatial proximity and the sharing of similar time zones reinforced Latin America's lead position in exporting inter-mediate inputs for electronic, automotive, and textile companies to the United States. However, China's entry into the WTO in 2001 challenged Latin America's standing. In Mexico alone, more than 900 maquiladora plants closed between 2001 and 2006. Low-wage competition from China and other emerging economies in Asia has led to questions about the competitiveness of Latin America in the production of unskilled-labor-intensive intermediate goods. Hence, one question drives this chapter's analysis. Has Latin American industry, built on low-wage assembly, lost an edge it can never reclaim?

Quintin (2004) of the Dallas Federal Reserve hypothesizes that China does not explain Mexico's recent difficulties, except in a few specific areas. In his view, the downturn in Mexican exports to the United States results primarily from the recent recession. Implicit in this hypothesis is that the situation will turn around once the US economy recovers. Another view claims that these changes are permanent. Gereffi (2009) states that China has surpassed Mexico in the battle for preeminence in the US market and believes that several factors, including China's significantly lower labor costs and stronger policies to promote knowledge-based industry, explain this reversal. The literature reviewed in this chapter shows that both the US recession and changes in trade policy have significantly transformed Mexico's place in the world.

The US recession in 2001 affected all maquiladoras while China's entry, that same year, into the WTO increased competition specifically for Mexican plants producing small electronics and textiles. In addition, the textiles sector in Mexico was hit by changes in trade policy that favored other countries. The CBI gave NAFTA parity to Caribbean countries in 2000, and the ending of the MFA in 2005 further strengthened China's hand. However, studies reviewed here show that although Mexican industry definitely lost ground in low-wage textiles and small-electronics sectors, it also found new ways to compete in the large-electronics and automotive sectors by becoming more technologically sophisticated and productive.

Carrillo and Hualde (1997) categorize production processes of maquiladoras by grouping them into three generations. First-generation maquiladoras are those that use mainly manual labor and do simple assembly 'assembled in Mexico'. Second-generation maquiladoras entail labor, manufacture, and the use of new technologies 'made in Mexico'. Third-generation plants are more knowledge intensive and do research and design in Mexico 'created in Mexico'. Carrillo (2009), comparing 1980, 1990, and 2000 data, reports a significant upgrading in the industry. In 1980, 100 percent of the maquiladoras in his sample were first-generation plants. In 1990, about 82 percent of the plants were first generation, and 18 percent were second generation. In 2000, only 18 percent were first generation, 55 percent were second generation, and 27 percent were third generation.

In 2006, the Mexican government stopped publishing maquiladora data. Other sources, however, reveal that Mexico continues to gain market share in the information and communication technology (ICT) sector. OECD data (2008) show that although China was the leading producer of electronics in 2008, Mexico is gaining ground as an ICT location. OECD figures show that electronics production increased 20 percent in Mexico between 2005 and 2008, and that Mexico, between 1996 and 2006, became increasingly specialized in the production of ICT goods, as measured by the share of ICT goods in total merchandise exports or by an index of 'revealed comparative advantages (RCA)'.[15] The OECD concludes that as the global restructuring of ICT production continued in 2007 and 2008, Mexico became an increasingly important producer and a new growth market.

It is only the lowest-paid and least-skilled maquiladoras that are disappearing. Other plants are upgrading production processes, and thus increasing their productivity. Cañas et al. (2007) find that as maquiladora recovery has moved forward, job growth has remained weak but real output has surged to new heights. Productivity, as measured by output per worker, increased nearly 60 percent from 2000 to 2005. Cañas and Gilmer (2009, p. 10) offer this view: 'As the industry evolved, it became apparent that permanent job losses were concentrated in the lowest-skill, lowest-wage sectors. With the maquiladora industry shifting to higher-wage, higher-productivity operations, the pace of recovery fell back on Mexico's long-standing competitive advantages, such as proximity to the US, an experienced and skilled workforce and a stable political system'. At the same time, the industry is diversifying and expanding as both US and Indian companies choose to offshore services from Latin America.

The United States is experiencing an increase in the offshoring of jobs in the service industry. Brazil and Mexico, the countries with the largest supply of engineers and scientists in Latin America, continue to capture an ever-larger share of intrafirm offshoring (affiliated US imports) of services. In addition, the two countries have developed clusters of IT startups that provide interfirm-offshoring services to US companies (unaffiliated US imports). Recent evidence shows that India is losing market share in service offshoring, which Latin America, given its geographical proximity to the United States and location within the same general time zone, appears to be gaining.

Latin America's continued vitality in global assembly and service industries is evident. First, Latin American countries, with more and more technological sophistication, continue to export electronic products, automotive parts, and IT services in spite of the slowdown in the US economy and competition from India and China. Second, small and large IT firms, capable of assembly and service operations for foreign clients, are rapidly emerging in the region. Third, Latin American countries are attracting Indian companies in growing numbers, who are using Latin America as a base to offshore IT services to US companies. In sum, instead of losing its ability to compete, Latin America is transforming itself into a vital location for not only offshore manufacturing but also offshore services.

NOTES

1. Maquiladoras, as they are known in Mexico, are export-oriented, labor-intensive assembly facilities. As Echeverri-Carroll (1994) explains, the term 'maquiladora' comes from an old Spanish word that used to describe the amount of corn paid by a farmer to a miller in exchange for grinding corn. Similarly today, the maquiladoras use parts and components provided by their US clients and return them in an assembled product.
2. While many countries participated in offshore assembly, the United States had by far the largest number of companies in the 1980s (Grunwald and Flamm, 1985).
3. 'Offshoring' is also defined as 'international outsourcing'.
4. Nominally, the 'North' refers to industrialized countries and the 'South' to developing countries.
5. Chapter 98, of the U.S. Harmonized Tariff Schedule (HTS), exempts duty on the value of US-made components returned as parts of items assembled abroad (9802.00.80), or as items of US-origin metal (except precious) imported for further processing (9802.00.60). Provision 9802.00.80 accounts for 95 percent of US imports under Chapter 98.
6. Chapter 98 data would significantly underestimate the size of the apparel sector's offshore production in Latin America before 2000, since the United States imports apparel products under several other duty-free programs (Tafoya and Watkins, 2005). For instance, it imported textiles and apparel duty free from Central American and Caribbean countries under the Caribbean Basin Initiative (CBI) and from Andean countries under the Andean Trade Preference Act (ATPA).
7. In 2003, maquiladoras obtained 97 percent of their material inputs from abroad and only 3 percent from national manufacturers (Anderson and Gerber, 2008, p. 100). Low wages and very few backward linkages with local suppliers explain the small value added in Mexico.
8. The CBI was a US program initiated by the 1983 Caribbean Basin Economic Recovery Act (CBERA). The CBI came into effect on January 1, 1984, aiming to provide several tariff and trade benefits to many Central American and Caribbean countries.
9. EPZs had become a leading source of exports and manufacturing employment in a number of Caribbean countries, of which the Dominican Republic is a prime example. In the mid-1990s, there were 430 companies employing 164,000 workers in 30 free-trade zones there; three-quarters of the firms were involved in textiles and apparel (Burns, 1995, p. 39).
10. The border zone includes the cities of Tijuana, Ciudad Juarez, and Piedras Negras, among others.
11. Brainard and Litan (2004, p. 2) note the discrepancy between BEA data and data published by the Indian government on services exports. They comment that the data on services collected by the BEA do not show any noticeable upticks in net imports in the services where outsourcing is believed to be prevalent. Countries, however, often use different methodologies to collect the same data, so straight comparisons between their data are generally difficult.
12. Luz (2008) explains how hyperinflation rates close to 2,500 percent in the early 1990s favored the development of IT-based banking systems that allowed for expedient cash transactions.
13. Data obtained on Softek are from the Mexico IT website at http://www.mexico-it.net
14. The Indian rupee's appreciation eroded the dollar's purchasing power in India, impacting Indian IT-service providers, who make an average of two-thirds of their revenue in US dollars but incur more than half of their costs in rupees (King, 2008).
15. The RCA measures whether, as an exporter, the ICT manufacturing industry performs better or worse in a given country than the average of its performance throughout the OECD area.

REFERENCES

Anderson, J. and Gerber, J. (2008), *Fifty years of change on the U.S.–Mexico Border: Growth, Development, and Quality of Life*, Austin, TX: University of Texas Press.

Bach, C.L. (2008), 'Annual Revision of the U.S. International Accounts, 1974–2007', *Survey of Current Business*, Washington, DC: Bureau of Economic Analysis, October.

Benjamin, D. (2008), 'Engineers' pay in India growing fast; China not so much', *Electronic Engineering Times*, November 6, available at: http://www.eetimes.com (accessed July 29, 2009).

Brainard, L. and Litan, R.E. (2004), '"Offshoring" service jobs: bane or boon – and what to do?', Policy Brief 132, Brookings Institution, Washington, DC.

Burns, J.G. (1995), 'Free trade zones: global overview and future prospects', *Industry, Trade and Technology Review*, September: 35–47.

Business Monitor International (2009), 'Mexico Information Technology Report Q1 2009', available at: http://www.marketresearch.com/product/display.asp?productid=2108618 (accessed August 28, 2009).

Cañas, J., Coronado, R. and Gilmer, R.W. (2007), 'Maquiladora recovery: lessons for the future', *Southwest Economy*, Federal Reserve Bank of Dallas, Issue 2, March/April 3–7.

Cañas, J. and Gilmer, W.G. (2009), 'The Maquiladora's changing geography', *Southwest Economy*, Federal Reserve Bank of Dallas, El Paso, Issue 2, 10–14.

Carrillo, J. (2009), 'Developing the U.S.–Mexico Border Region for a Prosperous and Secure Relationship: Innovative Companies and Policies for Innovation on the U.S.–Mexico Border', Binational Research Paper, James A Baker III Institute for Public Policy, Rice University, Houston, TX (accessed August 26, 2009).

Carrillo, J. and Hualde, A. (1997), 'Maquiladoras de Tercera Generación: El Caso Delphi-General Motors', *Comercio Exterior*, **47** (9): 771–9.

Echeverri-Carroll, E.L. (1994), 'Flexible linkages and offshore assembly facilities in developing countries', *International Regional Science Review*, **17** (1): 49–73.

Echeverri-Carroll, E.L. (1996), 'Flexible production, electronic linkages, and large firms: evidence from the automobile industry', *Annals of Regional Science*, **30** (1): 135–52.

Echeverri-Carroll, E.L. (1999), *Industrial Restructuring of the Electronics Industry in Guadalajara, Mexico: From Protectionism to Free Trade*, Austin, TX: Bureau of Business Research, University of Texas at Austin.

Echeverri-Carroll, E.L. (2008), 'The growth of knowledge-based small firms in Monterrey, Mexico', *Texas Business Review*, Bureau of Business Research, University of Texas at Austin.

Echeverri-Carroll, E.L. (2009), 'Las Pequeñas Empresas Basadas en el Conocimiento en Monterrey, México', *Comercio Exterior*, **59** (1): 111–15.

Echeverri-Carroll, E. and Ayala, S (2007), 'Does it matter where IT workers are located?', *Environmental and Planning C: Government and Policy*, **25** (5): 709–28.

Fernandez-Kelly, M.P. (1987), 'Technology and employment along the U.S.–Mexico border', in Cathryn L. Throup (ed.), *The United States and Mexico Face to Face with New Technology*, Washington, DC: Overseas Development Council and New Brunswick, NJ: Transaction Books, pp. 149–62.

Gallagher, K.P. and Zarsky, L. (2007), *The Enclave Economy – Foreign Investment and Sustainable Development in Mexico's Silicon Valley*, Cambridge, MA: MIT Press.

Gereffi, G. (2009), 'Development models and industry upgrading in China and Mexico', *European Sociological Review*, **25** (1): 37–51.

Glaeser, E.L. and Kohlhase, J.E. (2003), 'Cities, regions and the decline of transportation costs', Working Paper 9886, National Bureau of Economic Research, Cambridge, MA.

Government Accountability Office (GAO) (2004), *International Trade: Current Government Data Provide Limited Insight into Offshoring of Services*, GAO-04-932, Washington, DC.

Grossman, G.M. and Helpman, E. (2005), 'Outsourcing in a global economy', *Review of Economic Studies*, **72** (1): 135–59.

Grossman, G.M. and Rossi-Hansberg, E. (2006), 'The rise of offshoring: it's not wine for cloth anymore', Federal Reserve Bank of Kansas City, available at: http://works.bepress.com/esteban_rossi_hansberg/16 (accessed June 13, 2013).

Grossman, G.M. and Rossi-Hansberg, E. (2008), 'Trading tasks: a simple theory of offshoring', *American Economic Review*, **98** (5): 1978–97.

Grover, A. (2009), 'The Indian business process outsourcing industry: an evaluation of firm-level performance', Delhi School of Economics available at: http://artigrover.googlepages.com/Business_Process_Outsourcing_and_sup.pdf (accessed August 31, 2009).

Gruben, W.C. (2004), 'Have Mexico's Maquiladoras bottomed Out?', *Southwest Economy*, Federal Reserve Bank of Dallas, January–February, pp. 14–15.

Grunwald, J. and Flamm, K. (1985), *The Global Factory*, Washington, DC: Brookings Institution.

Hall, S. (2009), 'Offshoring takes off in Lation America, available at: http://www.itbusinessedge.com/cm/community/news/sou/blog/offshoring-takes-off-in-lation-america/?cs=31781 (accessed June 12, 2013).

Holmes, T.J. (2009), 'A theory of outsourcing and wage decline', Working Paper 14856, National Bureau of Economic Research, Cambridge, MA, available at: http://www.bakerinstitute.org/publications/LAI-pub-BorderSecCarrillo-051409.pdf http://www.bea.gov/scb/pdf/2008/10%20October/services_text.pdf (Accessed August 26, 2009).

Jensen, B.J. and Kletzer, L.G. (2008), '"Fear" and offshoring: the scope and potential impact of imports and exports of services', Policy Brief, Peterson Institute for International Economics, Washington, DC, January, available at: www.petersoninstitute.org (accessed June 13, 2013).

Junqueira-Botelho, A.J., Stefanuto, G. and Veloso, F. (2005), 'The Brazilian software industry', in A. Arora and A. Gambardella (eds), *From Underdogs to Tigers: The Rise and Growth of the Software Industry in Brazil, China, India, Ireland, and Israel*, Oxford: Oxford University Press, pp. 99–130.

King, R. (2008), 'The new economics of outsourcing', *Business Week*, April 7, available at: http://www.business week.com/stories/2008-04-07/the-new-economics-of-outsourcingbusinessweek-business-news-stock-market-and-financial-advice (accessed June 13, 2013).

Kirkegaard, J.F. (2005), 'Outsourcing and offshoring: pushing the European model over the hill, rather than off the cliff', IIE Working Paper 05-1, Institute for International Economics, Washington, DC.

Klier, T.H. and Rubenstein, J.M. (2008), 'Who really made your car?', *Chicago Fed Letter*, No. 255a, Chicago, IL: Federal Reserve Bank of Chicago, October.

Koncz, J. and Flatness, A. (2008), 'U.S. international services – cross border trade in 2007 and services supplied through affiliates in 2006', *Survey of Current Business*, October, 16–37.

Laszlo, K., Laszlo, A. and Defougères, L. (2008), 'Soft landing: Indian IT companies in Monterrey, Mexico', *Texas Business Review*, December.

Luz, D. (2008), 'An IT giant goes global', in Mark Kobayashi-Hillary (ed.), *Building a Future with BRICs: The Next Decade of Offshoring*, London: Springer-Verlag, pp. 17–24.

McCann, P. and Mudambi, R. (2005), 'Analytical differences in the economics of geography: the case of the multinational firm', *Environment and Planning A*, **37** (10): 1857–76.

Neoris (2009), 'IDC continues to rank Neoris among the largest IT consulting and systems integration companies in Latin America', *Neoris Practical Visionaries*, May 28 available at: http://www.neoris.com/Upload/ pdfPress/IDC%20Services%20Tracker%202008%20-%20English.pdf (accessed August 28, 2009).

Organisation for Economic Co-operation and Development (OECD) (2008), *OECD Information Technology Outlook*, Paris: OECD.

Quintin, E. (2004), 'Mexico's export woes not all China-induced', *Southwest Economy*, Federal Reserve Bank of Dallas, Issue 6, November, pp. 9–10.

Sklair, L. (1989), *Assembling for Development: The Maquila Industry in Mexico and the United States*, Boston, MA: Unwin Hyman.

Suarez-Villa, L. (1984), 'The manufacturing process cycle and the industrialization of the United States borderlands', *The Annals of Regional Science*, **18** (1): 1–23.

Tafoya, A. and Watkins, R. (2005), 'Production-sharing update: developments in 2003', *Industry Trade and Technology Review*, USITC Publication 3762, Washington, DC: United States International Trade Commission, December–January.

The Economist (2013), 'Here, there and everywhere. Special report: Outsourcing and offshoring', *The Economist*, January 19.

Van Welsum, D. and Reif, X. (2006), 'Potential offshoring: evidence from selected OECD countries', in S.M. Collings and L. Brainard (eds), *Offshoring White-Collar Work*, Brookings Trade Forum 2005, Washington, DC: Brookings Institute, pp. 165–94.

Ventura-Dias, V. and Duran-Lima, J. (2001), 'Production Sharing in Latin America: A Research Note', Series Comercio Internacional No. 2, CEPAL/ECLAC, Santiago, available at: http://www.eclac.org/publicaciones/ xml/9/9039/lcl1683i.pdf (accessed August 11, 2009).

Williamson, O.E. (1979), 'Transaction-cost economics: the governance of contractual relations', *Journal of Law and Economics*, **22** (2): 233–61.

Wilson, P. (1992), *Exports and Local Development: Mexico's New Maquiladoras*, Austin, TX: University of Texas Press.

World Bank (2001), *Global Economic Prospects – and the Developing Countries*, Washington, DC: International Bank for Reconstruction and Development/ World Bank.

World Trade Organization (WTO) (1998), *Annual Report 1998*, Geneva: WTO.

Yeats, A.J. (1998), 'Just how big is global production sharing?', Policy Research Working Paper 1871, World Bank, Washington, DC.

Zeile, W.J. (2003), *Trade in Goods Within Multinational Companies: Survey-based Data and Findings for the United States of America*, Washington, DC: US Bureau of Economic Analysis.

18 The global air transport industry: a comparative analysis of network structures in major continental regions
Aisling Reynolds-Feighan

18.1 INTRODUCTION

This chapter examines the global air transport industry in the 1998–2010 period. The air transport industry grew very rapidly during the second half of the twentieth century, with the US market being the dominant regional market. High overall growth levels in the twenty-first century have been sustained, accompanying the rapid economic growth and policy liberalization processes in the European and Asian markets in the 2000s. The air transport industry is a technology-rich sector with a heavy dependence on non-renewable fuel. The Boeing Airplane Company and Airbus industries' long-term forecasts both estimate that worldwide air traffic will continue its long-run growth rate of 5 per cent per annum to 2030 (Airbus, 2011; Boeing, 2011), despite the global economic downturn and sustained upward trend in fuel prices.

The chapter will present a comparative analysis of air transport trends in major global markets, focusing on recent network developments in the passenger air transport industry in these markets. Using a comprehensive and consistent global database, the network structures of the 10 largest carriers in each of seven global regions were examined in detail. Three main network structures are identified. The constraints associated with operational models found in the US market are discussed in relation to possible future scenarios for the growth of Chinese, other Asian and Latin American carriers.

Section 18.2 will look at the main drivers and influences on air passenger traffic trends, highlighting the key longer-term influences on air carrier behaviour and the accessibility for communities in the main global regional markets. Section 18.3 describes the data sources for global air transport analysis. In Section 18.4 an overview of regional air transport trends is presented, while in Section 18.5 the major global regions are described in terms of their airports' network structure and the competitiveness of their airline industry. A comparative analysis of key indicators concludes this section. In Section 18.6, the top 10 airports in each regional market are identified and compared, and in Section 18.7 the top 10 carriers in each region are selected. Differences in carrier network structures are highlighted and the implications for community accessibility are explained. Changing patterns of air traffic distribution across the airport networks of each region are measured and some general conclusions are set out in Section 18.8.

18.2   AIR TRANSPORT INDUSTRY TRENDS AND KEY DRIVERS

Global air traffic has grown consistently at 5–6 per cent per annum since the 1990s. The key driver of air traffic growth is economic growth. Improvements in productivity and reductions in transport costs have facilitated trade over ever-increasing distances and resulted in rising disposable incomes, both of which have increased the demand for air travel. The world's population has rapidly urbanized, with 67 per cent of the global population expected to live in cities by 2050 (United Nations, 2012). This concentration of the population and of economic activities in space has driven economic growth and development and acted as the focal point for the developing global air transport network. With the expansion in trade and increased mobility of the global population, these factors will continue to fuel increasing air passenger traffic demand, particularly in the emerging and developing economies of Asia, Latin America as well as in the Middle East and Africa.

Air transport services often involve the provision of passenger and freight services jointly. This is usually the case for long-haul services. In short-haul markets, however, with the faster turnaround times and limited cargo space in the belly-hold of passenger aircraft this means that passenger-only services are more typical. Since passenger and freight services have differing requirements in terms of routing preferences and space, the pricing and economic viability of services can be subject to strong cyclical trends. Increasing concerns about the security of air transport have also driven up costs in terms of both direct monetary charges and time costs due to delays.[1]

The liberalization of air service agreements between nation states affords air carriers the opportunity to develop new products and services and to streamline the organization of capacity in their networks in order to minimize costs and maximize yields on passenger and cargo services. Beginning in the 1970s in the US, the processes of air transport deregulation or liberalization have reduced the traditional tight government interventions that controlled the economic and legal operations of the air transport industry within and between nation states since the 1940s. The liberalization process has been applied in many domestic air transport markets as well as in international markets, and thus facilitated the growth and expansion of airline networks across the major global regions. This process is gradual and expanding at a varying pace in different global regions.

In Europe, the development of the Single European Market was accompanied by the development of a single air transport market during the 1990s. The European Common Aviation Area (ECAA) will cover the 28 EU member states by 2013 and 10 additional European states that lie outside the European Union.[2] In Asia, the Association of Southeast Asian Nations (ASEAN) agreed a programme of gradual multilateral liberalization of their air transport markets from 2010.[3] In China, the liberalization of pricing and market entry decisions from 1997, and reforms of the organization and structure of the industry from 2002 have facilitated the rapid growth and development of domestic and international air transport networks by Chinese carriers (Zhang and Round, 2008; Shaw et al., 2009). While liberalization is generally seen as a positive influence on air transport markets in terms of expanding access and service provision, the trend towards consolidation (mergers and takeovers) can work in the opposite direction and result in service reductions and withdrawal, especially for smaller-sized communities.

Fuel accounts for the largest share of an airline's direct operating costs. Spot jet fuel prices have been increasing steadily since the early 2000s. The possibilities for developing alternative fuels are more limited for air transport than for other transport modes because of the need for a pressurized fuselage and the weight constraints. Since air transport accounts for significant CO_2 emissions and noise externalities, it is expected that carbon taxes or emissions permits will add to the total fuel costs of airlines in the coming decades. Aircraft manufacturers have developed new aircraft and engines that have significantly reduced the fuel requirements per passenger-km travelled. The new generation of civil jet aircraft include the very large Airbus A380 passenger jet, with the capacity for up to 853 passengers depending on the cabin configuration selected. The world's two largest manufacturers of passenger aircraft have adopted alternative strategies in their development of new equipment to deal with expected passenger demand and increasing fuel costs: Boeing has gone for a medium-sized (up to 290 seats) long-range aircraft, while Airbus has opted for a very large long-range vehicle. The trade-offs between frequency, distance, capacity and unit costs will continue to pressure airlines in the coming decades.

18.3   AIR TRANSPORT DATA SOURCES

Consistent, reliable and up-to-date air transport data are difficult to source. The IATA (International Air Transport Association) and the ICAO (International Civil Aviation Organization) data presented are compiled from carrier-reported monthly traffic and capacity statistics relating to passenger and freight services for international scheduled operations. The IATA data cover 115 airlines and the dominant share of international scheduled air traffic. However, both the ICAO and IATA datasets cover a subset of airlines operating in regional markets, and access to the datasets is expensive. There is a delay of up to two years in the publication of the statistics. Detailed breakdowns of services by route and airport are not available for many carriers. While very detailed and extensive US data are compiled by the US Department of Transportation and Federal Aviation Administration, equivalent data for other global regions are not available.

In examining passenger air transport activity, the Official Airline Guide Historical MaxPlus (OAG) datasets give comprehensive coverage of *ex post* airline schedules for each year from 1996 to 2012 and cover scheduled and non-scheduled operations. Schedules are published one year ahead and the MaxPlus dataset presents the revised *ex post* schedules actually performed. The OAG coverage of airlines is far more extensive than either the ICAO's or the IATA's, and includes almost all passenger operators globally. The main problems with these datasets are that the activity measured is either seating or freight capacity available, rather than actual traffic performed, and the high access costs. However, the comprehensive and consistent coverage of domestic and international air transport activity globally allows for comparative analysis of major continental air passenger transport markets.

The OAG datasets were used to generate annual seating capacity and movement series for all airports and carriers operating jet equipment, including regional jets. The OAG

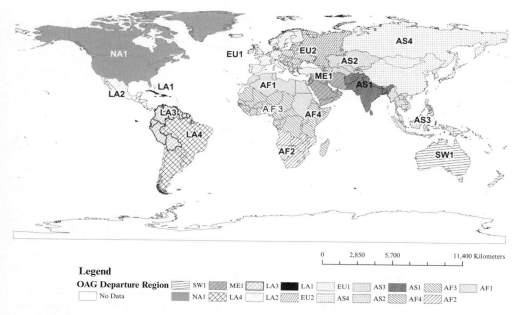

Legend

OAG Departure Region [diagonal lines] SW1 [hatch] ME1 [crosshatch] LA3 [solid black] LA1 [dotted] EU1 [dotted] AS3 [solid] AS1 [crosshatch] AF3 [dotted] AF1
[blank] No Data [gray] NA1 [crosshatch] LA4 [dotted] LA2 [diagonal lines] EU2 [dotted] AS4 [dotted] AS2 [crosshatch] AF4 [diagonal] AF2

Note: Regions were further combined to produce seven global regions: Latin America (LA) combines LA1, LA2, LA3 and LA4; Asia (AS) combines AS1, AS2, AS3 and AS4; Europe (EU) combines EU1 and EU2; Africa combines AF1, AF2, AF3 amd AF4. North America (NA1), Middle East (ME1) and Southwest (SW1).

Figure 18.1   Major global air transport departure regions in the OAG datasets based on IATA regional classifications, 2010

guide utilizes IATA and ICAO conventions in categorizing countries into global regions, and these will be used in the analysis in the rest of this chapter. The OAG datasets were used to generate annual air freight capacity and seating capacity variables for each of the top 10 Asian, European,[4] North American[5] Latin American, Middle East, Southwest and African carriers for the years 2000 to 2010. The OAG regional classification is illustrated in Figure 18.1.

18.4   REGIONAL DISTRIBUTION OF AIR TRAFFIC

Figure 18.2 presents the recent pattern of air traffic for the 190 member states of the ICAO between 1998 and 2010. The figure shows the total number of passengers carried and the passenger-km performed by carriers in the ICAO states during this period, indicating a long-term upward trend, with the average distance travelled increasing over the period. The impact of the 2001 and 2008 recessions (induced by the events of the 9/11 attacks in the US in 2001 and the global financial crisis of 2008) temporarily dampened the upward trend. Table 18.1 shows the regional breakdown of global scheduled air traffic for 2010. The main regions in terms of passengers carried are Europe, North America and Asia with 29, 30 and 28 per cent, respectively of total global traffic. The

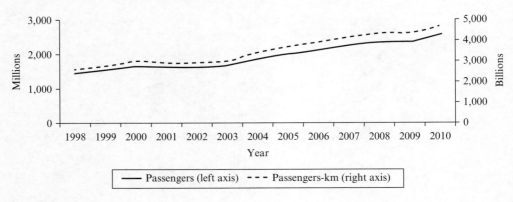

Source: ICAO.

Figure 18.2   Trends in global scheduled air traffic for ICAO states, 1998–2010

Table 18.1   Regional distribution of global scheduled air traffic, 2010

ICAO statistical region of airline registration	Aircraft km (billions)	Aircraft Departures (millions)	Passengers carried (millions)	Passenger-km performed (billions)	Passenger load factor (%)	Tonne-km performed Freight (billions)
Total	37.5	27.758	2,562	4,684	78	172
Percentage of world traffic						
Europe	26.6	28.3	29.2	27.9	77	25.9
Africa	3.3	2.7	2.4	2.6	68	1.3
Middle East	5.2	3.2	4.4	7.4	76	9.4
Asia and Pacific	25.7	22.5	27.7	27.4	76	36.5
North America	33.9	36.2	30	30.1	84	23.7
Latin America and Caribbean	5.4	7.1	6.3	4.5	70	3.2

Source: ICAO, *Annual Report to Council*, 2011.

North American market has a larger share of aircraft departures (36 per cent) reflecting the lower number of seats per movement. Significant differences arise depending on the metric of traffic used: the passenger-km measures give higher weight to airlines and countries with higher average route lengths; the number of movements gives greater weight to higher frequency carriers utilizing smaller aircraft. The Asian market in 2010 had the largest share of air freight activity as measured by tonne-km performed (36 per cent), followed by Europe (26 per cent) and North America (24 per cent). A detailed analysis of global air freight markets may be found in Reynolds-Feighan (2013).

   Table 18.2 gives details of the top 20 air traffic countries as measured by total tonne-km and passenger-km for carriers of ICAO member states. The US, China and

Table 18.2   *Top 20 countries (or groups of countries) by total tonne-km and by passenger-km performed on scheduled air services in 2010*

Country or group of countries	Passenger-km performed (millions)					
	Total operations (int'l & dom)			International operations only		
	Rank in 2010	2010	Change 2009–10 (%)	Rank in 2010	2010	Change 2009–10 (%)
United States	1	1,299,874	3	1	394,281	6
China	2	400,610	20	10	73,488	33
Hong Kong SAR		85,811	−4		85,811	−4
Macao SAR		2,106	1		2,106	1
Germany	4	202, 047	0	3	191,037	−1
United Arab Emirates	5	186, 821	21	4	186,821	21
United Kingdom	3	229,649	0	2	221,953	0
Republic of Korea	13	91,759	10	9	87,121	11
Japan	7	138,079	8	11	72,212	8
France	6	154,761	0	5	136,493	1
Singapore	17	87,674	4	8	87,674	4
Netherlands	16	87,696	4	7	87,695	4
Russian Federation	9	109,435	31	16	52,616	42
Canada	8	115,793	8	12	68,167	12
Australia	12	96,579	−4	19	46,902	−6
India	11	99,692	16	18	49,885	14
Brazil	14	90,846	23	25	22,777	10
Spain	15	88,300	10	13	68,079	14
Ireland	10	100,664	25	6	100,633	25
Thailand	19	57,201	6	14	53,257	8
Qatar	20	52,733	31	15	52,733	31
Turkey	18	64,800	13	17	51,475	15

Source: ICAO, *Annual Report to Council*, 2011.

Germany were the top-ranked countries in 2010, with the US carriers performing significantly more tonne-km and passenger-km than China. The US, China and Brazil have 30, 18 and 25 per cent of their passenger-km, respectively, performed on international operations (reflecting large domestic markets), while most other countries listed have at least half of all traffic performed internationally.

The rankings of countries in the table reflect a combination of population, higher incomes and the presence of larger airlines. Ireland is ranked 17th, for example, as Ryanair is an Irish registered carrier. The dramatic growth in air traffic volumes between 2009 and 2010 for China, Brazil, the Russian Federation and Korea are recorded in the table, though in many instances this reflects a recovery from declines in the 2008–09 period. Average passenger load factors increased by 10 per cent between 1998 and 2010, rising from 68 to 78 per cent. This increase in load factor has been driven by North American carriers who have cut capacity in their networks and consolidated services through merger and acquistion activities during this period.

Table 18.3   IATA top 10 carriers by number of passengers carried and by passenger-km, 2010

Top 10 carriers – passengers carried (m)			Top 10 carriers – passenger-km (bn)		
Rank	Airline	Millions	Rank	Airline	Billions
1	Delta Air Lines (USA)	111	1	Delta Air Lines (USA)	267
2	Southwest Airlines (USA)	106	2	American Airlines (USA)	202
3	American Airlines (USA)	86	3	United Airlines (USA)*	165
4	China Southern Airlines (China)	76	4	Emirates (Dubai)	144
			5	Lufthansa (Germany)	130
5	Ryanair (Ireland)+	71	6	Continental Airlines (USA)*	128
6	Lufthansa (Germany)	56	7	Southwest Airlines (USA)+	126
7	United Airlines (USA)	54	8	Air France (France)	125
8	US Airways (USA)	51	9	China Southern Airlines (China)	110
9	China Eastern Airlines (China)	50	10	British Airways (UK)	106
10	Air France (France)	47			

Notes:
* United Airline and Continental Airlines merged in 2010; the merger was completed in 2012 when the Continental Airlines brand ceased operations.
+ Ryanair and Southwest Airlines are considered to be low-cost carriers and do not offer air freight services.

Source: IATA, *World Air Transport Statistics*, 2010.

Table 18.3 shows the top 10 airlines in terms of passengers carried and passenger-km performed in 2010. The top three are US carriers, with a further two US carriers among the top 10. Ryanair and Southwest Airlines are two 'low-cost carriers' (LCCs), though this designation is quite vague. According to Airbus, LCCs are expected to account for one-third of all short-haul air traffic by 2030 (Airbus, 2011). The non-LCC carriers in Table 18.3 are ranked among the top 30 air freight carriers worldwide (air Cargo World, 2009). Several of the carriers listed in this table were involved in mergers during 2010: Northwest Airlines completed its merger with Delta Air Lines in December 2009; United Airlines and Continental Airlines merged in 2010; Southwest Airlines acquired the second-largest US LCC, AirTran in 2011; British Airways merged with the Spanish carrier Iberia in January 2011; USAir and American Airlines announced a merger in early 2013.

Beginning in the late 1990s, airline alliances were formed among small groups of airlines operating in different continents. The alliances vary considerably in how they function and in the degree of cooperation among the partners (Oum et al., 2000)). The alliances have facilitated the joint sourcing of maintenance services, the sharing of frequent flyer programmes, as well as code-sharing agreements, pricing arrangements in multi-carrier trips and cooperative passenger and baggage transfer arrangements that enable seamless intercontinental air travel. While these alliances have grown in size and extent in the 2000s, carrier network behaviour is driven by the individual airlines and the market environments in which they are operating.

18.5 GLOBAL REGIONAL AIR TRANSPORT MARKETS: STRUCTURE, ORGANIZATION AND COMPETITION

Using the OAG data series on air passenger movements and seating capacity, non-stop departure flights were counted in order to identify the main traffic flows. Figure 18.3 shows the main flows within and between the major regional markets in 2000 and 2010 as measured by the number of departure movements. The highest concentrations of flows are within each of the North American, European and Asian markets (that is, along

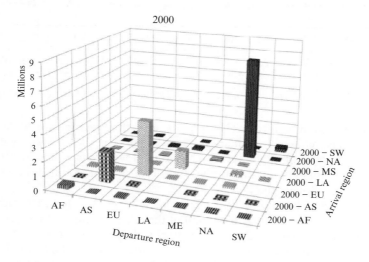

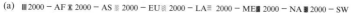

(a) ▥2000 − AF ▧ 2000 − AS ▒ 2000 − EU ▨ 2000 − LA ≡ 2000 − ME▦ 2000 − NA ▰ 2000 − SW

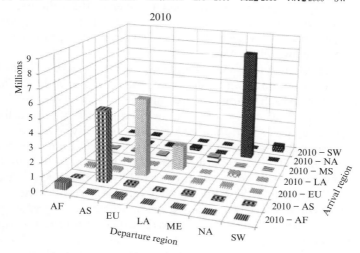

(b) ▥2010 − AF ▧ 2010 − AS ▒ 2010 − EU ▨ 2010 − LA ≡ 2010 − ME▦ 2010 − NA ▰ 2010 − SW

Figure 18.3 Global passenger departure movements in 2000 and 2010 by major region

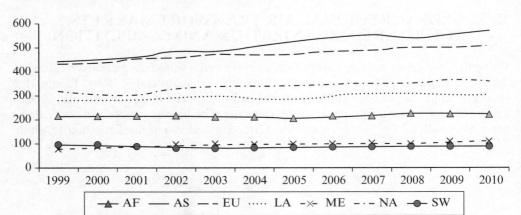

Figure 18.4   Number of airports in each global region receiving jet services, 1999–2010

the diagonal in both (a) and (b)). The dramatic growth in European and Asian traffic is clearly visible. The relatively small levels of traffic between the different regions are also evident in the figures, although more interregional flows are operated in 2010 compared with 2000. The availability of long-range aircraft has facilitated direct non-stop services between the major global regions.

Figure 18.4 shows the number of airports with jet services for each region between 1999 and 2010. This figure shows the extent of the infrastructure network supporting the air transport industry worldwide. There is very little change in the number of airports receiving jet services for most of the regions: the exceptions are the European and Asian markets where the numbers increased from 443 and 432 in Asia and Europe in 1999 to 571 and 506, respectively, in line with much bigger traffic volumes, as was shown in Figure 18.3. The European region here includes the Russian Federation west of the Urals. There were relatively few new airports constructed during this period, with most of the new airports being built in Asia.

The total number of air routes was computed for each of the years from 1996 to 2010 and the regional distribution of air routes is illustrated in Figure 18.5. The number of potential direct routes in each region can be computed as $N(N-1)$ where N is the number of airports in the region. The air routes are the product offerings of airlines and each product will have a separate flight number.[6] The vast majority of the routes offered are direct services, though the North American carriers offer significant numbers of indirect (or multi-stop) services. To illustrate this difference, the ratio of the number of flights offered to the number of non-stop services operated by carriers was computed for each region. Table 18.4 reports on these ratios. The North American carriers differ significantly from carriers in other regions in the manner in which air services are provided and this is reflected in the substantially higher ratios recorded in the table for North America.

The 'hub-and-spoke' nature of North American air services results in significant numbers of passengers travelling between their origin and destination indirectly by connecting through at least one 'hub' airport. The total number of non-stop segments offered in North America is substantially lower than in Europe, given the size of the airport network and the high overall traffic volume. Following deregulation in the US,

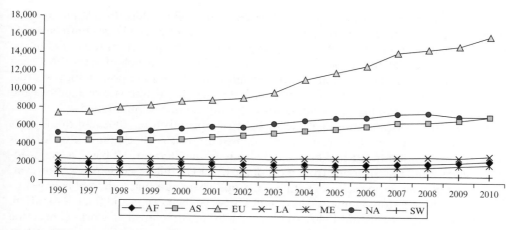

Figure 18.5   Number of non-stop routes operated by carriers in each global region, 1996–2010

Table 18.4   Ratio of flight/route offerings to non-stop air services for all carriers in each global region, 1999–2010

Year	AF	AS	EU	LA	ME	NA	SW
1999	1.50	1.34	1.25	1.84	1.47	3.26	1.67
2000	1.47	1.32	1.25	1.86	1.44	3.13	1.64
2001	1.45	1.32	1.25	1.92	1.43	3.02	1.54
2002	1.42	1.31	1.25	1.92	1.43	2.96	1.42
2003	1.42	1.32	1.24	1.85	1.43	2.87	1.35
2004	1.42	1.28	1.20	1.83	1.38	2.98	1.31
2005	1.42	1.28	1.16	1.83	1.36	2.89	1.28
2006	1.41	1.26	1.14	1.76	1.33	2.89	1.29
2007	1.36	1.25	1.11	1.74	1.29	3.16	1.27
2008	1.40	1.23	1.11	1.61	1.25	3.03	1.23
2009	1.34	1.24	1.11	1.56	1.23	3.28	1.20
2010	1.35	1.25	1.11	1.48	1.21	3.62	1.19

Note: Flight offerings are origin–destination pairs listed in the OAG schedules and offered by carriers directly for sale. Non-stop air services are the airport pair segments that carriers perform.

Source: Author's calculations from Official Airline Guide global schedules, 1999–2010.

the airlines made decisions about which cities to serve and where their key 'hubs' should be located. The number of small and medium-sized communities receiving scheduled jet services fell significantly in the decade following deregulation, thus reducing the number of potential routes (Reynolds-Feighan, 2010). The choice of hubs often reflected the historical origins of carriers (for example, Delta Air Lines being based at Atlanta). As the number of carriers reduced through mergers, takeovers and financial failures, so too did the number of hub airports. The greatly increased volume of traffic was channelled through a small number of airports, with feeder routes being added to sustain high frequencies between the main hubs. Because US carriers operate such large continent-wide networks, they can offer potentially any origin–destination pair from the nodes in the network as a service to customers. Because of the high frequency of service between hubs, customers can be accommodated through multiple routing possibilities. As fuel costs increase and landing taxes and environmental charges are imposed on landings and takeoffs, the sustainability of the hub-and-spoke model must be questioned.

The North American ratios in Table 18.4 rise significantly after 2008 and this reflects the increasing number of indirect services that Southwest Airlines and Delta Airlines offered for sale. Southwest had been cited widely in the literature as being a 'point-to-point' carrier and thus differing from most of the other US full service carriers. However, Southwest began offering services with multi-stops where passengers did not change aircraft but had short stops at intermediate nodes between their origin and final destination.

In Europe in the 1930s and 1940s, state-owned airlines developed networks connecting their home capital city or largest urban centres to other cities within Europe and further afield based on historical and economic ties. The interlinking of services was facilitated for customers through travel agents purchasing consecutive segments and designing routings that the airlines could not offer themselves, because they controlled more limited networks. With liberalization in the 1990s, many medium- and smaller-sized cities have begun receiving direct air services linking them to large and medium urban centres, within and beyond the continent. Many cities of equivalent size in the US would not have the number and range of direct routes available in Europe. The growth in the number of routes in Europe during the 2000s reflects the fragmented and small-scale nature of European air carrier networks, focused around national or regional centres. The carriers offer direct pairings if volumes are sufficient to support the service, even if the service operates less than daily.

The academic literature on airline network structures is very much dominated by the US market experience, with the emergence of hub-and-spoke network structures analysed extensively as one of the key impacts of domestic deregulation in terms of airline operations (see, for example, Borenstein, 1992; Brueckner et al., 1992; O'Kelly, 1998). The large size of the US domestic market and the availability of relatively cheap fuel enabled carriers to greatly expand their market pair offerings by offering indirect services, while only marginally increasing the number of non-stop segments that they operated. Passengers connect through one of a small number of key hubs in the carrier's network, where flights are coordinated in time so as to optimize the potential to transfer to departing segments within relatively short turnaround times. For a significant proportion of US customers, this increases the time costs and total distance travelled between origin–destination pairs. In comparing network structures across different global regions, the lack of detailed information on passenger connection rates hinders conclusions being drawn on the extent to which US-style hub-and-spoke operations are being practised.

Figure 18.6 shows the average number of seats per aircraft departure for each of the regions over the 1999–2010 period. The Asian and Middle Eastern markets have the highest seats per passenger movement (177 and 180, respectively), though the average has declined steadily since 2002 in both cases (196 and 187 in 1999). The average European departure movement has a capacity for 150 passengers in 2010, up

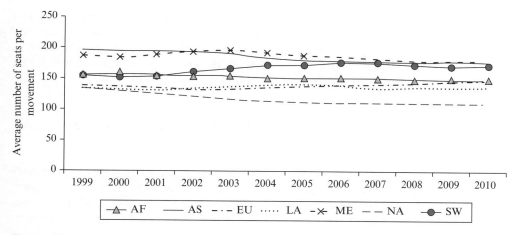

Figure 18.6 Average number of seats per flight departure by region, 1999–2010

Table 18.5 Percentage of routes originated in each global region by number of carriers, 2010

Region	Number of carriers per route					
	1	2	3	4	5	6 or more
AF	65.7	20.4	7.7	3.1	2.1	0.9
AS	54.3	20.9	10.4	6.6	4.1	3.7
EU	70.6	20.1	6.4	2.0	0.7	0.2
LA	58.5	26.3	11.0	3.1	0.8	0.4
ME	62.2	23.1	7.4	3.7	1.7	1.8
NA	64.3	26.6	6.9	1.7	0.3	0.1
SW	60.6	21.9	11.1	3.6	2.1	0.7

from 138 in 1999. The lowest average number of seats per departure is in the North American market at 111 per movement. The widespread introduction of regional jets and the use of single-aisle jet aircraft in the expanding domestic market resulted in this reduction in average seats per departure. The growth in the domestic US market was driven by the entry of LCCs during the 1990s and 2000s. These carriers have tended to employ a single type of aircraft and offered point-to-point rather than connecting services. The improved load factors achieved through the 2000s by North American carriers was noted above, and has contributed to improved economic performance of these airlines.

The extent of competition in regional markets and at more local levels is examined by measuring traffic distributions at the route and airport levels for the global air transport industry. Table 18.5 gives the percentage of routes in each major region with between one and five carriers providing direct air services in 2010. Carriers operating less than 20 movements per year were excluded from the analysis. For the 32,970 routes operated in 2010, 65 per cent had just a single carrier present, with a further 22 per cent having just two carriers. This pattern is reasonably consistent across all regions: Asian and Latin American routes have a higher proportion of routes with three or more carriers competing (25 and 15 per cent respectively). The European market has the highest number of routes (40 per cent of all non-stop routes in 2010 as shown in Figure 18.5) and the highest proportion with a single carrier (70 per cent of all European routes).

18.6   TRAFFIC DISTRIBUTION AT THE BUSIEST GLOBAL AIRPORTS

The traffic distributions at the top five airports in each of the study regions were examined in more detail in order to assess the extent of competition at the top of the international airport hierarchy. The number of passenger departures and number of routes operated from each airport are illustrated in Figures 18.7 and 18.8. Several measures

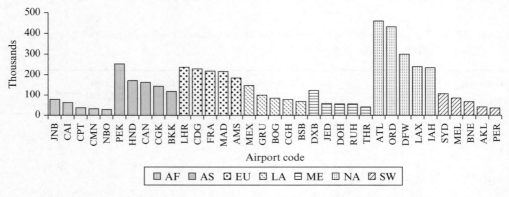

Figure 18.7   Passenger departures at the top five airports in global regions, 2010

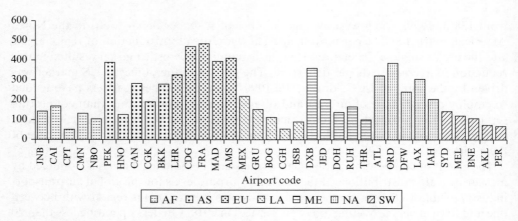

Figure 18.8   Number of routes operated from each of the top five airports in global regions, 2010

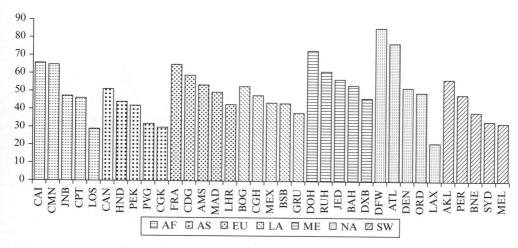

Figure 18.9   Traffic share of the largest carrier at the top five airports in global regions, 2010

of traffic concentration were computed for the airports and there is a high correlation between the Herfindahl–Hirschmann index, Gini index scores[7] and the traffic share (movements) of the top carrier at each airport. The last measure is illustrated for the airports in Figure 18.9. The very large size of the US airports is clear in Figure 18.7, with Atlanta (ATL), Chicago O'Hare (ORD) and Dallas-Fort Worth (DFW) handling far greater traffic volumes than any other airport in 2010.

The European and Asian airports have relatively similar traffic volumes (Figure 18.7), but the European airports have a greater number of non-stop routes than other airports (Figure 18.8). So the North American airports have larger volumes of traffic but these are spread over a smaller number of routes compared with European airports, reflecting the hub-and-spoke network strategy operated by most of the US carriers. The African, Latin American, Southwestern and Middle Eastern airports have smaller numbers of direct connections (less than 140) with the exception of Dubai International Airport (DXB) which had 359 originating routes in 2010. Many of the airports in Figures 18.7 and 18.8 are dominated by a single carrier and this is shown in Figure 18.9. The North American airports have the highest traffic shares operated by their top-ranked carriers: Dallas-Fort Worth Airport (DFW) is the top hub for American Airlines who performed 86 per cent of all movements from the airport in 2010; Atlanta (ATL) is the hub for Delta Airlines who performed 78 per cent of all departure movements in 2010. Chicago O'Hare Airport (ORD) has a lower percentage as it is a hub for both United Airlines and American Airlines.

The top five European airports in Figure 18.9 are the main airports serving the capital city or highest population centres in Germany, France, the UK, Spain and the Netherlands. Air France and KLM merged in 2004 but have continued operating the two airlines as separate brands.[8] In July 2010, a merger between BA and Iberia was approved by the European Commission and the merger was completed in January 2011. The process of airline consolidation is gathering pace in Europe and will result in

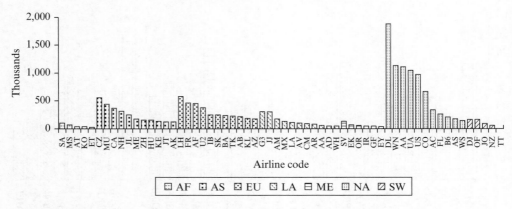

Figure 18.10   Total movements for selected carriers by global region, 2010

increasing levels of industry and spatial concentration. The assessment of airline mergers in Europe and in North America focuses on assessing the competitive impacts on routes where merging carriers currently overlap. The impact on carrier traffic shares at key airports is only considered indirectly if the merging carriers share one or more key hubs, and thus have significant numbers of overlapping routes. The recent experience has shown that mergers will be permitted if carriers have different main hubs, but blocked if they share main hubs.[9] Consolidation in Europe may result in the largest airports being dominated by a small group of carriers, as is the case in the US.

The Asian airports have generally lower traffic shares operated by the top-ranked carrier: Guangzhou Airport in China has the highest share as China Southern Airlines operated 51 per cent of the total departure movements in 2010. Despite the state-led consolidation in the Chinese airline industry in 2002, whereby nine airlines were regrouped into three (Air China, China Southern and China Eastern), carriers' shares at the largest airports in China are generally lower than in equivalent airports in the other global regions (Figure 18.10).

The largest Latin American airports have between 40 and 50 per cent of total movements operated by the top-ranked carriers. Countries with relatively high volumes of international traffic tend to have a greater presence of international carriers at their main airport(s), usually serving the capital city or largest city, and this reduces the share of traffic operated by nationally registered carriers.

18.7   CARRIER NETWORK STRUCTURES AND OPERATING CHARACTERISTICS

The top 10 carriers were selected for each of the major air transport regions, and the network structures were compared over a 10-year period. Selected summary 2010 operating characteristics and structural aspects of the carrier networks are presented for a selection of the carriers in the tables and figures.[10] Table 18.6 sets out summary statistics for each carrier. The carrier's top five airports are identified along with the traffic share and number of routes per airports. The main focus here is on identifying

Table 18.6 Top air passenger airports and network statistics for selected air passenger carriers, 2010

IATA region	Carrier name	Carrier IATA code	Total number of airports served	IATA airport code of top airport	Departure airport name	Departure country	Percentage of airline's total movements from top 2 airports		Number of top 5 airports in home country
AF1	Egyptair	MS	81	CAI	Cairo	Egypt	44.2	6.1	5
AF4	Ethiopian Airlines	ET	67	ADD	Addis Ababa	Ethiopia	31.7	3.9	1
AF4	Kenya Airways	KQ	51	NBO	Nairobi Jomo Kenyatta Int'l	Kenya	41.7	7.9	2
AF2	Royal Air Maroc	AT	89	CMN	Casablanca Mohammed V	Morocco	33.9	9.8	3
AF2	South African Airways	SA	53	JNB	Johannesburg Int'l	South Africa	35.8	17.0	5
AS4	Air China	CA	145	PEK	Beijing Capital	China	29.3	9.7	5
AS4	All Nippon Airways	NH	78	HND	Tokyo Haneda	Japan	24.6	6.8	5
AS4	China Eastern Airlines	MU	154	PVG	Shanghai Pudong Int'l	China	10.2	9.7	5
AS4	China Southern Airlines	CZ	187	CAN	Guangzhou	China	14.9	7.0	5
AS4	Hainan Airlines	HU	82	PEK	Beijing Capital	China	15.0	8.3	5
AS4	Japan Airlines Int'l	JL	81	HND	Tokyo Haneda	Japan	26.8	7.5	5
AS4	Korean Air	KE	108	ICN	Seoul Incheon Int'l	Korea	23.4	16.0	4
AS3	Lion Air	JT	36	CGK	Jakarta Soekarno-Hatta	Indonesia	33.8	10.3	5
AS4	Shenzhen Airlines	ZH	91	SZX	Shenzhen	China	19.8	9.6	5
AS4	Xiamen Airlines Company	MF	63	XMN	Xiamen	China	15.4	9.3	5
EU1	Air Berlin	AB	145	TXL	Berlin Tegel	Germany	13.0	10.6	4
EU1	Air France	AF	179	CDG	Paris Charles de Gaulle	France	27.4	10.7	5
EU1	British Airways	BA	165	LHR	London Heathrow	UK	34.9	7.4	4
EU1	Easyjet	U2	129	LGW	London Gatwick	UK	11.0	5.5	3
EU1	Iberia	IB	128	MAD	Madrid Barajas	Spain	40.0	8.0	5
EU1	KLM-Royal Dutch Airlines	KL	128	AMS	Amsterdam	Netherlands	48.7	1.8	1

Table 18.6 (continued)

IATA region	Carrier name	carrier IATA code	Total number of airports served	IATA airport code of top airport	Departure airport name	Departure country	Percentage of airline's total movements from top 2 airports		Number of top 5 airports in home country
EU1	Lufthansa German Airlines	LH	211	FRA	Frankfurt Int'l	Germany	22.6	16.1	5
EU1	Ryanair	FR	161	STN	London Stansted	UK	9.1	5.9	1
EU1	SAS Scandinavian Airlines	SK	91	CPH	Copenhagen Kastrup	Denmark	20.1	16.0	5*
EU1	Turkish Airlines	TK	174	IST	Istanbul Ataturk Airport	Turkey	38.6	9.9	5
LA4	Aerolineas Argentinas	AR	54	AEP	Buenos Aires Aeroparque	Argentina	38.0	8.4	5
LA2	Aeromexico	AM	74	MEX	Mexico City Juarez Int'l	Mexico	35.5	8.8	5
LA3	Avianca	AV	38	BOG	Bogota	Colombia	46.4	8.8	5
LA4	Azul Airlines	AD	27	VCP	Sao Paulo Viracopos	Brazil	40.2	9.7	5
LA2	Copa Airlines	CM	64	PTY	Panama City Tocumen Int'l	Panama	31.9	17.1	1
LA4	Lan Airlines	LA	64	SCL	Santiago Arturo Merino Benitez	Chile	28.7	7.6	2
LA2	Mexicana de Aviacion	MX	68	MEX	Mexico City Juarez Int'l	Mexico	36.5	8.7	5
LA4	TAM Linhas Aereas	JJ	66	GRU	Sao Paulo Guarulhos Intl	Brazil	12.9	12.2	5
LA4	VARIG-Gol	G3	63	CGH	Sao Paulo Congonhas	Brazil	12.6	9.6	5
LA4	Webjet	WH	13	GRU	Sao Paulo Guarulhos Intl	Brazil	17.9	13.6	5
ME1	Emirates	EK	99	DXB	Dubai Int'l	UAE	46.2	1.7	1
ME1	Etihad Airways	EY	66	AUH	Abu Dhabi Int'l	UAE	48.6	2.8	1
ME1	Gulf Air	GF	50	BAH	Bahrain	Bahrain	49.7	5.1	1
ME1	Iran Air	IR	63	THR	Tehran Mehrabad Int'l	Iran	33.5	7.7	5

	Airline	Code		Airport	Airport name	Country			
ME1	Qatar Airways	QR	93	DOH	Doha	Qatar	48.1	3.4	1
NA1	Air Canada	AC	129	YYZ	Toronto Lester B Pearson Intl	Canada	25.5	9.0	5
NA1	Airtran Airways	FL	71	ATL	Atlanta Hartsfield-Jackson Intl	USA	27.2	8.3	5
NA1	Alaska Airlines	AS	85	SEA	Seattle/Tacoma Int'l	USA	27.3	10.6	5
NA1	American Airlines	AA	243	DFW	Dallas/Fort Worth Intl	USA	21.6	13.8	5
NA1	Continental Airlines	CO	253	IAH	Houston G.Bush Intercontinental	USA	27.7	15.9	5
NA1	Delta Air Lines	DL	346	ATL	Atlanta Hartsfield-Jackson Intl	USA	18.2	8.4	5
NA1	JetBlue Airways	B6	63	JFK	New York J F Kennedy Int'l	USA	23.3	11.6	5
NA1	Southwest Airlines Corporation	WN	69	LAS	Las Vegas McCarran Int'l	USA	6.9	6.6	5
NA1	United Airlines	UA	208	ORD	Chicago O'Hare Int'l	USA	19.8	13.2	5
NA1	US Airways	US	193	CLT	Charlotte	USA	19.8	12.6	5
SW1	Air New Zealand	NZ	32	AKL	Auckland Int'l	New Zealand	37.4	18.3	4
SW1	Jetstar Airways	JQ	34	SYD	Sydney Kingsford Smith	Australia	17.2	14.7	4
SW1	Qantas Airways	QF	45	SYD	Sydney Kingsford Smith	Australia	21.9	17.0	5
SW1	Tiger Airways Australia	TT	24	MEL	Melbourne Airport	Australia	37.7	16.7	5
SW1	Virgin Blue	DJ	45	SYD	Sydney Kingsford Smith	Australia	22.2	17.6	5

Notes: * SAS Scandinavian Airlines (founded as Scandinavian Air Systems) was established to cooperatively provide long-haul air services and subsequently domestic and intra-European air services from Norway, Sweden and Denmark in 1946. The airline operates services from the three countries with similar traffic shares departing from the three national capitals. The top five airports served are located within the three Scandinavian countries.

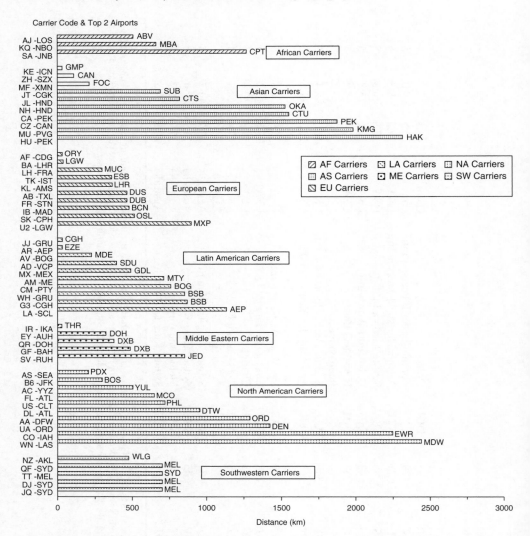

Figure 18.11 *Distance between top two airports for selected carriers in global regions in 2010*

common or different operating characteristics for groups of carriers across the different regions. Each region is briefly discussed before summary comparisons are presented. Figure 18.10 summarizes the 2010 traffic volume (measured as number of non-stop departure movements) for 55 carriers, while Figure 18.11 shows the distance between the top two airports in each carrier's network. This metric is important in distinguishing single-from multiple-hub networks. In Figure 18.12, stylized representations of a selection of carrier networks detailed in Table 18.6 are presented. These figures do not reflect the geographical location of nodes: they merely show the linkage structure between each carrier's set of nodes and non-stop flight segments.[11] The figures weight the nodes by the number of direct connections, making the identification of the key hub or hubs straight-forward. The diagrams also highlight the degree of interconnectedness in the network.

18.7.1   African Carriers

There were 87 carriers registered in African countries in 2010. The African carriers operate considerably smaller networks than carriers in other regions with the top five varying in size between 51 and 89 nodes. Egyptair and South African Airways (SAA) have all of their top five airports located within their country of registration. Ethiopian Airlines, Kenya Airways and Royal Air Maroc operate single-hub networks with their second-ranked airport being located in another country (Table 18.6). All of the carriers are the dominant airline at their top-ranked airport with only SAA having less than 50 per cent of its top-ranked airport's total movements. The networks of Egyptair, Kenya Airways and SAA are included in Figure 18.12 and clearly show the dominance of the main hub in these networks. All of the African carrier networks examined were single-hub networks.

18.7.2   Asian Carriers

There were 138 Asian registered carriers operating in 2010. The traffic volumes per-formed by the top 10 carriers are on a par with the volumes performed by the largest European carriers as can be seen in Figure 18.10. Six of the top 10 carriers are Chinese with networks focused on the largest urban centres of Beijing (Air China and Hainan Airlines), Shanghai (China Eastern Airlines), Guangzhou (China Southern Airlines), Shenzhen (Shenzhen Airlines) and Xiamen (Xiamen Airlines). Two Japanese carriers (JAL and All Nippon Airways (ANA)), Korean Airlines and Lion Air of Indonesia are also in the top 10. The absence of an Indian carrier in the top 10 is striking given the large population. The Japanese carriers' networks are both focused on Tokyo's Haneda Airport; the carriers each operate about one-quarter of Haneda's total movements. JAL also has a strong presence at Tokyo's Narita Airport and 34 per cent of all of the carrier's movements are performed from Tokyo. There is a high degree of interconnect-edness in the networks of the Japanese and the larger Chinese carriers and this can be seen in the network representation in Figure 18.12 for JAL, Air China, China Southern and China Eastern. The substantial distances between the carriers' top two airports and the numbers of routes operated from all of the top five airports suggesting multiple hub strategies, with the secondary hubs acting as focal points for provincial or regional networks.

In graph theory or social network analysis, a 'clique' consists of a subset of nodes that are adjacent (that is, all nodes are directly connected to one another), and there are no other nodes that are also adjacent to the members of the clique (Wasserman and Faust, 2006). Looking at the networks of the large Chinese and Japanese carriers, there are direct connections between all of the top-ranked airports. For Air China, China Eastern Airlines, Shenzhen Airlines and Xiamen Airlines, cliques of six airports are present in their networks; China Southern's network has 20 cliques of eight airports. The pres-ence of the cliques facilitates ease of transfer between nodes in the full network, and collectively the range of origin–destination pairs served by the large Chinese carriers is

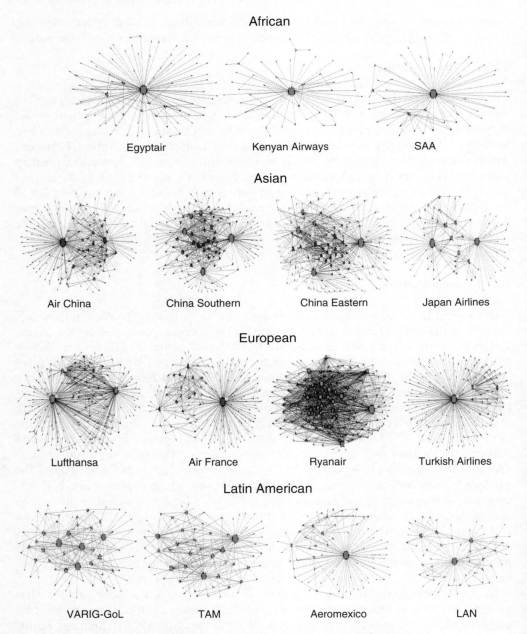

Figure 18.12   Stylized representations of selected carrier networks in 2010

greatly expanded. The Japanese carriers have smaller cliques of four and five nodes for ANA and JAL, respectively. Korean Air's network by contrast is focused largely on the two Seoul Airports (Incheon and Gimpo) and is a single-hub system, although there are many direct connections to China from Busan and Jeju.

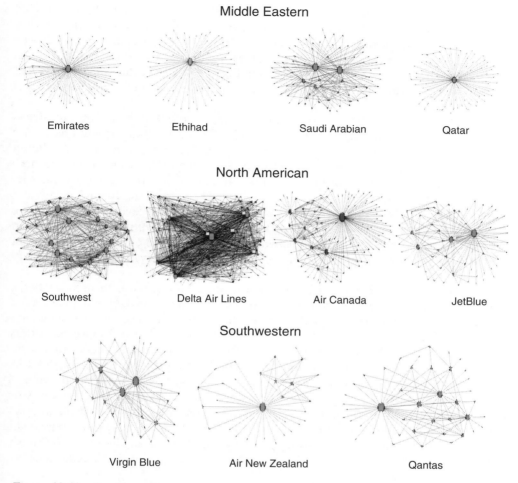

Figure 18.12   (continued)

18.7.3   European Carriers

Europe has a large number of nation states and a relatively high population density. There were a large number of airlines operating in 2010 (193). Table 18.6 gives details of the network characteristics of the top 10 carriers. Lufthansa is the largest European carrier and has its network focused around the five German cities of Frankfurt, Munich, Düsseldorf, Hamburg and Berlin, though Frankfurt and Munich very much dominate the linkage structure and account for almost 40 per cent of total departure movements. Lufthansa has recently completed acquisitions of several smaller European carriers: Swiss and Eurowings in 2005 and British Midland,[12] Austrian and SN Brussels Airlines in 2009. The linkage structure is illustrated in Figure 18.12. The Turkish Airlines network structure is similar to Lufthansa's in that it is focused around five large Turkish cities, with Istanbul and Ankara dominating the traffic flows: however 39 per cent of all departure movements in 2010 were performed from Istanbul. Like Germany, Turkey has a relatively large geographical area and air transport facilitates fast access between the main urban centres as well as connecting these centres to other European and global cities. Both carriers' networks are illustrated in Figure 18.12. The dual-hub strategies of the two carriers are discernible in the figure, though Turkish Airlines' Ankara hub makes a less visible impact.

The distance between the top two airports in the case of all of the European carriers is less than 500 km, with the exception of Easyjet. The LCCs Ryanair and Easyjet are ranked second and fourth in Europe in terms of passenger movements, with Air Berlin being the third LCC in the European top 10. The Ryanair and Easyjet networks are more dispersed (Ryanair is shown in Figure 18.12) than any of the other European carriers. Ryanair has its top five airports spread over four EU states (UK, Ireland, Spain and Italy) while Easyjet's top five are spread over three states (UK, Switzerland and Italy). Ryanair has several nine-node cliques, reflecting a high degree of interconnectedness in the carrier's network. The Air Berlin network is heavily focused on the German market but has a high volume of point-to-point services between nodes in its network with 19 six-node cliques.

Air France, KLM, Iberia and BA operate a single-hub network focused on Paris, Amsterdam, Madrid and London, respectively. Air France and BA split their traffic over two airports and have no flights between their two top-ranked airports: long-haul services are focused on the top-ranked airport in both cases. The Air France network is illustrated in Figure 18.12. Two Paris airports are clearly visible, but as they are just 35 km apart, they do not function as interacting hubs. The merger of Air France with KLM and BA with Iberia have to date had a relatively small impact on the network structure of these carriers. The relatively high levels of passenger and airport charges and taxes associated with many European airports have resulted in greater emphasis on direct air services rather than multi-stop services for travel within the European market. Scandinavian Airlines (SAS) evolved as a jointly owned carrier by the Norwegian, Swedish and Danish governments, with a route network focused around the three countries' capital cities.

18.7.4 Latin American Carriers

There were 55 Latin American carriers operating jet aircraft in 2010. Figure 18.11 shows that the distances between the top two airports for the top 10 carriers in Latin America is very similar to the distribution for European carriers. The distribution of movements between the top five airports and of seating capacity across the carriers' networks reflect the single-hub nature of the networks of Aerolineas Argentinas, Aeromexico, Avianca, Mexicana and Azul Airlines. Eight of the carriers have networks focused on their home country, with the capital city or most populous city airport dominating the traffic distribution in each case. TAM Linhas Aereas, VARIG-Gol and Aerolineas Argentinas (like Air France and BA) split their traffic between two airports in São Paulo and Buenos Aires. TAM and VARIG have multiple hubs with a high level of interconnections between several of the nodes in the network. Webjet was acquired by VARIG-Gol in 2011 and is also focused on São Paulo.

The Latin American carriers are small in global terms with VARIG-Gol and TAM the only carriers to operate in excess of 200,000 departure movements in 2010. Given the population and geographical size of the countries of Latin America, air transport is expected to grow rapidly in the next decade, particularly in Brazil and Mexico where economic growth and rising per capita incomes are expected to fuel demand for air travel. The networks of most Latin American carriers are currently nationally focused with international linkages to other Latin American countries, North America and Europe. There are very limited links to Asia as Figure 18.3 illustrated. The exception to this is LAN Airlines which operates several subsidiaries in Chile, Peru, Colombia, Ecuador and Argentina. In May 2012, LAN launched a share swap offer as the final stage in its takeover of TAM, the Brazilian carrier.[13] This will create the largest Latin American carrier with multiple hubs throughout Latin America. The LAN and TAM networks are illustrated in Figure 18.12 and show the existence of multiple hubs already in the networks.

18.7.5 Middle East Carriers

There were 40 carriers registered in Middle Eastern states in 2010. The top six carriers are described in terms of summary network characteristics in Table 18.6. The Middle East carriers operate smaller networks of fewer than 100 nodes with most having a single-hub network focused on the capital or largest city in their country of registration. Iran Air splits its traffic between the two airports in Tehran (Mehrabad International Airport (THR) and Imam Khomeini International Airport (IKA)). Saudi Arabian Airlines operates a two-hub strategy and has similar numbers of movements and routes operated from Riyadh and Jeddah which are 850 km apart. The carriers have grown rapidly in the 2000s and added numerous long-haul routes to their networks, connecting Europe, North America and Asia to the Middle East. All of the Middle Eastern carriers in Table 18.6 are government-owned flag carriers. Ethihad Airways and Qatar Airways have benefited from substantial government investment in recent years to enable rapid expansion of their operations internationally. These carriers, along with Emirates, are promoting their Middle Eastern hubs as transfer points between Asia, Australasia, the Americas and Europe for air passenger and cargo services. Emirates in 2012 was the largest operator of the Airbus A380 aircraft.

18.7.6 North American Carriers

There were 36 carriers operating jet aircraft and registered in North America in 2010. The carriers are the largest airlines globally in terms of departure movements performed, with the top six in North America being the top six globally. The mergers of Southwest Airlines with AirTran and Continental with United between 2010 and 2012 have further reduced the number of carriers in the North American market, as will the 2013 US Airways merger with bankrupt American Airlines, which is attempting to reorganize and rationalize its operations in order to remain in business. Figure 18.10 shows the scale of the US carriers relative to carriers in other global regions. Table 18.6 summarizes the network structures of the top 10 carriers in North America in 2010.

The Delta Airlines network is illustrated in Figure 18.12 and shows the multi-hub strategy employed by the carrier, with a high degree of interconnections between several nodes in the 346-node network.

A considerable literature exists examining the development and organization of US carrier networks (see, for example, Reynolds-Feighan, 1992; Morrison and Winston, 1995; Button and Stough, 2000). Following deregulation in 1978, the majority of the larger US carriers focused their networks around a small number of key transfer points or hubs. During the subsequent decades through mergers and acquisitions, the carriers have become extremely large with multiple hubs serving US regional markets and filtering intercontinental traffic through the interconnected hubs. The average distance between the top airports in most carrier systems has grown and this can be seen in Figure 18.10 where the distance between the top two airports is illustrated.

Alaskan Airlines continues to have a West Coast regional focus and has the smallest distance between its top two airports. JetBlue is a relatively new LCC (founded in 1999) with an east coast focus (JFK Airport in New York and Boston's Logan Airport are its top two airports) and a network consisting of 63 airports in 2010. The multi-hub strategy of JetBlue is illustrated in Figure 18.12. The Air Canada network (also shown in Figure 18.12) is focused on the largest Canadian cities of Toronto, Montreal and Vancouver and as with many of the national carriers in other regions, connects Canadian cities with a large number of other North American and global centres. Because of the geography and population distribution, a multi-hub network is operated with the top-ranked airport, Toronto's Lester Pearson Airport handling 25 per cent of all movements in the 129-node network.

Southwest and AirTran are LCCs and have relatively small networks with 69 and 71 nodes, respectively. The carriers operate point-to-point services, but also offer substantial connecting services where consecutive segments are listed with separate flight numbers. In 2010, Southwest Airlines offered half of all of its flight listings as multi-stop services. In Figure 18.12, the non-stop flights are illustrated and show a high degree of interconnectedness. Southwest Airlines operated two cliques of 11 nodes, the largest of any carrier included in this study. Unlike the network carriers, Southwest Airlines' network was focused exclusively on the domestic market; through the merger with AirTran, services to the Caribbean and Mexico will give Southwest an international network from 2013.

18.7.7 Southwest Region Carriers

The IATA Southwest region has the smallest population of the regional groupings discussed so far. The Southwest region had 20 airlines operating in 2010 and the network characteristics are summarized for the top six in Table 18.6. The carriers are small in terms of departure movements (fewer than 200,000 in 2010) and network size (45 or fewer airports). Virgin Blue and Qantas were the two largest carriers in the region in 2010, with networks focused on Sydney, Melbourne and Brisbane. Figure 18.12 includes representations of the Virgin Blue and Qantas air networks.

Air New Zealand operated a 32-node network in 2010 focused on its Auckland hub from where 37 per cent of the carrier's total movements were performed. In 2001, Air New Zealand had merged with Australia's second carrier at the time, Ansett. Following the collapse of Ansett, Air New Zealand was rescued through government re-capitalization, giving the state an 82 per cent ownership stake in the carrier.

18.8   SUMMARY AND CONCLUSIONS

Air passenger traffic has grown and is forecast to continue to grow at an annual rate of around 5 per cent for the next couple of decades. Economic growth and development is the key factor driving the increasing demand for air travel: increasing levels of economic activity result in rising income levels and generate demand for business and leisure air travel. Geography is also an important factor: countries with large land areas have a greater requirement for air transport for reasons of economic and social cohesion. The air transport mode has great flexibility: investment in airport infrastructure is relatively modest when compared with surface transport modes, and flow patterns can easily be reorganized and concentrated in particular corridors as circumstances change.

The number of airports receiving air services has expanded from 1,866 in 1999 to 2,161 in 2010. There are many more airports with the potential to handle jet air services: many small and medium-sized airports have experienced fluctuations in the level of service, or, withdrawal or rapid expansion of services depending on the needs and strategies of the airlines. In the US market following deregulation in 1978, the number of communities receiving jet air services declined in the decade following the regulatory change. In all other global regions, the effect of liberalization or deregulation has been to expand the number of airports receiving jet services, implying that regulation constrained the extent of air transport networks. On the other hand, the US experience has been extensively monitored, studied and discussed and there are many lessons to learn. However, it is important to examine the circumstances and responses to changing regulatory and economic environments in other global regions in order to identify new innovations in process, organization and strategy.

Air transport flows are very much dominated by domestic markets, with relatively small levels of traffic between the major continental regions of the world. The liberalization of international air service markets within Europe, within Asia and on transatlantic markets has demonstrated the potential for the rapid expansion of services and the linking or integration of air transport networks across borders. Europe has seen a very dramatic increase in the number of air routes in the decade since full liberalization was implemented, but the US network strategy of 'hub-and-spoke' operating models has not been replicated because of higher landing charges and fuel costs associated with landings and takeoffs, and because few carriers have expanded their networks across national boundaries to operate interacting hubs. The carriers that do operate European-wide networks are the LCCs, Ryanair and Easyjet, and their model has focused on expanding the direct service routings to communities that had not yet received jet air services before 2000. The geographical extent of the European market is small relative to the US, but with a far higher population density. The European governments have placed environmental policy issues high on their agenda and sustainability requirements will have a significant impact on the future shape of the European air transport industry. The interesting question arises for the Asian and Latin American markets as to whether the dominant North American carrier model or the European carrier model will play out in other regions given rising fuel costs, environmental concerns and political influences on the long-term development of air transport policy.

Despite the very high levels of growth in air traffic volumes, Asian markets have seen more modest expansions in the number of routings.

The average number of seats per passenger movement has declined marginally during the 2000s and particularly in the North American market. The deployment of smaller aircraft at higher frequencies, and the expansion of air services using single-aisle jet aircraft explain this trend. LCCs have played an important role in filling in gaps in the service networks offered by many of the older carriers.

Airline network strategies vary depending on (i) market size and potential; (ii) the regulatory environment; (iii) competition from national and international airlines; and (iv) technical and operational constraints. In examining the network structure and organization of 70 of the world's largest carriers, a number of conclusions may be drawn. The main network structures observed among the carriers were:

1. *Single hub with the majority of nodes in the network connecting to this central airport*   This network form is observed where airlines operate in relatively small domestic markets and are the dominant carrier at the capital city or largest urban centre in the state. Carriers with single-hub strategies will typically have more than one-third of their total movements performed from the hub. Carriers in this category include the African carriers in Table 18.6, Lion Air (Indonesia), KLM, Iberia, Avianca, Emirates, Qatar Airways, Ethihad Airways, Gulf Air and Air New Zealand. BA, Air France, Korean Airlines, Iran Air and JAL would also be included in this category since their traffic is split across two airports in the same urban centre, with no direct flights operated between the two nodes.

2. *Two- or three-hub networks with direct connections among hubs and substantial numbers of routes directly connected to each of the hub airports*   Carriers with two- or three-hub networks tend to operate in large geographical markets where the hubs are spaced at 500–1,000 km apart and will typically have a third or more of their total movements performed from the top two or three hubs. Examples would include Turkish Airlines, Air China, Qantas, Virgin Blue, Air Canada, SAS, Copa Airlines, LAN and Saudi Arabian Airlines.

3. *Large multi-hub networks with five or more hubs*   The hubs have direct connections to each other and have relatively large cliques of six or more nodes. These carriers operate in large geographical markets with substantial traffic volumes. Delta Airlines, American Airlines, Continental Airlines, Southwest Airlines, Ryanair, China Eastern and China Southern are examples of such multi-hub networks.

The term 'hub' is very loosely applied here and describes a key node in the network around which flows are concentrated. Since there is very little information about passenger connection rates available outside of the US, it is not possible to compare the operational aspects of the networks across regions. However, the ratios of listed flights to non-stop segment flows (presented in Table 18.4) would clearly indicate a difference between the North American carriers and carriers in other regions. The North American carriers offer many air services consisting of multiple flight segments, while such offerings are more limited by carriers in other regions. Travel agents and customers can and do combine flight segments and the formation of international airline alliances has facilitated this for long-haul travel.

As carriers expand operations through internal growth or because of mergers and acquisitions, their network strategies can change. Many of the LCCs began with small single- or dual-hub networks and have developed complex multi-hub networks as their traffic volumes have increased. Some of the US network carriers have had the experience of building traffic hubs within their networks and subsequently dismantling them. It was noted that several of the Middle Eastern carriers, operating single-hub networks, are developing long-haul services that connect through their main hubs and act as cross-over points between the main global regions. Strategic alliances and various code-sharing arrangements are being explored and tested by carriers in an effort to sustain profitable operations. The flexibility in air transport can result in very substantial shifts in air traffic flows: what may have 'worked' at a particular location and at a particular point in time may not work subsequently. Technological developments, binding energy constraints and growth in emerging markets will give rise to many new and innovative changes in the organization and structure of the air transport industry in the coming decades.

NOTES

1. In 2007, the US Congress passed the implementing recommendations of the 9/11 Commission Act (more commonly known as the 9/11 Act), which requires that all cargo transported on a passenger aircraft be screened for explosives as of 1 August 2010.
2. Norway, Iceland, Croatia, Macedonia, Albania, Bosnia and Herzegovina, Kosovo, Serbia, Montenegro and Moldova.
3. The ASEAN Multilateral Agreement on Air Services was signed in Manila, Philippines on 20 May 2009.
4. Europe is broadly defined and includes Austria, Belgium, Denmark, Faroe Islands, Finland, France, Germany, Gibraltar, Greece, Iceland, Ireland, Italy, Luxembourg, Malta, Monaco, Netherlands, Norway, Portugal, Spain, Sweden, Switzerland, United Kingdom, Cyprus, Turkey, Albania, Armenia, Azerbaijan, Bosnia and Herzegovina, Bulgaria, Belarus, Croatia, Czech Republic, Estonia, Georgia, Hungary, Latvia, Lithuania, Macedonia (Former Yugoslav Republic), Moldova Republic of, Montenegro, Poland, Romania, Russian Federation, Serbia, Slovenia, Slovakia, Ukraine. This categorization of Europe is based on IATA definitions of the region.
5. North America consists of Canada, USA, Greenland and Saint Pierre and Miquelon under the IATA regional classification. It is noted that this definition differs from the NAFTA region: Mexico is included in the IATA Latin America region.
6. Where code share agreements are in place between air carriers, the operating carrier is used to assign flight segments to regions in Figure 18.5 and Table 18.4.
7. The Gini index is a commonly used measure of concentration or dispersion in traffic distributions. It measures the extent to which an observed distribution differs from an equal share distribution (see Reynolds-Feighan, 2007).
8. See European Commission Case No COMP/M.3280-Air France/KLM.
9. Between 2004 and 2013, 13 mergers and a larger number of alliances have been examined in the European industry, with only three cases where the mergers were prohibited, namely Ryanair/Aer Lingus in 2007 and 2013 and Olympic/Aegean in 2010.
10. Several very small carriers operating in African, Middle Eastern and Southwestern markets made up the top 10 in these regions and have not been included in the summary tables and figures.
11. The NetDraw software associated with the social network measurement tool UCINET is used to generate stylized graphs of air carrier network linkage structures.
12. bmi was acquired by International Airlines group (owner of BA and Iberia) in 2012.
13. Reuters, Santiago, 9 May 2012.

REFERENCES

Air Cargo World (2009), 'IATA's top 50 cargo carriers', *Air Cargo World*, September, pp. 24–30.
Airbus (2011), 'Delivering the Future: Global Market Forecast 2011–2030', Airbus Industries, Available at: http://www.airbus.com/company/market/forecast/ (June 2012).

Boeing Airplane Company (2011), 'Current Market Outlook 2011–2030', Boeing, Available at: http://www.boeing.com/commercial/cmo/ (June 2012).

Borenstein, S. (1992), 'The evolution of U.S. airline competition', *Journal of Economic Perspectives*, **6** (2) (Spring), 45–73.

Brueckner, J.K., N. Dyer and P.T. Spiller (1992), 'Fare determination in airline hub-and-spoke networks', *RAND Journal of Economics*, **23** (3) (Autumn), 309–33.

Button, K.J. and R. Stough (2000), *Air Transport Networks: Theory and Policy Implications*, Cheltenham, UK and Northampton, MA, USA: Edward Elgar.

ICAO (2011), 'Annual Report of the Council 2010', International Civil Aviation Organisation (Doc 9952), Montreal.

Morrison, S. and C. Winston (1995), *The Evolution of the Airline Industry*, Washington, DC: Brookings Institution.

O'Kelly, M.E. (1998), 'A geographer's analysis of hub-and-spoke networks', *Journal of Transport Geography*, **6** (3), 171–86.

Oum, T.H., J.-H. Park and A. Zhang (2000), *Globalization and Strategic Alliances: The Case of the Airline Industry*, Amsterdam: Pergamon.

Reynolds-Feighan, A.J. (1992), *The Effects of Deregulation on U.S. Air Networks*, Heidelberg: Springer-Verlag.

Reynolds-Feighan, A.J. (2007), 'Competing networks, spatial and industrial concentration in the US airline industry', *Spatial Economics Analysis*, **2** (3), 239–59.

Reynolds-Feighan, A.J. (2010), 'Characterisation of airline networks: a North American and European comparison', *Journal of Air Transport Management*, **16** (3), 109–20.

Reynolds-Feighan, A.J. (2013 forthcoming) 'Comparative analysis of air freight networks in regional markets around the world', in James H. Bookbinder (ed.), *Handbook of Global Logistics*, International Series in Operations Research and Management Science, Vol. 181, New York: Springer Science & Business Media, pp. 325–66.

Shaw, S.-L., L. Feng, J. Chen and C. Zhou (2009), 'China's airline consolidation and its effects on domestic airline networks and competition', *Journal of Transport Geography*, **17** (4), July, 293–305.

United Nations (2012), *World Urbanization Prospects The 2011 Revision*, UN Department of Economic and Social Affairs Population Division (ESA/P/WP/224), March.

Wasserman, S. and K. Faust (2006), *Social Network Analysis*, New York: Cambridge University Press.

Zhang, Y. and D.K. Round (2008), 'China's airline deregulation since 1997 and the driving forces behind the 2002 airline consolidations', *Journal of Air Transport Management*, **14** (3), 130–42.

19 Innovation in New Zealand: issues of firm size, local market size and economic geography

Hong Shangqin, Philip McCann and Les Oxley

19.1 INTRODUCTION

The unique demographic, economic condition and geographical location makes New Zealand an interesting case study for understanding the processes which foster innovation. New Zealand is a small and isolated economy which, at least in a textbook sense, is institutionally almost ideal for promoting local entrepreneurship and innovation. Yet, in spite of a macroeconomic and institutional framework which should be ideal for promoting innovation, the observed innovation performance of New Zealand is poor, and this is particularly noticeable in comparison with other small isolated countries such as Israel and Finland. The reasons for this poor performance are as yet unclear. It may be that the awareness of best practice and state-of-the-art thinking on innovation issues is less in New Zealand than might be hoped. This scenario would call for better training and human capital development. Alternatively, there may be grounds for believing that some of the structural determinants of innovation in New Zealand are different from those in other countries. In this case, some of the recipes for promoting innovation which are adopted in other countries may not necessarily be appropriate in New Zealand.

This chapter aims to uncover the issues which drive innovation in New Zealand in order to assess the extent to which traditional innovation policy thinking is appropriate in the case of a small isolated economy. The approach of the chapter is to analyse both empirical and case-study data in order to provide a broad perspective on New Zealand's local innovation processes. This mixed-methods approach therefore combines both quantitative and qualitative analysis. A major element of the research presented here relates to the construction of a manufacturing-based Innovation Survey which was undertaken specifically as part of this research. Information including firm characteristics, innovation outcomes, innovation-related practices, general practices and market environment were collected by means of this survey, and a quantitative analysis was then applied to the data. Following the initial Survey, a number of in-depth case studies were then carried out in an attempt to resolve and explain some of the quantitative results and to elaborate on further issues not captured by the data. The major findings of the chapter are that New Zealand firms generally do demonstrate best practice and state-of-the-art thinking on innovation issues. Moreover, the local institutional environment for entrepreneurship and innovation is excellent. Yet, translating high levels of local entrepreneurship into innovation remains a problem. The chapter suggests that these observations can best be explained with reference to various structural features of the economy, which themselves cast doubt on some generally received wisdom regarding the role played by firm size in innovation processes.

The chapter is organized as follows. Section 19.2 describes the characteristics and features of the New Zealand economy and its innovation performance. Section 19.3 outlines the research method, the design of the survey and case studies. Section 19.4 presents the empirical results and Section 19.5 reports the observations from the in-depth case studies. Section 19.6 provides a discussion and some conclusions.

19.2   INNOVATION PERFORMANCE AND THE CHARACTERISTICS OF THE NEW ZEALAND ECONOMY

Since the economic reforms of the 1980s and early 1990s (Evans et al., 1996), New Zealand has maintained macroeconomic stability, with unemployment and inflation kept consistently among the lowest levels in the OECD (OECD, 2008a). New Zealand is now a relatively very open economy with a largely transparent institutional system, the third-strongest property rights in the world and the world's strongest investor protection environment (Porter et al., 2007), the seventh most flexible labour market in the world and the world's lowest labour firing costs (ibid.), the world's lowest number of procedures required to start a business (ibid.), high firm competition and turnover (Law and McLellan, 2005), and one of the world's most transparent and least corrupt institutional environments in the world (Porter et al., 2007). The result is that New Zealand has relatively very low levels of regulation and bureaucracy by OECD standards (Gerardin and Kerr, 2003; Hall and Casey, 2006). In comparison to other small advanced countries, New Zealand also has a relatively small public sector. New Zealand's relative share of social expenditure ranks only 21st highest in the OECD (OECD, 2008a) and its total tax revenue as a percentage of GDP ranks 15th out of 30 OECD countries, which is lower than for all but one of the small OECD countries (ibid.). Low levels of public sector intervention and regulation mean that New Zealand is consistently ranked as one of the world's most liberalized economies,[1] the second-best country in the world for doing business (World Bank, 2009), one of the best countries in the world for entrepreneurship,[2] the least corrupt country in the world,[3] the ninth best for overall institutions (Porter et al., 2007), with some of the world's lowest trade barriers (MED–Treasury, 2005), and one of the best locations for international capital investment.[4]

These beneficial features ought to mean that the level of local entrepreneurial activity in New Zealand is very high, and indeed on some measures it is the world's most entrepreneurial society (Acs and Szerb, 2009). Yet, as mentioned above, in spite of all of the very good macroeconomic and institutional characteristics of the economy, New Zealand's innovation performance is very poor. Although its innovation probability scores are good relative to OECD countries (MED–Treasury, 2005), patents per capita are ranked only 20th in the world and below both the OECD and EU averages (OECD, 2007a,b). Yet, even allowing for New Zealand's industry structure, the World Economic Forum (Porter et al., 2007) ranks the country only 27th in the world in terms of its overall capacity for innovation, which is the fourth-lowest ranking for any advanced economy. Institutionally New Zealand ought to be ideally suited to promoting entrepreneurship and innovation, yet its local innovation performance appears to be much weaker than expected. Part of the issue may be related to the role in the innovation process played by the size of firms, the size of local markets and the size of cities in New Zealand.

In terms of firm size, there is much international evidence which suggests that small firms have the highest propensity to innovate of all firm types (Acs and Audretsch, 1988), and a U-shaped innovation-size distribution is accepted by many scholars (Tether et al., 1997), reflecting the fact that the largest firms are also seen to exhibit high innovation propensities. Yet, translating these arguments to New Zealand may not be so straightforward because what is meant by 'large' and 'small' may be very different in different contexts.

The definition for small and medium-sized enterprises (SMEs) often varies between countries and generally uses numerical criteria such as staff numbers and a firm's assets or profit levels. In the case of New Zealand, the Ministry of Economic Development defines the firm size classification based on an enterprise's employment headcount, and considers firms with 19 or fewer employees to be an SME. This is a simpler definition than that which is used by the European Commission. On 1 January 2005 the European Commission adjusted the 1996 definition of an SME using updated thresholds, defining a medium-sized enterprise as a firm with fewer than 250 annual work units (AWUs),[5] an annual turnover[6] of no more than €50 million, or a firm which has an annual balance sheet total[7] of less than €43 million (European Commission, 2003). In the United States, the Small Business Administration (SBA) defines a small business size standard for every single private sector industry, thereby aiming to accurately reflect industry differences in firm-size distributions. The standard for a small or medium-sized firm is usually stated in terms of either number of employees or average annual receipts.[8] Within the manufacturing sector, the size standard for approximately 75 per cent of the industries is 500 employees, with the remaining industries having a higher threshold at 750, 1,000 or 1,500 employees. Compared to these thresholds, the vast majority of New Zealand's SMEs are therefore actually micro or nano firms, rather than small or medium-sized firms. In fact, on these definitions, very few firms in New Zealand would even be classed as medium-sized firms in the US.

The importance of very small firms to knowledge generation in New Zealand can be gauged by the fact that just under 50 per cent of its total business R&D is accounted for by firms of fewer than 50 employees and almost 80 per cent is accounted for by firms of fewer than 250 employees (OECD, 2007a). In both cases these are the highest relative R&D contributions by small firms of any OECD country. The equivalent numbers for the US are less than 10 per cent and less than 20 per cent, respectively (ibid.). Moreover, these figures are not necessarily typical for small countries. The total share of business R&D accounted for by firms with fewer than 50 employees in New Zealand is twice that of the next highest country, Australia, and five times that of Sweden, Finland and the Netherlands. Similarly, the total share of business R&D accounted for by firms with fewer than 250 employees is only 20 per cent in countries such as Finland and Sweden, and fewer than 30 per cent in Austria and Denmark.

Second, it is also found generally in the international literature that innovation propensities are increased when firms are located in large and diverse cities (Acs, 2002). Combining this observation with the above observations from the international literature regarding small firms suggests that large concentrations of small firms in large cities should promote innovation. Indeed, there is clear evidence from New Zealand which points to the role of cities in the promotion of innovation. In particular, Auckland is by far the largest city in New Zealand with a population three times that of the next city, and on some criteria the levels of entrepreneurial dynamism in Auckland relative to the national level are ranked as the highest in the OECD (Acs et al., 2008). Yet, with a population of 1.2 million people, Auckland is not even among the top 80 largest OECD cities (OECD, 2007c), and would only rank as a small to medium-sized city in the US. While urban areas are regarded as being beneficial for innovation promotion, absolute scale may also be critical. As such, once again there may be an urban population threshold above which being located in a city is advantageous for fostering innovation.

Third, market size may be important. New Zealand has the third-smallest national market in the OECD, with a total national market which is only equivalent in scale to a medium-sized urban market in the US. Yet, in terms of its accessibility to other national markets, New Zealand is also one of the two most geographically isolated countries in the world (IMF, 2004; OECD, 2008b,c). Many other small countries, and particularly those in the EU, are part of a much larger market, such that exporting increases the returns to innovation. In contrast, the nearest adjacent market for New Zealand firms is Australia which is more than 2,500 km away and accounts for only 20 million people in total. The fact that the net benefits of exporting diminish as distance costs increase implies that the positive effect of exporting on innovation may therefore also be smaller in New Zealand than for many other small countries. Once again, it may well be that there is a size threshold in terms of market accessibility, above which innovation propensities and innovation successes increase, and New Zealand may be only at the lower limit of this market-size threshold.

Finally, the small scale and isolation of the New Zealand economy means that there is always a higher risk premium attached to the New Zealand dollar than for almost all other currencies. The result is that interest rates are consistently among the highest in the world. As such, the optimal investment portfolio for businesses may be rather different in New Zealand compared with other countries with a greater relative preference for labour over capital investment. If technological progress means that innovation is also related to the embodied technology in capital deepening, then this may also inhibit New Zealand's innovation performance.

The objective of this chapter is to discover the main drivers of innovation for New Zealand firms. In particular, given the specific features and context of the economy, our aim is to identify whether or not similar issues and influences promote innovation in New Zealand as in other countries. In particular we also examine whether New Zealand's poor innovation performance is best explained by structural features or by issues related to awareness of the best practice and state-of-the-art thinking in terms of innovation. One of the major issues we focus on specifically in this chapter is the role in innovation promotion played by firm size.

19.3   RESEARCH METHODOLOGY AND DATA

We examine these issues by focusing on the New Zealand manufacturing sector. A mixed-method approach was adopted, which combines both quantitative and qualitative analysis. This type of approach was used successfully by Roper and Hewitt-Dundas (2008). The quantitative part of the analysis involves the design and implementation of an internet-based survey, and the qualitative analysis includes 15 in-depth company interviews.

19.3.1   The Innovation Survey

Since 2005, Statistics New Zealand (SNZ) has conducted a Business Operations Survey (BOS) in order to gain a better understanding of firm practices, performance and innovation processes. The integrated, modular BOS has assisted studies of innovation by providing an invaluable data source for a wide range of sectors. Due to the mandatory nature of the survey and its large sample size, high response rates are almost guaranteed. Using the BOS, Fabling and Grimes (2007) found that indicators of firm success, such as profitability, productivity and market share, are largely unrelated to the size, age or sector of the firm, and instead depend on the specific business practices of the firm, such as capital deepening, R&D, market research, and policies for enhancing labour skills. The only exception here is the case of export marketing, the effect of which tends to favour SMEs which have been in operation for less than 10 years. Similarly, industry structure also appears to be very important, with firms in highly competitive industries perceiving relatively greater barriers to innovation than firms in oligopolistic industries. Fabling (2007) also suggests that a broader use of innovation indicators which allows us to take account of the bundles of activities and competences that contribute to firm performance, rather than simply indicators of the higher-level outcomes, would represent a major step forward. Our development of a survey plus follow-up case studies is undertaken in this spirit.

In terms of arriving at more general conclusions regarding the drivers of innovation in New Zealand, the major limitation of the BOS is with regard to its target population. Most enterprises in the country are classified as SMEs and in New Zealand these firms have 19 or fewer employees by definition (MED 2007). Yet, the target population for BOS 2005 excludes firms with five or fewer employees, and this implies that 86.9 per cent of New Zealand's enterprises are not sampled by the survey. Hence, the BOS survey results are somewhat biased towards sampling what in New Zealand terms are described as being medium to large firms. For this reason in this research we construct a new survey that also includes much smaller firms in the analyses.

The Innovation Survey of the Manufacturing Sector which was undertaken for this research with the help of the New Zealand Manufacturers and Exporters Association (NZMEA), is therefore purposely designed to complement the official BOS, both in terms of its coverage and its information content. From hereon, we refer to the newly constructed survey as the 'Innovation Survey'. The questionnaire we developed for this research was designed to collect information on New Zealand businesses in terms of five different themes: firm characteristics; innovation outputs; innovation-related practices; general practices; and the market environment.

A total of 17 questions were included in the final version of the Innovation Survey questionnaire. Table 19.1 lists the content of the questions and according to the nature of the subject, the questions are distributed into each of the five themes. Some of the questions were also included in BOS 2005, and we also include the BOS question listings where relevant.

Unlike the official surveys, the responses to our Innovation Survey were all provided on a voluntary basis. In order to assist the response rates, the survey was designed to collect the required information as effortlessly as possible, in particular, categorical, multi-choice and numerical questions were widely used throughout the survey, with

Table 19.1   Innovation Survey questions by themes

Categories	Questions	Subject(s)	BOS
Firm characteristics	1	Export profile	Section A, Q11
	2	Input sources	N/A
	3	Staff number	Section A, Q30
	4	Firm age	Section A, Q46
	5	Number physical locations	N/A
Innovation output	8	Innovation activity	Section A, Q42
	9	Product innovation	Section B, Q3–6
	10	Process innovation	Section B, Q7–9
Innovation-related practices	11	Cooperation	Section B, Q21–25
	15	R&D activities	Section A, Q24
General practices	6	Specialization for different sites	N/A
	7	Staff movement between sites	
	12	New staff intake	Section A, Q34
	13	New staff's educational level	N/A
	14	New staff's work experience	
Market environment	16	Major competition	N/A
	17	Market structure	Section A, Q47

very few open-ended questions asked. In addition, instead of requesting actual figures for some of the numerical questions, respondents were asked to provide a percentage estimate. By sacrificing some accuracy, we not only encouraged the responses, but also respondents were more likely to reveal business characteristics, as various pieces of sensitive information, such as total sales and profit, were not requested. The Innovation Survey used the convenience sampling method by surveying all manufacturing firms, which are part of the NZMEA database. In November 2007 initial contact was made via a company e-mail, and survey invitations were addressed to either the managing director or the general/senior manager. Two hyperlinks were listed at the bottom of the e-mail invitation. Survey participants could access the online survey by clicking on the first hyperlink. If preferred, participants could also print a PDF version of the survey questionnaire, which could be downloaded via the second hyperlink, and then send back the completed survey by fax. The two-version collection method was proposed to encourage responses. The online survey was open for three weeks after the initial invitation, during which period two e-mail reminders were sent during the second and the third weeks. Survey invitations were sent to 1,274 manufacturing firms, out of which 75 responses were received by the end of the survey period, a response rate of 6 per cent. Identification was made optional for completion of the survey, and only 32 respondents identified themselves by name. The available information suggested that most of the respondent firms were located in the Auckland region in the North Island and the Christchurch (Canterbury) region in the South Island, with some respondents also from the Wellington, West Coast and Southland regions. Such a distribution of firms confirmed that the sample exhibits a reasonable geographical coverage of the manufacturing sector. The employment size distribution of the responding firms was as follows: 11 firms with 1–5 employees; 10 firms with 6–19 employees; 29 firms with 20–49 employees; 13

firms with 50–99 employees; five firms with 100–249 employees; five firms with 250–499 employees; and two firms with more than 500 employees. As such, 21 firms accounting for 28 per cent of the respondents are classified as small firms in New Zealand. However, in terms of the EU SME definitions, 68 firms accounting for 91 per cent of the sample would be classified as SMEs, and in terms of the US definition, 73 firms representing 97 per cent of the sample would be classified as SMEs.

Detailed descriptions were provided on the questionnaire concerning what the firms should regard as innovations, and here we followed the principles set out in the Oslo Manual (OECD, 2005). On the basis of the survey responses, for our analytical purposes in this chapter we developed three indicators of innovation: a qualified innovator (QI), a product-only innovator (PI), and an operational process-only innovator (OPI). Any firm which demonstrated some form of either product or process innovation during the last three financial years was classified as a QI. The definition of a QI is a firm which during the last three financial years has developed or introduced a new or significantly improved product, service, operational process, organizational process, or marketing method. We then divided the QIs into two subgroups, namely PIs and OPIs. The PI has a firm innovation focus solely on products and an OPI has a sole innovation focus on operational processes. The groups defined as PI and OPI are clearly both subsets of QI. Firms with no innovations in the previous three-year period are treated as our reference group.

The innovation group indicators, QI, PI and OPI, are categorical binary variables, which equal unity if a firm falls in the specified innovation group, and zero otherwise. Both linear and non-linear models can be used in this case. As already mentioned, when it comes to innovation and R&D issues the performance of New Zealand industry appears to be highly skewed relative to other international comparator cases. This observation, coupled with the fact that our sample size is not large, means that we have to allow for the possibility that our sample may also exhibit some small properties. For this reason we therefore estimate four different models, two of which are different types of linear probability models, plus a probit and a logit model.

19.3.2 Case Studies

Following our Innovation Survey, a series of follow-up studies were also undertaken, whereby additional detailed information on the innovative behaviour of New Zealand manufacturing business could be collected. This enables us to provide additional inputs to the quantitative analysis and also gain insights into the questions or issues which were not directly addressed in the survey. In particular, the major aim of the case studies was to ascertain the extent to which the motives and approaches to innovation in New Zealand reflect those in the international literature. As has already been mentioned, the innovation performance of New Zealand is relatively poor by OECD standards. Therefore, as well as using the Innovation Survey to identify the firm and industry characteristics which influence innovation behaviour, the case studies also allow us to assess the extent to which motives and perceptions may play a role. As is well known, motivations and opportunities are critical for entrepreneurship and innovation (Acs et al., 2008).

The case studies covered manufacturing firms in the Auckland and Christchurch regions. The focus on these two urban areas is because they are the two largest industrial centres with relatively high concentrations of manufacturing firms. The case participants were firms which had already responded to our online survey and were prepared to be involved in the study. Seven out of 24 willing companies were eliminated, as they were located outside of the targeted regions and two other firms, one from each city, were not able to be involved for other reasons. As a result, 15 company case studies were undertaken, which is an acceptable level of coverage for mixed-methods research of this type (Mariampolski, 2001). The case studies each took the form of semi-structured face-to-face interviews. The informants were typically the managing director or general manager of the company. A list of interview questions was sent to interviewee(s) two weeks prior to the interview session, and these questions focused upon four main areas of enquiry:

- the business perspective on innovation, and the extent to which the firm recognizes the difference between technological and non-technological-related innovations;
- the underlying motivation for innovation, and more specifically, what the firm perceives to be the major sources and drivers of innovation and what factors are regarded as being important for the innovation process;
- the role of staff and skills in innovation, and also the extent to which labour or skills shortages are a problem for the business; and
- the role played by market size, geography and exporting in promoting innovation.

Very little structure was imposed on the interviews. By asking open-ended questions the informants were able to express their opinions using their own constructs. As the interviews progressed, follow-up questions were asked to elicit greater detail or clarification. The interviews ranged from 40 to 90 minutes.

The interviewed firms have diverse profiles. As we see in Table 19.2, according to the Australian and New Zealand Standard Industrial Classification (ANZSIC) 2006 the sample of interviewed companies covers nine of 15 manufacturing subdivisions, with no obvious domination by any one particular subdivision. Table 19.3 displays the characteristics of interviewed firms in terms of the age of the firm, the number of employees, and the number of establishments or facilities operated by the firm. Eight of 15 companies were located in Auckland (North Island), and seven in Christchurch (South Island).

Table 19.2   Industrial coverage of the interviewed firms

ANZSIC Division C Manufacturing

Subdivision	Description	No. of firms
13	Textile, Leather, Clothing and Footwear Manufacturing	1
16	Printing	1
18	Basic Chemical and Chemical Product Manufacturing	1
19	Polymer Product and Rubber Product Manufacturing	2
20	Non-Metallic Mineral Product Manufacturing	1
21	Primary Metal and Metal Product Manufacturing	2
22	Fabricated Metal Product Manufacturing	2
24	Machinery and Equipment Manufacturing	3
25	Furniture and Other Manufacturing	2

Table 19.3   Characteristics of the interviewed firms

	Location/Island	Employment count	Age	No. of establishment
Firm A	South	318	42	1
Firm B	South	28	8	2
Firm C	South	22	12	1
Firm D	South	68	95	1
Firm E	South	3	6	1
Firm F	South	35	5	1
Firm G	South	4	1	1
Firm H	North	21	52	1
Firm I	North	47	40	1
Firm J	North	37	110	2
Firm K	North	434	40	3
Firm L	North	672	35	47
Firm M	North	17	25	1
Firm N	North	41	35	1
Firm O	North	45	24	2

Of the 11 companies who export, the split between Auckland and Christchurch is seven to four, respectively.

For confidentiality issues we have identified respondent firms as firms A to O. The largest firm included in the study employs 672 people, whereas the smallest firm has three paid staff. Eight out of the 15 companies fall into the 20–49 employment size group and three firms qualify as SMEs in New Zealand by MED's definition. The youngest firm has been in business for approximately a year and the oldest has an operating history of 110 years. The average firm age is 35 years. Of the 15 companies, five have more than one establishment.

19.4   REGRESSION MODELS AND EMPIRICAL RESULTS

The independent variables we employ in our regression models reflect the major themes in the international innovation literature and are listed in Table 19.4. Our variables capture the size of the firm in terms of its employment count, the age of the firm, as well as dummies which represent whether the firm engages in R&D or innovation cooperation with other firms, or undertakes exporting, as well as dummies which reflect whether the New Zealand market structure is highly competitive or rather more monopolistic or oligopolistic in nature.

The correlations between the independent variables are calculated using pairwise deletion.[9] As we see in Table 19.5 the 5 per cent significance-level firm size, measured in terms of employee numbers, is strongly correlated with age of the firm, and moderately correlated with employment of new staff and exporting. Exporters are more likely to have a longer operating history, employ new staff, and cooperate with other organizations. In addition, a moderate correlation was observed between R&D and cooperation arrangements.

Table 19.4   Description of the variables

Variable	Abbrev.	Details	Obs.
In (employment count)	In_ec	Logarithm total employment, measure on a headcount basis including both full- and part-time workers	75
Dummies for market structure	constant	operating within: monopoly and oligopoly environment	74
	monopolistic_comp	monopolistic competition	74
	perfect_comp	perfect competition	74
R&D	d_randd	Dummy for R&D	60
New employment	d_newstaff	Firm did/did not employ new staff in the last three financial years	74
In (age)	In_age	Logarithm of firm age	73
Cooperation	Co_operation	Firm did/did not have cooperation arrangement with other organization in the last three financial years	74
Exporter	d_exporter	Dummy for exporters	75

Table 19.5   Correlation matrix of the independent variables

	In_ec	monopolistic_comp	perfect_comp	d_randd	d_newsstaff	In_age	co_operation	d_exporter
In_ec	1.0000							
monopolistic_comp	0.1892	1.0000						
perfect_comp	0.0092	−0.5825*	1.0000					
d_randd	0.0969	0.1336	0.1753	1.0000				
d_newsstaff	0.2993*	0.0773	−0.0805	−0.0863	1.0000			
In_age	0.6081*	0.1160	0.1734	−0.0971	0.1242	1.0000		
co_operation	0.2019	0.0076	0.1592	0.2817*	0.1452	−0.1108	1.0000	
d_exporter	0.3161*	0.1991	−0.0805	0.0642	0.3148*	0.2942*	0.2716*	1.0000

Note: * Denotes significance at 5%.

As a pre-test, the pairwise correlations between each innovation group and the independent variables were also computed and reported in Table 19.6. At the 5 per cent level, all correlations were moderate in strength. Employment of new staff is significantly correlated with all innovation groups. Firm size has a stronger correlation with OPI, whereas cooperation is more related to PI.

Our first step is to estimate a multiple linear regression model with a binary dependent variable and this is referred to as the linear probability model (LPM). The model regresses a binary variable on a set of explanatory variables using OLS, whereby the response probability is linear in the parameters. In the context of this study, the linear model investigates whether factors such as firm characteristics, business practices and environment factors have significant effects on the probability of a firm exhibiting a certain type of innovation behaviour. Table 19.7 displays the results of three linear

Table 19.6   Pairwise correlation between innovation groups and variables

	QI	PI	OPI
In_ec	0.2369*	0.0864	0.4049*
monopolistic_comp	0.0469	0.0391	0.0710
perfect_comp	0.0101	0.0098	0.0069
d_randd	0.3208*	0.1654	0.1767
d_newsstaff	0.3187*	0.3801*	0.3328*
In_age	0.0036	−0.1089	0.0198
co_operation	0.2805*	0.3320*	0.2101
d_exporter	0.1589	0.2315*	0.1376

Note: * Denotes significance at 5%.

Table 19.7   Linear probability model estimates

	QI	PI	OPI
In (employment count)	0.021	−0.031	0.171**
	[0.712]	[0.640]	[0.011]
Monopolistic competition	−0.033	0.12	−0.016
	[0.813]	[0.454]	[0.918]
Perfect competition	−0.027	0.017	0.08
	[0.879]	[0.934]	[0.693]
R&D	0.450**	0.165	0.161
	[0.025]	[0.463]	[0.463]
New employment	0.355***	0.430***	0.241
	[0.010]	[0.007]	[0.115]
In (age)	0.007	−0.022	−0.094
	[0.931]	[0.799]	[0.274]
Cooperation	0.136	0.270*	0.045
	[0.291]	[0.072]	[0.766]
Exporter	−0.006	0.01	−0.004
	[0.965]	[0.953]	[0.983]
Constant	−0.031	0.09	−0.223
	[0.900]	[0.748]	[0.417]
R^2	0.311	0.304	0.326
Adjusted R^2	0.198	0.188	0.209
F-test (p-value)	0.013	0.018	0.013
Total obs.	58	57	55

Note: Stars denote significance at 10% (*), 5% (**) & 1% (***) level; p-values for t-test in square brackets are shown below the coefficients.

regressions. The model as a whole is highly significant with the F-tests giving a p-value of less than 0.05 for all regressions, and each explains over 30 per cent of the variance within the innovation groups. The adjusted R^2 is approximately 20 per cent.

New employment is the only significant variable at the 1 per cent level. Holding other

Table 19.8   Comparison of the p-*values in the two LPM models*

Variable	QI		PI		OPI	
	nonRobust	Robust	nonRobust	Robust	nonRobust	Robust
In (Employment count)	0.712	0.708	0.64	0.613	0.011**	0.005***
Monopolistic competition	0.813	0.836	0.454	0.481	0.918	0.932
Perfect competition	0.879	0.896	0.934	0.94	0.693	0.723
R&D	0.025**	0.054*	0.463	0.475	0.463	0.445
New employment	0.010***	0.025**	0.007***	0.008***	0.115	0.133
In (age)	0.931	0.937	0.799	0.81	0.274	0.393
Cooperation	0.291	0.189	0.072*	0.093*	0.766	0.804
Exporter	0.965	0.968	0.953	0.953	0.983	0.983
Constant	0.9	0.919	0.748	0.768	0.417	0.432

Note: Stars denote significance at 10% (*), 5% (**) & 1% (***).

factors fixed, a firm that hired new staff in the last three financial years is 35.5 per cent more likely to be a QI and 43 per cent more likely to be a PI compared with those firms that did not recruit new staff recently. Undertaking R&D activities also increases the probability of being in the QI group by 45 per cent, while cooperation arrangements are more likely to be associated with a PI, whereas the only issue affecting the probability of being an OPI is the size of the firm.

Compared with other binary response models, the linear model is simple to use and the results can be easily interpreted, although the model has some drawbacks. First, the fitted probabilities are not constrained to be between zero and one, and the model therefore works best if the independent variables take values which are near to the sample average. Second, the LPM's error term violates the assumption of homoscedasticity, as the disturbance can only take two possible values for a given set of **x** values due to the binary nature of the dependent variable.

To verify the validity of the variables' significance, a robust approach is applied which affects the calculation of the standard errors, leaving the coefficient estimates unchanged. The resulting *p*-values for each independent variable are listed in Table 19.8, which demonstrates the similarities between the robust and non-robust estimates.

Finally, we also have to allow for the fact that the relationship between the outcome probability and the independent variables may not be linear even as an approximation, and therefore we must also employ a non-linear model such as a probit or logit model to allow for this possibility.

The construction of both of these non-linear models is based upon a latent-variable approach. Here a variable y_i^* is the net benefit of taking a particular course of action and the outcome of the action y_i is dependent on y_i^* such that:

$$y_i = 0 \text{ if } y_i^* \leq 0 \text{ and } y_i = 1 \text{ if } y_i^* > 0.$$

However, only the binary outcome of the action (that is, the innovation group identity) can be observed, while y_i^* is a latent variable that can be directly explained by the set of explanatory variables:

$$y^*_i = \beta_i\, x_i + u_i.$$

Therefore:

$$\Pr(y^* > 0) = \Pr(u_i > -x\beta) = \Pr(u_i < x\beta) = \Pr(y_i = 1) = \Psi(y^*_i),$$

where $\Psi(\cdot)$ is a cumulative distribution function (CDF).

For the probit model, $\Psi(\cdot)$ is the CDF of the normal distribution and the logit model bases its estimates on a logistic distribution. The CDFs of the normal and logistic distribution are very similar to each other except in the tails.

Table 19.9 shows the marginal effects obtained from the non-linear models. The variables found to have a significant effect on each innovation group are the same in the LPM, but with slightly higher marginal effects. The likelihood ratio test results show that all regressions produce a p-value below 5 per cent, except for the QI probit regression, which passed the test at the 10 per cent level. The regressions produced pseudo-R^2 values of between 17.6 and 30 per cent, and values of 0.2 or above are regarded as being very good (McFadden, 1979; Louviere et al., 2000).

Based on the coefficient estimates reported in Tables 19.7 and 19.9, the predicted probabilities were calculated for each observation. Figure 19.1 illustrates the predicted probabilities at various percentiles of the predicted value. The LPM predicts the

Table 19.9   Probit and logit marginal effects

	Probit			Logit		
	QI	PI	OPI	QI	PI	OPI
In (employment count)	0.036	−0.048	0.255***	0.024	−0.052	0.256**
	[0.580]	[0.573]	[0.008]	[0.699]	[0.566]	[0.011]
Monopolistic competition	0.003	0.135	−0.085	−0.002	0.145	−0.079
	[0.982]	[0.475]	[0.646]	[0.991]	[0.448]	[0.687]
Perfect competition	−0.025	−0.014	0.032	−0.006	−0.008	0.032
	[0.895]	[0.954]	[0.894]	[0.973]	[0.977]	[0.900]
R&D	0.481*	0.207	0.195	0.491*	0.205	0.191
	[0.053]	[0.447]	[0.451]	[0.067]	[0.445]	[0.352]
New employment	0.378**	0.490***	0.279	0.389**	0.497***	0.288*
	[0.016]	[0.007]	[0.101]	[0.023]	[0.001]	[0.051]
In (age)	−0.003	−0.024	−0.148	0.003	−0.02	−0.146
	[0.971]	[0.822]	[0.139]	[0.970]	[0.857]	[0.185]
Cooperation	0.177	0.329*	0.057	0.17	0.346**	0.066
	[0.231]	[0.059]	[0.736]	[0.185]	[0.037]	[0.714]
Exporter	−0.054	−0.013	0.02	−0.039	−0.006	0.008
	[0.713]	[0.952]	[0.926]	[0.768]	[0.980]	[0.970]
LR test (p-value)	0.053	0.013	0.005	0.015	0.013	0.005
Pseudo R^2	0.176	0.247	0.300	0.285	0.247	0.298
Total obs.	58	57	55	58	57	55

Note: Stars denote significance at 10% (*), 5% (**) & 1% (***) level; p-values for t-test in square brackets are shown below the coefficients.

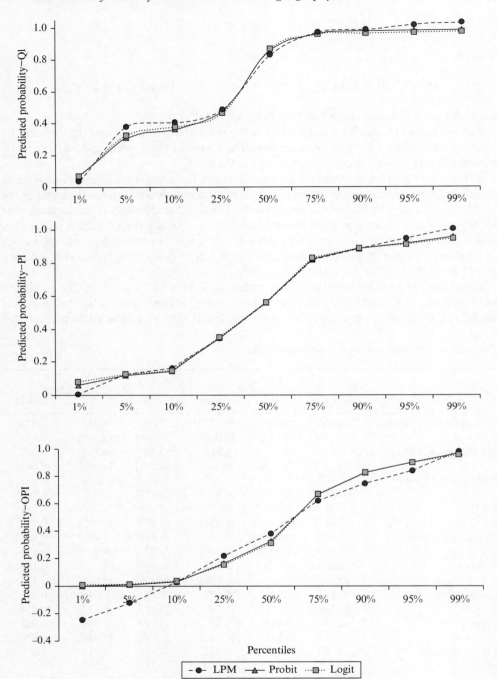

Figure 19.1   Linear versus non-linear models

probability to be outside the zero and one range in two out of three cases. The predictions from the probit and logit models almost follow the same path, only diverging at the extreme values, as would be expected by the constraints imposed by the model.

Based upon the regression results presented in Tables 19.7–9, the model suggests the following: R&D active firms which also hire new staff are more likely to be the QI qualified innovators; firms hiring new staff and those undertaking cooperation with other firms are more likely to produce product innovations; and greater firm size increases the probability of a firm producing OPI operational process innovations. Market structure and exporting appear to play little or no role in the likelihood of a firm exhibiting any particular form of innovation. Nor does the size of the firm appear to play any role in the likelihood of being either a QI or a PI. In contrast, being a larger firm increases the likelihood of exhibiting OPI organizational or process innovations. As such, there is no evidence here that being small promotes innovation. On the contrary, our results suggest that small firms in New Zealand are either no different to larger firms in their innovation performance or may actually be less likely to produce innovations than larger firms.

19.5 CASE-STUDY OBSERVATIONS

The case studies adopted a qualitative approach which involved a relatively small number of firms. The in-depth studies extended the insights from our innovation survey and were designed to further our understanding of the innovation practices of the New Zealand manufacturers. A large amount of information was collected during these case studies and after the transcription of the interviews, comments were sorted to identify common themes. In the discussion below, participating individuals will be identified by the codes corresponding to their respective companies so that, for example, the interviewee from firm A will be referred to as Informant A.

During the case studies, we aimed to detect whether there were any differences between the innovation awareness and practices in New Zealand in comparison to the major themes emerging from the international literature. The reason for this is that while institutionally New Zealand appears to be ideal for innovation, its international performance in innovation is relatively poor. Therefore, we aim to uncover whether differences in the aspirations, attitudes, awareness and practices towards innovation may play a role in this. We know that variations in these perceptions can explain some of the cross-country differences in the levels of entrepreneurship, so our intention is to see if this is also so in terms of innovation (Acs et al., 2008).

From our 15 case studies it became clear that the awareness of innovation as a concept appears to vary between firms. Larger firms seem to be relatively more familiar with the term 'innovation', while informants from the smaller firms often respond to the innovation question by first asking what the term 'innovation' meant. However, it is not clear that larger firms necessarily have a better understanding of the academic use of the term 'innovation'. When asked to give an example of recently introduced innovation, all businesses referred to new product development. Process and non-technological-related innovations were rarely mentioned. Informant C replied: 'our business is all about new ideas and delivering of the ideas to our customer in a product form'. This reflects a more general perception of innovation being related to products and services rather than to processes. Yet, firms are also aware that process, marketing and organizational innovations are often the inducements for product innovation, or alternatively they are often carried out in order to complement the introduction of new products and processes. In Informant D's words: 'new processes are often required for new product development, machines have to be built to specification, and development of the new market has to follow'. However, among the interviewed firms there still appears to be an emphasis on innovation being related mainly to marketed outputs rather than to processes.

The general importance of innovation for business growth was recognized by all those interviewed. Yet, only eight out of 15 companies plan their innovation formally, while others consider innovation to be an ongoing but informal process whereby the firms respond to the opportunities as they arise. It was also clear to all those interviewed that innovation must serve a recognizable purpose. For Firm A, 'a range of management practices have been introduced to reduce lead time, increase product activity, make the product development process transparent and more efficient, and expose the weakness at all stages of the manufacturing project'. For Firm B, innovation is also about ensuring long-term survival, profitability and competitiveness in the face of increasing global competition:

> Developing countries such as China and India, not only benefit from low labour costs, but they are often protected by tariffs and government subsidies. Considering the scale of their production, New Zealand manufacturers have no or very little chance to compete in terms of price competition. In order to survive under such huge competitive pressures, we need to find the right market and live in the niche.

The reason why New Zealand firms should focus innovations on niche markets is a question of scale. As Informant M points out, a 'typical niche market is generally ignored by the bigger players. It demands high value added, high quality products that are highly specialized, customized and potentially difficult to make'. Bigger firms will almost invariably come from other countries, so the much smaller New Zealand firms need to focus on niche markets in order to compete internationally. However, this focus on niche markets does not mean ignorance of the bigger markets. Informant I argues that 'a successful company will need to find a balance between the mainstream and the innovative market'. One way of achieving this, as Firm G does, is to try to access the larger markets using the so-called 'piggyback method' that first attracts customers using the specialized New Zealand niche product and then follows this up with a more conventional product when a supplier–customer relationship is firmly in place. Once the supplier–customer relationship is firmly established, the international customer may be willing to pay a slightly higher price in order to ensure convenience and a guaranteed quality of product from New Zealand. These types of approaches which focus on the exploitation of niche markets enable many small firms to better deal with market and economic uncertainties.

The sources of innovative ideas employed by the firms in the study were also very diverse. Both internal and external sources are important and characteristics such as creativity, ingenuity and forward thinking are regarded as invaluable for innovation. As Informant B argues: 'always think ahead, discover the profit potential in the sunshine industry and improve the production process to make it a more environmentally friendly product'. It is also regarded as being very important for a firm to continually update its understanding of its target market. Informant D states that: 'our sales person regularly receives feedbacks from existing customers and collects new ideas and market information from trade fairs'. Cooperation with other firms and exporting are also both regarded as providing additional innovation opportunities for New Zealand firms. Eleven of the 15 companies were exporters, and all of them consider Australia to be their major export market or the export market with the greatest growth potential for New Zealand firms. Four non-exporters within the group are either considering exporting in the near future or they are already part of an export value chain, which means that they supply goods and services to other exporters. Under various circumstances, these forms of cooperation can therefore be either a substitute or a complement to exports.

The final theme to emerge from all of the firms was the importance for innovation of face-to-face contact. All of the firms stressed the need for regular face-to-face contact with suppliers and customers in order to assess market developments and to acquire new knowledge, the basis for all innovations. As informant J noted: 'it is essential to be close to the market, face to face contact and networking is essential'. At the same time, the isolation and small scale of the local economy was mentioned by eight of the firms as being a major problem for growth and innovation. In order to help overcome these problems and to develop the business, three of the firms are explicitly aiming to increase their exports to Australia.

19.6   DISCUSSION AND CONCLUSIONS

The evidence obtained from the 15 case studies suggests that in general the innovation approaches in New Zealand are largely consistent with the benchmark approaches evident in the international literature. New Zealand firms acquire best-practice information from a wide variety of sources and their business practices are up to date with the types of discussion taking place in other countries. There is a generally high level of awareness of the importance of innovation and an awareness of the issues driving innovation. This general awareness of innovation issues is also reflected by the fact that the number of per capita scientific papers produced by New Zealand is high by international standards (OECD, 2007b). As well as a high level of awareness, the highly liberalized and transparent institutional environment is almost ideal for promoting entrepreneurship. The combination of awareness and institutions produces a society with the highest level of entrepreneurship in the world (Acs and Szerb, 2009). Yet, this high level of entrepreneurship is not translated into an equivalent innovation performance.

Although taking a broader perspective the innovation performance of New Zealand is probably stronger than many existing indicators imply (Fabling, 2007), there still appears to be a performance gap when moving from entrepreneurship to innovation. On the basis of this research, we would suggest that the likely reasons for this are related to the small size of the firms, the small size of the market, and the level of geographical isolation. While New Zealand's innovation performance is good if we control for market and firm size, distance and sectoral composition (Crawford et al., 2007), the point remains that the country's scale and geography may be disadvantageous in terms of translating entrepreneurship into innovation.

One particular aspect of this is that in the case of New Zealand the smallness and isolation of the economy appears to produce a different relationship between firm size and innovation performance in comparison to most other countries. As we have seen, our results suggest that New Zealand's small firms do not have an advantage in terms of the generation of innovations, and in some cases larger firms have an advantage. Our observation is also consistent with other New Zealand findings (Fabling and Grimes, 2007) which also suggest that firm success either is independent of firm size, or in some cases is positively related to the existence of oligopolistic structures. In contrast, our findings and those of Fabling and Grimes are rather different from the findings in many other countries in which small firms are found to be more innovative. While small firms may generally be considered to be advantageous for innovation in other countries, the weaker innovation performance of New Zealand suggests that there may still be a minimum-size threshold above which small scale is advantageous. As such, part of the reason why the innovation advantage of being small does not appear to operate in New Zealand might be an absolute scale issue. Being a small firm in New Zealand implies being a micro or a nano firm in many other countries, and it may be that these micro or nano firms are simply too small to maintain the levels of R&D and market research required in order to generate anything other than *ad hoc* occasional innovations rather than a large-scale continuous stream of innovations. In a country such as New Zealand, in order to promote increased innovation and exports it may be the case that public policy should therefore be geared towards increasing the size of firms rather than reducing them, and this has already been advocated elsewhere (Skilling and Boven, 2006).

Similar arguments also relate to the scale and isolation of the local market. Although we have not explicitly examined these issues econometrically, the case-study evidence indicates that the New Zealand economy is so small and isolated that the conventional arguments regarding the impacts of market structure, trade and size on innovation may also carry much less weight in this particular context. New Zealand is already very highly deregulated and competitive, with a large number of tiny firms. Yet, ironically, this combination of small national market size, small city size, small firm size distribution, and extreme geographical isolation (McCann, 2009) means that highly competitive markets may not be the ideal market structure for translating local entrepreneurship into local innovation. As such, in spite of an almost ideal institutional context for entrepreneurship and innovation, the relatively weaker innovation performance of New Zealand may therefore primarily be related to the specific set of structural and geographical features of the local economy. In New Zealand, it is questionable whether the classic U-shape relationship between innovation intensity and firm size, as suggested by the international literature, really holds.

NOTES

1. The Fraser Institute (2006) ranks New Zealand as the third-freest economy in the world (http://www.freetheworld.com/2006/EFWinternational-rls.pdf). The Heritage Foundation (2007) ranks NZ as the fifth-freest economy in the world (http://www.heritage.org/index/topten.cfm).
2. The Global Entrepreneurship Monitor (http://www.gemconsortium.org/).
3. Transparency International (www.transparency.org/layout/set/print/news_room/in_focus/2008/cpi2008/cpi_2008_table).
4. Forbes ranked NZ 10th out of 135 countries in 2006 in terms of capital 'hospitality' (http://www.forbes.com/lists/2006/6/CHI010.html) and (http://www.forbes.com/2006/01/24/capital-hospitality-index_06caphosp_land.html).

5. Similar to the full-time equivalent (FTE) measurement, a full-time worker is counted as one annual work unit, and part-time staff and seasonal workers are counted as fractions of one unit.
6. Income received in the reference year after rebate payouts, excluding value-added tax or other indirect taxes.
7. Refers to the value of the company's main assets.
8. Average of total income plus cost of goods sold for the latest three fiscal years; for exclusion receipts refer to SBA's website, http://www.sba.gov/services/contractingopportunities/sizestandardstopics/indexguide/index.html.
9. The default way of deleting missing data while calculating a correlation matrix is to exclude all cases that have missing data in at least one of the selected variables. Pairwise deletion is an alternative method, where a correlation between each pair of variables is calculated from all cases that have valid data on those two variables.

REFERENCES

Acs, Z.J. (2002), *Innovation and the Growth of Cities*, Cheltenham, UK and Northampton, MA, USA: Edward Elgar.

Acs, Z.J. and Audretsch, D.B. (1988), 'Innovation and large and small firms: an empirical analysis', *American Economic Review*, **78** (4), 678–90.

Acs, Z.J., Bosma, N. and Sterberg, R. (2008), '*The entrepreneurial advantage of world cities: evidence from Global Entrepreneurship Monitor data*', Working Paper H200810, SCALES, University of Utrecht and Netherlands Ministry of Economic Affairs.

Acs, Z.J. and Szerb, L. (2009), 'The Global Entrepreneurship Index (GEINEX) and the stages of economic development', Working Paper, Global Entrepreneurship Monitor.

Crawford, R., Fabling, R., Grimes, A. and Bonner, N. (2007), 'National R&D and patenting: is New Zealand an outlier?', *New Zealand Economic Papers*, **41** (1), 69–90.

European Commission (2003), *The New SME Definition: User Guide and Model Declaration*, Enterprise and Industry Publication, Brussels: European Commission.

Evans, L., Grimes, A., Teece, D. and Wilkinson, B. (1996), 'Economic reform in New Zealand 1984–95: the pursuit of efficiency', *Journal of Economic Literature*, **34**, 1856–902.

Fabling, R. (2007), 'How innovative are New Zealand firms? Quantifying and relating organizational and marketing innovation to traditional science and technology indicators', in *Science, Technology and Innovation Indicators in a Changing World: Responding to Policy Needs*, Paris: OECD, pp. 139–70.

Fabling, R. and Grimes, A. (2007), 'Practice makes profit: business practices and firm success', *Small Business Economics*, **29**, 383–99.

Gerardin, D. and Kerr, M. (2003), *Controlling Market Power in Telecommunications*, Oxford: Oxford University Press.

Hall, J. and Casey, A. (2006), 'International comparative surveys of regulatory impact', New Zealand Treasury Working Paper 06-05, Wellington.

IMF (2004), *New Zealand: Selected Issues*, IMF Country Report No. 04/127, International Monetary Fund, Washington, DC.

Law, D. and McLellan, N. (2005), 'The contributions from firm entry, exit and continuation to labour productivity growth in New Zealand', New Zealand Treasury Working Paper 05-01, Wellington.

Louviere, J.J., Hensher, D.A. and Swait, J.D. (2000), *Stated Choice Methods*, Cambridge: Cambridge University Press.

Mariampolski, H. (2001), *Qualitative Market Research: A Comprehensive Guide*, Thousand Oaks, CA: Sage.

McCann, P. (2009), 'Economic geography, globalisation and New Zealand's productivity paradox', *New Zealand Economic Papers*, **43** (3), 279–314.

McFadden, D. (1979), 'Quantitative methods for analysing travel behaviour of individuals', in Hensher, D.A. and Storper, P.R. (eds), *Behavioural Travel Modelling*, London: Croom Helm, pp. 279–318.

MED (2007), *Economic Development Indicators*, Ministry of Economic Development, The Treasury and Statistics New Zealand, Wellington.

MED–Treasury (2005), *Economic Development Indicators 2005: Growth Through Innovation*, Ministry of Economic Development and The Treasury, Wellington.

OECD (2005), *Oslo Manual: Guidelines for Collecting and Interpreting Innovation Data*, Paris: Organisation for Economic Co-operation and Development.

OECD (2007a), *OECD Science, Technology and Industry Scoreboard 2007*, Paris: Organisation for Economic Co-operation and Development.

OECD (2007b), *OECD Reviews of Innovation Policy: New Zealand*, Paris: Organisation for Economic Co-operation and Development.

OECD (2007c), *Competitive Cities in the Global Economy*, Paris: Organisation for Economic Co-operation and Development.

OECD (2008a), *OECD Factbook 2008: Economic, Environmental and Social Statistics*, Paris: Organisation for Economic Co-operation and Development.

OECD (2008b), *Economic Policy Reforms: Going for Growth*, Paris: Organisation for Economic Co-operation and Development.

OECD (2008c), 'The Contribution of Economic Geography to GDP per Capita', Economics Department Working Paper, Organisation for Economic Co-operation and Development, Paris.

Porter, M.E., Sala-i-Martin, X. and Schwab, K. (2007), *World Economic Forum: The Global Competitiveness Report*, Basingstoke: Palgrave.

Roper, S. and Hewitt-Dundas, N. (2008), 'Innovation persistence: survey and case-study evidence', *Research Policy*, **37**, 149–62.

Skilling, D. and Boven, D. (2006), 'Developing Kiwi global champions: growing successful New Zealand multinational companies', Discussion Paper 2006–03, New Zealand Institute, Auckland.

Tether, B.S., Smith, I.J. and Thwaites, A.T. (1997), 'Smaller enterprises and innovation in the UK: the SPRU innovations database revisited', *Research Policy*, **26**, 19–32.

World Bank (2009), *Doing Business 2009*, Washington, DC: World Bank.

20 They are industrial districts, but not as we know them!

Fiorenza Belussi and Lisa De Propris

20.1 INTRODUCTION

Beyond the lively debate on the weaknesses and decline of some Italian industrial districts, there is a documented reality of other dynamic localized industries that have not only embraced the opportunities of fast-changing markets and open production networks, but are also weathering the current economic crisis showing an enviable resilience. This chapter explores how close and how far such phenomena are from the *classic* Marshallian industrial districts of the Third Italy. Our analysis will draw on the literature that has looked at industrial districts as evolving, changing and adapting forms, but it goes beyond the common claim that the modern industrial districts are transforming themselves by mainly basing their competitive advantage on proximity (localized learning) and firm cooperation (trust-based organizations). Indeed, the sustained growth and related resilience of some historical Italian industrial districts is due to a combination of factors: (a) distance 'learning' and open models of innovation; (b) the emergence of brands and larger firms to create and control the final market; (c) the anchoring of the value creation stages to locally embedded creativity; and finally (d) the adoption of specific strategies to maintain and to regenerate the skills of the local workforce, in order to translate local firms' research into new applications and innovations. The chapter will present a review of the current trends across 'weak' and 'resilient' industrial districts complemented by detailed case studies. New parameters to define 'evolved and open industrial districts' will be suggested.

20.2 THE PARAMETERS OF MARSHALLIAN INDUSTRIAL DISTRICTS

The concept of the 'Marshallian industrial district' (MID) emerged in the 1990s inspired by the scholarly work of Becattini (Becattini, 1990; Becattini et al., 2009). The MID is defined as a locality where there is a community of people and an agglomeration of small and medium-sized firms specialized in a particular production activity. Looking at industrial districts (IDs) scattered across industrialized England, Marshall (1920) observed that the organization of production in such localized industries was able to generate external economies as the complementarities of firms' specializations were integrated along the local value chain. Agglomeration forces enabled the creation of a pool of skilled and specialized labour and the development of an 'industrial atmosphere', namely a localized industrial culture. The MID model draws on Marshall's conceptualization. In the MID model, the co-location of firms and the centripetal forces of industrial specialization also create socioeconomic relationships that are intertwined, facilitated by trust and social capital, and mediated by proactive and dedicated local institutional actors. A crucial byproduct of both external economies and the thick industrial atmosphere is the emergence of a mechanism of collective learning and innovation prompted by knowledge spillovers as well as opportunities for collective actions.

In evolutionary terms, an MID can be defined as 'a learning system producing localised knowledge, strongly based on local culture and the capabilities of local actors' (Belussi and Sedita, 2009:508). As a live form, an MID follows a life cycle from birth, to growth, maturity and decline (De Propris and Lazzeretti, 2009). As evidenced in Belussi and Sedita (2009), decline and death are not inevitable: their meta-analysis shows that the evolution of Italian MIDs can unfold along multiple paths, albeit starting from the same origin. Key issues for the endurance of MIDs are first, whether they contain mechanisms and resources to identify growth opportunities and jump onto ascending paths; and second, whether the technology (driven by the innovation process and learning), the social fabric and the production system, are able to co-evolve harmoniously. Recent responses to both the opportunities and threats of globalization and the emergence of new technological paradigms have decided the fortune of most IDs. Those which have avoided decline are those where individual firms, as well as collectively the aggregate socio-productive networks, have been able to absorb, adapt and outline avenues of potential growth, drawing upon internal and external resources.

Our analysis goes beyond the common claim that the modern IDs are evolving by largely basing their competitive advantage on proximity (localized learning) and firm cooperation (trust-based organizations). In particular, we would argue that the endurance of IDs rests on a combination of factors: (a) upstream and downstream functional upgrading, including the introduction of new international distributive channels or new international alliances for product commercialization; (b) a strong drift towards the intensification of innovation and creativity (Osservatorio Nazionale dei Distretti Industriali, 2012a) leading to a strategy of continuous product upgrading, demand-driven innovations, and customization; (c) a novel and diffused consciousness regarding the need for local firms to pursue specific firm investments with regard to brand recognition (see within the Italian districts, for instance, the cases of Geox, Tecnica and Natuzzi), within a long-term process that is seeing the emergence of ID leaders; and (d) the experimentation of distance 'learning' and open models of innovation.

The need to pursue all or some of the above factors could not leave IDs unchanged. The most successful IDs have both undergone, and are still undergoing, a process of restructuring. We could question whether, at the end of these processes, what is left is still an MID. Or we could discuss whether there are still some crucial parameters defining the existence of a 'true' MID. These issues will be disentangled in the following sections. After an overview of some key indicators to help capture and appreciate the current trends and trajectories of MIDs, we shall relate them to the impact of globalization, suggesting in some depth the transformation of the parameters defining the current evolutionary trends.

20.3   EVIDENCE ON THE RECENT PERFORMANCE OF INDUSTRIAL DISTRICTS

Despite a lively debate on the crisis in some Italian IDs – and for some it has indeed led to unavoidable decline – there is ample evidence to suggest that some IDs have been able to maintain their competitive edge and are performing exceptionally well, given that the international economic outlook in 2012 is still bleak four years into the crisis. Overall, Italian ID exports have experienced sustained growth in 2011, with a 15 per cent rise to non-EU countries and an 8.3 per cent rise to EU countries, taking the overall ID export value back to the pre-crisis 2008 level (Osservatorio Nazionale dei Distretti Industriali, 2012b). In 2010–11, the best-performing sectors were high-tech machinery and equipment with a 15 per cent increase; leather products (17 per cent rise) textiles and garments (12 per cent rise) and home design (5% per cent rise) (ibid). Furthermore food and wine exports grew by almost 11 per cent in 2010–11 despite the long-lasting global downturn (Fondazione Edison, 2012). The positive trend of their export value reflects the increased specialization of IDs in high value-added or high-tech content sectors, the demand for which is somewhat inelastic and where price competition is minimal. However, such performance is in stark contrast to employment contractions across most IDs. Productivity growth has absorbed many low-skilled jobs (continuous automation, standardization and modularity, process innovations and labour-saving restructuring) and a torpid entrepreneurial climate has not been able to create enough new jobs to compensate for those also lost due to the relocation abroad of labour-intensive functions. Across IDs, employment has dropped by 7 per cent between 2001 and 2007 (ibid.). The composition of skills in IDs is also changing as more highly skilled jobs are in demand over low-skill job contracting. A study on productivity shows that white-collar workers are, however, less productive in IDs than in urban areas (this is probably due to the sectoral composition of tertiary activity, whose hierarchical localization moves the highest value-added functions – R&D, financial services, advertising and marketing, and knowledge-intensive business services – towards urban centres such as Milan and Rome), while blue-collar workers are comparatively more productive in IDs (Di Giacinto et al., 2012). Therefore, the IDs' manufacturing hollowing-out is likely to coincide with the possible future loss of relatively precious manual skills.

Indicators of competitiveness for IDs produce a mixed picture. If export flows are strong and still expanding, productivity and value-added trends are of concern. Productivity (measured as total factor productivity: TFP) is greater for firms in IDs than for those outside IDs. However, firms in urban areas are relatively more productive than those in IDs: cross-sector spillovers (Jacobian economies) and especially the co-location with a critical mass and a mix of service firms emerge as a source of productivity (Osservatorio Nazionale dei Distretti Industriali, 2012b). As such, IDs' manufacturing specialization is likely to hamper such efficiency gains. Indeed, once the presence of service activities within an ID reaches a tipping point – a point at which Jacobian advantages are likely to emerge – the tight criteria for defining an MID tend to slip and what was before classified as an MID becomes then a more broadly defined local production system. Thus, over time the level of specialization decreases and related varieties of activities tend to grow. This causes an underestimation of the productivity level and growth in IDs overall. In terms of trends, district firms' productivity has also been found to be declining over the 1995–2006 period (Di Giacinto et al., 2012) suggesting that the relocation strategies have reached a point where the shift to high value-added functions is complete. Despite the sustained growth of export flows, value-added growth has also fallen over the 1995–2009 period in regions typically characterized by the presence of IDs such as the northwestern and northeastern regions, albeit such levels have consistently been above the national average (Osservatorio Nazionale dei Distretti Industriali, 2012b). More broadly, the manufacturing sectors accounted for 15 per cent of the overall economy in 2011, with services having the largest share of 73 per cent, dropping from 21 per cent in 1992 (ISTAT, 2012). This indicates a shift of the economy towards the service activities, namely towards the so-called 'knowledge economy'.

20.4   THREATS AND OPPORTUNITIES

In the last decade, threats and opportunities for IDs have come from the changing role of the globalization process, and also the changing nature and role of innovation in the production processes.

20.4.1   Globalization

New competition coming from Asian, and Chinese manufacturers in particular, has shaken what in the past were considered to be largely stable market positions, while also offering low-cost production bases for the production networks which are spreading globally. Indeed, the emergence of China as the 'workshop of the world' (Gao, 2011) runs in parallel with the emergence of multinational corporations and the importance of branding in these increasingly affluent economies. In a very short period this turmoil has changed not only the dynamics of competition, but also the organization of production.

The flooding of poor-quality but cheap manufacturing goods coming from low-wage countries has wiped out firms producing in the same low end of markets. This has led to a deterioration of the competitive position of so-called 'weak districts', namely those with a low level of firm innovativeness and a high degree of institutional and productive lock-in. However, simultaneously, globalization has also offered significant growth opportunities to those districts that have been able to expand their production organization beyond the national borders by constructing *external linkages* abroad. In recent years, evidence has shown that district firms are going abroad to look for new forms of cooperation in production and to seek innovative alliances with suppliers, scouting for intelligence on new knowledge, technology or fashion trends.

The weaving of ID production along global networks (Belussi and Sammarra, 2010) has changed the sources of IDs' economies. Those external economies that were internal to the ID are now external to the ID but internal to its value chain, and are increasingly extending worldwide. Furthermore, the governance of the production process is assuming more hierarchical features: high value-added functions *vis-à-vis* volume productions; customized innovations *vis-à-vis* scale economies; the search for cost-cutting *vis-à-vis* the commitment to quality and innovation; finally, the power and visibility of final firms and brands *vis-à-vis* labour-intensive but concealed subcontractors. Social interaction and shared customs no longer underpin all economic relations. Local linkages might maintain such important features, albeit disrupted by the offshoring of chunks of the production process and by the increased diversity of the labour force. On the other hand, the local institutional framework which is so important for the renewability of the ID in relation to the provision of collective public goods (Bellandi, 2006) still has a very local remit. It is more complex to organize initiatives supporting the internationalization of firms and the formation of transnational alliances than the mere provision of local services.

20.4.2 Innovation and Learning

The innovation process in IDs is characterized by diffused localized learning (Belussi and Pilotti, 2002a) where combinations of tacit and codified knowledge have enabled mechanisms of knowledge creation and transfer. The competitive advantage of IDs, especially in their 'golden period', had been to deliver product variety and short product life cycles thanks to production flexibility and incremental innovation capabilities. Such strengths were particularly relevant in the household and personal goods markets, where consumers' tastes and fashions changed regularly. The sources of such a dynamic incremental innovativeness stemmed from inside the ID, where firms utilized their own embedded knowledge together with the shared knowledge that emerges through firms' value chain interactions.

In Italy, IDs were always found to lack competitiveness in high-tech sectors, where innovation was reliant on R&D activities. This is largely due to the weakness of the national innovation system. At the height of the knowledge economy period, the emphasis placed on radical technological innovations and science-based sectors introduced a competitive challenge to IDs. Radical innovations appear to be more prominent in relation to the translation of innovation into a competitive advantage. In this context, the ID model can be juxtaposed with other basic-research-driven models, which were arguably better at capturing the need for systemic innovation – for example, university-centred clusters and regional innovation systems (Becattini et al., 2009). In Italy, in general, the experience of IDs remains relegated within the so-called 'traditional' sectors, such as garments, textiles, furniture, footwear, or ceramics. Not all IDs evolved towards an advanced model of knowledge creation and transfer necessary for enforcing the innovation capability of the local system. The IDs' past innovativeness had somewhat drawn the contours of their competitive advantage. Indeed, what was an advantage at one point had turned into a constraint at another. Such contours have, however, proved to be less fixed than was once thought.

Some Italian IDs have in fact proved able to transform themselves into dynamic evolving systems, to renew their competitive advantage, and more recently to weather the economic crisis. This has been realized in different ways. Some more traditional IDs have undergone functional and inter-sectoral upgrading (Humphrey and Schmitz, 2002); others have been successful in product upgrading and in securing the top segment of the market; finally, more high-tech IDs have maintained their market leadership thanks to innovation and customization. Our analysis stresses three main issues.

First, functional and inter-sectoral upgrading is triggered by the so-called 'Heckscher–Ohlin' effect, whereby the growth of IDs coincides with the spawning within the same locality of industrial specializations along the value chain. As the value chain becomes more complex and populated by diverse agents, evidence shows that the core specialization of the ID might change over time: some competences become dominant at the expense of others, or some come to the fore as others lose competitiveness. Exemplary cases in this respect include the Arzignano district (Belussi and Sedita, 2009) where leather machinery production became as important as the more traditional leather manufacturing, or the shoe machinery district in Vigevano and textile machinery in the Biella textile district (De Arcangelis and Ferri, 2005). The creation of the specialized machinery and equipment manufacturing segment has diversified the traditional district model, pushing forward an important renewal. As already mentioned, district firms have been found to be more productive than non-district ones, and this can be explained by their superior performance in product as well as in process innovation (Cainelli, 2008). Indeed, the product customization refers to a specific ability which is spread among the ID firms, given their sophisticated specialization in dealing with their buyers' needs.

Second, for many IDs, their competitive advantage needs to be redrawn in the context of the so-called 'experience economy'. Such a move is driven by a better understanding of the sources of value creation (for instance, the economic value of softer forms of innovation associated with entrepreneurial creativity). In this context, the distinction between radical and incremental innovation loses its explanatory power once we consider innovation in relation, for instance, to design. The ability to invent and transform the invention into a radically new innovation – product or service innovation – now applies also to non-science-based industries. The competitive advantage of some IDs stems therefore from the innovative, but more precisely, from the creative content of the so-called 'Made in Italy' production. These are the fashion and design-intensive industries. What was before a traditional activity, is therefore now a high value-added function, based on intangible products.

Two considerations are worth mentioning in relation to the above. One is that the origin of such strengths is in the anchoring of local firms in the embedded creativity of the IDs. Thus, the real driver of their innovation/creativity is in the local industrial culture. The authenticity of the cumulated knowledge (Crevoisier and Jeannerat, 2009) and the privilege to draw on such pools of knowledge to create generative learning (Belussi and Pilotti, 2002b) enables firms to proactively respond to differentiated demands by shaping their requests and tastes. The non-Schumpeterian nature of radical creativity guarantees a larger space for the introduction of novelties which are not necessarily based on technological innovations. The source of this type of creativity stems from the wealth of old knowledge, and this process is in continuity with the old district. This creativity cannot be defined within a pure branding strategy. It is a more complex dynamic, since it has to recombine the existing competences of local international leading firms, with the local industrial competences and culture. Often radical shifts take place because local firms are able to cover new market segments and to improve the quality of their products. Important changes in this sense are introduced once local firms open their supply chains to foreign firms, spreading their production stages geographically around the world to maintain a tighter control over costs. These organizational innovations can imply the introduction of new forms of functional and inter-sectoral upgrading (Humphrey and Schmitz, 2002). Another related point is that the opportunity to acquire a higher competitiveness has neither happened by chance nor been a painless process. While the creation of new capabilities has drawn on the IDs' inner knowledge and learning together with the use of external linkages created by the local firms, the dynamic advantage for firms has been triggered by an important process of district restructuring taking place through several organizational innovations. This latter process coincides with the emergence of visible leading firms, as well as the pursuit of cost reduction strategies. Typically, a painstaking process of manufacturing hollowing-out (Bailey, 2003) involves the more labour-intensive tasks.

Third, despite the historical specialization of Italian IDs in low- and medium-tech sectors, it is worth noting that some IDs are shifting their specialization towards products with a higher technological content. In addition, there is evidence of a new generation of IDs that have started to operate quite successfully in high-tech sectors. An example is the Etna Valley district, whose activities are connected to the subcontracting of the Franco-Italian firm STMicroelectronics. Here, around 500 local firms are specialized in microelectronic components, and district export flows grew by 9 per cent in the first part of 2011. Another example is the biomedical district of Mirandola, near Modena, whose quite spontaneous, development was the result of crucial upgrading starting from already existing mechanical competences which were applied to the production of medical equipment (for example, artificial kidneys). Italy has neither a national innovation system capable of creating and anchoring new technological sectors differently from northern European countries (Finland, Denmark, and Norway), nor universities that are able to trigger processes of knowledge transfer and new venture creations. Such Italian high-tech districts moved from traditional specializations into new high-tech competences thanks to the spillover effects deriving from the localization of some multinationals or national champions acting as anchors (De Propris and Crevoisier, 2011), as, for example, in the case of Mirandola and the Etna Valley. An interesting consideration is whether the emergence of distance 'learning' and open models of innovation will enable such high-tech IDs to grow, regardless of the weak Italian research infrastructure.

20.5   NEW PARAMETERS

Visible trends in the evolution of IDs are the emergence of medium-sized firms (Mediobanca, 2012) as lead firms and points of contact with the final market. Such firms often embody a brand value, and they are very active in the creation of business groups (Cainelli and Iacobucci, 2007). In particular, since the 1970s, the demography of Italian firms has shown a steady increase of medium-sized firms: already in 1991 60 per cent of firms had between 10 and 499 employees (Colli, 2010). The consolidation of this dynamic core was the result of a thinning out of both micro and larger firms. In particular 62 per cent of medium-sized firms produce the so-called 'Made in Italy' sectors typical of IDs. Changes in the governance of IDs have also led to the emergence of business groups endowed with the managerial and financial capacity to manage a multi-located value chain and to penetrate valuable foreign markets. Indeed, one can observe the extension of IDs' production systems beyond their own locality, as lead firms become and behave in a manner similar to pocket multinationals coordinating multi-local production networks (Zucchella, 2006). The most important ID enterprises have started to be engaged in global subcontracting chains, especially in emerging countries such as China and India, but also in the closer Eastern Europe regions. The translocality of the organization of production – the mimicking of multinationals' global value chains – has brought about dramatic changes in the composition of competences in IDs which are increasingly focused on high value-added functions, as well as the governance of the global supply chains (Mudambi, 2007, 2008). Lead firms and groups are now on the front line as the most dynamic actors of the Italian IDs. They act as an interface between the ID and the global economy, and as knowledge gatekeepers for the local firms (Belussi et al., 2011).

Another trend is the enrichment of the manufacturing specialization of IDs with immaterial functions, namely the high value-added tasks of research and development, communication and marketing, logistics, and direct management of the international distributive channels or retail chains. Some argue that IDs are becoming an internationally interconnected community of practice, comprising stable localized and global firm networks, and emergent localized and global temporary organizations (Belussi and Sedita, 2012). Our understanding of an ID as a community was originally introduced by Dei Ottati (1994), so it has always been an element in the organizational complexity of an ID. However, in the modern IDs the role of the communities crosses the district boundaries through the systematic participation of entrepreneurs, workers and local associations in international initiatives (such as exhibitions, trade fairs, collective missions to explore new markets, contacts with foreign firms and so on).

We observe a process of the 'tertiarization' of Italian IDs. New sectors are emerging within evolving and resilient IDs involving service-based industries, and these are contributing to the enduring competitiveness of some IDs. However, they are also tainting the *manufacturing purity* instilled in the MID conceptualization. The conundrum is to what extent a value chain approach that included both manufacturing and service activities would meaningfully capture the MID model, which clearly endorses the manufacturing nature of the economic activities of a district. However, we would argue that to capture the current changes in full we need instead to combine a 'place-based' with an 'industry life-cycle' approach (Martin and Sunley, 2011). This would mean mapping and weighting the spectrum of material and non-material activities that characterize a specific local system. Indeed, the manufacturing and service activities found in a specific local system are likely be linked to a nexus of core activities whose life cycle determines the IDs' evolutionary pattern at different points in time.

We would therefore suggest a model in which some of the parameters defining MIDs are relaxed in order to better understand and explain what an ID will look like at the maturity stage, when only resilient activities remain, and the ID has constantly renewed its competitive advantage. This means that the proposed model would describe an *open ID*, accommodating companies that have become leaders in their market niche, commanding rather inelastic demand schedules, which could be business groups or home-grown pocket multinationals. These cases reflect situations where the ID has become the hub of a multi-local knowledge and production network, and where the local *industrial atmosphere* has been complemented by a web of international linkages. In these cases the ID becomes more specialized in non-material functions that are co-located with lower value-added tasks related to the manufacturing stages.

20.6 CASE STUDIES

The case studies presented here are based on a meta-analysis of a sample of nine IDs and draw on academic contributions as well as press information and data made available by national newspapers and magazines. The analysis will address the issues discussed above in the context of real and evolving local realities regarding exactly what transformation district firms have been undergoing in response to the globalization of markets. What have been their main drivers of change?

The IDs selected are the textile clothing district in Prato, the footwear district in Riviera del Brenta (Venice), the tannery district in Arzignano, the 'sport-system' in Montebelluna, the Matera leather sofa district, the spectacle frame district in Agordo (Belluno), the ceramic tile district in Sassuolo (Bologna), the packaging machinery district in Bologna and, finally, the biomedical technology district in Mirandola.

The analysis follows the coordinates highlighted above, focusing on five areas.

20.6.1 Manufacturing Relocation Process

The processes of manufacturing relocation activity have occurred in all nine IDs except for Arzignano, Bologna and Sassuolo. In these IDs, the relocation process has not completely eroded the 'volume of activities' previously taking place in the districts, because it was mainly limited to the most labour-intensive value-added tasks, but it has reduced the activities related to local subcontracting. Thus, in general, there has been a reduction both in the number of firms previously localized in the district and in the workforce. The three districts that did not follow the path of the international relocation of the production were all specialized in continuous process manufacturing activity. Thus the main production was anchored, or immovable, because it was attached to large fixed investments (as in the cases of Sassuolo and Arzignano) or based on large standalone customer-based machinery production (as in the case of Bologna). In some cases the relocation process was organized within a context of high-speed internationalization. For instance, in the Montebelluna sport-system (Belussi and Asheim, 2010), the internationalization process has been ongoing for a long time. It began in the 1970s with the shift of the production of tennis shoes to Vietnam. During the 1980s the district moved en masse to Timisoara in northern Romania (Belussi, 2010). This was accompanied by a bandwagon shift of local public and private institutions as well as the opening in Timisoara of Italian bank branches. The result is that a 'satellite' district has emerged in Timisoara to handle the standardized labour-intensive tasks of shoe assembly. In Montebelluna, the local economy has gradually been able to absorb the labour redundancy created by the transfer of activities abroad. While in the past the local ID employed more than 8,000 workers, now the number has dropped to about 5,000. Many local subcontractors initially located in the Montebelluna area have moved to Romania, while others are supplying larger firms that also control subcontracting activities in Romania. It can be argued that Montebelluna has been able to seize the opportunities of internationalizing its production process over a period of more than three decades. But more importantly, it has managed to translate the shock of relocation into an element of strength for the local ID rather than a threat. The slowness of the process and the anchoring in the district of firms' innovation activity have both guaranteed its renewing success.

The shock of globalization was inauspicious for many newly formed IDs, for whom the sudden relocation abroad of the manufacturing activities of the majority of local firms resulted in a threat to their very existence. Such is the case of the Matera leather sofa district. The difficulty of managing the process of relocation has led to the demise of one of the district's three major companies, Nicoletti spa, as it attempted to move the more labour-intensive activities to Romania. At the same time, the district has experienced the crisis of another local leader, namely Natuzzi spa. Natuzzi accounts for about 55 per cent of the Italian sofa production and about 11 per cent of the international leather sofa production. Natuzzi moved a significant portion of its activity to three factories in China, but has encountered severe organizational difficulties in managing distant markets such as, for instance, the US. Over the last few years, Natuzzi has been obliged to deal with the disruption of many of its commercial contracts in the US, due to serious delays in delivering orders. Recently, in order to address these difficulties, it suddenly relocated to Shanghai within an exporting area created by the Chinese government to attract foreign investors. Despite receiving significant help from the Chinese government in the form of US$64 million in cash as part of a welcome pack, Natuzzi is still in crisis – some 3,500 employees in its factories located in the South of Italy are supported by the Wages Guarantee Fund. Overall, between 2001 and 2010 the district lost about 50 per cent of its labour force and the number of firms halved from 14,000 to 7,000. The crisis in the Italian furniture market has severely damaged the relatively young ID, where, in contrast to other IDs for which cyclical crises were the norm, firms had never before experienced such turbulent markets.

20.6.2   Entry of Foreign Multinationals

Examples of the entry of foreign multinationals which have acquired numerous dynamic and innovative local firms are the biomedical technology district of Mirandola, where foreign firms started to enter in the 1980s, and more recently, the district of the Riviera del Brenta, near Venice, which specializes in high-quality fashionable ladies' shoes. The first large acquisition in the latter district was that of one of the once leading local firms, Calzaturificio Luigino Rossi, Rossimoda. For many years Rossimoda's most important client was the French luxury holding LVMH. When the owner retired, LVMH acquired the firm's entire stock. During the last decade LVMH also acquired Monique and Arcad, two well-known traditional ladies' producers of fashion footwear. Furthermore, during the last decade, Prada, Armani and Gucci (through the firm PPR) started to take over local small footwear producers. Guardi was acquired by Armani in 2002, Iris by the Gibò Group in 2005, Corrado Maretto by LVMH in 2002, and Lamos by Prada in 2000, to cite the most famous cases. The district in Riviera del Brenta is now partially hierarchical, although it still contains many autonomous producers, subcontractors and specialized firms. The local association of entrepreneurs, ACRIB, is still very active in supporting the export of luxury goods to advanced and emerging markets. This district is still vibrant and economically very strong, and is focused on branded products. It comprises about 1,000 firms employing about 14,000 employees, producing 22 million pairs of shoes a year corresponding to some €1.7 billion in sales, of which 89 per cent is exported.

20.6.3 Emergence of Home-grown Multinational Firms

Another largely understudied issue is the emergence of home-grown multinational firms. During the phase of expansion in the 1980s, the most dynamic Italian IDs saw some of their final-output firms grow to the point of becoming true multinationals. This is certainly the case of the spectacle frame district in Agordo (Belluno) with Luxottica; the Matera leather sofa district with Natuzzi; the sport-system in Montebelluna with brands that include Tecnica, Salomon, Scarpa, Invicta and Geox; the tannery district in Arzignano with the Mastrotto Group; and the ceramic tile district in Sassuolo (Bologna) with the Marazzi Group. In some cases, the decision of these firms (which in the past were smaller in size) to relocate some manufacturing functions abroad and thereby to create a firm-specific international subcontracting chain, proceeded hand in hand with their growth. This is particularly the case of Montebelluna, where companies have thereby decreased the risk of internationalization and are better at controlling the so-called 'liability of foreignness'. The emergence of home-grown multinationals occurred through conspicuous flows of foreign acquisitions. For instance, Luxottica acquired the Ray-Ban company in 1999, and Oakley, the technological leader in ophthalmic lens manufacture, in 2007. In China, Luxottica has created an important distributive chain. At the same time, between 1997 and 2006 LenCrafters acquired and restructured two large Chinese plants in Dong Guan City (3,500 workers) and Gabobu Town (1,600 workers). This has not hampered the ability of the spectacle frame district in Agordo (Belluno) to grow: the district actually has about 600 firms and 12,000 workforce units.

20.6.4 Access to External Knowledge

The novel access to external knowledge that IDs have been experiencing is also evidenced in the case studies. To the original Marshallian conceptualization of IDs, where 'knowledge was in the air' and ID firms were expected to make only minor innovations, we juxtapose the reality of some Italian IDs which during the 1980s and 1990s were radically innovative and able to introduce Schumpeterian innovations new to the market. This is the case of the plastic boots industry in Montebelluna, the machinery for plastic frame moulding in Belluno, the industrialization of sofas in Matera, the new tanning machinery in Arzignano, the single-oven technology introduced in Sassuolo for ceramic tiles, and the innovative artificial kidneys in Mirandola – to mention a few. Indeed, the district innovation capacity was once a self-contained process, where the process of local creativity and innovation was activated by interactive learning across ID firms. However, more recently, as these firms have become increasingly open to international stimuli, they have been scouting, scanning and exploring new external sources of innovation, external both to the firm and to the district. To this end, the local institutions seem to have been playing a more central role than in the past. For example, the Polytechnic Institute of Footwear in Riviera del Brenta, near Venice, is offering courses for designers and design experts who have been taken on by NIKE. To support local businesses the Polytechnic has received EU funding to develop automated technology that can use a robotic 'montage chain' for the assembly of stylish ladies' footwear.

Another interesting case comes from the ceramic district of Modena-Sassuolo. In the Sassuolo ceramic tile district, for instance, until recently local expertise had been sufficient to support a series of radical innovations in both process and product – such as the single-oven technology introduced by Marazzi in the 1970s, or the 'Made in Italy' brand and designer ceramic tiles of the 1980s. However, currently district firms are hampered by Italy's lack of a national innovation system. Radical innovations in this sector have mostly come from Japanese companies who have introduced, for instance, self-cleaning tiles and antibacterial treatments for tiles. These innovations were introduced in the last decades as a result of collaborations between the public laboratory of the University of Tokyo – Fujishima Laboratory – and the producer TOTO Ltd. The result is that for the first time in their history Italian ID firms have to buy science-based innovations from abroad and acquire the patents from the Japanese firms.

Another observable phenomenon, in the case of the medical technology district in Mirandola, is the collaboration over innovation between branches of foreign multinationals located within the district and their respective R&D foreign headquarters. Thus, the process of innovation is becoming less local and more global in nature.

20.6.5   The Role of Migrant Labour in IDs

Good examples of the role of migrant labour are the textile district in Prato and the tannery district in Arzignano (Belussi and Sedita, 2010). Italy is experiencing a wave of incoming migrant labour, which has penetrated some localities more than others depending on the need for relatively cheaper manual labour. In particular, 50 per cent of the employers in the tanneries in Arzignano are now foreigners. Likewise, the Prato textile district first experienced the penetration of Chinese labour, and then the opening or take-over of local businesses by Chinese entrepreneurs. Currently, Chinese-owned businesses employ around 30–40,000 – mostly Chinese – employees and have geared their activities towards garment production using their links with China to import lower-cost textiles. This has led to the formation of a new garment district adjacent to the traditional textile district, albeit in reality completely separate.

20.7   CONCLUSIONS

It would be wrong to think that the crisis in the Italian economy is due to its specialization and the presence of IDs. The truth is somewhat different. Indeed, the best-performing IDs have shown remarkable resilience and endurance despite some structural domestic growth-hindering factors such as bureaucracy, taxation, the aftermath of the 2008 crisis and the contracting effect of the macro-austerity measures. The present discussion shows that, as vibrant organizational forms, IDs have been constantly evolving to adapt to and to withstand exogenous and endogenous shocks. We find that the existence of a district life cycle does not automatically imply a linear growth path, because decline and death are not inevitable. Despite the existence of similar initial conditions, together with the allocation of resources and widespread opportunities for development, we observe extremely heterogeneous models of development. Every ID seems to have reacted differently to the same external shocks, and has evolved differently depending on the unique learning capabilities of its local firms. Indeed, considering the evolution of IDs over the last decade, we find that they have proceeded along a multiplicity of paths driven by different strategies, including product differentiation, diversification into technologically contiguous niches, product quality upgrading and the continuous introduction of technological innovations.

Despite IDs' unique evolutionary trajectories, we have identified common underlying success factors. These include the emergence of district leaders or brands – either medium-sized enterprises or business groups – the insertion of the IDs' production into global production networks, and the shift of manufacturing specializations with non-material functions. Effective responses to endogenous and exogenous factors have included the ability to tap into growing international demand, the capability to introduce original technological innovations, a trend towards diversification, and a renewed role played by local institutions and vocational training institutes in constantly updating the necessary skills.

The meta-analysis of nine IDs shows that their ability to maintain a competitive advantage rests on their capacity to change while retaining control over their *industrial* core. Touched by all the forces that have shaken certainties over the last decade, the most successful IDs have evolved organically, building on their existing strengths while getting to grips with their weaknesses. We would therefore point to a model where some of the parameters defining MIDs are relaxed in order to better understand and explain what a mature but resilient ID looks like: as open IDs, they are indeed still IDs, but not as we know them.

REFERENCES

Bailey D. (2003), 'Explaining Japan's Kūdōka [hollowing out]: a case of government and strategic failure?', *Asia Pacific Business Review*, **10** (1), 1–20.

Becattini, G. (1990), 'The Marshallian district as a socio-economic notion', in F. Pyke, G. Becattini and W. Sengenberger (eds), *Industrial Districts and Inter-firm Collaboration in Italy*, Geneva: International Institute for Labor Studies, pp. 37–51.

Becattini, G., Bellandi, L. and De Propris, L. (2009), *The Handbook of Industrial Districts*, Cheltenham, UK and Northampton, MA, USA: Edward Elgar.

Bellandi, M. (2006), 'A perspective on clusters, localities and specific public goods', in C. Pitelis, R. Sugden and J.R. Wilson (eds), *Clusters and Globalisation: The Development of Economies*, Cheltenham, UK and Northampton, MA, USA: Edward Elgar, pp. 96–113.

Belussi, F. (2010), 'Transfering entrepreneurialship: the making of the cluster of Timişoara', in Belussi and Sammarra (eds), pp. 172–85.

Belussi, F. and Asheim, B. (2010), 'Industrial districts and globalisation: learning and innovation in local and global production systems', in Belussi and Sammarra (eds), pp. 246–65.

Belussi, F. and Pilotti, L. (2002a), 'Learning and innovation by networking within the Italian industrial districts: the development of an explorative analytical model', *Sinergie*, 58/02, 3–43.

Belussi, F. and Pilotti, L. (2002b), 'Knowledge creation, learning and innovation in Italian industrial districts', *Geografiska Annaler*, **84**, 19–33.

Belussi, F. and Sammarra, A. (eds) (2010), *Business Networks in Clusters and Industrial Districts: The Governance of the Global Value Chain*, London: Routledge.

Belussi, F. and Sedita, S.R. (2009), 'Life cycle vs. multiple path dependency in industrial districts', *European Planning Studies*, **17** (4), 505–28.

Belussi, F. and Sedita, S.R. (2010), 'The evolution of the district model: "reverse relocation" and the case of the leather-tanning district of Arzigano', *European Review of Industrial Economics and Policy*, **1**, 15 July, available at: http://testrevel.unice.fr/eriep/index.html/id=3067.

Belussi, F. and Sedita, S.R. (2012), 'Industrial districts as open learning systems: combining emergent and deliberate knowledge structures', *Regional Studies*, **46** (2), 165–84.

Belussi, F., Sedita, S. Aage, T. and Porcellato, D. (2011), 'Inwards flows of information and knowledge in low-tech industrial districts: contrasting the "few firms gatekeeper" and "direct peer" model', in P.L. Robertson,

D. Jacobson (eds), *Knowledge Transfer and Technological Diffusion*, Cheltenham, UK and Northampton, MA, USA: Edward Elgar, pp. 64–90.

Cainelli, G. (2008), 'Spatial agglomeration, technological innovations, and firm productivity: evidence from Italian industrial districts', *Growth and Change*, **39** (3), 414–35.

Cainelli, G. and Iacobucci, D. (2007), *Agglomeration, Technology and Business Groups*, Cheltenham, UK and Northampton, MA, USA: Edward Elgar.

Colli, A. (2010), 'Dwarf giants, giant dwarfs: reflections about the Italian "industrial demography" at the beginning of the new millennium', *Journal of Modern Italian Studies*, **15** (1), 43–60.

Crevoisier, O. and Jeannerat, H. (2009), 'Territorial knowledge dynamics: from the proximity paradigm to the multi-location paradigm', *European Planning Studies*, **17** (8), 1223–41.

De Arcangelis, G. and Ferri, G. (2005), 'The specialization of the districts: from typical final goods to machinery for making them?', in Banca d'Italia, *Local Economies and Internalisation in Italy*, Rome: Banca d'Italia, pp. 421–36.

De Propris, L. and Crevoisier, O. (2011), 'From regional anchors to anchoring', in B. Asheim, R. Boschma, P. Cooke and R. Martin (eds), *Handbook of Regional Innovation and Growth*, Cheltenham, UK and Northampton, MA, USA: Edward Elgar, pp. 167–80.

De Propris, L. and Lazzeretti, L. (2009), 'Measuring the decline of a Marshallian industrial district: the Birmingham jewellery quarter', *Regional Studies*, **43** (9), 1135–54.

Dei Ottati, G. (1994), 'Trust, interlinking transactions and credit in the industrial district', *Cambridge Journal of Economics*, **18** (6), 529–46.

Di Giacinto, V., Gomellini, M., Micucci, G. and Pagnini M. (2012), *Mapping Local Productivity Advantages in Italy: Industrial Districts, Cities or Both?*, Rome: Banca d'Italia.

Fondazione Edison (2012), *Il Settore del Vino: Un Pilastro del Made in Italy*, Milan.

Gao, Y. (2011), *China as the Workshop of the World: An Analysis at the National and Industrial Level of China in the International Division of Labour*, London: Routledge.

Humphrey, J. and Schmitz, H. (2002), 'How does insertion in global value chains affect upgrading in industrial clusters?', *Regional Studies*, **36** (9), 1017–27.

ISTAT (2012), *Annual Report*, Rome: ISTAT.

Marini, D. and Toschi, G. (2012), 'Imprese distrettuali e processi di innovazione', Osservatorio Approfondimento A, Distretti Italiani, Osservatorio Nazionale Distretti Italiani.

Marshall, A. (1920), *Principles of Economics*, 8th edn, London: Macmillan.

Martin, P. and Sunley, P. (2011), 'Conceptualising cluster evolution: beyond the life cycle model?', *Regional Studies*, **45** (10), 1299–318.

Mediobanca-Unioncamere (2012), *Le Medie Imprese Industriali Italiane (2000–2009)*, Milan: Ufficio Studi Mediobanca e Centro Studi Unioncamere.

Mudambi, R. (2007), 'Managing global offshoring strategies: a case approach', *Journal of International Business Studies*, **38**, 206–10.

Mudambi, R. (2008), 'Location, control and innovation in knowledge-intensive industries', *Economic Geography*, **8**, 699–725.

Osservatorio Nazionale dei Distretti Industriali (2012a), 'Approfondimento A', in *Rapporto*, Distretti Italiani, Osservatorio Nazionale Distretti Italiani.

Osservatorio Nazionale dei Distretti Industriali (2012b), *Rapporto*, Distretti Italiani, Osservatorio Nazionale Distretti Italiani.

Zucchella, A. (2006), 'Local cluster dynamics: trajectories of mature industrial districts between decline and multiple embeddedness', *Journal of Institutional Economics*, **2**, 21–44.

Index

Titles of publications are shown in *italics*.